HOMELAND SECURITY AND TERRORISM

Readings and Interpretations

RUSSELL D. HOWARD

Brigadier General, U.S. Army (Ret.)

JAMES J. F. FOREST

Assistant Professor, West Point

JOANNE C. MOORE

Major, U.S. Army

McGraw-Hill
New York Chicago San Francisco Lisbon
London Madrid Mexico City Milan New Delhi
San Juan Seoul Singapore Sydney Toronto

The McGraw·Hill Companies

Copyright © 2006 by The McGraw-Hill Companies, Inc. All rights reserved. Printed in the United States of America. Except as permitted under the United States Copyright Act of 1976, no part of this publication may be reproduced or distributed in any form or by any means, or stored in a database or retrieval system, without the prior written permission of the publisher.

1 2 3 4 5 6 7 8 9 0   FGR / FGR   0 9 8 7 6 5

ISBN 0-07-145282-6

McGraw-Hill books are available at special quantity discounts to use as premiums and sales promotions, or for use in corporate training programs. For more information, please write to the Director of Special Sales, Professional Publishing, McGraw-Hill, Two Penn Plaza, New York, NY 10121-2298. Or contact your local bookstore.

 This book is printed on recycled, acid-free paper containing a minimum of 50% recycled, de-inked fiber.

Library of Congress Cataloging-in-Publication Data

Howard, Russell D.
   Homeland security and terrorism: readings and interpretations/by Russell Howard, James Forest, Joanne Moore.—1st ed.
      p. cm.
   Includes bibliographical references.
   ISBN 0-07-145282-6
   1. Terrorism—United States—Prevention. 2. Civil defense—United States. 3. National security—United States. 4. Civil rights—United States. I. Forest, James F. II. Moore, JoAnne. III. Title.
   HV6432.H72 2005
   363.32'0973—dc22
                                       2005009859

Contents

Preface

Homeland Security and Terrorism: Readings and Interpretations is the third in a series of books edited by the staff of the Combating Terrorism Center at West Point and published by McGraw-Hill. The first, *Terrorism and Counterterrorism: Understanding the New Security Environment: Readings and Interpretations,* is in its second printing. *Terrorism and Counterterrorism* aims to give the reader a comprehensive understanding of the most crucial security problems facing modern society. It presents the philosophical, political, and religious roots of terrorist activities—past and present—discusses their national, regional, and global effects, and suggests responses and defenses. As textbooks go, *Terrorism and Counterterrorism* is a best-seller, used in graduate and undergraduate courses around the world. However, students are not the book's only audience. Sales figure show that the general public has purchased an approximately equal number of copies—rather unusual for a textbook.

The general reader was taken into account when *Defeating Terrorism: Shaping the New Security Environment* was edited and published in 2003. The second McGraw-Hill/Combating Terrorism Center collaboration, *Defeating Terrorism* presents original contributions not only by well-known scholars and practitioners but also by several "out-of-the-box" thinkers who offers cutting-edge thinking about how to fight and win the war against terrorism. *Defeating Terrorism* applies theory to practice in ways that are useful for all who want to be better informed about the threat of terrorism.

Homeland Security and Terrorism: Readings and Interpretations, our new collaboration, is, we think, an important book. Defense of the homeland is the primary responsibility of the federal government and is the core of its national security strategy. This book's premise is that, while much has been done to secure the American homeland since 9/11, much more remains to be done, not only by the federal government but also by state and local governments, the private sector, and ordinary citizens.

Organization

Homeland Security: Readings and Interpretations is a collective volume, written by noted terrorism experts, homeland security practitioners, government officials, police and fire officials, military officers, educators, business executives, medical personnel, lawyers, and other citizens with relevant expertise. It is organized in five parts. Part I describes the threat to the homeland from terrorists waging a type of warfare not well understood in the business towers of New York, the fields of Nebraska, the coasts of Maine and California, or even (some would say) the halls of government in Washington DC. Part II reviews a diverse group of particularly vulnerable U.S. targets. Aviation, transportation, cyberspace, and infrastructure targets are analyzed, along with less obvious vulnerabilities such as food, water, and porous borders. Part III addresses the ability of national, state, and local agencies to respond to acts of terrorism. Contributions from a state governor, a city police detective, and a metropolitan fire chief add a sense of operational realism to this section. The importance of interagency coordination is discussed, and a spirited debate about the effectiveness of the newly established Department of Homeland Security is included. Part IV deals with the complicated issue of civil liberties in a democratic nation under attack. It explores the tension sometimes encountered in assuring both the personal freedoms guaranteed to Americans by the Constitution and the Bill of Rights and the safety of American citizens from terrorist attacks. The role of the media, law enforcement, and intelligence services in an open society come in for discussion, while three chapters—one pro, one con, and one somewhere in between—address the USA PATRIOT Act. Part V asks whether the lessons learned from natural and man-made disasters, such as the blackout of 2003 and the outbreak of the SARS and West Nile viruses, can be used to better prepare the nation for certain types of terrorist attacks.

Part I

Part 1 consists of six chapters. The first, "The New Terrorism and Homeland Security," outlines seven ways in which today's terrorism differs from that of the Cold War era. For example, the American homeland was not at risk for acts of terrorism during the Cold War, while now it is very much at risk. The new terrorism is more violent and better financed. Al Qaeda, their surrogates, and their followers operate globally, are better trained, and more difficult to penetrate. Unlike previous groups, they are very keen to acquire and use weapons of mass destruction. This chapter discusses the advantages present-day terrorists, particularly the al Qaeda and like-minded groups, have in targeting the United States.

"Terrorism and Counterterrorism since 9/11: Understanding Past, Present and Future Trends" was written for this volume by Kate Marquis, a counterterrorism analyst for the U.S. Government. She argues that al Qaeda and its supporters see the 9/11 attacks as simply one battle in an ongoing campaign, which also includes subsequent attacks in Bali, Turkey, Madrid, and Iraq. The perception that all these events are part of a unified effort to achieve a single goal, strengthens the terrorists' commitment. The counterterrorist coalition, on the other hand, has a more fragmented view of the war. Fewer strategists have assimilated the fact that 9/11 is of a piece with the later attacks, and that this string of apparently discrete events requires a unified response. The tendency, however understandable, to see 9/11 as unique, may therefore be hindering the U.S. from combating the overall threat as effectively as possible.

In "Putting WMD Terrorism into Perspective," John Parachini argues that our fear of terrorists using WMD, while justified, should not be exaggerated. "Focusing on a particular means of attack must not come at the expense of adequate attention to broader diplomatic, border control, intelligence, and law enforcement measures to counter terrorism." Moreover, counterterrorism efforts should not focus solely on al Qaeda but should also address broader terrorist trends and a variety of other groups.

"Invasive Species: The Biological Threat to America" explains that a biological attack may not come in the form of anthrax or other known biological agents that governments now spend millions to protect against. Instead, Robert J. Pratt warns, the attacks could be in the form of an invasive species or a disease pathogen. Pratt explores the history of invasive attacks and concludes that the United States is not prepared to counter the intentional and hostile introduction of invasive species or disease pathogens. The government's Invasive Species Management Plan is not adequate and will not be until the Department of Homeland Security takes the lead and embeds invasive species management into its homeland security strategy.

According to Dr. Bruce Hoffman in "The Logic of Suicide Terrorism," the tactics of terrorism, particularly suicide bombing, have a strategic logic of their own. Suicide bombings are inexpensive, accurate, and effective. They are the ultimate smart bomb: they guarantee media coverage and are less complicated and compromising than other kinds of terrorist operations. Hoffman takes Israel as his case study in this chapter and claims that if Americans can learn from the Israeli experience, we will substantially reduce the threat of suicide bombing here. And in the final chapter of this section, Robert Page draws on extensive research to explain how suicide terrorism follows a strategic logic, one specifically designed to coerce modern liberal democracies to make significant territorial concessions.

Part II

Part II consists of eight chapters highlighting specific areas of vulnerability to terrorist attack in the United States. Choosing these eight articles from the more than fifty we considered was a difficult undertaking. So much in America is at risk that prioritizing by group, time, location, vulnerability, or effect is virtually impossible. Instead, we chose these articles based on the ability of the authors to make their points succinctly and with authority. Some of the authors, such as Brian Jenkins and Larry Wortzel, are noted terrorism experts. Others, such as Barbara Bruemmer, Claudia Copeland and Betsy Cody, are experts in other areas who have applied their special knowledge to conceptualizing the impact of terrorist attacks. "Aviation Security: Promise or Reality," updated for this book by Joseph S. Szyliowicz, analyzes the state of aviation security, beginning with the unique characteristics of the air transportation system that complicate the security effort there. Szyliowicz also reflects on the security situation before 9/11 and the changes since. Unfortunately, he concludes, no adequate overall security program has yet been put in place.

"Improving Public Surface Transportation Security" is by Brian Michael Jenkins, a respected terrorism expert and former special forces practitioner. As aviation security improves, Jenkins argues, terrorists will most likely turn to surface transportation, which offers them much easier access. He points out that lessons learned in the area of aviation security are not necessarily transferable to ground transportation. "Threat levels differ, the potential consequences of terrorist attacks are different and the systems themselves differ greatly, as do the means of providing security." And although much has been done to improve ground transportation security since 9/11, what remains will be more difficult and much more expensive.

"Border Security: Closing the Ingenuity Gap" describes the globalization paradox and the difficulties of protecting America's borders. According to Frank Hoffman, "the ever-increasing degree of global interconnectivity and the rising volume and velocity of goods and services moving between societies that are the hall marks of globalization are one side of the paradox." These same intricate networks, high concentrations of critical infrastructure, and large volumes of unsecured economic activity expose advanced states to crippling acts of ultra-terrorism. Bin Laden, for example, cunningly used the openness of America's society and infrastructure against itself. To protect our borders will take ingenuity, something Hoffman fears is presently in short supply.

Frank Cilluffo and Paul Byron Pattak's essay, "Cyber Threats: Ten Issues to Consider," was written before 9/11 but is still very relevant and instructive. Presciently, the authors point out that since few adversaries would care to confront the United States in a conventional war on a conventional battlefield, they might well turn to terrorism and other asymmetric forms of conflict—including virtual ones—as more effective ways of attacking the U.S. where it is most vulnerable. "Bits and bytes will never completely replace bullets and bombs," say Cilluffo and Pattak, but they can be synergistically combined. Imagine if 9/11 or the Oklahoma City bombing had been accompanied by electronic disruptions of federal, state, and local emergency and public-safety communications systems. "Ten Items to Consider" helps frame the policy debate in this underappreciated area.

"Securing America's Critical Infrastructures: A Top Priority for the Department of Homeland Security," was authored by Larry M. Wortzel, a retired Army colonel and intelligence expert. Wortzel explains what critical infrastructure is and why it is difficult to protect. While the Department of Homeland Security must take the lead in this area, he acknowledges, unprecedented cooperation and coordination across government and private-sector boundaries is required. Private industry owns and operates approximately 85 percent of the critical infrastructure and key assets in America. In this area, "the new front line of defense has become the communities and individual institutions that make up our critical infrastructure sector."

"Seacurity: Improving the Security of the Global Sea-Container Shipping System" is a collaboration by Maarten van de Voort, Kevin A. O'Brien, Adnan Rahman, and Lorenzo Valeri. According to the authors, there is a threat of terrorists using containers to transport dangerous materials or weapons, and even of using containers themselves as weapons of mass destruction. A systematic review of global container commerce security is urgently required, and better methods of inspecting and securing containers must be implemented.

"Terrorism and Security Issues Facing the Water Infrastructure Sector" was written by Claudia Copeland and Betsy Cody, both specialists in natural resources and environmental policy. Copeland and Cody explain how vulnerable the nation's water supply and water quality infrastructure is, describe the security-related actions taken by government and the private sector since 9/11, and discuss a number of other policy issues and responses in this area.

Rounding out Part II is "Food Supply and Bioterrorism" by Barbara Bruemmer, a dietician with an interest in terrorism and security issues. Dr. Bruemmer shows how the food supply in the United States could be compromised and how best to prepare for possible food-related terrorism. Registered dietitians, she believes, are in a unique position to help formulate a global approach to the provision of a safe food supply.

Part III

Part III examines how government agencies at several levels are responding to the terrorist threat. All six chapters look particularly at intergovernmental and interagency cooperation, or the lack therof. Louise Comfort begins by presenting a model to improve coordination in response to extreme events, such as a natural disaster or terrorist attack. John Sullivan describes an interagency model developed in Los Angeles County to assess the information needed to manage terrorist threats or acts. Reid Sawyer and Joseph Pfeiffer recount the lessons learned since 9/11 by the New York City Fire Department. Former Oklahoma governor Frank Keating reminds us that not all terrorist attacks are conducted by international non-state actors like al Qaeda. Finally, Seth Jones and Chris Hornbarger debate the relative merits of the Department of Homeland Security, America's newest and most important experiment in interagency and intergovernmental coordination. In "Managing Intergovernmental Responses to Terrorism and Other Extreme Events," Louise Comfort examines the performance of the intergovernmental system. Dr. Comfort proposes a model of "auto-adaptation," based on the concept of individual, organizational,and collective learning in environments exposed to recurring risk and guided by a shared goal.

In "Terrorism Early-Warning Groups: Regional Intelligence to Combat Terrorism," John P. Sullivan, a sergeant with the Los Angeles Sheriff's Department, describes Los Angeles's interagency model. In "Strategic Planning for First Responders: Lessons Learned from the New York City Fire Department," Reid Sawyer, a noted counterterror expert, and Joe Pfeifer, the onsite New York Fire Department commander on 9/11, address the pressing need to build capacity within first-responder organizations. They present a framework for identifying the need for change in an organization prior to a crisis and examine themes such as crisis management in a first-responder context and how organizations should adapt to the changing security environment.

In "Catastrophic Terrorism: Local Response to a National Threat," former Oklahoma Governor Frank Keating reminds us that some terrorism is home-grown. Based on his experience during the April 19, 1995, Oklahoma City bombing and his later participation in the *Dark Winter* exercise in 2002, Gov. Keating provides useful conclusions and findings and makes recommendations for first-responders in the event of a terrorist attack.

Completing Part III are two chapters that discuss the newly established Department of Homeland Security. In "Terrorism and the Battle for Homeland Security," Seth Jones argues that until the Department of Homeland Security (DHS) has authority to "synthesize and analyze homeland security intelligence from multiple sources," it will not be able to fulfill its three primary objectives: (1) prevent terrorist attacks in the U.S., (2) reduce America's vulnerability to terrorism, and (3) respond to any terrorist attacks and natural disasters. Jones contends that the effectiveness of DHS has been greatly diminished by the reluctance of the FBI and CIA to relinquish significant intelligence gathering powers.

Chris Hornbarger takes a different view. In "National Strategy: Building Capability for the Long-Haul," Hornbarger argues that the nation's homeland security policies are on track and that the next administration should stay the course. Hornbarger contends that *National Strategy for Homeland Security,* in concert with other Presidential policies, has provided meaningful direction to federal, state, local and private sector homeland security activities.

Part IV

Part IV features six chapters discussing civil liberties and citizen support for homeland security issues during the war on terror. All of the contributors take note of occasional tensions between the imperative for government to provide domestic security against the

x   *Preface*

threat of terrorist attack and the equal imperative of ensuring that individual rights and liberties are protected. Amanda J. Dory begins Part IV with the assertion that civil defense measures taken during the Cold War should again be implemented. Public support and participation, notes Dory, is crucial to homeland security. In chapters written specifically for this book, Jim Robbins discusses the freedom of the press and the challenges it sometimes entails, and Elizabeth Robbins offers a possible framework for better government-media relations. Three chapters address the relative merits of the PATRIOT Act. Nancy Chang, an outspoken critic, says the Act is an attack on the Bill of Rights. Brian Hook, Margaret Peterlin, and Peter Walsh disagree, arguing that intelligence and information-sharing among governmental agencies will not occur without many of the provisions of the Act. Roger Dean Golden weighs both the positive and negative aspects of the Act. Golden concludes that the Act represents a shift toward security at the cost of potential loss of freedom, but that a majority of Americans appear willing to accept this shift.

In "American Civil Security: The U.S. Public and Homeland Security," Amanda Dory posits that increased government attention to the role of the public in the war on terrorism is crucial. She finds a historical precedent in civil defense measures taken during the Cold War and advocates a new "civil security" program to involve the American public more fully in homeland defense. "Inherent Conflict of Interests Between the Media and National Security," by Jim Robbins, suggests that terrorism and the media have a symbiotic relationship. One important challenge to homeland security is to prevent terrorists from making use of the media. For a variety of reasons (such as media culture, competition for news, and new information technologies), this is becoming more difficult. This chapter examines how the enemy seeks to exploit the media and the extent to which, when they succeed in doing so, the mass media are a something of a force multiplier for terrorism.

Elizabeth Robbins contends that the media can nevertheless greatly assist public officials during domestic crises. Her chapter, while acknowledging that the media are driven far more by profit than public service, offers suggestions on how to craft government-media relations that serve the government's need to provide the public with updated, actionable, immediate guidance.

The final three chapters in Part IV address the PATRIOT Act. "The USA PATRIOT Act: What's So Patriotic about Trampling on the Bill of Rights?" by Nancy Chang, is a stinging critique. In Chang's view, the Act confers vast and unchecked powers on the executive branch and fails to respect the democratic values that define our nation. It should therefore be repealed.

In reply, "White Paper on Anti-terrorism Legislation *Intelligence and the New Threat: The USA PATRIOT Act and Information Sharing Between the Intelligence and Law Enforcement Communities*," by Brian H. Hook, Margaret J. A. Peterlin, and Peter L. Welsh, notes that the security environment has changed substantially since the Cold War, imposing a greatly increased necessity for intelligence sharing. The PATRIOT Act ensures an indispensable measure of cooperation and information-sharing between the intelligence and law enforcement communities.

Attempting to strike a balance, Roger Dean Golden's "What Price Security? The USA PATRIOT Act and America's Balance Between Freedom and Security" examines the tensions that arise in the wake of the Act between protecting the openness of American society and making it more secure. According to Golden, the Act represents a shift toward security at the expense of some loss of personal freedom. At present, it appears that the

American public supports this trade-off, though how long this support will last is open to debate.

Part V

The contributors to Part V agree that our previous experience in mitigating natural and technological disasters and disease outbreaks has great utility in preparing for possible future terrorist attacks. The first three chapters examine past emergencies—the Northeast blackout, the West Nile virus epidemic, and the SARS crisis—with an eye to managing terrorist attacks. The final chapter considers U.S. population responses to a range of natural and technological disasters—the 1918 Spanish influenza pandemic for example—and suggests that by learning from previous catastrophic events, citizens can prepare for and mitigate terrorist attacks with resourcefulness, civility, and mutual aid.

According to Randolph May in "Preventing a Communications Blackout: The Need for Telecom Redundancy," the events of September 11 and the Northeast blackout of August 14, 2003, demonstrated the need for redundant telecommunications networks, operable during emergencies and with sufficient capacity to handle peak call volumes. May points to government policies that are needed to increase the reliability and security under stress of America's telecommunication's infrastructure.

"Risk Communication, the West Nile Virus Epidemic, and Bioterrorism: Responding to the Communication Challenges Posed by the Intentional or Unintentional Release of a Pathogen in an Urban Setting" is a collaborative effort by Vincent T. Covello, Richard G. Peters, Joseph G. Wojteki, and Richard C. Hyde. The authors recognize that the introduction of pathogens in an urban setting—intentional or unintentional—will present severe communication problems to first responders and government officials. Using the 1999 and 2000 New York City West Nile Virus epidemics as case studies, they advocate adoption of a "risk communication" model to increase communications effectiveness in times of emergencies. According to Covello et al, the model applies not only to the unintentional introduction of pathogens, as in the West Nile Virus case, but also to a bioterrorism event.

"How Business Can Defeat Terrorism: Global Financial Firms Battle the SARS Outbreak in Hong Kong" has been updated especially for this volume. Kelly Hicks begins by describing what appears to be a dastardly terrorist event. In reality, however, it is the SARS outbreak, which brought Hong Kong to its knees. Hicks uses Hong Kong's response to SARS to explain both how a bioterrorist attack could unfold and, more important, how business, government, and the international community can respond successfully.

"Bioterrorism and the People: How to Vaccinate a City Against Panic," by Thomas A. Glass and Monica Schoch-Spana, reviews lessons learned from previous terrorist attacks and national health emergencies, Drs. Glass and Schoch-Spana conclude that the public can prepare for, and help mitigate, a bioterrorist attack. In fact, it is vital that health officials and other leaders view the public as active participants in any bioterror response.

Acknowledgements

This book is dedicated to H. Ross Perot, without whose support, none of this would have been possible.

Homeland Security and Terrorism: Readings and Interpretations is the product of broad collaboration among several policymakers, scholars, and security professionals. We note our appreciation to all the staff at the Combating Terrorism Center at West Point for their assistance and support including Bruce Hoffman, Rohan Gunaratna, and John Ellis, the Center's talented Senior Fellows who continue to provide critical guidance for all our initiatives. Members of the Office of the Dean and the Association of Graduates also played an important contributing role in this effort. Our thanks also go to all the contributors to this volume. Throughout this project, we have been blessed with an abundance of authors dedicated to our shared goal of understanding and improving homeland security. And finally, to our partners—Paula, Ken, and Alicia—we offer our sincere appreciation for the incredible patience and support you have shown us throughout this project.

Permissions

Copyright and original publication information for the chapters of this volume, where relevant, is provided below:

Chapter 1: An earlier version of this discussion was published as "Understanding Al Qaeda's Application of the New Terrorism-The Key to Victory in the Current Campaign." In *Terrorism and Counterterrorism: Understanding the New Security Environment, Readings and Interpretations*, ed. R. Howard and R. Sawyer. New York: McGraw-Hill, 2002. It has been updated and revised for this volume.

Chapter 2: Originally authored for this volume.

Chapter 3: Originally published as "Putting WMD Terrorism into Perspective," *The Washington Quarterly* 26 (4) (Autumn 2003): 37–50. Copyright © 2003 by The Center for Strategic and International Studies and the Massachusetts Institute of Technology. The views expressed here are those of the author and do not represent the views of RAND, Corp. or its research sponsors.

Chapter 4: Originally published as "Invasive Threats to the American Homeland," *Parameters* (Spring 2004): 44–61. Copyright © 2004 U.S. Army War College.

Chapter 5: Originally published as "The Logic of Suicide Terrorism: Lessons from Israel That America Must Learn," *The Atlantic Monthly* (June 2003). Copyright © 2003 Bruce Hoffman.

Chapter 6: Originally published as "The Strategic Logic of Suicide Terrorism," *American Political Science Review* 97 (3) (August, 2003).

Chapter 7: An earlier version of this discussion was published as "Aviation Security: Promise or Reality," *Studies in Conflict and Terrorism* 27 (2004): 47–63. Copyright © 2004 Taylor & Francis, Inc. It has been revised and updated for this volume.

Chapter 8: Originally published as "Improving Public Surface Transportation Security: What Do We Do Now?" Arlington, VA: Lexington Institute, 2001.

Chapter 9: An earlier version of this discussion was published as "Border Security: Closing the Ingenuity Gap." Arlington, VA: Lexington Institute, 2003. It has been revised and updated for this volume.

Chapter 10: Originally published as "Cyber Threats: Ten Issues To Consider," *Georgetown Journal of International Affairs* 1 (1) (Winter/Spring 2000): 41-50

Chapter 11: Originally published as "Securing America's Critical Infrastructures: A Top Priority for the Department of Homeland Security," *Heritage Lectures* no. 787 (May

7, 2003). Washington, DC: The Heritage Foundation. Copyright © 2003, Kathryn and Shelby Cullom Davis Institute for International Studies.

Chapter 12: Originally published as "Seacurity: Improving The Security Of The Global Sea-Container Shipping System," RAND Europe. Copyright © 2003, RAND, Inc. It has been revised for this volume. RAND's publications do not necessarily reflect the opinions or policies of its research sponsors.

Chapter 13: Originally published as "Terrorism and Security Issues Facing the Water Infrastructure Sector: A CRS Report for Congress." Washington, DC: Resources, Science, and Industry Division of the Congressional Research Service, March 9, 2004. It has been revised and updated for this volume.

Chapter 14: Originally published as "Food Biosecurity: Food Supply and Bioterrorism," *Journal of the American Dietetic Association* (June 2003). Copyright © 2003, the American Dietetic Association.

Chapter 15: Originally published as "Managing Intergovernmental Response to Terrorism and Other Extreme Events," *Publius: The Journal of Federalism* 32 (4) (Fall 2002): 29-49.

Chapter 16: Originally authored for this volume.

Chapter 17: Originally authored for this volume.

Chapter 18: Originally published as "Catastrophic Terrorism: Local Response to a National Threat," *Journal of Homeland Security* (2002). www.homelandsecurity.org. Copyright © 2002, Frank Keating.

Chapter 19: Originally published as "Terrorism and the Battle for Homeland Security," Foreign Policy Research Institute, E-Notes, May 21, 2004, www.fpri.org. Copyright © 2001, Foreign Policy Research Institute, Philadelphia, PA.

Chapter 20: Originally authored for this volume.

Chapter 21: Originally published as "American Civil Security: The U.S. Public and Homeland Security," *The Washington Quarterly* 27(1) (Winter 2003-04): 37–52. Copyright © 2003 by The Center for Strategic and International Studies and the Massachusetts Institute of Technology.

Chapter 22: Originally authored for this volume.

Chapter 23: Originally authored for this volume.

Chapter 24: Originally published as "The USA PATRIOT Act: What's So Patriotic About Trampling on the Bill of Rights?" by the Center for Constitutional Rights (December, 2001), as an excerpt from Nancy Chang's book, *Silencing Political Dissent: How Post-September 11 Antiterrorism Measures Threaten Our Civil Liberties* (Seven Stories Press, 2002).

Chapter 25: Originally published as "Intelligence and the New Threat: The USA PATRIOT Act and Information Sharing Between the Intelligence and Law Enforcement Communities." White Paper on Anti-terrorism Legislation. Federalist Society for Law and Public Policy Studies (December, 2001).

Chapter 26: Originally published as "What Price Security? The USA PATRIOT Act and America's Balance Between Freedom and Security." In *The Homeland Security Papers: Stemming the Tide of Terror,* ed. M. W. Ritz, R. G. Hensley, and J. C. Whitmire. Maxwell Air Force Base, AL: USAF Counterproliferation Center, 2004.

Chapter 27: Originally published as "Preventing a Communications Blackout: The Need for Telecom Redundancy," *Progress on Point: Periodic Commentaries on the Policy*

Debate #10.24 (December, 2003). Washington, DC: The Progress and Freedom Foundation. It has been revised and updated for this volume. The views expressed here are those of the authors, and do not necessarily represent the views of the Foundation, its Board of Directors, officers or staff.

Chapter 28: Originally published as "Risk Communication, the West Nile Virus Epidemic, and Bio-terrorism: Responding to the Communication Challenges Posed by the Intentional or Unintentional Release of a Pathogen in an Urban Setting," *Journal of Urban Health. Bulletin of the New York Academy of Medicine* 78 (2) (June, 2001): 382-391.

Chapter 29: An earlier version of this discussion was published as "How Business can Defeat Terrorism: Global Financial Firms Battle the SARS outbreak in Hong Kong." In *Defeating Terrorism: Shaping the New Security Environment*, ed. R. Howard and R. Sawyer. New York: McGraw Hill, 2003. It has been revised and updated for this volume.

Chapter 30: Originally published as "Bioterrorism and the People: How to Vaccinate a City Against Panic," *Clinical Infectious Diseases* 34 (January 15, 2002): 217–23. Copyright © 2002 by the Infectious Diseases Society of America.

Contributors

Brigadier General Russell D. Howard (chapter 1) is a career Special Forces officer, is now a professor and department head at the United States Military Academy. His recent publications include *Terrorism and Counterterrorism: Understanding the New Security Environment: Readings and Interpretations* (2002), and *Defeating Terrorism: Shaping the New Security Environment* (2003), both published by McGraw-Hill.

Kate Marquis (chapter 2) is a counterterrorism analyst for the U.S. government and served as a fellow in residence at the Combating Terrorism Center at West Point.

John V. Parachini, Ph.D. (chapter 3) is a policy analyst at RAND in Virginia, and has directed a variety of projects on the propensity of terrorists to acquire chemical, biological, radiological, and nuclear weapons. The views expressed here are those of the author and do not represent the views of RAND or its research sponsors.

Colonel Robert J. Pratt (chapter 4) is a colonel in the Illinois Army National Guard, commanding the 66th Infantry Brigade and a graduate of the US Army Command and General Staff College and the US Army War College. In addition to his military service, he manages a 550-acre farm in central Illinois.

Bruce Hoffman, Ph.D. (chapter 5) is director of the RAND Corporation's Center for Middle East Public Policy. He is an internationally-recognized expert on terrorism, who has written extensively in both academic and popular journals and serves as Editor-in-Chief of *Studies in Conflict and Terrorism,* the leading scholarly journal in the field.

Robert A. Pape, Ph.D. (chapter 6) is Associate Professor in the Department of Political Science at the University of Chicago, specializing in international security affairs.

Joseph S. Szyliowicz, Ph.D. (chapter 7) is Professor in the Graduate School of International Studies at the University of Denver.

Brian Michael Jenkins (chapter 8) is senior advisor to the president of the RAND Corporation and one of the world's leading authorities on terrorism. A former Army captain who served with Special Forces in Vietnam, Jenkins has served on several national commissions and has provided testimony at numerous Congressional hearings on homeland security matters.

Frank G. Hoffman (chapter 9) is currently an employee of EDO Corporation and works as a research fellow at the Marine Corps Center for Emerging Threats and Opportunities. He previously served as a national security analyst on various commissions and on the Defense Science Board. He was a staff member on the U.S. National Security Commission (Hart-Rudman Commission).

Frank J. Cilluffo, Ph.D. (chapter 10) is deputy director of the Global Organized Crime Project at the Center for Strategic and International Studies (CSIS) in Washington, DC, where he directs task forces on transnational threats and organized crime. Co-author **Paul Byron Pattak** is president of the Byron Group, Ltd. in Alexandria, Virginia. He has served as a senior consultant to the President's Commission on Critical Infrastructure Protection (PCCIP).

Larry M. Wortzel, Ph.D. (chapter 11) is vice president and director of the Kathryn and Shelby Cullom Davis Institute for International Studies at The Heritage Foundation. His chapter is based on comments delivered at a conference, Infrastructure and Homeland Security: Public Policy Implications for Business, which was sponsored by the U.S. Chamber of Commerce on April 23, 2003.

Maarten van de Voort (chapter 12) and his co-authors **Kevin A. O'Brien, Adnan Rahman, and Lorenzo Valeri** are affiliated with RAND Europe's *General SeaCurity* initiative. RAND Europe is an independent, non-profit policy research organization working with European governments, institutions, and private sector entities on a variety of public policy and security issues.

Claudia Copeland (chapter 13) is a specialist in resources and environmental policy in the Resources, Science, and Industry Division of the Congressional Research Service (CRS). Her co-author **Betsy Cody** is a specialist in natural resources policy in the same division of CRS.

Barbara Bruemmer, Ph.D., RD (chapter 14) is a lecturer in the Department of Epidemiology, Nutritional Sciences Program at the University of Washington in Seattle.

Louise K. Comfort, Ph.D. (chapter 15) is a professor in the Graduate School of Public and International Affairs at the University of Pittsburgh.

John P. Sullivan (chapter 16) is a sergeant with the Los Angeles Sheriff's department. He is co-founder of the Los Angeles Terrorism Early Warning (TEW) group and coordinates many of its activities. He has a master of arts in Urban Affairs and Policy analysis from the New School for Social Research in New York and a bachelor of arts in Government from the College of William and Mary in Virginia.

Major Reid L. Sawyer (chapter 17) is a career military intelligence officer in the U.S. Army and executive director of the Combating Terrorism Center at the U.S. Military Academy. His recent publications include *Terrorism and Counterterrorism: Understanding the New Security Environment: Readings and Interpretations* (2002) and *Defeating Terrorism: Shaping the New Security Environment* (2003), both published by McGraw-Hill. His co-author Deputy Assistant Chief **Joseph Pfeifer** is currently the chief of planning and strategy at the New York City Fire Department and was the first chief to arrive at the World Trade Center on 9/11.

Frank Keating (chapter 18) is the former governor of Oklahoma. He is currently the president of the American Council of Life Insurers in Washington, DC. Following the terrorist attack in downtown Oklahoma City on April 19, 1995, Gov. Keating led his state's response, organizing rescue and recovery operations and ensuring that those affected by the bombing received prompt assistance. Gov. and Mrs. Keating were honored by the Salvation Army with the prestigious William Booth Award as recognition for their outstanding contributions to the recovery effort.

Seth G. Jones (chapter 19) is an associate political scientist at the RAND Corp. and adjunct professor at Georgetown University's Edmund A. Walsh School of Foreign Service. From 2002–2003 he was an analyst for the Gilmore Commission (formally called the Advisory Panel to Assess Domestic Response Capabilities for Terrorism Involving Weapons of Mass Destruction).

Major Chris Hornbarger (chapter 20) is a career aviation officer in the U.S. Army and instructor in the Department of Social Sciences at the U.S. Military Academy. He has previously served as director for policy and plans (and later director for military programs) in the Homeland Security Council at the White House.

Amanda J. Dory (chapter 21) works in the Homeland Defense Office within the Office of the Secretary of Defense. She was a 2002–2003 council on foreign relations international affairs fellow at CSIS when she wrote the article on which this chapter is based.

James S. Robbins, Ph.D. (chapter 22) is a professor of International Relations at the National Defense University in Washington, DC and senior fellow for National Security Affairs at the American Foreign Policy Council. He is also a contributing editor for *National Review Online*.

Major Beth Robbins (chapter 23) is currently a media relations officer assigned to Army Public Affairs, The Pentagon. Commissioned in the Corps of Engineers, she served in bridging, construction, and training units prior to earning a masters of public policy at Duke University. Returning to West Point, she served as an instructor and assistant professor of American Politics, Civil-Military Relations, and Mass Media.

Nancy Chang (chapter 24) is the senior litigation attorney at the Center for Constitutional Rights, a progressive non-profit legal and educational organization in New York City.

Brian H. Hook (chapter 25) is advisor to the International Law and American Sovereignty Project, Department of Justice, Office of Legal Policy. Co-author **Margaret J. A. Peterlin** is editor-in-chief of the *Chicago Journal of International Law,* and additional co-author **Peter L. Welsh** is a practicing attorney with the firm of Ropes and Gray in Boston, MA.

Roger Dean Golden, Ph.D. (chapter 26) is currently chief of the Matrixed Contract Support Division, HQ Standard Systems Group, Acquisitions Directorate, Maxwell Air Force Base.

Randolph J. May (chapter 27) is senior fellow and director of communications policy studies at The Progress and Freedom Foundation. The views expressed are his own and do not necessarily reflect those of the foundation, its officers, or board of directors.

Vincent T. Covello, Ph.D. (chapter 28) is director of the Center for Risk Communication, New York and an internationally recognized expert in communicating during high concern, sensitive, controversial, or emotionally charged situations. Co-author **Dr. Richard G. Peters** is a fellow with the center, where he provides strategic communication guidance and support for a wide range of clients, and has held academic positions at the Massachusetts Institute of Technology and William Paterson University. Co-author **Joseph G. Wojtecki** is a fellow with the center, and has over 30 years of experience in communications and public affairs, including the public and private sectors. Co-author **Richard C. Hyde** is a senior visiting fellow and also Executive Vice President of Hill & Knowlton, where he directs their U.S. crisis communication management team.

Kelly Hicks (chapter 29) is a retired Lieutenant Colonel from the U.S. Army and is now global head of crisis management, Goldman Sachs and Company.

Thomas A. Glass, Ph.D. (chapter 30) is a professor and physician at the Center on Aging and Health and the Department of Epidemiology, Johns Hopkins University and at the Bloomberg School of Public Health, Baltimore, Maryland. His co-author **Dr. Monica Schoch-Spana** is senior fellow with the Center for Biosecurity of the University of Pittsburgh Medical Center (UPMC) and an assistant professor in the University of Pittsburgh School of Medicine.

Editors

Brigadier General (Ret.) Russell D. Howard, a career special forces officer, is the former head of the Department of Social Sciences at the United States Military Academy. As a special forces officer, Colonel Howard served at every level of command, including: A Detachment Commander in the 7th Special Forces Group to Group B, Detachment Commander in the 1st Special Forces Group, Battalion Commander in the Special Warfare Center and School and Commander of the 1st Special Forces Group. In preparation for his academic position, Colonel Howard earned degrees from San Jose State University, the University of Maryland, the Monterey Institute of International Studies, and Harvard University. Presently, he is finishing a Ph.D. in international security studies at the Fletcher School of Law and Diplomacy. During the course of his career, Colonel Howard has had antiterror and counterterror responsibilities and has taught and published articles on terrorism subjects.

Dr. James J. F. Forest is the director of Terrorism Studies and assistant professor of Political Science at the U.S. Military Academy. His duties in the Combating Terrorism Center at West Point include developing counterterrorism education programs for junior officers and security personnel and teaching courses on terrorism and counterterrorism, international relations theory, comparative politics, African political development and information warfare/cyberterrorism. Dr. Forest has published several books and journal articles, addressing a broad range of issues related to organizational learning and knowledge transfer, technology, globalization, and strategic analysis. He holds degrees from De Anza College, Georgetown University, Stanford University, and Boston College.

Major Joanne C. Moore is a career Army officer currently stationed in Atlanta, Georgia. She recently served as an assistant professor of political science at West Point, teaching courses in American Politics and Homeland Security and directing the Combating Terrorism Center. As a military police officer, she has served in Korea, Haiti, Central America, Kosovo, Iraq, and the US. She holds a bachelor's degree from West Point in International Relations and a master's degree in Public Administration from Columbia University.

Foreword

As this book goes to press, four years have passed since September 11, 2001. In these intervening years it is easy to see that the attacks on the World Trade Center and the Pentagon fundamentally changed this nation. That day's terrorist attack changed the way Americans think about and involve themselves in national security issues. Americans simply view the world differently now. September 11 precipitated military operations in Afghanistan, Iraq, and elsewhere around the world; created new alliances; and strained long-standing international partnerships. The United States awoke to the growing threat posed by terrorist organizations with global reach, and to the probability of additional attacks on U.S. soil of a potential magnitude dwarfing the infernos of Pearl Harbor and 9/11 combined.

No longer an abstract concept about conflicts fought in far-away lands, national security now includes safeguarding our public spaces, our economic infrastructure, our transportation and information networks, and our public confidence. Because American infrastructure interconnects industry, public services, and private citizens, an attack on a single point causes ripple effects for all Americans. Our government's central role and focus must become the collective security of the American people at home.

Indeed, American government thinking is changing. *The National Security Strategy,* published in 2003, sets defense of the homeland as its foundation while applying other elements of national power to defeat terrorist organizations and their supporters abroad. While military operations and law enforcement actions in Afghanistan, Iraq, Pakistan and around the globe grab headlines by capturing or killing known terrorists, the remainder of the U.S. government quietly undergoes a reformation, the scope of which has not been seen since the aftermath of World War II and the National Security Act of 1947. The creation of the Department of Homeland Security (DHS) represents the largest federal government restructuring since the late 1940s, and Washington still struggles to adjust to the massive displacements involving the Executive and Legislative branches. The new department has accomplished much by improving airline passenger security, tightening standards for immigration and visa applications, incorporating disparate agencies into more rational organizations, and engaging other federal departments and organizations in the homeland security mission; however, a dysfunctional Congressional oversight structure which retains ancient committee power and prerogative—irrationally aligned with a new single department—greatly impedes full realization of its potential.

Organizational reform alone will not make America impervious to deadly terrorist attacks. Organizations are made up of people, and people will continue to create informal networks for dealing with one another. Even with sound organizational design, leaders must work to ensure that problems are addressed and decided at the proper level, and that accountability is ensured.

This new security environment cannot become the sole purview of the federal government. States, localities, private enterprise, civic organizations, and private persons all have important roles. As exemplified by the passengers and crew of Flight 93, terrorists will be defeated by attentive, informed citizens. Organizational reform and cooperation among a wide variety of groups and individuals will help set the homeland security foundation for the global war on terror. To that end, thousands of people—including civil servants, first responders, military officers, public health officials, local police and fire departments, academics, industry leaders, and concerned citizens—have taken on increased responsibility to improve our national capacity to defend against terrorist attack and respond appropriately when another attack occurs. The offerings included in this book highlight the achievements of the last several years, as well as the vulnerabilities that continue to require the combined attentions of government, public and private sectors, and concerned citizens.

This volume, the third in a series produced by the staff of the Combating Terrorism Center at West Point, provides the reader with a brief overview of the terrorist threat and then highlights both current and enduring issues surrounding homeland security. These pages illuminate controversies surrounding the federal government's creation of the Department of Homeland Security and the powers granted to government in the USA PATRIOT Act, as well as current issues regarding security of vulnerable infrastructure and lessons learned from recent experience. The volume includes both long-standing voices in the field of terrorism as well as newcomers. In no other volume to date will the ideas, experiences, and opinions of such a wide variety of talents be represented. In this respect, it is an extraordinarily important contribution to the national dialogue on terrorism and homeland security.

General Charles G. Boyd, USAF (Ret.)
President and CEO
Business Executives for National Security

Section I

The Threat

America is a target; the homeland is under threat. While Americans have been targets of terrorist attacks for quite some time, September 11, 2001, awoke the nation to the reality that we are vulnerable in our homes, in our places of work and worship, and in our means of public transportation. Understanding this new threat—its origins, forms, and potential capabilities—is vital before we can effectively develop and implement measures to secure the homeland.

Thus, we begin this volume with a chapter by Russ Howard, a U.S. Army retired brigadier general with extensive Special Forces experience. This chapter presents a framework for understanding the new model of terrorism. Howard's discussion highlights key factors that justify the nation's overarching concern for the threat posed by the al-Qaida terrorist network. These factors include the fact that al-Qaida has a global reach and strategic objectives, as demonstrated by its ability to successfully attack the United States homeland in 2001; that this enemy is a wealthy, multinational organization with several income streams and a strict adherence to its networked, cellular structure which, makes penetrating al-Qaida extremely difficult; and finally, and most worrisome, that al-Qaida is determined to acquire nuclear, radiological, chemical, and biological weapons of mass destruction. Howard argues that the nexus of these elements creates an enemy that is difficult to find, difficult to defeat, and very dangerous.

In thinking about this more dangerous world, it is important to understand how terrorism has changed so that we can move to a better understanding of how to address the problem in a comprehensive manner. Howard's framework is the starting point for such an analysis.

In the following chapter, intelligence analyst Kate Marquis examines terrorism since the attacks of 9/11, with particular attention to the events surrounding the attacks in Madrid in March 2004. She argues that al-Qaida and its extremist supporters view attacks such as those in Bali, Turkey, Madrid, and Iraq as equally important as the 9/11 attacks in their ongoing campaign. However, few national security strategists have recognized the relationships among these attacks, which she believes may demonstrate America's inability to fully contain the homeland security threat.

John Parachini follows with a balanced discussion on weapons of mass destruction. He notes that when it comes to these kinds of weapons, a nuanced, multidimensional approach is needed to address the complex and varied relationships between states and terrorist groups. While terrorist organizations may have significant difficulties acquiring unconventional weapons with catastrophic potential, weak or supportive states can help them alleviate these difficulties. The implications for U.S. counterterrorism policy are striking.

The next chapter in this section, by Colonel Robert J. Pratt, examines the unique and potentially disastrous threat to the homeland from a biological attack. He argues that the United States is not adequately prepared for such an attack and highlights a number of historical and hypothetical examples of how even the accidental introduction of an invasive biological species can have a devastating impact on life and commerce. Given the goals of terrorist organizations like al-Qaida, it is clear to see why they are attracted to the idea of a biological attack. Pratt argues for a set of policy recommendations and actions to better secure the homeland against this unconventional threat.

The threat of suicide bombers is front and center for individuals at all levels of government—from city police and fire departments to the Department of Homeland Security. Thus, the last two chapters in this section deal with the unique threat of suicide bombers. In recent years, the world has seen suicide bombers in Israel, Saudi Arabia, Indonesia, and Colombia, to name but a few countries. Most Americans find it particularly difficult to understand how any human being willfully strap explosives to their body in order to murder unarmed civilians. For help in understanding, this volume presents the perspectives of Bruce Hoffman, head of terrorist research at the RAND Corporation, and Robert Pape, a professor at the University of Chicago. In the first of these chapters, Hoffman provides rare insights into this very dangerous and potentially imminent threat to the United States.

Ultimately, "suicide terrorism is embraced as a psychological weapon designed to induce paralysis in one's opponent," explains Hoffman. Through an examination of Palestinian suicide bombers, Hoffman offers the reader insight into what other countries may be able to expect and the challenges faced in defending against such attacks.

In the following chapter, Robert Pape contributes to our understanding of suicide terrorism by exploring the strategic motivations of terrorists worldwide. He argues that while suicide terrorism is rising around the world, the most common explanations do not help us understand why. Religious fanaticism does not explain why the world leader in suicide terrorism is the Tamil Tigers in Sri Lanka, a group that adheres to a Marxist/Leninist ideology, Pape notes. He goes on to point out that while existing psychological explanations have been contradicted by the widening range of socioeconomic backgrounds of suicide terrorists.

To advance our understanding of this growing phenomenon, Pape analyzes 188 suicide terrorist attacks worldwide from 1980 to 2001 and finds that suicide terrorism follows a strategic logic, one specifically designed to coerce modern liberal democracies into making significant territorial concessions. Pope concludes that, over the past two decades, suicide terrorism has been on the rise largely because terrorists have learned that it pays. Suicide terrorists sought to compel American and French military forces to abandon Lebanon in 1983, Israeli forces to leave Lebanon in 1985, Israeli forces to quit the Gaza Strip and the West Bank in 1994 and 1995, the Sri Lankan government to create an independent Tamil state from 1990 on, and the Turkish government to grant autonomy to the Kurds in the late 1990s. In all but the case of Turkey, the terrorists' political cause made more gains after the resort to suicide operations than it had before. Therefore, Pape argues, Western democracies should pursue policies that teach terrorists that the lesson of the 1980s and 1990s no longer holds. These policies may have more to do with improving homeland security than with offensive military action.

Terrorist organizations could expand their powers of destruction through a host of methods. Together, these chapters highlight the clear and present danger to America posed by terrorist organizations. The challenges and questions raised by these essays frame the importance of the remaining sections in this volume. The threat we face is not insurmountable, but we must work to counter the rapid change of techniques and procedures used by the terrorists. Clearly, we must develop better tools for understanding and managing the threat if we are to have any hope of securing the homeland.

Chapter 1

Homeland Security and the New Terrorism

Russ Howard[1]

Bruce Hoffman, head of terrorism research at the RAND Corporation and arguably one of the world's leading experts, put it this way: "I don't mean to sound perverse, but there is maybe a certain nostalgia for the old style of terrorism, where there wasn't the threat of loss of life on a massive scale . . . It's a real commentary on how much the world has changed."[2]

In much the same way that many cold warriors miss the predictability and transparency of the U.S.-Soviet confrontation, many intelligence professionals, military operators, pundits, and academics miss the familiar type of terrorism that, although quite dangerous, in the end was merely a nasty sideshow to the greater East-West conflict.[3] Much of this Cold War terrorism was inspired by Marxist-Leninist ideology; its perpetrators sought to draw attention to their cause and to gain political concessions. They were motivated by secular rather than apocalyptic ends and were quick to claim responsibility for their attacks.[4] The commando-style terrorism waged by the likes of Andreas Baader and Ulrike Meinhof of the German extreme left Rote Armee Faction or by Abu Nidal of the Fatah National Council (who was killed in Baghdad in 2002), was ruthless. But it was not nearly as deadly as the threat the world faces today.[5] Now the old, predominantly state-sponsored terrorism has been supplanted by a religiously and ethnically motivated terrorism that "neither relies on the support of sovereign states nor is constrained by the limits on violence that state sponsors observed themselves or placed on their proxies."[6]

This new terrorism has a much greater potential to cause harm to America, the West, and all secular countries, including those in the Muslim world. Led by al-Qaida and Usama bin Ladin, the new terrorism "is built around loosely linked cells that do not rely on a single leader or state sponsor." It is transnational, borderless, and prosecuted by nonstate actors, and it is very, very dangerous.[7]

The old and new styles of terrorism are distinguishable in seven different ways:

1.   The September 11, 2001, attacks effectively shattered the illusion of an invulnerable U.S. homeland, protected by two oceans and bordered by friendly or weak neighbors. In the past, the nation was not vulnerable to terrorists except for the homegrown, mainly right-wing variety such as the Oklahoma City bomber. Now, the American homeland is very much at risk.

"When, not if," is how many terrorism experts regard the likelihood of another 9/11-type attack.

2. The new terrorism is more violent. Under the old paradigm, terrorists wanted attention, not mass casualties. Now they want both.

3. Unlike their Cold War counterparts, who were usually small, local groups trying to effect change in local politics, today's terrorists are transnational, non-state actors who operate globally and want to destroy the West and all Islamic secular states.

4. The new terrorists are much better financed than their predecessors, who relied mainly on crime or the largesse of state sponsors. Today's terrorists have income streams from legal and illegal sources and are not accountable to state sponsors—or anybody else.

5. Today's terrorists are better trained than those in past decades. We know this from the materials captured in al-Qaida's training camps in Afghanistan and from the training materials of other Muslim extremist groups found in Europe and Central Asia.

6. This generation's terrorist groups are more difficult to penetrate than those of previous generations. The networked, cellular structure used by al-Qaida and its allies is especially difficult to penetrate for a hierarchical security apparatus like that of the United States. Bribes and sex traps could catch terrorists for prosecution and information in the old days; it is difficult to "turn" religious extremists with these methods. The $50-million reward on bin Ladin has yet to be collected, and it is unclear how successful other methods have been in getting bin Ladin's followers to talk.

7. In the 1980s we were concerned about small arms, explosives (particularly plastique), rocket propelled grenades, and the occasional shoulder-fired anti-aircraft missile. Today, the availability of weapons of mass destruction (WMD) means we must be concerned about nuclear, radiological, chemical, and biological weapons—all with catastrophic, massive killing potential.

This chapter discusses these seven distinguishing characteristics of the new terrorism and argues that they must be understood and addressed if the United States hopes to win the war. Usama bin Ladin's al-Qaida is the case study because his ideology, organization, surrogates, and followers epitomize the new terrorism and are the number-one threat to America's security.

America at Risk

September 11 shattered the illusion that Americans are safe from troubles originating beyond our shores, which traditionally have been protected by geography and by weak or friendly neighbors. The attacks forced American citizens and policymakers to accept new security needs to learn how to fight a new kind of war.

Some have compared September 11, 2001, to December 7, 1941, the only other occasion since the War of 1812 that American territory has been attacked.[8] There are many similarities. Both were surprise attacks. Boths were predictable and possibly avoidable, were extraordinarily costly in life and national treasure, and were defining points in

American history. However, as David Halberstam notes in *War in a Time of Peace*, there are also many differences.

According to Halberstam, the historical demarcation point that the United States crossed on September 11 is even greater than the one it crossed with the bombing of Pearl Harbor.[9] The post–Pearl Harbor war was easily understood. The enemy was a state and warfare was traditional, definable, and susceptible to American's industrial and technological advantages. Today's enemy is not a state but a transnational, nonstate actor. Its method of warfare is not traditional: it is elusive, operates in the shadows, often at a great distance, sometimes right among us with secret cells and aliases, and it exploits America's industrial and technological advantages.[10]

Different, too, seems the resolve of the American people to wage war. Throughout our history, Americans have traditionally displayed an extraordinary degree of resourcefulness and self-sacrifice in times of war.[11] The best example of that tradition is World War II, when the war effort became an immediate extension of America's national will and purpose.[12] Today, says national security expert Stephen Flynn, "we are breaking with that tradition. Our nation faces grave peril, but we seem unwilling to mobilize at home to confront the threat before us."[13] Why are the American people unwilling to rally the troops? Two reasons come to mind. First, they understand conventional war but not the war on terror. Second, they fail to realize the security implications of globalization and information technology.

The war on terror is not like engaging an enemy that is massed on a foreign battlefield. Destroying or confiscating the enemy's battlefield capabilities and dispersing its troops will not ensure victory.[14] Today, as Halberstam explains, "the more visible the enemy is, the further he is from the magnetic field of our intelligence operations and any potential military strike."[15]

> It is not that America, as it enters a very different kind of battle, lacks weaponry; it is that the particular kind of weaponry we specialize in lacks targets. This will be a difficult military-intelligence-security challenge: What we do best, they are not vulnerable to. What we do least well, they are vulnerable to. What they do best, we are—to a considerable degree—vulnerable to.[16]

Combating terrorism, particularly the al-Qaida variety, is as much about fighting an international idea as an organized military force maneuvering within defined geographical boundaries. Managing the danger that al-Qaida, its followers and its surrogates pose cannot be achieved by relying primarily on military campaigns overseas. As Stephen Flynn observes, "there are no fronts in the war on terrorism."[17]

> The 9/11 attacks highlighted the fact that our borders offer no effective barrier to terrorists intent on bringing their war to our soil. Nor do their weapons have to be imported, since they have proven how easy it is to exploit the modern systems we rely upon in our daily lives and use them against us.[18]

These modern systems are the sophisticated networks that move people, goods, energy, money, and information at increasingly higher volumes and greater velocities each year[19]—the very systems that ensure America's competitive edge in the age of globalization. For years, our growing dependence on these networks has not been matched by a parallel focus on securing them.[20]

> The architects of these networks have made efficiency and diminishing costs their highest priority. Security considerations have been widely perceived as annoying speed bumps in achieving their goals. As a result, the systems that underpin our prosperity are soft targets for those bent on challenging U.S. power.[21]

The attacks on the World Trade Center and Pentagon ended a unique historical span for the United States as a great power. For nearly a century, America has been a major player in the world. Until 9/11, however, the homeland had escaped the ravages of modern warfare and weaponry because of its unique geographical position and unparalleled industrial technological base. When confronted with threats, the United States dealt with them on our adversaries' or allies' turf. Except for the occasional disaster and heinous crime, life in America had been terror-free. It has taken a group of rebels without a country—a ghost nation as it were—to become a threat to America and our way of life.[22]

More Violent

In the past, "terrorists wanted a lot of people watching, not a lot of people dead."[23] As terrorism expert Rohan Gunaratna has observed, "Unlike the terrorists of the 1960s to the 1990s, who generally avoided high-casualty attacks for fear of the negative publicity they would generate, al-Qaida is not in the least concerned by such matters."[24] Terrorists in past decades did not want large body counts because they wanted converts; they also wanted a seat at the table. Today's terrorists are not particularly concerned about converts, and rather than wanting a seat at the table, "they want to destroy the table and everyone sitting at it."[25] In fact, religious terrorists, al-Qaida in particular, want casualties—lots of them.[26]

In the past, civilians most often became victims of terrorist operations either because they were captives of hostage-taking events or because they happened to be in the wrong place at the wrong time. Terrorists took hostages for three reasons: attention for their cause, the release of imprisoned comrades, or ransom (profit). The odds were—96 percent of the time in the 1980s—that hostages would survive the event. Victims of terrorist operations were generally casualties because they happened to be in the proximity of an explosion, ambush, or bank robbery. However, the motive was to get attention or money, not cause the deaths of civilians. Today, however, mass casualties are a primary aspect of bin Ladin's strategy:

> By causing mass casualties on a regular basis [bin Laden] could hope to persuade the Americans to keep clear of overseas conflicts. There was also a retributive element to the strategy . . . the militants of al-Qaeda and like-minded groups clearly wanted to punish the Americans for a whole range of policies, particularly for those it pursued in the Middle East, as well as for what they saw as its irreligious decadence.[27]

Despite successes against al-Qaida by coalition military forces in Afghanistan and police agencies around the world, some predict that the "frequency and reach of al-Qaida's attacks will continue to increase, even though their lethality may decrease slightly."[28]

Truly Global: Conducted by Transnational, Nonstate Actors

In the 1970s and 1980s, terrorism was mostly local. The terrorists were small, local groups intent on overturning a state's political and/or economic system. Today, there has been a shift from localized terrorist groups, supported by state sponsors, to loosely organized, global networks. This parallels a change from primarily politically motivated terrorism to one that is, to a large degree, religiously motivated.[29]

Al-Qaida's global network consists of permanent or independently operating semi-permanent cells of trained militants that have been established in more than 76 countries.[30] In fact, since September 11, more than 3,300 al-Qaida operatives, hailing from 47 countries, have been arrested in 97 countries.[31]

There is also growing evidence that al-Qaida is now subcontracting work to like-minded terrorists. According to renowned terrorism expert Jessica Stern:

> Bin Laden's organization has also nurtured ties with and works closely with a variety of other groups around the world, including: Ansar al Islam, based mainly in Iraq and Europe, Jemaah Islamiah in Southeast Asia, Abu Sayyaf and the Moro Islamic Liberation Front in the Philippines, and many Pakistani jihadi groups.[32]

These affiliated or like-minded groups have the capacity to carry out attacks and inflict pain on the United States under al-Qaida's banner, says Bruce Hoffman. In fact, new revelations about the emerging al-Qaida network—the depth of its ranks and its ties to "franchise" terrorists in up to 70 countries—shows that the intent to attack America, the West, and secular states around the world has not gone away.[33] According to some, successes against al-Qaida in Afghanistan and elsewhere may have made defeating the organization more difficult. Once al-Qaida lost its sanctuary in Afghanistan, Jason Burke believes, "there is no longer a central hub for Islamic militancy."[34] Instead, the al-Qaida worldview, or "al-Qaidaism," is what sustains acts of terrorism against the West and the United States.[35]

> This radical internationalist ideology—sustained by anti-Western, anti-Zionist, and anti-Semitic rhetoric—has adherents among many individuals and groups, few of whom are currently linked in any substantial way to bin Laden or those around him. They merely follow his precepts, models, and methods. They act in the style of al Qaeda, but they are only part of al Qaeda in the very loosest sense.[36]

Perhaps most troubling is recent evidence that al-Qaida—a Sunni organization—is now cooperating with Hizballah, a Shiite group considered by many to be the most sophisticated terrorist organization in the world.[37] As Jessica Stern notes, "Hizballah, which enjoys backing from Syria and Iran, is based in southern Lebanon and in the lawless 'tri-border' region of South America, where Paraguay, Brazil, and Argentina meet."[38]

Al-Qaida's targeting is global, which is also different from the local, tactical focus of earlier terrorist groups. Now, not only are targets selected to cause casualties without limit, they are selected to undermine the global economy. As Stern observes, "they might be called strategic acts of destruction, rather than the tactical terrorist acts of the past."[39] According to Air Marshall Sir Timothy Garden, "it may have been possible for the international community to live with occasional acts of local terrorism around the world; it is much more difficult to live with non-state actors who have a mission to destroy a large part of the global system."[40]

In summary, we have seen the emergence of a new breed of terrorism that is not ideological in a political sense but is inspired by religious extremists working in cells, small groups, and larger coalitions.[41] They do not answer completely to any government; they operate across national borders; and they have access to funding and advanced technology.[42] Such groups are not bound by the same constraints or motivated by the same goals as nation-states. And unlike state-sponsored groups, religious extremists such as al-Qaida are not susceptible to traditional diplomacy or military deterrence. There is no state with which to negotiate or against which to retaliate.

Well-Financed

Al-Qaida learned from some of the failings of previous terrorist groups, such as the Baader Meinhof gang, the Red Brigades, and the Abu Nidal group, all of which were perennially undercapitalized. According to Bruce Hoffman, al-Qaida under bin Ladin saw the need to be much more flexible and to maintain a steady supply of money, which is crucial to lubricate the wheels of terrorism.[43]

Estimates of bin Ladin's personal wealth range from $18 million to as high as $200 million, but "it is most commonly agreed that bin Ladin inherited approximately $57 million at age 16."[44] Bin Ladin has been able to leverage his millions into a global financial empire by investing in legitimate businesses, taking advantage of the globalized financial system, abusing the Islamic banking (*hawala*) system, and coercing an entire network of Islamic philanthropic and charitable institutions. The total net worth of the al-Qaida financial empire is unclear—likely in the hundreds of millions of dollars.

Between September 11, 2001, and October 2002, more than 165 countries enacted blocking actions against terrorist assets, and approximately $112 million of these assets have been frozen worldwide ($34 million in the United States and $78 million overseas).[45] Nevertheless, these successes have not forced al-Qaida to cease operations, which is indicative of its deep, well-lined pockets.

Usama bin Ladin's entrepreneurial skills are legendary. During his five-year stint in Sudan, he cornered the market on gum Arabic, the basic ingredient in fruit juices produced in the United States.[46] According to terrorism scholar Robin Wright, bin Ladin also "started an Islamic Bank, built a tannery, created an export company, launched construction projects, and developed agricultural schemes."[47] Other business ventures included a trading company in Kenya and a ceramic plant, a publishing outlet, and a appliance firm in Yemen.[48]

Al-Qaida's misuse of the *hawala* underground banking system, which allows money transfers without actual money movement, is particularly instructive. Seemingly custom-made for al-Qaida, the *hawala* is an ancient system that originated in South Asia and is still used worldwide to conduct legitimate business as well as for money laundering. The components of *hawala* that distinguish it from other parallel remittance systems are trust and the extensive use of connections, such as family relationships or regional affiliations. Unlike traditional banking, *hawala* makes minimal use of any sort of negotiable instruments or documentation. Transfers of money take place based on communications between members of a network of *hawaladars*, or *hawala* dealers.[49] A recent Council on Foreign Relations study illustrates how the *hawala* system works:

> Customers in one city hand their local *hawaladar* some money. That individual then contacts his counterpart across the world, who in turn distributes money out of his own resources to the intended recipient. The volume of transactions flowing through the system in both directions is such that the two *hawaladars* rarely have to worry about settlement.[50]

Hawaladars charge their customers a nominal cash transaction fee for the service. They are willing to carry each other's debts for long periods of time because they are often related through familial, clan, or ethnic associations.[51]

Other methods of moving funds include cash smuggling and moving assets in the form of precious metals and gemstones. The gold trade and the *hawala* are especially symbiotic, as they flourish in the same locales and offer complementary services to those moving assets across borders. Al-Qaida operatives also use traditional smuggling routes and methods favored by international drug traffickers, arms dealers, and other organized criminal groups.[52]

Charities and philanthropic organizations have also been sources of al-Qaida funding. A recent investigation by the *New York Times* revealed that "since December 2001, the assets of more than a dozen Islamic charities worldwide have been frozen, three of them based in the United States."[53] For example, U.S. authorities have designated the U.S.-based Benevolence International Foundation (BIF) a terrorist financier with links to the al-Qaida network, and its assets have been frozen in the United States, Canada, and Bosnia. The bin Ladin network is not the only terrorist element skimming funds from U.S.-based charities.[54] In fact, the U.S. Treasury Department found overwhelming evidence that the Holy Land Foundation for Relief and Development, the self-proclaimed largest Muslim charity in the United States, was an arm of HAMAS, a radical Islamic organization that operates in the West Bank and Gaza strip.[55]

Well-Trained

Formalized terrorist training during the Cold War was generally conducted by the states sponsoring terrorist groups. It is known, for instance, that the former Soviet Union ran terrorism training camps at Simferpol in the Crimea, Ostrova in Czechoslovakia, and Pankow in East Germany. Captured PLO terrorist Adnan Jaber has given a comprehensive account of his Soviet training:

> He did a six-month course there, during which Russian military and civilian instructors covered propaganda methods, political affairs, tactics and weapons. Other such courses dealt with advanced explosives work, bomb-making, and training in biological and chemical warfare.[56]

However, it would be incorrect to assume that most terrorists during the Cold War years went through such formal training. Many went into action without such instruction and simply learned by doing.[57]

This is not at all the case today. In fact, graduating from training camp is the common denominator and a rite of passage for al-Qaida operatives and their allies. The camps have trained both formal al-Qaida members and members of allied Islamist organizations.[58]

Al-Qaida manuals and records captured in Afghanistan training camps portray a comprehensive program that emphasizes paramilitary training, Islamic studies, and current politics. All members of al-Qaida and its associated groups are required to have the following personality traits and qualifications, before becoming an Islamist military operative:

> Knowledge of Islam, ideological commitment, maturity, self-sacrifice, discipline, secrecy and concealment of information, good health, patience, unflappability, intelligence and insight, caution and prudence, truthfulness wisdom, and the ability to observe and analyze, and the ability to act.[59]

Aspiring operatives are also taught forgery, assassination techniques, and the conducting of maritime or vehicle suicide attacks.[60]

An al-Qaida manual, *Military Studies in the Jihad Against the Tyrants*, which was seized in Manchester, England, at the home of a bin Ladin follower, is a condensed version of the thousands of pages of al-Qaida training materials seized in Afghanistan. An English translation of the 180-page Arabic document was placed into evidence during the recent Kenya and Tanzania bombing trials in New York City. The manual is extraordinarily comprehensive and instructs terrorist operatives on an array of terrorist techniques, including jihad (Holy War), military organization, financial precautions and forged documents, security measures in public transportation, special operations and weapons, guidelines for beating and killing hostages, how to assassinate with poisons, spoiled food and feces, and methods of physical and psychological torture.[61]

Al-Qaida's training is eclectic and comprehensive; its tacticians and trainers have taken much from the special operations forces of several nations, including the United States, United Kingdom, and Russia. Indeed, al-Qaida fighters are as well or better trained than those of many national armies (as was the case in Afghanistan). What is more startling is its intelligence and "black operations" acumen. "Unlike the rag-tag terrorist groups of the Cold War period," says Rohan Gunaratna, "sophisticated terrorist groups of the post-Cold Ward period, such as al-Qaida, have developed intelligence wings comparable to government intelligence agencies."[62]

Difficult to Penetrate

Another difference between old and new terrorism is that the latter has adopted a networked and less hierarchical form. British terrorism expert Michael Whine has noted that "both the anti-capitalist and national liberation terrorist groups of the 1970s and 1980s mostly had hierarchical forms and chains of command."[63] In response to improvements in counterterror capabilities and increased cooperation among governments, groups like al-Qaida have adopted networked structural models instead of hierarchical structures. Rapid advances in digital communication have also increased the viability of these networks, although they are not totally dependent on the latest information technology. As noted in a recent report distributed to members of the U.S. military, information technology has made networks more effective, but low-tech means, such as couriers and landline telephones, can enable networks in certain circumstances.[64]

Network structures will obviously be more likely to achieve long-term effectiveness if their members share a unifying ideology, common goals, or mutual interests, as is the case with al-Qaida.[66] Networks are most effective when they distribute the responsibility for operations and provide redundancies for key functions. In their groundbreaking discussion of the so-called netwar concept, John Arquilla and David Ronfeldt note that "operating cells need not contact or coordinate with other cells except for those essential to a particular operation or function."[67] Avoiding unnecessary coordination or approval provides deniability to terrorist leaders and enhances the security of terrorist operations.

Strict adherence to a flat, diffused, cellular, networked structure has allowed al-Qaida to maintain a high degree of secrecy and security. Research on terrorism indicates that these cells are independent of other local groups that al-Qaida may be aligned with and range in size from 2 to 15 members.[65] Using code, targets are announced in the general media and individuals or independent cells are expected to use initiative, stealth, and flexibility to destroy them.

Though weakened by the disruption of its finances and communications, its base destroyed, and its leaders in flight, al-Qaida is still dangerous and very difficult to penetrate.[68] Although its membership may share a common militant Islamic ideology, the organization has become a loose and "ever-shifting alliance of like-minded groups."[69] Instead of large, well orchestrated attacks like those of September 11, al-Qaida operations are now smaller and less ambitious. The organization remains extremely dangerous, however, and its "killer cells" seem to be growing and spawning imitations around the world.[70]

Access to Weapons of Mass Destruction

The seventh way the new terrorists differ from old is the most worrisome: they are determined to obtain and use nuclear, radiological, chemical, and biological weapons of mass destruction (WMD). With a single act, terrorists using a weapon of mass destruction can cause the deaths of thousands, even millions of people.[71] Acquiring WMD has been made easier by Information-Age technologies and the availability of suppliers.[72] Recent discoveries in Afghanistan have confirmed that al-Qaida and other terrorist groups are actively pursuing biological agents for use against the United States and its allies.[73] According to United Nations weapons inspector David Kaye, this should not be a surprise:

> Only a blind, deaf and dumb terrorist group could have survived the last five years and not been exposed at least to the possibility of the use of WMD, while the more discerning terrorists would have found some tactically brilliant possibilities already laid out on the public record.[74]

"We must be prepared for new types of attacks; anything could happen," says Koichi Oizumi, an international relations professor at Nihon University in Tokyo, the city where the Aum Shinrikio used saran nerve gas to kill 12 and injure 250 in the first major use of a chemical agent in a terrorist attack.[75]

Steven Miller, director of the International Security Program at Harvard's Kennedy School, says that policy makers should be particularly concerned about terrorist access to nuclear weapons He notes specifically that "opportunities for well-organized and well-financed terrorists to infiltrate a Russian nuclear storage facility are greater than ever."[76] Miller believes that there have been more than two dozen thefts of weapons-grade materials in the former Soviet Union in recent years. Although "several suspects have been arrested in undercover sting operations," he wonders about those who may have gotten away.[77] These thefts go back to at least 1994, "when 350 grams of plutonium were smuggled on board a Lufthansa flight from Moscow to Munich. Fortunately, SWAT teams confiscated the material as soon as it arrived."[78]

In the past, any state that allowed a terrorist group it sponsored to use WMD against the United States knew it would be committing suicide, and the fear of nuclear retaliation was ample motivation for sponsors to keep the lid on. Today, any terrorist group with a known base of operations, even if it does not have a state sponsor, would similarly risk annihilation for waging a WMD terrorist attack. But al-Qaida, has no state sponsor and is a loosely organized global network, which makes retaliation much more problematic.

Conclusion

To recap, seven key factors differentiate the al-Qaida terrorist network from the terrorist organizations of more recent generations. First, al-Qaida attacked the United States homeland, seriously undermining American's sense of security and well-being. The attack raised serious questions about the ability of the United States to respond to radically different threats and to meet "the paramount responsibility of any government—assuring the security of all persons, citizens or not, who legally reside within its sovereign territory."[79] Second, terrorism today is more violent. It has been responsible for the most lethal terrorist attack in history and has achieved the highest death-rate per attack ever.[80]

Third, while earlier terrorist organizations had local aspirations, al-Qaida has global reach and strategic objectives. Its operators are transnational, nonstate actors whose allegiance is to a cause, not a state. This is problematic because the traditional forms of state interaction—diplomatic, economic, and military—to solve differences prior to conflict are difficult to apply in a nonstate actor context. When things get testy, with whom do you negotiate, who do you sanction, and who do you threaten with force? And if a transnational, nonstate actor like bin Ladin uses a weapon of mass destruction against you, who do you nuke?

Fourth, al-Qaida is a wealthy, multinational organization with several income streams. It has investments and concealed accounts around the world, many in the Western societies bin Ladin most despises.[81] He and his followers will use their wealth to continue to leverage (coerce) governments for access and safe haven, just as they have done in the Sudan and Afghanistan. They will also pay to subcontract and franchise the services of like-minded terrorist organizations, all for the purpose of killing Americans.

Fifth, as Rohan Gunaratna says, al-Qaida is not a ragtag outfit. Al-Qaida operatives are well trained in military, special operations, and intelligence functions. Notwithstanding the coalition's victory in Afghanistan, the allies learned what made the al-Qaida global terrorist network a daunting foe—in the words of global reporter Ann Tyson, "a relatively sophisticated, well-trained, and well-financed organization that drew on ongoing grass-roots support and a fanatical willingness to fight to the death."[82]

Sixth, strict adherence to its networked, cellular structure makes penetrating al-Qaida extremely difficult. Composed of many cells whose members do not know one another, never assemble in one place together, and use strict communication discipline, al-Qaida is more than a match for Western intelligence agencies that rely mainly on technical means of intelligence collection.[83] "America's new enemies," notes columnist Glenn Sacks, "can't be bought, bribed, or even blackmailed."[84] They want to kill Americans and will do so at any cost.

Seventh, and most worrisome, is al-Qaida's determination to acquire nuclear, radiological, chemical, and biological weapons of mass destruction. The potential for acquiring these weapons is greater because of globalization, information technology, and the availability of shady suppliers. Indeed, the new terrorism has a global reach today that it did not have before the information revolution and globalization. It can ride the back of the Web, using advanced communications to move immense financial flows from Sudan to the Philippines or from Australia to banks in Florida.[85] And any Internet surfer can find information resources for growing deadly bacteria. Shady suppliers come from many countries, particularly Russia, which cannot offer employment to many ex-Soviet scientists and weaponeers. In fact, there are many reports of plutonium for sale across Eastern Europe and of Russian scientists who once worked in Soviet labs linked to germ warfare selling their services in the Middle East for hefty fees.[86]

As envisioned by al-Qaida, the "perfect new warfare" would entail multiple attacks against America, each designed to produce the greatest number of casualties. For maximum effect, these attacks would take place almost simultaneously and at several locations, much like the attacks of September 11 in New York City, Washington DC, and a field in Pennsylvania.[87]

One might say that America's war against the new terrorism is far colder than the Cold War ever was—"cold" as in the "cold-blooded murder" of September 11. At least with the Soviets, we always knew who was in charge and that we couldn't be attacked without his orders. In fact, the U.S. president had a direct line to Soviet leaders and could work through difficult moments with them personally. By contrast, on September 11, 2001, we lost thousands of people; we know bin Ladin ordered the killing but have no direct line to him or anyone else in his leadership. We also know that he and his followers will continue to hit the United States, its allies, and secular Islamic states again and again until he and his network are stopped.

It has been said that generals always make the mistake of preparing for the last war instead of the next one. This chapter has emphasized changes in the terrorist threat from the Cold War of decades ago so that today's generals and their civilian masters can understand how to fight and win the current war, and in the hope that having won it, we will never have to fight a war like this again.

Notes

1. The views expressed herein are those of the author and do not purport to reflect the position of the United States Military Academy, the Department of the Army, or the Department of Defense.

2. "Terror Cells of Today Hard to Combat," *New York Times,* August, 20, 2002, www.nytimes.com/aponline/international/AP-Evolution-of-Terror.html.

3. John Mearsheimer, "Why We Will Soon Miss the Cold War," *Atlantic Monthly*, August 1990. See also, Glenn Sacks, "Why I Miss the Cold War," October 2, 2001, www.glennsacks.com.
4. Brian H. Hook, p. 3.
5. Brian Murphy, "The Shape of Terrorism Changes," *Fayetteville Observer*, August 21, 2002.
6. Steven Simon and Daniel Benjamin, "America and the New Terrorism," *Survival*, 42 no. 1 (Spring 2000): 69.
7. Ibid.
8. Some in the Southwest may include Pancho Villa's excursion into New Mexico as an attack.
9. David Halberstam, *War in Time of Peace* (New York, Simon and Schuster: 2001), p. 498.
10. Ibid., p. 496–497.
11. Stephen Flynn, *America the Vulnerable* (New York, Harper Collins: 2004), p. x.
12. Halberstam, *War in Time of Peace*, p. 496
13. Flynn, *America the Vulnerable*, p. x.
14. Brian H. Hook, Margaret J. A. Peterlin, Peter L. Welsh, "Intelligence and the New Threat: The USA PATRIOT Act and Information Sharing Between the Intelligence and Law Enforcement Communities." See *Federalist Society for Law and Public Policy Studies*, December 2001., p. 3. Chapter 25 in this volume.
15. Halberstam, *War in Time of Peace*, p. 497.
16. Ibid.
17. Flynn, *America the Vulnerable*, p. x.
18. Ibid.
19. Ibid., p. 5.
20. Ibid.
21. Ibid., p. 5
22. Halberstam, *War in Time of Peace*, p. 498.
23. Quote attributed to Brian Jenkins in 1974. See Jessica Stern, "Loose Nukes, Poisons, and Terrorism: The New Threats to International Security," June 19, 1996.
24. Rohan Gunaratna, *Inside Al Qaeda—Global Network of Terror* (New York: Columbia University Press), p. 91.
25. Quote attributed to James Woolsey, 1994.
26. Bruce Hoffman, *Inside Terrorism* (New York: Columbia University Press, 1998), p. 205.
27. Lawrence Freeman, "Out of Nowhere—Bin Laden's Grievances," BBC Online, www.bbc.co.uk/history/war/sept_11/build_up_05.shtml.
28. Bruce Newsome, "Executive Summary," *Mass-Casualty Terrorism: Second Quarterly Forecast by the University of Reading Terrorism Forecasting Group* (University of Reading, June 13, 2003), p. 3, www.rdg.ac.uk/GSEIS/University_of_Reading_Terrorism_Forecast_2003Q2.pdf.
29. Michael Whine, "The New Terrorism,"www.ict.org.il/articles/articledet.cfm?articleid=427.
30. Jerrold M. Post, "Killing in the Name of God: Osama Bin Laden and Al Qaeda," in *Know Thy Enemy: Profiles of Adversary Leaders and Their Strategic Cultures*, ed.

Barry R. Schneider and Jerrold M. Post (Maxwell Air Force Base: USAF Counterproliferation Center), p. 33.

31. Conversation with Dr. Rohan Gunaratna, November 15, 2002, Garmisch, Germany.

32. Jessica Stern, "The Protean Enemy," *Foreign Affairs*, July-August 2003, p. 33.

33. See Ann Tyson, "Al Qaeda Broken, but Dangerous," *Christian Science Monitor*, June 24, 2002, www.csmonitor.com/2002/0624/p01s02-usgn.htm.

34. Jason Burke, "Al Qaeda," *Foreign Policy*, May/June 2004, p. 18.

35. Ibid.

36. Ibid.

37. Jessica Stern, "The Protean Enemy (Al Qaeda)," p. 31.

38. Ibid., p. 32.

39. Ibid.

40. Timothy Garden's weblog, "Security and the War Against Terrorism," *Foreign and Security Policy,* www.tgarden.demon.co.uk/writings/articles/2002/020320riia.html.

41. Stephen A. Cambone, *A New Structure for National Security Policy Planning,* (Washington, DC: GPO, 1996), p. 43.

42. Gideon Rose, "It Could Happen Here—Facing the New Terrorism," *Foreign Affairs*, March-April, 1999, p. 1.

43. Discussion with Bruce Hoffman.

44. Multiple conversations with John Dorschner. See also John Dorschner, "A Shadowy Empire of Hate was Born of a War in Afghanistan," *Knight Ridder Newspapers,* September 24, 2001.

45. Center for Defense Information, *CDI Primer: Terrorist Finances,* October 25, 2002, www.cdi.org/terrorism/finance_primer-pr.cfm.

46. Robin Wright, *Sacred Rage* (New York: Simon and Schuster, 2001), p. 252.

47. Ibid.

48. Ibid.

49. Patrick M Yost and Harjit Singh Sandhu, The *Hawala* Alternative Remittance System and Its Role in Money Laundering (Interpol General Secretariat, January 2002), www.interpol.int/Public/FinancialCrime/MoneyLaundering/hawala/default.asp.

50. Maurice Greenberg, "Terrorist Financing," *Council on Foreign Relations Report,* 2002, p. 11.

51. Ibid.

52. Ibid.

53. Neil A. Lewis, "The Money Trail—Court Upholds Freeze on Assets of Muslim Group Based in U.S." *New York Times*, June 21, 2003.

54. "US Accuses Charity of Financing Terror," *BBC Online*, November 20, 2002.

55. Neil A. Lewis, "The Money Trail."

56. Christopher Dobson and Ronald Payne, *The Terrorists, Their Weapons, Leaders and Tactics* (New York: Facts on File, 1982), p. 80.

57. Ibid.

58. Jerrold M. Post, "Killing in the Name of God: Osama Bin Laden and Al Qaeda," p. 35.

59. Rohan Gunaratna, *Inside Al Qaeda,* p. 73.

60. Ibid.

61. Abdullah Ali Al-Salama, *Military Espionage in Islam*, www.skfriends.com/bin-laden-terrorist-manual.htm.

62. Rohan Gunaratna, *Inside Al Qaeda-Global Network of Terror*, p. 76.

63. Michael Whine, "The New Terrorism."

64. *A Military Guide to Terrorism in the Twenty-First Century,* Version 1.0, May 13, 2003, p. 40.

65. Ibid., p. 33.

66. John Arquilla and David Ronfeldt, ed., *Networks and Netwars* (Santa Monica: RAND, Corp., 2001), p. 9.

67. *A Military Guide to Terrorism in the the Twenty-First Century*, 2003, p. 40.

68. "Al-Qaeda, An Ever-Shifting Web," *The Economist*, October 19–25, 2002, p. 26.

69. Ibid.

70. Ibid.

71. Richard B. Myers, "Fighting Terrorism in an Information Age," International Information Programs (U.S. Department of State, August 19, 2002), p. 2, usinfo.state.gov/regional/nea/sasia/text/0819info.htm.

72. Ibid.

73. Judith Miller, "Lab Suggests Qaeda Planned to Build Arms, Officials Say," *New York Times*, September 14, 2002.

74. David Kay, "WMD Terrorism: Hype or Reality," in *The Terrorism Threat and US Government Response: Operational and Organizational Factors,* ed. James M. Smith and William C. Thomas (Boulder, CO: US Air Force Academy, 2001), p. 12.

75. "Terror Cells of Today Hard to Combat."

76. Doug Gavel, "Can Nuclear Weapons be Put Beyond the Reach of Terrorists?" *Kennedy School of Government Bulletin*, Autumn 2002, p. 43.

77. Ibid. p. 45.

78. Ibid, p. 48.

79. Richard H. Ullman, "9/11 a New Day for Counterterrorism?" in *Great Decisions Briefing Book* (Washington, DC: Foreign Policy Association, 2002), p. 5.

80. Bruce Newsome, "Executive Summary," p. 3.

81. Robin Wright, *Sacred Rage,* p. 253.

82. Ann Tyson, "Al Qaeda, Resilient and Organized" *Christian Science Monitor*, March 7, 2002.

83. Rohan Gunaratna, *Inside Al Qaeda,* p. 76.

84. Glenn Sacks, "Why I Miss the Cold War."

85. Paul Mann, "Modern Military Threats: Not All They Might Seem?" *Aviation Week & Space Technology,* April 22, 2002, p. 1.

86. For example, see the 1997 National Academies Press report, "Proliferation Concerns: Assessing U.S. Efforts to Help Contain Nuclear and Other Dangerous Materials and Technologies in the Former Soviet Union."

87.   "A Military Assessment of the al Qaeda Training Tapes," June 28, 2003. Internet: www.strategypage.com/articles/tapes/5.asp.

Chapter 2

Did 9/11 Matter? Terrorism and Counterterrorism Trends: Present, Past, and Future

Kate Marquis[1]

The terrorist attacks of Tuesday, September 11, 2001, forced U.S. security professionals to face the vulnerability of the U.S. homeland to attack by Islamic extremist terrorists in a new way. Three years after the attack, however, the U.S. counterterrorist mission is still overwhelmingly inspired and shaped by the September 11 attacks themselves. The specter of that day remains so central that it may prevent security professionals from seeing that the September 11 al-Qaida attack was only one of many jihadist terrorist threats. With the support of a broad community of ideological supporters, jihadist terrorists are working every day to find new ways to strike the United States.

The range of factors that inspire jihadist terrorists and Islamic extremist communities worldwide started before, and have continued after, September 11. The terrorists that pose the greatest threat to U.S. homeland security today are not motivated by a single attack whose repercussions have already been overtaken by events—they are drawn to enlist in a nonstate army to prosecute a global insurgency that spans nations and decades. The context for their volunteerism is rich and deeply populated with heroes and battles won and lost. Some of the most powerful factors shaping their anti-U.S. worldview are their perceptions of U.S. policy and actions, including homeland security initiatives.

In order to assess the current threat situation, counterterrorists must understand—and comprehend the relationship between—jihadist terrorist groups, Islamic extremist social and political movements, and counterterrorist policies and actions.[2] U.S. counterterrorism strategists must assess these critically interrelated areas as components of a dynamic system rather than as discrete elements. To understand the system, counterterrorism professionals must analyze each component in depth, assessing carefully how the people and groups in each component act, what motivates them, and how they interact within the bounds of their component. At the same time, however, because the components are connected in a dynamic system, counterterrorists must also weigh how developments in one component will influence trends in each of the others. Omitting one component from an analysis of the system may yield partial or false conclusions. Ultimately, unless U.S. homeland security strategy reflects the complete system of terrorist trends—including how terrorist trends are necessarily shaped by (and shape) homeland security policies—U.S. homeland security measures will be inadequate, even counterproductive, in addressing the jihadist threat.

Understanding the Threat

A full assessment of the threat system is beyond the scope of this chapter. Rather, this analysis will focus on four elements of the threat system that are critical for counterterrorist professionals to consider:

- Decentralization of the jihadist terrorist network, which poses a far more complex problem than some analysts have considered and is a serious hurdle for building long-term operational success against those networks.
- Developments in widely held interpretations of jihadist ideology, which increasingly include the United States as a primary target in the campaign to destroy corrupt, un-Islamic regimes throughout the world and replace them with a Muslim state.
- Jihadist willingness to conduct unpredictable attacks against official and civilian targets, using a full array of weapons, from small arms to explosives to WMD.
- Increased prominence of worldwide Islamic extremist social and political movements, which act as enablers for terrorist activity and pose a significant threat to U.S. interests in and of themselves.

Ultimately, unless counterterrorists master these, as well as dozens of other elements of the threat system, U.S. counterterrorism will be ineffective, if not counterproductive.

Decentralization

One of the most commonly cited—but most difficult to understand—trends in jihadist terrorism is the decentralization of the loosely knit worldwide network of jihadist terrorists and their associates. It is a hybrid network,[3] decentralized overall but with centralized components and functions.

The fact is that many jihadist groups, including portions of al-Qaida, many of its associates, and many of the Islamic charities that have provided financial support to al-Qaida and associated groups, are highly centralized. These centralized groups exhibit some or all of the features of an organized business: they have recognized leaders, a relatively clear chain of command, designated responsibilities for given personnel, central accounting procedures, and clear membership rules.

Even the jihadist training camp system active in Afghanistan in the late 1990s had formal characteristics.[4] Each training camp offered a relatively well-structured curriculum for its trainees. Most focused on basic Islamic extremist indoctrination, small-arms familiarization, and physical fitness, but some offeredspecialized training in assault tactics, surveillance, or even chemical and biological warfare. The camps were carefully organized and administered, often with clear chains of command, distinct administrative procedures, and carefully planned daily schedules of activity. Central planning and organization were as crucial to camp operations as hierarchical organization patterns were to al-Qaida's leadership and terrorist planners.

Nevertheless, al-Qaida and the camps benefited from operating within a larger, decentralized context. The Afghan camps accepted students on the basis of word-of-mouth referrals from trusted camp alumni, thereby tapping a diverse, worldwide pool of recruits and freeing camp administrators from the need to conduct worldwide recruiting. Students often paid their own way, minimizing the financial burden on camp managers. Students who were either too advanced or not skilled enough for a given program often could be sent to a better-suited program elsewhere in the region, ensuring that those volunteers were retained in the jihadist network rather than turned away if the initial match was not right. Ultimately, because it brought students in through informal, decentralized processes from all parts of the globe, the formal camp system served as much to create dense networks of unstructured ties between alumni—a sort of jihadist "old boy network"—as to instruct students in jihad. Alumni, in turn, established both formal and *ad hoc* procedures to send future students or equipment to the camps or to recruit students into their own organizations.

Centralized jihadist terrorist groups, like Al-Qaida, also benefited from operating in a decentralized network. For example, cherry-picking recruits from Taliban training camps, or piggybacking their operational money transfers with donations for other causes, freed them from having to rely on their internal recruitment or financial systems for all their needs.

The decentralized nature of the jihadist network is exemplified at the individual level as well.[5] For example, individual jihadists may participate in multiple jihadist activities, perhaps working with a loose association of insurgents in one region, a strictly hierarchical group of jihadists focused on a terrorist plot elsewhere, and in jihadist recruitment activities in their hometowns. Some of the organizations they associate with may be legitimate social, political, or religious organizations. Some of their tasks may be ancillary to terrorism at most, or even involve perfectly legal work with Muslim community organizations. Each jihadist may divide each of their days between these endeavors or dedicate weeks at a time to one project or another. No single ideologue, jihadist leader, or organizational framework determines their involvement in jihad, and they are free to build relationships across the global network of jihadists as they choose. If they have a disagreement with the members of any of the jihadist groups, they can quit or the groups can expel them. Replacements may be drawn from an entirely different part of the jihadist world.

This phenomenon is significant for counterterrorist planners in several ways. It suggests that a successful counterterrorist operation against one component of the jihadist network—a key financier or human trafficker, for example—may actually affect several other interconnected components of the network, including all the terrorist groups the financier funded, together with private businesses, or a pool of new terrorist recruits awaiting transfer to training camps, or the camps themselves. Nevertheless, the success against any of those components may be short-lived if remaining operatives are able to draw on their dense network of associates to find a replacement operative or service provider to meet their needs. Ultimately, this complicates U.S. counterterrorists' efforts to identify meaningful metrics of success in the overall campaign against terrorism as it is difficult to assess the full range of jihadist capabilities disrupted by any given arrest or to gauge how much time it may pass before the network recovers.

This is particularly evident in the case of the Afghan training camps. The counterterrorist coalition, in a few short weeks in late 2001, completely destroyed the Afghan camp infrastructure and in the ensuing months ensured that the operating environment would not permit future training there. Over the long run, however, this has not ended jihadist recruitment or training. The majority of post-9/11 jihadist volunteers may never have been to Afghanistan, but they are finding formal and informal alternatives elsewhere. Long-standing jihadist training camps continued operations in the Philippines after 9/11, prompting a demarche from the U.S. Ambassador to the Philippine government as recently as June 2004.[6] At the other end of the spectrum, a small group of volunteers for the Pakistani terrorist group Lashkar-e-Tayyiba were convicted in 2004 on charges of conducting small-arms familiarization at a paintball facility in Virginia to prepare for potentially joining the jihad in Kashmir.[7] Reports about jihadist training for participation in the Iraqi jihad are few, but as Operation Iraqi Freedom (OIF) continues, it seems highly likely that programs will emerge to train future volunteers for this conflict as well.

Decentralization has not only minimized the long-term effect of the destruction of the Afghan training camps. It also has mitigated the effect on the jihadist terrorist network of direct counterterrorist successes against specific terrorist groups. U.S. and coalition partners have arrested and killed dozens of senior al-Qaida members and severely disrupted its operations. Nevertheless, the continuing stream of terrorist attacks by jihadist organizations—Bali in 2002, Istanbul in 2003, and Madrid in 2004—are signs that other parts of the network are continuing to operate. Some are even taking up al-Qaida's longstanding role of conducting spectacular terrorist attacks to maintain momentum in the global jihad.

Effective disruption of a jihadist network requires not only the arrest or capture of the key members that execute and directly support terrorist acts. It also requires disruption of the network on the periphery of the core terrorist members to ensure that new operatives do not simply replace their captured colleagues. This is particularly challenging for U.S. counterterrorists when legal or regulatory constraints prohibit action against targets or operatives in ancillary or support roles who have not yet committed crimes.

In the end, counterterrorists must target their disruption operations against the jihadist network with an eye to the ripple effects their actions will have. This will require a long-term commitment by U.S. counterterrorism planners to struggle with difficult analytic challenges. In the interim, counterterrorist professionals will have to maintain their operational tempo over a sustained campaign in order to eliminate terrorist operatives as they come to the fore in the wake of each counterterrorist success.

Unified Doctrine and Strategy

What has enabled jihadists to operate a complex decentralized network so effectively is not the presence of a central organization but rather a compelling doctrine based on a shared ideology. Even though they do not answer to a central authority that coordinates their operational efforts, the common Salafi jihadist ideology underlying Islamic extremist terrorism has guided disparate jihadists to compatible doctrines for implementing their ideological agenda.

At its root, the ideology that motivates many jihadists today is a reactionary vision for political, social, and religious reform, expressed using rhetoric that draws heavily from multiple Islamic traditions. Jihadists have identified a set of grievances in the modern world that they believe spring primarily from the economic and political repression of the Muslim third world by corrupt local governing elites and global hegemonic powers, most notably the United States. The jihadist solution to their perceived ills is to overthrow these corrupt and imperialistic powers by force in order to clear the way for a new regime that will be governed by a just *caliph* (ruler). Jihadists believe that the caliph, led by guidance from Allah as delivered in the Koran and exemplified by the lives of the first Muslim leaders, will then lead the Islamic world to a political, social, and religious revival. Salafi doctrine calls for the Caliph to ultimately liberate all countries in the world from un-Islamic rule and bring them into the sphere of godly Muslim prosperity.

Although U.S. counterterrorism professionals have followed developments in jihadist ideology since 9/11, the basic principles of contemporary jihad draw on decades of earlier Islamic extremist political activity. Abdullah Azzam, often credited as one of the most influential figures in promoting modern jihad, laid the critical ideological framework for today's jihadism in the late 1970s, when he began urging Muslims around the world to take personal responsibility for supporting Afghan Muslims in their jihad against the Soviets. Modern jihadist ideas have become deeply embedded in Islamic political thought in the 25 years since then.

Disparate jihadists emphasize slightly different interpretations of basic jihadist ideology or doctrine, however, and therefore adopt different operational strategies for realizing their goals. One point of strategic debate that has been particularly significant among jihadist terrorists is whether jihad should be focused primarily on the *near enemy*—the local and national governments in the Muslim world that jihadists accuse of abusing their power at the expense of citizens—or on the *far enemy*—the hegemonic powers like the United States that provide critical support to those hated local and national governments. Prior to September 11, 2001, al-Qaida was nearly alone in pursuing a strategy of attacking the far enemy above all others. Most other jihadists were focused on a near enemy, for example Chechen separatists against Russia, or the Salafist Group for Call and Combat (GSPC) against Algerian authorities and their supporters in France. Since late 2001, however, there has been a sweeping shift to include the far enemy in campaigns against the near enemy, or even to concentrate fully on the far enemy regardless of the near enemy's status.

This is arguably the most significant trend in terrorism to emerge since the 9/11 attacks, although some U.S. counterterrorist planners were slow to recognize it at first. The shift of the jihadist terrorist network toward a far-enemy strategy has had an important effect on the threat system. Previously, jihadist victories in the struggle against a given near enemy encouraged primarily those jihadists active in that region, thus localizing the positive effects (such as on morale). Today, however, jihadists' new commitment to a unified struggle against near and far enemies ensures that any jihadist's action against any enemy is seen as a direct victory for jihadists everywhere, thus boosting morale and ongoing dedication to the cause worldwide.

The trend of focusing efforts on the far enemy is of great significance for U.S. counterterrorist professionals. More and more jihadists who might previously have preferred to target their home governments now seek to target the United States. Examples of groups that in the past few years have adopted the far enemy doctrine include Jemaah Islamiya, which in 2001 planned attacks against U.S. and U.K. embassies in Singapore and in 2002 executed an attack against a popular Australian tourist spot in Bali. Pakistani jihadist groups in 2002 also perpetrated far-enemy campaigns with a car bombing against the U.S. consulate in Karachi and a grenade attack at a church affiliated with the U.S. embassy in Islamabad.

Americans generally have not viewed these attacks as strikes against themselves. Nevertheless, U.S. counterterrorist planners must include the attacks in their threat assessments in order to capture the full scope of the jihadist threat. Americans must remember that the losses in the overall conflict against terrorism include not only the 3,000 killed in New York City, Pennsylvania, and Washington DC in 2001. On August 7, 1998, 437 people were killed and 5,000 others wounded in attacks on the U.S. embassies in Nairobi and Dar es Salaam. Twelve U.S. citizens were killed on that day, but it is the toll on the African population, particularly in Kenya, that demonstrates the magnitude of that attack. Similarly, it is only casualties outside the United States that demonstrate the continued threat from jihadist terrorism since 9/11, including those killed and maimed in Bali, Istanbul, Madrid, and dozens of other locations over the past three years. As jihadists increasingly define their mission in global terms, counterterrorist planners in the United States and around the world must also assess the threat globally to shape their national security responses appropriately.

Rules of Engagement, Means, and Methods of Attack

The particulars of a given jihadist's doctrinal interpretation are significant not only in determining whether he will focus his jihad against the near or far enemy but also in shaping what types of targets he will select and how he will approach them. Some Salafi jihadist groups have confined their efforts to attacking only official representatives of the enemy government, permitting attacks against target nations' soldiers or civilian employees of key policy, intelligence, and military agencies. Other jihadists hold doctrinal interpretations that permit targeting civilians within certain limits, including sometimes targeting only non-Muslim citizens of the target nation or local third countries. Still other groups permit a total war, up to and including attacks on Muslim citizens of the target nation. For example, the GSPC in Algeria has denounced targeting civilians in the Algerian civil war and focused its attention on attacks against official government personnel. The millennium attacks planned at international hotels in Jordan demonstrated a preference for targeting tourists and non-Muslims, although it allowed for the possibility that Jordanian Muslim passersby would be victims of the planned attack. On the far end of the spectrum, the Armed Islamic Group (GIA) has massacred thousands of local Muslim citizens in the course of the Algerian civil war.

Ideology also dictates what tactics jihadists will adopt, including assassination, non-lethal attacks against infrastructure targets, or mass-casualty attacks. Over the past few years, jihadists around the world have broadened their tactics to include a full range of low- and mass-casualty attacks against near and far enemy targets. Recent attacks demonstrate a trend in jihadist terrorism of high-casualty attacks against soft targets, such as recreation and business areas, including the March 11, 2004, attack in Madrid against commuter trains and the suicide bombings at concerts and key shopping areas in Moscow in 2003 and 2004.

Once they have chosen a target, jihadists choose from a wide variety of means and methods to attack it. The list of preferred terrorist means and methods is all too familiar from newspaper headlines: suicide attacks using truck bombs or improvised explosive devices (IEDs); stand-off attacks using pre-positioned IEDs or small arms such as rocket-propelled grenades; kidnappings and hostage scenarios; assassinations; and even attempted attacks using WMD. Ironically, some of the most effective jihadist attacks of the past few years have been among the simplest, for example the persistent roadside attacks against coalition convoys in Iraq, the simultaneous truck bombings of the British consulate and bank in Istanbul in November 2003, and repeated hijackings over the past decade—France in 1994, the United States in 2001, and Russia in 2004.

Terrorists continue to develop capabilities to use new techniques as well. The disruption of several planned unconventional attacks over the past year suggests jihadists will not be content to rely on familiar means and methods. Separate arrests in January 2003 and March 2004 show that jihadist terrorist cells in England may have been preparing ricin to use in poisoning attacks against unknown targets,[8] and plotting what they believed would be a toxic chemical attack.[9] There is significant debate within the homeland security establishment over the jihadist ability to employ unconventional WMD against the United States, but it is clear that some jihadists believe it is worth trying. At the very least, jihadists have already demonstrated that they are seeking new and more dangerous weapons.

The obvious implication for counterterrorism professionals is that no U.S. target is safe if jihadists continue to adhere to a doctrine that permits using a vast range of means and methods to kill men, women, and children of all faiths at any time regardless of their affiliations. A more complex consequence of jihadists' preparedness to use innovative tactics against any target is that counterterrorist professionals may never be able to fully eliminate ambiguity and uncertainty about the details of pending jihadist plots. Instead of basing a homeland security strategy on the hopes of being able to identify and defuse every individual terrorist plot against the United States, counterterrorism planners must expect the unexpected. U.S. counterterrorists must be as imaginative as the jihadists in anticipating attacks by any variety of mean and method, from sniper attacks to low- or perhaps mass-casualty biological attacks. The large-scale attacks against the United Nations compound in Iraq in 2003 and the increasingly brutal targeting of individual aid workers, contractors, and journalists there throughout 2003 and 2004 are only the latest examples of the range of situations the U.S. security community must prepare to face as, or perhaps even before, they emerge.

Critical Role of the Extremist Community

Understanding the terrorist picture and where it may lead is only one challenge. Even less well understood, but potentially even more important, is the influence of Islamic extremist ideas in shaping the political and social views of Muslims around the world. The general Islamic extremist movement is motivated by the same basic ideology as jihadist terrorists, although its adherents may not endorse the requirement or option to use violence to support their cause. The movement is strongly anti-American, anti-hegemonic, and anti-imperialist.

The Islamic extremist movement itself is nonstate; members identify politically and socially with the *ummah,* the body of all Muslim believers around the world, rather than with their state or even, sometimes, their ethnic group. The movement generally has embraced modern communications technology, and adherents use the Internet and other propaganda tools to communicate closely with like-minded Muslims around the world. These characteristics are not necessarily a threat, of course. At their most benign, Islamic extremist groups have promoted community unity in the face of economic and social disruption and campaigned for government accountability at home and abroad. This trend is evidenced by the growth of Islamic education programs in elementary and secondary schools throughout the world, and by the adoption of conservative traditions, such as wearing headscarves and beards as symbols of personal piety.[10]

At their worst, however, Islamic extremist groups promote fascist social and political agendas, reactionary black-and-white analyses of critical policy issues, and sectarian hatred. It is these ideas that fuel tacit and vocal support for terrorist activity, provide an enabling environment for terrorist operations, and may, in the long run, pose a greater threat to international stability than the activities of terrorists themselves.

As with the terrorist movement, Islamic extremist movements have been present for far longer than commonly recognized. They have been inspired by conflicts such as the *intifadah*, Bosnia, Chechnya, and by local issues around the world. The second *intifadah* may be particularly noteworthy in this case, since as early as 2000, the increased use of suicide bombings in the Middle East forced Muslims around the world to choose whether they accepted these attacks as martyrdom or condemned them as suicide. Many Muslim communities adopted the more politically charged label for these activities and began moving down a slippery slope. Very swiftly, the Israeli-Palestinian crisis became a powerful unifying issue for Islamic extremists worldwide. Muslims associated with Islamic extremist communities began identifying themselves as partisans in a trans-state struggle between Muslims and non-Muslims, and Islamic extremist political and social organizations like Hizb al-Tahrir and Jamaat al-Tabligh were reinvigorated as their increasingly popular mandate began to crystallize.

The greatest recent catalysts for encouraging Muslims to endorse the Islamic extremist movement, however, have been the U.S. and coalition counterterrorist efforts Operation Enduring Freedom (OEF) and Operation Iraqi Freedom (OIF). The United States tends to consider these actions in Afghanistan and Iraq as legitimate counterstrikes against al-Qaida, its Taliban sponsors, and other terrorists. Interestingly, many Muslims—including some Islamic extremists—were initially dismayed and disgusted with the 9/11 attacks, which they deemed had stepped beyond the pale in killing so many innocent people. However, Muslims around the world overwhelmingly believed that the U.S. conduct in OEF, including massive bombings by the world's most advanced army against an essentially medieval state, represented U.S. desire for hegemony over Muslim regimes and global resources. Thus, U.S. retaliatory actions after 9/11 seemed only to confirm the Islamic extremist interpretation of history as a global struggle between oppressed Muslims and corrupt, conspiratorial, un-Islamic powers.

Therefore, while the counterterrorist efforts in Afghanistan were successful against the Taliban and al-Qaida's set infrastructure, they have has generated tremendous negative opinion about the United States throughout the Muslim world. Incidentally, by curtailing al-Qaida's operations, OEF ended al-Qaida's dominant role in shaping global jihadist rhetoric at the same time as other organized Islamic extremist groups, such as Hizb al-Tahrir and al-Mouhajiroun, increased their production of powerful pro-jihadist rhetoric. These groups' message has filled the gap left by the disruption of al-Qaida's propaganda efforts and has been well received in communities around the world. The groups now benefit from a mutually reinforcing process, whereby they increase their own profiles and influence through propaganda and recruitment that, in turn, promote the popularity of the Islamic extremist movement worldwide. Many of these groups are now leading the Islamic extremist public campaign against OIF, which was perceived by many Islamic extremist communities as a completely unjustified act of aggression against a Muslim country. The invasion and occupation of Iraq, and the continued prominence of U.S. troops there, has driven U.S. popularity among Islamic extremists to further lows.

Islamic extremists are also very sensitive to perceived imperialist or hegemonic abuses of power, especially to perceived U.S. mistreatment of Muslims. The use of counterterrorist tactics, such as extended detentions, harsh interrogation practices, deportations, and immigration exclusions, for example, has generally exacerbated Islamic extremists' already negative views of the United States. Deep criticism of U.S. hegemony can be found in many Muslim societies worldwide, not only in poor areas, but even in Western universities and elite communities.[11] This is not to say that U.S. counterterrorism policy should not include strong action against terrorist operatives and their sponsors. Certainly, one of the keys to defending against a terrorist attack is to defuse terrorist networks and reduce the context for terrorist support. Nevertheless, U.S. counterterrorism professionals must recognize that their actions have repercussions and be sure to account for them in their operational and strategic planning.

Counterterrorism: Catching up to Terrorist Trends

While many factors shape jihadist and Islamic extremist movements, the 9/11 attacks remain one of the single most influential factors shaping U.S. counterterrorist planning. In one regard, the commonly held passion among U.S. counterterrorism professionals about the events of that day serves almost the same function as Salafi ideology does for jihadists and Islamic extremists: it provides a powerful unifying cause for U.S. counterterrorists and citizens and focuses their political will to support counterterrorism measures. On the other hand, the continued centrality of that day must not prevent counterterrorism planners from challenging the assumptions that sprang from those attacks three years ago about the terrorist threat. Counterterrorism planners must look beyond 9/11 and recognize that the threat is constantly evolving. They must constantly adopt new lenses to see more clearly the jihadist and societal trends that led to 9/11 and to understand which elements have shaped jihadism and Islamic extremism since then.

One critical challenge will be for counterterrorism planners to step beyond 9/11, even beyond U.S.-centric views entirely, in order to see the threat system from jihadist and Islamic extremist perspectives. Seeing events through enemies' eyes will be especially valuable in helping counterterrorists to appreciate how jihadists and extremists will react to U.S. counterterrorism actions. This is not to say that U.S. counterterrorist strategy should not take aggressive, preemptive measures when appropriate. It is critical, though, that counterterrorism strategists consider how their actions will affect the future threat system and plan accordingly. They must consciously evaluate the potential reactions to planned counterterrorism measures and prepare follow-on strategies in advance to address expected negative effects as (or before) they occur.

Counterterrorists can also benefit from considering elements of the threat system, such as jihadist decentralization and ideology, and questioning how they create challenges and opportunities for counterterrorist policy. The range of options open to jihadist terrorists in choosing targets and attack plans is another crucial element of the threat system, because it is the root of the uncertainty in our threat assessments. Rigorously assessing the widest possible implications of developments in this element may help counterterrorists plan more effectively for a surprise attack.

Counterterrorism planners must also consider the role of Islamic extremist communities in enabling and supporting jihadist terrorism and in countering perceived U.S. hegemonic policies in the Muslim world. Although the movement began decades ago, elements of this component of the threat system have become increasingly important since OEF, particularly in light of Muslim receptivity to anti-imperialist rhetoric. The rise of these elements is a significant and negative consequence of U.S. counterterrorism successes against al-Qaida and the training camp network in Afghanistan.

Ultimately, counterterrorists need to build a deep understanding of each component of the threat system—including jihadist terrorism, Islamic extremism, and counterterrorism—as well as a broad understanding of how each component relates to the others. If U.S. counterterrorist planning fails to address the complete threat system, U.S. counterterrorism policy will continue to disrupt many jihadist terrorist plots, but it will likely not stop the jihadist threat. At worst, U.S. counterterrorism policy could exacerbate the threat and might even serve as the catalyst for the next attacks.

Notes

1.   The author wishes to thank MAJ Reid Sawyer, Executive Director of the Combating Terrorism Center at West Point, and Ms. Amy Keyser for assistance above and beyond the call of duty in the preparation of this chapter. Dr. Rohan Gunaratna, Senior Fellow at the Combating Terrorism Center, also made very generous intellectual contributions to this work. Final thanks are due to Dr. Eric Silla and Mr. Jarret Brachman, who offered valuable comments during the conceptualization of several of the arguments presented here. This work has been approved for publication by the U.S. government but does not represent the views of the U.S. government or denote U.S. government endorsement of any position stated herein.

2.   Because the primary threat to the U.S. homeland currently stems from Salafi jihadist terrorists, this chapter will focus on that realm. However, to understand an ever fuller picture of the terrorist threat facing U.S. interests, analysts could include nationalist, rightist, leftist, and other issue-oriented terrorisms and their supporters in their assessments of a total threat system facing the United States.

3.   The concept of a "hybrid network" is presented in John Arquilla and David Ronfeldt, *The Advent of Netwar*, (RAND, Santa Monica, CA), 1996. This work remains one of

the most useful studies available on how terrorism can be shaped by terrorists' organizational structures.

4. There are several excellent sources on the history of the Afghan jihadist camps, including Rohan Gunaratna, *Inside al Qaeda: Global Network of Terror*, (Berkeley Books, NY; 2002); Jason Burke, *al Qaeda: Casting a Shadow of Terror*, (I.B. Tauris, London; 2003); and Peter L. Bergen, *Holy War, Inc.: Inside the Secret World of Osama bin Ladin*, (The Free Press, New York), 2001, among others. Key primary sources for each of these analyses include testimony from the trials of al-Qaida operatives in the cases of the 1993 World Trade Center attack and the 1998 East African Embassy attacks.

5. Illustrations of this phenomenon have appeared in numerous reports about investigations against jihadists like Abu Hamza, the prominent London-based cleric, or Kamal Derwish, of the Lackawanna Six investigation. Both of these men filled an overt role of publicly promoting jihadist ideology in their local communities but had separate, clandestine roles in the broader jihadist network. Details of Abu Hamza's jihadist career have been widely reported in international news media. An excellent accounting of the Lackawanna case is available in "Unclear Danger: Inside the Lackawanna Terror Case," *New York Times,* October 12, 2003.

6. For information about some of the camps that have recently offered training to international jihadists in the Philippines, see Maria Ressa, *Seeds of Terror: An Eyewitness Account of al-Qaeda's Newest Center of Operations in Southeast Asia,* (The Free Press, New York, NY), 2003, especially pp. 7–9, which illustrate the continued activity of the camps through at least December 12, 2002. For information about the U.S. demarche, see Agence-France Presse, "U.S. expresses concern over JI training camps in Mindanao," accessed at www.inq7.net/brk/2004/jul/06/brkpol-11-1.htm on September 1, 2004, or other news wire reports on the Ambassador's public statement about the issue.

7. See coverage of the trial, including "Judge Convicts Three in 'Va. Jihad' Case, U.S. Linked Defendants to Terrorists," *Washington Post*, March 5, 2001, p. A01.

8. For an assessment of this possible plot, see Jeffrey M. Bale, Anjali Bhattacharjee, Eric Croddy, Richard Pilch, "Ricin Found in London: An al-Qa'ida Connection?" Center for Nonproliferation Studies Report, January 23, 2003. Available at the Center for Nonproliferation Studies Web site. Accessed at cns.miis.edu/pubs/reports/ricin.htm.

9. See "Report: London Gas Plot Foiled," CBS/AP, April 6, 2004, accessed at www.cbsnews.com/stories/2004/03/30/terror/main609272.shtml.

10. The parallel to increased politicization of other traditionally apolitical or moderately political communities—including Christian, environmentalist, Jewish, and many others—should not be overlooked. These disparate movements share striking commonalities in their doctrinal and rhetorical stances, suggesting that the increased popularity of the Islamic extremist movement may stem from the same root causes as contending political movements in other realms.

11. The truly global influence of the Islamic extremist movement, especially in the United States, has serious implications for homeland security. The transnational

Islamic extremist movement is present throughout the United States, and its influence in many areas has been powerful for decades. U.S. counterterrorist and homeland security planners must consider that the next jihadist terrorist attack against the U.S. homeland may be perpetrated by Americans—perhaps including members of the security community—who will come to believe, or already believe, that the U.S. government must be challenged.

Chapter 3

Putting WMD Terrorism into Perspective

John Parachini

What would you do? The FBI's National Infrastructure Protection Center (NIPC) warned that "Al Qaeda and affiliated groups continue to enhance their capabilities to conduct effective mass-casualty chemical, biological, radiological, and nuclear (CBRN) attacks" and that al-Qaida possesses "at least a crude capability to use" CBRN weapons.[1] As a policymaker, doubts about the quality, interpretation, and inherent uncertainty of intelligence continue to gnaw at you with each day that passes. For example, you are faced with unanswered questions about the extent, history, and even location of Iraq's forbidden weapons of mass destruction (WMD) arsenal, much less more furtive transnational threats.

Rewarded for decisiveness as policymakers are, the instinctive route is to play it safe and extrapolate worst-case conclusions from imperfect information, even if serious consequences for government resource allocation result. Although constantly making pessimistic interpretations of imperfect data clearly has its disadvantages, such an approach seems prudent when assessing the threat of CBRN terrorism. The September 11 attacks and a series of other al-Qaida or al-Qaida–inspired attacks—from Bali to Mombassa, and Riyadh to Casablanca—all combine to elevate the perceived potency of the al-Qaida threat. Even though al-Qaida consistently has used conventional explosives in these attacks, movement adherents may also be willing to use CBRN weapons on a grand scale. The degree to which they have actually acquired the capability to do so, however, remains unknown. How should we assess this risk?

Limited as it is, the historical record cautions against axiomatically suggesting that the al-Qaida movement or any other terrorist group will inevitably successfully use CBRN weapons in a catastrophic attack against the United States. Moreover, although hedging against terrorists exploiting the catastrophic potential of CBRN weapons is an essential task of government, resources and the public's patience are finite.

Focusing on a particular means of attack must not come at the expense of adequate attention to broader diplomatic, border control, intelligence, and law enforcement efforts to counter terrorism. Attention cannot simply result in obsessing over CBRN effects but also must produce improved understanding of the motives, vulnerabilities, capabilities, and context for actual attacks, not just expressions of interest.

Moreover, as if all this were not complicated enough, counterterrorism efforts must not focus solely on al-Qaida, as amorphous as it is, but must address broader terrorist trends and a variety of other groups including Hizballah, the Revolutionary Armed Forces of Colombia (FARC), and less well identified, armed rebel factions in Chechnya, Indonesia, and the Congo—to name a few that we know of today.

Fighting in the Dark

The few historical cases of terrorist interest in and acquisition of CBRN weapons make for a comparatively small data set to formulate general observations about the potential for terrorists to use unconventional weapons successfully. Furthermore, the details of many of these cases are sketchy and often ambiguous, which only further complicates the task of accurately portraying the scope and magnitude of the threat. With these uncertainties, many people will understandably hedge against the unknown and err on the side of finding the threat potential high.

A close reading of the February 2003 FBI alert mentioned earlier and a May 2003 unclassified CIA report entitled "Terrorist CBRN: Materials and Effects" reveals the nuanced language of intelligence analysts who weigh the meaning of ambiguous information.[2] The CIA's Directorate of Intelligence asserts that al-Qaida "has crude *procedures* for making mustard agent, sarin, and VX."

Elsewhere in the same CIA publication, however, the caption beneath a drawing copied from a document taken from an al-Qaida safe house in Afghanistan describes "*interest* in the production of more effective chemical agents such as mustard, sarin, and VX."[3] In the FBI's NIPC Information Bulletin, al-Qaida is alleged to have "*experimented* with procedures for making blister (mustard) and nerve (sarin and VX) chemical agents."[4] The conclusion that experiments, standard procedures, and interest in preparing these chemical agents existed may be based on a very different set of facts.

The dual-use nature of chemical, biological, and radioactive materials opens up the possibility that innocent, naturally occurring events are mistaken for pernicious weapons-development activities. For example, reputable media organizations reported findings of Iraqi clandestine weapons programs throughout the recent hostilities, which only proved to be false alarms on further inspection, not the smoking gun that officials and private experts expected to find. Homeland security officials and experts face similar challenges, bedeviled by the anticipated clandestine CBRN terrorist activity they consistently expect to find.

Al-Qaida's interest in and willingness to use unconventional weapons are not in question, but evidence of al-Qaida's capabilities is fragmentary and reveals the difficulty of finding conclusive proof of a threatening capability. Demonstrating interest in something is far different both from, first, experimenting with it and, second, mastering the procedures to execute an attack. Gaining access to materials is certainly a major barrier, but it is not the only one. Delivering toxic materials to targets in sufficient quantities to kill in the same fashion as explosives is not easy.

Journalists repeatedly asked Gen. Tommy Franks and Secretary of Defense Donald Rumsfeld whether U.S. forces had found evidence of al-Qaida CBRN weapons capabilities in Afghanistan; they consistently responded that forces discovered evidence of considerable interest, even some equipment that could be used for biological weapons development, but no hard physical evidence of weapons production. The difficulty of finding evidence of al-Qaida's unconventional weapons capabilities in Afghanistan foreshadowed the difficulty of finding clandestine weapons programs in Iraq. In both cases, the perceived intentions of al-Qaida and Iraq led to the suspicion and strong presumption of their capabilities, but hard evidence of capabilities commensurate with perceived and indeed stated intent has proven elusive.

The use of unconventional weapons by terrorists has fortunately been rare. In the last 25 years, there have been only four significant attacks by terrorists using poison, disease, or radioactive material as weapons and a few instances where groups or individuals showed interest in using such weapons. The first incident was in 1984, in Oregon, when a religious cult sought to depress voter turnout in a local election by clandestinely contaminating restaurant salad with salmonella, sickening at least 751 people. In 1990, in northern Sri Lanka, the Liberation Tigers of Tamil Eelam (LTTE) attacked a Sri Lankan Armed Forces (SLAF) base with chlorine gas, injuring more than 60 military personnel and enabling the LTTE to rout the fort. An attack on the Tokyo subway with liquid sarin in 1995 and the 2001 anthrax attacks in the United States are the other two incidents.[5]

The March 1995 attack by Aum Shinrikyo—a Japanese religious cult—on the Tokyo subway using sarin liquid, catapulted concern about terrorist use of unconventional weapons to the front burner of U.S. security policymaking. The dramatic Tokyo attack occurred at a time marked by significant concerns about loose nuclear weapons and materials in the former Soviet Union, as well as revelations of covert unconventional weapons programs in Iraq, the 1993 terrorist attack on the World Trade Center, and the April 1995 Oklahoma City bombing.

The cumulative impact of a terrorist group using a chemical weapons agent in a society as orderly as Japan's, major conventional terrorist attacks on the U.S. homeland, and a series of revelations about hidden weapons programs both in Iraq and the former Soviet Union, led to a number of new presidential directives and new legislative initiatives. Federal officials worried about the danger of a similar subway incident in the United States, and the challenge such an attack would pose for emergency responders. Would the United States be able to respond any better than Japan had, or would the loss of life be even worse?

These events in the early 1990s fundamentally changed how federal officials, particularly in the White House, perceived the safety of the U.S. homeland. Previously, terrorism was an evil that occurred far away from U.S. shores. The early and mid-1990s, however, demonstrated not only the willingness of foreign and U.S. terrorists to strike on U.S. soil, but also that terrorists, even if they were not yet targeting U.S. soil, were willing to do what once had been taboo: kill indiscriminately with large quantities of explosives, or even use poison or disease as a weapon. These events led the executive branch and Congress to increase counterterrorism funding significantly and initiate several new presidential directives, numerous governmental and private studies, expert commissions, and a plethora of new programs to increase the capabilities of local responders, particularly when faced with CBRN attacks.[6]

The nature of terrorism seemed to have changed fundamentally. Terrorists no longer seemed bound by previous limits, when they sought attention to their cause rather than deaths. By the 1990s, terrorists sought mass and indiscriminate killing and justified it by invoking higher, religious authorities. Bruce Hoffman, a well-known terrorist expert, noted in 1993 that, because "[r]eligious terrorist violence inevitably assumes a transcendent purpose and therefore becomes a sacramental or divine duty, [it] arguably results in a significant loosening of the constraints on the commission of mass murder."[7] With moral restraints loosening, Richard Falkenrath, who has since joined the White House Office of Homeland Security, predicted in 1998 that "[i]t is certain that more and more non-state actors will become capable of NBC (nuclear, biological, and chemical weapons) acquisition and use."[8]

More recently, the U.S. National Strategy for Homeland Security warned that the "expertise, technology, and material needed to build the most deadly weapons known to mankind—including chemical, biological, radiological, and nuclear weapons—are spreading inexorably."[9] Similarly, two former senior government counterterrorism officials argued that the confluence of religiously inspired terrorism and technological diffusion "will impel terrorists to overcome technical, organizational and logistical obstacles to WMD use."[10]

If these policymakers and scholars are correct, why have terrorists not yet attacked the United States with unconventional weapons? Although evidence exists that some terrorists are willing to attack the United States, some are willing to kill indiscriminately, some are willing to use WMD, and some are even able to do so (with limited success), combining these trends into one coherent threat conflates a series of loosely related events in the 1990s. It is not unreasonable to draw such conclusions, but these insights are best gauged against a systematic examination of the historical—albeit surprisingly small—record of terrorist cases involving unconventional weapons.

The Sparse Historical Record

A series of 28 case studies, sponsored by the Monterey Institute's Center for Nonproliferation Studies, spanning the last 50 years and compiled by more than a dozen researchers, provides an empirical foundation to assess the motivations, behavior, and patterns related to terrorist interest, or alleged interest, in unconventional weapons. The same analytic questions were applied to each case, allowing for comparison across the entire set,[11] and strongly emphasized primary source material. When possible, the authors interviewed the perpetrators and arresting officials, reviewed court documents, and read the writings of the perpetrating groups.

Upon this rigorous inspection, several of the empirical cases frequently cited in the media and scholarly literature proved to be apocryphal.[12] The initial set of case studies raised doubts about the alleged claims of terrorist interest in, or use of, chemical and biological weapons. New evidence and a more thorough investigation of old evidence still underscored the difficulty of assessing incomplete and complicated data of sensitive security cases.

Considering the entire body of case study work, three other observations provide some conceptual framework for assessing the phenomena of terrorist acquisition and use of unconventional weapons. First, groups that seek to acquire and use unconventional weapons share a few key factors, such as the mindset of the group leaders, the opportunities they seized, and the technical capabilities they possessed. Second, exogenous and internal restraints do prevent some groups that engage in indiscriminate and often mass violence from pursuing unconventional weapons. Several factors inhibit terrorist and insurgency movements from pursuing CBRN weapons as their means of violence. Accounting for and understanding the impact of these restraints and disincentives to terrorist acquisition and use of unconventional weapons is critical. Bolstering the appropriate disincentives may serve as a critical component to a counterterrorism campaign.

Finally, although religion in part orients some groups toward extreme violence, it does not necessarily lead groups to use poison, disease, or radioactive material as weapons. Group leaders who pursue unconventional weapons are just as likely to be obsessed with particular types of weapons, such as poison, for unconnected reasons, demonstrating behavior more akin to a serial poisoner than to a mass casualty terrorist. Alternatively, terrorist groups are just as likely to use unconventional weapons to capitalize on what they perceive as a practical opportunity to accomplish a desired end.

For example, when the Tamil Tigers ran low on conventional weapons, they took chlorine containers from a nearby paper mill to use in the 1990 attack on an SLAF fort. Their immediate battlefield needs drove their use of toxic material as a weapon, not any unique fascination with chlorine as a weapon.[13]

More than anything else, the observations made during these case studies convey that the mindset of leadership, opportunity, and technical capacity are the factors that most significantly influence a group's propensity to seek to acquire and to use unconventional weapons.

The Mindset of Leadership

Although it may include a religious orientation, the mindset of leadership may also include other facets. For example, Aum Shinrikyo leader Shoko Asahara prophesized the destruction of the Japanese government and the creation of a future world in which Asahara and his followers would rule—catalyzed by the use of nuclear, chemical, and biological weapons. Although Asahara's worldview entailed the use of unconventional weapons to spark an apocalyptic change, Aum's actual use of sarin—in Matsumoto against judicial officials (to thwart a judicial proceeding against them), and on Tokyo subway lines leading to many government ministries (to disrupt moves by law enforcement authorities to arrest them)—was more tactical.

The sarin attacks were also in large part a result of Asahara's obsession with poison as a weapon. In a poem Asahara wrote, he celebrated the beauty of the deadly power of sarin.[14] The case studies involving Larry Wayne Harris, James Dalton Bell, and Masumi Hiyashi focus on individuals who sought to use poison or biological agents for their personal or political ends;[15] like Asahara and his Aum followers, these individuals harbored a fascination with poison and disease. Unlike Harris, Bell, and Hiyashi, however, who largely acted alone, Asahara's Aum included scientists and considerable assets that enabled him to achieve a serious scale of operations that posed a major threat to public security.

Usama bin Ladin and al-Qaida have demonstrated a tremendous interest in unconventional weapons but have not necessarily been obsessed with them. There is a cult-like quality to how bin Ladin inspires his followers with his pattern of speech, mimicking Koranic Arabic spoken in another era, and with his goal of reestablishing a golden era of Islam and expelling the United States, Israel, and all other infidels from the Middle East. Yet, bin Ladin's worldview does not depend on the use of unconventional weapons, unlike Ashara's apocalyptic vision of the future. Attacks with explosives or crashing jetliners into buildings will suffice.

Both Asahara and bin Ladin exhibit more than mere leadership power. They motivate group members to take actions that they would not necessarily do on their own and that are widely perceived as outside the norms of social behavior. Asahara's command over his followers extended to ritualistic practices of having them drink his bath water and bathe in scalding hot water. Although bin Ladin motivated people to kill themselves in the process of killing thousands of others, the practice of suicide attacks has a history in the minds of its practitioners as legitimate violence; Aum's bizarre practices and its widespread use of poison to kill others, however, has no analog.

Opportunity

Rather than obsession, opportunity best explains the Tamil Tigers' use of chlorine against an SLAF fort in June 1990. The Tigers released the chlorine gas so that it drifted over the fort, where it injured more than 60 government soldiers. The gas enabled the Tigers to take the fort, but it also drifted back over them. For more than a decade after this incident, despite the continuing conflict, the Tigers never used chemicals in this fashion again. Interviews with former Tamil Tiger cadre and Sri Lankan intelligence officials revealed that the Tamil Tigers feared the loss of support from Tamil constituents as well that of the Tamil diaspora communities that are critical for the organization's fundraising.[16] They used chlorine in this one instance not out of some religious ideology but merely because it was available and met a battlefield need.

Aum Shinrikyo, al-Qaida, and the Tamil Tigers all operated in permissive environments, where they could utilize the power of unconventional weapons without much interference from their host state. The Japanese government's National Police Agency, for example, proved ineffective at investigating Aum, and the group hid behind laws protecting religious organizations from government interference. Where law enforcement authorities of most countries would have investigated, intervened, and arrested, Japanese authorities waited to accumulate enough evidence for an overwhelming case. Tragically, they waited too long.

Al-Qaida was a strong terrorist group operating in Afghanistan on the territory of a weak state that was beholden to it. Al-Qaida operatives provided money to Taliban ministries to keep them operating, and its 055 Brigade was the most effective fighting force in the Taliban military. Al-Qaida was able to do as it pleased without any interference from the Taliban government and, as a non-state actor, was able to act outside the norms of state behavior. Al-Qaida's operations in Afghanistan included an extensive network of terrorist training camps, some of which conducted research and provided instruction in the clandestine use of chemical and biological materials.

The FARC also enjoyed freedom of operations in the sanctuary the Colombian government permitted it. Although the few allegations of FARC having used chemical agents remain obscure, the group's deep involvement in the drug trade brings it in contact with a variety of toxic chemicals that can add a nasty toxic component to their bombs.[17] Although the group's government-designated sanctuary was revoked in 2002, the jungle of Colombia's interior allows the FARC to conduct much of its activities free from government control.

Technical Hurdles

The third explanation for the paucity of terrorist attacks using unconventional weapons is the technical hurdles involved. The technical capacity of groups to produce or acquire and effectively deliver unconventional weapons varies considerably. Achieving catastrophic outcomes with unconventional weapons requires a considerable scale of operations. Only in a very few cases have groups been able to amass the skills, knowledge, material, and equipment to perpetrate attacks with unconventional weapons on a scale that comes close to that of the danger posed by terrorist attacks with conventional explosives.

To date, only Aum Shinrikyo and al-Qaida have been able to achieve the scale of operations required to mount serious unconventional weapons programs, but even these two groups have encountered difficulties. Aum Shinrikyo, which had considerable financial resources, front companies, and members with scientific talents, failed in all 10 of its biological weapons attacks.[18] Similarly, the group's sarin attack on the Tokyo subway caused roughly the same number of fatalities as the average Palestinian suicide bomber attack.[19] Aside from some minor efforts to develop the toxin ricin, al-Qaida and its affiliated groups tend to use explosives delivered by suicide attackers as its weapon of choice. During the last 25 years, terrorist attacks with unconventional weapons have inflicted far fewer casualties and fatalities than indiscriminate terrorist bombings or suicide hijackings,[20] the tragic toll of the September 11 attacks being the most pronounced example.

In cases where terrorists have used unconventional weapons in the past, they mainly have used crude toxic materials, not sophisticated, military-grade weapons. Aum is the one group that developed a chemical agent that is commonly found in military arsenals. Otherwise, most cases have involved limited efforts to use industrial materials or industrial by-products as weapons. Toxic warfare can pose considerable security challenges, but on balance, these types of threats pale in comparison to the catastrophic terrorist attacks for which government authorities prepare in tabletop exercises.[21] In a survey of 60 tabletop exercises for federal departments and agencies, only a handful involve non–military-grade weapons agents.

An apparent lack of interest on the part of terrorist groups in acquiring unconventional weapons also helps explain why unconventional weapons attacks are so rare. In the case studies on the Irish Republican Army (IRA), the FARC, and HAMAS, political vision, practical military utility, and moral codes all restrained them in part from seeking and using unconventional weapons. In some cases, group leaders indicated to members that the use of chemical or biological weapons would not be legitimate to their struggle. HAMAS[22] leader Abu Shannab, for one, stated that the use of poison was contrary to Islamic teachings.[23] Although HAMAS is a religiously based organization, its struggle to establish a Palestinian state on Israeli territory and to eliminate Israel as a state is decidedly political.

In another instance, FARC Southern Bloc commander Joaquin Gomez asked, "What is the point of using acid? We use the bombs to destroy the buildings, as we do not have artillery or tanks. Acid is of no use against concrete or bricks."[24] In contrast to the occasion when the Tamil Tigers used chlorine gas because they were short on small arms, Gomez perceived no value in using chemical agents in his insurgency struggle; explosive firepower is what he deemed important.

Finally, despite a few allegations of interest by the IRA in purchasing nuclear material and wanting to poison certain targets, neither the Provisional IRA, other IRA factions, nor the political wing Sinn Fein was willing to jeopardize the embryonic peace process leading to the goal of acquiring political power by wielding unconventional weapons.[25] The discovery of any attempt by an IRA group to acquire such nuclear material would only hurt the movement with financial supporters and likely elicit a ferocious crackdown from the British. Although many of the factions of the Irish Republican movement have considerable technical skills, abundant financial resources, and extensive contacts with organized criminal organizations and states seeking unconventional weapons, they have eschewed opportunities to obtain such capabilities because such efforts would only jeopardize their chances for success.[26]

Thus, a complex group of factors shape a group's propensity to acquire and use unconventional weapons. Religion is an important one, but not the only one. Although religion can provide a dangerous motivating component, the greatest danger occurs when the group also has technical capabilities, easily exploitable opportunities, and a minimum of restraints. Groups need technical capacity, including knowledge, skill, critical weapons material, production equipment, and sometimes even sheer serendipity, to acquire and use unconventional weapons.

Use of an unconventional weapon also risks the demise of a group's leadership. Most of Aum's leaders were imprisoned and have since been released. Others, including Shoko Asahara, still face the drawn-out Japanese legal process. The group has renamed itself Aleph and appears to be living a peaceful existence, although there have been some reports of suspicious information-collection activities. Al-Qaida, in contrast, continues to be interested in these weapons, but is also willing and able to conduct significant, multiple, and near simultaneous attacks with conventional means.

Implications for U.S. Counterterrorism Policy

Combating terrorism in all its forms and protecting against attacks with the range of possible weaponry terrorists might assemble remains a high priority challenge for the U.S. government. Given the empirical importance of permissive environments in facilitating the technical capacity needed for terrorist groups to seek and utilize unconventional weapons, the role of states is critical. A central component of the Bush administration's strategy to combat terrorism has been to apply a variety of diplomatic and military tools to state sponsors of terrorist groups. A more nuanced understanding of the relationships between states and terrorist groups may provide the United States with additional policy tools. Strong states supporting terrorist groups present different policy problems than do weak states, from which strong terrorist groups operate. Weak, failing, or supportive states not only enable terrorist groups to thrive but also enable their ability to acquire unconventional capabilities with sufficient scale for truly catastrophic attacks. This finding holds important implications for U.S. counterterrorism policy.

Eliminating all possibility of terrorist groups or individuals using CBRN weapons is impossible. Trying to limit the scope and scale of a group's activities, however, may prevent it from achieving the freedom of action that proved critical in several cases in the past. One option is to restrict the physical sanctuary within a state where a terrorist group operates to impinge on its scale of operations. Collapsed or abruptly transitioning states present a more extreme danger. In such instances, whatever remains of a governing authority may not be able to exercise control over terrorist activities on its territory. The unstable state may also possess military or dual-use materials that terrorists or insurgency movements willing to use unconventional weapons could exploit or steal. Given these dangers, a range of diplomatic, economic, and military policies to shore up weak and failing states are crucial to reducing the terrorist threat.

Another policy option is to declare publicly that state sponsors who transfer unconventional weapons capabilities to nonsovereign, subnational groups will be in violation of a fundamental norm of the international system and will run the most severe risks to their security. U.S. military action against the Iraqi regime demonstrated only one unequivocal way to bolster the taboo against such transfers; there are other ways to bolster the norm and crush the offending regime.

U.S. diplomacy should also encourage friends and allies to underscore the seriousness of such potential transfers with states such as Syria, Iran, Libya, and North Korea. Pressure from other nations, such as China, Russia, and Japan, may be as effective with these states as U.S. diplomatic pressure.

Recognizing that the so-called new terrorists may not always escalate to unconventional weapons is the first step to achieving a better balance on the nature of the terrorist threat and how to combat it. Focusing inordinately on the prospect of terrorist attacks with unconventional weapons unduly limits authorities' focus and resource allocation. Contrary to one scholar's assertion that "the only way to prevent" terrorist use of CBRN weapons is "to implement far greater police control than the United States has ever known,"[27] policymakers need to refocus the core of governmental attention and resources on preventing and preempting terrorist attacks from occurring in the first place.

In addition, policymakers need to seek opportunities for dual-use measures that benefit society on a daily basis and also help prevent terrorism. Merely improving the ability to manage consequences by broadening training for first responders,[28] the police and firefighters likely to be on the scene in the event of an attack, prematurely gives up on the task of preventing attacks before they occur, regardless of their weaponry or mode of operation.

The United States may have difficulty sustaining a twin-track policy of preemptive military engagement and reactive homeland defense, focused on detecting and responding to the consequences of a CBRN terrorist attack. Both approaches are important components of a strategy, but a range of other measures that focus on preempting terrorist operations themselves must complement them.

The United States must strike a balance between preparing to address attacks with unconventional or CBRN weapons materials and conventional attacks that may also have dramatic consequences. Tragically, precious little of the millions of dollars used for first-responder training in the last five years proved valuable following the September 11 attacks because so few survived the attack. This is not to suggest that the training was not valuable—it was, but not necessarily in these incidents. The new Department of Homeland Security and other federal agencies need to pay particular attention to finding the right balance in their budgets for new research and new capabilities.

A greater focus on how to prevent terrorist attacks from happening in the first place—regardless of the means we fear they may use—is needed. Inordinate attention on the comparatively unique challenges of coping with unconventional weapons draws scarce resources away from the more basic but essential activities of law enforcement, intelligence, border and customs control, diplomacy, and military action.

Notes

1.   National Infrastructure Protection Center, *Homeland Security Information Update: Al Qa'ida Chemical, Biological, Radiological, and Nuclear Threat and Basic*

Countermeasures, Information Bulletin 03–003, February 12, 2003, www.nipc.gov/publications/infobulletins/2003/ib03–003.htm (accessed May 13, 2003). Hereinafter NIPC Information Bulletin.

2.   Central Intelligence Agency (CIA), *Terrorist CBRN: Materials and Effects (U),* CTC 2003–40058, May 2003.

3.   Ibid. Emphasis added.

4.   NIPC Information Bulletin. Emphasis added.

5.   See W. Seth Carus, "The Rajneeshees (1984)," in *Toxic Terror: Assessing Terrorist Use of Chemical and Biological Weapons,* ed. Jonathan B. Tucker (Cambridge, MA: MIT Press, 2000), pp. 55–70; Bruce Hoffman, "Tamil Tigers," in *Motives, Means, and Mayhem: Terrorist Acquisition and Use of Unconventional Weapons,* ed. John Parachini (forthcoming); Bruce Hoffman, "Terrorism and Weapons of Mass Destruction: An Analysis of Trends and Motivations," RAND Document P-8039, 1999, pp. 44–50.

6.   "United States Policy on Counterterrorism," Presidential Decision Directive 39, www.ojp.usdoj.gov/odp/docs/pdd39.htm (accessed July 12, 2003) (unclassified synopsis); "Protection Against Unconventional Threats to the Homeland and Americans Overseas," PDD-62, www.ojp.usdoj.gov/odp/docs/pdd62.htm (accessed July 12, 2003). For information on the increases in U.S. government spending to combat terrorism, as well as a useful basis for congressional and public review of the executive branch's policies and programs, see the report submitted by the director of the Office of Management and Budget (OMB) pursuant to section 1051 of the Fiscal Year 1998 National Defense Authorization Act (Public Law 105–85) entitled "Director of the Office of Management and Budget's Annual Report to Congress on Combating Terrorism" and the Bush administration's first annual report to Congress on combating terrorism, "Including Defense Against Weapons of Mass Destruction/Domestic Preparedness and Critical Infrastructure Protection," May 2001. For an analysis of the changes in funding to combat terrorism, see John Parachini, "Combating Terrorism: Assessing Threats, Risk Management, and Establishing Priorities," statement before the House Government Reform Subcommittee on National Security, Veterans Affairs, and International Relations, July 26, 2000, cns.miis.edu/pubs/reports/paraterr.htm (accessed July 12, 2003).

7.   Bruce Hoffman, *'Holy Terror': The Implications of Terrorism Motivated by a Religious Imperative,* RAND Document P-7834. (Santa Monica, CA: RAND, Corp., 1993).

8.   Richard A. Falkenrath, "Confronting Nuclear, Biological and Chemical Terrorism," *Survival* 40 no. 3 (Autumn 1998): 53.

9.   Office of Homeland Security, *National Strategy for Homeland Security* (Washington, DC: Office of Homeland Security, July 2002), p. ix.

10. Steven Simon and Daniel Benjamin, "America and the New Terrorism," *Survival* 42 no. 1 (Spring 2000): 72.

11. In addition to the 12 case studies contained each in *Toxic Terror* and in *Motives, Means, and Mayhem,* additional cases on the PKK, Chechen rebels, an anthrax hoaxer in California, and Kashmiri separatists were included.

12. Jonathan B. Tucker, "Lessons Learned," in *Toxic Terror: Assessing Terrorist Use of Chemical and Biological Weapons*, ed. Jonathan B. Tucker (Cambridge, MA: MIT Press, 2000), pp. 249–252.

13. Hoffman, "Tamil Tigers."

14. To see the text of Asahara's "Song of Sarin," see D. W. Brackett, *Holy Terror: Armageddon in Tokyo* (Weatherhill: New York, 1996), p. 119.

15. See Jessica Eve Stern, "Larry Wayne Harris (1998)," in *Toxic Terror: Assessing Terrorist Use of Chemical and Biological Weapons*, ed. Jonathan B. Tucker (Cambridge, MA: MIT Press, 2000). See also Jessica Stern and Darcy Bender, "James Dalton Bell," in *Motives, Means, and Mayhem: Terrorist Acquisition and Use of Unconventional Weapons*, ed. John Parachini (forthcoming); Masaaki Sugishima, "Poisonings in Japan," in *Motives, Means, and Mayhem: Terrorist Acquisition and Use of Unconventional Weapons*, ed. John Parachini (forthcoming).

16. Hoffman, "Tamil Tigers."

17. Jeremy McDermott, "FARC," in *Motives, Means, and Mayhem: Terrorist Acquisition and Use of Unconventional Weapons*, ed. John Parachini (forthcoming).

18. Milton Leitenberg, "The Widespread Distortion of Information on the Efforts to Produce Biological Warfare Agents by the Japanese Aum Shinrikyo Group: A Case Study in the Serial Propagation of Misinformation," *Terrorism and Political Violence* 11 no. 4 (winter 1999). For a list of Aum attacks with biological agents, see David E. Kaplan, "Aum Shinrikyo (1995)," in *Toxic Terror: Assessing Terrorist Use of Chemical and Biological Weapons*, ed. Jonathan B. Tucker (Cambridge, MA: MIT Press, 2000), p. 221.

19. Bruce Hoffman, "The Logic of Suicide Terrorism: Lessons from Israel that America Must Learn," *Atlantic Monthly* (June 2003): p. 43.

20. John V. Parachini, "Comparing Motives and Outcomes of Mass Casualty Terrorism Involving Conventional and Unconventional Weapons," *Studies in Conflict & Terrorism* 24 (2001): 401. See Falkenrath, "Confronting Nuclear, Biological and Chemical Terrorism," p. 52.

21. For the types of challenges toxic warfare can pose, see Theodore Karasik, *Toxic Warfare* (Santa Monica, CA: RAND, 2002). For further information on government tabletop exercises, see U.S. General Accounting Office, "Combating Terrorism: Analysis of Federal Counterterrorist Exercises," *Briefing Report to Congressional Committees*, GAO/NSIAD-99–157BR (Washington, DC: GAO), June 1999, www.gao.gov/archive/1999/ns99157b.pdf (accessed July 30, 2003).

22. In Arabic, HAMAS is an acronym for "Harakat Al-Muqawama Al-Islamia"—Islamic Resistance Movement—and a word meaning courage and bravery.

23. Magnus Ranstorp, "Hamas," in *Motives, Means, and Mayhem: Terrorist Acquisition and Use of Unconventional Weapons*, ed. John Parachini (forthcoming).

24. McDermott, "FARC."

25. Roger Davies and Michael Dolamore, "PIRA," in *Motives, Means, and Mayhem: Terrorist Acquisition and Use of Unconventional Weapons*, ed. John Parachini (forthcoming).

26. For reports on potential IRA-FARC chemical cooperation, see David Sharrock, "Rebel Weapons 'Have IRA Hallmark,'" *Times* (London), February 8, 2003, p. 20; Andrew

Selsky, "U.S. Investigation of Deaths of Colombian Police Discovers Trace of Cyanide," Associated Press, August 21, 2002.

27. Jessica Stern, "Terrorist Motivations and Unconventional Weapons," in *Planning the Unthinkable: How New Powers Will Use Nuclear, Biological and Chemical Weapons*, eds. Peter R. Lavoy, Scott D. Sagan, and James J. Wirtz (Ithaca and London: Cornell University Press, 2000), p. 229.

28. Ibid.

Chapter 4

Invasive Species:
The Biological Threat to America

Robert J. Pratt

Defending our nation against its enemies is the first and fundamental commitment of the federal government. Today, that task has changed dramatically. Enemies in the past needed great armies and great industrial capabilities to endanger America. Now, shadowy networks of individuals can bring great chaos and suffering to our shores for less than it costs to purchase a single tank.

—President George W. Bush,
National Security Strategy of the United States, September 2002

Before September 11, 2001, when American leaders prepared for war, they envisioned enemies using bombs, tanks, guns, military force, and other traditional armaments. The attacks on that fateful day forever changed the way the United States and the world would view the nature of war. Using four hijacked commercial jetliners, terrorists attacked the United States, killing some 3,000 men and women.

This surprise attack was not a symmetric attack, but an asymmetric one.[1] Furthermore, a non-state entity conducted this attack at a relatively low cost of under $500,000.[2] However, that may have been just the beginning of the asymmetric threats we face. The success of the attack, and the devastation inflicted on the nation at a relatively low cost, will doubtless inspire our adversaries to continue to employ asymmetric methods to threaten and weaken the United States. Among those methods may be the introduction of an invasive species, a disease pathogen, or some other biological threat.

Introducing Invasive Species

Presidential Executive Order 13112 defines invasive species as "a species that is (1) non-native (or alien) to the ecosystem under consideration and (2) whose introduction causes or is likely to cause economic or environmental harm or harm to human health."[3] An invasive species can be a microbe, plant, animal, or other organism. These invaders may be moved from their natural habitat and introduced to a new environment, either purposefully or by accident. The simple act of moving a species not indigenous to the area to a new habitat does not make it invasive. For centuries people have moved species around the world for agricultural and other purposes. Examples of noninvasive species are numerous—from livestock to grain crops to ornamental plants. Most of these species are non-threatening and benign, but some species can be threatening because of their adverse impact on their new environment. Their introduction may threaten the natural balance in the ecosystem because of their competitive nature, may threaten human and agricultural plant and animal health, and may cause economic damage through the cost of controlling or managing the species. These threatening species are "invasive species."

Historically, the introduction of an invasive species has not been intentional, nor has it been the purposeful act of an adversary to weaken or attack the United States. Typically, invasive species have been accidentally introduced when they were imported for ornamental purposes, escaped from captivity, or were carelessly released into the environment. Often invasive species arrived by means of ocean vessels' ballasts, or in pallets, produce, or plant nursery stock. Additionally, animals and other agricultural products have transported them to the United States.[4]

The new species may flourish and rapidly expand, as they typically have few or no natural enemies in their new environment. Parasites, pathogens, or predators that would inhibit or limit their spread may be few or nonexistent. In addition, the new environment often provides a better medium for growth and reproduction than the species' original surroundings.[5] With these advantages, native species may find it difficult to compete and survive against a new, more energetic and prolific neighbor.

A 1999 study by Cornell University estimated that approximately 50,000 foreign species have invaded the United States since the 1700s, and the number in the last 30 years has increased at an alarming rate.[6] Ten to 15 percent of these foreign species are considered threatening or invasive. Their effects range from being a nuisance to causing economic damage, health problems, and endangerment of native species. In fact, 42 percent of "endangered" or "threatened" species are at risk because of invasive species.[7] One hundred million acres of the United States are covered by invasive plants, and the rate of spread is 14 percent per year—an area twice the size of Delaware.[8] Since 1985, the U.S. Department of Agriculture's Animal and Plant Health Inspection Service (APHIS) has intercepted 7,400 species of plant pests at our country's borders.[9] The U.S. Department of Transportation estimates that every day 4,600 acres of land are colonized by invasive species in the United States.[10] Every 60 seconds, oceangoing vessels release 40,000 gallons of foreign ballast water in American waters, often releasing invasive species.[11]

Historical Examples

History offers many examples of invasive species damaging their new parent environment. Four revealing examples include (1) the invasion of multiple species in San Francisco Bay, (2) the glassy-winged sharpshooter, (3) "foot-and-mouth" disease (aphthovirus), and (4) the brown tree snake.

The San Francisco Bay plays an important role in American commerce. Many ocean-going vessels bring in foreign goods through the Bay's ports to trade with the United States. In addition to bringing in foreign goods, these transports also inadvertently bring in foreign invasive species; the Bay is invaded by a new species an average of once every 12 weeks.[12] From 1940 to 1969, the Bay saw a doubling of the number of entering invasive species. From 1970 to 1995, the rate jumped to almost a fivefold increase.[13] The

San Francisco Bay is now home to over 240 non-indigenous species.[14] In some areas of the Bay, it is difficult to find a native organism.[15]

In October 1986, three small clams were collected from the Bay by a college biology class and later identified as a foreign species from Asia: potamocorbula amurinsis. In 1996, this species reached densities of 50,000 clams per square meter, a density that filters the entire water in the Bay at least once and up to two times a day. These prolific clams virtually eliminated phytoplankton, the base of the food chain in the Bay. Although the final effects have yet to be determined, this disruption in the food chain can only be detrimental.[16]

The second example is the glassy-winged sharpshooter, an invasive insect that hosts the bacterium xylella fastidiosa. The insect was first detected in California in 1990. Although it is uncertain how it arrived in California, it is believed to have arrived on imported plants. The bacterium xylella fastidiosa causes Pierce's Disease in grapes, which infects and kills the grapevine. The glassy-winged sharpshooter transmits and spreads the disease when it feeds on the plant. Severe outbreaks of the disease necessitated destruction of diseased plants and a major replanting of grapevines, resulting in a reduction in grape production.[17] Tourism and grape-related industries are collectively worth $35 billion in California. The bacteria-carrying insect has cost a $40-million overall loss in California's grape, wine, and raisin industry, and an undisclosed amount in the tourism industry.[18]

A third example is foot-and-mouth disease (aphthovirus), a highly infectious disease that infects cloven-hoofed animals. The disease struck Britain in 2001 with a vengeance, killing over a thousand livestock,[19] with millions more voluntarily killed or destroyed to prevent the spread of the disease.[20] Furthermore, to prevent the disease from spreading from Great Britain, the European Union placed an embargo on British meat. In turn, the United States placed a temporary ban on meat imports from the entire European Union and Chile. To control the spread of the disease in Britain, limits were placed on movement of people and equipment throughout the area. Overall, foot-and-mouth disease cost British companies the equivalent of $30 billion, with a $300,000 average loss to large businesses and a $75,000 average loss to small businesses.[21]

A fourth and powerful example of the effect of invasive species is the accidental introduction of the brown tree snake into Guam. The brown tree snake was probably brought into Guam during World War II by military ships arriving from the South Pacific. Its introduction eventually resulted in 1,200 incidents of power outages and the extinction of several native species, including 10 of the 13 native bird species, 2 of the 3 native bat species, and 6 of the 12 native lizard species.[22] The snake is indeed a public nuisance; it has spread across the island at a rapid rate and achieved densities of 12,000 snakes per square mile.[23] The snakes are very aggressive and have been reported to attack small children while they sleep. One in every thousand visits to the emergency room is the result of snakebite from the slightly venomous snake.

As a result, Guam, which was once a popular tourist site, has lost most of its tourism business. Before the brown tree snake's invasion, tourism ranked third as a revenue source, surpassed only by federal government and military expenditures. Transportation and shipping have slowed to ensure no further spread of the snake. Healthcare costs on the island have risen due to snakebites. The snake has gravely affected agriculture, where production and revenues have steadily declined since the snake was introduced in 1945. The snake's predation pressure on both live animals and eggs makes it almost impossible to raise poultry. Insect species that were formerly controlled by species eliminated by the brown tree snake are now damaging fruits and vegetables. Increased insect populations demand more pesticides, which increases the cost of agricultural production. Direct damages in losses of overall productivity in the country are estimated at between $1 million and $4 million per year, with estimated research and control costs of the brown tree snake at an additional $4 million.[24]

In all, the introduction of the brown tree snake has had a more negative ecological impact on the island of Guam than all of the heavy fighting and naval bombardment that leveled the island's forests in World War II. The island's ecology recovered from World War II with time, but time offers no chance for recovery of the extinct species lost to the brown tree snake.[25]

Prospects for an Attack

Terrorist adversaries will not overlook the overwhelming impact that invasive species could have on the United States. An adversary could use invasive species as an asymmetric method of attack to weaken the country by inflicting tremendous economic and psychological damage. Such an attack could ultimately weaken the will of the people and affect national policy by straining the economy, tainting America's food supply, or endangering the health of the populace. In addition, adversaries could strike a strong blow while avoiding any symmetric retaliation.

Adversaries may seek to weaken the United States as a way to achieve a more equitable political, economic, and military balance of power. Today, the United States is the world's only true superpower, so dominating that it is sometimes referred to as a "hyperpower."[26] To attack the United States directly in a symmetric manner would defy logic and result in the rapid destruction of a weaker adversary.

Additionally, the United States is increasing its dominance through constant incorporation of state-of-the-art technology and advanced information systems. Few adversaries will be able and willing to commit the resources necessary to build a force that is a symmetric peer competitor of the United States. An asymmetric attack, however, could delay the United States' transformation of military forces and continued buildup of military and national power. This could allow an adversary the opportunity for a buildup of its own, to permit a direct, symmetric confrontation at a later time when the correlation of forces and the balance of military strength might be more favorable. A successful asymmetric attack also would provide a more favorable position for an adversary to use in negotiating for desired goals.

Terrorists also have other reasons for using invasive species. Traditionally, terrorists have used violence and fear as a means of political coercion to "undermine the legitimacy of the targeted government and garner support among a disaffected populace." Other nonpolitical objectives include using "indiscriminate violence to create a general environment of fear and chaos prior to a general overthrow of Western political order or . . . even simply [to] seek anarchy as a goal." An example of this is the subway sarin attack in Tokyo by the Aum Shinrikyo group, which took no credit for the attack.[27]

Yet another reason for terrorists' use of an invasive species is the new "war paradigm."[28] Paradigmatic theorists assert that since terrorist groups typically lack the ability to confront their adversary directly, they will take a more indirect, less confrontational approach to conducting terrorist acts. This long-term approach does not advance specific demands but intends to inflict damage to wear down an adversary over time. Consider the strategy of Usama bin Ladin and the al-Qaida organization. The bombings in the 1990s of the World Trade Center, of the embassies in Nairobi and Dar-es-Saalam, and of U.S. military forces at the Khobar Towers, exemplify this protracted war paradigm.[29] They are not isolated events. Rather, they are a loosely coordinated series of attacks designed to confuse, disrupt, and demoralize the U.S. government and its citizens over time.

Invasive species could be used to support all three of these terrorist motives. The introduction of fast-spreading invasive species and pathogens, such as smallpox and other microbes that threaten human health or food safety, would directly support the terrorist tactics of causing violence and instilling fear to undermine the legitimacy of government or to support anarchical objectives. However, the use of most other invasive species would support the latter, "protracted war" paradigm. Most of these are slower in their effects and would require some time to cause damage. Such a slower, covert attack might go undetected for years until the species are well implanted and impossible to counter. The long-term economic, health, and psychological effects of using invasive species could strike a tremendous blow at the United States by exhausting resources and national will over time.

Potential Effects

One of the primary effects of a terrorist introduction of an invasive species would be economic damage. The 1999 Cornell University study estimated the cost of invasive species to be $138 billion annually in their effects and control measures in the United States.[30] This equates to more than one-third of the funding allocated to the total military budget in the 2003 National Defense Authorization Act.

In addition, according to the Congressional Budget Office, discretionary spending for defense as a percentage of the total GDP has been decreasing from 1962 to 2001. Domestic needs compete heavily for tax dollars. Given the drastic increases forecast in spending for Social Security, Medicare, and Medicaid in the years ahead, expenditures for national defense will undoubtedly be constrained.

If an adversary chooses the right invasive species, the costs to counter its effects could be dramatic. Coupled with a strained economy and a tight budget, it could become difficult to sustain the funds to fully man and equip U.S. military forces at current levels. It might become extremely difficult to fund the kind of costly transformation needed to better prepare our armed forces to tackle this threat. Therefore, the second- or third-order effects of an invasive species attack could mean less money for discretionary spending, and ultimately, a weakened military.

Second, military resources could also be diverted to meet an emerging crisis. Military forces could be needed to cordon off infested areas or to assist in caring for the ill from an invasive bacteria or virus. Consider an outbreak of Ebola or smallpox. National Guard forces would be diverted for homeland security missions and thus not be available for contingencies elsewhere or to support major regional wars. Military forces likely also would suffer direct casualties from such an attack, as the same invasive microbes or pathogens that attack the civilian population would attack military personnel. Whole Army divisions and specialized units could be rendered physically ineffective from an invasive disease. The ensuing psychological impact on both the military and the country would be immense.

Third, invasive species could diminish the industrial capability and productivity of the United States to support a war. Resources used to mobilize the nation's industrial base, conceivably would be diverted to control the effects of the invasive species. Personnel needed to support industry and augment military forces could be incapacitated, or be unwilling to work in areas where they would be exposed to infectious bacteria. Invasive species might directly attack timber or other natural resources used as raw material for industry, thereby forcing the United States to rely on imports or other expensive alternatives for raw materials.

Fourth, illness could be spread rampantly by an invasive disease. A biological attack could begin with one infected person or the release of toxins in a highly populated area, such as a subway or a sports stadium. Victims probably would not initially know they were infected. The first victims might report to their doctors with common flu-like complaints, and their symptoms could easily be misdiagnosed. Even after suspicion of a deliberate attack, it would take time for the Centers for Disease Control to identify the agent. Meanwhile, the contagious disease would spread, leading to widespread illness and public panic. Critical community services, where available, would be strained. Officials might consider quarantining affected communities. But quarantines are very difficult, if not impossible, to enforce on a large scale. In the end, the disease could spread in epidemic proportions.[31]

Health care costs for an invasive contagious disease in this scenario would be phenomenal. The health care system would be greatly stressed in terms of its capacity to handle patients, and the money, facilities, and professionals available to support the population's health care needs. The cost of providing such massive care would eventually be placed on the consumer, further straining the economy.

Fifth, the agricultural sector and a reliable food supply could be deeply affected. A recent U.S. government report asserted that the "U.S. agricultural sector is especially vulnerable to agro terrorism . . . and a successful attack could result in local or regional economic destabilization," ultimately affecting international commerce.[32] Citizens have come to expect a safe and cheap food supply. Although American agriculture is diverse and spread over many states, large portions of it are concentrated in local areas. The top five agricultural states account for 34 percent of the nation's total agricultural production. Some crops are far more concentrated in specific regions than others.

For example, California produces 100 percent of the nation's almonds, 92 percent of its grapes, 78 percent of its lettuce, 75 percent of its strawberries, 47 percent of its tomatoes, and 34 percent of its oranges. Such concentrations can be further localized. Forty-one percent of California's strawberry production is concentrated in two contiguous counties. Seventy percent of its cattle production is concentrated in a 200-mile radius. Such concentration makes our agricultural assets especially vulnerable to a terrorist attack using an invasive species.[33]

The cost to agriculture from the introduction of one or several invasive species is difficult to predict, but it could be extraordinary. The attack would not only affect the producer, but the entire producer-consumer chain, from the grower and those employed in agriculture-related fields, through packagers and distributors, and ultimately the consumer. In 1999, farming and its related industries accounted for 16 percent of the U.S. gross national product. In the same year, agriculture employed 17 percent of the U.S. work force, some 24 million people.[34] In 1997, U.S. farmers sold $208 billion in agricultural products.[35] The amount of economic damage from an invasive species attack would vary considerably depending on the extent of infestation, the crops or livestock affected, the response, and the ability to counter, contain, or destroy the species. Effects also would be dependent on the availability of substitute products, the elasticity of supply, and on the ability to ramp up production elsewhere.[36]

Last, but certainly not least, as *Joint Vision 2020* notes, there would be psychological and political costs resulting from the introduction of an invasive species; "The psychological impact of an attack might far outweigh the actual physical damage inflicted."[37] The apparent inability of the government of the United States to protect its people and resources would have severe detrimental effects on the social contract between the government and the people. The government would lose credibility, with a resulting loss of confidence and productivity from its citizens.[38]

Historically, affecting consumer confidence has been the objective of attacks on agriculture.[39] For example, in 1989, a previously unknown group called the Breeders threatened to spread the Medfly to damage crops in California if the state did not stop aerial spraying of pesticides. Although no one was caught or prosecuted, that season's dense Medfly population confirmed that a deliberate infestation was being conducted. Although their attack may not have been successful, the Breeders attracted much publicity by destroying crops and reducing consumer confidence.[40]

Another example is the West Nile Virus. First detected in 1999 in the state of New York, by 2000 it had spread up and down the East Coast. In 2001, it spread north and further into the central part of the United States. In 2002, it was reported in 32 states, in Canada, and was suspected to be in Mexico. As of September 2002, there had been 1,965 West Nile cases resulting in 94 deaths.[41] West Nile Virus is non-native, and it is not known how it was introduced into the United States. As the number of cases and deaths continue to increase and further affect public health (and possibly our blood supply), it is uncertain what psychological effects will result and what effects it will have on everyday life. If it continues to spread, will the elderly or people who are not in good health avoid outdoor activity? If it is determined that the introduction of West Nile virus was intentional, would it be wise to inform the public? Such an announcement of an intentional infestation could spread panic, fear, lack of trust in the government and its services, and in turn support the goals of the perpetrator.[42]

An invasive species coupled with other forms of asymmetric warfare also would have a synergistic effect. If an enemy focused on creating maximum economic impact and attacked along multiple, low-profile paths, he would be more likely to generate overwhelming effects. Such an attack could include an invasive species coupled with a cyber attack, the use of weapons of mass destruction such as a "dirty bomb," or the use of more standard terrorist bombing techniques. Likewise, invasive species could be coupled with more symmetric methods of conventional force-on-force warfare. Such multifaceted attacks would have a greater chance of destroying or severely damaging American national power. If two or more methods proved successful, the combined synergistic effect could be much greater, producing more physical and psychological damage.

Production and Introduction

Invasive species are relatively cheap and easy to produce or acquire, and introduce into the environment. Large numbers need not be introduced, only enough to start a population base. Introduction at multiple locations in numbers large enough to begin colonization would reduce the risk of both detection, and the failure of one or two clusters to colonize and establish a population base for the species' spread. Introduction in multiple locations also would decrease the amount of time needed to establish and spread the invasive species to dangerous levels. Most microbes can be easily produced.

Kathleen Bailey, who interviewed pharmaceutical manufacturers, professors, and graduate students, noted that, "Several biologists with only $10,000 worth of equipment could produce a significant quantity of biological agents. The required site equipment would fit in a small room, and the glassware, centrifuges, growth media, etc., can all be manufactured by virtually any country."[43]

Detection, particularly at American borders, would be extremely difficult. The mere fact that billions of dollars of illegal drugs are smuggled annually into the United States speaks for itself. Border inspectors have difficulty finding unintentional smuggling violations, let alone detecting the purposefully concealed smuggling of invasive species. Insects, plant seeds, or a vial of microbes could be easily hidden. Most likely, inspectors would not even know what to look for.

Once an invasive species is established, it would be extremely difficult to discern who had implanted it unless the perpetrator or group claimed credit for the attack. In turn, it would be virtually impossible to track it to its source. If the United States could not identify who introduced the species, it would be difficult to counter or apply national power in retribution for such an attack. With all the accidental introduction of so many invasive species, how could we legitimately and credibly blame a suspected adversary? A current example is the West Nile Virus. As previously noted, no one knows how it was introduced to this country. Some, though, including at least one analyst at the Center for Defense Information, suspect it was brought to the United States as a terrorist act.[44]

Once an invasive species becomes established, it is difficult if not impossible to exterminate it without a huge expenditure. Our history is replete with failures to control invasive species once they are established. The gypsy moth, zebra mussel, purple loosestrife, and Kudzu are just a few examples. The foot-and-mouth disease outbreak in England is an example of an invasive disease being controlled, but at a high cost ($30 billion).[45] The Asian long-horned beetle is another example. Thought to have been carried into this country in wooden pallets from China, it was detected in New York City and Chicago in 1996. The United States has been battling the beetle ever since. In 1996, the cost to control it was $4 million in New York alone. Total annual revenue from all New York related industries affected is $11 billion, and the total for the affected U.S. industries is $138 billion. In response, Secretary of Agriculture Dan Glickman declared a state of emergency, authorizing $5.5 million to aid in the prevention, detection, control, and eradication of the pest in 2001. Even with all this expenditure of effort and resources, however, the Asian long-horned beetle has yet to be exterminated.[46]

Genetic Engineering

Genetic engineering is defined as "the directed alteration of genetic material by intervention in genetic processes." Adversaries of the United States may modify the genetics of an invasive species to increase its competitiveness, virulence, lethality, or resistance to control measures. Subtle changes in gene and DNA sequencings can have drastic effects on the characteristics of an organism.

Genetic engineering is a common practice in agriculture. Plants are engineered to be hardier, more chemical-tolerant, and more resistant to insects. For example, Bacillus thuringiensis, a bacterium commonly known as "Bt," is used as a natural insecticide. The toxin gene, which makes it an effective insecticide, was identified by scientists and inserted into agricultural crops such as field corn to make them resistant to corn borers. When the corn borer ingests plant material, it dies from the toxic gene.[47]

Another example is glyphosate, the active ingredient in Roundup herbicide. Glyphosate is a broad-spectrum herbicide used to kill most herbaceous plants. Microbiologists inserted a glyphosate-resistant gene into corn, soybeans, and other agricultural crops, enabling farmers to liberally spray glyphosate and kill all other plants except the resistant variety. Inserting these same genes into an aggressive invasive plant would nullify many of the chemicals used to control unwanted plants, and even make them resistant to some natural biological insect controls, thereby making the invasive species a more lethal, faster-spreading, asymmetric weapon.

Another example is the laboratory mouse on display in the Smithsonian Institution which scientists genetically modified to be susceptible to cancer. Scientists identified and inserted the gene to aid in cancer research. If scientists can modify the mouse's genetic makeup, they can modify an invasive species to make it more competitive, resilient, or tailored for a particular need.

Adversaries with technological and scientific support could genetically modify all types of organisms. If the technology or the scientific support is not available, they could purchase or acquire it through the black market.

Alastair Hay, an expert on biological warfare from the University of Leeds in the United Kingdom, debriefed defecting scientists from Biopreparat (a clandestine group of facilities spread across Russia and Kazakhstan). From these interviews, it is apparent he believes genetically modified organisms currently exist. One of them is a form of the plague that is resistant to 16 different antibiotics.[48] Stephen Block, a biophysicist at Stanford University and the leader of JASON (a study of a group of scientists hired by the U.S. government for technical advice), commenting on the possibilities of genetic engineering, observed, "If you put a bunch of biologists in a room and asked them to brainstorm, you'd come up with countless possibilities."[49]

In the wrong hands, genetic engineering technology applied to an already competitive or virulent invasive species would make control methods difficult, if not impossible. New methods of control would have to be developed, tested, and fielded to defeat the genetically modified organism. Serums would be less effective, and diagnosis of human pathogens could change and become harder to recognize. It would take a considerable amount of time to isolate, test, and determine what control or treatment methods would be necessary to battle the organism.[50] Additionally, production and distribution of counter-mechanisms in large numbers would take significant time and resources.

Hypothetical Attack

What would an attack with an invasive species or a group of invasive species look like? What effects might it have? There are many possibilities, but let's consider one hypothetical nightmare: The year is 2025. America remains a strong military power, but her national power is waning. Adversaries of the United States have subversively smuggled invasive species and pathogens into the country and attacked her in the first decades of the twenty-first century. The attacks were designed to weaken the U.S. economy and diminish America's influence around the world. Asian long-horned beetles have decimated the American forests and severely weakened the related $138 billion timber industry.[51] The brown tree snake was introduced in Hawaii and the population is rapidly growing, nearing densities of 12,000 per square mile, as was seen in Guam in 2002.[52] Hawaii's tourist industry and economy are faltering. American agriculture and its food supply are also in jeopardy. Foot-and-mouth disease has killed many livestock, and hundreds of thousands of livestock were destroyed before the disease could be contained. Most countries have banned American exports of meat due to concerns about the spread of disease. Similar problems have occurred in the grain industry after a contagious rust was identified on summer and winter wheat. West Nile Virus deaths continue to rise. A "small" outbreak of smallpox left five million Americans dead, requiring vaccination for the remainder of the population, and further stressing the health care system. No country or organization takes credit for the attacks, nor has the United States been able to determine who or what organization is responsible. The American economy is in a full depression. America has shifted what little discretionary funds remain in the federal budget away from defense spending. The military has abandoned its technological transformation to maintain current military strength and programs. Adversaries are rapidly approaching parity in military strength and should surpass America's military prowess in the near future. America's national security is threatened.

Executive Order 13112

That distressing scenario indicates that the detrimental effects of invasive species and pathogens are potentially insurmountable. Local governments, state governments, environmental groups, farmers, ranchers, and scientists collectively have urged the federal government to coordinate the defensive effort and to make invasive species control a higher-priority issue. In 1999, in response to this pressure, President Clinton issued Executive Order 13112 on invasive species.[53] It was designed to coordinate and enhance federal activities "to prevent the introduction of invasive species and provide for their control and to minimize the economic, ecological, and human health impacts that invasive species cause."[54]

Executive Order 13112 established the National Invasive Species Council, whose members include the Secretary of State, the Secretary of the Treasury, the Secretary of

Defense, the Secretary of the Interior, the Secretary of Agriculture, the Secretary of Commerce, the Secretary of Transportation, and the Administrator of the Environmental Protection Agency.[55] The purpose of the Invasive Species Council is to prepare and oversee a "National Invasive Species Management Plan," which would detail the requirements, goals, objectives, and efforts of involved federal agencies.[56] Additionally, the council was established to "provide national leadership on invasive species; see that their federal efforts are coordinated and effective; promote action at local, state, tribal, and ecosystem levels; identify recommendations for international cooperation; [and] facilitate a coordinated network to document and monitor invasive species for federal agencies to use in implementing the National Environmental Policy Act."[57]

The Invasive Species Council developed a national management plan within the 18-month period set by the executive order. The plan identified nine interrelated and equally important areas of concern for addressing invasive species issues and countering their potentially devastating spread (leadership, coordination, prevention, research, early detection and rapid response, international cooperation, information management, education, and public awareness); the coordinated activities emanating from these areas thus comprise the defense of the United States against invasive species.

Evaluation and Recommendations

Executive Order 13112 makes an excellent start toward development of a much-needed national plan for invasive species control. The establishment of the Invasive Species Council's National Management Plan continues the movement in the right direction. Despite this good start, however, there remains much to do. Al-Qaida terrorists continue to threaten the United States, and could be introducing invasive species to weaken this country even at this moment.

First, we must prepare for the purposeful introduction of invasive species. The National Invasive Species Management Plan and the General Accounting Office's report to Congress on the matter do not currently consider the intentional introduction of an invasive species as a security threat. Identification of all asymmetric threats and pathways should be anticipated in order to defend the U.S. homeland, to include an adversary's use of invasive species. Potential pathways should be identified and analyzed in the council's prioritizing of invasive species problems. Adversaries may choose methods of introduction that are considerably different from those that happen by accident.

Second, the plan conveys no sense of urgency. The management plan is not being implemented fast enough, particularly to counter a known hostile threat. The plan's timeline should be accelerated to quickly mobilize the resources and efforts of all agencies involved. As with any new plan, deficiencies surface and problems arise during implementation. The plan was issued in 2001, and many of the proposed programs have yet to be implemented. The sooner the plan is fully implemented, the sooner its deficiencies and problems can be identified and fixed. Rapid identification and response is critical to success in controlling invasive species. If the plan is not fully implemented, invasive species may become established and spread before proposals to control them are fully implemented.

A third deficiency of the plan is the development and implementation of a comprehensive national system for detecting all types of invasive species infestations and responding to them. All levels of government, national through local, will need to work together under one national system to adequately detect and combat invasive species and protect the homeland. Both the GAO report and the National Invasive Species Management Plan identify this weakness. According to the GAO report this "system could provide (1) integrated planning to encourage partnerships, coordinate funding, and develop response priorities; (2) technical assistance and other resources; and (3) guidance on effective response measures."[58]

The Invasive Species Council's Management Plan adequately identified this need, recommending by July 2003 the development of a program of coordinated rapid response and support. Again, this is a slow process, with nothing yet produced. The Centers for Disease Control's reaction plan to an invasive disease dangerous to human health offers a good model for responding to invasive species. The council's plan indicates that insufficient resources, lack of funding, jurisdictional issues, limited technology, and other factors are the prominent reasons for lack of a national system.[59]

The fourth deficiency is rapid response. Officials from the Departments of Agriculture, Interior, Commerce, and Defense have reported that, "rapid response needs have not been and are not being adequately met."[60] Reasons for this include lack of resources, lack of attention to the problem, not detecting infestations in their early stages of spread, insufficient understanding about the potential risk, and lack of technology to thwart the colonization of the invasive species. In addition, the nation needs a systematic national approach with criteria to determine when a rapid crisis response is needed. Many agencies stated they did not know when or what criteria to use when requesting a rapid response. Rapid response criteria should be based on a fair risk analysis. Currently, responses to invasive species on agricultural land receive a higher priority than on non-agricultural land or native areas. This may not be the right priority for a terrorist attack. Rapid response decisions should be based on common risk criteria, and these risks should include intentional introductions of invasive species.[61]

Adequate funding is currently unavailable for an aggressive invasive species program. Implementing the strategies identified in the Invasive Species National Management Plan will be costly. In fiscal year 2000, the total expenditure of the federal government on invasive species-related activities was over $611 million. The Department of Agriculture spent over $556 million—90 percent of the total federal outlay—to fight invasive species. The Department of Interior spent over $30 million, and the Department of Defense spent over $12 million.[62] Of the $611 million budgeted, rapid response costs were less than one-quarter, resourced at $148.7 million. This is not adequate.[63] More funding is necessary to support the plan. If the federal government cannot handle the monetary burden, then the tasks should be shifted to the state and local levels. An official from the Bureau of Land Management aptly observed, "You can pay now or later, but you will eventually pay sometime."[64]

The Invasive Species Management Plan does not address invasive pathogens that affect human health. However, such pathogens fall under the Presidential Executive Order 13112 definition of an invasive species and should be included in the Management Plan. If not, then the definition should be changed to exclude human disease pathogens. This must be made clear to determine who responds and who manages an outbreak of such pathogens. The Centers for Disease Control currently responds to the introduction of invasive human pathogens, but its efforts are not integrated into the Invasive Species

Management Plan. Nor is the Department of Health and Human Services or the Centers for Disease Control represented on the council. The plan simply does not include all of the needed agencies.

Last, the Department of Homeland Security ought to be integrated into the council and, indeed, assume the lead agency role. Although the Department of Homeland Security is new, the executive order should be amended to add the department as a full, leading member. Invasive species management is a homeland security issue. The new department should lead the council's efforts to integrate inspection, detection, prevention, and crisis response capabilities across government agencies. Invasive species management should be embedded into the homeland security strategy.

Conclusion

An adversary's purposeful introduction of invasive species or disease pathogens into the United States presents a potentially devastating threat. Currently, the United States is not adequately prepared for such an attack. The council's plan is designed more to protect U.S. agriculture from accidental introductions of invasive species than to counter intentional, hostile introductions. To better protect the United States from an attack, we need to prepare now.

Recommendations to improve protection from an adversary's use of invasive species should include timely national identification of the employment of an invasive species as a potential weapon and appropriate planning and preparation to counter its use as a weapon. Additionally, the federal government must speed up the process for full implementation of the council's plan to fully implement a comprehensive national system for management and control of this potential threat. The council should develop and implement criteria for rapid response based on risk correlation. The plan should be fully resourced and actively supported at an accelerated pace. Mitigation measures should include invasive human disease pathogens as part of the plan, or else the definition should be changed to exclude such pathogens. The Department of Health and Human Services and the Department of Homeland Defense should participate on the National Invasive Species Council. Finally, invasive species protection and management should be made a key part of the homeland security strategy.

Despite America's status and strength as a superpower, the United States was tragically vulnerable to attack on September 11, 2001. That attack came not from cruise missiles, ballistic missiles, bombing, or other conventional weapons but by unconventional, asymmetric means. Today, the homeland is vulnerable to a different type of asymmetric attack; a biological attack from invasive species. We should act now to strengthen our defenses to protect ourselves from such attacks. Our future and our children's future may depend on it.

Notes

1. Asymmetric threats are defined by the Pentagon's 1999 *Joint Strategy Review* as attempts to "circumvent or undermine U.S. strengths while exploiting U.S. weaknesses, using methods that significantly differ from the United States' expected method of operations." In other words, symmetry implies an enemy's use of force for

which we have anticipated some form of defense, while asymmetry implies a coordinated attack on targets (and using weapons) which we have not anticipated (typically on noncombat or civilian targets).

2. Daniel Rubin and Michael Dorgan, "Terrorists' Sept. 11 Plot a Many-Tentacled Creature," *Knight Rider Newspapers*, September 9, 2002, www.tallahassee.com/mld/tallahassee/news/special_packages/attack_ on_america/4020169.

3. National Invasive Species Council (NISC), "National Management Plan: Executive Summary," www.invasivespecies.gov/council/execsumm.shtml, p. 1.

4. Ibid.

5. Tim Abbey, "University of Connecticut; Integrated Peat Management—Check Those Plants for Unwanted Pests," Connecticut Agricultural Experiment Station, Windsor, Conn., 2001, www.hort.uconn.edu/ipm/nursery/htms/invasives.htm.

6. Lori Lach et al., "Environmental and Economic Costs Associated with Non-Indigenous Species in the United States," College of Agriculture and Life Sciences, Cornell University, Ithaca, N.Y., June 12, 1999, www.news.cornell.edu/releases/Jan99/species_costs.html.

7. Ibid.

8. US Department of Agriculture (USDA), Animal and Plant Health Inspection Service, "Invasive Species," April 2003, www.aphis.usda.gov/lpa/pubs/fsheet_faq_notice/fs_aphisinvasive.html.

9. Abbey, "Check Those Plants."

10. US Department of Transportation, Federal Highway Administration, *Guidance: Implementing Executive Order on Invasive Species,* June 20, 2001, www.fhwa.dot.gov/environment/em_inv.htm.

11. National Oceanic & Atmospheric Administration (NOAA), *America's Ocean Future,* www.publicaffairs.noaa.gov/pdf/ocean_rpt.pdf.

12. USDA, *Invasive Species.*

13. NISC, *National Management Plan,* www.invasivespecies.gov/council/nmptoc.shtml, p. 17.

14. NOAA, *America's Ocean Future.*

15. NISC, *National Management Plan,* www.invasivespecies.gov/council/intro.shtml.

16. NISC, *National Management Plan,* p. 17.

17. Mark Souder, "Small Carriers Deliver Big Worries to Local Agriculture," *Farm Bureau Bulletin*, April 2000, www.slofarmbureau.org/OldNews/april00.html.

18. NISC, "What Are the Invasive Species: Impacts of Invasive Species?," www.invasivespecies.gov/impacts.shtml.

19. Gavon Cameron and Jason Pate, "Covert Biological Weapons Attacks Against Agriculture Targets, Assessing the Impact Against U.S. Agriculture," in *Terrorism and Counterterrorism, Understanding the New Security Environment*, ed. Russell D. Howard and Reid L. Sawyer (Guilford, CT: McGraw Hill, 2003), p. 254.

20. John Leatherbury, "Living Through the FMD Outbreak," *Country Spirit* (Summer 2002): 13.

21. NISC, "What Are the Invasive Species: Impacts of Invasive Species?"

22. Ibid.

23. U.S. Geologic Service, "Safety and Health of Pacific Island Residents and Tourists," The Brown Tree Snake on Guam, www.mesc.usgs.gov/resources/education/bts/impacts/safety.asp.

24. U.S. Geologic Service, "Economic Damages from the Brown Tree Snake," The Brown Tree Snake on Guam, www.mesc.usgs.gov/resources/education/bts/invasion/intro_pred.asp.

25. U.S. Geologic Service, "Introduced Predators on Formerly Snake Free Oceanic Islands," The Brown Tree Snake on Guam, www.mesc.usgs.gov/resources/education/bts/impacts/economic.asp.

26. G. John Ikenberry, "Getting Hegemony Right," *National Interest*, 63 (Spring 2001): p. 17.

27. Gregory J. Rattray, "The Cyberterrorism Threat," in Howard and Sawyer, p. 224.

28. Caleb Carr, "Terrorism as Warfare," *World Policy Journal* 13 (Winter 1996–1997): 1–12.

29. Rattray, "The Cyberterrorism Threat," pp. 224–25.

30. Lach, "Enviornmental and Economic Costs."

31. Frank Cilluffo, Sharon Cardash, and Gordon N. Lederman, *Combating Chemical, Biological, Radiological, and Nuclear Terrorism: A Comprehensive Strategy: A Report of the CSIS Homeland Defense Project* (Washington, DC: CSIS Press, 2001), p. 5.

32. Gilmore Commission, "First Annual Report to the President and the Congress of the Advisory Panel to Assess Domestic Response Capabilities for Terrorism Involving Weapons of Mass Destruction, I: Assessing the Threat," December 15, 1999, www.rand.org/nsrd/terrpanel/terror.pdf, p. 12.

33. Cameron and Pate, pp. 258–59. Also, see the chapter in this volume by B. Bruemmer.

34. U.S. Congress, Senate, Committee on Appropriations, Subcommittee on Agriculture, Rural Development, and Related Agencies, "Statement of Keith Collins, Chief Economist, U.S. Department of Agriculture," May 17, 2001, www.usda.gov/oce/speeches/051701co.html.

35. Cameron and Pate, p. 258.

36. Ibid., p. 250.

37. Director for Strategic Plans and Policy, *Joint Vision 2020* (Washington, DC: GPO, June 2000), p. 5.

38. Ibid.

39. Ibid., p. 260.

40. Ibid., p. 253.

41. "US Senator Richard Durbin (D-IL) Holds Joint Hearing With Senate Health, Education, Labor and Pensions Committee on West Nile Virus," September 24 2002, environmentalrisk.cornell.edu/WNV/WNVEducDocs/SenateHearing 9–24–02.html.

42. Cameron and Pate, "Covert Biological Weapon Attacks," p. 257.

43. Jessica Stern, "Getting and Using the Weapons," in T*errorism and Counterterrorism: Understanding the New Security Environments,* ed. Russell D. Howard and Reid L. Sawyer (Guilford, CT: McGraw-Hill, 2003), p. 159.

44. Seva Gunitskiy, "Iraq and the West Nile Virus: A Possible Connection?" Center for Defense Information, Terrorism Project, October 28, 2002, www.cdi.org/terrorism/west-nile.cfm.

45. NISC, "What Are the Impacts of Invasive Species?"

46. USDA, Agricultural Research Service, *From East to West: The Asian Longhorned Beetle Has Landed,* www.ars.usda.gov/is/np/mba/apr00/asian.htm.

47. Jim Deacon, "The Microbial World: *Bacillus thuringiensis,*" Institute of Cell and Molecular Biology, University of Edinburgh, helios.bto.ed.ac.uk/bto/microbes/bt.htm.

48. Carina Dennis, "The Bugs of War," *Nature*, May 17, 2001, p. 232, www.nature.com/cgi-taf/DynaPage.taf?file=/nature/journal/v411/n6835/full/411232a0_fs.html.

49. Ibid.

50. Ibid., pp. 232–35.

51. USDA, *From East to West: The Asian Longhorned Beetle Has Landed.*

52. NISC, "What Are the Impacts of Invasive Species."

53. NISC, "Executive Summary."

54. Executive Order no. 13112, Invasive Species, February 3, 1999, ceq.eh.doe.gov/nepa/regs/eos/eo13112.html.

55. Ibid.

56. USDA, *Invasive Species.*

57. NISC, "Executive Summary."

58. General Accounting Office, *Invasive Species: Obstacles Hinder Federal Rapid Response to Growing Threat* (Washington, DC: GPO, 2001), p. 20.

59. NISC, *National Management Plan,* p. 5.

60. General Accounting Office, *Invasive Species*, p. 17.

61. Ibid., pp. 27–34.

62. Ibid., p. 4.

63. Ibid., p. 12.

64. Ibid., p. 20.

Chapter 5

The Logic of Suicide Terrorism

Bruce Hoffman

First you feel nervous about riding the bus. Then you wonder about going to a mall. Then you think twice about sitting for long at your favorite café. Then nowhere seems safe. Terrorist groups have a strategy—to shrink to nothing the areas in which people move freely—and suicide bombers, inexpensive and reliably lethal, are their latest weapons. Israel has learned to recognize and disrupt the steps on the path to suicide attacks. We must learn too.

Nearly everywhere in the world, it is taken for granted that one can simply push open the door to a restaurant, café, or bar, sit down, and order a meal or a drink. In Israel, however, the process of entering such a place is more complicated. There one often encounters an armed guard who, in addition to asking prospective patrons whether they themselves are armed, may quickly pat them down, feeling for the telltale bulge of a belt or a vest containing explosives. Establishments that cannot afford a guard or are unwilling to pass on the cost of one to customers simply keep their doors locked, responding to knocks with a quick glance through the glass and an instant judgment as to whether this or that person can be admitted safely. What would have been unimaginable a year ago is now not only routine, but reassuring. It has become the price of a redefined normality.

In the United States, in the months and years since 9/11 we, too, have had to become accustomed to an array of new, often previously inconceivable security measures, in airports and other transportation hubs, hotels, office buildings, sports stadiums, and concert halls. Although some are more noticeable and perhaps more inconvenient than others, the fact remains that they have redefined our own sense of normality. They are accepted because we feel more vulnerable than before. With every new threat to international security, we become more willing to live with stringent precautions and reflexive, almost unconscious wariness. With every new threat, that is, our everyday life becomes more like Israel's.

The situation in Israel, where an intensified suicide-bombing campaign changed the national mood and people's personal politics, is not analogous to that of the United States today. But the organization and the operations of the suicide bombers are neither limited to Israel and its conflict with the Palestinians nor unique to its geo-strategic position. The fundamental characteristics of suicide bombing and its strong attraction for the terrorist organizations behind it are universal: Suicide bombings are inexpensive and effective. They are less complicated and compromising than other kinds of terrorist operations. They guarantee media coverage. The suicide terrorist is the ultimate smart bomb. Perhaps most important, coldly efficient bombings tear at the fabric of trust that holds societies together. All these reasons doubtlessly account for the spread of suicide terrorism from the Middle East to Sri Lanka, to Turkey, Argentina, Chechnya, Russia, Algeria, and to the United States.

To understand the power that suicide terrorism can have over a populace—and what a populace can do to counter it—one naturally goes to the society that has been most deeply affected. As a researcher who has studied the strategies of terrorism for more than 25 years, I recently visited Israel to review the steps the military, the police, and the intelligence and security services have taken against a threat more pervasive and personal than ever before.

I looked at x-rays with Dr. Shmuel Shapira in his office at Jerusalem's Hadassah Hospital. "This is not a place to have a wristwatch," he said, as he described the injuries of a young girl who had been on her way to school one morning last November when a suicide terrorist detonated a bomb on her bus. Eleven of her fellow passengers were killed, and more than 50 others were wounded. The blast was so powerful that the hands and case of the bomber's wristwatch had turned into lethal projectiles, lodging in the girl's neck and ripping a major artery. The presence of such foreign objects in the bodies of his patients no longer surprises Shapira. "We have cases with a nail in the neck, or nuts and bolts in the thigh . . . a ball bearing in the skull," he said.

Such are the weapons of war in Israel today: nuts and bolts, screws and ball bearings, any metal shards or odd bits of broken machinery that can be packed together with homemade explosive and then strapped to the body of a terrorist dispatched to any place where people gather—bus, train, restaurant, café, supermarket, shopping mall, street corner, promenade. These attacks probably cost no more than $150 to mount, and they need no escape plan—often the most difficult aspect of a terrorist operation. And they are reliably deadly. According to data from the RAND Corporation's chronology of international terrorism incidents, suicide attacks on average kill four times as many people as other terrorist acts.

Perhaps it is not surprising, then, that this means of terror has become increasingly popular. The tactic first emerged in Lebanon in 1983. A decade later it came to Israel, and it has been a regular security problem ever since. Fully two thirds of all such incidents in Israel have occurred in the past two and a half years—that is, since the start of the second *intifada* in September 2000. Indeed, suicide bombers are responsible for almost half of the approximately 750 deaths in terrorist attacks since then.

In December 2002, I walked through Jerusalem with two police officers, one of them a senior operational commander, who show me the sites of suicide bombings in recent years. They described the first major suicide-terrorist attack in the city, which occurred in February 1996, early on a Sunday morning, the beginning of the Israeli work week. The driver of the No. 18 Egged bus was hurrying across a busy intersection at Sarei Yisrael Street as a yellow light turned red. The bus was about halfway through when an explosion transformed it into an inferno of twisted metal, pulverized glass, and burning flesh. A traffic camera designed to catch drivers running stop lights captured the scene on film. Twenty-five people were killed, including two U.S. citizens, and 80 were wounded.

The early years of suicide terrorism were a simpler time, the officers explained. Suicide bombers were—at least in theory—easier to spot then. They tended to carry their bombs in nylon backpacks or duffel bags rather than in belts or vests concealed beneath their clothing as they do now. They were typically male, age 17 to 23, and unmarried. Armed with these data, the authorities could simply deny work permits to Palestinians most likely to be suicide bombers, thus restricting their ability to cross the Green Line (Israel's pre-1967 border) into Israel proper from the West Bank or the Gaza Strip.

Today, however, suicide bombers are middle-aged or young, married or unmarried, and some of them have children. Some of them, too, are women, and word has it that even children are being trained for martyrdom. "There is no clear profile anymore—not for terrorists and especially not for suicide bombers," an exasperated senior officer in the Israel Defense Forces told me last year.

Sometimes the bombers disguise themselves: male *shaheed* (Arabic for martyrs) have worn green IDF fatigues, have dressed as *haredim* (ultra-Orthodox Jews), complete with yarmulkes and tzitzit (the fringes that devout Jews display as part of their everyday clothing), or have donned long-haired wigs in an effort to look like hip Israelis rather than threatening Arabs. A few women have tried to camouflage bombs by strapping them to their stomachs to fake pregnancy. Contrary to popular belief, the bombers are not drawn exclusively from the ranks of the poor but have included two sons of millionaires. (Most of the September 11 terrorists came from comfortable middle- to upper-middle-class families and were well educated.) The Israeli journalist Ronni Shaked, an expert on the Palestinian terrorist group HAMAS, who writes for *Yedioth Ahronoth*, an Israeli daily, has debunked the myth that it is only people with no means of improving their lot in life who turn to suicide terrorism. "All leaders of HAMAS," he told me, "are university graduates, some with master's degrees. This is a movement not of poor, miserable people, but of highly educated people who are using [the image of] poverty to make the movement more powerful."

Buses remain among the bombers' preferred targets. Winter and summer are the better seasons for bombing buses in Jerusalem, because the closed windows (for heat or air-conditioning) intensify the force of the blast, maximizing the bomb's killing potential. As a hail of shrapnel pierces flesh and breaks bones, the shock wave tears lungs and crushes other internal organs. When the bus's fuel tank explodes, a fireball causes burns, and smoke inhalation causes respiratory damage. All this is a significant return on a relatively modest investment. Two or three kilograms of explosive on a bus can kill as many people as 20 to 30 kilograms left on a street or in a mall or restaurant. But as security on buses has improved and passengers have become more alert, the bombers have been forced to seek other targets.

The terrorists are lethally flexible and inventive. A person wearing a bomb is far more dangerous and far more difficult to defend against than a timed device left to explode in a marketplace. This human weapons system can effect last-minute changes based on the ease of approach, the paucity or density of people, and the security measures in evidence. On a Thursday afternoon in March of last year, a reportedly smiling, self-satisfied bomber strolled down King George Street in the heart of Jerusalem, looking for just the right target. He found it in a crowd of shoppers gathered in front of the trendy Aroma Café near the corner of Agrippas Street. In a fusillade of nails and other bits of metal, two victims were killed and 56 wounded. Similarly, in April of last year, a female suicide bomber tried to enter the Mahane Yehuda open-air market—the fourth woman to make such an attempt in four months—but was deterred by a strong police presence. As a result, she simply walked up to a bus stop packed with shoppers hurrying home before the Sabbath and detonated her explosives, killing six and wounding 73.

Suicide bombing initially seemed the desperate act of lone individuals, but it is not undertaken alone. Invariably, a terrorist organization such as HAMAS (the Islamic Resistance Movement), the Palestine Islamic Jihad (PIJ), or the al Aqsa Martyrs Brigade has recruited the bomber, conducted reconnaissance, prepared the explosive device, and identified a target—explaining that if it turns out to be guarded or protected, any crowded place nearby will do. "We hardly ever find that the suicide bomber came [alone]," a police officer explained to me. "There is always a handler." In fact, in some cases a handler has used a cell phone or other device to trigger the blast from a distance. A policeman told me, "There was one event where a suicide bomber had been told all he had to do was to carry the bomb and plant explosives in a certain place. But the bomb was remote-control detonated."

The organizations behind the Palestinians' suicide terrorism have numerous components. Quartermasters obtain the explosives and the other materials (nuts, bolts, nails, and the like) that are combined to make a bomb. Now that bomb-making methods have been so widely disseminated throughout the West Bank and Gaza, a merely competent technician, rather than the skilled engineer once required, can build a bomb. Explosive material is packed into pockets sewn into a canvas or denim belt or vest and hooked up to a detonator—usually involving a simple hand-operated plunger.

Before the operation is to be launched, minders sequester the bomber in a safe house, isolating him or her from family and friends—from all contact with the outside world—during the final preparations for martyrdom. A film crew makes a martyrdom video, as much to help ensure that the bomber can't back out as for propaganda and recruitment purposes. Reconnaissance teams have already either scouted the target or received detailed information about it, which they pass on to the bomber's handlers. The job of the handlers, who are highly skilled at avoiding Israeli army checkpoints or police patrols, is to deliver the bomber as close to the target as possible.

I talked to a senior police-operations commander in his office at the Russian Compound, the nerve center of law enforcement for Jerusalem since the time when the Turks and then the British ruled this part of the world. It was easy to imagine, amid the graceful arches and the traditional Jerusalem stone, an era when Jerusalem's law-enforcement officers wore tarbooshes and pressed blue tunics with Sam Browne belts rather than the bland polyester uniforms and blue baseball-style caps of today. Although policing this multifaith, historically beleaguered city has doubtless always involved difficult challenges, none can compare with the current situation. "This year there were very many events," my host explained, using the bland generic noun that signifies terrorist attacks or attempted attacks. "In previous years we considered 10 events as normal; now we are already at 43." He sighed. There were still three weeks to go before the end of the year. Nineteen of these events had been suicide bombings. In the calculus of terrorism, it doesn't get much better. "How easy it has become for a person to wake up in the morning and go off and commit suicide," he observed. Once there were only "bags on buses, not vests or belts" to contend with, the policeman said. "Everything is open now. The purpose is to prove that the police can do whatever they want but it won't help."

This, of course, is the age-old strategy of terrorists everywhere—to undermine public confidence in the ability of the authorities to protect and defend citizens, thereby creating a climate of fear and intimidation amenable to terrorist exploitation. In Jerusalem, and in Israel as a whole, this strategy has not succeeded. But it has fundamentally changed daily behavior patterns—the first step toward crushing morale and breaking the will to resist.

The terrorists appear to be deliberately homing in on the few remaining places where Israelis thought they could socialize in peace. An unprecedented string of attacks in the first four months of 2002 illustrated this careful strategy, beginning at bus stops and malls and moving into more private realms, such as corner supermarkets and local coffee bars. In March, for example, no one paid much attention to a young man who was dressed like an ultra-Orthodox Jew and standing near some parked cars as guests left a bar mitzvah celebration at a social hall in the ultra-Orthodox Jerusalem neighborhood of Beit Yisrael. Then he blew himself up, killing nine people, eight of them children, and wounding 59. The tight-knit religious community had felt that it was protected by God, pointing to the miraculous lack of injury a year before when a booby-trapped car blew up in front of the same hall. Using a strategy al-Qaida has made familiar, the terrorists revisited the site.

Less than a month after the Beit Yisrael attack, the suicide bombers and their leaders drove home the point that Israelis cannot feel safe anywhere by going to the one large Israeli city that had felt immune from the suspicion and antipathy prevalent elsewhere—Haifa, which has successful mixture of Jews, Christian and Muslim Arabs, and followers of the Bahai faith. The University of Haifa has long had the highest proportion of Arab students of any Israeli university. The nearby Matza restaurant, owned by Jews but run by an Israeli Arab family from Galilee, seemed to embody the unusually cordial relations that exist among the city's diverse communities. Matza was popular with Jews and Arabs alike, and the presence of its Arab staff and patrons provided a feeling of safety from attack. That feeling was shattered at 2:30 on a quiet Sunday afternoon, when a suicide bomber killed 15 people and wounded nearly 50.

As we had tea late one afternoon in the regal, although almost preternaturally quiet, surroundings of Jerusalem's King David Hotel, Benny Morris, a professor of history at Ben Gurion University, explained, "The Palestinians say they have found a strategic weapon, and suicide bombing is it. This hotel is empty. The streets are empty. They have effectively terrorized Israeli society. My wife won't use a bus anymore, only a taxi." It is undeniable that daily life in Jerusalem, and throughout Israel, has changed as a result of last year's wave of suicide bombings. Even the police have been affected. "I'm worried," one officer told me in an aside—whether in confidence or in embarrassment, I couldn't tell—as we walked past Zion Square, near where some bombs had exploded. "I tell you this as a police officer. I don't come to Jerusalem with my children anymore. I'd give back the settlements. I'd give over my bank account to live in peace."

By any measure, 2002 was an astonishing year for Israel in terms of suicide bombings. An average of five attacks a month were made, nearly double the number during the first 15 months of the second *intifada*—and that number was itself more than 10 times the monthly average since 1993. Indeed, according to a database maintained by the National Security Studies Center at Haifa University, there were nearly as many suicide attacks in Israel in 2002 (59) as there had been in the previous eight years combined (62). In

Jerusalem alone there were nine suicide attacks during the first four months of 2002, killing 33 and injuring 464. "It was horrendous," a young professional woman living in the city told me. "No one went out for coffee. No one went out to restaurants. We went as a group of people to one another's houses only."

Again, terrorism is meant to produce psychological effects that reach far beyond the immediate victims of the attack. "The Scuds of Saddam [in 1991] never caused as much psychological damage as the suicide bombers have," says Ami Pedahzur, a professor of political science at Haifa University and an expert on political extremism and violence who manages the National Security Studies Center's terrorism database. As the French philosopher Gaston Bouthoul argued three decades ago in a theoretical treatise on the subject, the "anonymous, unidentifiable threat creates huge anxiety, and the terrorist tries to spread fear by contagion, to immobilize and subjugate those living under this threat."[1]

This is precisely what the Palestinian terrorist groups are trying to achieve. "The Israelis . . . will fall to their knees," Sheikh Ahmad Yassin, the spiritual leader of HAMAS, said in 2001. "You can sense the fear in Israel already; they are worried about where and when the next attacks will come. Ultimately, HAMAS will win."[2]

The strategy of suicide terrorists is to make people paranoid and xenophobic, fearful of venturing beyond their homes even to a convenience store. Terrorists hope to compel the enemy society's acquiescence, if not outright surrender, to their demands. This is what al-Qaida hoped to achieve on 9/11 in one stunning blow—and what the Palestinians seek as well, on a more sustained, if piecemeal, basis.

After decades of struggle, the Palestinians are convinced that they have finally discovered Israel's Achilles' heel. Ismail Haniya, another HAMAS leader, was quoted in March 2002 in *The Washington Post* as saying that Jews "love life more than any other people, and they prefer not to die."[3] In contrast, suicide terrorists are often said to have gone to their deaths smiling. An Israeli policeman told me, "A suicide bomber goes on a bus and finds himself face-to-face with victims and he smiles and he activates the bomb— but we learned that only by asking people afterwards who survived." This is what is known in the Shia Islamic tradition as the *bassamat al-farah*, or "smile of joy"—prompted by one's impending martyrdom. It is just as prevalent among Sunni terrorists. (Indeed, the last will and testament of Mohammed Atta, the ringleader of the September 11 hijackers, and his "primer" for martyrs, *The Sky Smiles, My Young Son*, clearly evidence a belief in the joy of death.)

This perceived weakness of an ostensibly powerful society has given rise to what is known in the Middle East as the "spider-web theory," which originated within Hizballah, the Lebanese Shia organization, following a struggle that ultimately compelled the Israel Defense Forces to withdraw from southern Lebanon in May 2000. The term is said to have been coined by Hizballah's secretary general, Sheikh Hassan Nasrallah, who described Israel as a still formidable military power whose civil society had become materialistic and lazy, its citizens self-satisfied, comfortable, and pampered to the point where they had gone soft. IDF Chief of Staff Moshe "Boogie" Ya'alon paraphrased Nasrallah for the Israeli public in an interview published in the newspaper *Ha'aretz* last August.

The Israeli army is strong, Israel has technological superiority and is said to
have strategic capabilities, but its citizens are unwilling any longer to sacri-

fice lives in order to defend their national interests and national goals. Therefore, Israel is a spider-web society: it looks strong from the outside, but touch it and it will fall apart.

Al-Qaida, of course, has made a similar assessment of United States' vulnerability.

A society facing such a determined foe can respond. Israel, with its necessarily advanced military and intelligence capacities, was able in the first four months of 2002, to meet the most concerted effort to date by Palestinian terrorists to test the resolve of its government and the mettle of its citizens. Twelve Israelis were killed in terrorist attacks in January, 26 in February, 108 in March, and 41 in April. The population of the United States is roughly 47 times that of Israel, meaning that the American equivalent of the March figure would have exceeded 5,000—another 9/11 but with more than 2,000 additional deaths.

After April of 2002, however, a period of relative quiet settled over Israel. The number of suicide attacks, according to the National Security Studies Center, declined from 16 in March to six in April, six in May, five in June, and six in July, before falling still further to two in August, and similarly small numbers for the remainder of the year. "We wouldn't want it to be perceived [by the Israeli population] that we have no military answers," a senior IDF planner told me. The military answer was Operation Defensive Shield, which began in March and involved both the IDF's huge deployment of personnel to the West Bank and its continuing presence in all the major Palestinian population centers that Israel regards as wellsprings of the suicide campaign. This presence has involved aggressive military operations to preempt suicide bombing, along with curfews and other restrictions on the movement of residents.

The success of the IDF's strategy is utterly dependent on regularly acquiring intelligence and rapidly disseminating it to operational units that can take appropriate action. Thus the IDF must continue to occupy the West Bank's major population centers so that Israeli intelligence agents can stay in close—and relatively safe—proximity to their information sources, and troops can act immediately, either to round up suspects or to rescue the agent should an operation go awry.

"Military pressure facilitates arrests, because you're there," one knowledgeable observer explained to me. "Not only do you know the area, but you have [covert] spotters deployed, and the whole area is under curfew anyway, so it is difficult for terrorists to move about and hide without being noticed, and more difficult for them to get out. The IDF presence facilitates intelligence gathering, and the troops can also conduct massive sweeps, house to house and block to block, pick up people, and interrogate them."

The IDF units in West Bank cities and towns can amass detailed knowledge of a community, identifying terrorists and their sympathizers, tracking their movements and daily routines, and observing the people with whom they associate. Agents from Shabak, Israel's General Security Service (also known as the Shin Bet) work alongside these units, participating in operations and often assigning missions. "The moment someone from Shabak comes with us, everything changes," a young soldier in an elite reconnaissance unit told me over coffee and cake in his mother's apartment. "The Shabak guy talks in Arabic to [the suspect] without an accent, or appears as an Arab guy himself. Shabak already knows everything about them, and that is such a shock to them. So they are afraid, and they will tell Shabak everything." The success of Defensive Shield and the subsequent Operation Determined Way depends on this synchronization of intelligence and operations. A junior officer well acquainted with this environment says, "Whoever has better intelligence is the winner."

The strategy—at least in the short run—is working. The dramatic decline in the number of suicide operations since last spring is proof enough. "Tactically, we are doing everything we can," a senior officer involved in the framing of this policy told me, "and we have managed to prevent 80 percent of all attempts." Another officer said, "We are now bringing the war to them. We do it so that we fight the war in *their* homes rather than in *our* homes. We try to make certain that we fight on their ground, where we can have the maximum advantage." The goal of the IDF, however, is not simply to fight in a manner that plays to its strength; the goal is to actively shrink the time and space in which the suicide bombers and their operational commanders, logisticians, and handlers function— to stop them before they can cross the Green Line—by threatening their personal safety and putting them on the defensive.

Citizens in Israel, as in America, have a fundamental expectation that their government and its military and security forces will protect and defend them. Soldiers are expected to die, if necessary, in order to discharge this responsibility. As one senior IDF commander put it, "It is better for the IDF to bear the brunt of these attacks than Israeli civilians. The IDF is better prepared, protected, educated." Thus security in Israel means to the IDF an almost indefinite deployment in the West Bank—a state of ongoing low-level war. For Palestinian civilians it means no respite from roadblocks and identity checks, cordon-and-search operations, lightning snatch-and-grabs, bombing raids, helicopter strikes, ground attacks, and other countermeasures that have turned densely populated civilian areas into war zones.

Many Israelis do not relish involvement in this protracted war of attrition, but even more of them accept that there is no alternative. "Israel's ability to stand fast indefinitely is a tremendous advantage," says Dan Schueftan, an Israeli strategist and military thinker who teaches at Haifa University, "since the suicide bombers believe that time is on their side. It imposes a strain on the army, yes, but this is what the army is for."

Indeed, no Israeli with whom I spoke on this visit doubted that the IDF's continued heavy presence in the West Bank was directly responsible for the drop in the number of suicide bombings. And I encountered very few who favored withdrawing the IDF from the West Bank. This view cut across ideological and demographic lines. As we dined one evening at Matza, which has been rebuilt, a centrist graduate student at Haifa University named Uzi Nisim told me that Palestinian terrorists "will have the power to hit us, to hurt us, once [the IDF] withdraws from Jenin and elsewhere on the West Bank." Ami Pedahzur of Haifa University, who is a leftist, agreed. He said, "There is widespread recognition in Israel that this is the only way to stop terrorism." I later heard the same thing from a South African couple, relatively new immigrants to Israel, who are active in a variety of human-rights endeavors. "Just the other day," the husband told me, "even my wife said, 'Thank God we have Sharon. Otherwise I wouldn't feel safe going out.'"

Nevertheless, few Israelis believe that the current situation will lead to any improvement in Israeli-Palestinian relations over the long run. Dennis Zinn, the defense correspondent for Israel's Channel 1, told me, "Yes, there is a drop-off [in suicide bombings].

When you have bombs coming down on your heads, you can't carry out planning and suicide attacks. But that doesn't take away their motivation. It only increases it."

Suicide Terrorism and Homeland Security in the United States

Given the relative ease and the strategic and tactical attraction of suicide bombing, it is perhaps no wonder that after a five-day visit to Israel last fall, Louis Anemone, the security chief of the New York Metropolitan Transit Authority, concluded that New Yorkers and, by implication, other Americans face the same threat. "This stuff is going to be imported over here," he declared—a prediction that Vice President Dick Cheney and FBI Director Robert Mueller had already made.

In March 2004, Secretary of Homeland Security Tom Ridge also referred to the threat, saying in an interview with Fox News that we have to "prepare for the inevitability" of suicide bombings in the United States. Anemone even argued that "today's terrorists appear to be using Israel as a testing ground to prepare for a sustained attack against the U.S."

In fact, Palestinians had tried a suicide attack in New York four years before 9/11; their plans to bomb a Brooklyn subway station were foiled only because an informant told the police. When they were arrested, the terrorists were probably less than a day away from attacking. According to law-enforcement authorities, five bombs had been primed. "I wouldn't call them sophisticated," Howard Safir, the commissioner of police at the time, commented, "but they certainly were very dangerous." That suicide bombers don't need to be sophisticated is precisely what makes them so dangerous. All that's required is a willingness to kill and a willingness to die.

According to the RAND Corporation's chronology of worldwide terrorism, which begins in 1968 (the year acknowledged as marking the advent of modern international terrorism, whereby terrorists attack other countries or foreign targets in their own country), nearly two thirds of the 144 suicide bombings recorded have occurred in the past two years. No society, least of all the United States, can regard itself as immune from this threat. Israeli Foreign Minister Benjamin Netanyahu emphasized this point when he addressed the U.S. Congress nine days after 9/11. So did Dan Schueftan, the Israeli strategist, when I asked him if he thought suicide terrorism would come to America in a form similar to that seen in Israel this past year. He said, "It is an interesting comment that the terrorists make: we will finish defeating the Jews because they love life so much. Their goal is to bring misery and grief to people who have an arrogance of power. Who has this? The United States and Israel. Europe will suffer too. I don't think that it will happen in the U.S. on the magnitude we have seen it here, but I have no doubt that it will occur. We had the same discussion back in 1968, when El Al aircraft were hijacked and people said this is your problem, not ours."

The United States, of course, is not Israel. However much we may want to harden our hearts and our targets, the challenge goes far beyond fortifying a single national airline or corralling the enemy into a territory ringed by walls and barbed-wire fences that can be intensively monitored by our armed forces. But we can take precautions based on Israel's experience, and be confident that we are substantially reducing the threat of suicide terrorism here.

The police, the military, and intelligence agencies can take steps that work from the outside in, beginning far in time and distance from a potential attack and ending at the moment and the site of an actual attack. Although the importance of these steps is widely recognized, they have been implemented only unevenly across the United States:

- Understand the terrorists' operational environment. Know their *modus operandi* and targeting patterns. Suicide bombers are rarely lone outlaws; they are preceded by long logistical trails. Focus not just on suspected bombers, but on the infrastructure required to launch and sustain suicide-bombing campaigns. This is the essential spadework. It will be for naught, however, if concerted efforts are not made to circulate this information quickly and systematically among federal, state, and local authorities.
- Develop strong, confidence-building ties with the communities from which terrorists are most likely to come and mount communications campaigns to eradicate support from these communities. The most effective and useful intelligence comes from places where terrorists conceal themselves and seek to establish and hide their infrastructure. Law-enforcement officers should actively encourage and cultivate cooperation in a nonthreatening way.
- Encourage businesses from which terrorists can obtain bomb-making components to alert authorities if they notice large purchases of, for example, ammonium nitrate fertilizer, pipes, batteries, wires, or chemicals commonly used to fabricate explosives. Information about customers who simply inquire about any of these materials can also be extremely useful to the police.
- Force terrorists to pay more attention to their own organizational security than to planning and carrying out attacks. The greatest benefit is in disrupting pre-attack operations. Given the highly fluid, international threat the United States faces, counterterrorism units, dedicated to identifying and targeting the intelligence-gathering and reconnaissance activities of terrorist organizations, should be established here within existing law-enforcement agencies. These units should be especially aware of places where organizations frequently recruit new members and the bombers themselves, such as community centers, social clubs, schools, and religious institutions.
- Make sure ordinary materials don't become shrapnel. Some steps to build up physical defenses were taken after 9/11—reinforcing park benches, erecting Jersey barriers around vulnerable buildings, and the like. More are needed, such as ensuring that windows on buses and subway cars are shatterproof, and that seats and other accoutrements are not easily dislodged or splintered. Israel has had to learn to examine every element of its public infrastructure. Israeli buses and bus shelters are austere for a reason.
- Teach law-enforcement personnel what to do at the moment of an attack or an attempt. Prevention comes first from the cop on the beat, who will be forced to make instant life-and-death decisions affecting those nearby. Rigorous training is needed for identifying a potential suicide bomber, confronting a suspect, and responding and securing the area around the attack site in the event of an explosion. Is the officer authorized to take action upon sighting a

suspected bomber, or must a supervisor or special unit be called first? Policies and procedures must be established. In the aftermath of a blast, the police must determine whether emergency medical crews and firefighters may enter the site; concerns about a follow-up attack can dictate that first responders be held back until the area is secured. The ability to make such lightning determinations requires training—and, tragically, experience. We can learn from foreign countries with long experience of suicide bombings, such as Israel and Sri Lanka, and also from our own responses in the past to other types of terrorist attacks.

America's enemies are marshaling their resources to continue the struggle that crystallized on 9/11. Exactly what shape that struggle will take remains to be seen. But a recruitment video reportedly circulated by al-Qaida as recently as spring of 2002 may provide some important clues. The seven-minute tape, seized from an al-Qaida member by U.S. authorities, extols the virtues of martyrdom and solicits recruits to Usama bin Ladin's cause. It depicts scenes of *jihadists* in combat, followed by the successive images of 27 martyrs with their names, where they were from, and where they died. Twelve of the martyrs are featured in a concluding segment with voice-over that says, "They rejoice in the bounty provided by Allah. And with regard to those left behind who have not yet joined them in their bliss, the martyrs glory in the fact that on them is no fear, nor have they cause to grieve." The video closes with a message of greeting from the Black Banner Center for Islamic Information.

The greatest military onslaught in history against a terrorist group crushed the infrastructure of al-Qaida in Afghanistan, depriving it of training camps, operational bases, and command-and-control headquarters; killing and wounding many of its leaders and fighters; and dispersing the survivors. Yet this group still actively seeks to rally its forces and attract recruits. Ayman Zawahiri, bin Ladin's chief lieutenant, laid out a list of terrorist principles in his book, *Knights Under the Prophet's Banner* (2001), prominent among them the need for al-Qaida to "move the battle to the enemy's ground to burn the hands of those who ignite fire in our countries." He also mentioned "the need to concentrate on the method of martyrdom operations as the most successful way of inflicting damage against the opponent and the least costly to the mujahideen in terms of casualties."

That martyrdom is highlighted in the recruitment video strongly suggests that suicide attacks will continue to be a primary instrument in al-Qaida's war against—and perhaps in—the United States. Suleiman Abu Gheith, al-Qaida's chief spokesman, has said as much. In rhetoric disturbingly reminiscent of the way that Palestinian terrorists describe their inevitable triumph over Israel, Abu Gheith declared, "Those youths that destroyed Americans with their planes, they did a good deed. There are thousands more young followers who look forward to death like Americans look forward to living."

Notes

1. Gaston Bouthoul, *Traité de Polémologie: Sociologie des Guerres [The Treaty of Polémologie: The Sociology of Wars]* (Paris: Payot, 1970).

2. Burhan Wazir, "Suicide Bombing Is Democratic Right, Says the 'Soul' of Hamas." *The Observer* (UK), August 19, 2001.
3. Lee Hockstader, "Suicide Bomber Kills At Least 19," *Washington Post*, March 28, 2002.

Chapter 6

The Strategic Logic of Suicide Terrorism

Robert A. Pape

Terrorist organizations are increasingly relying on suicide attacks to achieve major political objectives. For example, spectacular suicide terrorist attacks have recently been employed by Palestinian groups in attempts to force Israel to abandon the West Bank and Gaza, by the Liberation Tigers of Tamil Eelam to compel the Sri Lankan government to accept an independent Tamil homeland, and by al-Qaida to pressure the United States to withdraw from the Saudi Arabian Peninsula.

Moreover, these attacks are increasing both in tempo and location. Before the early 1980s, suicide terrorism was rare but not unknown (Lewis, 1968; O'Neill, 1981; Rapoport, 1984). However, since the attack on the U.S. embassy in Beirut in April 1983, there have been at least 188 separate suicide terrorist attacks worldwide—Lebanon, Israel, Sri Lanka, India, Pakistan, Afghanistan, Yemen, Turkey, Russia, and the United States. The rate has increased from 31 in the 1980s to 104 in the 1990s to 53 in 2000–2001 alone (Pape, 2002). The rise of suicide terrorism is especially remarkable, given that the total number of terrorist incidents worldwide fell during this same period from a peak of 666 in 1987 to a low of 274 in 1998, with 348 in 2001 (Department of State, 2001).

What accounts for the rise in suicide terrorism, especially the sharp escalation from the 1990s onward? Although terrorism has long been part of international politics, we do not have good explanations for the growing phenomenon of suicide terrorism. Traditional studies of terrorism tend to treat suicide attack as one of many tactics that terrorists use and so do not shed much light on the recent rise of this type of attack (e.g., Hoffman, 1998; Jenkins, 1985; Laqueur, 1987). The small number of studies addressed explicitly to suicide terrorism tend to focus on the irrationality of the act of suicide from the perspective of the individual attacker. As a result, they focus on individual motives—either religious indoctrination (especially Islamic fundamentalism) or psychological predispositions that might drive individual suicide bombers (Kramer, 1990; Merari, 1990; Post, 1990).

The first-wave explanations of suicide terrorism were developed during the 1980s and were consistent with the data from that period. However, as suicide attacks have mounted from the 1990s onward, it has become evident that these initial explanations are insufficient to account for which individuals become suicide terrorists and, more importantly, why terrorist organizations are increasingly relying on this form of attack (Institute for Counter-Terrorism, 2001).

First, although religious motives may matter, modern suicide terrorism is not limited to Islamic fundamentalism. Islamic groups receive the most attention in Western media, but the world's leader in suicide terrorism is actually the Liberation Tigers of Tamil Eelam (LTTE), a group that recruits from the predominantly Hindu Tamil population in northern and eastern Sri Lanka and whose ideology has Marxist/Leninist elements. The LTTE alone accounted for 75 of the 186 suicide terrorist attacks from 1980 to 2001. Even among Islamic suicide attacks, groups with secular orientations account for about a third of these attacks (Merari, 1990; Sprinzak, 2000).

Second, although study of the personal characteristics of suicide attackers may someday help identify those individuals whom terrorist organizations are likely to recruit for this purpose, the vast spread of suicide terrorism over the last two decades suggests that there may not be a single profile. Until recently, the leading experts in psychological profiles of suicide terrorists characterized them as uneducated, unemployed, socially isolated, single men in their late teens and early 20s (Merari, 1990; Post, 1990). Now we know that suicide terrorists can be college educated or uneducated, married or single, men or women, socially isolated or integrated, from age 13 to age 47 (Sprinzak, 2000). In other words, although only a tiny number of people become suicide terrorists, they come from a broad cross section of lifestyles, and it may be impossible to pick them out in advance.

In contrast to the first-wave explanations, suicide terrorism follows a strategic logic. Even if many suicide attackers are irrational or fanatical, the leadership groups that recruit and direct them are not. Viewed from the perspective of the terrorist organization, suicide attacks are designed to achieve specific political purposes: to coerce a target government to change policy, to mobilize additional recruits and financial support, or both. Crenshaw (1981) has shown that terrorism is best understood in terms of its strategic function; the same is true for suicide terrorism. In essence, suicide terrorism is an extreme form of what Thomas Schelling (1966) calls "the rationality of irrationality," in which an act that is irrational for individual attackers is meant to demonstrate to a democratic audience that still more and greater attacks are sure to come. As such, modern suicide terrorism is analogous to instances of international coercion. For states, air power and economic sanctions are often the preferred coercive tools (George et al., 1972; Pape, 1996; 1997). For terrorist groups, suicide attacks are becoming the coercive instrument of choice.

To examine the strategic logic of suicide terrorism, this article collects the universe suicide terrorist attacks worldwide from 1980 to 2001, explains how terrorist organizations have assessed the effectiveness of these attacks, and evaluates the limits on their coercive utility.

Five principal findings follow. First, suicide terrorism is strategic. The vast majority of suicide terrorist attacks are not isolated or random acts by individual fanatics but, rather, occur in clusters as part of a larger campaign by an organized group to achieve a specific political goal. Groups using suicide terrorism consistently announce specific political goals and stop suicide attacks when those goals have been fully or partially achieved.

Second, the strategic logic of suicide terrorism is specifically designed to coerce modern democracies to make significant concessions to national self-determination. In general, suicide terrorist campaigns seek to achieve specific territorial goals, most often the withdrawal of the target state's military forces from what the terrorists see as national homeland. From Lebanon to Israel to Sri Lanka to Kashmir to Chechnya, every suicide terrorist campaign from 1980 to 2001 has been waged by terrorist groups whose main goal has been to establish or maintain self-determination for their community's homeland by compelling an enemy to withdraw. Further, every suicide terrorist campaign since 1980 has been targeted against a state that had a democratic form of government.

Third, during the past 20 years, suicide terrorism has been steadily rising because terrorists have learned that it pays. Suicide terrorists sought to compel American and French military forces to abandon Lebanon in 1983, Israeli forces to leave Lebanon in 1985, Israeli forces to quit the Gaza Strip and the West Bank in 1994 and 1995, the Sri Lankan government to create an independent Tamil state from 1990 on, and the Turkish government to grant autonomy to the Kurds in the late 1990s. Terrorist groups did not achieve their full objectives in all these cases. However, in all but the case of Turkey, the terrorist political cause made more gains after the resort to suicide operations than it had before.

Leaders of terrorist groups have consistently credited suicide operations with contributing to these gains. These assessments are hardly unreasonable given the timing and circumstances of many of the concessions and given that other observers within the terrorists' national community, neutral analysts, and target government leaders themselves often agreed that suicide operations accelerated or caused the concession. This pattern of making concessions to suicide terrorist organizations over the past two decades has probably encouraged terrorist groups to pursue even more ambitious suicide campaigns.

Fourth, although moderate suicide terrorism led to moderate concessions, these more ambitious suicide terrorist campaigns are not likely to achieve still greater gains and may well fail completely. In general, suicide terrorism relies on the threat to inflict low to medium levels of punishment on civilians. In other circumstances, this level of punishment has rarely caused modern nation states to surrender significant political goals, partly because modern nation states are often willing to countenance high costs for high interests and partly because modern nation states are often able to mitigate civilian costs by making economic and other adjustments. Suicide terrorism does not change a nation's willingness to trade high interests for high costs, but suicide attacks can overcome a country's efforts to mitigate civilian costs.

Accordingly, suicide terrorism may marginally increase the punishment that is inflicted and so make target nations somewhat more likely to surrender modest goals, but it is unlikely to compel states to abandon important interests related to the physical security or national wealth of the state. National governments have, in fact, responded aggressively to ambitious suicide terrorist campaigns in recent years, events which confirm these expectations.

Finally, the most promising way to contain suicide terrorism is to reduce terrorists' confidence in their ability to carry out such attacks on the target society. States that face persistent suicide terrorism should recognize that neither offensive military action nor concessions alone are likely to do much good and should invest significant resources in border defenses and other means of homeland security.

The Logic of Suicide Terrorism

Most suicide terrorism is undertaken as a strategic effort directed toward achieving particular political goals; it is not simply the product of irrational individuals or an expression of fanatical hatreds. The main purpose of suicide terrorism is to use the threat of punishment to coerce a target government to change policy, especially to cause democratic states to withdraw forces from territory terrorists view as their homeland. The record of suicide terrorism from 1980 to 2001 exhibits tendencies in the timing, goals, and targets of attack that are consistent with this strategic logic but not with irrational or fanatical behavior.

Defining Suicide Terrorism

Terrorism involves the use of violence by an organization other than a national government to cause intimidation or fear among a target audience (Department of State, 1983–2001; Reich, 1990; Schmid and Jongman, 1988). Although one could broaden the definition of terrorism to include the actions of a national government to cause terror among an opposing population, adopting such a broad definition would distract attention from what policy makers would most like to know: how to combat the threat posed by subnational groups to state security. Further, it could also create analytic confusion. Terrorist organizations and state governments have different levels of resources, face different kinds of incentives, and are susceptible to different types of pressures. Accordingly, the determinants of their behavior are not likely to be the same and, thus, require separate theoretical investigations.

In general, terrorism has two purposes—to gain supporters and to coerce opponents. Most terrorism seeks both goals to some extent, often aiming to affect enemy calculations while simultaneously mobilizing support for the terrorists cause and, in some cases, even gaining an edge over rival groups in the same social movement (Bloom, 2002). However, there are tradeoffs between these objectives, and terrorists can strike various balances between them. These choices represent different forms of terrorism, the most important of which are demonstrative, destructive, and suicide terrorism.

Demonstrative terrorism is directed mainly at gaining publicity for any or all of three reasons: to recruit more activists, to gain attention to grievances from soft-liners on the other side, and to gain attention from third parties who might exert pressure on the other side. Groups that emphasize demonstrative terrorism include the Orange Volunteers (Northern Ireland), National Liberation Army (Columbia), and Red Brigades (Italy) (Clutterbuck, 1975; Edler Baumann, 1973; St. John, 1991). Hostage taking, airline hijacking, and explosions announced in advance are generally intended to use the possibility of harm to bring issues to the attention of the target audience. In these cases, terrorists often avoid doing serious harm so as not to undermine sympathy for the political cause. Brian Jenkins (1975, 4) captured the essence of demonstrative terrorism with his well-known remark, "Terrorists want a lot of people watching, not a lot of people dead."

Destructive terrorism is more aggressive, seeking to coerce opponents as well as mobilize support for the cause. Destructive terrorists seek to inflict real harm on members of the target audience at the risk of losing sympathy for their cause. Exactly how groups strike the balance between harm and sympathy depends on the nature of the political goal. For instance, the Baader-Meinhoft group selectively assassinated rich German industrialists, which alienated certain segments of German society but not others. Palestinian terrorists in the 1970s often sought to kill as many Israelis as possible, fully alienating Jewish society but still evoking sympathy from Muslim communities. Other groups that emphasize destructive terrorism include the Irish Republican Army, the Revolutionary Armed

Forces of Colombia (FARC), and the nineteenth-century anarchists (Elliott, 1998; Rapoport, 1971; Tuchman, 1966).

Suicide terrorism is the most aggressive form of terrorism, pursuing coercion even at the expense of losing support among the terrorists' own community. What distinguishes a suicide terrorist is that the attacker does not expect to survive a mission, and often employs a method of attack that requires the attacker's death in order to succeed (such as planting a car bomb, wearing a suicide vest, or ramming an airplane into a building). In essence, a suicide terrorist kills others at the same time that he kills himself.[1]

In principle, suicide terrorists could be used for demonstrative purposes or could be limited to targeted assassinations.[2] In practice, however, suicide terrorists often seek simply to kill the largest number of people possible. Although this maximizes the coercive leverage that can be gained from terrorism, it does so at the greatest cost to the basis of support for the terrorist cause. Maximizing the number of enemies killed alienates those in the target audience who might be sympathetic to the terrorists cause, while the act of suicide creates a debate and often loss of support among moderate segments of the terrorists' community, even if also attracting support among radical elements. Thus, while coercion is an element in all terrorism, coercion is the paramount objective of suicide terrorism.

The Coercive Logic of Suicide Terrorism

At its core, suicide terrorism is a strategy of coercion, a means to compel a target government to change policy. The central logic of this strategy is simple: suicide terrorism attempts to inflict enough pain on the opposing society so as to overwhelm their interest in resisting the terrorists' demands and to cause either the government to concede, or the population to revolt against the government. The common feature of all suicide terrorist campaigns is that they inflict punishment on the opposing society, either directly by killing civilians or indirectly by killing military personnel in circumstances that cannot lead to meaningful battlefield victory. As we shall see, suicide terrorism is rarely a one-time event but often occurs in a series of suicide attacks. As such, suicide terrorism generates coercive leverage both from the immediate panic associated with each attack and from the risk of civilian punishment in the future.

Suicide terrorism does not occur in the same circumstances as military coercion used by states, and these structural differences help to explain the logic of the strategy. In virtually all instances of international military coercion, the coercer is the stronger state and the target is the weaker state; otherwise, the coercer would likely be deterred or simply unable to execute the threatened military operations (Pape, 1996). In these circumstances, coercers have a choice between two main coercive strategies: punishment and denial. Punishment seeks to coerce by raising the costs or risks to the target society to a level that overwhelms the value of the interests in dispute. Denial seeks to coerce by demonstrating to the target state that it simply cannot win the dispute regardless of its level of effort and, therefore, fighting to a finish is pointless—for example, because the coercer has the ability to conquer the disputed territory.

Hence, although coercers may initially rely on punishment, they often have the resources to create a formidable threat to deny the opponent victory in battle and, if necessary, to achieve a brute force military victory if the target government refuses to change its behavior. The Allied bombing of Germany in World War II, American bombing of North Vietnam in 1972, and Coalition attacks against Iraq in 1991 all fit this pattern.

Suicide terrorism (and terrorism in general) occurs under the reverse structural conditions. In suicide terrorism, the coercer is the weaker actor and the target is the stronger. Although some elements of the situation remain the same, flipping the stronger and weaker sides in a coercive dispute has a dramatic change on the relative feasibility of punishment and denial. In these circumstances, denial is impossible, because military conquest is ruled out by relative weakness. Even though some groups using suicide terrorism have received important support from states and some have been strong enough to wage guerrilla military campaigns as well as terrorism, none has been strong enough to have serious prospects of achieving their political goals by conquest. The suicide terrorist group with the most significant military capacity has been the LTTE, but it has not had a real prospect of controlling the whole of the homeland that it claims, which includes the eastern and northern provinces of Sri Lanka.

As a result, the only coercive strategy available to suicide terrorists is punishment. Although the element of suicide is novel and the pain inflicted on civilians is often spectacular and gruesome, the heart of the strategy of suicide terrorism is the same as the coercive logic used by states when they employ air power or economic sanctions to punish an adversary: to cause mounting civilian costs to overwhelm the target state's interest in the issue in dispute and so to cause it to concede to the terrorists' political demands. What creates the coercive leverage is not so much actual damage as the expectation of future damage. Targets may be economic or political, military or civilian, but in all cases the main task is less to destroy the specific targets than to convince the opposing society that it isvulnerable to more attacks in the future. These features also make suicide terrorism convenient for retaliation, a tit-for-tat interaction that generally occurs between terrorists and the defending government (Crenshaw, 1981).

The rhetoric of major suicide terrorist groups reflects the logic of coercive punishment. Abdel Karim, a leader of Al Aksa Martyrs' Brigades, a militant group linked to Yasir Arafat's Fatah movement, said the goal of his group was "to increase losses in Israel to a point at which the Israeli public would demand a withdrawal from the West Bank and Gaza Strip" (Greenberg, 2002). The infamous fatwa signed by Usama bin Ladin and others against the United States reads, "The ruling to kill the Americans and their allies—civilians and military—is an individual duty for every Muslim who can do it in any country in which it is possible to do it, in order to liberate the al-Aqsa Mosque and the holy mosque [Mecca] from their grip, and in order for their armies to move out of all the lands of Islam, defeated and unable to threaten any Muslim" (World Islamic Front, 1998).

Suicide terrorists' willingness to die magnifies the coercive effects of punishment in three ways. First, suicide attacks are generally more destructive than other terrorist attacks. An attacker who is willing to die is much more likely to accomplish the mission and to cause maximum damage to the target. Suicide attackers can conceal weapons on their own bodies and make last-minute adjustments more easily than ordinary terrorists. They are also better able to infiltrate heavily guarded targets because they do not need escape plans or rescue teams. Suicide attackers are also able to use certain especially destructive tactics such as wearing "suicide vests" and ramming vehicles into targets.

The 188 suicide terrorist attacks from 1980 to 2001 killed an average of 13 people each, not counting the unusually large number of fatalities on September 11 and also not counting the attackers themselves. During the same period, there were about 4,155 total terrorist incidents worldwide, which killed 3,207 people (also excluding September 11), or less than one person per incident. Overall, from 1980 to 2001, suicide attacks amount to 3 percent of all terrorist attacks but account for 48 percent of total deaths due to terrorism, again, excluding September 11 (Department of State, 1983–2001).

Second, suicide attacks are an especially convincing way to signal the likelihood of more pain to come because suicide itself is a costly signal, one that suggests that the attackers could not have been deterred by a threat of costly retaliation. Organizations that sponsor suicide attacks can also deliberately orchestrate the circumstances around the death of a suicide attacker to increase further expectations of future attacks. This can be called the "art of martyrdom" (Schalk, 1997).

The more suicide terrorists justify their actions on the basis of religious or ideological motives that match the beliefs of a broader national community, the more the status of terrorist martyrs is elevated, and the more plausible it becomes that others will follow in their footsteps. Suicide terrorist organizations commonly cultivate "sacrificial myths" that include elaborate sets of symbols and rituals to mark an individual attacker's death as a contribution to the nation. Suicide attackers' families also often receive material rewards both from the terrorist organizations and from other supporters. As a result, the art of martyrdom elicits popular support from the terrorists' community, reducing the moral backlash that suicide attacks might otherwise produce, and so establishes the foundation for credible signals of more attacks to come.

Third, suicide terrorist organizations are better positioned than other terrorists to increase expectations about escalating future costs by deliberately violating norms in the use of violence. They can do this by crossing thresholds of damage, by breaching taboos concerning legitimate targets, and by broadening recruitment to confound expectations about limits on the number of possible terrorists. The element of suicide itself helps increase the credibility of future attacks, because it suggests that attackers cannot be deterred. Although the capture and conviction of Timothy McVeigh gave reason for some confidence that others with similar political views might be deterred, the deaths of the September 11 hijackers did not, because Americans would have to expect that future al-Qaida attackers would be equally willing to die.

The Record of Suicide Terrorism, 1980 to 2001

To characterize the nature of suicide terrorism, this study identified every suicide terrorist attack from 1980 to 2001 that could be found in Lexis Nexis's online database of world news media (Pape, 2002).[3] Examination of the universe shows that suicide terrorism has three properties that are consistent with strategic logic but not with irrational or fanatical behavior:

1. *timing*—nearly all suicide attacks occur in organized, coherent campaigns, not as isolated or randomly timed incidents;
2. *nationalist goals*—suicide terrorist campaigns are directed at gaining control of what the terrorists see as their national homeland territory, specifically at ejecting foreign forces from that territory; and

3.   *target selection*—all suicide terrorist campaigns in the last two decades have been aimed at democracies, which make more suitable targets from the terrorists' point of view. Nationalist movements that face nondemocratic opponents have not resorted to suicide attack as a means of coercion.

Timing. As Table 6-1 indicates, were been 188 separate suicide terrorist attacks between 1980 and 2001. Of these, 179, or 95 percent, were parts of organized, coherent campaigns, while only nine were isolated or random events. Seven separate disputes have led to suicide terrorist campaigns: the presence of American and French forces in Lebanon; Israeli occupation of West Bank and Gaza; the independence of the Tamil regions of Sri Lanka; the independence of the Kurdish region of Turkey; Russian occupation of Chechnya; Indian occupation of Kashmir; and the presence of American forces on the Saudi Arabian Peninsula.

Overall, however, there have been 16 distinct campaigns, because, in certain disputes, the terrorists elected to suspend operations one or more times, either in response to concessions or for other reasons. Eleven of the campaigns ended and five were ongoing as of the end of 2001. The attacks comprising each campaign were organized by the same terrorist group (or, sometimes, a set of cooperating groups as in the ongoing second *intifada* in Israel/Palestine), clustered in time, publicly justified in terms of a specified political goal, and directed against targets related to that goal.

The most important indicator of the strategic orientation of suicide terrorists is the timing of the suspension of campaigns, which most often occurs based on a strategic decision by leaders of the terrorist organizations that further attacks would be counterproductive to their coercive purposes—for instance, in response to full or partial concessions by the target state to the terrorists' political goals. Such suspensions are often accompanied by public explanations that justify the decision to opt for a "cease-fire." Further, the terrorist organizations' discipline is usually fairly good. Although there are exceptions, such announced cease-fires usually do stick for a period of months at least, normally until the terrorist leaders make a new strategic decision to resume in pursuit of goals not achieved in the earlier campaign. This pattern indicates that both terrorist leaders and their recruits are sensitive to the coercive value of the attacks.

As an example of a suicide campaign, consider HAMAS's suicide attacks in 1995 to compel Israel to withdraw from towns in the West Bank. HAMAS leaders deliberately withheld attacking during the spring and early summer in order to give PLO negotiations with Israel an opportunity to finalize a withdrawal. However, when HAMAS leaders came to believe that Israel was backsliding and delaying withdrawal in early July, HAMAS launched a series of suicide attacks. Israel accelerated the pace of its withdrawal, after which HAMAS ended the campaign. Mahmud al-Zahar, a HAMAS leader in Gaza, made this announcement following the cessation of suicide attacks in October 1995:

> We must calculate the benefit and cost of continued armed operations. If we can fulfill our goals without violence, we will do so. Violence is a means, not a goal. HAMAS's decision to adopt self-restraint does not contradict our aims, which include the establishment of an Islamic state instead of Israel. . . . We will never recognize Israel, but it is possible that a truce could prevail between us for days, months, or years (Mishal and Sela 2000, p. 71).

TABLE 6-1. Suicide Terrorist Campaigns, 1980–2001

Date	Terrorist Group	Terrorists' Goal	No. of Attacks	No. Killed	Target Behavior
Completed Campaigns					
1. Apr–Dec 1983	Hizballah	U.S./France out of Lebanon	6	384	Complete withdrawal
2. Nov 1983–Apr 1985	Hizballah	Israel out of Lebanon	6	96	Partial withdrawal
3. June 1985–June 1986	Hizballah	Israel out of Lebanon security zone	16	179	No change
4. July 1990–Nov 1994	LTTE	Sri Lanka accept Tamil state	14	164	Negotiations
5. Apr 1995–Oct 2000	LTTE	Sri Lanka accept Tamil state	54	629	No change
6. Apr 1994	HAMAS	Israel out of Palestine	2	15	Partial withdrawal from Gaza
7. Oct 1994–Aug 1995	HAMAS	Israel out of Palestine	7	65	Partial withdrawal from West Bank
8. Feb–Mar 1996	HAMAS	Retaliation for Israeli assassination	4	58	No change
9. Mar–Sept 1997	HAMAS	Israel out of Palestine	3	24	Hamas leader Released
10. June–Oct 1996	PKK	Turkey accept Kurd autonomy	3	17	No change
11. Mar–Aug 1999	PKK	Turkey release jailed leader	6	0	No change
Ongoing Campaigns, as of December 2001					
12. 1996–	al-Qaida	U.S. out of Saudi Peninsula	6	3,329	TBD[a]
13. 2000–	Chechen Rebels	Russia out of Chechnya	4	53	TBD
14. 2000–	Kashmir Rebels	India out of Kashmir	3	45	TBD
15. 2001–	LTTE	Sri Lanka accept Tamil state	6	51	TBD
16. 2000–	Several	Israel out of Palestine	39	177	TBD
Total incidents	188				
No. in campaigns	179				
No. isolated	9				

Source: Pape (2002).
[a]To be determined.

If suicide terrorism were mainly irrational or even disorganized, we would expect a much different pattern in which either political goals were not articulated (e.g., references in news reports to "rogue" attacks), or the stated goals varied considerably even within the same conflict. We would also expect the timing to be either random or event driven in response to particularly provocative or infuriating actions by the other side, but little if at all related to the progress of negotiations over issues in dispute that the terrorists want to influence.

Nationalist Goals. Suicide terrorism is a high-cost strategy, one that would only make strategic sense for a group when high interests are at stake and, even then, only as a last resort. The reason is that suicide terrorism maximizes coercive leverage at the expense of support among the terrorists' own community and so can be sustained over time only when there already exists a high degree of commitment among the potential pool of recruits. The most important goal that a community can have is the independence of its homeland (population, property, and way of life) from foreign influence or control. As a result, a strategy of suicide terrorism is most likely to be used to achieve nationalist goals, such as gaining control of what the terrorists see as their national homeland territory and expelling foreign military forces from that territory.

In fact, every suicide campaign from 1980 to 2001 has had as a major objective—or as its central objective—coercing a foreign government that has military forces in what they see as their homeland to take those forces out. Table 6-2 summarizes the disputes that have engendered suicide terrorist campaigns. Since 1980, there has not been a suicide terrorist campaign directed mainly against domestic opponents or against foreign opponents who did not have military forces in the terrorists' homeland. Although attacks against civilians are often the most salient to Western observers, actually every suicide terrorist campaign in the past two decades has included attacks directly against the foreign military forces in the country, and most have been waged by guerrilla organizations that also use more conventional methods of attack against those forces.

Even al-Qaida fits this pattern. Although Saudi Arabia is not under American military occupation per se and the terrorists have political objectives against the Saudi regime and others, one major objective of al-Qaida is the expulsion of U.S. troops from the Saudi Peninsula, and there have been attacks by terrorists loyal to Usama bin Ladin against American troops in Saudi Arabia. To be sure, there is a major debate among Islamists over the morality of suicide attacks, but within Saudi Arabia there is little debate over al-Qaida's objection to American forces in the region, and over 95 percent of Saudi society reportedly agrees with bin Ladin on this matter (Sciolino, 2002).

Still, even if suicide terrorism follows a strategic logic, could some suicide terrorist campaigns be irrational in the sense that they are being waged for unrealistic goals? The answer is that some suicide terrorist groups have not been realistic in expecting the full concessions demanded of the target, but this is normal for disputes involving overlapping nationalist claims and even for coercive attempts in general.

Rather, the ambitions of terrorist leaders are realistic in two other senses. First, suicide terrorists' political aims, if not their methods, are often more mainstream than observers realize; they generally reflect the quite common, straightforward, nationalist self-determination claims of their community. Second, these groups often have significant support for their policy goals versus the target state, goals that are typically much the same as those of other nationalists within their community. Differences between the terrorists and more "moderate" leaders usually concern the usefulness of a certain level of violence and—sometimes—the legitimacy of attacking additional targets besides foreign troops in the country, such as attacks in other countries or against third parties and civilians. Thus, it is not that the terrorists pursue radical goals and then seek others' support. Rather, the

TABLE 6-2. Motivation and Targets of Suicide Terrorist Campaigns, 1980–2001

Region Dispute	Homeland Status	Terrorist Goal	Target a Democracy?
Lebanon, 1983–86	U.S./F/IDF military presence	U.S./F/IDF withdrawal	Yes
West Bank/Gaza, 1994–	IDF military presence	IDF withdrawal	Yes
Tamils in Sri Lanka, 1990–	SL military presence	SL withdrawal	Yes (1950)[a]
Kurds in Turkey, 1990s	Turkey military presence	Turkey withdrawal	Yes (1983)[a]
Chechnya, 2000–	Russia military presence	Russian withdrawal	Yes (1993)[a]
Kashmir, 2000–	Indian military presence	Indian withdrawal	Yes
Saudi Peninsula, 1996–	U.S. military presence	U.S. withdrawal	Yes

Sources: Pape (2002). Przeworski et al. (2000) identifies four simple rules for determining regime type: (1) The chief executive must be elected, (2) the legislature must be elected, (3) there must be more than one party, and (4) there must be at least one peaceful transfer of power. By these criteria all the targets of suicide terrorism were and are democracies. Przeworski et al. codes only from 1950 to 1990 and is updated to 1999 by Boix and Rosato (2001). Freedom House also rates countries as "free," "partly free," and "not free," using criteria for degree of political rights and civil liberties. According to Freedom House's measures, Sri Lanka, Turkey, and Russia were all partly free when they were the targets of suicide terrorism, which puts them approximately in the middle of all countries, a score that is actually biased against this study since terrorism itself lowers a country's civil liberties rating (freedomhouse.org).

[a]Date established as a democracy (if not always a democracy).

terrorists are simply the members of their societies who are the most optimistic about the usefulness of violence for achieving goals that many, and often most, support.

The behavior of HAMAS illustrates the point. HAMAS terrorism has provoked Israeli retaliation that has been costly for Palestinians while pursuing the—apparently unrealistic—goal of abolishing the state of Israel. Although prospects of establishing an Arab state in all of "historic Palestine" may be poor, most Palestinians agree that it would be desirable if possible. HAMAS's terrorist violence was in fact carefully calculated and controlled. In April 1994, as its first suicide campaign was beginning, HAMAS leaders explained that "martyrdom operations" would be used to achieve intermediate objectives, such as Israeli withdrawal from the West Bank and Gaza, while the final objective of creating an Islamic state from the Jordan River to the Mediterranean might require other forms of armed resistance (Shiqaqi, 2002; Hroub, 2000; Nusse, 1998).

Democracies as the Targets. Suicide terrorism is more likely to be employed against states with democratic political systems than against authoritarian governments for several reasons. First, democracies are often thought to be especially vulnerable to coercive punishment. Domestic critics and international rivals, as well as terrorists, often view democracies as "soft," usually on the grounds that their publics have low thresholds of cost tolerance and high ability to affect state policy. Even if there is little evidence that democracies are easier to coerce than other regime types (Horowitz and Reiter, 2001), this image of democracy matters. Since terrorists can inflict only moderate damage in comparison to even small interstate wars, terrorism can be expected to coerce only if the target state is viewed as especially vulnerable to punishment.

Second, suicide terrorism is a tool of the weak, which means that, regardless of how much punishment the terrorists inflict, the target state almost always has the capacity to retaliate with far more extreme punishment or even by exterminating the terrorists' community. Accordingly, suicide terrorists must not only have high interests at stake, they must also be confident that their opponent will be at least somewhat restrained. While there are infamous exceptions, democracies have generally been more restrained in their use of force against civilians, at least since World War II.

Finally, suicide attacks may be harder to organize or publicize in authoritarian police states, although these possibilities are weakened by the fact that weak authoritarian states are also not targets.

In fact, the target state of every modern suicide campaign has been a democracy. The United States, France, Israel, India, Sri Lanka, Turkey, and Russia were all democracies when they were attacked by suicide terrorist campaigns, even though the last three became democracies more recently than the others. To be sure, these states vary in the degree to which they share "liberal" norms that respect minority rights. Freedom House rates Sri Lanka, Turkey, and Russia as "partly free" (3.5–4.5 on a seven-point scale) rather than "free" during the relevant years, partly for this reason and partly because terrorism and civil violence themselves lower the freedom rating of these states. Still, all these states elect their chief executives and legislatures in multiparty elections and have seen at least one peaceful transfer of power, making them solidly democratic by standard criteria (Boix and Rosato, 2001; Huntington, 1991; Przeworski et al., 2000).

The Kurds, who straddle Turkey and Iraq, illustrate the point that suicide terrorist campaigns are more likely to be targeted against democracies than authoritarian regimes. Although Iraq has been far more brutal toward its Kurdish population than has Turkey, violent Kurdish groups have used suicide attacks exclusively against democratic Turkey and not against the authoritarian regime in Iraq. There are plenty of national groups living under authoritarian regimes with grievances that could possibly inspire suicide terrorism, but none has. Thus, the fact that rebels have resorted to this strategy only when they face the more suitable type of target counts against arguments that suicide terrorism is a nonstrategic response, motivated mainly by fanaticism or irrational hatreds.

Terrorists' Assessments of Suicide Terrorism

The main reason suicide terrorism is growing is that terrorists have learned that it works. Even more troubling, the encouraging lessons that terrorists have learned from the experiences of the 1980s and 1990s are not, for the most part, products of wild-eyed interpretations or wishful thinking. They are, rather, quite reasonable assessments of the outcomes of suicide terrorist campaigns during this period.

To understand how terrorists groups have assessed the effectiveness of suicide terrorism requires three tasks: (1) explanation of appropriate standards for evaluating the effectiveness of coercion from the standpoint of coercers; (2) analysis of the 11 suicide terrorist campaigns that have ended as of 2001 to determine how frequently target states made concessions that were, or at least could have been, interpreted as due to suicide attack; and (3) close analysis of terrorists' learning from particular campaigns. Because some analysts see suicide terrorism as fundamentally irrational (Kramer, 1990; Merari, 1990; Post, 1990), it is important to assess whether the lessons that the terrorists drew were reasonable conclusions from the record. The crucial cases are the HAMAS and Islamic Jihad campaigns against Israel during the 1990s, because they are most frequently cited as aimed at unrealistic goals and therefore as basically irrational.

Standards of Assessment

Terrorists, like other people, learn from experience. Since the main purpose of suicide terrorism is coercion, the learning that is likely to have the greatest impact on terrorists' future behavior is the lessons that they have drawn from past campaigns about the coercive effectiveness of suicide attack.

Most analyses of coercion focus on the decision making of target states, largely to determine their vulnerability to various coercive pressures (George, 1972; Pape, 1996). The analysis here, however, seeks to determine why terrorist coercers are increasingly attracted to a specific coercive strategy. For this purpose, we must develop a new set of standards, because assessing the value of coercive pressure for the coercer is not the same problem as assessing its impact on the target.

From the perspective of a target state, the key question is whether the value of the concession that the coercer is demanding is greater than the costs imposed by the coercive pressure, regardless of whether that pressure is in the form of lives at risk, economic hardship, or other types of costs. However, from the perspective of the coercer, the key question is whether a particular coercive strategy promises to be more effective than alternative methods of influence and, so, warrants continued (or increased) effort. This is especially true for terrorists who are highly committed to a particular goal and so are willing to exhaust virtually any alternative rather than abandoning it. In this search for an effective strategy, coercers' assessments are likely to be largely a function of estimates of the success of past efforts; for suicide terrorists, this means assessments of whether past suicide campaigns produced significant concessions.

A glance at the behavior of suicide terrorists reveals that such trade-offs between alternative methods are important in their calculations. All the organizations that have resorted to suicide terrorism began their coercive efforts with more conventional guerrilla operations, nonsuicide terrorism, or both. Hizballah, HAMAS, Islamic Jihad, the PKK, the LTTE, and al-Qaida all used demonstrative and destructive means of violence long before resorting to suicide attack. Indeed, looking at the trajectory of terrorist groups over time, there is a distinct element of experimentation in the techniques and strategies used by these groups, and distinct movement toward those techniques and strategies that produce the most effect. Al-Qaida actually prides itself for a commitment to even tactical learning over time—the infamous "terrorist manual" stresses at numerous points the importance of writing "lessons learned" memoranda that can be shared with other members to improve the effectiveness of future attacks.

The most important analytical difficulty in assessing outcomes of coercive efforts is that successes are more ambiguous than failures. Whenever a suicide terrorist campaign or any coercive effort ends without obtaining significant concessions, presumably the coercers must judge the effort as a failure. If, however, the target state does make policy changes in the direction of the terrorists' political goals, this may or may not represent a coercive success for suicide attack in the calculations of the terrorists. The target government's decision could have been mainly or partly a response to the punishment inflicted by the suicide attacks, but it also could be a response to another type of pressure (such as an ongoing guerrilla campaign), or to pressure from a different actor (such as one of the target state's allies) or a different country, or the target's policy decision may not even have been intended as a concession but could have been made for other reasons that only coincidentally moved in a direction desired by the terrorists. Different judgments among these alternatives yield different lessons for future usefulness of suicide attack.

Standard principles from social psychology suggest how terrorists are likely to resolve these ambiguities. Under normal conditions, most people tend to interpret ambiguous information in ways that are consistent with their prior beliefs, as well as in ways that justify their past actions (Jervis, 1976; Lebow, 1981). Suicide terrorists, of course, are likely to have at least some initial confidence in the efficacy of suicide attack, or else they would not resort to it. Of course, the fact of having carried out such attacks gives them an interest in justifying that choice. Thus, whenever targets of suicide terrorism make a real or apparent concession, and it is a plausible interpretation that it was due to the coercive pressure of the suicide campaign, we would expect terrorists to favor *that* interpretation, even if other interpretations are also plausible.

This does not mean that we should simply expect terrorists to interpret virtually all outcomes, regardless of evidence, as encouraging further terrorism; that would not constitute learning and would make sense only if the terrorists were deeply irrational. To control for this possibility, it is crucial to consider the assessments of the same events by other well-informed people. If we find that when suicide terrorist leaders claim credit for coercing potential concessions, their claims are unique (or nearly so), then it would be appropriate to dismiss them as irrational. If, on the other hand, we find that their interpretations are shared by a significant portion of other observers across a range of circumstances and interests—from target state leaders to others in the terrorists' community, to neutral analysts—then we should assume that their assessments are as rational as anyone else's and should take the lessons they draw seriously.

In making these judgments, the testimony of target state leaders is often especially telling; although states like the United States and Israel virtually never officially admit making concessions to terrorism, leaders such as Ronald Reagan and Yitzhak Rabin have, at times, been quite open about the impact of suicide terrorism on their own policy decisions.

Finally, understanding how terrorists assess the effectiveness of suicide terrorism should also be influenced by our prior understanding of the fanatical nature of the specific terrorists at issue. If the most fanatical groups also make what appear to be reasonable assessments, then this would increase our confidence in the finding that most terrorists would make similar calculations. HAMAS and Islamic Jihad are the most crucial case, because these groups have been considered to be fanatical extremists even among terrorists (Kramer, 1996). Thus, detailed examination of how HAMAS and Islamic Jihad leaders assessed the coercive value of suicide attacks during the 1990s is especially important.

The Apparent Success of Suicide Terrorism

Perhaps the most striking aspect of recent suicide terrorist campaigns is that they are associated with gains for the terrorists' political cause about half the time. As Table 6-1 shows, of the 11 suicide terrorist campaigns that were completed during 1980–2001, six closely correlate with significant policy changes by the target state toward the terrorists' major political goals. In one case, the terrorists' territorial goals were fully achieved (Hizballah v. US/F, 1983); in three cases, the terrorists territorial aims were partly achieved (Hizballah v. Israel, 1983–85; HAMAS v. Israel, 1994; and HAMAS v. Israel, 1994–95); in one case, the target government entered into sovereignty negotiations with the terrorists (LTTE v. Sri Lanka, 1993–94); and in one case, the terrorist organization's top leader was released from prison (HAMAS v. Israel, 1997). Five campaigns did not lead to noticeable concessions (Hizballah's second effort against Israel in Lebanon, 1985–86; a HAMAS campaign in 1996 retaliating for an Israeli assassination; the LTTE v. Sri Lanka, 1995–2002; and both PKK campaigns). Coercive success is so rare that even a 50 percent success rate is significant, because international military and economic coercion, using the same standards as above, generally works less than a third of the time (Art and Cronin, 2003).

There were limits to what suicide terrorism appeared to gain in the 1980s and 1990s. Most of the gains for the terrorists' causes were modest, not involving interests central to the target countries' security or wealth, and most were potentially revocable. For the United States and France, Lebanon was a relatively minor foreign policy interest. Israel's apparent concessions to the Palestinians from 1994 to 1997 were more modest than they might appear.

Although Israel withdrew its forces from parts of Gaza and the West Bank and released Sheikh Yassin, during the same period Israeli settlement in the occupied territories almost doubled, and recent events have shown that Israel is not deterred from sending forces back in when necessary. In two disputes, the terrorists achieved initial success but failed to reach greater goals. Although Israel withdrew from much of Lebanon in June 1985, it retained a six-mile security buffer zone along the southern edge of the country for another 15 years, which a second Hizballah suicide terrorist campaign failed to dislodge. The Sri Lankan government did conduct apparently serious negotiations with the LTTE from November 1994 to April 1995 but did not concede the Tamil's main demand for independence, and since 1995, the government has preferred to prosecute the war rather than consider permitting Tamil secession.

Still, these six concessions, or at least apparent concessions, help to explain why suicide terrorism is on the rise. In three of the cases, the target government policy changes are clearly due to coercive pressure from the terrorist group. The American and French withdrawal was perhaps the most clear-cut coercive success for suicide terrorism. In his memoirs, President Ronald Reagan (1990, 465) explained the U.S. decision to withdraw from Lebanon:

> The price we had to pay in Beirut was so great, the tragedy at the barracks was so enormous. . . . We had to pull out. . . . We couldn't stay there and run the risk of another suicide attack on the Marines.

The IDF withdrawal from most of southern Lebanon in 1985 and the Sri Lankan government decision to hold negotiations with the LTTE were also widely understood to be a direct result of the coercive punishment imposed by Hizballah and LTTE respectively. In both cases, the concessions followed periods in which the terrorists had turned more and more to suicide attacks, but since Hizballah and the LTTE employed a combination of suicide attack and conventional attack on their opponents, one can question the relative weight of suicide attack in coercing these target states.

However, there is little question in either case that punishment pressures inflicted by these terrorist organizations were decisive in the outcomes. For instance, as a candidate in the November 9, 1994, presidential election of Sri Lanka, Mrs. Chandrika Kumaratunga explicitly asked for a mandate to redraw boundaries so as to appease the Tamils in their demand for a separate homeland in the island's northeast provinces, often saying, "We definitely hope to begin discussions with the Tamil people, with their representatives— including the Tigers—and offer them political solutions to end the war. . . . [involving] extensive devolution." This would, Kumaratunga said, "create an environment in which people could live without fear" (Sauvagnargues, 1994; "Sri Lanka", 1994).

The other three concessions, or arguable concessions, are less clear-cut. All three involve HAMAS campaigns against Israel. Not counting the ongoing second *intifada*, HAMAS waged four separate suicide attack campaigns against Israel, in 1994, 1995, 1996, and 1997. One, in 1996, did not correspond with Israeli concessions. This campaign was announced as retaliation for Israel's assassination of a HAMAS leader; no particular coercive goal was announced, and it was suspended by HAMAS after four attacks in two weeks.

The other three all do correspond with Israeli concessions. In April 1994, HAMAS began a series of suicide bombings in retaliation for the Hebron Massacre. After two attacks, Israel decided to accelerate its withdrawal from Gaza, which was required under the Oslo Agreement but which had been delayed. HAMAS then suspended attacks for five months. From October 1994 to August 1995, HAMAS (and Islamic Jihad) carried out a total of seven suicide attacks against Israel. In September 1995, Israel agreed to withdraw from certain West Bank towns that December, which it earlier had claimed could not be done before April 1996 at the soonest. HAMAS then suspended attacks until its retaliation campaign during the last week of February and first week of March 1996. Finally, in March 1997, HAMAS began a suicide attack campaign that included an attack about every two months until September 1997. In response Israeli Prime Minister Netanyahu authorized the assassination of a HAMAS leader. The attempt, in Amman, Jordan, failed and the Israeli agents were captured. To get them back, Israel agreed to release Sheikh Ahmed Yassin, spiritual leader of HAMAS. While this was not a concession to the terrorists' territorial goals, there is no evidence that HAMAS interpreted this in anyway different from the standard view, that this release was the product of American and Jordanian pressure. Accordingly the key HAMAS campaigns that might have encouraged the view that suicide terrorism pays were the 1994 and 1995 campaigns that were associated with Israel's military withdrawals from Gaza and the West Banks. Terrorists' assessments of these events are evaluated in detail.

The Crucial Case of HAMAS

The HAMAS and Islamic Jihad suicide campaigns against Israel in 1994 and 1995 are crucial tests of the reasonableness of terrorists' assessments. In each case, Israel made significant concessions in the direction of the terrorists' cause, and terrorist leaders report that these Israeli concessions increased their confidence in the coercive effectiveness of suicide attack. However, there is an important alternative explanation for Israel's concessions in these cases—the Israeli government's obligations under the Oslo Accords.

Accordingly, evaluating the reasonableness of the terrorists' assessments of these cases is crucial because many observers characterize HAMAS and Islamic Jihad as fanatical, irrational groups, extreme both within Palestinian society and among terrorists groups in general (Kramer, 1996). Further, these campaigns are also of special interest because they helped to encourage the most intense ongoing campaign, the second *intifada* against Israel, and also may have helped to encourage al-Qaida's campaign against the United States.

Examination of these crucial cases demonstrates that the terrorist groups came to the conclusion that suicide attacks accelerated Israel's withdrawal in both cases. Although the Oslo Accords formally committed to withdrawing the IDF from Gaza and the West Bank, Israel routinely missed key deadlines, often by many months, and the terrorists came to believe that Israel would not have withdrawn when it did, and perhaps not at all, had it not been for the coercive leverage of suicide attack. Moreover, this interpretation of events was hardly unique. Numerous other observers and key Israeli government leaders themselves came to the same conclusion. To be clear, HAMAS may well have had motives other than coercion for launching particular attacks, such as retaliation (De Figueredo and Weingast, 1998), gaining local support (Bloom 2002), or disrupting negotiated outcomes it considered insufficient (Kydd and Walter, 2002). However, the experience of observing how the target reacted to the suicide campaigns appears to have convinced terrorist leaders of the coercive effectiveness of this strategy.

To evaluate these cases, we need to know (1) the facts of each case, (2) how others interpreted the events, and (3) how the terrorists interpreted these events. Each campaign is discussed in turn.

Israel's Withdrawal from Gaza, May 1994

The first HAMAS case, in 1994, involved a series of suicide attacks and Israeli territorial concessions to the Palestinians. A significant number of outside observers attributed the concessions to the coercive pressure of suicide terrorism, as did the terrorist leaders themselves.

The Facts. Israel and the Palestinian Liberation Organization (PLO) signed the Oslo Accords on September 13, 1993. These obligated Israel to withdraw its military forces from the Gaza Strip and the West Bank town of Jericho, beginning on December 13 and ending on April 13, 1994. In fact, Israel missed both deadlines. The major sticking points during the implementation negotiations in fall and winter of 1993–1994 were the size of the Palestinian police force (Israel proposed a limit of 1,800, while the Palestinians demanded 9,000), and jurisdiction for certain criminal prosecutions, especially whether Israel could retain a right of hot pursuit to prosecute Palestinian attackers who might flee into Palestinian ruled zones. As of April 5, 1994, these issues were unresolved. HAMAS then launched two suicide attacks, one on April 6 and another on April 13, killing 15 Israeli civilians. On April 18, the Israeli Knesset voted to withdraw, effectively accepting the Palestinian positions on both disputed issues. The suicide attacks then stopped and the withdrawal was actually conducted in a few weeks starting on May 4, 1994.[4]

These two suicide attacks may not originally have been intended as coercive, since HAMAS leaders had announced them in March 1994 as part of a planned series of five attacks in retaliation for the February 24 Hebron massacre in which an Israeli settler killed 29 Palestinians and had strong reservations about negotiating a compromise settlement with Israel (Kydd and Walter, 2002). However, when Israel agreed to withdraw more promptly than expected, HAMAS decided to forgo the remaining three planned attacks. There is thus a circumstantial case that these attacks had the effect of coercing the Israelis into being more forthcoming in the withdrawal negotiations, and both Israeli government leaders and HAMAS leaders publicly drew this conclusion.

   Israeli and Other Assessments. There are two main reasons to doubt that terrorist pressure accelerated Israel's decision to withdraw. First, one might think that Israel would have withdrawn in any case, as it had promised to do in the Oslo Accords of September 1993. Second, one might argue that HAMAS was opposed to a negotiated settlement with Israel. Taking both points together, therefore, HAMAS' attacks could not have contributed to Israel's withdrawal.

   The first of these arguments, however, ignores the facts that Israel had already missed the originally agreed deadline and, as of early April 1994, did not appear ready to withdraw at all if that meant surrendering on the size of the Palestinian police force and legal jurisdiction over terrorists. The second argument is simply illogical. Although HAMAS objected to surrendering claims to all of historic Palestine, it did value the West Bank and Gaza as an intermediate goal, and certainly had no objection to obtaining this goal sooner rather than later.

   Most important, other observers took explanations based on terrorist pressure far more seriously, including the person whose testimony must count most, Israeli Prime Minister Yitzhak Rabin. On April 13, 1994, Rabin said:

> I can't recall in the past any suicidal terror acts by the PLO. We have seen by now at least six acts of this type by Hamas and Islamic Jihad. . . . The only response to them and to the enemies of peace on the part of Israel is to accelerate the negotiations. (Makovsky and Pinkas, 1994).

On April 18, 1994, Rabin went further, giving a major speech in the Knesset explaining why the withdrawal was necessary:

> Members of the Knessett: I want to tell the truth. For 27 years we have been dominating another people against its will. For 27 years Palestinians in the territories. . . get up in the morning harboring a fierce hatred for us, as Israelis and Jews. Each morning they get up to a hard life, for which we are also, but not solely responsible. We cannot deny that our continuing control over a foreign people who do not want us exacts a painful price. . . . For two or three years we have been facing a phenomenon of extremist Islamic terrorism, which recalls Hezbollah, which surfaced in Lebanon and perpetrated attacks, including suicide missions. . . . There is no end to the targets Hamas and other terrorist organizations have among us. Each Israeli, in the territories and inside sovereign Israel, including united Jerusalem, each bus, each home, is a target for their murderous plans. Since there is no separation between the two populations, the current situation creates endless possibilities for Hamas and the other organizations.

Independent Israeli observers also credited suicide terrorism with considerable coercive effectiveness. The most detailed assessment is by Efraim Inbar (1999, 141–42):

> A significant change occurred in Rabin's assessment of the importance of terrorist activities. . . . Reacting to the April 1994 suicide attack in Afula, Rabin recognized that terrorists activities by Hamas and other Islamic radicals were "a form of terrorism different from what we once knew from the PLO terrorist organizations. . . ." Rabin admitted that there was no "hermitic" solution available to protect Israeli citizens against such terrorist attacks. . . . He also understood that such incidents intensified the domestic pressure to freeze the Palestinian track of the peace process. Islamic terrorism thus initially contributed to the pressure for accelerating the negotiations on his part.

Arab writers also attributed Israeli accommodation to the suicide attacks. Mazin Hammad wrote in an editorial in a Jordanian newspaper:

> It is unprecedented for an Israeli official like Y. Rabin to clearly state that there is no future for the settlements in the occupied territories. . . . He would not have said this [yesterday] if it was not for the collapse of the security Israel. . . . The martyrdom operation in Hadera shook the faith of the settlers in the possibility of staying in the West Bank and Gaza and increased their motivation to pack their belongings and dismantle their settlements ("Hamas Operations" 1994).

Terrorists' Assessments. Even though the favorable result was apparently unexpected by HAMAS leaders, given the circumstances and the assessments voiced by Rabin and others, it certainly would have been reasonable for them to conclude that suicide terrorism had helped accelerate Israeli withdrawal, and they did.

HAMAS leader Ahmed Bakr (1995) said that "what forced the Israelis to withdraw from Gaza was the *intifada* and not the Oslo agreement," while Imad al- Faluji judged that

> all that has been achieved so far is the consequence of our military actions. Without the so-called peace process, we would have gotten even more. . . . We would have got Gaza and the West Bank without this agreement. . . . Israel can beat all Arab Armies. However, it can do nothing against a youth with a knife or an explosive charge on his body. Since it was unable to guarantee security within its borders, Israel entered into negotiations with the PLO. . . . If the Israelis want security, they will have to abandon their settlements . . . in Gaza, the West Bank, and Jerusalem ("Hamas Leader," 1995).

Further, these events appear to have persuaded terrorists that future suicide attacks could eventually produce still greater concessions. Fathi al-Shaqaqi (1995), leader of Islamic Jihad, said:

> Our jihad action has exposed the enemy weakness, confusion, and hysteria. It has become clear that the enemy can be defeated, for if a small faithful group was able to instill all this horror and panic in the enemy through confronting it in Palestine and southern Lebanon, what will happen when the nation confronts it with all its potential. . . . Martyrdom actions will escalate in the face of all pressures . . . [they] are a realistic option in confronting the

unequal balance of power. If we are unable to effect a balance of power now, we can achieve a balance of horror.

Israel's Withdrawal from West Bank Towns, December 1995

The second HAMAS case, in 1995, tells essentially the same story as the first. Again, a series of suicide attacks was associated with Israeli territorial concessions to the Palestinians, and again, a significant fraction of outside observers attributed the concessions to the coercive pressure of suicide terrorism, as did the terrorist leaders themselves.

The Facts. The original Oslo Accords scheduled Israel to withdraw from the Palestinian populated areas of the West Bank by July 13, 1994, but after the delays over Gaza and Jericho, all sides recognized that this could not be met. From October 1994 to April 1995, HAMAS, along with Islamic Jihad, carried out a series of seven suicide terrorist attacks that were intended to compel Israel to make further withdrawals. The attacks were suspended temporarily at the request of the Palestinian Authority after Israel agreed on March 29, 1995, to begin withdrawals by July 1. Later, however, the Israelis announced that withdrawals could not begin before April 1996 because bypass roads needed for the security of Israeli settlements were not ready. HAMAS and Islamic Jihad then mounted new suicide attacks on July 24 and August 21, 1995, killing 11 Israeli civilians. In September, Israel agreed to withdraw from the West Bank towns in December (Oslo II), even though the roads were not finished yet. The suicide attacks then stopped, and the withdrawal was actually carried out in a few weeks starting on December 12, 1995.[5]

Israeli and Other Assessments. Although Israeli government spokesmen frequently claimed that suicide terrorism was delaying withdrawal, this claim was contradicted by, among others, Prime Minister Rabin. Rabin (1995) explained that the decision for the second withdrawal was, like the first in 1994, motivated in part by the goal of reducing suicide terrorism:

> *Interviewer:* Mr. Rabin, what is the logic of withdrawing from towns and villages when you know that terror might continue to strike at us from there?

> *Rabin:* What is the alternative, to have double the amount of terror? As for the issue of terror, take the suicide bombings. Some 119 Israelis . . . have been killed or murdered since 1st January 1994, 77 of them in suicide bombings perpetrated by Islamic radical fanatics . . . All the bombers were Palestinians who came from areas under our control.

Similarly, an editorial in the Israeli daily *Yediot Aharonot* ("Bus Attack" 1995) explained:

> If the planners of yesterday's attack intended to get Israel to back away from the Oslo accord, they apparently failed. In fact, Prime Minister Y. Rabin is leaning toward expediting the talks with the Palestinians. . . . The immediate conclusion from this line of thinking on Rabin's part—whose results we will witness in the coming days—will be to instruct the negotiators to expedite the talks with the Palestinians with the aim of completing them in the very near future.

Terrorists' Assessments. As in 1994, HAMAS and Islamic Jihad came to the conclusion that suicide terrorism was working. HAMAS's spokesman in Jordan explained that new attacks were necessary to change Israel's behavior:

> Hamas, leader Muhammad Nazzal said, needed military muscle in order to negotiate with Israel from a position of strength. Arafat started from a position of weakness, he said, which is how the Israelis managed to push on him the solution and get recognition of their state and settlements without getting anything in return (Theodoulou, 1995).

After the agreement was signed, HAMAS leaders also argued that suicide operations contributed to the Israeli withdrawal. Mahmud al-Zahhar (1996), a spokesman for Hamas, said:

> The Authority told us that military action embarrasses the PA because it obstructs the redeployment of the Israeli's forces and implementation of the agreement. . . . We offered many martyrs to attain freedom. . . . Any fair person knows that the military action was useful for the Authority during negotiations.

Moreover, the terrorists also stressed that stopping the attacks only discouraged Israel from withdrawing. An early August HAMAS communiqué (No. 125, 1995) read:

> They said that the strugglers' operations have been the cause of the delay in widening the autonomous rule in the West Bank, and that they have been the reason for the deterioration of the living and economic conditions of our people. Now the days have come to debunk their false claims . . . and to affirm that July 1 [a promised date for IDF withdrawal] was no more than yet another of the "unholy" Zionist dates. . . . Hamas has shown an utmost degree of self-restraint throughout the past period. . . . but matters have gone far enough and the criminals will reap what their hands have sown.

Recent Impact of Lessons Learned. In addition to the 1994 and 1995 campaigns, Palestinian terrorist leaders have also cited Hizballah experience in Lebanon as a source of the lesson that suicide terrorism is an effective way of coercing Israel. Islamic Jihad leader Ramadan Shallah (2001) argued:

> The shameful defeat that Israel suffered in southern Lebanon and which caused its army to flee it in terror was not made on the negotiations table but on the battlefield and through jihad and martyrdom, which achieved a great victory for the Islamic resistance and Lebanese People. . . . We would not exaggerate if we said that the chances of achieving victory in Palestine are greater than in Lebanon. . . . If the enemy could not bear the losses of the war on the border strip with Lebanon, will it be able to withstand a long war of attrition in the heart of its security dimension and major cities?

Palestinian terrorists are now applying the lessons they have learned. In November 2000, Khalid Mish'al explained HAMAS's strategy for the second *intifada*, which was then in its early stages:

Like the *intifada* in 1987, the current *intifada* has taught us that we should move forward normally from popular confrontation to the rifle to suicide operations. This is the normal development. . . .We always have the Lebanese experiment before our eyes. It was a great model of which we are proud.

Even before the second *intifada* began, other HAMAS statements similarly expressed this:

The Zionist enemy . . . only understands the language of Jihad, resistance and martyrdom, that was the language that led to its blatant defeat in South Lebanon and it will be the language that will defeat it on the land of Palestine (HAMAS Statement, 2000).

The bottom line is that the ferocious escalation of the pace of suicide terrorism witnessed in the past several years cannot be considered irrational or even surprising. Rather, it is simply the result of the lesson that terrorists have quite reasonably learned from their experience of the previous two decades: Suicide terrorism pays.

The Limits of Suicide Terrorism

Despite suicide terrorists' reasons for confidence in the coercive effectiveness of this strategy, there are sharp limits to what suicide terrorism is likely to accomplish in the future. During the 1980s and 1990s, terrorist leaders learned that moderate punishment often leads to moderate concessions and so concluded that more ambitious suicide campaigns would lead to greater political gains. However, today's more ambitious suicide terrorist campaigns are likely to fail. Although suicide terrorism is somewhat more effective than ordinary coercive punishment, for example, using air power or economic sanctions, it is not drastically so.

Suicide Terrorism Is Unlikely to Achieve Ambitious Goals

In international military coercion, threats to inflict military defeat often generate more coercive leverage than punishment. Punishment, using anything short of nuclear weapons, is a relatively weak coercive strategy because modern nation states generally will accept high costs rather than abandon important national goals, while modern administrative techniques and economic adjustments over time often allow states to minimize civilian costs. The most punishing air attacks with conventional munitions in history were the American B-29 raids against Japan's 62 largest cities from March to August 1945. Although these raids killed nearly 800,000 Japanese civilians—almost 10 percent died on the first day, the March 9, 1945, firebombing of Tokyo, which killed over 85,000—the conventional bombing did not compel the Japanese to surrender.

Suicide terrorism makes it more difficult for state leaders to reduce potential damage than when faced with military coercion or economic sanctions. However, it does not affect the target state's interests in the issues at stake. As a result, suicide terrorism can coerce states to abandon limited or modest goals, such as withdrawal from territory of low strategic importance or, as in Israel's case in 1994 and 1995, a temporary and partial withdrawal from a more important area. However, suicide terrorism is unlikely to cause targets to abandon goals central to their wealth or security, such as a loss of territory that would weaken the economic prospects of the state or strengthen the rivals of the state.

Suicide terrorism makes punishment more effective than international military coercion. Targets remain willing to countenance high costs for important goals, but administrative, economic, or military adjustments to prevent suicide attacks are harder, while suicide attackers themselves are unlikely to be deterred by the threat of retaliation. Accordingly, suicide attack is likely to present a threat of continuing limited civilian punishment that the target government cannot completely eliminate, and the upper bound on what punishment can gain for coercers is recognizably higher in suicidal terrorism than in international military coercion.

The data on suicide terrorism from 1980 to 2001 support this conclusion. While suicide terrorism has achieved modest or very limited goals, it has so far failed to compel target democracies to abandon goals central to national wealth or security. When the United States withdrew from Lebanon in 1984, it had no important security, economic, or even ideological interests at stake. Lebanon was largely a humanitarian mission and not viewed as central to the national welfare of the United States. Israel withdrew from most of Lebanon in June 1985 but remained in a security buffer on the edge of southern Lebanon for more than a decade afterward, despite the fact that 17 of 22 suicide attacks occurred in 1985 and 1986. Israel's withdrawals from Gaza and the West Bank in 1994 and 1995 occurred at the same time that settlements increased and did little to hinder the IDF's return. Thus, these concessions were more modest than they may appear. Sri Lanka has suffered more casualties from suicide attack than Israel but has not acceded to demands that it surrender part of its national territory. Thus, the logic of punishment and the record of suicide terrorism suggest that, unless suicide terrorists acquire far more destructive technologies, suicide attacks for more ambitious goals are likely to fail and will continue to provoke more aggressive military responses.

Policy Implications for Containing Suicide Terrorism

While the rise in suicide terrorism and the reasons behind it seem daunting, there are important policy lessons to learn. The current policy debate is misguided. Offensive military action or concessions alone rarely work for long. For more than 20 years, the governments of Israel and other states targeted by suicide terrorism have engaged in extensive military efforts to kill, isolate, and jail suicide terrorist leaders and operatives, sometimes with the help of quite good surveillance of the terrorists' communities. Thus far, they have met with meager success. Although decapitation of suicide terrorist organizations can disrupt their operations temporarily, it rarely yields long-term gains. Of the 11 major suicide terrorist campaigns that had ended as of 2001, only one—the PKK versus Turkey—did so as a result of leadership decapitation, when the leader, in Turkish custody, asked his followers to stop. So far, leadership decapitation has also not ended al-Qaida's campaign. Although the United States successfully toppled the Taliban in Afghanistan in December 2001, al-Qaida launched seven successful suicide terrorist attacks from April to December 2002, killing some 250 Western civilians, more than in the three years before September 11, 2001, combined.

Concessions are also not a simple answer. Concessions to nationalist grievances that are widely held in the terrorists' community can reduce popular support for further terrorism, making it more difficult to recruit new suicide attackers and improving the standing of more moderate nationalist elites who are in competition with the terrorists. Such benefits can be realized, however, only if the concessions really do substantially satisfy the nationalist or self-determination aspirations of a large fraction of the community.

Partial, incremental, or deliberately staggered concessions that are dragged out over a substantial period of time are likely to become the worst of both worlds. Incremental compromise may appear—or easily be portrayed—to the terrorists' community as simply delaying tactics and, thus, may fail to reduce, or actually increase, their distrust that their main concerns will ever be met. Further, incrementalism provides time and opportunity for the terrorists to intentionally provoke the target state in hopes of derailing the smooth progress of negotiated compromise in the short term, so that they can re-radicalize their own community, and actually escalate their efforts toward even greater gains in the long term.[6] Thus, states that are willing to make concessions should do so in a single step if at all possible.

Advocates of concessions should also recognize that even if they are successful in undermining the terrorist leaders' base of support, almost any concession at all will tend to encourage the terrorist leaders further about their own coercive effectiveness. Thus, even in the aftermath of a real settlement with the opposing community, some terrorists will remain motivated to continue attacks and, for the medium term, may be able to do so, which in turn would put a premium on combining concessions with other solutions. Given the limits of offense and of concessions, homeland security and defensive efforts generally must be a core part of any solution. Undermining the feasibility of suicide terrorism is a difficult task. After all, a major advantage of suicide attack is that it is more difficult to prevent than other types of attack. However, the difficulty of achieving perfect security should not keep us from taking serious measures to prevent would-be terrorists from easily entering their target society.

As Chaim Kaufmann (1996) has shown, even intense ethnic civil wars can often be stopped by demographic separation because it greatly reduces both means and incentives for the sides to attack each other. This logic may apply with even more force to the related problem of suicide terrorism, since, for suicide attackers, gaining physical access to the general area of the target is the only genuinely demanding part of an operation, and as we have seen, resentment of foreign occupation of their national homeland is a key part of the motive for suicide terrorism.

The requirements for demographic separation depend on geographic and other circumstances that may not be attainable in all cases. For example, much of Israel's difficulty in containing suicide terrorism derives from the deeply intermixed settlement patterns of the West Bank and Gaza, which make the effective length of the border between Palestinian and Jewish settled areas practically infinite, and have rendered even very intensive Israeli border control efforts ineffective (Kaufmann, 1998). As a result, territorial concessions could well encourage terrorist leaders to strive for still greater gains, while greater repression may only exacerbate the conditions of occupation that cultivate more recruits for terrorist organizations. Instead, the best course to improve Israel's security may well be a combined strategy: abandoning territory on the West Bank along with an actual wall that physically separates the populations.

Similarly, if al-Qaida proves able to continue suicide attacks against the American homeland, the United States should emphasize improving its domestic security. In the short term, the United States should adopt stronger border controls to make it more difficult for suicide attackers to enter the United States. In the long term, the United States should work toward energy independence and thus reduce the need for American troops in the Persian Gulf countries, where their presence has helped recruit suicide terrorists to attack America. These measures will not provide a perfect solution, but they may make it far more difficult for al-Qaida to continue attacks in the United States, especially spectacular attacks that require elaborate coordination.

Perhaps most important, the close association between foreign military occupations and the growth of suicide terrorist movements in the occupied regions should give pause to those who favor solutions that involve conquering countries in order to transform their political systems. Conquering countries may disrupt terrorist operations in the short term, but it is important to recognize that occupation of more countries may well increase the number of terrorists coming at us.

Acknowledgments

I thank Robert Art, Mia Bloom, Steven C'y'cala, Alex Downs, Daniel Drezner, Adria Lawrence, Sean Lynn-Jones, John Mearsheimer, Michael O'Connor, Sebastian Rosato, Lisa Weeden, anonymous reviewers, and the members of the program on International Security Policy at the University of Chicago for their superb comments. I especially thank James K. Feldman and Chaim D. Kaufmann for their excellent comments on multiple drafts. I would also like to acknowledge encouragement from the committee for the Combating Political Violence paper competition sponsored by the Institute for War and Peace Studies at Columbia University, which selected an earlier version as a winning paper.

Appendix

Suicide Terrorist Campaigns, 1980–2001

Date	Weapon	Target	Killed
		Completed Campaigns	
Campaign #1: Hizballah vs. U.S., France			
1. April 18, 1983	car bomb	U.S. embassy, Beirut	63
2. Oct 23, 1983	car bomb	U.S. Marine barracks, Beirut	241
3. Oct 23, 1983	car bomb	French barracks, Beirut	58
4. Dec 12, 1983	grenades	U.S. embassy, Kuwait	7
5. Dec 21, 1983	car bomb	French HQ, Beirut	1
6. Sept 12, 1984	truck bomb	U.S. embassy, Beirut	14
Campaign #2: Hizballah vs. Israel			
1. Nov 4, 1983	car bomb	IDF post, Tyre, Lebanon	50
2. Jun 16, 1984	car bomb	IDF post, south Lebanon	5
3. Mar 8, 1985:	truck bomb	IDF post	12
4. Apr 9, 1985:	car bomb	IDF post	4
5. May 9, 1985:	suitcase bomb	Southern Lebanese Army checkpoint	2
6. June 15, 1985:	car bomb	IDF post, Beirut	23
Campaign #3: Hizballah vs. Israel and South Lebanon Army			
1. July 9, 1985	car bombs	2 SLA outposts	22
2. July 15, 1985	car bomb	SLA outpost	10
3. July 31, 1985	car bomb	IDF patrol, south Lebanon	2
4. Aug 6, 1985	mule bomb	SLA outpost	0
5. Aug 29, 1985	car bomb	SLA outpost	15
6. Sept 3, 1985	car bomb	SLA outpost	37
7. Sept 12, 1985	car bomb	SLA outpost	21
8. Sept 17, 1985	car bomb	SLA outpost	30
9. Sept 18, 1985	car bomb	SLA outpost	0
10. Oct 17, 1985	grenades	SLA radio station	6
11. Nov 4, 1985	car bomb	SLA outpost	0
12. Nov 12, 1985	car bomb	Christ. militia leaders, Beirut	5**
13. Nov 26, 1985	car bomb	SLA outpost	20
14. April 7, 1986	car bomb	SLA outpost	1
15. July 17, 1986	car bomb	Jezzine, south Lebanon	7
16. Nov 20, 1986:	car bomb	SLA outpost	3
Campaign #4: Liberation Tigers of Tamil Eelam vs. Sri Lanka			
1. Jul 12, 1990	boat bomb	naval vessel, Trincomalee	6
2. Nov 23, 1990	mines	army camp, Manakulam	0
3. Mar 2, 1991	car bomb	defense minister, Colombo	18**
4. Mar 19, 1991	truck bomb	army camp, Silavathurai	5
5. May 5, 1991	boat bomb	naval vessel	5

6. May 21, 1991	belt bomb	Rajiv Gandhi, Madras, India	1**
7. June 22, 1991	car bomb	defense ministry, Colombo	27
8. Nov 16, 1992	motorcycle bomb	navy commander, Colombo	1**
9. May 1, 1993	belt bomb	president of Sri Lanka, Colombo 2	3**
10. Nov 11, 1993	boat bomb	naval base, Jaffna Lagoon	0
11. Aug 2, 1994	grenades	air force helicopter, Palali	0
12. Sept 19, 1994	mines	naval vessel, Sagarawardene	25
13. Oct 24, 1994	belt bomb	Presidential candidate, Colombo 5	3**
14. Nov 8, 1994	mines	naval vessel, Vettilaikerny	0

Campaign #5: LTTE vs. Sri Lanka

1. Apr 18, 1995	scuba divers	naval vessel, Trincomalee	11
2. Jul 16, 1995	scuba divers	naval vessel, Jaffna peninsula	0
3. Aug 7, 1995	belt bomb	government bldg, Colombo	22
4. Sep 3, 1995	scuba divers	naval vessel, Trincomalee	0
5. Sep 10, 1995	scuba divers	naval vessel, Kankesanthurai	0
6. Sep 20, 1995	scuba divers	naval vessel, Kankesanthurai	0
7. Oct 2, 1995	scuba divers	naval vessel, Kankesanthurai	0
8. Oct 17, 1995	scuba divers	naval vessel, Trincomalee	9
9. Oct 20, 1995	mines	2 oil depots, Colombo	23
10. Nov 11, 1995	belt bombs	army HQ, crowd, Colombo	23
11. Dec 5, 1995	truck bomb	police camp, Batticaloa	23
12. Jan 8, 1996	belt bomb	market, Batticaloa	0
13. Jan 31, 1996	truck bomb	bank, Colombo	91
14. Apr 1, 1996	boat bomb	navy vessel, Vettilaikerni	10
15. Apr 12, 1996	scuba divers	port building, Colombo	0
16. Jul 3, 1996	belt bomb	government motorcade, Jaffna	37
17. Jul 18,1996	mines	naval gunboat, Mullaittivu	35
18. Aug 6, 1996	boat bomb	naval ship, north coast	0
19. Aug 14, 1996	bicycle bomb	public rally, Kalmunai	0
20. Oct 25, 1996	boat bomb	gunboat, Trincomalee	12
21. Nov 25, 1996	belt bomb	police chief vehicle, Trincomalee	0**
22. Dec 17, 1996	motorcycle bomb	police unit jeep, Ampara	1
23. Mar 6, 1997	grenades	air base, China Bay	0
24. Oct 15, 1997	truck bomb	World Trade Centre, Colombo	18
25. Oct 19, 1997	boat bomb	naval gunboat, northeastern coast	7
26. Dec 28, 1997	truck bomb	political leader, south Sri Lanka	0**
27. Jan 25, 1998	truck bomb	Buddhist shrine, Kandy	11
28. Feb 5, 1998	belt bomb	air force headquarters, Colombo	8
29. Feb 23, 1998	boat bombs	2 landing ships off Point Pedru	47
30. Mar 5, 1998	bus bomb	train station, Colombo	38
31. May 15, 1998	belt bomb	army brigadier, Jaffna peninsula	1
32. Sep 11, 1998	belt bomb	mayor of Jaffna	20**
33. Mar 15, 1999	belt bomb	police station, Colombo	5
34. May 29, 1999	belt bomb	Tamil rival leader, Batticaloa	2
35. Jul 25, 1999	belt bomb	passenger ferry, Trincomalee	1
36. Jul 29, 1999	belt bomb	Tamil politician, Colombo	1**
37. Aug 4, 1999	bicycle bomb	police vehicle, Vavuniya	12
38. Aug 9, 1999	belt bomb	military commander, Vakarai	1
39. Sep 2, 1999	belt bomb	Tamil rival, Vavuniya	3**

40. Dec 18, 1999	belt bombs	president of Sri Lanka, Colombo	38**
41. Jan 5, 2000	belt bomb	prime minister of Sri Lanka, Colombo	11**
42. Feb 4, 2000	sea diver	naval vessel, Trincomalee	0
43. Mar 2, 2000	belt bomb	military commander, Trincomalee	1**
44. Mar 10, 2000	belt bomb	government motorcade Colombo	23
45. Jun 5, 2000	scuba diver	ammunition ship, northeast coast	5
46. Jun 7, 2000	belt bomb	industries minister, Colombo	26**
47. Jun 14, 2000	bicycle bomb	air force bus, Wattala Town	2
48. Jun 26, 2000	boat bomb	merchant vessel, north coast	7
49. Aug 16, 2000	belt bomb	military vehicle, Vavuniya	1
50. Sep 15, 2000	belt bomb	hospital, Colombo	7
51. Oct 2, 2000	belt bomb	political leader, Trincomalee	22**
52. Oct 5, 2000	belt bomb	political rally, Medawachchiya	12
53. Oct 19, 2000	belt bomb	Cabinet ceremony, Colombo	0
54. Oct 23, 2000	boat bombs	gunboat/troop carrier, Trincomalee	2

Date	Group	Weapon	Target	Killed
Campaign #6: HAMAS vs. Israel				
1. Apr 6, 1994	HAMAS	car bomb	Afula	9
2. Apr 13, 1994	HAMAS	belt bomb	Hadera	6
Campaign #7: HAMAS/Islamic Jihad vs. Israel				
1. Oct 19, 1994	HAMAS	belt bomb	Tel Aviv	22
2. Nov 11, 1994	Islamic Jihad	bike bomb	Netzarim, Gaza	3
3. Dec 25, 1994	HAMAS	belt bomb	Jerusalem	0
4. Jan 22, 1995	Islamic Jihad	belt bomb	Beit Lid Junction	21
5. Apr 9, 1995	Islamic Jihad	2 car bombs	Netzarim, Gaza	8
6. July 24, 1995	HAMAS	belt bomb	Tel Aviv	6
7. Aug 21, 1995	HAMAS	belt bomb	Jerusalem	5
Campaign #8: HAMAS vs. Israel				
1. Feb 25, 1996	HAMAS	belt bomb	Jerusalem	25
2. Feb 25, 1996	HAMAS	belt bomb	Ashkelon	1
3. Mar 3, 1996	HAMAS	belt bomb	Jerusalem	19
4. Mar 4, 1996	HAMAS	belt bomb	Tel Aviv	13
Campaign #9: HAMAS vs. Israel				
1. Mar 21, 1997	HAMAS	belt bomb	cafe, Tel Aviv	3
2. Jul 30, 1997	HAMAS	belt bomb	Jerusalem	14
3. Sept 4, 1997	HAMAS	belt bomb	Jerusalem	7
Campaign #10: Kurdistan Workers Party (PKK) vs. Turkey				
1. Jun 30, 1996		belt bomb	Tunceli	9
2. Oct 25, 1996		belt bomb	Adana	4
3. Oct 29, 1996		belt bombs	Sivas	4

Campaign #11: PKK vs. Turkey

1. Mar 4, 1999	belt bomb	Batman	0
2. Mar 27, 1999	grenade	Istanbul	0
3. Apr 5, 1999	belt bomb	governor, Bingol	0
4. Jul 5, 1999	belt bomb	Adana	0
5. Jul 7, 1999	grenades	Iluh	0
6. Aug 28, 1999	bomb	Tunceli	0

Ongoing Campaigns

Campaign #12: al-Qaida vs. United States

1. Nov 13, 1995	car bomb	U.S. military base, Riyadh, SA	5
2. Jun 25, 1996	truck bomb	U.S. military base, Dhahran SA	19
3. Aug 7, 1998	truck bombs	U.S. embassies, Kenya/Tanzania	250
4. Oct 12, 2000	boat bomb	USS Cole, Yemen	17
5. Sep 9, 2001	camera bomb	Ahmed Shah Massoud, Afghanistan	1**
6. Sep 11, 2001	hijacked airplanes	WTC/Pentagon	3,037

Campaign #13: Chechen Separatists vs. Russia

1. Jun 7, 2000	truck bomb	Russian police station, Chechnya	2
2. Jul 3, 2000	truck bomb	Argun, Russia	30
3. Mar 24, 2001	car bomb	Chechnya	20
4. Nov 29, 2001	belt bomb	military commander, Chechnya	

Campaign #14: Kashmir Separatists vs. India

1. Dec 25, 2000	car bomb	Srinagar, Kashmir	8
2. Oct 1, 2001	car bomb	Legislative assembly, Kashmir	30
3. Dec 13, 2001	gunmen	Parliament, New Delhi	7

Campaign #15: LTTE vs. Sri Lanka

1. Jul 24, 2001	belt bomb	international airport, Colombo	12
2. Sep 16, 2001	boat bomb	naval vessel, north	29
3. Oct 29, 2001	belt bomb	PM of Sri Lanka, Colombo	3**
4. Oct 30, 2001	boat bomb	oil tanker, northern coast	4
5. Nov 9, 2001	belt bomb	police jeep, Batticaloa	0
6. Nov 15, 2001	belt bomb	crowd, Batticaloa	3

Campaign #16: HAMAS/Islamic Jihad vs. Israel

1. Oct 26, 2000	Islamic Jihad	bike bomb	Gaza	0
2. Oct 30, 2000	HAMAS	belt bomb	Jerusalem	15
3. Nov 2, 2000	Al Aqsa	car bomb	Jerusalem	2
4. Nov 22, 2000	Islamic Jihad	car bomb	Hadera	2
5. Dec 22, 2000	Al Aqsa	belt bomb	Jordan valley	3
6. Jan 1, 2001	HAMAS	belt bomb	Netanya	10
7. Feb 14, 2001	HAMAS	bus driver	Tel Aviv	8
8. Mar 1, 2001	HAMAS	car bomb	Mei Ami	1
9. Mar 4, 2001	HAMAS	belt bomb	Netanya	3
10. Mar 27, 2001	HAMAS	belt bomb	Jerusalem	1
11. Mar 27, 2001	HAMAS	belt bomb	Jerusalem (2nd attack)	0
12. Mar 28, 2001	HAMAS	belt bomb	Kfar Saba	3

13. Apr 22, 2001	HAMAS	belt bomb	Kfar Saba	3
14. Apr 23, 2001	PFLP	car bomb	Yehuda	8
15. Apr 29, 2001	HAMAS	belt bomb	West Bank	0
16. May 18, 2001	HAMAS	belt bomb	Netanya	5
17. May 25, 2001	Islamic Jihad	truck bomb	Netzarim, Gaza	2
18. May 27, 2001	HAMAS	car bomb	Netanya	1
19. May 30, 2001	Islamic Jihad	car bomb	Netanya	8
20. Jun 1, 2001	HAMAS	belt bomb	nightclub, Tel Aviv	22
21. Jun 22, 2001	HAMAS	belt bomb	Gaza	2
22. Jul 2, 2001	HAMAS	car bomb	IDF checkpt, Gaza	0
23. Jul 9, 2001	HAMAS	car bomb	Gaza	0
24. Jul 16, 2001	Islamic Jihad	belt bomb	Jerusalem	5
25. Aug 8, 2001	Al Aqsa	car bomb	Jerusalem	8
26. Aug 9, 2001	Islamic Jihad	belt bomb	Haifa	15
27. Aug 12, 2001	Islamic Jihad	belt bomb	Haifa	0
28. Aug 21, 2001	Al Aqsa	car bomb	Jerusalem	0
29. Sept 4, 2001	HAMAS	belt bomb	Jerusalem	0
30. Sept 9, 2001	HAMAS	belt bomb	Nahariya	3
31. Oct 1, 2001	HAMAS	car bomb	Afula	1
32. Oct 7, 2001	Islamic Jihad	car bomb	North Israel	2
33. Nov 26, 2001	HAMAS	car bomb	Gaza	0
34. Nov 29, 2001	Islamic Jihad	belt bomb	Gaza	3
35. Dec 1, 2001	HAMAS	belt bomb	Haifa	11
36. Dec 2, 2001	HAMAS	belt bomb	Jerusalem	15
37. Dec 5, 2001	Islamic Jihad	belt bomb	Jerusalem	0
38. Dec 9, 2001	???	belt bomb	Haifa	0
39. Dec 12, 2001	HAMAS	belt bomb	Gaza	4

Isolated Attacks

1. Dec 15, 1981	???	car bomb	Iraqi embassy, Beirut	30
2. May 25, 1985	Hizballah	car bomb	Emir, Kuwait	0***
3. Jul 5, 1987	LTTE	truck bomb	army camp, Jaffna Peninsula	18
4. Aug 15, 1993	???	motorcycle bomb	Interior Minister, Egypt	3
5. Jan 30, 1995	Armed Islamic Group	truck bomb	crowd, Algiers	42
6. Nov 19, 1995	Islamic Group	truck bomb	Egyptian embassy, Pakistan	16
7. Oct 29, 1998	HAMAS	belt bomb	Gaza	1
8. Nov 17, 1998	???	belt bomb	Yuksekova, Turkey	0
9. Dec 29, 1999	Hizballah	car bomb	South Lebanon	1

Note: Several reports of PKK suicide in May and June 1997 during fighting between PKK and Kurdish militias in Iraq, but coverage insufficient to distinguish suicide attack from suicide to avoid capture.

* Not including attacker(s).

** Assassination target killed.

*** Assassination target survived.

??? Unclaimed.

Notes

1. A suicide attack can be defined in two ways: a narrow definition limited to situations in which an attacker kills himself and a broad definition that includes any instance in

which an attacker fully expects to be killed by others during an attack. An example that fits the broad definition is Baruch Goldstein who continued killing Palestinians at the February 1994 Hebron Massacre until he himself was killed, who had no plan for escape, and who left a note for his family indicating that he did not expect to return. My research relies on the narrow definition, partly because this is the common practice in the literature and partly because there are so few instances in which it is clear that an attacker expected to be killed by others that adding this category of events would not change my findings.

2.   Hunger strikes and self-immolation are not ordinarily considered acts of terrorism because their main purpose is to evoke understanding and sympathy from the target audience and not to cause terror (Niebuhr 1960).

3.   This survey sought to include every instance of a suicide attack in which the attacker killed himself except those explicitly authorized by a state and carried out by the state government apparatus (e.g., Iranian human wave attacks in the Iran–Iraq war were not counted). The survey is probably quite reliable, because a majority of the incidents were openly claimed by the sponsoring terrorist organizations. Even those that were not claimed were, in nearly all cases, reported multiple times in regional news media, even if not always in the U.S. media. To probe for additional cases, I interviewed experts and officials involved in what some might consider conflicts especially prone to suicide attacks, such as Afghanistan in the 1980s, but this did not yield more incidents. According to the CIA station chief for Pakistan from 1986 to 1988 (Bearden 2002), "I cannot recall a single incident where an Afghan launched himself against a Soviet target with the intention of dying in the process. I don't think these things ever happened, though some of their attacks were a little hare-brained and could have been considered suicidal. I think it's important that Afghans never even took their war outside their borders—for example they never tried to blow up the Soviet Embassy in Pakistan."

4.   There were no suicide attacks from April to October 1994.

5.   There were no suicide attacks from August 1995 to February 1996. There were four suicide attacks from February 25 to March 4, 1996, in response to an Israeli assassination and then none until March 1997.

6.   The Bush administration's decision in May 2003 to withdraw most U.S. troops from Saudi Arabia is the kind of partial concession likely to backfire. Al-Qaida may well view this as evidence that the United States is vulnerable to coercive pressure, but the concession does not satisfy al-Qaida's core demand to reduce American military control over the holy areas on the Arab peninsula. With the conquest and long-term military occupation of Iraq, American military capabilities to control Saudi Arabia have substantially increased, even if there are no American troops on Saudi soil itself.

References

al-Shaqaqi, Fathi. "Interview with Secretary General of Islamic Jihad." *Al-Quds*. 11 April. 1995 Foreign Broadcast Information Service (FBIS)-NES-95-70, 12 April 1995. Hereinafter cited as FBIS.

al-Zahhar, Mahmud. "Interview." *Al-Dustur* (Amman), 19 February 1996, FBIS-NES-96-034, 20 February 1996.

Art, Robert J., and Patrick M. Cronin. *The United States and Coercive Diplomacy*. Washington, DC: United States Institute of Peace, 2003.

Bakr, Ahmed. "Interview." *The Independent* (London), 14 March 1995. FBIS-NES-95-086, 4 May 1995.

Bearden, Milton. Personal correspondence. University of Chicago, March 26, 2002.

Bloom, Mia. "Rational Interpretations of Palestinian Suicide Bombing." Paper. Program on International Security Policy, University of Chicago, 2002.

Boix, Carlos, and Sebastian Rosato. "A Complete Dataset of Regimes, 1850–1999." Typescript. University of Chicago, 2001.

"Bus Attack Said to Spur Rabin to Speed Talks." *Yediot Aharonot*. FBIS-NES-94-142, 25 July 1995.

Clutterbuck, Richard. *Living with Terrorism*. London: Faber & Faber, 1975.

Crenshaw, Martha. "The Causes of Terrorism." *Comparative Politics* (July 1981): 397–99.

De Figueiredo, Rui, and Barry R. Weingast. "Vicious Cycles: Endogenous Political Extremism and Political Violence." Paper. American Political Science Association, 1998.

Edler Baumann, Carol. *Diplomatic Kidnappings: A Revolutionary Tactic of Urban Terrorism*. The Hague: Nijhoff, 1973.

Elliott, Paul. *Brotherhoods of Fear*. London: Blandford, 1998.

George, Alexander, et al. *Limits of Coercive Diplomacy*. Boston: Little, Brown, 1972.

Greenberg, Joel. "Suicide Planner Expresses Joy Over His Missions," *New York Times*, 9 May 2002.

Hamas Communique No. 125. *Filastin al-Muslimah*. London. FBIS-NES-95-152, 8 August 1995.

"Hamas Leader Discusses Goals." *Frankfurter Runschau*. FBIS-NES-95-086, 4 May 1995.

"Hamas Operations Against Israel Said to Continue." *Al-Dustur* (Amman), 4 April 1994, FBIS-NES-94-072, 14 April 1994.

Hamas Statement. *BBC Summary of World Broadcasts*, 23 July 2000.

Hoffman, Bruce. *Inside Terrorism*. New York: Columbia University Press, 1998.

Horowitz, Michael, and Dan Reiter. "When Does Aerial Bombing Work? Quantitative Empirical Tests, 1917–1999." *Journal of Conflict Resolution* 45 (2001): 147–73.

Hroub, Khaled. *Hamas: Political Thought and Practice*. Washington, DC: Institute for Palestine Studies, 2000.

Huntington, Samuel P. *The Third Wave: Democratization in the Twentieth Century*. Norman: University of Oklahoma Press, 1991.

Inbar, Efraim. *Rabin and Israel's National Security*. Baltimore: John's Hopkins University Press, 1999.

Institute for Counter-Terrorism (ICT). *Countering Suicide Terrorism*. Herzliya, Israel: International Policy Institute for Counter-Terrorism, 2001.

Jenkins, Brian N. *Will Terrorists Go Nuclear?* RAND Report P-5541. Santa Monica, CA: RAND Corp, 1975.

———. *International Terrorism*. Santa Monica, CA: RAND Corp, 1985.

Jervis, Robert. *Perception and Misperception in International Politics*. Princeton, NJ: Princeton University Press, 1976.

Kaufmann, Chaim D. "Possible and Impossible Solutions to Ethnic Civil Wars." *International Security* 20 (Spring 1996): 136–75.

———. "When All Else Fails: Ethnic Population Transfers and Partitions in the Twentieth Century." *International Security* 23 (Fall 1998): 120–56.

Kramer, Martin. "The Moral Logic of Hizballah." In *Origins of Terrorism*, ed. Walter Reich. New York: Cambridge University Press, 1990.

———. "Fundamentalist Islam at Large: Drive for Power." *Middle East Quarterly* 3 (June 1996): 37–49.

Kydd, Andrew, and Barbara F. Walter. "Sabotaging the Peace: The Politics of Extremist Violence." *International Organization* 56 no. 2 (2002): 263–96.

Laqueur, Walter. *The Age of Terrorism*. Boston: Little, Brown, 1987.

Lebow, Richard Ned. *Between Peace and War: The Nature of International Crisis*. Baltimore, MD: Johns Hopkins University Press, 1981.

Lewis, Bernard. *The Assassins*. New York: Basic Books, 1968.

Makovsky, David, and Alon Pinkas. "Rabin: Killing Civilians Won't Kill the Negotiations." *Jerusalem Post*, 13 April 1994.

Merari, Ariel. "The Readiness to Kill and Die: Suicidal Terrorism in the Middle East." In *Origins of Terrorism*, ed. Walter Reich. New York: Cambridge University Press, 1990.

Mish'al, Khalid. "Interview." *BBC Summary of World Broadcasts*, 17 November 2000.

Mishal, Shaul, and Avraham Sela. *The Palestinian Hamas*. New York: Columbia University Press, 2000.

Niebuhr, Reinhold. *Moral Man and Immoral Society*. New York: Scribner, 1960.

Nusse, Andrea. *Muslim Palestine: The Ideology of Hamas*. Amsterdam: Harwood Academic, 1998.

O'Neill, Richard. *Suicide Squads*. New York: Ballantine Books, 1981.

Pape, Robert A. *Bombing to Win: Air Power and Coercion in War*. Ithaca, NY: Cornell University Press, 1996.

———. "Why Economic Sanctions Do Not Work." *International Security* 22 (Fall 1997): 90–136.

———. "The Universe of Suicide Terrorist Attacks Worldwide, 1980–2001." Typescript. University of Chicago, 2002.

Post, Jerrold M. "Terrorist Psycho-Logic: Terrorist Behavior as a Product of Psychological Forces." In *Origins of Terrorism*, ed. Walter Reich. New York: Cambridge University Press, 1990.

Przeworski, Adam, Michael E. Alvarez, Jose Antonio Cheibub, and Fernando Limongi. *Democracy and Development: Political Institutions and Well-Being in the World, 1950–1990*. Cambridge, UK: Cambridge University Press, 2000.

Rabin, Yitzhaq. "Speech to Knessett." *BBC Summary of World Broadcasts*, 20 April 1994.

———. "Interview." *BBC Summary of World Broadcasts*, 8 September 1995.

Rapoport, David C. *Assassination and Terrorism*. Toronto: CBC Merchandising, 1971.

———. "Fear and Trembling: Terrorism in Three Religious Traditions." *American Political Science Review* 78. (September) 1984, 655–77.

Reagan, Ronald. *An American Life*. New York: Simon and Schuster, 1990.

Reich, Walter, ed. *Origins of Terrorism*. New York: Cambridge University Press, 1990.

Sauvagnargues, Philippe. "Opposition Candidate." Agence France Presse, 14 August 1994.

Schalk, Peter. "Resistance and Martyrdom in the Process of State Formation of Tamililam." In *Martyrdom and Political Resistance*, ed. Joyed Pettigerw. Amsterdam: VU University Press, 1997, 61–83.

Schelling, Thomas. *Arms and Influence*. New Haven, CT: Yale University Press, 1966.

Schmid, Alex P., and Albert J. Jongman. *Political Terrorism*. New Brunswick, NJ: Transaction Books, 1998.

Sciolino, Elaine. "Saudi Warns Bush." *New York Times*, 27 January 2002.

Shallah, Ramadan. "Interview." *BBC Summary of World Broadcasts*, 3 November 2001.

Shiqaqi, Khalil, et al. *The Israeli-Palestinian Peace Process*. Portland, OR: Sussex Academic Press, 2002.

Sprinzak, Ehud. "Rational Fanatics." *Foreign Policy* no. 120 (September/October 2000): 66–73.

"Sri Lanka Opposition Leader Promises Talk with Rebels." *Japan Economic Newswire*, 11 August 1994.

St. John, Peter. *Air Piracy, Airport Security, and International Terrorism*. New York: Quorum Books, 1991.

U.S. Department of State. *Patterns of Global Terrorism*. Washington, DC: Department of State, 1983–2001.

Theodoulou, Michael. "New Attacks Feared." *Times* (London), 21 August 1995. FBIS-NES-95–165, 25 August 1995.

Tuchman, Barbara W. *The Proud Tower*. New York: Macmillan, 1996.

World Islamic Front. "Jihad Against Jews and Crusaders." Statement. 23 February 1998.

Section II

Specific Areas of Vulnerability in Homeland Security

In this section, a collection of subject-matter experts and scholars of terrorism explore America's vulnerabilities in critical areas such as aviation, public transportation, borders, critical infrastructure, ports and maritime commerce, the water and food supplies. In the first of these, Professor Joseph Szyliowicz analyzes the state of aviation security, beginning with the characteristics of the air transportation system that complicate the achievement of a high level of security. He examines the situation that existed prior to 9/11 and then evaluates the changes that have occurred since, concluding that no overall systematic program has yet been put in place to deal with the threats that terrorism poses to the various elements of aviation. He also argues that aviation security—and indeed homeland security—requires incorporating antiterrorism into foreign policy and ongoing attempts to deal with the underlying factors that promote terrorism.

Following this analysis, Brian Michael Jenkins explores specific vulnerabilities of the nation's surface transportation system. He begins with a review of the threat and then discusses some of the broader aspects of implementing homeland security. In reviewing the progress made in improving surface transportation security—and problems that persist—he notes that operators and local authorities have done the things they could easily do. However, effective security for surface transportation consists of more than deterrence and prevention—both of which are difficult, given the volume of passengers and the ease of accessibility of surface transportation facilities. Effective security must also include mitigation through design, construction, and rapid response, all of which can save lives as well as minimize disruption. Further, Jenkins argues, the federal government should focus on developing an overall strategic approach to transportation security, guiding and supporting research and development, evaluating new technologies, and disseminating information to end users.

Frank Hoffman follows with an analysis of security at the nation's borders. He explores the impact of globalization—particularly economic interconnectivity and the growing volume of transnational trade in goods and services—on our ability to adequately secure the nation's ports and land borders. His belief that September 11 was a direct attack on global interconnectivity is shared by a significant number of policy analysts. However, he argues that we have yet to develop and implement new, innovative ways to ensure an open and safe border system, and we must engage the private sector in doing so.

In the next chapter, Frank Cilluffo and Paul Byron Pattak explore the overlapping threats of information warfare, cyber crime, and cyber terrorism, arguing that the United States must come to a new understanding of conflict and the rules of engagement in cyberspace. The involvement of nonstate actors, public opinion, and the media in this new form of conflict underscores the role of individuals in the national security arena, and suggests that the nation's security focus is strategically misplaced. Their analysis concludes that federal, state, and local government agencies must establish a genuine partnership with private industry and the general public in order to adequately secure the U.S. from the cyberthreat.

Larry Wortzel, a retired Army colonel and intelligence expert, argues that the level of security required in the new environment demands unprecedented levels of cooperation and coordination across government and private-sector boundaries. He notes that private industry owns and operates approximately 85 percent of the critical infrastructure and key assets in America. The role of the private sector is thus vital; responsibility for securing an element of critical infrastructure ultimately belongs to the operator or owner of the technology. A vibrant and responsible public-private partnership is thus critical to homeland security.

Maritime security is the focus of the following chapter, authored by RAND analysts Maarten van de Voort, Kevin A. O'Brien, Adnan Rahman, and Lorenzo Valeri. They explore the threat of terrorists using commercial shipping containers to transport dangerous materials and weapons, or using containers themselves as weapons of mass destruction. Their stark analysis reveals an urgent need for better methods of inspecting and securing containers throughout the global shipping industry, and they offer 18 specific policy recommendations for consideration.

The chapter by Claudia Copeland and Betsy Cody explores the vulnerabilities of the nation's water supply and water quality infrastructure, including contamination (especially of water and wastewater treatment systems), damage to physical assets (pumps and valves, for example), and loss of service to customers. A number of security related actions have been taken by federal, state and local government agencies—as well as the private sector—since September 11, 2001, to prevent terrorist attacks on this vital resource. However, their analysis suggests additional policy recommendations for both government leaders and local resource managers.

In a similar vein, Barbara Bruemmer notes that the nation's food supply is vulnerable, particularly to a biological or chemical attack. A compromised food supply would have potentially disastrous physical, psychological, political, and economic consequences. Her analysis suggests that public-health preparedness plans and responses should incorporate registered dietitians, who are in a unique position to provide assistance because of their special training and expertise.

In each of these chapters, the authors illuminate specific areas of critical vulnerability to terrorist attacks in the United States, and in doing so, inform our understanding of the overarching homeland security challenges we face today. As a whole, this section reveals the need for increased vigilance and public-private cooperation throughout the country, and underscores the importance of the daily decisions made by every policymaker and individual citizen.

Chapter 7

Aviation Security:
Promise or Reality?

Joseph S. Szyliowicz

The catastrophic events of September 11, 2001, have often been referred to as a wake-up call. It is obvious that this tragedy has had a profound impact on all aspects of our lives, including our approach to transportation security generally and aviation security specifically. But it was not the first wake-up call, although it was the first that yielded truly significant change. The list of terrorist attacks involving aviation is a long and bloody one. Aviation has always represented an appealing target, and terrorists have not hesitated to strike at the planes and airports of many countries.[1]

Aviation facilities are not only of symbolic significance, they are also of great functional importance, and their destruction wreaks widespread economic effects. Aviation is a critical part of local and national economies around the globe. In the United States, aviation is estimated to account for 6 percent to 7 percent of the nation's gross domestic product (GDP). Airports are often busy and crowded and have become even more attractive targets since the trend in terrorist attacks has shifted toward inflicting mass casualties. But aviation provides more than just tempting targets. Its vehicles can be used as weapons, as was demonstrated dramatically on 9/11, when a horrified nation watched hijacked planes plunge into the Pentagon and the World Trade Center.

In short, the existence of a serious threat to aviation has been obvious for years. After the 1988 Pan Am 103 disaster over Lockerbie, Scotland, the worst security-related disaster in the history of U.S. civil aviation until then, a proliferation of cries for action led to the adoption of important steps designed to enhance the security of the U.S. aviation system. These measures did not, unfortunately, prevent the destruction of the World Trade Center, the damage to the Pentagon, and the loss of so many innocent lives. This chapter addresses three related theses. First, the character of modern aviation systems makes security highly difficult to attain. Second, important steps have been taken to eliminate the security shortcomings that existed prior to 9/11, but serious weaknesses still remain. Third, given the nature of the terrorist threat, an emphasis on prevention and law enforcement, though essential, can be only part of an overall strategy that incorporates the vital but often overlooked foreign policy dimension.

The Nature of Modern Aviation Systems

Modern aviation functions in ways that make it especially difficult to safeguard. First, it is a vast and complex system consisting of three main branches—commercial aviation, general aviation, and air cargo, each of which poses separate and complex security challenges. Furthermore, its infrastructure is extensive and widespread. It involves airports and the supporting assets, including aircraft and the national air space that relies on complex command, control, and communications technologies. The latest report of the President's Commission on Critical Infrastructure identified the following vulnerabilities of the commercial passenger and freight segments (2003, 54–55):

1. *Volume.* There are 97 U.S. carriers that transport over 650 million passengers annually to and from 506 major airports that have 1,000 screening points and handle more than 2.5 billion handheld and checked bags.
2. *Limited capabilities and available space.* The number, capability, and ease of use of existing detection technologies is inadequate.
3. *Economic sensitivity.* The shift to just-in-time delivery by many firms has made the U.S. economy vulnerable to delays in cargo shipments.
4. *Security versus convenience and cost.* The need to minimize congestion and delays while maintaining security has major financial implications.
5. *Accessibility.* Airports are public spaces and are easily accessible from highways.

To this list must be added the security issues posed by general aviation (discussed later), as well as those resulting from the rapidly changing nature of commercial aviation. Two trends are especially critical. First, aviation has become increasingly integrated with other modes, especially with light and heavy rail as the landside capacity of airports has become increasingly strained. Currently 10 airport-rail links are being built and another 10 are in the planning stages, so that by 2010 20 of the country's top 30 airports will be served by rail. Such facilities pose some new security challenges, starting with their design and extending to such issues as ensuring effective communication between rail transit, airport, FAA, and other personnel, so that they understand their proper roles in the security program and can manage it effectively (Boyd and Caton, 2001).

Second, increased linkages between telecommunications and aviation compound the security problem. Because disruptions of telecommunications networks have profound consequences for global, regional, and national aviation systems, aviation security cannot be addressed as if it were independent of telecommunications. Of particular concern is the national airspace system, which is rapidly becoming modernized in order to deal with increasing traffic. Its obsolete, isolated subsystems are being replaced with an open systems architecture that will permit extensive data interchange and is thus highly vulnerable to cyber attacks. Any attempt to enhance security must, accordingly, pay close attention to the ever-present threat of hacking into computer databases. But cyber security is difficult to achieve. Even the U.S. government agencies have pervasive weaknesses that place their databases and systems at risk; the publicly known number of cases involving computer security rose from 9,850 in 1999 to 52,658 in 2001 to 73,359 for the first 9 months of 2002, and it is estimated that up to 80 percent of such incidents are never reported (Dacey, 2002).

Third, aviation security is an international as well as national issue. U.S. airlines are heavily involved in international travel and are becoming more and more intertwined through code sharing and other arrangements with foreign airlines. Thus, the issue of U.S.

aviation security must be viewed in its global context. It is instructive that the bomb that destroyed Pan Am 103 was loaded in Frankfurt, through an intramodal movement from a foreign airline originating in still another country by yet another country's intelligence service and that the tragedy itself occurred in the skies of a fifth country. Thus, even if the United States succeeds in deterring attacks against its aviation facilities, foreign airlines still can be used to attack targets in America.

The problem arises from the absence of any international authority that can enforce regulations and mandates. The International Civil Aviation Organization (ICAO), which has some 184 member states, attempted to deal with the issue of security by establishing overall standards and practices through Annex 17. Although the annex includes important measures and represents an accepted international standard subject to implementation by state authorities, it is considered by experts to establish at best only a minimum, not especially stringent, standard. Over time it has become obvious that most host governments, with the exception of Israel, were either incapable or unwilling to provide the level of security necessary to counter terrorist actions against U.S. aviation. Accordingly, in 1984 and 1990 (following the Pan Am 103 disaster), the United States enacted legislation providing for measures, including assessments, to provide additional security at high threat locations.

Since 9/11, various measures have been undertaken to strengthen aviation security throughout the world. ICAO (2002) recently adopted an aviation security plan of action that calls for "regular, mandatory, systematic and harmonized audits . . . in order to identify and correct deficiencies in the implementation of ICAO security related standards." However, implementation of this plan is estimated to cost $17 million, of which $15 million is to be derived from voluntary contributions Despite such efforts and activities by other international organizations, significant problems remain at the global level.

The Pre-9/11 Situation

The magnitude of the threat to air transportation posed by terrorism prompted the U.S. government to accord this mode priority attention. However, the FAA proved to be a reactive agency that acted sporadically in ways designed to prevent a specific kind of attack that had been carried out successfully in the past. The first threat, hijackings, was successfully met in the United States and abroad by the development and installation of passenger screening devices and processes at all major airports. But terrorists soon acquired more sophisticated and lethal technologies—automatic weapons and such deadly plastic explosives as SEMTEX that are easily shaped into innocuous-looking objects, such as suitcases and radios, so armed attacks and bombings against airports proliferated.

The Aviation Security Improvement Act of 1990, which resulted from the outcry that followed the Pan Am 103 disaster, wrought many changes, especially within the FAA, but did little to transform the agency. On the one hand, it was supposed to represent the passengers and the overall security interests of the country; on the other, it remained concerned with the financial well-being of the airlines. Thus, the FAA only made the rules (with an eye to their economic impacts on the industry); corporations (airlines) and municipalities (airport operators) retained responsibility for such activities as passenger and baggage screening arrangements, usually subcontracted to a private firm. Even in the areas that fell directly under the FAA's jurisdiction, security lapses were common. A security audit at four major airports in 1993 found that unauthorized personnel had succeeded in gaining access to secure areas in 15 out of 20 attempts. A subsequent GAO report concluded that "the Federal Aviation Administration (FAA) oversight of airport security systems . . . was not aggressive and enforcement actions were limited" (Del Valle, 1997).

When the FAA did move aggressively, it often did so without giving due consideration to the utility, costs, and efficacy of the new technologies, systems, and procedures that it mandated. The most glaring example of hasty actions in the late 1980s was the decision by the secretary of transportation, following the destruction of Pan Am Flight 103, to require the 100 main airports in the United States to install new thermal neutron analysis (TNA) machines, without assessing adequately the capabilities of the TNA explosives detectors. Nor did the FAA develop any coherent, effective policy to safeguard America's skies. Its operational practices and culture remained seriously flawed. As the *New York Times* noted following the October 1994 crash of a turboprop in which 68 people died, "The Federal Aviation Administration had for years brushed aside repeated warnings from pilots and experts, and from the behavior of the plane itself, that something was awry. The failure to heed those warnings raises troubling questions that go beyond the Roselawn crash, questions about the procedures and safeguards of the agency itself" (U.S. DOT, 2003). Two years later, when the crash of a ValuJet plane killed 110 persons, the head of the FAA, David Hinson, announced, "The airline is safe to fly. I would fly it." Subsequently, Mary Schiavo, the former Inspector General of the U.S. DOT, noted: "The FAA didn't fall down just on ValuJet. It was incompetent at virtually all of its inspection responsibilities" (Gleick, 1996).

Whether the tragedy of 9/11 could have been avoided remains a controversial point, but there is no doubt that the FAA failed to act promptly and decisively to implement the recommendations of the White House (Gore) Commission on Aviation Safety and Security established in 1996 following the crash of TWA 800 off Long Island, New York. By September 11, 2001, few of the 31 recommendations had been implemented—in particular, the United States had not yet embraced more sophisticated profiling, passenger-bag matching, mandatory improvements in screening company performance, enhanced background checks for screeners and airport employees, or measures to deal with cargo threats. Although the FAA claimed that 25 of the suggestions had been "completed," in actuality "most were still in development; some remained entangled in interagency squabbles and bureaucratic delays." The Commission's staff director commented "It's a governmental failure. . . . We specifically said the FAA had to change, and they've proved resistant to change" (Pasternak, 2002; Public Citizen, 2001).

The airlines contributed greatly to this situation. Focused on attracting and retaining passengers, they tended to view additional security measures and procedures as inconveniences that would alienate passengers and cost more than they were worth, particularly given the difficulties many of these firms have had turning even a modest profit. Thus security generally, and additional security measures especially, ranked relatively low on the list of priorities, as is evident from the airlines' expenditures. One estimate, for example, placed the amount the airlines spent on security and food in the 1990s at 65 cents and $6.50, respectively. Essentially "the logic of collective action" was in play—no single airline had an incentive to enhance its security by making costly investments because effective security requires an integrated approach, and the lower standards of its competitors would continue to endanger it (Kunreuther, Heal, and Orszag, 2002). The historical record is clear and it is not a pretty one: numerous warnings, reports, and studies identified the problems that had to be resolved, but the structure and culture of the key players, the policy context, and the nature of the aviation sector itself, created an environment where a disaster was almost inevitable.

The Contemporary Scene

The tragedy of September 11 spurred a widespread reassessment of the state of aviation security, and the implementation of a range of policy responses designed to minimize what remains a very serious threat to U.S. national security. The most dramatic move has been the Bush administration's reluctant decision to yield to outside pressures and create a Department of Homeland Security, as originally advocated by Gary Hart and Warren Rudman in the final report of the National Commission that they chaired (U.S. Commission on National Security, 2001). The largest governmental reorganization in decades, involving 22 agencies and 170,000 employees (including critical transportation-related agencies such as the Transportation Security Administration (TSA), which was established in November 2001 as part of the U.S. DOT), the new Homeland Security Department (HSD) became fully functional in early 2004.

The first major steps naturally have involved renewed and more stringent attempts to prevent hijackings. These have included reinforcing cockpit doors and placing specially trained air marshals on many flights. Following considerable discussion, it has been decided to allow pilots to carry guns, but the TSA has created outrage among pilots when it announced publicly that the guns would not be available until the pilots were in the cockpit and the door was closed. The TSA has also appointed 158 Federal Security Directors who are responsible for all 429 major airports. Here too, the TSA has come under criticism for hiring persons who may have security backgrounds, but do not possess any extensive knowledge of aviation.

The most visible change implemented by the TSA has been the replacement of the much-criticized system of having private contractors provide passenger screening by poorly paid, badly trained, and inefficient personnel, with a force of 60,000 federal workers. The TSA succeeded in hiring and deploying this large force in less than a year and greatly improved the screening procedures. The screeners behave professionally and courteously, and often go out of their way to help passengers, especially the elderly, when they are selected for further screening. Furthermore, there is an abundance of screeners so that bottlenecks seldom occur and problems can be resolved quickly.

Most important, they are implementing the rules and regulations rigorously, as anyone who has had to remove their shoes recognizes. In about a year, they confiscated almost 5 million items, including 1.4 million knives, 1,101 guns, 15,666 clubs, almost 40,000 box cutters, and such unusual items as a trailer hitch, a kitchen sink pipe, and a circular saw. The TSA proudly claims that this achievement enhances security. The significance of these results, however, is debatable, because a large percentage of the items are probably things that people forgot about (Miller, 2003b), nor is it obvious how much of a threat a smuggled box cutter actually represents. In the present climate, it is hard to imagine a hijacker wielding such a weapon not being tackled by a horde of passengers.

One can also query how many potential weapons were not intercepted. To cite but one example, the author's daughter passed successfully through at least a dozen screenings since 9/11 with a small Swiss army knife she had forgotten about before it was finally confiscated. That this was not a unique case is reflected in the GAO's report that guns, bombs, and dynamite had eluded screeners 25 percent of the time at 32 major airports. The porousness of screening has been demonstrated by various enterprising reporters, most recently by one who carried explosives past the screeners at Denver International Airport. Significant traces of the chemical were placed on his belt buckle, shoes, and coat, his carry-on bag, and on a laptop computer. He was selected for further examination. The screener found a dark powdery substance on the individual's hands, told the reporter that his bag was dirty, and politely cleaned it. The screener then used the explosive trace detector, which failed to obtain a positive reading even though significant amounts of the chemical remained. On the next three tries, the reporter again passed through without the explosives being detected. The TSA spokesperson called these results "unrealistic and alarmist," and went on to say "screeners performed their jobs exactly as trained and proper screening procedures were followed" (Sallinger, 2003).

The TSA originally awarded a $107 million contract to hire and train the new federal screeners, but the cost quickly rose to about $700 million. A review of how $18 million of that total was spent revealed that "one-third to one-half was attributed to wasteful and abusive spending practices." The problem extended well beyond this one contract. As the U.S. DOT's Inspector General testified in a congressional hearing, "we have $8.5 billion of contract and a limited infrastructure in place for overseeing them . . . the lack of infrastructure contributed to gaps in contract oversight that, in turn, led to tremendous growth in some contract costs." He also noted the heavy burden that was being imposed on the airlines and airports at a time when the industry was suffering tremendous financial losses (Miller, 2003a).

This army of screeners, whose contribution to aviation security is questionable, continues to be a very expensive item. Thus the question arises whether the present system is financially viable. In its budget request for fiscal year 2004, the TSA requested a total of about $5 billion, $1.8 billion of which was allocated to passenger screening. Will (or can), given the present budgetary climate, this level of expenditures continue? If layoffs take place, how will morale and efficiency be affected? The TSA has already announced plans to reduce the number of screeners (which ballooned from a projected 30,000 to 40,000 persons, to 48,000 to 51,000 in fiscal year 2004).

The TSA's second priority involved attempts to prevent bombs from being smuggled on board airplanes. Prior to 9/11, detection systems (the CTX 5000, manufactured by InVision and first certified in December 1994, and a similar machine manufactured by L3 Communications) had been installed in about 10 percent of the country's airports. These machines were underutilized, checking but a very small number of bags per day. Most of the baggage that was examined belonged to persons who fit the Computer Assisted Passenger Prescreening System (CAPPS) profile. In November 2000, the airlines were required, by law, to expand the use of the machines for random searches. The use of bomb-sniffing dogs also became commonplace. The FAA planned to achieve 100 percent baggage screening only by 2014 but Congress mandated that this be achieved by December 31, 2002.

This measure, which the TSA struggled to implement, aroused considerable controversy. Most major airport executives lobbied hard against the proposal, arguing that the large expense involved—each Computerized Tomography (CT) machine cost $1 million, plus maintenance—was not warranted because the certified technology was inadequate in terms of throughput and accuracy, and new technologies were likely to render it obsolete in a short time. New neutron scanning and "fused technology" systems that combine X-ray and neutron technologies are being developed, and the Heimann Systems Corporation had already produced a high throughput machine that combined the dual energy technology of EDS units with the volumetric density analysis of the CT that the FAA was expected to begin testing in May 2002. In the spring of 2003, Denver International Airport became a test bed for the EDtS. In addition, the short time frame and the physical layout of many baggage systems meant that the machines (which take up 600 sq. ft. each) would have to be installed in already crowded terminals, thus causing major delays and inconvenience for travelers.

All objections were brushed aside and the deadline was officially met, though to what extent 100 percent baggage screening was actually realized remains controversial because, in order to meet the deadline, the TSA agreed to various makeshift arrangements that have to be amended in the future. Most obvious is the need to move these SUV-sized machines from lobby areas and to integrate them into the baggage handling systems. Doing so will require an estimated $5 billion, less than 10 percent of which is presently available, and it is not anticipated that the Bush administration and Congress will provide any additional funds.

Furthermore, questions have been raised about the ways in which the $508 million contract signed with Boeing on June 7, 2002, was implemented. Boeing assumed responsibility for installing the machines, training the operators, renovating the airports, and maintaining the equipment, but airport officials claim that they had to make large investments of their own, in part to correct Boeing's mistakes. The U.S. DOT's Inspector General is currently investigating the contract to determine the degree of waste and abuse (Miller, 2003b).

In addition to the waste and the economic and physical burdens placed on the airports, the efficacy of the machines remains in doubt. It is not clear that the $2 billion that was spent on the machines, plus the additional billions needed to install them, has enhanced the security of the flying public to a significant degree. The machines produce monochromatic X-ray pictures that have to be interpreted by a skilled operator and yield a high percentage of "false positives," perhaps as high as 30 percent. Some experts have acidly noted that these pictures "cannot distinguish between a block of plastic explosives or a wedge of cheese" (Eng, 2003). Clearly, serious questions continue to be raised about the wisdom of this decision and the manner in which it was implemented by the TSA.

Even if the promise of the EDtS machine is realized, and an accurate and reliable technology is deployed, the issue of baggage liability remains. Thefts, including organized looting, have been known to occur, but the TSA assigns responsibility to the airlines that operate under a series of international rules and conventions. Essentially the system divides responsibility in a manner that makes it difficult for passengers whose belongings have been stolen to hold someone accountable; but there is no easy solution. If TSA were to assume responsibility, many questions remain. Would the baggage handlers be federalized or replaced? Would they handle the baggage or merely watch it? And, to what extent would a change actually decrease present theft levels?

Given the volume, effective screening—whether of passengers or of baggage—is fundamentally dependent on careful profiling in order to identify potential terrorist threats, who can then receive more detailed security checks. Originally developed in 1994, the CAPPS system utilizes a number of specific factors to identify individuals who fit a particular profile, such as how and where the ticket was purchased and whether the traveler is a member of a frequent flyer program. Civil libertarians have often expressed concern about possible discrimination against particular groups even though such factors as race, religion, and ethnicity are apparently not included. Because of such concerns, the Gore Commission asked the Justice Department to review the program. In 1997, it reported that CAPPS did not discriminate, but suggested a number of precautions.

CAPPS II is an enhanced version, developed by the TSA, to better evaluate the risk posed by the flying public. Many, including the American Civil Liberties Union viewed it as potentially an enormous intrusion on personal privacy since it would "data mine" commercial data bases that contained credit information, telephone records, automobile registrations, and the like. Every U.S. airline would provide reservation and ticketing information on its passengers. This information is then checked against a variety of commercial and governmental databases in order to uncover clues about potential threats even before the day of departure. Thousands of personal details about each passenger would be analyzed, using predictive software, in order to arrive at a threat index that would be used to rank passengers. Those who rated high would then be selected for additional investigation. This system, which was expected to take years before it became fully operational, was expected to enhance security and reduce the hassles that many travelers now endure because a much smaller number of passengers would have to undergo further scrutiny (O'Harrow, 2003).

CAPPS II was to be implemented in a manner that would protect individual rights by providing individuals, should a controversy arise, access to an ombudsman. Nevertheless, civil rights groups and many individuals, including some members of Congress, remained concerned about the potential abuse of this system, so that although CAPPS II was tested in the spring of 2003 and was scheduled to be operational by the summer of 2004, the government decided in July 2004 not to proceed with its deployment. Instead, the TSA announced that it was "reshaping and repackaging" the system so that it would rely only on governmental databases that would be integrated. Although the CAPPS II project could be legitimately criticized for, among other reasons, its reliance on databases that could contain inaccurate information and the potential for data abuse, it would have reduced the number of passengers undergoing secondary screenings from 14 percent to 4 percent, led to cost savings, and more effective and efficient screening of people and baggage (Wald, 2004). At present, it is not clear how quickly the new system will be implemented, or how effective it will be in identifying high risk passengers.

A related problem is that of airport workers and staff. Airports are cities—their personnel engage in a variety of activities and represent vocations ranging from salespeople to mechanics to cleaners. This diversity of people provides terrorists with numerous opportunities and, in order to forestall them, the FAA requires checks of previous employment records and the wearing of badges. These measures, however, have not ensured the security of particular areas. Terrorists can forge badges, although forging computerized badges is a far more difficult task requiring insider collaboration or access to the computerized database and badging process. Terrorists can follow a potentially riskier path: using threats to family members to pressure employees or simply bribing them to gain access. This is not as farfetched as it might first seem. Security at airports and other transportation nodes has always been a problem at the personnel level, suggested by the sheer amount of drugs that regularly flow undetected through these hubs (DEA, 2003; Kidwell, 1999).

New ID systems based on biometric information that is shared between various federal databases are being developed. Preliminary tests of a new technology that uses "smart" ID cards containing digitized photos, signatures, and biographical information, have yielded promising results and are scheduled for use in 100 land, sea, and air entry points within a year (Lee, 2003). The need for such systems was recently highlighted by the results of a test by government officials equipped with false birth certificates and driver's licenses that they had created using standard computer software. Claiming to be U.S. citizens, they successfully passed the INS inspection at Miami International Airport (Chardy, 2003).

The ever increasing reliance on interacting databases inevitably raises the issue of cybersecurity. As noted earlier, cyberwarfare is of direct relevance to transportation, given the new national airspace architecture and the accelerating dependence on modern information, tracking, and data processing systems by transportation companies and agencies. This is also an international issue because hacking knows no borders and there have been numerous attempts to break into computers from abroad. Yet transportation databases remain highly vulnerable. A recent study by the GAO of the situation in various governmental agencies concluded that all continue to have "significant information security weaknesses that place a broad array of federal operations and assets at risk of fraud, misuse, and disruption" (p. 3). The Department of Transportation (which has been subject to many such efforts—its Web sites have been defaced and over 25,000 attacks were recorded in 2002) ranked last with a score of 28 points out of a possible 100. Nor can one overlook the high probability that private sector computer systems are also extremely vulnerable (GAO, 2001).

Combating an Innovative Adversary

All of the hundreds of millions of dollars that have been spent on the measures discussed earlier apply primarily to commercial aviation. Yet even in regard to this mode, the response mounted by the Bush administration and the TSA cannot be considered to have truly minimized the terrorist threat. Its actions are not, and could not, be either systematic or comprehensive, because of the ways in which aviation security had been dealt with in the past. In the words of an expert panel, ". . . after the attacks, federal policymakers, seeking to secure commercial aviation and regain public confidence in air travel, did not have a well-designed security system in place that could be assessed methodically to identify gaps that needed to be filled" (TRB, 2002, 2).

Perhaps of more immediate concern is that the major measures taken to date are directed against known threats, even though al-Qaida has already demonstrated its innovativeness, and it is easy to imagine a possible shift from explosives and hijackings to the use of biological, chemical, and radiological weapons. Although such weapons can be used against commercial aviation, they are also relevant to general aviation, the vulnerabilities of which will be discussed later.

Most experts are even more worried about a second threat—the use of shoulder-launched surface-to-air missiles, officially known as MANPADS (man-portable air defense systems). These have a four-mile range, can travel up to 15,000 feet, and have been used on a number of occasions to bring down commercial aircraft in various countries. Airline flights make attractive targets for they adhere to rigid schedules and, since the 1970s, 42 civil aircraft have been attacked, of which 29 were brought down. The latest attack, an unsuccessful one, was launched against an Israeli plane in Mombasa, Kenya, in November 2002 (Caffera, 2002). Thousands of these portable missiles are scattered throughout the world, having been mass produced by the United States, whose Stinger missile was extensively used in Afghanistan and by the U.S.S.R., countries that also distributed these weapons to many states. Many have entered the black market and are freely available for a relatively small price; an estimated 27 separate terrorist organizations are believed to have acquired them. Many may already be hidden within the United States, for the U.S. military failed to maintain tight inventory control of its MANPADS and, because they are small, they can easily be smuggled into this country. Although the threat is well known—it has been labeled by one expert as "aviation's dirty little secret"—few if any countermeasures have been adopted by the government and the airlines (Caffera, 2002; Phelps, 2003). Another expert noted "The threats are real and the countermeasures exist. . . . Some of us are perplexed as to why a greater urgency hasn't been demonstrated in securing our airspace" (Caffera, 2002).

Such reticence may be analogous to the airlines' unwillingness to address the cockpit door issue prior to 9/11 because of potentially increased exposure to liability and increases in insurance costs. Today, such concerns are even more daunting. The airlines' perilous financial situation increases their reluctance to equip their planes with antimissile capabilities, and there is no evidence that serious governmental actions will be forthcoming, though the TSA has recently taken notice of this threat and taken some modest actions.

Securing Air Cargo

The other elements of the aviation system also pose very real threats. Air cargo represents a potential threat not only to the freight carriers but also to passenger planes, which also carry large amounts of cargo. Freight passes through many transfer points in its journey from the shipper to a plane, so that opportunities for tampering are quite extensive. Furthermore, cargo planes are just as powerful weapons as loaded passenger planes. However, cargo pilots are not permitted to carry guns, there are no federal marshals on cargo flights, cockpit doors are weak, if they exist at all, and the cargo ramps are insecure in comparison to passenger ramps; thousands of people, many strangers, few if any with background checks, work on loading and unloading air cargo. Although some claim that the "trusted shipper" program ensures safety, the high level of air cargo theft, drug smuggling, and other illegal activities indicates the degree to which the system is vulnerable (GAO, 2002a). A terrorist attack aimed at blowing up several cargo planes simultaneously would have very damaging consequences for the U.S. economy and for global trade generally.

These and numerous other security risks involving cargo have been recognized for some time, and various measures have been implemented in the past decade by the FAA and the air cargo companies. However, air freight continues to be accorded a lower security priority than passengers. A recent report noted that such measures as work on explosive detection or cargo profiling are at best ongoing, but that no comprehensive cargo security plan has been developed by the FAA or the TSA. The importance of such a plan is summarized as follows:

> Without a comprehensive plan that incorporates a risk management approach and sets deadlines and performance targets, TSA and other federal decision-makers cannot know whether resources are being deployed as effectively and efficiently as possible (GAO, 2002a).

General Aviation

A second critical element of the aviation system that has received scant attention is general aviation. This is an enormous enterprise involving some 550,000 pilots, 200,000 private planes, and over 5,000 airports. Safeguarding these facilities would require billions of dollars and, although some modest steps have been taken, access to these airports and their planes remains relatively open. The Aircraft Owners and Pilots Association (AOPA), a powerful lobby, cites the government's decision to permit general aviation to continue to function as proof that general aviation does not present a major threat. Furthermore, their industry has voluntarily taken steps to enhance security, small airports are inherently secure because strangers would be noticed immediately, and the planes, most of which are small craft that are not easily stolen, cannot cause significant damage. It has therefore opposed various measures proposed by the TSA such as rules regarding the denial, suspension, or revocation of pilot certificates to individuals considered potential security risks (AOPA, 2003).

AOPA's optimistic view, however, is not shared by most experts. A simulated attack on the United States' "Silent Vector" revealed what its planners called a "gaping hole" in aviation security—the charter services that operate small and medium jets. It is a simple matter to charter a plane with intercontinental range and sophisticated navigation equipment and to include a large bomb in the luggage, thus transforming the plane into the equivalent of a cruise missile (Waterman, 2003). Nor can one dismiss the threat posed by smaller planes, for it is possible to do considerable damage with even a small aircraft. It would not be a difficult matter for a terrorist to purchase a commercial sprayer, load a couple of drums with dangerous chemicals (such as sulfur mustard) onto the plane, and release them in a way that would terrorize people. At present, stealing a small plane is not a difficult task. Even crop dusters are vulnerable for they are typically left in a hangar and merely tied down. Many farmers who do crop dusting have a little plane parked next to their combine. It is not even necessary to steal a plane, for all that is required to rent a plane is a government-issued photo ID, a license, and a credit card.

In short, the use of general aviation to cause serious damage and to create panic might require planning, but is certainly possible. It is, therefore, appropriate to consider at least two additional measures to make it more difficult for terrorists to gain access to planes. First, in order to ensure that only reliable persons be permitted to rent a plane, enhanced background checks should be required. Second, because it is presently relatively easy to steal a plane, available technologies, notably a sophisticated form of ignition with embedded biometric data, should be installed to make thefts more difficult.

Given the complexity of the challenge that safeguarding aviation requires, it is obviously necessary to mount a sophisticated and nuanced response. Any integrated, innovative approach to aviation security depends on the development and implementation of a carefully developed and comprehensive strategy that recognizes the weaknesses of each element and develops well-thought-out systematic measures based on careful assessments. It has been suggested that this should be the mandate of the TSA—that it should assume a strategic systems-oriented research and planning role with a strong evaluative capability in key areas, especially technology, and that its activities be closely linked to relevant national and international actors (TRB, 2002, 3–7).

Successfully implementing this approach and these recommendations will be no easy matter given the massiveness of the bureaucratic reorganization that is now underway, the need to change organizational cultures, and the many traditional obstacles that have to be overcome. Indeed, one knowledgeable observer, a former staff director for the White House Commission on Aviation Safety and Security, has written, ". . . the strategic role . . . propose(d) for the TSA cannot be accomplished by the current organization with the current staff and under the existing legislation" (Kauver, 2002) because lobbyists influence departmental R & D programs, and policymakers override the conclusions of researchers. Nor will the new Department of Homeland Security be able to carry out the analytical tasks suggested earlier given the immediate needs with which it must deal. Accordingly, he proposes assigning this task to academia and the private sector (Kauver, 2002).

The Future

Obviously, much remains to be done to safeguard the aviation system from terrorist threats. How vulnerable the system remains has already been documented here, as has the need for a new approach to planning, operations, and enforcement. Until now, the focus has been on safeguarding assets—airplanes and airports—but there are simply too many facilities to safeguard and too many potential attack scenarios ranging from cyber to physical to biological, chemical, or nuclear. Furthermore, the costs of a successful attack will vary greatly depending on the event. The loss of an airplane is tragic; the disruption of the U.S. economy could be catastrophic. Accordingly, many experts have suggested that the focus should shift to the consequences of a successful attack not only at the system level, but at the national as well.

U.S. national security is dependent on complex interconnected systems, and the more complex the system (as is the case for international aviation), the greater the vulnerability. One element contributing to this complexity is the large number of actors, many of whom are in the private sector. Their cooperation is essential if appropriate levels of security are to be achieved but, as noted earlier, the airlines and other private sector firms have not been interested, historically, in investing in security measures, apart perhaps from theft prevention, and have resisted efforts to enhance the level of aviation security. If this pattern is to change, incentives that will motivate the private sector to adopt different policies will have to be devised.

The goal should be to create a situation where the private sector achieves economies while security is enhanced. Obviously, every effort must be made to safeguard existing systems, by reducing vulnerabilities. What is required is an approach that is systematic and comprehensive rather than a continuation of the former "guards, guns, and gates" strategy that failed so dismally to prevent the 9/11 catastrophe. As a TRB panel of experts noted, "By defeating one . . . perimeter defense—passenger screeners intended to intercept handguns—the September 11 attackers were able to defeat the entire security regime." Accordingly, a "layered system" (one with many security arrangements that are interconnected) should be developed because:

> Layered systems cannot be breached by the defeat of a single security feature—such as a gate or guard—as each layer provides backup for the others, so that impermeability of individual layers is not required. Moreover, the interleaved layers can confound the would-be terrorist (TRB, 2002, 2).

Deploying such a layered system will require the cooperation of many actors, but achieving such coordination continues to be as difficult to obtain as ever. Only limited progress has so far been achieved in implementing the technology-related measures that were recommended by a National Academy of Science committee in 1999. These dealt with such issues as bulk and trace explosives, passenger screening, and operator effectiveness. Though various technologies have been developed and implemented, it is clear that much remains to be done as evidenced by such comments as "needs improvement," "needs to be more comprehensive," and "deployment schedules have not been maintained." The five-year plan which was to be prepared "in cooperation with all stakeholders," remains "in development with only two subplans having been completed so far." There are numerous reasons for this situation, ranging from lack of adequate funding and personnel from the FAA to the large number of actors involved in aviation security, which greatly complicates coordination and stakeholder involvement (NAS, 2002, 5).

It is also necessary to begin to think creatively about designing systems that are less vulnerable than the ones that have been built heretofore. Such systems should be loosely coupled, resilient, flexible, possess redundant capacity, and not be based on resources whose flow can be easily disrupted (Winner, 2002). Widespread changes in all aspects of aviation—in planning, design, implementation, and operation—are required, if such a system is to emerge. The goal should be to incorporate security into every element of the system to the extent possible. Such a focus means a new approach to the planning, design, and operation of aviation. New concepts like robustness, flexibility, and redundancy will have to be operationalized and integrated into the planning process. Accepted ideas will have to be reexamined. For example, is remote check-in at transit stations desirable? Should the trend toward intermodal terminals, where several modes converge be reversed? Should people and baggage be handled separately?

At the core of such a reappraisal would be a decision process based on clearly defined goals. At present, such definition is not apparent. Is the goal of all the security measures enacted by the TSA to decrease the overall risk to passengers? If so, then more stringent measures should be enacted. Is it to enhance the well-being of the airlines? If so, airlines should not be expected to bear the high costs. Is it to protect the national economy? If so, air cargo requires more attention. Is it to prevent the release of chemical or biological agents? If so, general aviation requires more attention. Is it to increase consumer confidence? If so, the least invasive procedures are probably desirable. Because some of these goals are contradictory, attempting to achieve them all leads to conflicting policies.

Once goals and objectives are specified, risk assessment methodologies that relate actions to potential threats and to costs can be utilized. These should be based on a realistic appraisal of the potential threat that evaluates such basic factors as the terrorists' training, skill levels, resources, attack methods, and weapons—including chemical, biological, radiological, and nuclear, as well as the more traditional ones. On the basis of this type of analysis, it is possible to raise such basic questions as the following (Polzin, 2002; Gale and Husick, 2003):

1. What are the consequences of both the proposed action and the failure to act?
2. What adverse security effects would be avoided if the proposal is enacted and which ones are unavoidable?
3. What are the alternatives to the proposed action, the expected criteria for decision making, and why is the proposed action the preferred choice?
4. What are the costs of the proposed action (including those imposed on the nation) as compared to a successful attack?
5. What are the estimated costs of the proposed action and what is the estimated net present value of the investment required to take the proposed action?

Science and technology will inevitably comprise important elements in such a strategy. There is no doubt that technology can reduce the vulnerability of aviation in many important ways. Indeed, great hopes are being placed on research and development to identify new methods of safeguarding telecommunications systems, of detecting biological, chemical, and nuclear agents, of checking baggage for explosives, and of tracking and protecting containers. Ideally, the new technologies will increase efficiency at the same time they enhance security. Such technologies are obviously more likely to be accepted rapidly by the many actors who are involved in the aviation system.

Yet it is not clear that the high hopes will be realized. The Department of Homeland Security is composed of agencies that are not known for their experience in this area, and the amounts devoted to R & D are quite small. Only $0.5 billion was allocated to R & D in the HSD's fiscal year 2003 budget of $37.5 billion, and the TSA's fiscal year 2004 budget allocated only $75 million out of a total of $5 billion. What is required is a national science and technology strategy for homeland security (of which aviation should be an important part), but at least one expert believes that "for some period of time more reliance will have to be placed on private initiative and resources" (Branscomb, 2002).

Even if an appropriately funded national strategy is devised and implemented, it must be recognized that technology is not a panacea that can provide a "fix" to the problem of terrorism. Such a perspective has often been lacking in the past; as noted earlier, federal agencies such as the FAA have rushed to deploy technologies whose efficacy was limited and whose financial and other costs were very high. Furthermore, for some threats such as biological and chemical or radiological weapons of mass destruction, breakthrough technologies are not available.

Even when technologies appear promising, long lead times are often involved in bringing them to market, they are often costly, do not always yield anticipated results, and have social and economic consequences. For example, the use of biometric technology to screen people at airports and other entry points is being discussed. These technologies can tie individuals accurately to travel documents, thus, greatly reducing, if not eliminating, problems of identity theft and forgery; but their implementation has significant implications for increased processing times and, thus, the flow of tourists and business travelers, especially though not exclusively, to border communities. Furthermore, Americans traveling abroad may be required to provide biometric samples to foreign governments (GAO, 2002b). Accordingly, it is essential to apply the risk analytical approach outlined earlier when making decisions regarding technology.

Science and technology can also play an important role in enhancing consequence management, which must also become a part of aviation security planning. Important steps have been taken in this regard, but much remains to be done, given the financial limitations and the problems of coordinating the many actors involved, especially given the frequent lack of compatibility. Denver International Airport, for example, had an emergency evacuation plan that called for, in the case of a major power failure, sending people to nearby hotels. When consultants met with the State Police, however, they learned that its plans called for closing the highway leading from the airport to the hotels. Of particular concern is the importance of preparing for effective communication with the public to avert panic.

Public education is but one dimension of the education and training needs that are required. Technology ultimately depends on people. It is human beings who operate the technologies who must interpret the results that technological tools provide. Ample evidence of this point can be found in the many tests at various airports that demonstrated the ease with which weapons could be smuggled past the screeners. Because every aspect of aviation (its planning, design, operation, and maintenance) requires organizational and technological change, professionals with appropriate skills and perspectives will be required. Only recently have educational security issues received any attention, so that few transportation professionals in either the public or the private sector possess an appropriate understanding of the issues or the relevant skills required to function effectively in the new environment.

An appropriate level of security will be achieved when all levels of all aviation-related organizations assume ownership of security. However, this will take time and be dependent on improving the technical and conceptual skills of all members of the aviation sector, from truck drivers delivering cargo to clerical staff opening the mail and entering data, to corporate-level executives and government officials planning and implementing policy. Developing a coherent strategy to tackle such educational and training needs is no simple matter, but it is an issue of great urgency.

Reducing the vulnerability of the aviation system, therefore, requires that the following measures be taken as rapidly as possible:

- Restructure the TSA so that it becomes an effective, efficient agency that is held accountable for its performance. Appropriate planning and budgetary mechanisms should be developed, as well as an organizational culture that emphasizes anticipatory rather than reactive behavior to terrorist threats.
- Develop and implement a comprehensive strategic plan based on risk management principles that specifies goals and objectives, priorities, targets and

deadlines, and has built-in evaluative mechanisms. Allocate adequate funds and human resources to ensure its implementation.

- Enhance the security of all computer systems, especially those dealing with Air Traffic Control.
- Utilize appropriate technologies to strengthen airport perimeter security.
- Deploy biometric and other technologies to prevent unauthorized persons from gaining access to aircraft on the tarmac and such facilities as cargo, postal, food, fuel farm and pipeline, electrical systems, etc.
- Develop comprehensive airport emergency plans with contingency and damage mitigation components.
- Implement an acceptable and effective method of computerized passenger screening to identify high risk persons, and establish enhanced screening procedures for them and their carry-on and checked baggage.
- Establish a "Trusted Traveler" Program so as to release resources for other security needs.
- Implement procedures and technologies for the screening of air cargo in a way that recognizes the specific nature of various carriers and does not impose undue economic costs upon them.
- Develop and implement more effective policies to control access to general aviation planes and facilities.

Such measures, however, must be supplemented by detailed attention by law-enforcement agencies and an effective intelligence apparatus capable of providing officials with the kind of information necessary to prevent terrorist designs. Apprehending, convicting, and imprisoning terrorists will prevent them from staging new attacks and may temporarily dislocate their organizations. Such actions may disrupt or even prevent terrorist operations, but committed terrorist organizations will rally and reorganize, as recent history tragically demonstrates.

Accordingly, it is also necessary to deny these groups the ability to establish themselves in secure bases from which they can plan attacks, obtain the necessary weapons and intelligence, and recruit followers with the appropriate training to carry them out. A preventative strategy would aim at identifying, as thoroughly as possible, the members of terrorist organizations, discouraging states from supporting them covertly, denying terrorists access to skills and resources (especially weapons of mass destruction), and limiting their appeal and ability to recruit new members (Heymann, 2001).

Such a policy requires that all foreign policy decisions incorporate a counterterrorist perspective. Priority should be given to using all available methods to disrupt terrorist infrastructures, to aiding states to deal with terrorist networks. Given the diversity of terrorist threats, it is essential not to rely too heavily on any single method and to adapt policies to meet different terrorist challenges. Although sometimes necessary, vivid rhetoric such as denouncing rogue states as an "axis of evil" and punishing state sponsors are instruments that may isolate and further alienate such countries. Efforts to encourage change by engagement of various sorts, either unilaterally or working with other governments, may well be more productive. Public diplomacy, too, has an important role to play in educating people about terrorism, but it is important to do so without accidentally enhancing their appeal (Pillar, 2001). The history of U.S.

efforts to forge an effective policy toward Iran and North Korea reflects these complexities.

Allies are essential in any integrated approach to counterterrorism. The cooperation of foreign states will obviously be required, but achieving such cooperation is seldom easy, given the character of the international system and the widespread hypocrisy and application of double standards that often characterize state behavior. The United States has not been immune from such practices, especially when strategic interests such as the flow of oil are concerned.

Further complicating efforts to gain support and cooperation in the struggle against terrorism is the Bush administration's willingness to avoid participating in international treaties and to forsake the multilateral approach of its predecessors in favor of unilateralism. The newly declared U.S. security policy that emphasizes the right of preemption aroused further concerns about American leadership abroad, and the decision to topple Saddam Hussein's regime in Iraq resulted in the deepest rift between the United States and many of its traditional European allies, perhaps in history. The greater the growth of negative attitudes towards the United States—and these seem to have reached extraordinarily high levels all over the globe—the more difficult it is to find allies who will cooperate fully and wholeheartedly in the struggle against terrorism.

Crafting and implementing a policy that contributes in a positive way to the struggle against terrorism is perhaps easier than making even modest improvements in resolving ethnic and other conflicts. Ameliorating, let alone eliminating grievances, whether real or perceived, is no simple matter but efforts to do so are urgently needed because the overwhelming majority of terrorists perceive themselves, rightly or wrongly, as injured individuals who have to resort to terrorism to gain attention or to achieve specific political goals. Identifying and attempting to assuage these motivations does not mean that terrorist attacks are condoned or excused; they are still violent, illegal actions that must be condemned and, if possible, prosecuted. Nevertheless, any comprehensive approach to the aviation security challenge must incorporate policies that are designed to deal with social and political factors.

Despite the appeal and possible contribution of short-term measures (which are preferred by policymakers and political leaders seeking quick results), a commitment to slow, patient, long-term action aimed at underlying factors can make major contributions to enhancing security. When ethnic and other conflicts are, if not resolved, at least moved away from violent confrontations, terrorism related to that conflict inevitably declines. Northern Ireland, where steps toward reconciliation have led to a dramatic decrease in inter-communal violence, provides a textbook case.

On the other hand, when conflicts continue to rage as is the case with Palestinians and Israelis and in Kashmir, violent attacks continue to be mounted against aviation and other targets. Resolving such complex issues, which have been characterized by violence for decades, is likely to be an aspiration toward which policymakers can only strive. Progress, if any is achieved, will be slow and probably marked by frustrating setbacks. But if tensions can be lowered and the foundations laid for possible accommodation, then aggrieved parties will be less likely to utilize terrorist tactics to advance their cause.

It remains to be seen whether the U.S. political system can successfully develop and implement the kind of integrated and systematic domestic and foreign policies that are outlined in this article. Well before 9/11, the precarious state of aviation security was apparent. Hopefully the reforms that have been initiated since then, and the measures that are forthcoming, will greatly improve the situation. Clearly, much remains to be done. Prior to the destruction of the World Trade Center, two scholars wrote:

> . . . designing an effective strategy to meet the problems posed by transportation security is no simple matter. It requires fresh thinking and new, integrated approaches. . . . While (terrorist) threats can never be eliminated completely, they are likely to increase over time unless they are addressed adequately (Szyliowicz and Viotti, 1997, 393–394).

Those words are as true today as they were in 1997.

Notes

1. This article draws on my previous work in this area, "The International Dimensions of Transportation Security," prepared for Terrorism and Transportation Symposium; V. R. Johnston, ed., *Review of Policy Research*, 20(2) (2003); and J. Szyliowicz and Paul Viotti, "Transportation Security," *Transportation Quarterly* (1997). A preliminary version was presented at the CUNY Aviation Institute, Inaugural Conference: Strategies and Skills for Revitalizing Aviation," York College March 31, 2003 and was published in the conference proceedings.

References

AOPA Online. *General Aviation and Homeland Security* and *Regulatory Brief: FAA and TSA Security Direct Final Rules*. 2003. www.aopa.org/whatsnew/regulatory/reg_ security.html.

Boyd, A., and J. Caton. *Securing Intermodal Connections*. Boyd, Caton and Grant Transportation Group. 2001. www.bcgtrans.com.

Branscomb, Lewis. Comments. Homeland Security Conference. University of Colorado, October 2002.

Caffera, P. J. "The Air Industry's Worst Nightmare." *Salon*, 25 December 2002. www.iasa.com.au/folders/Security_Issues/dosamspose-1.html.

Chardy, A. "Lax Security at MIA." *Miami Herald*, 31 January 2003.

Dacey, R. F. "Computer Security: Progress Made, but Critical Federal Operations and Assets Remain at Risk." Statement before the Subcommittee on Government Efficiency, Financial Management and Intergovernmental Relations, U.S. House Committee on Government Reform, 19 November 2002.

Del Valle, C. "Was the FAA Asleep at the Joystick." *Business Week*, 14 April 1997.

Drug Enforcement Agency (DEA). *Drug Trafficking in the United States*. 2003. www.dea.gov./ concern/drug_trafficking.html.

Eng, Paul. "Neutron Bomb Sniffer," 4 February 2003. www.ABCnews.com.

Gale, S., and L. Husick. "From MAD to MUD: Dealing with the New Terrorism." *FPRI Wire* 11 no. 1 (February 2003).

General Accounting Office (GAO). Information Security, GAO-01-1004T. 2001. www.gao.gov.

———. 2002a. *Using Biometrics for Border Security.* November 2002. www.gao.gov.

———. 2002b. *Vulnerabilities and Potential Improvements for the Air Cargo System.* December 2002. www.gao.gov.

Gleick, E. "Human Error May Have Caused the Crash but the FAA may also Tolerate High Risk for Low Cost Airlines." *Time*, 27 May 1996.

Heymann, P. "Dealing with Terrorism, an Overview." *International Security* 26 no. 3 (December 2001): 24–39.

ICAO. Aviation Security Plan of Action. 2002. www.icao.org/applications/search/Results.cfm.

Kauvar, G. B. "Transportation Security." *Issues in Science and Technology,* Fall 2002, p. 6.

Kidwell, David. "Drug Ring Busted at Airport." *Miami Herald*, 26 August 1999.

Kunreuther, H., G. Heal, and P. Orszag. *Interdependent Security: Implications for Homeland Security and Other Areas.* Policy Brief 108. The Brookings Institution. 2002. www.brookings.org/comm/policybriefs/pb108.htm.

Lee, J. "Progress Seen in Border Tests of ID System," *The New York Times,* 7 February 2003.

Miller, L. 2003a. "Airports: Baggage Screening Needs Work," Associated Press, 5 February 2003.

———. "U.S. Airport Screeners Tally 4.8 million Seized Items," *The Denver Post*, 11 March 2003.

National Academy of Sciences. "Second Report: Progress Toward Objectives." *Assessment of Technologies Deployed to Improve Aviation Security.* Washington, DC: National Academy of Sciences, 2002. Summary available at www.books.nap.edu/books/NI000396/htm/7.html.

O'Harrow, R. Jr. "Intricate Screening of Fliers in Works." *Washington Post*, 1 February 2003.

Pasternak, J. "FAA, Airlines Stalled Major Security Plans," *New York Times*, 14 December 2002.

Phelps, Mark. "Do SAMs Pose a Real Threat to Civil Aviation?" *Aviation International News.* 2003. www.iasa.com.au/folders/Security_Issues/dosamspose.html.

Pillar, Paul. *Terrorism and U.S. Foreign Policy.* Washington, DC: The Brookings Institution Press, 2001.

Polzin, S. "Security Considerations in Transportation Planning," Southeastern Transportation Center, 2002.

President's Commission on Critical Infrastructure. *National Strategy for the Physical Protection of Critical Infrastructure and Key Assets.* 2003. www.iwar.org.uk/eip/resources/physical-cip/national-strategy.htm.

Public Citizen. *Delay, Dilute and Discard: How the Airline Industry and the FAA have stymied Aviation Security Recommendations.* 2001. www.citizen.org.

Sallinger, R. "Explosive Traces Evade DIA Security." *News4*. 2003. www.news4Colorado.com/global/story.asp?s=1142555.

Szyliowicz, J., and P. Viotti. "Transportation Security." *Transportation Quarterly* 51 (1997): 79–95.

Transportation Research Board (TRB). *Deterrence, Protection and Preparation: The New Transportation Security Imperative.* Special Report 270. Washington, DC: Transportation Research Board, 2002.

U.S. Commission on National Security/21st Century. *Road Map for National Security: Imperative for Change: Phase 3 Report.* 2001. www.nssg.gov/PhaseIIIFR.pdf.

U.S. Department of Transportation. *Report on Audit of Federal Aviation Administration's Airport Security Program.* U.S. Department of Transportation: Office of the Inspector General, 1993.

Wald, Matthew L. "A Plan for Screening at Airports Is Dropped." *New York Times,* 25 July 2004, section 5.

Waterman, Shaun. "Huge U.S. Aviation Gap." *Washington Politics and Policy Desk,* 2003. www.upi.com/view.cfm?StoryID=20030307–024411–3954r.

Winner, L. "Complexity, Trust and Terror." *Tech Knowledge Revue*, 3.1, 2002. www.praxagora.com/stevet/netfuture/2002/Oct2202_137.html#

Chapter 8

Improving Public Surface Transportation Security: What Do We Do Now?

Brian Michael Jenkins

Like almost everything recently written on security, this chapter takes September 11, 2001, as its starting point. On that date, the most lethal terrorist attack in history profoundly affected how Americans view security. However, this essay draws upon research that began much earlier. That research addressed the protection of surface transportation systems against terrorist attacks. It focused particularly on identifying the best security practices, and by September 11, had already produced several reports. These were quickly summarized after the attacks on the World Trade Center and the Pentagon and were disseminated through various government-sponsored and industry association forums.[1] While this essay specifically deals with surface transportation security, it also touches upon the broader issues of homeland security and national transportation strategy. It begins with a review of the threat and then discusses some of the broader aspects of implementing homeland security. Next, it reviews the progress made in improving surface transportation security and discusses remaining problems. It then examines ways to approach the problem (and ways not to). A final section summarizes the conclusions.

The Threat

The terrorist threat to surface transportation is real: contemporary terrorists have made it a major theater of operations. Initially, the primary terrorist targets were commercial airliners because they were widely available symbols of nations and policies despised by the terrorists, portable containers of victims or hostages, and sometimes a means of escape. But as aviation security improved, the total number of attacks on commercial aircraft declined, and terrorists increasingly turned to attacks on surface transportation: bombing trains, stations, depots, and buses. A softer target than aviation, surface transportation offers terrorists easy access and little security to penetrate. In addition, the large crowds of strangers at surface transportation facilities guarantee anonymity for the attackers and facilitate their escape.

Transportation systems are the nervous systems of large cities. Attacking them produces profound psychological effects and economic disruption. Concentrations of people in contained environments also enhance the effects of explosives and chemical weapons, and offer venues for the spread of biological agents—all attractions to terrorists who are determined to kill in quantity, and willing to do so indiscriminately.

Clearly, killing is the objective of many terrorists who attack surface transportation targets. Such attacks have been almost twice as lethal as terrorist attacks overall. An analysis of nearly 1,000 attacks on surface transportation revealed that two-thirds were intended to kill and 37 percent resulted in fatalities. The goal was often slaughter; 74 percent of the deadly attacks involved multiple fatalities and 23 percent involved ten or more deaths.[2] To be sure, many of these attacks occurred in the midst of ongoing civil wars, but a third of them took place outside of identified conflict zones.

Although many of the attacks are isolated incidents, major terrorist campaigns have targeted surface transportation. The Irish Republican Army (IRA) waged a 25-year terrorist campaign against London's Underground and British railroads. Between 1991 and 1999, IRA terrorists planted 81 explosive devices; during the same period, British transportation authorities had to deal with more than 6,000 bomb threats and had to inspect more than 9,000 suspicious objects.[3] From 1995 to 1996, terrorists in France carried out a bombing campaign aimed at the Paris Metro, local commuter trains, high speed intercity trains, and other surface transportation targets. For the past two years, suicide bombers in Israel have frequently targeted buses. Terrorists connected with al-Qaida planned to carry out attacks on Singapore's metro.

In the United States, the 1993 bombing of New York's World Trade Center blasted the train stations beneath the towers, although the attack was not aimed specifically at the subways. In 1995, a still unidentified saboteur derailed Amtrak's Sunset Limited in Arizona. In 1997, terrorists planned to carry out suicide bombings on New York's subways, but the plot was foiled when one of the groups informed police. The September 11, 2001, attack completely destroyed the New York Transport Authority (NYTA) and Port Authority Trans-Hudson (PATH) train stations at the World Trade Center. After September 11, a mentally disturbed individual attacked the driver of a Greyhound bus, causing it to crash, and killing seven persons.

The following two charts, drawn from research conducted by the Mineta Transportation Institute, show that attacks on surface transportation have historically been divided almost evenly between trains and buses, with bombing being the most common tactic (excluding bomb threats). The deadliest incidents have resulted from explosions or deliberately initiated fires in crowded stations, trains, or buses and from train derailments.

Today, European authorities worry about chemical or biological attacks on local subways. Terrorist use of chemical, biological, or radiological weapons in surface transportation is a real, not a theoretical, threat. In 1995, members of Japan's Aum Shinrikyo sect released nerve gas on Tokyo's subways, killing 12 persons; 5,500 people sought medical treatment and millions were terrified. Recent arrests in Europe of extremists connected with al-Qaida who were engaged in manufacturing ricin and the discovery of a container of ricin in a Paris train station renewed fears that terrorists might try to disperse lethal chemicals or release biological agents at transportation facilities. Even a radiological attack is not unprecedented. In 1974, a mentally disturbed individual spread small quantities of radioactive isotopes on train coaches in Austria.

Large-scale attacks involving chemical or biological substances would be very difficult to carry out, but even a small-scale attack could produce widespread panic and, as demonstrated in the anthrax attacks in the United States in 2001, it could deny use of

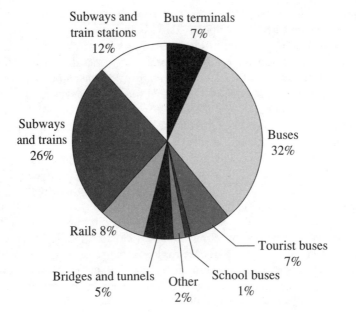

FIGURE 8-1.   Targets of Attacks on Public Surface Transportation Systems (1920–2000)

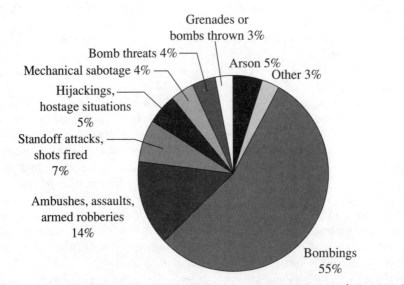

FIGURE 8-2.   Tactics Used Against Public Surface Transportation Systems (July 1997–December 2000)

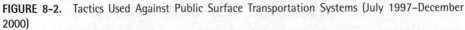

transportation facilities for a lengthy period and result in costly cleanups. As the Tokyo subway experience shows, rapid diagnosis of an attack can be vital to limiting casualties and contamination, and can assist in discerning hoaxes, thereby reducing unnecessary shutdowns and disruptions. Bio-detectors can alert public health authorities to the dissemination of dangerous pathogens that otherwise might not become apparent for days, i.e., until symptoms developed and medical diagnosis was confirmed. Development of effective monitoring systems and portable devices is an area of intensive research, particularly in government-sponsored laboratories. Chemical and biological detectors were recently installed in the Washington, DC, Metro on an experimental basis. These detectors are, of course, useful for dealing with natural outbreaks of disease as well as terrorist attacks.

Implementing Homeland Security

Security against terrorism has improved greatly since September 11. With allied help, the United States has launched a global campaign against terrorism, and at home, Americans have embraced the concept of "homeland security"—providing for the common defense—as a national mission. The government has created a new Department of Homeland Security to coordinate the federal response, and a new military command has been created to coordinate the Defense Department's supporting role. Security has been significantly increased nationwide, largely by using local resources such as the National Guard, police, and private security. Specific new measures have also been implemented to enhance the security of commercial air travel and the shipment of containerized cargo. The vaccination of soldiers and health workers against smallpox has begun, and sufficient vaccine is being stockpiled to inoculate the entire nation. New vaccines and antidotes to deal with other biological weapons are rapidly being developed, but thus far have failed to reverse the decline in U.S. public health and emergency medical treatment capabilities. Because of constrained local budgets, public health capabilities are, in fact, being reduced and emergency treatment centers are closing.

Intelligence collection efforts have increased and federal agencies are getting better at sharing information. A system has been developed to consolidate all available intelligence and communicate judgments about threat levels. In addition, the federal government has recently created a combined intelligence analysis center. However, the government still has difficulty communicating threat information to the public in a way that does not lend itself to provoking panic or derision. And it has failed to effectively exploit the vast intelligence capabilities of the local police. With additional training and support, both technological and financial, local police departments could become part of a national terrorism intelligence network to supplement the current "hub and spoke" system in which intelligence is passed to the federal government and then fed back to local agencies.

Despite a great deal of rhetoric and some exchange of information, the federal government and the private sector have yet to achieve a true operating partnership. Problems lie on both sides. The government is understandably reluctant to share sensitive threat information (what little it has) or to offer specific advice. Corporations have increased their security, but they are reluctant to share proprietary information and they have not launched business-sector initiatives outlining workable security solutions. The surface transportation industry is a significant exception.

Clearly, many problems remain. The approach to homeland security, especially in the transportation sector, is regulatory and rule-based, implemented by enforcement—a "gates and guards" approach. This approach may be necessary to prod industries that are reluctant to divert precious resources to security, but regulatory approaches are seldom imaginative, and with their emphasis on prevention rather than resiliency, they are dangerously predictable and rarely efficient.

Paradoxically, a society that incorporates into its national myth the minuteman, the self-reliant pioneer and the armed citizen, has failed to effectively engage the public in homeland security. Ordinary people are warned what to expect, but they are not instructed as to what they can do.

Progress in Transportation Security

The September 11 attacks prompted a profound review of transportation security. Understandably, the initial focus was on commercial aviation. The Transportation Security Agency (TSA) was established by the Aviation Security Act of 2001 to take over airline security, but it soon began addressing security for other transportation modes. Subsequently the TSA was moved from the Department of Transportation to the newly created Department of Homeland Security.

A review of events on and immediately after September 11 showed that local surface transportation systems were profoundly affected by the attack, but also that they played a vital role in evacuation, rescue, communications, and recovery. Prompt action by stationmasters saved lives by preventing the unloading of passengers at the New York subway and PATH train stations under the World Trade Center. Additional commuter trains were mobilized to help evacuate New York City, and Washington's Metro and bus system similarly assisted in the evacuation around areas of the capital. At the same time, the Metropolitan Transportation Authority (MTA) in New York played a major role in getting emergency personnel into the city and to Ground Zero. The MTA's own emergency personnel and heavy equipment provided major support to the rescue effort, while its communication system was used to augment New York's damaged and overloaded emergency communications systems. The MTA also used its own Web site and staff to communicate directly with the public.

Following September 11, the Department of Transportation's Federal Transit Administration reviewed security measures and discussed improvements with industry associations and state governments. Systems operators and local police implemented the easy measures first. They increased the presence of uniformed and plainclothes security staff and conducted more frequent patrols. The public was asked to remain vigilant for suspicious activity and abandoned packages. Doors leading to vital systems were locked, and stations were tidied to reduce hiding spaces. Crisis plans were reviewed and responses exercised.

In 2002, the National Academies created a Committee on Science and Technology for Countering Terrorism. Actually, this was a committee of committees; one panel, jointly sponsored by the National Academies and the Transportation Research Board, addressed the specific issue of transportation. The panel recognized that responsibility for the security of surface transportation rests with state and local law enforcement authorities as well as the public and private entities that own and operate the transportation infrastructure and assets. However, it noted that the creation of the TSA represents an opportunity to build security into the nation's transportation sector in a more systematic way. The TSA could be more than a mere regulatory and enforcement arm, although to fulfill a strategic role it would need to establish a strategic research and planning office. The panel also recommended that the TSA establish an in-house capability to support its operations and evaluate new technologies for systems operators.

In late 2002, the General Accounting Office (GAO) conducted a survey of transit agencies to determine their security needs and to identify ways the federal government could best assist them. The GAO took note of the difficulties in securing public surface transportation: inherent vulnerabilities and high passenger volume make surface transportation systems both attractive targets and difficult to protect. Much progress had been made since September 11, but most of the improvements have addressed the easy things. Further significant improvements would cost billions. "Insufficient funding," the GAO reported, "is the most significant challenge in making transit systems as safe and secure as possible."[4]

In their constrained local budget environments, transit systems operators have looked to the federal government for help, but at the federal level, they would have to engage in fierce competition for finite dollars. Moreover, federal expenditures would have to be prioritized. The GAO concluded that a comprehensive risk-management approach would be the most effective way to improve surface transportation security.

The same themes were echoed in a broader GAO report issued in April 2003,[5] which repeated the need to develop a comprehensive risk-management approach. The report went on to recommend ensuring that transportation security funding needs be identified and prioritized, establishing effective coordination among the public and private entities responsible for transportation security, ensuring adequate work force competence, and implementing security standards for transportation facilities. It is this final recommendation that merits close attention. The GAO believes that setting and enforcing security standards "will ensure that operators improve their security practices in modes where lax security could make surface transportation facilities attractive targets to terrorists." (This specific comment was made in the context of pipelines, but it would also apply to other transportation modes.) The GAO would require the Department of Transportation to prescribe standards for security and then approve or disapprove the operators' programs on the basis of adherence to these standards.

Operators, of course, would prefer a non-regulatory approach that gives them flexibility in designing security programs for specific facilities. The GAO itself recognized that there is little precedent for enforcement of standards in entities as large, complex, and diverse as surface transportation systems. Moreover, setting standards presupposes that we know how much security is enough when, in fact, this is extremely difficult to determine. Finally, while goals and some performance measures are necessary, words such as *standards, prescribe,* and *enforce* have a decidedly regulatory ring. It is necessary to find a balance between exhortation and rule making, and we have to remain realistic about risk.

What Do We Do Now?

We tend to review transportation security mode by mode: commercial aviation, ports and container shipping, transport of hazardous cargo, public surface transportation, pipelines, bridges and tunnels. Each mode has its own requirements, but in treating each separately we may miss some broader strategic issues. Security must be assessed across the entire spectrum of transportation systems. Such an across-the-board look could lead to new and innovative security solutions.

Historically, security considerations in times of war have been major factors in the development of America's transportation system. George Washington's early unsuccessful military expeditions over Indian trails that did not allow the passage of cannons and wagons provided impetus for the new federal government to build the national road from Cumberland to Wheeling, West Virginia. While commerce was the main reason for improving the internal road network, British blockades in the War of 1812 further underscored the need. The great difficulty in moving troops and munitions to western New York provided an additional strategic reason for digging the Erie Canal. Railroads were built to open up the west, but it was the Civil War that demonstrated their strategic importance. In return for land grants, railroads were obliged to transport troops at half fare.

Poor roads plagued Pershing's expedition into Mexico. In World War I, shipping sufficient numbers of horses to Europe and enough fodder to feed them on the way obliged the American Expeditionary Force to switch to motorized transport, for which existing U.S. roads were inadequate; the vehicles could not be driven to embarkation ports, and instead had to be ferried by rail. American security required good highways, an imperative renewed in World War II, ultimately leading to the federally subsidized interstate highway system. In the post-September 11-security environment, it is appropriate to contemplate a national transportation security strategy.

At present, there is no such strategy. Creating one would require identifying and ranking overall objectives: preventing the loss of life; minimizing long-term risks to health; and limiting social upheaval, environmental catastrophe, and economic disruption. Because these concerns transcend the specific topic of transportation, the next step would be to determine the unique vulnerabilities of transportation systems and their potential consequences.

Airliners hijacked by suicidal pilots clearly represent the biggest terrorist threat to national security, since they can produce an order of magnitude more casualties than the bloodiest incidents of airline sabotage or truck bombs, and they can result in orders of magnitude more economic disruption. It could be argued that the security of commercial aviation therefore, merits a larger share of the national resources devoted to security, whether paid for out of general tax revenues or special taxes on air travel. Clandestinely delivered weapons of mass destruction, the principal concern in container security, could also produce large-scale casualties and destruction, making this another priority area. Attacks on other transportation modes would have local effects, although the psychological effects could be felt nationally.

After September 11, many travelers switched from commuter flights to passenger trains, where available, or to private automobiles. Airlines understandably lamented the loss of revenue, but was this truly a negative development? Putting aside other factors, such as the efficient use of energy and environmental impact, one could argue that the shift actually favored security. Trains run on rails; unlike hijacked airliners, they cannot be turned into piloted missiles. Theoretically, fewer flights would represent a security gain. Such considerations should be factored into a national transportation security strategy. Protecting one set of targets against terrorist attacks that can just as easily be carried out anywhere else, may still be desirable for occupants and owners, but it represents no gain in overall national security—it merely displaces the risk. Some transportation targets may offer terrorists unique opportunities—for example, major train stations through which millions of passengers pass daily may present unique opportunities for chemical or biological threats. Tunnels also may have unique vulnerabilities.

Vulnerable bridges can be upgraded and protected at a cost, or, if they are near obsolescence, they can be replaced with new, physically stronger structures. The system could also be augmented with additional bridges to make it less vulnerable overall. Rather than merely becoming a continuing operational expense, security could be the basis for the reconstruction of the U.S. national transportation infrastructure.

Surface Transportation Requires its Own Security Model

The commercial aviation model of security cannot be applied to surface transportation. There are differences in the threat, the consequences of attacks, the ability to provide security, and the economics of the two modes. The terrorist threat to both is high; commercial aviation has remained a preferred terrorist target since the late 1960s, although improved security measures and international treaty agreements to extradite or prosecute hijackers have reduced the number of attacks. And according to government sources, approximately one-third of all terrorist attacks are directed against surface transportation.

The risk to individual passengers in either aviation or surface transportation is very low. A total of 246 passengers died in the four aircraft hijacked on September 11. Since there are more than 700 million passenger boardings annually in the United States, the risk to an individual on any flight in 2001 was approximately one in several million. Considering a longer time span—say, 10 years—would change the odds of perishing on an aircraft hijacked or sabotaged by terrorists to one in tens of millions. Every year, nine billion passengers use public surface transportation in the United States, so the odds of becoming a victim of terrorism in this venue are infinitesimal—one in tens of millions, or close to one in a hundred million if a longer-term horizon is used for an actuarial chart.

The consequences of attacks, however, do differ. A hijacked airliner with a suicide pilot at the controls can bring death to thousands, potentially tens of thousands. Damage can run to the tens of billions of dollars, with economic disruption in the hundreds of billions. It can be argued that with the new aviation security measures in place, especially locked reinforced cockpit doors, this is no longer a viable tactic, unless the pilot in place is suborned. And even before the new doors were in place, the tactic had already failed: On September 11, realizing what was happening, passengers on United Airlines Flight 92 took action against the hijackers and became part of the security system. Facing certain death if they do not take action, determined passengers are likely to behave the same way again; or when an aircraft is known to have been hijacked, Air Force planes might be ordered to bring it down. At least terrorist planners can no longer count on a permissive environment inside or outside the plane.

The situation is different with surface transportation. Trains and buses cannot be flown into skyscrapers, so the casualties that occur in a surface transportation attack are likely to be confined to the passengers themselves. And whereas the deadliest terrorist attacks on passenger aircraft have killed several hundred (325 in the 1985 sabotage of an Air India flight, 270 in the sabotage of Pan Am 103, and 189 in the sabotage of a 1989

UTA French airline flight), the five deadliest train derailments each killed between 25 and 95 people, the ten deadliest bombings on trains or in stations each killed between 20 and 80 persons, and the deadliest attacks on buses each killed fewer than 40 persons. But while approximately 10,000 flights take off every day—perhaps fewer now as a consequence of recent cutbacks—the number of potential targets in the surface transportation system is probably in the hundreds of thousands.

Thus, the approach to security must be different for surface transportation. In commercial aviation security, the emphasis is on deterrence and prevention. If the layers of security have been breached, there is seldom much that can be done other than to use blast-resistant cargo containers to provide some protection against bombs smuggled inside checked bags or to implement schemes that override cockpit controls and remotely bring hijacked aircraft to safe landings. Mitigation is not much of an option—an airline crash allows few opportunities for lives to be saved, even with rapid response.

Public surface transportation offers easier access and higher volumes of passengers than aviation. Some deterrence of terrorist attacks may be possible, but prevention is extremely difficult in the absence of screening measures that, given the volume of users, the vast number of access points, the absence of advance ticket purchases, and the low cost of fares, are unrealistic. Nearly 60,000 federal employees are needed to screen 700 million passengers a year at airports, and waits at check points can be as long as an hour. How many security personnel would be needed to conduct even a rudimentary screening of nine billion surface transport users? And what kind of delays would screening introduce? It is significant that when faced with long-term terrorist threats to surface transportation, neither the United Kingdom nor Israel has adopted airport-style passenger screening procedures (except at Israeli central bus depots).

Neither do the finances support the application of commercial aviation security to surface transport. Airline passengers now pay a security tax of $2.50 per trip segment to offset total security costs. This represents a small percentage of a several hundred-dollar airline ticket. A similar percentage of surface transportation fares—which are typically a dollar or two—would not provide anywhere near the funds needed to support airport-style screening.

Security emphasis therefore must shift to mitigation through station and vehicle design, quick diagnosis of threats, prompt intervention, and rapid response. In other words, surface transportation security has to be more reactive than proactive. Commercial aviation is a network, whereas surface transportation is a mosaic. A terrorist bent upon attacking commercial aviation must penetrate security at one of 430 commercial airports in the United States. Once inside the security, however, the terrorist's target range is national. Surface transportation offers almost unlimited access points, but once a terrorist is on board, his target range is local.

Because it is a single system, commercial aviation may be viewed as a single target, with the same security measures in effect at all airports. Surface transportation, in contrast, comprises diverse modes—subways, elevated trains, light rail, and buses—and as a result, standardized procedures are harder to sustain or to justify.

Finally, the federal government's role in aviation is different from its role in surface transportation. In commercial aviation, the government has a broad mandate to dictate security measures. After September 11, Congress, in no mood to listen to industry opposition, created the TSA and instructed it to take direct charge of airport security. There is still concern that the federal government, driven by political considerations, may impose additional requirements that are disruptive, costly and that contribute only marginally to overall security. Given the airline industry's traditional reluctance to implement security measures that affect operations or the bottom line, an adversarial relationship has developed between the government and the industry.

The federal government has far less authority in dealing with surface transportation, and we do not envision the creation of a national transport police like the force in the United Kingdom. Instead, we are likely to see an altogether different but still significant federal role, which we will discuss later.

A "Best Practices" Approach Rather Than Uniform Rules

A surface transportation security strategy must reflect the diversity of the transportation networks. These complex networks range from long-distance rail and bus systems, to commuter and city transit systems. They include trains, light rail, elevated trains, subways, stations, buses, terminals, thousands of miles of rail line itself, bridges, and tunnels. (For the purpose of this discussion, we are excluding freight and pipelines.) Operations range in size from multi-modal urban systems to rural bus lines.

Transportation security has two objectives: preventing casualties and minimizing disruption. Therefore, a broader definition of "security" is required. Effective security must consist of more than deterrent and preventive measures; it must encompass all efforts to mitigate casualties, damage and disruption, and to facilitate rapid restoration of operations. Attributes of effective surface transportation security include flexibility, the ability to increase and decrease efforts according to threat conditions, an emphasis on technology rather than personnel and given limited prevention possibilities, a focus on crisis planning and response training.

The terrorist threat must be viewed in national terms. Terrorists can attack anything, anywhere, anytime. It is not inconceivable that domestic terrorists or terrorists who are sent or inspired from abroad could carry out an attack in any surface transportation venue anywhere in the country. At the same time, the threat is not the same everywhere in the country. In fact, terrorists tend to carry out their attacks in nearby, familiar surroundings; most terrorist bombings occur within an hour's drive of the terrorist's home. Historically, the vast majority of terrorist attacks in the United States have occurred in six major metropolitan areas: New York, Washington, Miami, Chicago, San Francisco, and Los Angeles. The threat is not the same for Duluth as it is for the District of Columbia. Nor is it the same for a small rural bus line as it is for a major urban transportation network. National threat alerts imply a uniformity of threat, which simply does not exist, although no one can argue that "it won't happen here."

There is also considerable diversity in the way security is provided. Some large urban systems, such as the New York City MTA, have their own police forces. A few of the larger police departments have special transit divisions to deal with crime on trains and buses. In many systems, security is provided by a private security force, proprietary or contracted, which may operate under the auspices of a small proprietary police unit or a director of security. In some cases, local police provide security for the systems within their jurisdiction. Combinations of these are common, especially where transportation systems cross two or more police jurisdictions.

Given the diversity of the systems, the differences in the threat, and the ways in which security is provided, transportation security cannot easily be mandated according to uniform standards and rules. A best-practices approach may be a more effective alternative. In such an approach, terrorist events are constantly reviewed for lessons learned—what worked, what didn't work—to identify best practices, and supporting security technologies are evaluated. The findings are then passed on through reports and industry symposia.

Without compromising sensitive intelligence sources and methods, government agencies attempt to pass the best available information about possible threats, as well as general information about terrorist tactics and targeting, to local jurisdictions and operators. But getting this intelligence to local police and transport operators remains a challenge, one not yet met satisfactorily. The system could work better if local police departments throughout the nation were enlisted in terrorist intelligence collection and given the resources, training, technology, and connectivity to become part of a national network. In a best-practices approach, system operators and local jurisdictions armed with good terrorist intelligence can decide on the investment and procedures that best fit local conditions. There are no universally applied standards. Security for surface transportation becomes goal-oriented rather than rule-based.

Without minimum standards, there will inevitably be different levels of security. However, best practices, when published, have a way of becoming minimum standards. Certainly, no operator wants to operate at less than best practices; if an incident were to occur, the operator would be vulnerable to charges of incompetence or negligence, and could be subject to liability litigation. But best practices remain a menu, not a prescribed diet.

The Division of Responsibilities

A best-practices approach does require coordination among the stakeholders—federal, state, and local, public sector and private sector. The operating entity has direct responsibility for security, for immediate response to threats, for crisis planning, and for restoration of operations. Local authorities (i.e., the police) share responsibility for providing overall security, passing intelligence along, conducting investigations, providing immediate response to threats, and participating in crisis planning.

In a best-practices approach, the federal government does not dictate security measures, but supports ongoing research to conduct case studies that identify the best practices. The federal government funds research and development on new security technologies such as chemical-biological detection systems. It could provide a further valuable service by evaluating new security technologies coming onto the market. In some cases, the federal government could fund the deployment of experimental technology, and it could augment efforts by industry associations and state transportation agencies to disseminate best practices.

In addition to passing threat information to the local police, the federal government sometimes participates in the investigation of terrorist-related crimes. It supports emergency response and, depending on the circumstances, may provide specialized expertise and equipment (for example, in dealing with chemical, biological, or radiological threats).

This role is consistent with the recommendations of the Transportation Research Board panel that was convened in 2002.[6]

The federal government also contributes to the ongoing security costs incurred by state and local governments, although this remains a problem area. The increased security costs incurred since September 11, 2001, have imposed an enormous burden on already strapped local governments. In extraordinary circumstances, the federal government could directly augment security at transportation facilities, as both the British and French did on occasion during terrorist campaigns in their countries. To date, this function has been carried out in the United States by the National Guard.

Conclusions

The terrorist threat to surface transportation is real, and it will increase as terrorists seek ways to kill large numbers of people. However, the threat is difficult to quantify, and it is therefore difficult to determine the right level of security.

Increased security measures implemented since September 11 have made surface transportation safer—somewhat. Operators and local authorities have done the things they could easily do. Much more remains to be done, but significant gains in security will require significant funding. It is not clear where the money will come from. Riders cannot provide significant funds for security without dramatic fare increases, which would affect use. Local and state governments now subsidize public transportation, but many of these governments are in dire financial straits and are looking for ways to cut budgets. The federal government can assist through research and development (R&D) funding, direct subsidies, and tax incentives, but there is fierce competition for finite federal dollars. In the end, Americans may be obliged to accept some risk.

Effective security for surface transportation consists of more than deterrence and prevention, both of which are difficult in any case, given the volume of passengers and the ease of accessibility of surface transportation facilities. Effective security must also include mitigation through design and construction and rapid response, both of which can save lives as well as minimize disruption.

Surface transportation is not a single national system. It is a complex quilt of networks that vary in size, mode, and means of providing security. There is no single solution. Immediately after September 11, government agencies and industry associations were able to provide useful security advice quickly, thanks to the availability of research that was conducted prior to September 11. This research examined terrorist tactics, distilled lessons learned from case studies of earlier terrorist attacks, and identified best security practices.

Indeed, a best-practices approach may be the most effective model for surface transportation security, since it would allow operators and local authorities to decide what works for them. The aviation security model is definitely not applicable to surface transportation. Threat levels differ, the potential consequences of terrorist attacks are different, and the systems themselves differ greatly, as do the means of providing security. There is no national mandate to set and enforce security standards for surface transportation, but given the diversity of the systems, a strict regulatory approach probably would not work anyway.

Crisis management and rapid response are essential ingredients in any security program. Crisis management plans can be improved and tested without a large financial investment, but response remains a problem because of resource constraints at the local level. Further gains in security can also be achieved with the deployment of new technologies. The detection of chemical and biological weapons is a priority area for research.

The federal government should focus on developing an overall strategic approach to transportation security, guiding and supporting research and development, evaluating new technologies, and disseminating information to end users. The creation of a Homeland Security Department reaffirms the constitutional duty of the federal government to "provide for the common defense." Its greatest shortcoming thus far has been the failure to provide adequate resources to local authorities who are on the front line.

The transfer of the Transportation Security Agency from the Department of Transportation to the Department of Homeland Security, while reasonable from the standpoint of consolidating security functions, separates transportation security strategy from broader transportation strategy considerations. It could encourage enforcement strategies while failing to consider other ways to mitigate risks and disruptions, e.g., through design of the transportation system. At the very least, the consolidation poses a new challenge for cooperation. Close cooperation between operators and local or state authorities may be easier to achieve than cooperation with federal authorities. It is easy to sort out the respective roles and responsibilities of the operators, the local and state authorities, and the federal government, but achieving a truly collaborative effort is far more difficult. There is no obvious answer here.

The terrorist threat is dynamic. Research must continue, not only on the development of new technology, but on monitoring trends in terrorism, anticipating novel means of attack, distilling lessons learned from past incidents, and continually updating best practices.

Notes

1. Norman Y. Mineta, ed. *Terrorism in Surface Transportation: A Symposium* (San Jose: Norman Y. Mineta International Institute for Surface Transportation Studies, 1996); Brian Michael Jenkins, et al., *Protecting Surface Transportation: Systems and Patrons from Terrorist Activities: Case Studies of Best Security Practices and a Chronology of Attacks* (San Jose: Norman Y. Mineta International Institute for Surface Transportation Studies, 1997); Brian Michael Jenkins and Larry N. Gersten, *Protecting Public Surface Transportation Against Terrorism and Serious Crime: Continuing Research on Best Security Practices* (San Jose: Norman Y. Mineta International Institute for Surface Transportation Studies, 2001); and Brian Michael Jenkins, *Protecting Public Surface Transportation Against Terrorism and Serious Crime: An Executive Overview* (San Jose: Norman Y. Mineta International Institute for Surface Transportation Studies, 2001).
2. Jenkins and Gersten, *Protecting Public Surface Transportation.*
3. Ibid.
4. General Accounting Office, *Mass Transit: Federal Action Could Help Transit Agencies,* GAO 03–263 (Washington, DC: General Accounting Office, 2002).

5. General Accounting Office, *Transportation Security: Post-September 11th Initiatives and Long-Term Challenges,* GAO 03-616T (Washington, DC: GAO, 2003).

6. Transportation Research Board, *Deterrence, Protection, and Preparation: The New Transportation Security Imperative,* Special Report 270 (Washington, DC: Transportaion Research Board, 2002).

Chapter 9

Border Security:
Closing the Ingenuity Gap

Frank Hoffman

Globalization has many advocates, and no small number of detractors and discontents. For the past decade, most of the world has benefited from expanded markets and free trade in a rapidly growing global economy. Only a small minority has rejected globalization, and even fewer have warned of its darker side. Oddly, Usama bin Ladin was one of globalization's major beneficiaries, although we can safely presume he will not show up at the annual Davos Economic Summit anytime soon.

Bin Ladin perceptively understood that globalization presents a paradox of Gordian proportions. Today's global interconnectivity, with its rising volume and velocity of goods moving between societies, is one side of this paradox, as are the economic interactions, diffusion of technology, and the profusion of ideas and intellectual property that are the core of the global economy. These characteristics have helped many achieve economic prosperity.

But at the same time, globalization's fast-paced interconnectivity, coupled with the spread of advanced technologies, poses a threat to modern societies. Intricate networks, high concentrations of critical infrastructure, and large volumes of unsecured economic activity expose the soft underbelly of advanced states to crippling acts of "ultra-terrorism."[1] Bin Ladin recognized the paradox of the modern global economy, and struck at America's Achilles' heel—its porous borders, transportation networks, and vulnerable economic portals.[2] With extraordinary cunning, bin Ladin used the openness of American society and its own infrastructure as a weapon against itself.

In an insightful book on the nature of modern society, Thomas Homer-Dixon argues that the complexity, unpredictability, and pace of events in our world has accelerated to the point where the capacity of our government and experts to understand, much less control, events is diminishing. In his book, *The Ingenuity Gap*, Homer-Dixon contends that the challenges facing society—ranging from financial crises, global climate change, pandemics, and technological changes—have unleashed a set of dynamics that increase our need for better governance while simultaneously decreasing our ability to govern.[3]

Thus, we face what he called an ingenuity gap, a shortfall between our rapidly rising need for ingenuity and an inadequate supply. To Homer-Dixon, better and more sophisticated institutions and more competent government mechanisms are critical forms of social ingenuity needed to close this gap. There is no greater need for ingenuity, nor a more important "governance gap" to resolve, than the American border security system.

The Scope of the Problem

While the ongoing global war against terrorism is focused on "draining the swamp,"—that is, reducing the sanctuaries overseas within which terrorists hide—our most daunting domestic challenge is posed by the open nature of America's society: borders and transportation networks. Our borders and airports were designed to facilitate travel and trade, not enforce security. The hallmarks of this transportation system are its openness, accessibility, ubiquity, efficiency, diversity, and competitiveness.[4]

Responsibility for overseeing critical aspects of security over the components of global trade was fragmented across nearly a dozen federal departments and agencies. The major agencies, the Customs Service, the Coast Guard, and the Immigration and Naturalization Service, were distributed over three separate departments, often with competing agendas and programs. Their operations were redundant, competitive, and uncooperative. They were not integrated by any common strategy, doctrine or information networks. In fact, all three agencies were barely functional, with severe funding shortfalls for operations and overdue capitalization projects for information technology and platforms. The border agencies were struggling to stay afloat in the riptide created by globalization, but they remained unwanted step-children within large Federal bureaucracies that answer to other priorities. Overwhelmed by globalization, and an ever-increasing volume and speed of trade, U.S. border security mechanisms—until September 2001—manifested a decade of malign neglect.[5]

The nature of the problem does not have to be exaggerated. With some 90,000 miles of coastline, 5,000 miles of intercoastal waterways, and 9,000 miles of land borders, access into America is almost limitless. The 4,500-mile border between the U.S. and Canada was wide open, virtually unguarded. On September 11, the 9,000-plus strong U.S. Border Patrol had only 334 agents along the Canadian border, which is twice as long as the U.S.-Mexican border. The Great Lakes region was, and is, equally exposed. More than 360 ports and major points of entry for international travelers stretch the capacity of the federal government to maintain even an appearance of control. In 2001, half a billion people, 125 million cars, 12 million trucks, and 33 million overseas shipments—including nearly 6 million shipping containers, 800 million planes, 2 million railcars, and over 200,000 ships—went through U.S. borders. Those 6 million maritime containers equate to 21,000 containers a day, or one container passing through a port every 20 seconds.

The economic value of this activity is equally impressive. About 90 percent of America's non-North American trade arrives by sea in containers. Almost 25 percent of the American GDP, some $2.4 trillion worth, is related to international trade.[6] Over $8.8 billion worth of goods are processed daily at U.S. entry points nationwide, of which $1.4 billion is processed at our major ports.

The volume of U.S. international trade, measured in terms of dollars and containers, has doubled since 1990. Depending on how well the global economy recovers, it could double again in the next decade, which would materially contribute to the lives and economic prosperity of this nation. Yet the border agencies do not have the resources to examine more than 2 percent of the cargo that comes into the country. They do not have the data to identify what is coming in; they do not possess the analytical capability to discern what to inspect and what to pass through; they do not have the information systems to rapidly update databases and incorporate intelligence from other agencies; and they do not have the people to conduct meaningful inspections. Finding the terrorist needle in the proverbial haystack was not important in the past. Now we seem to recognize that we have to somehow reduce the number of haystacks or make the needles easier to find.

A recent war game highlights the potential impacts of an attack that targets our maritime trade and existing system of port security. A group of 85 experts from government and industry went through a detailed scenario based on a simulated attack against U.S. ports to see how they reacted, and how a public-private partnership might react to the devastating implications of such an attack on our transportation and supply chain. In the game, a number of containers entered the United States with simulated "dirty bombs," conventional bombs packed with radiological materials or nuclear waste. A few were detected and some were intercepted, but one got through the system and exploded in a Chicago freight yard. The players ended up closing U.S. ports for eight days, causing a tremendous backlog that seriously constipated the entire supply chain. Even when the ports were reopened for full operations, the experts estimated it would take more than two months for port, shipping and manufacturing activity to return to normal. The "ripple" effect of the port closure generated an economic cost of $58 billion to the U.S. economy.[7] In a world in which loose nuclear materials and shoddy security in other countries are a concern, such scenarios are not limited to Hollywood's screenwriters.[8]

Improved Governance

What is the Administration doing in the face of the riptides of globalization? Actually, quite a bit is being done. The most important achievement has been the promulgation of the nation's first *National Strategy for Homeland Security*. The need for this strategy had been identified by several commissions and advisory panels. One panel stressed to Congress that despite wide agreement on the seriousness of the threat in government, they could find "no coherent, functional strategy for combating terrorism."[9] This conclusion was repeatedly echoed by other commissions and studies.[10]

The strategy, issued by the White House on July 16, 2002, is remarkable compared to typical Beltway policy pronouncements. Unlike most strategic documents, the homeland security strategy goes well beyond platitudes and generalities. It does not shy away from identifying ends, and articulates many steps towards those goals. Even more startling, it talks about priorities. However, it is not as comprehensive as it should be, contains few if any measurable program objectives, nor is it a complementary component of the *National Security Strategy*, as we will discuss later. However, it does acknowledge the unique dimensions of the homeland security problem that cut across traditional geographic and institutional boundaries, and how these require national (versus federal) solutions and intensive collaboration with private industries.

On the plus side, the strategy identifies Border and Transportation Security as a critical mission area. It also acknowledges that the United States must:

> . . . rethink and renovate fundamentally its systems for border and transportation security. Indeed, we must now begin to conceive of border security and transportation security as fully integrated requirements, because our domestic transportation systems are inextricably intertwined with the global transport infrastructure.[11]

Supporting this critical mission area are a number of logical initiatives the Bush administration intends to pursue, including:

- Ensuring accountability in border and transportation security
- Creating "smart borders"
- Increasing international shipping container security
- Implementing the Aviation and Transportation Security Act
- Recapitalizing the Coast Guard
- Reforming immigration services

These initiatives represent a new recognition of their importance at the strategic level. But before we can congratulate the Administration, we should explore how these tasks are being executed by the responsible agencies at the operational level. A number of major programs have been initiated to operationalize the strategy.

Container Security Initiative

One of the first steps taken by the U.S. Customs Service to enhance maritime trade and border security has been its Container Security Initiative (CSI). As part of this initiative, launched in January 2004 by Commissioner Robert Bonner, the Customs Service is negotiating agreements with the customs agencies of our major trading partners to establish uniform procedures for screening and inspecting cargo before loading aboard U.S.-bound vessels.[12] As part of these agreements, U.S. customs officials are being "forward deployed" to major overseas shipping ports, and being granted access to shipping manifests and to observe loading procedures. Under certain situations, U.S. officials can intercept and screen suspicious cargos before they are placed into containers. The CSI has been aggressively pursued by Customs, and has met near universal acceptance. Currently, 18 of the world's top 20 seaports—representing nearly 70 percent of all the containers shipped to U.S. seaports—have signed agreements with American customs officials to help secure international trade from terrorism (see Figure 9- 1).

The CSI consists of four key components: (1) using automated information to identify and target high-risk containers; (2) pre-screening those containers identified as high-risk before they arrive at U.S. ports; (3) using detection technology to quickly pre-screen high-risk containers; and (4) using smarter, tamper proof containers. This four-part program is designed to achieve the objective of a vastly more secure maritime commercial environment while still meeting legitimate needs for efficiency and throughput in a global economy.

This is the first step in a series of initiatives designed to sharply enhance security within the various transportation systems that are the foundation of global trade, without inhibiting commerce and without creating an inspection regime at each border.[13] A critical element in the success of this program will be the availability of advance information to perform sophisticated targeting using risk management principles instead of pure chance or an inspector's intuition. To further support this requirement for timely information, Customs published a new rule requiring carriers to file cargo manifests 24 hours before loading containers aboard any ship that is bound for unloading in the United States. This rule is an integral part of the CSI, and became effective at the end of January 2003.

FIGURE 1. Top Ten Trading Ports for Exports and Imports

Top Ten Foreign Ports (Exports to U.S.)	Top Ten U.S. Ports (Imports)
1. Hong Kong	1. New York
2. Shanghai, China	2. Los Angeles
3. Singapore	3. Long Beach
4. Kaohsiung	4. Charleston
5. Rotterdam, Netherlands	5. Seattle
6. Pusan, Republic of Korea	6. Norfolk
7. Bremerhaven, Germany	7. Houston
8. Tokyo, Japan	8. Oakland
9. Genoa, Italy	9. Savannah
10. Yantian, China	10. Miami

Source: U.S. Customs Service

Customs-Trade Partnership Against Terrorism

A corollary with CSI is the Customs-Trade Partnership Against Terrorism (C-TPAT), a public-private endeavor between the Customs Service and the trading industries, to develop and maintain effective security processes throughout the global supply chain. In November 2001, Commissioner Bonner introduced the C-TPAT program at the Customs Trade Symposium, and challenged the trade and shipping community to cooperatively design a new approach to supply chain security in order to simultaneously strengthen our borders, and facilitate the rapid movement of trade. Within a little more than a year, the C-TPAT program had been implemented extensively throughout the trade community, with more than 1,600 carriers, brokers, shippers, and freight forwarders voluntarily participating. The program established clear benefits for participants. Those companies involved in the supply chain that establish practices to enhance their own security get reviewed and validated by Customs.

When C-TPAT is fully implemented, these businesses are given expedited Customs processing at U.S. ports of entry. To date, of the 1,600 companies that have agreed to participate in the program, 300 are certified members and eligible for swifter processing benefits. In a tight competitive market, where time and security are both important variables, C-TPAT is an ingenious way to narrow the governance gap by engaging private sector market dynamics and encouraging security investments.[14]

Automated Commercial Environment (ACE)

Another long overdue step has been the initiation of the information technology architecture that sustains the U.S. government's ability to manage its role in our international trade. The Customs Service cannot fulfill its mission of overseeing the rapid processing of lawful international commerce—while protecting the health and safety of U.S. citizens—without a modern, functional, and interoperable automated data system to process commercial trade information. The Automated Commercial System (ACS), Customs' current system, was designed in 1984, and was unable to meet the greater (and more complex) volume and velocity of modern trade. This requirement is increasingly impacted by the growth in trade, enforcement responsibilities, and legislation.

The Automated Commercial Environment (or ACE) will streamline data entry and exchanges between Customs and the trade community by automating time-consuming and labor-intensive transactions, and by moving goods through the ports, on to markets faster and at lower cost. Simultaneously, it will increase information access and increase time for analysis of data. By providing the right information and support tools, ACE will be a critical element for trade enforcement and in preventing cargo from becoming an instrument of terrorism.

Consequently, Customs has lobbied for several years for a priority IT modernization project, replacing ACS with the ACE, which was projected to cost at least $1.5 billion. However, funding for this critical system was not provided at the necessary level by either the Treasury Department or Congress. Prior to September 11, at planned funding levels, it would have taken at least a decade to finally design, test, and field ACE. Our Customs efforts would remain inefficient and hampered during this entire period. However, funding for ACE has substantially increased, doubling in fiscal year 2003 to $331 million and even higher in the current budget request. While many homeland security IT investments have been put on hold, the ACE has gone forward, and will be substantially fielded by fiscal year 2005.[15]

Operation Safe Commerce (OSC)

Another positive step is the initiation of Operation Safe Commerce, under the auspices of the Department of Transportation (DOT) and U.S. Customs Service. This initiative provides a live experimental test-bed for a series of new techniques to increase the security of container shipments. DOT and Customs are using this experiment to identify existing vulnerabilities in the supply chain, and to test improved techniques for enhancing security for goods either entering or leaving the United States. Congress, in the 2002 Supplemental Appropriations Act, provided $28 million for OSC to improve the security of container shipments through pilot projects involving the United States' three largest container ports of entry (Los Angeles/Long Beach, New York/New Jersey, and Seattle/Tacoma).

OSC is designed to provide a "virtual laboratory" to test the utility and efficacy of a number of security products, including electronic seals for containers, sensors, and tracking systems. Such technologies will help validate security at points of origin, increase security as cargo moves through the supply chain, and vastly increase our ability to monitor containers in transit. Upon validation and further consultation with the private sector, the successful and cost effective security methods under the program could then be recommended for implementation system-wide.[16]

This experimentation/pilot program will go a long way toward assuring the various trade groups and associated industries that these security initiatives will measurably improve security, while at the same time not impose unreasonable costs and delays to trade. There may be additional security costs for the private sector to absorb, but these could be offset by reduced theft and liability losses, as well as lower insurance costs.

Maritime Transportation Security Act

The executive branch has not been acting entirely on its own, as Congress has historically maintained a close interest in trade matters. This interest is seen in the final version of the Maritime Transportation Security Act of 2002. This bill eventually passed both houses, but only after a bruising conference committee and extensive lobbying over implementation costs. The act was signed into law by President Bush on November 25, 2002. The major provisions of this act are summarized in Figure 9-2.

U.S. Coast Guard

One of the more important steps forward has been the increased awareness of the need to recapitalize the Coast Guard. A highly disciplined force with multiple missions, it performs maritime search and rescue tasks, manages vessel traffic, enforces U.S. environmental and fishery laws, and interdicts and searches vessels suspected of carrying illegal aliens, drugs, and other contraband. In a time of war, the Coast Guard also works with the Navy to protect U.S. ports from attack, and supports the military overseas.

FIGURE 9-2. Major Provisions of The Maritime Transportation Security Act of 2002

Domestic Facility and Vessel Vulnerability Assessments. Tasks the Coast Guard with conducting an initial assessment of vessel types and United States facilities to identify high risks. These assessments include critical assets and infrastructures, identification of the threats, and weaknesses in physical security, passenger and cargo security, communications systems, transportation infrastructure, and contingency response.

Maritime Transportation Security Plans. Requires a National Maritime Transportation Security Plan for deterring and responding to transportation security incidents. These plans "shall provide for efficient, coordinated, and effective action to deter and minimize damage from a transportation security incident."

Vessel and Facility Security Plans. Requires an owner or operator of a vessel or facility to prepare and submit a security plan for the vessel or facility, for deterring a transportation security incident. Such plans are to include provisions for

1. Establishing and controlling access to secure areas of the vessel or facility;
2. Procedural security policies;
3. Communications systems; and
4. Training and periodic unannounced drills.

Transportation Security Cards. These cards help enforce new access regulations to prevent individuals from entering areas of a vessel or facility designated as a secure area.

Security Grants. Establishes a grant program for port authorities, and State and local agencies that contribute to implementing Area Maritime Transportation Security Plans and facility security plans. Included are costs for acquisition, operation, and maintenance of security equipment, security gates and fencing, marine barriers for security zones, lighting systems, remote surveillance, video systems, security vessels, and other infrastructure.

Foreign port assessment. Directs the government to assess the effectiveness of the antiterrorism measures at foreign ports from which foreign vessels depart on a voyage to the United States; as well as any foreign port believed to pose a security risk to maritime commerce.

Container Security. Requires the DHS to maintain a cargo tracking, identification and screening system for shipping containers shipped to and from the United States. Requires the establishment of standards to enhance the physical security of shipping containers, including seals and locks. Contains other important security enhancements for crew identification, Sea marshals, and vessel transponders to track vessels in U.S. waters.

The Coast Guard has an increasingly important role to play in homeland security, but its ships and aircraft are aging and technologically obsolete. As a result, they have excessive operating and maintenance costs, and lack essential capabilities in speed, sensors, and interoperability. The Coast Guard cutter fleet is older than 39 of the world's 41 major naval fleets. Under-appreciated for far too long, the Coast Guard must be equipped and trained so that it can perform its key homeland defense role with confidence and greater capability.

The Coast Guard is willing, but its hardware is outmoded and updating is absolutely necessary. The Administration belatedly recognized this, increasing funds for the Coast Guard's primary modernization program, known as Deepwater. This $17 billion program will materially enhance the Coast Guard's ability to secure U.S. trade and ports, conduct navigation and public safety missions, and enforce U.S. laws.[17]

The Deepwater Program passed a significant milestone in June 2002, when the Coast Guard Commandant, Admiral Thomas H. Collins, announced the contract award of the largest acquisition program in the history of the Coast Guard to Integrated Coast Guard Systems (ICGS), a joint venture created by Lockheed Martin and Northrop Grumman. When fully implemented, the interoperable ICGS system will be comprised of three modern classes of cutters, a new fixed-wing aircraft fleet, a refurbished helicopter fleet, and new manned helicopters and unmanned air vehicles. These highly capable assets are linked with a new suite of Command, Control, Communications and Computers, Intelligence, and Surveillance and Reconnaissance (C4ISR) systems to extend the Coast Guard's capacity to detect and identify all activity in the maritime arena. This capability, known as "maritime domain awareness," is needed to intercept and engage those activities that pose a direct threat to U.S. sovereignty and security.[18]

The Coast Guard's most critical missions—countering terrorist threats, rescuing mariners in distress, catching drug smugglers, stopping illegal migrants, and protecting the marine environment—demand forces able to operate effectively across a broad geographic spectrum, from inter-waterways, rivers, ports, and coastal regions, out to the U.S. Exclusive Economic Zone. The Deepwater program supports the first line of a layered defense against threats to America's homeland.[19]

Visitor/Immigration Processing

To improve security and screening of travelers, DHS has implemented the U.S. Visitor and Immigrant Status Indicator Technology (VISIT) program, by which visitors have their photographs and fingerprints taken to confirm their identity and validate their entry into, and exit from, the United States. Already more than two million visitors have been documented. VISIT is in place in 130 airports and seaports, with plans to expand it further. Yet few resources are in place to go after those who do not leave, and instead join the estimated eight million illegal aliens loose inside the United States. The program also has a gaping hole, since visitors from 27 allied countries are exempt from participation. Many prospective terrorists have traveled to the United States via these countries.

Another new tool is the Computer Assisted Passenger Pre-Screening System or CAPPS II. This system uses routine passenger information and matches it against government databases to prescreen flight lists and identify "high risk" travelers. The Transportation Security Administration plans to collect this data from airlines to score passengers, and assign a color code to passenger boarding passes. High-risk passengers with high threat indicators could be barred from flying, or subjected to intensive searches. DHS has not yet satisfied its critics that this program is cost effective, or that privacy and due process concerns are being addressed.

Assessment

By any standard, the nation is more secure today than it has been in the past. President Bush and Secretary Ridge deserve much of the credit for this, and many others in all branches of government deserve applause. Yet, while we are safer, we are not as safe as we need to be. With respect to border security there is much more to be done before we can claim that we've done everything that needs to be done to provide for the common defense and preserve our way of life. There are deficiencies at the strategic planning level, and in the allocation of resources, which remain to be resolved. There are also issues with respect to program implementation, technology requirements, and organizational structure. These five areas form the framework for the subsequent assessment, which will be graded using the Homeland Security Threat Advisory color code system.

Strategy: High (Orange)

There are many definitions of strategy, but the best formulation defines it as "the process by which ends are related to means, intentions to capabilities, [and] objectives to resources."[20] If you accept that definition, then President Bush's *National Security Strategy* is probably not the new gold standard for strategic statements.[21] It provides no guidance to the subordinate *National Strategy for Homeland Security*, and it completely fails at drawing priorities or linking objectives between foreign policy, international trade, defense, and domestic security.

In many respects, the *National Security Strategy* appears to have been written before September 11, as if the National Security Council was in a time bottle. Aside from incorporating preemption and anticipatory action as a necessary arrow in our strategic quiver, it neglects the realities of the highly interconnected world we live in.[22] It makes only one reference to homeland security, and that comes across as a backhanded aside.[23] Homeland security should be a core element of an overarching national security strategy. If one believes that government's first duty is to provide for the common defense, as the President has claimed, then one would expect to find that the security of the American homeland is *the* primary national security mission of the U.S. government. You should be able to discern this from both the strategy and the agenda of the national security staff supporting the Chief Executive.[24]

Rather than integrate and prioritize our foreign policy, economic programs, and military strategy, and link them together with our agenda for securing the homeland, the Bush Administration's first crack at a national security strategy pigeonholes homeland security as a peripheral function in a separate strategy document, with little connection to either the grand strategy, or major crisis management processes of the National Security Council, the President's primary vehicle for integrating foreign policy, economic, and domestic security issues. Such a peripheral status is not warranted given the key objectives and interest of the United States.

The *National Security Strategy* identifies, *inter alia*, four major action steps:

1. Strengthen alliances to defeat global terrorism and work to prevent attacks against us;
2. Prevent our enemies from threatening us with weapons of mass destruction;
3. Ignite a new era of global growth through free markets and free trade; and
4. Transform America's national security institutions to meet the challenges and opportunities of the twenty-first century.[25]

Despite these clear objectives, the *National Security Strategy* does not acknowledge that "to defeat global terrorism" and to work on preventing attacks mandates a strong border security regime. "Preventing our enemies from threatening us with weapons of mass destruction" has many components, including advanced detection systems to preclude such a weapon being placed into a shipping container and delivered by our own economic lifeline. Igniting "a new era of global growth" is certainly a worthy strategic initiative, but so is recognizing that our economic system is frightfully exposed to corruption from criminals, smugglers, drug dealers, and—potentially—terrorists with weapons of mass destruction. The strategy does not suggest that transforming our national security institutions includes the Department of Homeland Security or other contributors. It only explicitly mentions the intelligence community and the military services, suggesting that other institutions are not part of the national security architecture.[26] This is a strategic oversight. If 9/11 proved anything, it's that we need to transform far more than just the Defense Department.[27]

While it does not appear to be a complementary supporting strategy, the homeland security strategy itself is a much better document that comes a lot closer to Gaddis' definition of a good strategy. While the strategy tries to link ends to means, and articulates many intentions and initiatives, it *does not* do a good job of defining objectives, nor does it provide any empirical measures or metrics to grade progress or success. We are once again falling into the trap of defining strategic aims in terms of inputs (like funding levels and numbers of personnel), instead of discrete objectives and measures of performance.[28]

The *National Strategy for Homeland Security* does define major objectives, lists initiatives, and even details budget priorities. It breaks down the homeland security functions of the country, and includes border and transportation security mechanisms as a critical mission area. However, funding priorities are not clearly aligned with the strategy at all. The strategy argues for protecting Americans and preventing attacks, but the funding priorities lean towards consequence management and post-attack responses. Thus, the strategy's emphasis for prevention and protection are not being followed. The implications of these misplaced priorities on resources will be shown in the next section.

Adding to strategic confusion has been the plethora of glossy strategic documents that have been issued. President Bush's *National Security Strategy* appears to provide no guidance to the subordinate *National Strategy for Combating Terrorism* or the *National Strategy for Homeland Security*. In fact, it is not clear that any of these documents have been integrated or tied to contributing activities including foreign policy, intelligence, international trade, threat reduction, or nonproliferation programs.

In effect, homeland security has been downgraded to a supporting role in an overall counter-terrorism strategy that seeks first the *defeat* of terrorists and their organizations, to *deny* them sponsorship or sanctuary, then to *diminish* the causes or conditions that they exploit, and only last, to *defend* U.S. citizens. This "4 D" strategy is based on a doubtful American sports adage that "the best defense is a good offense." As President Bush stated in a speech "We must take the battle to the enemy, disrupt his plans, and confront the worst threats before they emerge." Such an approach fits America's strategic culture and the belief that only the offensive approach can produce decisive results. While the strategy may fit the American culture, it is not necessarily a winning strategy. As any student of American football knows, a good defense wins Super Bowls.

Until clear linkages between grand strategy and homeland security are established, until funding priorities are reestablished for each element of the strategy, with measurable metrics for assessing progress, this report card must assess a "High Threat" to strategic planning.

Resources: Severe Threat (Red)

The strategy's misplaced priorities, and its bifurcation between traditional national security institutions and the need to dramatically transform other governmental agencies, leads to the next shortfall—insufficient resources. In the immediate aftermath of 9/11, substantial amounts of money were allocated to help victims and their communities recover. Additional funds were employed to help out industries—like the aviation industry—which were adversely impacted. Substantial resources were needed to get the Transportation Security Administration off the ground. Many security experts assumed that after September 11, the clear vulnerabilities of the U.S. domestic security system would receive a substantial cash infusion, at least equal to increases for more traditional security needs like the military.[29] This has not occurred, however, and resources have not been forthcoming to the rest of the homeland security team.

Spending on domestic security *has* appreciably increased since 9/11. Total government spending on homeland security, including supplemental budgets for domestic security, totaled over $33 billion in fiscal year 2002. The Administration's first post-attack budget requested a 25 percent increase in federal spending, a total of $41 billion for fiscal year 2003.[30] The President's fiscal year 2004 budget proposal, though, requested a 1 percent increase, raising resources for total homeland security and domestic counter-terrorism to $41.3 billion,[31] and his proposed fiscal year 2005 budget of $47.4 billion for homeland security represents a nearly 15 percent increase in annual homeland security spending—all within a political climate where every other non-Defense portion of the discretionary federal budget has remained constant or seen considerable decrease. However, before the budget was even released, many analysts and members of Congress claimed that the President was shortchanging domestic security.[32]

There are numerous claimants for additional resources, and in the absence of a clear vulnerability assessment—as well as a national intelligence estimate—it is difficult to determine who should be given these resources. Arguably, border and maritime security mechanisms should have first priority on the nation's treasure, since they promote prevention and our economic strength and prosperity. However, the *National Strategy for Homeland Security* lists securing America's borders as a priority of equal importance as "support for first responders" and bioterrorism defense.[33] America's priorities should seek to protect its way of life and its economic strength by *preventing* attacks, rather than building up its capacity to *respond* to the consequences of an attack *after* it occurs. Consequence management and mitigation should be part of our strategy, but do little to prevent incidents of mass effect and disruption or protect the American people. Furthermore, the enormous public-private assets in the nation's public safety, public health, emergency care, and disaster relief agencies are already substantial, nearly twice as much as the entire federal homeland security budget.[34] They are not properly orchestrated for the challenges of the twenty-first century, but the existing capabilities are significant.

The same cannot be said for the nation's border security assets. While three of the eight priorities listed in the *National Strategy for Homeland Security* deal with border security, budget spending on this area of security remains insufficient. The President's commitments to first responders and to preparing for acts of bioterrorism are clearly evident in the changes in budgets between fiscal year 2002 and fiscal year 2003. As displayed in Figure 9-3, funding for first responders were almost tripled, while investments in public health infrastructure and research for biological defenses remained on the rise. This funding level is preserved for fiscal year 2004.

However, like the rest of the homeland security budget, border security funding remains flat despite higher operational tempos, increased mission requirements, and neglected modernization needs. As shown in Figure 9-3, the budget for Customs and border protection rises slightly, by $180 million, and immigration and customs enforcement tasks also receive an additional $110 million for fiscal year 2005. The Coast Guard will receive a healthy 10 percent increase. In absolute terms, the increases sound impressive. But in real terms, they reflect decreases in operating funds. After considering inflation, personnel pay raises, and higher costs, total real program growth for border and transportation security is actually negative. This does not begin to account for new legislative requirements, support from the Coast Guard to ongoing military operations in the Persian Gulf

FIGURE 9-3. Selected Homeland Security Budget Elements

	FY02 Appn	FY02 Supplement	FY03 Budget Request	FY04 Budget Request
First Responders	291	1,000	3,500	3,500
Bioterror	1,408	4,730	5,898	6,000
Border Security				
Customs and Border Protection	4,063	870	5,466	5,649
Immigration and Customs Enforcement	2,127	179	2,375	2,488
U.S. Coast Guard	4,129	464	6,174	6,789
Technology	90	77	561	803
Aviation Security	1,543	5,335	5,338	4,812

Source: Securing the Homeland and Strengthening the Nation, Washington, White House, Feb., 2002, and DHS budget at www.whitehouse.gov/omb/fy2004/homeland.html.

area of operations, or the taxing of the various agencies to establish the new Department of Homeland Security and its regional structure and offices.

The fiscal year 2004 budget proposal is quite simply too small. Thus, many potential investments in maritime, container inspection, and port security are unfunded or underfunded. Presidential commissions and industry experts have agreed that securing the country's major ports could cost from $10 to $50 million each, for a total of $2.2 billion.[35] Congress has put up just over $300 million to date, which will only cover assessments and planning efforts, and few security enhancements. Likewise, other security mandates in the Maritime and Transportation Security Act are largely unfunded since there was no agreement in Congress on the division of responsibility among myriad users and beneficiaries. Discussed elsewhere in this chapter are significant IT system upgrades and new data fusion techniques that are desperately needed.

The Administration weakened its own case in February 2004 when it rolled out the fiscal year 2005 budget for the Department of Homeland Security and trumpeted it as a 10 percent increase. Mr. Ridge defended the $40.2 billion budget before the U.S. Senate as demonstration of the President's commitment, but lost a great deal of credibility when the 10 percent raise was shown to be an accounting gimmick that included increased user fees and taxes, and incorporated the multi-year $2.5 billion BioShield Program as a single year's appropriation. Secretary Ridge admitted that discretionary spending for his fledgling department was less than 4 percent, which would barely cover inflation and expected pay raises for his 180,000 employees. However, overall spending for Homeland Security—including Defense Department and intelligence spending—did represent an overall 1.7 percent increase.[36]

The biggest losers in the strategy/budget mismatch seem to be the principal border security agencies, Customs and the Coast Guard. Both have been recognized by outside studies as candidates for substantial retooling and recapitalization.[37] Both are identified in the President's strategy, but apparently there are those in OMB with a different sense of the strategic priorities.[38] If future budgets do not address these concerns, a severe readiness crunch will impact these agencies, and substantially widen our vulnerabilities to further attack. The Coast Guard's Deepwater Program is designed to ensure that the nation can capably defend against maritime threats far out to sea, well before they can reach U.S. territory. To preserve our ability to enforce laws, protect our citizens in the maritime environment, and prepare for more challenging homeland security threats, the Coast Guard's modernization account must be increased above the fiscal year 2003 and fiscal year 2004 budget ($500 million).

Accelerating the Deepwater Program also appears to be an efficient expenditure of the taxpayer's dollar, even in fiscally constrained times. Instead of stretching out this program over 20 years, compressing it to a 15-year program will reduce costs over the long haul. At least $800 million a year in constant dollars is needed to make this happen. Furthermore, rather than continuing to see the Coast Guard's performance erode, and our public safety and security suffer, a modest end strength increase and higher operating cost baseline are warranted. The cost efficiencies and increased operational capability for accelerating the Coast Guard's principal modernization program have been subsequently validated by the RAND Corporation in a major analytical effort.[39]

The Customs Service has similar claims to meet higher operating costs and badly needed modernized equipment for processing shipping containers quickly and detecting contraband materials, including explosives or nuclear material. With sufficient funding, America's ability to safeguard homeland and maritime security will be secured for generations to come. But it cannot be achieved on the cheap. We have increased annual security spending at least $150 billion since fiscal year 2001, and the traditional claimants in DOD and the intelligence community have garnered almost 85 percent of that funding.[40] The Pentagon, with the military engaged in many dark spots around the world, has a justifiable claim on resources. There is no reason that the country cannot afford to spend 4 percent of its GDP on defense. This is especially needed since we deferred investments in the 1990s that have delayed a much needed modernization of a worn-out force.

We have been skirting with a train wreck for quite some time.[41] But it is not consistent with the *National Security Strategy* to hold the top line on other national security institutions at a mere fraction of defense. We risk a greater train wreck, or more appropriately, another ship wreck or aviation disaster, if we continue to hold back homeland security spending to current levels (less than 0.4 percent of GDP). Given the sorts of unconventional threats we face in the twenty-first century, is it difficult to conclude that a ten-to-one ratio between traditional military spending and homeland security is the right mix. A 10 percent increase in homeland security funding, largely devoted to border security modernization, is necessary to correct a decade of neglect. Because of the resource shortfall relative to where we need to be, this remains a most severe threat to homeland security.

Technology: Elevated Threat (Yellow)

Another area to assess is our use of technology. President Bush observed, "in the war against terrorism, America's vast science and technology base provides us with a key advantage."[42] The *National Strategy for Homeland Security* is predicated on an ability to leverage technology to enhance security. Our current position in world affairs is built upon the creativity, imagination and ingenuity of our people. Our strategic culture and our way of life are profoundly influenced by our ability to solve problems and significantly increase productivity by the application of advanced technology. Our economy, our prosperity, and our significant edge in military operations are all based on a foundation of technology.

However, we have only just begun to think about how we can apply our decisive edge in technology development to the new security challenges posed by catastrophic terrorism and asymmetric warfare. As noted by a very distinguished group of Americans in a report sponsored by the Markle Foundation:

> America has become a potential battlefield for major assaults. Yet, though our military has deeply integrated intelligence and information technology into war fighting, we have not developed a similarly sophisticated use of information and information technology to protect Americans from attacks at home.[43]

There are many potential applications for advanced technology to close our "ingenuity gap." We have rudimentary capabilities fielded in many domains of homeland security already, and scores of proposed initiatives to develop an array of new devices, systems, and sensors. These proposals include biometric devices to improve personal identification and reduce visa fraud, explosive, chemical, and nuclear material sensors for detecting bombs and weapons of mass destruction, unmanned aerial vehicles for improving border security and area surveillance, electronic locks and seals for enhancing container and cargo security, and tracking systems to monitor cargo and increase asset visibility. There is no shortage of useful ideas being generated on how to fix specific challenges,[44] but technology is not a panacea. As we have painfully learned in our military operations over the past few decades, technology is only as good as the strategy it is supporting, the design of the processes it facilitates, and the people who employ it.[45]

The most important and the most difficult challenge, though, will be in the development of a strategy, and the design of information systems that will be the central nervous system of our homeland security operations. The strategy that has been promulgated, the department's design, and the programs put in place so far are all predicated upon our ability to amass, process, distribute, and analyze vast amounts of bits and bytes. Visa applications, watch lists, passenger profiles, ticket purchases, cargo manifests, shipping documents, bills of lading, and freight bills are all being absorbed in various forms. In the past, much of this was done haphazardly, manually, by stove-piped organizations. In today's global economy, no business would be successful with such a slow, nonintegrated, inefficient, and manpower-intensive approach. Nor will our new security imperatives be met by the same bureaucratic approach. We will need to significantly increase the government's ability to apply advanced information technology (IT) solutions to this problem.

As noted by the National Academy of Sciences:

> All phases of counter-terrorism efforts require that large amounts of information from many sources be acquired, integrated, and interpreted. Given the range of data sources and data types, the volume of information each source provides, and the difficulty of analyzing partial information from single sources, the timely and insightful use of these inputs is very difficult.[46]

Thus, a major focus on preventing future incidents of terrorism is going to be based on techniques that facilitate data integration, fusion, and mining. The various components that now comprise the border and transportation security directorate at DHS all have crucial IT programs that require review and resources. INS has been tasked once again to create an automated Entry-Exit system, and the administration requested $362 million in fiscal year 2003, and nearly $480 million in fiscal year 2004, to ramp up this element of our immigration/visa monitoring program. INS faces many other IT shortfalls if it is to upgrade antiquated and costly information processing functions. TSA has equally daunting challenges, starting with creating its own management and information architecture from scratch. Much attention has been placed on its explosive detection and screening machines, which will continue to require investment as we expand to the cargo side of the industry. Customs received $313 million in the fiscal year 2003 budget for its ACE program. The Coast Guard has equally daunting shortfalls, and must increase its interoperability with both its new partners in DHS as well as its wartime teammates in the Navy. Many (if not all) of these systems require integration with the DHS as a whole, and also require significant information sharing and interface with other Federal Departments (State, DOE, EPA, DOD, Justice, HHS, etc.) and nongovernmental sources, such as maritime industry components, and municipal and local port authorities.

The scale and complexity of the IT challenge looms large, although the opportunity is widely recognized.[47] The DHS has a crucial management hurdle before it as it goes through the throes of integrating the people, cultures, practices, and tasks of 22 odd agencies and nearly 170,000 employees. The Administration proposed an overall IT budget of $1.7 billion for DHS, but only a total of $200 million to fund the information integration challenge. This is out of an IT budget of roughly $4.2 billion of the nearly $38 billion allocated for homeland security. Congress has not been very supportive of this critical integration element in the budget.[48]

This poses a major challenge to Secretary Ridge and the new Department of Homeland Security, one that they are very much aware of. With few exceptions, the U.S. government has not been very adept at acquiring and managing large, integrated, information systems that share massive databases across multiple owners and actors. Our government's arcane acquisition processes, shortage of human capital, and inconsistent support for critical infrastructure improvements, have hampered the federal government's ability to match the private sector's success in IT.[49]

The Administration has a very solid team of CIOs looking at this problem, but will need continued support from OMB and the Congress to bring about a remarkably difficult but essential system and data integration challenge.[50] The fusion of information is the linchpin in the entire approach to deterring, preventing, or intercepting attacks through our transportation networks. Without the ability to cross-check information between agencies and offices, the intelligence processing and analytical function inherent to all of the border security programs will remain limited. It will ultimately be a fool's errand to have created the various muscle groups of the Department if they cannot be integrated by a central nervous system to thwart the complex, adaptive enemies we now face.[51]

The Markle Foundation Task Force was correct. We have not yet brought the same degree of sophisticated IT applications to mitigate the threat to our homeland that we have to our military operations overseas. We can no longer just excel at military "away games" however. Our approach to homeland security requires what is known in the Pentagon as Network Centric Warfare, which is predicated upon our capacity to share data from a variety of sources—including sensors, reconnaissance personnel, and imagery—and use it to conduct precise, decisive, and decentralized operations faster and with more agility than our adversaries.[52] Until it creates its own network, DHS will not be able to conduct Network Centric Warfare or the defensive "home game" it has been created to fulfill. Until DHS achieves a higher degree of network integration, the threat remains "elevated" in this area.

Structure: Low Threat (Green)

The one area where the Bush Administration deserves great credit is in tackling the domestic security organizational chaos that evolved in this country over a long time. Strategy is far more than merely identifying ends or allocating funding; it also includes an organizational dimension.[53] Policy aims and resources are requisites, but so are the structural means for implementation. Policy without resources is a common delusion in Washington, but policy without an effective framework for execution is an all too frequent failure of government. Several formal assessments—by special commissions, industry experts, and by the Bush Administration—have found the pre-existing HLS organizational framework too disjointed and incoherent to execute the new strategy and supporting programs.[54]

The Administration deserves great credit for moving past standard governmental responses such as rhetorical policy pronouncements, increased staff oversight, interagency meetings, more commissions and studies, and the like. The president's team eventually grasped the need for substantive change, and undertook the difficult burden of dealing with bureaucratic habit and encrusted fiefdoms, for which it gets a well-deserved "A+" for both strategic vision and courage.

The establishment of a homeland security department, with the bulk of the border management agencies embedded within it, is a critical first step to enhancing border security. Some highly regarded defense experts thought that such a bold initiative was unnecessary or premature.[55] Others thought that the entire debate over the new department was a distraction or a dangerous exercise in over-centralization.[56] The Administration could have consigned proposals like the Hart-Rudman Commission to "the dust bin of Commission libraries" as some terrorism advisors prematurely concluded.[57]

Quite the contrary, the new organizational structure is both vital and timely. Rather than a distraction that took our attention away from other imperatives, the debate over the Department generated a necessary awareness of the problem and a consensus on the necessary institutional architecture we needed to ensure our security in the twenty-first century. Absent such a debate, the United States would still be throwing money into a variety of stovepipes, and we would certainly never achieve the degree of seamless processes, information sharing, and efficiency that the new Department potentially offers. Historically, such major undertakings are poisoned by bureaucratic politics and infighting, like the origins of the pieces encapsulated in the 1947 National Security Act. This can produce national security institutions that are flawed by design, and hobbled at birth.[58] The debate over the DHS was healthy, informative, and constructive. Quite frankly, as one national expert quipped, anyone who contends that we could meet the imperatives of the homeland security strategy without a major realignment of the principal agencies is engaged in "an exercise in wishful thinking."[59] As one panel noted, the government's capacity to deal with terrorism has been "fragmented, uncoordinated, and politically unaccountable."[60] As the 9/11 Commission highlighted, the degree of fragmentation and poor coordination is not limited to just border security.[61]

Bringing the border agencies together under one department roof knits their individual capabilities into a stronger, sophisticated surveillance system, and creates synergistic effects not possible under the existing design. Given that most of the global transportation system is based on common intermodal links and containers between air, truck, and shipping lines, it makes little sense to have three separate stovepipes. It makes even less sense when these agencies do not have interoperable databases and communications networks. This bold structure adjustment responds to calls from industry experts to overhaul the existing organizational maze which was unclear, uncooperative and inadequate to execute a unified strategy.[62] Aside from making the system more transparent to users, and more accountable, it precludes potential adversaries from exploiting the archaic "seams" and gaps within today's domestic security apparatus.

The challenge before Secretary Ridge is to extend the inherent logic of the Departmental structure beyond the Beltway and achieve an effective and efficient regional structure that harnesses the potential synergies of the consolidated Department. Ultimately, we should begin to see greatly enhanced tactical capabilities at our borders and entry portals, and far greater efficiencies.

However, the scale of this undertaking poses potential concerns, and policy experts who warn that the new Department's design may be unduly complex have a point.[63] The scale of DHS is principally a function of its border security functions. Bringing about increased integration to these previously separate entities is not an easy task. Anyone familiar with the history of the Department of Defense (DOD) and its long road toward increased Jointness knows how difficult this portion of DHS's challenge will be. Thus, the structural dimension of the border security merits continued review and inclusion in our "threat advisory," but only as a "low level" threat.

Border Security Programs: Guarded (Blue)

The major programs that have been initiated to date—the Container Security Initiative, Port Security assessments, the Customs-Trade Partnership Against Terrorism, and Operation Safe Commerce—appear to be well-designed and consistent with the functional imperatives of homeland security. We cannot construct a Maginot Line or Fortress America. This would be a self-defeating strategy that would only accomplish bin Ladin's agenda by weakening us and changing who we are. Defending physical borders is extraordinarily difficult, if not impossible, and only piles up everything at a customs point—a crippling event in a finely tuned and highly integrated economic system like ours. These economic links and transportation networks have been refined to support a "just-in-time" manufacturing system that is extremely efficient, but intricately connected. It is just as fragile if interrupted.

The only way to eventually resolve the dilemma of simultaneously enhancing security while facilitating a high volume of trade flow is to reengineer the system from end-to-end, with security built into the entire network, not just at national borders. Increased security and accountability of assets and people throughout the entire network is key to achieving this end-to-end security system.

Contrary to reports, we do not face a Hobbesian choice between keeping the commercial lifeblood of our economy flowing or preventing bloodshed of innocent Americans by terrorism. This is a false choice. Solutions for the paradoxes of globalization must bridge our need for security and trade at the same time. Tightening up on security and freedom of movement at the expense of our economic success weakens us in the long run. Looking the other way, ignoring the security risks posed by globalization is equally dangerous since it leaves U.S. citizens and their way of life dangerously exposed to another attack by ultra-terrorism.

Instead of attempting to reinforce a Maginot Line, the United States should be (and is) encouraging its partners—our trading partners and industry, via tools such as tax credits and "fast pass" benefits—to a) enhance security at overseas loading docks, ports and warehouses; b) conduct background checks on shipping personnel and crews; and c) establish automated information systems and databases to identify and track shipping throughout the entire transit pipeline.

This combination of initiatives offers a layered approach for in-depth defense. It pushes out our borders and helps up identify threats far from our own cities. This is not about securing our perimeter, nor is it a "nation-centric" viewpoint.[64] In fact, it's just the opposite. The approach taken to date is an international and a systems (or network) perspective. Instead of focusing merely on borders, an outdated concept, our government is working with its trading partners and the private sector to establish "systems of security" throughout the major transportation systems.

While it is not possible to search every container, truck, package, and person entering the United States, a more closely coordinated team effort by all the federal agencies involved—supported by sufficient resources and advanced technology—could overcome these obstacles and give law enforcement a better shot at early warning and identification. Instead of merely guessing about which haystack to examine based on pure chance, improving our ability to identify which dozen of the thousands of haystacks entering the country might contain a needle is the way forward. In the long run, we may not increase the number of containers searched—roughly 2 percent of the 21,000 containers that enter the country every day. However, we will end up ensuring that we inspect the right 2 percent, which may make all the difference in deterring attacks or detecting threats.

In this area of the assessment, the Administration gets high marks for program design, for the way they have phased programs in, and for the urgency in which the various agreements have been negotiated. The experiments embedded in Operation Safe Commerce can also be applauded. Many shippers and carriers are concerned about the relative effectiveness and costs of the required enhanced security measures, and OSC provides a test for various technologies and begins the process of shared learning by which both the public and private sector adapt to better secure our trade.[65] The new directorate for border and transportation security must maintain these programs and follow through. Overall, border security programs receive a guarded grade until greater buy-in is achieved with the private sector, and until these programs are funded adequately. If we are going to achieve any significant progress in border and transportation security, we must begin to shape the market dynamics by offering both carrots and sticks in order to incorporate security as an element throughout the entire transportation network.

The Administration has not provided enough money to help port authorities meet the mandate from the Maritime and Transportation Security Act to assess vulnerabilities in ports and vessels, and address the gaps. The Coast Guard estimated the first year of the plan alone will cost $1.25 billion ($7 billion over ten years), yet the Administration proposed no funding for port security and Congress added only $125 million to the 2004 budget. At the current rate, the United States will finish assessing weaknesses in port and maritime security by the end of the decade, without materially investing in additional real security capability.

We have to move from "malign neglect" to fundamentally reforming our border management practices to be able to "filter out the good from the bad."[66] In all of this, our goal is to remain an open, economically dynamic, and globally engaged society. The alternative is to become "a nation trapped behind the modern versions of moats and castles."[67]

Conclusion

Speaking at the U.S. Military Academy in June 2002, President Bush appropriately declared that, "the gravest danger to freedom lies at the crossroads of radicalism and technology."[68] What he did not say is that this grave danger to our freedom will most likely occur at the crossroads of our economic lifelines, at our borders and the vulnerable transportation networks that intersect them.

If we are going to close the ingenuity gap, we have to overcome both old habits and the sense of complacency that will ultimately return as the vivid pictures of 9/11 fade from our collective memory. We have nothing to be complacent about—the threat is persistent and undiminished.[69] America's connectedness to world events and a global economy militate against turning inward. We cannot dismiss the world's problems as something that occurs "over there," when the end result shows up right on our doorstep, or more accurately, right in our mailboxes and office buildings. In many respects, September 11 was a direct attack on global interconnectivity and ushered in a new way of warfare.

We need to face up to the realities of this type of warfare. Our economy and way of life benefit from—and are ultimately dependent upon—an open and safe border system and secure and efficient transportation networks. The positive aspects of globalization provide us with economic prosperity and freedom. The dark side, however, exposes us to harm. To resolve this paradox, we must undertake a necessary "strategic adjustment," including difficult institutional reforms, to preserve the well being of our citizenry, our economic lifeblood, and our fundamental security interests.[70] The preceding assessment suggests we have a way to go. Progress has been made, but we must continue making progress, and do so with a greater sense of urgency, as reflected by a Council on Foreign Relations' task force report, appropriately titled, *America: Still Unprepared—Still In Danger.*[71]

We will remain in danger until we come to grips with our ingenuity gap. If we do not close this gap, another catastrophic event could seriously impact the lives of many Americans, derail a fragile economy, or disrupt our way of life in a truly profound way. It is important to remember that terrorists seek to undermine the public's trust in its government. Correspondingly, our public has an expectation that their government will protect them. The structure we had to deal with this problem in the past was unsuited for today's imperatives or tomorrow's challenges. The task before us is to determine how to wisely refashion Cold War structures and reflexive habits, and stimulate the private sector elements of the security equation, to meet this demand. Until we do so, America will remain unprepared, and therefore still in danger. We have overcome stark threats in the past. With sufficient ingenuity, we can do so again.

Notes

1. For an overview on global dynamics and modern security concerns, see U. S. Commission on National Security/21st Century, *New World Coming: American Security in the 21st Century, Phase 1* (Washington, DC: 1999). On the nature of modern terrorism, see Jessica Stern, *The Ultimate Terrorists* (Cambridge, MA: Harvard University Press, 1999), and Bruce Hoffman, *Inside Terrorism* (New York: Columbia University Press, 2000). On the dark side of globalization as it relates to economic and border security, see Stephen E. Flynn, "America the Vulnerable," *Foreign Affairs*, January/February 2002, pp. 60–74.
2. Thomas Homer-Dixon, "The Rise of Complex Terrorism," *Foreign Policy*, January/February 2002, pp. 52–56.

3. Thomas Homer-Dixon, *The Ingenuity Gap: Facing the Economic, Environmental, and Other Challenges of an Increasingly Complex and Unpredictable World* (New York: Vintage, 2002).

4. These characteristics were drawn from a major study by the National Academy of Sciences, *Making the Nation Safer: The Role of Science and Technology in Countering Terrorism* (Washington, DC: National Research Council, 2002), pp. 212–213.

5. Stephen E. Flynn, "Border Security: A Decade of Malign Neglect," in *How Did This Happen? Terrorism and the New War*, ed. James F. Hoge, Jr. and Gideon Rose (New York: Public Affairs, 2002).

6. Today's $11 trillion American economy includes $1.35 trillion in imports and $1.0 trillion in exports. See Office Homeland Security, *National Strategy for Homeland Security*, Department of Homeland Security (Washington, DC:, 2002), p. 21.

7. Gary Fields, "War Game Scenario Shows Economic Impact of Terror," *Wall Street Journal*, December 4, 2002.

8. Michael Dobbs, "Russian Official Reveals Attempt Made to Steal Nuclear Materials," *Washington Post*, November 13, 2001; Steven Erlanger, "Lax Nuclear Security in Russia Is Cited as Way for Bin Laden to Get Arms," *New York Times*, November 12, 2001; Jeanne Whalen, "Uranium Bust Heightens Fears About Russia's Nuclear Material," *Wall Street Journal*, December 10, 2001; and James Kitfield, "Nuclear Nightmares," *National Journal*, December 15, 2001.

9. See Advisory Panel to Assess Domestic Response Capabilities for Terrorism Involving Weapons of Mass Destruction, *Toward a National Strategy for Combating Terrorism*, *Phase 2 Report*, December 15, 2000, p. 2, www.rand.org/nsrd/terrpanel. The panel was chaired by former Virginia governor James Gilmore. Also see Frank J. Cilluffo, *Combating Chemical, Biological, Radiological, and Nuclear Terrorism: A Comprehensive Strategy* (Washington, DC: Center for Strategic and International Studies, 2001), p. 1.

10. U.S. Commission on National Security/21st Century, *Road Map for National Security: Imperatives for Change, Phase 3 Report* (Washington, DC: GPO, 2001).

11. Office of Homeland Security, *National Strategy for Homeland Security*, p. vii.

12. For further details on these initiatives see Remarks of U.S. Customs Commissioner Robert C. Bonner, July 15, 2002, The Heritage Center; and Remarks of U.S. Commissioner Robert C. Bonner, Center for Strategic and International Studies, August 26, 2002, www.customs.gov/about/speeches.

13. The intellectual foundation for these initiatives can be found in Stephen E. Flynn, "Beyond Border Control," *Foreign Affairs*, November/December 2000, pp. 57–68.

14. For more information, see www.customs.gov/xp/cgov/import/commercial_enforcement/ctpat.html.

15. For current information on this program, see www.customs.gov/xp/cgov/toolbox/about/modernization.

16. Additional insights on this innovative program can be found in Jason Peckenpaugh, "In Transit," *Government Executive*, July 2002, pp. 71–77.

17. The Deepwater homepage contains background on this modernization program and can be accessed at www.uscg.mil/deepwater.

18. James M. Loy and Robert G. Ross, "Global Trade: America's Achilles' Heel," *Defense Horizons* 7 (February 2002).

19. For additional insights into the contributions of the U.S. Coast Guard see Colin S. Gray, "Keeping the Coast Guard Afloat," *The National Interest*, accessed at www.uscg.mil/overview/article-keep%20afloat.html, and Christopher Lehman and Scott Truver, "Coast Guard More Important Than Ever," *Washington Times*, November 13, 2001, p. 19.

20. John Lewis Gaddis, *Strategies of Containment, A Critical Appraisal of Postwar American National Security Policy* (New York: Oxford University Press, 1982), p. viii.

21. Office of Homeland Security, *The National Security Strategy of the United States of America*. The National Security Strategy, by law, is an annual public document, mandated by the Goldwater-Nichols Defense Reorganization Act of 1986.

22. Preemption and the costs of inaction are discussed in Office of Homeland Security, *National Security Strategy*, p. 15. For a concise assessment of the National Security Strategy, see Ivo H. Daalder, James M. Lindsay, and James B. Steinberg, *The Bush National Security Strategy: An Evaluation*, Brookings Policy Paper, October 4, 2002, www.brookings.edu/views/papers/daalder/20021004.htm.

23. "While we recognize that our best defense is a good offense, we are also strengthening America's homeland security to protect against and deter attack." Office of Homeland Security, *National Security Strategy*, p. 6.

24. U.S. Commission on National Security, 21st Century, *Road Map for National Security: Imperatives for Change*, p. 9.

25. Deparment of Homeland Defense, *National Security Strategy*, pp. 1–2.

26. Ibid., pp. 29–31.

27. See F. G. Hoffman, "Transform *Security*, Not Just Defense," *Strategic Review*, Spring 2001, pp. 59–60.

28. For excellent advice on the contents of a comprehensive strategy, see Advisory Panel to Assess Domestic Response Capabilites for Terrorism Involving Weapon of Mass Destruction, *Toward a National Strategy, Phase 2 Report*, pp. 1–6.

29. Kurt M. Campbell and Michele A. Flournoy, *To Prevail: An American Strategy for the Campaign Against Terrorism* (Washington, DC: Center for Strategic and International Studies, 2001), p. 128.

30. There is not always agreement regarding budget figures for homeland security. For example, in a recent interview with the editors of this volume, Chris Hornbarger noted that the president's first post-attack budget (FY2003), proposed $37.7 billion for homeland security, up from $19.5 billion (after the creation of critical mission areas, OMB recomputed the pre-9-11 budget as $20.6 billion).

31. See FY04 Summary Tables, S-5 Homeland Security Funding by Agency, 2004, www.whitehouse/omb/ budget/fy2004/tables.html.

32. Philip Shenon, "White House Accused of Shortchanging Security Budget," *New York Times*, February 3, 2003.

33. Office for Homeland Security, *National Strategy for Homeland Security*, p. xii. It is important to note that when 9/11 happened, the FY2003 budget was largely done. The president and his still tiny OHS staff had to identify priorities, and build them into the 2003 request in an incredibly short period of time; they managed to come up with four priorities which are listed in no particular order in terms of funding priority.

34. Ivo H. Daalder, et al, *Protecting the American Homeland, One Year On* (Washington, DC: Brookings Institution, 2003), p. 3.

35. This estimate was originally developed by the Interagency Commission on Crime and Security at U.S. Seaports, prior to September 11, 2001. The U.S. Coast Guard estimates that the Maritime and Transportation Security Act mandates total just under $1B for the first year and an annual recurring cost of $535M. See www.aapa.org/govrelations/aapa_security_position.pdf.

36. Steven M. Kosiak, *Overview of the Administration's FY2005 Request for Homeland Security* (Washington, DC: Center for Strategic and Budgetary Assessments, 2004).

37. U.S. Commission on National Security, *Road Map for National Security*, pp. 15–16; Daadler, *Protecting the American Homeland*, pp. 21–27.

38. Office of Homeland Security, *National Strategy for Homeland Security*, p. 23.

39. Birkler et al., *The U.S. Coast Guard's Force Modernization Program*, 2004, accessed www.rand.org/publications/MG/MG114/MG114.pdf.

40. Steven M. Kosiak, *Funding for Defense, Homeland Security and Combating Terrorism Since 9–11: Where Has All the Money Gone?* (Washington, DC: Center for Strategic and Budgetary Assessments, 2003); and David Isenberg, *Less Talk, More Walk: Strengthening Homeland Security Now* (Washington, DC: Center for Defense Information, 2002), pp. 6–7.

41. Daniel Goure and Jeffrey M. Ranney, *Averting the Defense Train Wreck in the New Millennium* (Washington, DC: Center for Strategic and International Studies, 1999).

42. George W. Bush, Address to the Nation, June 6, 2002, www.whitehouse.gov/news/release/2002/06/20020606–8.html.

43. Zoe Baird and James Barksdale, *Protecting America's Freedom in the Information Age* (New York: The Markle Foundation, 2002), p. 1.

44. On biometrics, see John D. Woodward, Jr., *Biometrics: Facing Up to Terrorism* (Santa Monica, CA: RAND, Corp., 2002); on UAVs, see Toby Eckert, "A New Tool for Homeland Security?" *San Diego Union-Tribune,* December 22, 2002.

45. National Academy of Sciences, *Making the Nation Safer: The Role of Science and Technology in Countering Terrorism* (Washington, DC: National Academy Press, 2002), p. 147.

46. Ibid., p. 11.

47. See Lee Holcomb in Anne Plummer, "Officials Work Overtime to Develop IT Infrastructure for New Agency," *Inside the Pentagon,* January 23, 2003, pp. 11–12; Government Accounting Office, *Homeland Security: Information Technology Funding and Associated Management Issues,* GAO report 03–250 (Washington, DC: GPO, 2002).

48. For an overview on Federal IT programs and homeland security related projects, see Judi Hasson, "This Means War," *Federal Computer Week*, February 18, 2002, pp. 18–24.

49. Baird and Barksdale, *Protecting America's Freedom in the Information Age*, pp. 37–38.

50. For insights on the scope of this challenge, see Paul Byron Pattak, "Homeland Issues Give Federal IT Officers Critical Role," *Defense News*, August 26, 2002, pp. 14–15.

51. For additional insights on the contributions of information technology to homeland security and a unique approach to accelerating critical programs, see Jan M. Lodal and James J. Shinn, *Red Teaming the Data Gap,* CFR Independent Task Force on America's Response to Terrorism (New York: Council on Foreign Relations, 2002).

52. Arthur K. Cebrowski and John J. Gartska, "Network Centric Warfare: Its Origin and Future," *Naval Institute Proceedings*, January 1998, pp. 28–35, and David S. Alberts, John J. Garstka, and Frederick P. Stein, *Network Centric Warfare: Developing and Leveraging Information Superiority* (Washington, DC: Department of Defense, 1999).

53. Eliot A. Cohen and John Gooch, *Military Misfortunes: The Anatomy of Failure in War* (New York: Free Press, 1990), p. 231.

54. U.S. Commission on National Security 21st Century, *Road Map For National Security*, p. 9. That commission, which included a dozen prominent Americans with extensive public service with both executive and legislative branch experience, concluded that "The United States *is today very poorly organized to design and implement any comprehensive strategy to protect the homeland."*

55. Kurt M. Campbell and Michele A. Flournoy, *To Prevail: An American Strategy for the Campaign Against Terrorism* (Washington, DC: Center for Strategic and International Studies, 2001) p. 329.

56. Ivo H. Daalder and I.M. Destler, "Advisors, Czars and Councils: Organizing for Homeland Security," *The National Interest*, Summer 2002, pp. 66–78.

57. Daniel Benjamin and Steven Simon, *The Age of Sacred Terror* (New York: Random House, 2002), p. 367.

58. For an in depth assessment of the National Security Act, see Amy B. Zegart, *Flawed by Design: The Evolution of the CIA, JCS, and NSC* (Stanford, CA: Stanford University Press, 1999). For comparisons to the trials and tribulations of the Defense Department. See also James Jay Carafano, *Prospects for the Homeland Security Department: The 1947 Analogy,* Backgrounder (Center for Strategic and Budgetary Assessments, Washington, DC: 2002).

59. Stephen E. Flynn, "Creating the Department of Homeland Security: Rethinking the Ends and Means," Issue Brief, 2002, p. 2, www.homelandsec.org.

60. Advisory Panel to Assess Domestic Response Capabilities for Terrorism Invovling Weapons of Mass Destruction, *Toward a National Strategy: Phase 2 Report,* p. 4.

61. The National Commission on Terrorist Attacks Upon the United States, *The 9/11 Commission Report* (New York: Norton, 2004). See Chapter 13, "How to Do It? A Different Way of Organizing the Government," pp. 399–428, in this regard.

62. Statement of Christopher Koch, President and CEO of the World Shipping Council, to U.S. House Transportation and Infrastructure Committee, March 13, 2002.

63. Daalder et al., *Protecting the American Homeland,* p. 1.

64. John J. Hamre, "Homeland Defense, A Net Assessment," *Planning to Win*: *A Report on Homeland Security From the Aspen Strategy Group* (Washington, DC: Aspen Institute, 2002), p. 20.

65. Jeff Sparshott, "Transport Firms Fear Anti-Terror Measure," *Washington Times*, January 16, 2003.

66. Stephen E. Flynn, "America The Vulnerable," *Foreign Affairs*, January/February 2002, p. 60–74. For greater detail and proposals on border security, see Stephen Flynn, *America the Vulnerable: How Our Government is Failing to Protect Us From Terrorism* (New York: HarperCollins, 2004), pp. 81–110.

67. Gary Hart and Warren B. Rudman, *America—Still Unprepared, Still in Danger* (New York: Council on Foreign Relations, 2002), p. 9.

68.   President George W. Bush, Remarks at West Point, New York, June 1, 2002, www.whitehouse.gov.

69.   Barton Gellman, "In U.S., Terrorism's Peril Undiminished," *Washington Post*, December 24, 2002.

70.   Peter Trubowitz, Emily O. Goldman, and Edward Rhodes, *The Politics of Strategic Adjustment: Ideas, Institutions and Interests* (New York: Columbia University Press, 1998).

71.   Hart and Rudman, *America—Still Unprepared, Still in Danger*.

Chapter 10

Cyber Threats:
Ten Issues to Consider

Frank Cilluffo and Paul Byron Pattak[1]

As the United States hurtles into the Information Age, we are forced to grapple with a new set of national security problems heretofore not contemplated. Distance, time, and geography have been reduced to the point of irrelevancy. Information networks have given the United States an unrivaled, perhaps unsurpassable, lead over the rest of the world in virtually every facet of modern life. To an unprecedented degree, American national security and economic well-being depend upon critical infrastructures, such as banking and finance, electric power, information and communications, oil and gas production, transportation, water supply, emergency services, and the continuity of government services. These infrastructures, in turn, depend upon telecommunications and networked information systems. Along with the clear rewards of information systems come new risks and a host of unintended consequences that need to be better understood by corporate and government leaders.

The United States faces threats from peer nations, trading partners, hostile countries, non-state actors, terrorists, organized crime, insiders, and teenage hackers. While few adversaries would attempt to confront the United States in a conventional war on the traditional battlefield, its adversaries recognize that terrorism and other asymmetric forms of conflict, such as cyber attacks, are more effective methods of striking the United States where it is most vulnerable. Bits and bytes will never completely replace bullets and bombs, but they can be synergistically combined. Imagine if the Oklahoma City bombing had been accompanied by electronic disruptions of federal, state, and local emergency and public safety communications systems, including Emergency-911.

The ability to network has far outpaced the ability to protect networks. When the Internet was created, it was designed with "openness" and accessibility as guiding principles. Most information systems have been engineered in the most economically efficient manner, and are therefore dependent upon a small number of critical nodes, making them vulnerable to attack. As computer systems become increasingly interdependent, damage to one can potentially cascade and impact others.

America's vulnerabilities were dramatized during a 1997 Joint Chiefs of Staff exercise, code-named "Eligible Receiver." The purpose of the exercise was to test the United States' ability to respond to cyber attacks. The results opened the eyes of skeptics. Using software widely available from hacker websites, the 35-person team showed how they could have disabled elements of the U.S. electric power grid by exploiting Supervisory

Control and Data Acquisition (SCADA) systems (which allow remote control of the systems). They also demonstrated how to incapacitate portions of U.S. military command-and-control systems in the Pacific, and Emergency-911 systems in the United States.

In response to the emerging threat of cyber terrorism, on May 22, 1998, Presidential Decision Directive (PDD-63) authorized the creation of a National Infrastructure Protection Center (NIPC). The NIPC is now housed within the Federal Bureau of Investigation (FBI) and serves as a lookout for attempted intrusions and to monitor cyber attacks. PDD-63 also led to the establishment of the Critical Infrastructure Assurance Office (CIAO), within the Department of Commerce, to serve as a policy coordination staff for infrastructure assurance issues within the Executive Branch.

While the U.S. government has taken these important steps, a more holistic, high-level policy debate is required. Information warfare, cyber crime, and cyber terrorism all overlap, yet require different domain expertise and varied responses. At present it is impossible to refer to clearly delineated rules. Before committing ourselves to policies with enormous potential for adverse results and misspent taxpayer dollars, the United States must first fully understand the dangers of cyber threats. Ten issues require thoughtful consideration.

1. Defining Conflict in Cyberspace

Cyber warfare raises serious questions about how future conflicts and wars are prosecuted. What constitutes an act of war? How does one differentiate between a terrorist attack and a financial crime committed with a computer? What is the adequate balance between protecting civil liberties, businesses, and national security? To a large extent, determining whether the United States is at war depends on the antagonist. A cyber attack by China's People's Liberation Army requires a substantially different series of responses than an attack by teenagers from China, although American victims of an attack might never know the difference.

In late January and early February 1998, as the United States considered deploying forces to the Persian Gulf, hackers attacked scores of Defense Department networks. Pentagon and FBI investigators thought that these intrusions might have been launched in response to a military build-up in the Persian Gulf. Fearing the worst, senior Defense officials informed the White House that an Iraqi information warfare campaign may have been underway. Their fears were substantiated because the hackers used foreign Internet service providers, including one located in the United Arab Emirates, as a staging point for their attacks.

After several days of investigating, the FBI learned that two California-based teenagers, mentored by an 18-year-old Israeli national, had conducted the attack. They were able to preserve the anonymity of their attack by routing it through a host of computer systems around the world. They successfully breached U.S. military computer defenses and gained access to the Defense Department's unclassified (yet important) logistics networks. The attack and the subsequent investigation, dubbed "Solar Sunrise," were characterized by John Hamre, Deputy Secretary of Defense, as "the most organized and systematic attack" on U.S. defense networks discovered thus far.

Cyber warriors can systemically attack vital American networks in relative anonymity. The person on the other end could just as easily be a child, a competitor, or a foreign intelligence service. A few months after "Solar Sunrise," a Massachusetts teenager was charged with disabling the FAA control tower at Worcester Regional Airport for six hours. Incoming planes could not use the runway lights. Later in 1998, a man in Toborg, Sweden managed to disable major portions of South Florida's Emergency-911 system.

To date, most of these denial-of-service incidents have either been perpetrated by insiders or hackers, and are best characterized as annoyances. Hackers, largely thrill-seeking young people, have demonstrated that vulnerabilities can be exploited by those with hostile intent. Any one of the increasing number of groups and individuals hostile to U.S. interests could exploit these vulnerabilities to harm those interests.

Current U.S. policy does not draw clear distinctions between these various scenarios. Without established rules of engagement, there is no battle plan in place to address the dangers raised by the various attacks. Likewise, because of the virtual nature of cyberspace, conventional force projection will not preempt or prevent cyber assaults. As we are by and large dealing with "actors without addresses," conventional military projection will not prevent a cyber assault. But a well-defined policy and an established strategy would go a long way towards showing our adversaries that the United States is willing and able to respond both in kind and conventionally. In the final analysis, the nation's best deterrent may be the ability to quickly reconstitute our damaged systems, regardless of the perpetrator.

2. Rules of Engagement

National planners need to define carefully the criteria for U.S. rules of engagement for cyberspace. In short, they must determine how the United States selects information warfare targets, as well as who and what are fair game. In turn, this may be a harbinger of how U.S. systems will be targeted by adversaries.

According to U.S. media reports, President Clinton issued a highly classified finding authorizing the CIA to use covert means to undermine Serbian President Slobodan Milosevic. The President allegedly authorized government agencies to conduct cyber operations against President Milosevic by tapping into his bank accounts. Intelligence sources believe President Milosevic secreted money in Swiss, Russian, Greek, Cypriot, and Chinese banks. A compelling reason to support this effort is that it personalized the target and did not result in collateral damage—in this case innocent Serbian civilians.

The problem with this particular "covert" action is that it ceased to be covert upon the public's awareness of its occurrence. Accordingly, it is substantially more difficult to execute this type of plan when the would-be target is aware of the action. The first rule of covert action is to keep it clandestine and maintain plausible deniability. An information arms race does not bode well for the United States given its unparalleled dependence on critical infrastructures. In many ways, it is the reverse of Cold War nuclear deterrence policy—America's ability to defend ourselves is now more important than its ability to project power.

3. Non-State Actors

The increased availability of advanced technology has strengthened the capabilities of hostile non-state actors. The situation will only worsen as the requisite level of knowledge and skill decreases while the power and technological sophistication of these cyber attack tools increase exponentially. As a result, terrorists have become empowered and have moved away from the fringes of world affairs toward the center stage.

Cyber warfare can also be a tool to collect intelligence in support of terrorist operations and campaigns, and to communicate and disseminate propaganda. Given today's state of technology and dual-use applications, terrorist groups can easily acquire an inexpensive, yet robust, communications intelligence (COMINT) collection capability. First, terrorists can intercept valuable political, economic, and military secrets; run counter-surveillance on law enforcement; and perform profiling analyses to identify individuals who can be bribed, co-opted, coerced, or "neutralized." Much of this work can be done anonymously, diminishing the risk of reprisal and increasing the likelihood of success. Second, terrorists can use advanced technology for communication and tradecraft. The Internet and other information systems provide terrorist groups a global and near real-time command, control, and communications capability. The availability of sophisticated encryption devices and anonymous re-mailers also provides relatively secure communications or stored data.[2]

Nearly all major terrorist organizations have a Web site, including the Shining Path, HAMAS, the Revolutionary Armed Forces of Columbia (FARC), the Liberation Tamil Tigers of Eelam (LTTE), and the Irish Republican Army (IRA). They look to the Internet largely to disseminate communiqués, fundraise, and recruit. The United States' most-wanted transnational terrorist, Usama bin Ladin, uses laptops with satellite uplinks and encrypted messages to conduct operations and maintain links across national borders with his terrorist network.

There is no shortage of terrorist "cookbooks" on the Internet, step-by-step recipes for hackers, crackers (criminal hackers), and cyber terrorists.[3] An adversary can circumvent national militaries completely, armed only with automated "weapons of mass disruption." It is only a matter of time before there is a convergence between those with hostile intent and those with techno-savvy—where the real bad guys exploit the real good stuff.

4. Public Opinion

Malfeasants can easily hide in cyberspace's void and lash out either precisely or indiscriminately. The Internet also provides the perfect medium for people to communicate their ideas, organize initiatives, and execute activities on a distributed basis.[4] This raises the possibility that adversaries could organize covertly on an unprecedented scale. The activities of "hacktivists" such as the J18 and the Electronic Disturbance Theater (EDT) begin to illustrate the potential for global organization and mobilization.

On June 18, 1999, demonstrators organized a global protest, with manifestations in major cities on several continents and along a broad spectrum of agendas. Groups were implored to demonstrate against the rubric of globalization, but without a unified theme or format.

The result was simultaneously orchestrated global disruptions and Internet attacks. In London, individuals described in the media as "evil savages" and "masked thugs," assembled in the financial district in a rampage against capitalism. Stilt-walkers, magicians, jugglers, and musicians lined the streets, targeting the London International Financial Futures and Options Exchange. Dismissed locally as a drunken mob, the "New Age guerrillas" managed to disrupt the ebb and flow of business.

Meanwhile, on the same day in Austin, Texas, a bicycle ride by a group called Critical Mass arrived at a particular coffee shop to be part of a global "reclaim the street" project. As the first set of bikers started to arrive, they encouraged others to stand in the street, which had been barricaded to interrupt traffic. The organizers managed to briefly address the crowd and hand out fliers before the police arrived and dispersed them.

While people protested, the Electronic Disturbance Theater organized a "virtual sit-in," a denial-of-service attack that called on people around the world to point their Internet browser toward the Zapatista Floodnet URL between 4:00 P.M. and 10:00 P.M. (GMT). The computers continually sent reload commands to the Floodnet site. Floodnet then redirected these requests to the Mexican Embassy in London. Thus, much like the previous two examples, the Internet "streets" were crowded with "people." The results of the virtual sit-in were even more impressive than the physical demonstrations: 18,615 unique contributors from 46 countries were part of the assault.

The events of June 18, 1999, raise frightening possibilities. Protesters in more than 40 countries mobilized on the same day, physically and virtually. If the protests had existed for a single organized purpose, the results could have been devastating. These events further illustrate that the Internet can be both a tool and a target. J18 passed largely unnoticed by the media, which to date has focused only on highly visible activities, while ignoring many of cyber warfare's subtle dangers.

The November 1999 World Trade Organization (WTO) meetings became the site of the most recent iteration of Internet-mobilized protests. Under the same anti-globalization banner, chief organizer Michael Dolan used the Internet to organize and mobilize a large unrelated group of protesters under the collective banner of "NO2WTO." The protesters represented a panoply of issues. Everyone from animal rights activists to supporters of the Zapatistas in Mexico came from all across North America to voice their grievances. The result was the "Battle in Seattle." Individual messages were lost in the ensuing violence. Through their Web site, a group calling themselves the "Electrohippies" organized a virtual sit-in, shorthand for a denial-of-service attack, just as other groups had done with J18.

J18 and NO2WTO were successful protests in that they succeeded in disrupting that day's, and even that week's, events. They illustrate a new model or principle dubbed "disorganization," or decentralization by experts. This precept encourages many simultaneous local protests addressing specific concerns. Protesters thereby benefit from "demonstrations of scale."

NO2WTO also introduced new faces to the protest crowd. It showed the appeal of being not only able to reach a wider audience, but also in drawing from a larger pool. In many ways, however, this was a one-trick pony. Groups with an established constituency and a defined message, like the AFL-CIO, clearly suffered some loss in legitimacy by association with violent protests. While future protests may lose several better-known organizations, the more radical elements have everything to gain by joining forces and in this paradoxical global-local protest.

5. Media Misunderstanding

The most visible attacks on American systems result in a disproportionate amount of media attention. Indeed, there has been no shortage of headlines with the recent battle between federal officials and computer intruders. Web sites maintained by the Senate, the FBI, the Interior Department, the White House, the U.S. Army, and the North Atlantic

Treaty Organization (NATO), to name a few, were defaced in 1999. The transgressions were usually nothing more than graffiti and unsightly annoyances. Meanwhile, a number of truly dangerous incidents have passed relatively unnoticed.

The recent spate of hacker events has drawn a great deal of publicity. The media focused on the attacks against the FBI and Senate Web pages and dutifully reported that a top U.S. Justice Department official labeled the attacks as "serious." On June 2, 1999, apparently in retaliation for FBI raids against their peers, hackers overwhelmed the agency's Web site and left messages criticizing the FBI's investigation of the hacker incidents. They were limited to the Web pages and did not penetrate the FBI's main computer systems. These attacks were serious in that they disrupted the government's ability to effectively communicate its message to the population at large, but they are not the most serious threats. While the perpetrators should be punished, they do not warrant the highest level of coverage or attention.

Young hackers want to show off, and hacktivists seek to use the Internet as simply another means to draw attention to their respective causes. What both groups have in common is a desire for attention, and the media is happy to oblige. Insufficiently covered in press reports are the discreet and often silent efforts by serious adversaries to develop tools, techniques, and doctrines for conducting information warfare against the United States and its interests. The imbalance of reporting must change in order for the American public to better understand the extent of the emerging threats.

Despite the extensive coverage of Web hacks and Web site vandalism, they amount to mere graffiti in cyberspace. While it is essential that the media act responsibly and not panic the citizenry, they play a crucial role in educating the public as to the dangers, both overt and subtle, presented by information warfare.

6. Lessons from Y2K

Insiders and internal saboteurs, either disgruntled employees or moles, are perfectly positioned to wreak havoc within organizations. Moreover, these people know where the most sensitive information is stored, how to access it, and what to steal or damage. Insiders are ideal candidates for subversion by foreign governments or terrorist organizations. Pressure to solve the Y2K dilemma led the United States government and private industry to emphasize expediency over safety in many cases. As a result, thousands of Y2K consultants have been given unprecedented access to systems that are otherwise strictly protected.

Most crisis managers knew a lot about the Y2K problem, but not enough about its possible consequences. There are some issues that have not generated much media interest, but which present possible national security hazards. Aside from the counterintelligence concerns, backdoor Y2K access can be exploited for theft or disruption. Some of the programmers contracted to exterminate the Y2K bug may have exploited their position by leaving a "backdoor," granting them the ability to subsequently access the system undetected. The profile of likely perpetrators in such a scenario would be a highly skilled software engineer who worked on Y2K remediation efforts and understands both the information systems and the business processes of the enterprise that hired them.

Ideally, the Y2K experience should serve as both a wake-up call and a training exercise so that industry and government can use the lessons learned to become better informed about the potential effects and consequences of cyber threats. Hopefully, Y2K will inspire both industry and government to strengthen information protection and infrastructure assurance. Success is possible with plans in place and a course of action.

7. Cyber Invasion

Currently, several countries possess offensive information warfare capabilities comparable to those of the United States. Most of these nations, however, would be foolish to take down U.S. systems, as this would compromise a valuable intelligence collection method for them. Nevertheless, they are conducting surveillance, mapping critical nodes that can be exploited during future crises.

The ability to identify and reconnoiter such targets is today possible due to the Internet and powerful search engines on the World Wide Web. Moreover, information warfare extends the battlefield to incorporate all of society. In the same way that we can no longer rely upon Fort Knox's steel and concrete to protect U.S. financial assets, Americans can no longer rely upon the two oceans to prevent a mainland invasion.

The myth persists that the continental United States has not been invaded since 1812. In reality, invasion through cyberspace has become a daily occurrence. Currently, an Internet-connected computer or server in the United States is broken into every 20 seconds. While an assailant can penetrate borders in a matter of nanoseconds, the law enforcement official charged with their apprehension must stop at these borders and cannot adequately pursue the attacker. In essence, we have created a "global village" without a police department.

Enemies also have the luxury of choosing between civilian and military targets. As military targets become better protected, assailants will naturally turn to more vulnerable prey. Industry and government need to solidify their partnership in the face of this reality.

8. Public and Private Overlap

Due to financial considerations and efficiency principles, military and civilian sectors are interdependent. The U.S. military is becoming increasingly dependent on applications developed by the civilian world. Specifically, U.S. forces rely on commercial off-the-shelf (COTS) technology, and commercial systems and services. U.S. forces also count on commercial transportation services and facilities for mobilization and logistics support. These all have an information technology component, be they air traffic control or ground transportation. These systems are largely under civilian control and are responsible for ensuring the delivery of people and machines from place to place.

About 95 percent of Defense Department communications travel over commercial networks, services, and lines. The substance of the communiqués can be protected through encryption, which can better protect confidentiality of information, and to a lesser extent, the integrity of the information. All of the encryption in the world, however, cannot prevent denial-of-service attacks. The physical connections—the satellite links, glass fibers, metal wires, and microwave stations—go relatively unprotected. Additionally, in embracing COTS, the Pentagon is now more likely to purchase hardware, software, and firmware from various domestic and overseas sources. Similar risks occur in business with just-in-time delivery and reliance on electronic information transfers.

9. Privacy vs. National Security

The delicate balance between privacy and security is an ever-present tension in American society. One hundred years ago, government employees did not undergo background investigations for security clearances in the same manner as today. However, over the course of the tumultuous twentieth century, background investigations, security clearances, and loyalty oaths became the necessary price that many Americans have paid to serve in critical civilian and military positions.

As government and other organizations compile databases to track everything from driver's licenses to medical histories, Americans have become more sensitive to privacy issues and the specter of numerous "Little Brothers" in addition to "Big Brother." Serious debates are also raging on such matters as encryption technology and the ability to track and trace cellular phones.

Tools that ensure privacy and convenience for the United States do the same for its adversaries. The encryption software that protects sensitive financial information also allows a terrorist to conceal a destructive plot. The ability to track cellular phones may prove critical in stopping or capturing those who are conducting hostile operations. The key issue here is not whether a line must be drawn, but rather, where it will be drawn. The United States must reallocate and manage intelligence assets in order to ensure that policymakers develop an accurate, comprehensive understanding of the threat posed by information warfare. Information must not be trapped in narrow channels, but should instead flow to all sources that may be affected, including business concerns. We do not have to choose between privacy and national security—we can have both.

10. The Rule of Law

Almost all of the issues discussed in this chapter have legal implications, yet the United States has only just begun to consider the necessity of amending existing laws and passing new ones. Laws that do not necessarily appear to have a direct application to national security are relevant. Unless changes are made to the Freedom of Information Act and certain anti-trust statutes, it will be virtually impossible for industry and government to share information that would help defend against cyber threats.

Almost all U.S. national security legislation is based on American operations in air, on land, on water, and in space. And it is not surprising that a large percentage of U.S. laws concern physical property and associated rights. Many of these laws, and the entities that enforce them, have their authority based upon, and limited by, geography. But with the movement of conflict to the electronic domain, the United States, without delay, must conform its statutes to reflect the corresponding jurisdictional issues. Our legislative and legal mechanisms are admittedly cautious in a world that is moving with ever-increasing speed. Mindful of the tradeoff between these deliberative processes and the rapid development of cyber threats, the United States cannot effectively address twenty-first-century crimes armed only with nineteenth-century laws.

Concluding Thoughts: Community and Defense

The United States has faltered in the face of cyber threats because, despite considerable efforts, the national focus is strategically misplaced. The media misdirects the nation's attention, using more ink to report hacker exploits than the substantive national security threats made possible by information technology. This same technology has also enhanced the role of individuals in the national security arena. Gone are the days when one needed to raise an army, build a command structure, train soldiers, and purchase weapons to attack an adversary. The price of entry is at an all-time low. Widespread destruction can be perpetrated from the comfort of one's living room with inexpensive tools, or over telecommunications networks designed, ironically, for collective convenience.

Industry and government must establish a genuine partnership. In some way, we must introduce the "sandals" to the "wingtips." The Department of Defense should not be the only entity concerned with defending American interests in cyberspace. Government no longer has the luxury of having all the knowledge or assuming that it will be in a position to provide all of the answers. If we are to ensure that all relevant parties have a seat at the table, a bigger table must be furnished.

The administration should be applauded for its initial first efforts with PDD-63. However, to truly enhance national security, such efforts must extend beyond the government-centered parameters of PDD-63. The United States must make an irrevocable commitment in terms of education, awareness, sensible application of technology, and decisive action.

Perhaps the old notion that security begins in the communities—neighbors watching out for each other—is more significant now than ever before. Interconnectedness will become the *sine qua non* of everyday life now that everyone has a vested interest in community protection. As interdependence among institutions and individuals grows, particularly in the realm of cyberspace, the distinctions between public and private, industry and government, and "your" and "my" responsibility fade, and are replaced by "our" responsibility.

President John F. Kennedy once said, "The best time to fix the roof is when the sun is shining." The time to begin thinking about, and addressing, the challenges posed by cyber threats is now.

Notes

1. The authors would like to acknowledge the substantial contributions made by George C. Salmoiraghi, a third-year student at the University of Richmond Law School.
2. For a more in-depth review, see Frank J. Cilluffo and Curt H. Gergely, "Information Warfare and Strategic Terrorism," *Terrorism and Political Violence* 9 no. 1 (Spring 1997): 84–94.
3. For a more in-depth review, see Frank Cilluffo and Bruce Berkowitz, eds., *Cybercrime, Cyberterrorism, and Cyberwarfare: Averting and Electronic Waterloo* (Center for Strategic and International Studies, 1998).
4. For a more in-depth review, see John Arquilla and David Ronfeldt, eds., *In Athena's Camp: Preparing for Conflict in the Information Age* (Santa Monica, CA: RAND Corp., 1997).

Chapter 11

Securing America's Critical Infrastructures: A Top Priority for the Department of Homeland Security

Larry M. Wortzel

The aftermath of the September 11, 2001, attacks on the Pentagon and the World Trade Center illustrates the high vulnerability of America's infrastructure to terrorist attacks, and the massive consequences of not protecting it. While the terrorists were able to utilize deficiencies in America's overall approach to intelligence sharing and aviation security, similar vulnerabilities exist in every infrastructure vital to the security, economy, and survival of the nation, such as computer networks, energy supplies, and transportation systems.

Today, the federal government and most Americans recognize that responsibility for protecting critical infrastructure from terrorism does not rest solely with any one level of government. While the new Department of Homeland Security (DHS) will take the lead in many of these efforts, the level of security required demands unprecedented levels of cooperation and coordination across government and private-sector boundaries. Adequate protection of America's critical infrastructures and key assets will rest on the ability of the federal, state, and local governments to cooperate with each other and the private sector.

Strategic Approach to Protecting Critical Infrastructures

Securing the nation's critical infrastructure has rightly become an increasingly vital component of a post–September 11 homeland security strategy. The USA PATRIOT Act defines critical infrastructure as "systems and assets, whether physical or virtual, so vital to the United States that the incapacity or destruction of such systems and assets would have a debilitating impact on security, national economic security, national public health or safety, or any combination of those matters."

As a result of the increased attention to this issue since September 11, the Administration has recognized the importance of establishing a national strategy to protect and defend America's critical infrastructure components, while placing an increased reliance on the private sector to assist and guide this process. The release of the *National Strategy for the Physical Protection of Critical Infrastructures and Key Assets* was a very important step in advancing this mission and ensuring nationwide coordination and cooperation.

As evidenced by September 11, terrorists are flexible, creative, and resourceful, and have learned to target areas of particular vulnerability, while avoiding those that are more protected and predictable. By targeting America's critical infrastructures, these terrorists seek to advance their goal of disrupting and imposing financial consequences on the government, society, and the economy. Our technology and sophisticated society are therefore excellent targets for terrorists, and must rise to this unprecedented challenge with security improvements and infrastructure protection in a way not currently being done.

Meeting this challenge will require cooperation and coordination across government and commercial boundaries. Yet the nature of the threat also requires a degree of decentralization since the task of homeland defense is too large, complex, and expensive for one isolated federal department to control.

While homeland security and traditional national security issues have much in common, there are some important differences that greatly vary the process by which they are implemented. National security has traditionally been recognized as the responsibility of the federal government, relying on the collective efforts of the military, the foreign policy establishment, and the intelligence community. Homeland security, however, is a shared responsibility that cannot be accomplished by the federal government alone. During the Cold War era, many government and private-sector operations isolated themselves and their infrastructures as a matter of security.

This antiquated approach to the safety of the American public is no longer appropriate or acceptable. The current culture and increased threats facing our nation require unprecedented levels of trust and collaboration between public and private stakeholders. They require coordinated action on the part of federal, state, and local governments, with increasing reliance on the private sector, as well as concerned citizens all across the country. This is especially important in the context of protecting our nation's critical infrastructures and key assets.

Private industry owns and operates approximately 85 percent of our critical infrastructures and key assets. Therefore, much of the expertise and many of the resources required for planning and taking better protective measures lie outside the federal government. The new front line of defense for America's critical infrastructure has become the communities and individual institutions that make up our critical infrastructure sector.

More can and must be done to ensure that this remains a priority in the long term within homeland security planning. The nation's critical infrastructures must be more clearly defined and identified, followed by a comprehensive assessment of how best to protect them and eliminate vulnerabilities.

The federal government is responsible for issuing standards and "best practices" to ensure a coordinated approach among all aspects of critical infrastructure protection. In addition, we must focus more attention on the interconnectivity of infrastructure and its ability to operate effectively in emergency situations. A successful critical infrastructure protection strategy also depends on clearly defined and attainable expectations, as well as cooperation and coordination across all levels of government and all business sectors.

Defining Government and Private Sector Roles and Responsibilities

Since the creation of the new DHS, many lawmakers and policymakers have begun to question the roles that the private sector should play in helping to secure America's critical infrastructure. Some of these people have falsely assumed that placing more responsibility on the private sector—or allowing it to take more responsibility—is the wrong approach.

In fact, the opposite is likely true. Permitted enough flexibility, the private sector can respond much more quickly and effectively to many homeland security threats than government agencies can.

Historically, many barriers have impeded the public–private partner relationship. Many of these barriers are attitudes from a bygone era of mistrust and bad interactions between the government and businesses. Today's fluid marketplace and vulnerability to terrorism in a post-9/11 world demand a new, more cooperative set of attitudes and relationships.

There remain many challenges to overcome in ensuring cooperation, but it is important to recognize that these challenges and roles are often different for industry and the government. Because most of America's critical infrastructure is owned or operated by the private sector, these businesses and companies face a greater degree of threat than the government, and should therefore feel a greater incentive to engage in increased protection and security.

The private sector is driven by bottom lines, consumer and shareholder confidence, and market forces, which are strong incentives for increased security. But a change in focus is necessary for this process to succeed. Businesses around the nation should view the government's demands on their expertise not just as a cost, but also as an opportunity.

The government can assist to some degree in this process and, in fact, has the obligation to do so. The government should not inhibit any industry's efforts to protect itself; instead, it should ensure that businesses have the tools necessary to do so. However, it will be impossible for the government to pay for all of the necessary security improvements to the level required by the current threat. The assessment of who will foot the bill must be done on a case-by-case basis.

If industry fails to implement the appropriate levels of protection, then the government will likely have to intervene and enforce stricter regulations. The airline industry after 9/11 is a recent example of the government intervention required because of the private sector's failure to respond to the threat. This should not be the case with America's critical infrastructures and key assets.

This process could become a slippery slope only if industry chooses not to fulfill its responsibilities to meet the current threat. The ball is in the court of each of our nation's key industries and companies, and responsibility ultimately lies with them to implement their own security improvements, using the federal government as a guiding and motivating source.

Facilitating the Communication of Security Information

Since most of America's critical infrastructure is owned or operated by the private sector, it is important to ensure that industry is willing to engage the government in cooperating to implement the appropriate levels of protection and security. However, legal concerns and a lack of detailed information can limit the extent to which the private sector is willing to be involved in federal efforts.

The Administration and Congress should work together to allow federal agencies that rely on the private sector for infrastructure information to maintain Freedom of

Information Act (FOIA) exemptions. Many private firms are reluctant to provide extensive information on vulnerability because they fear that this information could become public, and therefore adversely affect public or shareholder confidence. Such fears are major roadblocks to a dialogue with the private sector and could severely diminish levels of cooperation.

Public accountability must be preserved, but access to sensitive information must be restricted. For example, information on the weak areas of a chemical plant should *not* be posted on the Web for a terrorist to download and then use to attack that chemical plant. Instead, a cleansed vulnerability assessment should be made available to those who live or do business around that particular area.

Congress should provide narrowed antitrust exemptions for companies that share information on infrastructure protection. When corporations work together, concerns inevitably arise that they are trying to subvert the market. Antitrust laws, which try to prevent such practices, also inhibit companies from sharing information on the vulnerability of the infrastructure or the means to protect it.

Cooperation on protecting critical infrastructure and information sharing should be exempt from antitrust laws in order to protect companies from unjust lawsuits. Similarly, independent private sector mechanisms for sharing information, known as Information Sharing and Analysis Centers (ISACs), should also be exempt from these antitrust laws. Any legislation to accomplish this goal will have to be carefully crafted in order to prevent it from being used to achieve anti-competitive objectives.

Congress should also seek to reduce the liability for service providers who adopt best-practice security measures. Such a move would allow additional incentives for businesses to adopt new standards of security and participate in information sharing.

Congress should further assist in this process by removing tax penalties that make it more difficult for the private sector to invest in security. They should instead enact a reform that would allow infrastructure owners to deduct the full cost of security-related spending in the year such expenses are incurred. Allowing industries to write off security spending all at once will reduce the significant costs, thereby improving the all-important bottom line for companies investing in security.

Lead federal agencies should work with companies and businesses to develop new and improved security standards for industry. Federal agencies should also assist in creating risk assessment programs for the private-sector companies involved in infrastructure protection. Though the government can advise owners and operators of infrastructure of a suspected threat, it cannot assess the risk, vulnerability, or survivability of each asset.

Lead agencies should use a best-practices model for the private sector that enables them to conduct more accurate assessments. Such a model would allow industry to address security necessities by meeting a set of performance standards instead of firm government specifications. The Defense Department's internal assessment program would be a useful guide for beginning this process.

Working with the Department of Homeland Security

While the private sector should play a leading role in securing America's critical infrastructures, the burden will also rest heavily on the new DHS. The DHS's organization and structure will serve as a critical vehicle in ensuring and initiating communication across all levels of government, and between federal agencies, while also greatly improving the opportunities for government–industry cooperation.

The DHS also provides a streamlined and consolidated approach to homeland security, which will be especially important in working with the private sector to secure America's critical infrastructure. The integration of critical infrastructure protection and intelligence analysts under a single Undersecretary within the DHS should provide for a more focused agenda than the disjointed and inefficient organization previously spread throughout the federal government.

As time passes and the DHS gains the experience and authority it needs to better guide the nation's security and protection efforts, this process is likely to become much more efficient. It is important to remember that improving security to the level that this new post-9/11 world requires is a *process*. This cannot happen overnight and will likely result in two steps forward and one step back along the way. It took 50 years for the United States to develop our national security program to its current level. Unfortunately, terrorists will not wait for us to get our government in order before attacking us again, so homeland security must be accomplished as quickly and efficiently as possible.

The efforts of the DHS are already helping to make our nation's critical infrastructures safer from the many unconventional threats of terrorism. They are engaged in several important functions, such as serving as the primary liaison and facilitator for coordination among other federal departments, state and local governments, and the private sector.

The DHS is also beginning to build and maintain a complete, current, and accurate assessment of national-level critical assets, systems, and functions, while also beginning to assess vulnerabilities and protective postures across the critical infrastructure sectors. These assessments are vital to evaluating threats, providing timely warnings to threatened infrastructures, and building capabilities to evaluate preparedness across government jurisdictions. In addition, the DHS plays an important role in collaborating with other federal agencies, state and local governments, and private-sector businesses to define and implement complementary structures and coordination processes.

In order to fulfill these missions, the DHS should rely on the valuable models for cooperation that already exist within their structure. The Federal Emergency Management Agency (FEMA), which is now part of the new Department, has extensive experience coordinating and working with multiple federal agencies, the private sector, and local authorities in responding to natural disasters. The government's efforts to secure and prepare the cyber sector for the Y2K issue should also provide valuable "lessons learned" for doing similar efforts on a much larger and more significant scale. These and other successful models of cooperation will serve as important starting points for the DHS in working to incorporate the private sector in securing our nation's homeland from the threat of terrorism.

As noted above, companies interested in working with the DHS should consider this an opportunity, not a cost. The new threat environment demands unprecedented levels of partnership and cooperation, so businesses should be more willing than ever before to bring their experience and expertise to the table as requested. They should view the creation of the DHS as a more streamlined and direct opportunity to engage with the government. This shift in the government's organizational culture can help to eliminate many of the prior complications and frustrations felt by the private sector when working with the government.

In particular, the DHS has created the Office of Private Sector Liaison, which will provide America's business community with a direct line of communication to the DHS, and help foster dialogue on the full range of issues and challenges faced by America's business sector in the post-9/11 world. This office will deal specifically with America's critical industry sectors as outlined in the President's National Strategy for Homeland Security, as well general business matters and concerns related to the DHS.

Perhaps most important, the DHS will give the private sector one primary contact, instead of many different ones, for coordinating protection activities with the federal government, that include vulnerability assessments, strategic planning efforts, and exercises. Such changes will help to ensure that the DHS establishes a long-term working relationship with the private sector that will help to eliminate vulnerabilities, and secure America's critical infrastructures and key assets.

Recommendations to Clarify Public and Private-Sector Roles

While progress has certainly been made in securing and identifying America's critical infrastructure, this process is far from complete. A critical step is for the federal government to issue a set of guiding principles or "best practices" to ensure that a coordinated and efficient approach is taken by critical infrastructure sectors. Leadership and guidance at the federal level will provide an increased incentive for the private sector to come on board and cooperate in protecting America's critical infrastructures. To be effective, these best practices must be reinforced by incentives to encourage maximum and responsive cooperation by the private sector.

Another vital component of critical infrastructure protection is information sharing. The DHS should expedite its development of a "threat integration center"—something that The Heritage Foundation began calling for immediately after September 11—that will communicate and disseminate important intelligence information regarding terrorist threats quickly and efficiently across all levels of government, as well as to the relevant private-sector entities. The critical infrastructure components of the DHS must then be linked to this threat integration center, which will greatly improve the government's ability to conduct adequate threat analysis and make the appropriate security enhancements at the nation's most vulnerable and critical locations.

Ultimately, responsibility for securing an element of critical infrastructure belongs to the operator or owner of the technology. In business environments, market forces are typically much more effective than government regulation in effecting timely, efficient, and effective change. Through tax relief, reduced liability, and a framework of business-friendly regulation, Congress can use market forces to enhance the private sector's inherent sense of self-preservation and encourage the private sector to address homeland security needs.

However, as the process of securing the homeland proceeds, Congress and the Administration must be willing to step in to fill the gaps that the private sector cannot address. Acting in the best interests of homeland security is in the economic, political, and regulatory interests of both individual companies and government agencies.

Chapter 12

Seacurity: Improving the Security of the Global Sea-Container Shipping System

Maarten van de Voort, Kevin A. O'Brien,
Adnan Rahman, and Lorenzo Valeri

In light of the new terrorism, the security of the global sea-container shipping system needs to be reviewed and systematically analyzed. A systematic review of global container commerce with an eye to improving system wide security is required. As part of this larger effort, a first step should be a consultation involving relevant stakeholders to identify the major issues and perspectives, the results of which will be used to increase awareness about security issues among the stakeholders, as well as to formulate a research agenda and a research effort to improve the security of global container commerce.

Background and Problem Definition

Approximately 90 percent of all cargo moves in containers. Approximately 250 million containers are shipped annually. This massive flow of containers around the world is, in some sense, the lubricant for the world's economy. Thus, the global shipping system is a critical infrastructure for the global economy; it is, however, also very vulnerable. Estimates are that the contents of less than 2 percent of all containers are checked to verify that what is inside these containers is actually what is said to be inside the containers. In fact, containers are used by criminals to transport all sorts of banned goods, and even people.

The problem of the illegal transport of goods and people takes on particularly worrying proportions in light of recent terrorist activities. Terrorists could, for example, use containers to transport dangerous materials or weapons, or use the containers themselves as weapons of mass destruction. The potential threat of terrorists using containers poses a large risk to our economies and to our societies. How large is this risk, and what is the most effective way to reduce these risks to acceptable levels?

Answering these questions requires a system analysis for several reasons. First, there is a clear need for an integrated assessment of global threats, risks, and existing and potential security measures with regard to costs and benefits of such measures. Second, all technical and non-technical factors and their interdependencies may potentially act as weak spots in the entire complex system. Third, implementation strategies should be tested for feasibility with regard to political, legal, economic, cultural, and other contextual aspects. Fourth, the development and implementation of additional security measures—if any—that stood the test of the analysis, would still require a major investment of stakeholders, which have yet to be identified.

Securing the global sea-container shipping system is clearly a major undertaking requiring a systematic approach. Such a major undertaking has been suggested to the European Commission as an Expression of Interest[1] to conduct an integrated project in the EU's VI Framework Program,[2] among other initiatives. But the approach should also be careful, with small initial steps to gain support among the various stakeholders in the international community. Also, the current security situation and the threat of terrorism requires swift action. Under such circumstances, it is wise to take the initiative to gather a group of experts and think the problem through in a logical and systematic way, identifying the major issues in preparation and anticipation of next steps.

Based on a series of consultations with stakeholders, this discussion identifies the major issues in securing the global sea-container shipping system, and suggests strategies to build support for addressing the issue of maritime security.

The Threat

Several dimensions of the threat must be considered, including the strategic actions of terrorists, and information-sharing challenges between public and private entities.

Terrorists' Actions

Certain patterns can be distinguished in the ways terrorists choose concepts and targets for their attacks. It is generally acknowledged that terrorists will choose the way of least resistance; this is, however, a theoretical situation as it implies that terrorists would need perfect information on all possible targets to be able to select the weakest link, which—of course—is not the case. This is one of the reasons the maritime system and container transport so far have not been targeted by terrorists' actions; terrorists do not yet appear to have the information they need in order to infiltrate the container system. Besides perfect or sufficient information, knowledge and experience in and with possible targets also seems to be a driver for terrorists with regard to target selection. Once a target has been identified as a weak spot, it will pose a more likely target for future attacks.

This can be illustrated through the air travel sector, which frequently remains a terrorists' target, even though security measures have been taken after earlier attacks. A most likely reason for terrorists to keep falling back in their usual patterns is that the results and consequences of these kinds of attacks are known to both the terrorists as well as to the general public. Another specific driver that can be identified for terrorists to choose their targets is media coverage. This coverage is most likely to be provided through attacks resulting in many casualties.

Attacks aimed at disturbing the container supply chain have the potential of creating worldwide chaos in that supply chain, but are less likely to inflict a high number of casualties. This is where a clear distinction can be made in threat analysis. Terrorists can both target the maritime sector itself or (mis)use its open character and effectiveness to import/export terrorism. Both threats are fundamentally different and therefore require fundamentally different solutions. For instance, if the maritime system were not considered as a target itself but only as a means, container inspection at the port of destination would be possible. If, however, port infrastructures are considered possible terrorist targets, securing these by having containers checked at the port of origin results in a more complex and far more costly system. If a terrorist was to blow up a container at a certain time or at a certain location, he would most probably rely on remote control instead of on a timer or e-tracking, since these ways would be far less precise.

Based on these drivers, the September 11 attacks do not diverge from previous patterns. It can therefore be argued that the container supply chain does not pose a likely target, since it has not been one in the past. However, some terrorist groups like the LTTE (the Liberation Tigers of Tamil Eelam) have been known to attack maritime targets and make use of waterborne mines. From their past actions, it would not be a drastic turn to using container transport as a means of distributing terror.

Public Ownership

Since September 11, 2001, the awareness of terrorists' actions has clearly risen. This increase, however, has not been as substantial in all fields as it has been in the air transport sector. As far as the maritime sector is concerned, initiatives have been started, budgets have been raised, and a few coordinated counter-measures have been put into place. Ultimately, this means that the maritime sector, and specifically the container transport sector, remain wide-open to the terrorist threat, with the key issue in this being responsibility and ownership of the problem. So far, there has not been one single stakeholder who can clearly be identified as being responsible for implementing counter-measures. For instance, in the United States, approximately nine governmental agencies have some role in national security regarding the maritime sector, but so far none has taken control over the problem. Ever since the creation of the Department of Homeland Security was announced, all initiatives from current security-related agencies have been delayed until the make-up and stance of the new department has been determined. This does, however, mean that maritime security will be far from perfect at least until this department becomes operational.

In Europe, there currently are no plans for setting up a comparable coordinating body; similarly, no clear ownership of the problem can be identified in Europe. The structure of current European cooperation is such that security remains a national issue. These national interests are therefore protected through bilateral agreements with the United States in the Container Security Initiative (CSI) agreement.

Another U.S. initiative, which is implemented on a bilateral basis, is the new Customs-Trade Partnership Against Terrorism (CTPAT); an initiative in which ports within a complying country obligate themselves to have containers sealed before they arrive in the United States. This, however, does not provide actual security, as the container can now be sealed at the port of departure, keeping it unsealed during its transfer to the port of origin—this while land-based transport is considered to be the most vulnerable phase in the container's move, as they are known to be left unguarded at parking lots and at shunting yards. Though once arrived at a port, a container is usually relatively well protected due to terminal fences, guarded gates and (camera) surveillance. In addition, another weakness in the CTPAT initiative is that there is no standard for applying seals or for the type of seals. It can, therefore be concluded that generally, the existing U.S. programs are poorly integrated with European ones.

The European Commission strongly opposes these bilateral agreements since they will scatter European interests creating dissension, increasing competitiveness amongst ports and countries, and thus reducing European cooperation and the European Commission's authority. Thus far, the European Commission has not outlined concrete proposals to oppose the terrorist threat. Since the Commission's initiative in this field is lacking, member-states are now launching their own individual (occasionally collective on a bilateral basis) initiatives and solutions. Besides security, there is also the countries' ports' competitive positions at stake here. If the United States is planning on expanding CTPAT into their "safe ports" initiative, it is likely that complying European ports could greatly benefit from this. Individual countries might be able to adapt a system of checks at their ports which would be—for the time being—satisfactory to the United States without providing a supply chain-wide security coverage system. U.S.-authorized countries and ports will, however, gain a pseudo-oligarchic position, giving them considerable competitive advantages.

The resulting lack of ownership, awareness and cooperation between the United States and Europe, as well as within Europe itself, leaves such initiatives scattered, the research budget marginal, and the maritime system wide open to the terrorist threat.

Private Ownership

One of the key challenges presented by the overwhelming private ownership of the majority of the container supply chain is that a container changes hands several times on its way from its origin to its destination, causing multiple parties to be responsible and liable for the container's contents. A way around this, in order to achieve involvement by fewer parties in the transport of a container, would be logistics-chain integration. By reducing the number of supply-chain participants, the number of handovers and seal inspections can similarly be reduced.

The current system is, in fact, problematic from the start; although forwarders, transporters, and carriers do accept responsibility and liability for a container, they are dependant on information provided by the shipper, while not being allowed to open the container. In some cases, the shipper also demands to facilitate the transport from the container's origin to the terminal, leaving the forwarder or carrier in the dark even on the actual origin of the container. They now are fully dependant on the data provided in the Bill of Lading. It therefore does not make sense to place responsibility in the hands of a carrier.

A solution for this problem could be found by making one body responsible for the container's transport. It would be logical that, since this party has to be present at both the point of origin where the container is sealed and the point of destination where the cargo is received, this party is either the shipper or the receiver. If the seal is compromised during transport, the transporting party at that moment should reseal the container, thus taking responsibility for its load. In the current system, liability is only considered applicable to determine which party should approach its insurance company in order to get stolen property refunded. The party that is liable is the party that is shipping or storing the container at the moment of theft.

To verify whether a seal has been tampered with, its number should be compared (or read) with the number on the Bill of Lading. A problem with seals under the current regime is that they are only "read" occasionally, since reading them costs money. For example, the seals of containers arriving at the Port of Rotterdam by rail, truck, or barge are not checked/read. This means the port takes responsibility for these containers without verifying their status. In most cases where seals are read and do not match the numbers on the documents, the mismatch is caused simply by a lack of enforced discipline in the chain, instead of by illicit activities. If Customs, for example, opens a container to inspect its contents, they afterwards reseal the container with a different seal, and therefore a different seal number. If this is not properly documented, mismatches will occur.

The majority of containers are currently sealed through a passive, indicative seal. This is a seal that does not physically prevent entry into a container as a lock would, but merely indicates that the container door at one point has been opened. Active seals can incorporate several options, from communicating with close proximity readers on the container's status, to signaling a control center on the container's status and whereabouts. The active, close proximity seals costs approximately $3.00 to $5.00, which is significantly more than the passive seals at $0.50. Besides this, the cost of development of the active seals is also high.

Summarizing Threats

The system is perceived to be poorly defended against misuse and terrorism due to its global and open nature. There is no clear set of safety and security criteria from both the United States and the European Commission, leading to individual EU member-states taking their own uncoordinated initiatives. A way of dealing with this in Europe could be the establishment of a European coordinating body. If such a body is not founded, Europe risks an additional delay and continued problematic approaches to this challenge, comparable with ones the United States is now experiencing due to fragmented responsibilities of agencies.

The International Maritime Organization (IMO)[3] has served as a market place for ideas thus far and should continue to do so in the future. At its December 2003 Diplomatic Conference on Maritime Security held in London, the IMO adopted a number of amendments to the 1974 Safety of Life at Sea Convention (SOLAS), the most far-reaching of which enshrines the new International Ship and Port Facility Security Code (ISPS Code). The Code contains detailed security-related requirements for Governments, port authorities and shipping companies in a mandatory section (Part A), together with a series of guidelines about how to meet these requirements in a second, non-mandatory section (Part B).

The Conference also adopted a series of resolutions designed to add weight to the amendments, encourage the application of the measures to ships and port facilities not covered by the Code, and pave the way for future work on the subject. These new measures will enter into force in July 2004 as part of a series of measures to strengthen maritime security and prevent and suppress acts of terrorism against shipping, which will be of crucial significance not only to the international maritime community but the world community as a whole, given the pivotal role shipping plays in the conduct of world trade. The measures represent the culmination of just over a year's intense work by IMO's

Maritime Safety Committee and its Intersessional Working Group, since the terrorist atrocities in the United States in September 2001.

In the United States as well as in Europe, there is a distinct lack of awareness of the threat, especially in the private sector; if there is any concern within the private sector, it is for counter-measures taken by governments that will adversely affect container throughput—affecting the commercial imperative. Ultimately, greater enforced discipline of uniform application to container security throughout the supply and transport chain would go a long way to obviating much of the non-malicious threat.

Solutions

For reducing (not eliminating) the terrorist threat, several methods can be identified.

1. Risk analysis
2. Container integrity
3. Container tracking and tracing
4. Container load verification

Risk Analysis

Risk analysis forms a strong tool to detect suspicious cargo in order to be able to intercept it. It is, however, only as strong as the algorithms and information behind it. Risk analysis, as it is currently performed in many ports, frequently does not incorporate sufficient data to be able to detect the bulk of illicit trade. An expansion of criteria, enhancement of algorithms, more information exchange within the logistics chain as well as between ports, and more extensive use of computerized search tools, would increase the effectiveness of risk analysis.

The European Commission's Joint Research Centre has, in cooperation with the European Anti-fraud Office, OLAF, developed a software tool named Contraffic, capable of performing a risk analysis on the likeliness that a container is transporting illicit material. In the Contraffic system, this is done by keeping track of the ports-of-call of both the container *and* the ship used in the container's transport. In most of the current risk analyses, only the last port-of-call is registered, whereas Contraffic registers the actual origin of the container and all ports-of-call on its way to its final destination. Based on the results of a pilot that was performed with Contraffic, it can be concluded that this way of conducting risk analysis forms a valuable extension to the current aspects. The algorithms incorporated in Contraffic focus on the detection of the evasion of anti-dumping taxes; algorithms focusing on other aspects can be developed using the same principle of origin-destination analyses.

Currently, a large portion (approximately 50 percent to 70 percent) of the containers that are inspected in both the United States and Europe, are inspected randomly, without any risk profiling. Random checks severely disturb the logistics chain at the ports and, therefore, need to be minimized. These kinds of random checks are necessary though, as they provide a benchmark to assess the effectiveness of risk profiling. Furthermore, they are able to point out weak points in the risk analyses and new or other types of contraband trafficking. For these purposes, randomly checking a 10 percent part of the total should be sufficient.

Risk analysis is a relatively cost-effective way to retrieve illegal cargo, especially financially-motivated contraband trafficking. Unfortunately, it is by no means foolproof, and is by definition vulnerable to terrorists' contraband, as it relies on patterns which can be assessed by terrorists in order to ensure that their shipments do not match these patterns. It can even be argued that, if risk analysis algorithms are not complicated enough to avoid pattern-recognition based on the analysis' outcome, they can be a threat instead of a cure regarding terrorists' contraband.

Container Integrity

The integrity of a container during its transport from Point A to Point B in the logistics chain cannot be assured. Given sufficient time, opportunity, and a remote location, people will be able to open a container and tamper with its contents. The easiest way of gaining access to a container is to break the container's seal and open the doors; however, this can be easily identified and the container's contents can be examined before it is allowed to be shipped again. To avoid attracting attention to the container, criminals will try to leave the seal intact when opening the container. There are several ways to do this, many of which are even illustrated on the Internet.[4]

A problem in sealing containers is posed by the fact that a container is not as standardized as it may seem. This lack of standardization contributes to the lack of sealing standards. Furthermore, the way in which many seals are attached is susceptible to unnoticed container tampering; for example, it is believed that an experienced thief can take cargo from a sealed container without noticeably tampering with it, within 20 minutes. A more effective way of sealing a container would be to attach a string/seal around both locking bars, or to apply a seal on the inside of a container. The quality of the seal does not have anything to do with the possibilities of working around it; the bottom line of sealing a container is maximizing the time that is needed to circumvent it. Indeed, if criminals are given sufficient time and opportunity they can also cut through the side or the hinges of the container giving them access. In order not to attract suspicion, these parts would afterwards have to be repainted, which can result in differences in color that stand out.

The container's integrity can also be assessed through electronic systems that are installed inside the container. Since these systems are in general quite costly, only containers carrying high value loads currently are equipped and protected this way. These systems are able to detect movement within the container, including the opening of the door. They can be set in such a way that they will send out a signal to a control center on opening or send out this signal if opened at another position other than its predetermined destination. These options incorporate GPS (Global Positioning System) and GSM (Global System for Mobiles) technologies, and are ascending the container integrity function towards container tracking. Many of these systems dispose of integrity assurance as well as tracking and tracing abilities.

Clearly not all possibilities for sealing containers have been carefully studied since it has not received top priority due to the costs this would introduce to the chain.

Container Tracking and Tracing

As mentioned before, there are systems which (although quite costly) are able to give the position of a container. A distinction can be made between systems giving a time-to-time or a continuous update on the container's position, and systems that signal status-changes, like the opening of the door or movement within the container. Currently, these systems do not yet provide global coverage. This is not because of technical feasibility, but instead a result of the moderate number of current system's users.

If the control center is notified of a non-planned incident, such as deviation from the planned route or opening of the container's door prior to reaching its destination, it will in turn notify local authorities. Experiences with these systems so far indicate that theft is practically non-existent after the system's application, and local authorities quickly respond to a control center's notification. If these systems were less costly, for instance because of advantages of producing them in larger numbers, they would definitely improve the security of the container supply chain.

Container Load Verification

There currently are two ways of physical verification of a container's load. The term "physical verification" refers to the actual opening of a container and manually verifying its contents with the Bill of Lading. This process of unpacking takes—depending on the number of (Customs) officials who are performing the task—approximately eight hours. This, of course, results in significant delays for containers and introduces uncertainties in the logistics chain. It also does not offer a structural solution to the problem, as it causes delays due to manpower, container terminal space, and the resulting container handling backlog—therefore, it is impossible to open every container for load verification.

A form of container load verification that has come into use in recent years is an X-ray scanner. These scanners are capable of giving a fairly accurate image of the container's contents. Scanners have been known to generate such a large amount of taxes from confiscated contraband that they can be regarded as a profitable investment instead of a costly expenditure. For X-ray scanners to work properly within a terminal's handling process and to reach a high utilization, terminal space needs to be reserved for their placement. This is one of the reasons why a number of European terminals do not yet use an X-ray scanner.

Although organic substances are fairly easy to identify in a container scan, there are ways to keep these substances from showing up. Scanners are, for instance, unable to penetrate cans and lead within a container, causing materials inside boxes or tins to remain unverified. In addition, Customs officials interpreting the X-ray image have to be trained in what they should look for; it is suggested, for example, that if a weapon of mass destruction (WMD) is taken apart and transported in pieces in a container, Customs officials would probably not be able to distinguish them from auto-parts. Research is being done to improve scanning, including the ability to scan for different types of loads, such as nuclear, biological, and radioactive cargo. In the United States, the container scanning process is focusing on radioactive material. This again illustrates that there will always be a focus on some type of illicit good since a radiation scanner will not be able to detect drugs; one machine cannot scan for everything, and it is not feasible to put a container through 10 different kinds of scanners.

In the United Kingdom, 4 percent to 7 percent of imported containers are checked based on a risk analysis, which is well above the European and United States average of 2 percent. If a scan does not result in a clear and satisfactory image (on average, this is the case for 1 in every 150), the container is unpacked.

For contraband, it is virtually impossible to forecast which percentage of contraband remains undetected. If such a forecast could be made, it should be made per illicit good, since there are large differences in the ways goods are smuggled in, and the degree of success this smuggling has. It is anticipated, for example, that approximately 10 percent of smuggled drugs are intercepted.

Integration

Since all of the measures mentioned above form parts of solutions, clearly an integration of measures is required. An integrated solution that is often referred to is the "intelligent container." This means a container should be perceived to have the ability to scan its own contents and detect certain illicit and dangerous cargo. The container should then be able to contact and warn authorities. Although there already is sufficient technology available to oppose numerous threats, and technical implementation of these measures in a container is feasible, financially we still have a long way to go.

Issues of Ownership

Although most of the solutions that were thought up so far serve more than one security/legal aspect, they usually do focus on theft prevention, smuggling prevention, or security enhancement. It is clear that if the problem's ownership is to be shifted to the private sector, and a private company such as a forwarder is to invest in one of these fields, theft prevention will be the most likely choice since there is at least some form of benefit to be gained. If theft is not a major problem to the company, there will be little financial incentive for further research.

The initiative to take container security to the next level is currently with companies manufacturing security related products such as seals. Since there are globally thought to be over 15 million containers in circulation which provide for approximately 250 million moves per year, the container securing business has the potential to be a very high value and therefore lucrative. If these manufacturers would come up with a system that would have a positive return on investments within a reasonable period of time, there would be a potential market of 15 million containers to apply this solution to. A possible outcome to the security and its solution funding problem could be the introduction of a security tax, as is already in place at airports. There, an amount of $20 is charged per passenger to finance security measures.

Although the public and some governmental bodies are willing to pay (a certain amount) for security improvements, the majority of security measures places costs with the shippers and carriers. Of course this is not insurmountable, but does again raise a barrier for improvements.

Conclusions

Our consultations with stakeholders revealed considerable challenges to securing the global sea-container shipping system.[5] Our analysis leads to the following conclusions and suggested strategies for addressing the issue of maritime security:

1. There was a wide range of views among the stakeholders on the magnitude of the threat posed by terrorists to container shipping. There was agreement that the magnitude and nature of this threat are not well understood. The participants also agreed on the need to study and understand the nature and magnitude of the threats posed by terrorists, and the potential consequences of terrorist actions.

2. There was a consensus that the flow of containers is vulnerable to terrorist action. The transport chain for containers is quite fragmented and involves many different organizations. This makes the chain quite "leaky" and easy to penetrate, and makes it difficult to secure the transport chain.

3. The transport of containers is not sufficiently transparent, i.e., the information about what is being transported, by whom, and from where is not easy to check. The flow of information accompanying the flow of containers is not good. Even when the information is available, there is little Customs can do, short of physically opening and inspecting the container, to check its validity. Only 1 percent to 2 percent of all containers are physically opened and inspected.

4. Physically opening and inspecting containers, while possible, is considered to be too expensive to do on a routine basis. Most inspections are based on intelligence gained about the contents of containers.

5. An alternative to physically opening and inspecting containers is to X-ray the container. However, the available X-ray devices are not foolproof by a long shot. Assuming that X-ray machines are able to detect suspicious loads, the issue of what to do next remains.

6. Ports are reluctant to unilaterally undertake security measures that slow down the processing of arriving containers. In part, this reluctance is fostered by the low margins with which the industry operates. This makes ports very reluctant to unilaterally do anything that would raise their costs and hence prices. as they see this as hurting their competitive position vis-à-vis other ports.

7. It is difficult to track the journey of a container. There are several ways in which, if one wants, the real origin of a container can be hidden from officials at the destination point. This is usually made possible with the help of corrupt officials at intermediate ports who are willing to change or falsify the necessary documents.

8. The issue of who is liable for the contents of a container is potentially a very important issue. As of now, the person (organization) whose cargo is being shipped is liable. However, it is quite easy for someone to falsify the information needed for transporting a shipment in a container. Given that all the liability rests with shippers, ports and ship owners, there is little incentive for ports, shipping companies, and ship owners to verify the information they are

provided with. The risks of damage caused to the assets of port operators or ship owners are covered by insurance.

9. There seems to be some issue about who controls the ports; most ports are not owned and operated by national governments. This makes it difficult for the national governments to force the ports to do something that the national governments want, but the port itself does not want to do. The lack of policy instruments for exerting any leverage in the area of port security was also noted as hindering efforts to improve port security.

10. Ports are extremely worried about the competitive position vis-à-vis other ports. In short, they are extremely price sensitive and are willing to gloss over security concerns when these are in conflict with their commercial interests. This observation seems to hold for the entire freight transportation sector.

11. National governments of EU member-states are concerned about potential actions being taken by the U.S. government, actions which would adversely affect the position of ports in their countries. The EU is concerned that member-states may negotiate bilateral agreements with individual member-states. These concerns are a potential cause of friction between the European Commission and the governments of member-states.

12. Solutions should cover the complete logistics chain, should incorporate some form of risk analysis, and should make use of the latest available technology (such as electronic seals, positioning technology, sensors, etc.).

13. Awareness—in both governmental offices and private companies—about the need to improve security against potential threats was perceived as low; it was suggested that actions should be undertaken to raise the level of awareness about these issues.

14. The importance of having timely and reliable information was mentioned many times. The available information about containers and their contents needs to be addressed. Several reasons cause the lack of timely and reliable information. Steps to standardize and digitize information provision would go a long way in remedying this state of affairs.

15. A clear definition of the possible threats and the likeliness of their occurrence should be defined. Many threats and their solutions are in some way interrelated, causing solutions to emerge that are not tackling the threats that they are supposed to.

16. There should be a single European body that deals with port and maritime security. This body should:

    •   Coordinate European efforts to improve maritime security.
    •   Ensure post-attack measures are thoughtfully applied; just like halfway measures can bring about more attacks, the 9/11 attacks teach that drastic counter-measures can easily be just as harmful as the attacks themselves.
    •   Set security criteria for all European ports to comply with; these criteria should include risk boundaries assessing which containers to scan—in all likelihood, this will cause the number of checks to increase.
    •   Check the degree to which the security criteria are complied with.

17. An effort should be made to further standardize containers. Container seals should be applied in a standard way, which should ensure the container's doors cannot be opened without damaging the seal. Efforts should also be made to incorporate advanced electronic container integrity systems in the container transport business.
18. Risk analysis challenges include:

    - The criteria used in risk analysis should be expanded to be able to target more types of contraband.
    - Container manifests should be pre-announced digitally so risk profiling can also be done digitally.
    - Random checks should be limited to approximately 10 percent.

While these observations and recommendations by no means represent the complete scope of maritime security challenges, they are offered here as research-based contributions to the overall mission of homeland security. Further, this discussion provides some useful ideas for how the public and private sector worldwide can more effectively collaborate in the global war on terrorism.[6]

Notes

1. This Expression of Interest is entitled "Securing the sea-container shipping system" and can be found at eoi.cordis.lu/dsp_details.cfm?ID=26447.
2. For more information on the Framework VI Program, see www.cordis.lu/fp6/whatisfp6.htm. FP6 is the result of the call by EU governments at the March 2000 EU summit in Lisbon for a better use of European research efforts through the creation of an internal market for science and technology–a "European Research Area" (ERA). FP6 is the financial instrument to help make the ERA a reality through funding research across Europe in a broad range of subjects and disciplines.
3. For more information on the IMO, see www.imo.org.
4. See, for example, "Break into a Container in Under 2 Minutes!" www.sealock.com/problem/problem.htm and "Hide the Evidence of a Break-In in Under 1 Minute!" www.sealock.com/problem/problem2.htm; see also 09/06/1997 Reference Number: 199777, www.maritimesecurity.org/asa1997.htm and 02/03/2001 Reference Number: 2001–75, www.maritimesecurity.org/asa2001.htm.
5. On behalf of RAND Europe, we would like to thank the consultation's attendees for their participation and ideas, and hope that the material that was brought up through this initiative will result in a strong take-up from all stakeholders.
6. Final paragraph of this conclusion added by volume editors. For more information about RAND Europe or this document, please contact: *General SeaCurity,* RAND Europe, Maarten van de Voort, voort@rand.org, Newtonweg 1, 2333 CP Leiden, Phone: +31 71 524 5151, fax: +31 71 524 5192. reinfo@rand.org. www.randeurope.org. RAND Europe, is an independent, not-for-profit, policy research organization that serves the public interest by improving policy-making and informing the public debate. RAND Europe's work is for European governments, institutions, and private sector entities with a need for rigorous, impartial and multidisciplinary analy-

sis of the hardest problems they face. This report has been peer-reviewed in accordance with RAND's quality assurance standards (see www.rand.org/about/standards/) and therefore may be represented as a RAND Europe product.

Chapter 13

Terrorism and Security Issues Facing the Water Infrastructure Sector

Claudia Copeland and Betsy Cody

The September 11, 2001, attacks on the World Trade Center and the Pentagon have drawn attention to the security of many institutions, facilities, and systems in the United States, including the nation's water supply and water quality infrastructure.[1] These systems have long been recognized as being potentially vulnerable to terrorist attacks of various types including physical disruption, bioterrorism/chemical contamination, and cyber attack. Damage or destruction by terrorist attack could disrupt the delivery of vital human services in this country, threatening public health and the environment, or possibly causing loss of life. This chapter presents an overview of this large and diverse sector, describes security-related actions by the government and private sector since September 11, and discusses additional policy issues and responses, including congressional interest.

The potential for terrorism is not new. In 1941, Federal Bureau of Investigation Director J. Edgar Hoover wrote, "It has long been recognized that among public utilities, water supply facilities offer a particularly vulnerable point of attack to the foreign agent, due to the strategic position they occupy in keeping the wheels of industry turning and in preserving the health and morale of the American populace."[2] Water infrastructure systems also are highly linked with other infrastructures, especially electric power and transportation, as well as the chemical industry which supplies treatment chemicals, making security of all of them an issue of concern. These types of vulnerable interconnections were evident, for example, during the August 2003 electricity blackout in the northeastern United States; wastewater treatment plants in Cleveland, Detroit, New York, and other locations that lacked backup generation systems lost power and discharged millions of gallons of untreated sewage during the emergency, and power failures at drinking water plants led to boil water advisories in many communities.

Background

Broadly speaking, water infrastructure systems include surface and ground water sources of untreated water for municipal, industrial, agricultural, and household needs; dams, reservoirs, aqueducts, and pipes that contain and transport raw water; treatment facilities that remove contaminants from raw water; finished water reservoirs; systems that distribute water to users; and wastewater collection and treatment facilities. Across the country, these systems comprise more than 75,000 dams and reservoirs; thousands of miles of pipes, aqueducts, water distribution, and sewer lines; 168,000 public drinking water facilities (many serving as few as 25 customers); and about 16,000 publicly owned wastewater treatment facilities. Ownership and management are both public and private; the federal government has ownership responsibility for hundreds of dams and diversion structures, but the vast majority of the nation's water infrastructure is either privately owned or owned by non-federal units of government.

The federal government has built hundreds of water projects, primarily dams and reservoirs for irrigation development and flood control, with municipal and industrial water use (M&I) as an incidental, self-financed, project purpose. Many of these facilities are critically entwined with the nation's overall water supply, transportation, and electricity infrastructure. The largest federal facilities were built and are managed by the Bureau of Reclamation (Bureau) of the Department of the Interior and the U.S. Army Corps of Engineers (Corps) of the Department of Defense.

Bureau reservoirs, particularly those along the Colorado River, supply water to millions of people in southern California, Arizona, and Nevada via Bureau and non-Bureau aqueducts. Bureau projects also supply water to 9 million acres of farmland and other municipal and industrial water users in the 17 western states. The Corps operates 276 navigation locks, 11,000 miles of commercial navigation channels, and approximately 1,200 projects of varying types, including 609 dams. It supplies water to thousands of cities, towns, and industries from the 9.5 million acre-feet of water stored in its 116 lakes and reservoirs throughout the country, including service to approximately one million residents of the District of Columbia and portions of northern Virginia. The largest Corps and Bureau facilities also produce enormous amounts of power. For example, Hoover and Glen Canyon dams on the Colorado River represent 23 percent of the installed electrical capacity of the Bureau of Reclamation's 58 power plants in the west, and 7 percent of the total installed capacity in the western United States. Similarly, Corps facilities and the Bureau's Grand Coulee Dam on the Columbia River provide 43 percent of the total installed hydroelectric capacity in the west (25 percent nationwide).

A fairly small number of large drinking water and wastewater utilities located primarily in urban areas (about 15 percent of the systems) provide water services to more than 75 percent of the U.S. population. Arguably, these systems represent the greatest targets of opportunity for terrorist attacks, while the larger number of small systems that each serve fewer than 10,000 persons are less likely to be perceived as key targets by terrorists who might seek to disrupt water infrastructure systems. However, the more numerous smaller systems also tend to be less protected and, thus, are potentially more vulnerable to attack, whether by vandals or terrorists. A successful attack on even a small system could cause widespread panic, economic impacts, and a loss of public confidence in water supply systems.

Attacks resulting in physical destruction to any of these systems could include disruption of operating or distribution system components, power or telecommunications systems, electronic control systems, and could cause actual damage to reservoirs and pumping stations. A loss of flow and pressure would cause problems for customers and would hinder firefighting efforts. Further, destruction of a large dam could result in catastrophic flooding and loss of life. Bioterrorism or chemical attacks could deliver widespread contamination with small amounts of microbiological agents or toxic chemicals, and could endanger the public health of thousands. While some experts believe that risks to water systems actually are small, because it would be difficult to introduce sufficient quantities of agents to cause widespread harm, concern and heightened awareness of potential problems are apparent. Factors that are relevant to a biological agent's potential as a weapon include its stability in a drinking water system, virulence, culturability in the quantity required, and resistance to detection and treatment. Cyber attacks on computer operations can affect an entire infrastructure network, and hacking into water utility systems could result in theft or corruption of information, or denial and disruption of service.

Responses to Security Concerns

Federal dam operators went on "high-alert" immediately following the September 11 terrorist attacks. The Bureau closed its visitor facilities at Grand Coulee, Hoover, and Glen Canyon dams. Because of potential loss of life and property downstream if breached, security threats are under constant review, and coordination efforts with both the National Guard and local law enforcement officials are ongoing. The Corps also operates under continued high defense alert and temporarily closed all its facilities to visitors after September 11, although locks and dams remained operational; most closed facilities later reopened, but security is being reassessed. Following a heightened alert issued by the federal government in February 2003, the Bureau implemented additional security measures which remain in effect at dams, power plants, and other facilities. These measures include limited access to facilities and roads, closure of visitor centers, and random vehicle inspections.

Although officials believe that risks to water and wastewater utilities are small, operators have been under heightened security conditions since September 11. Local utilities have primary responsibility to assess their vulnerabilities and prioritize them for necessary security improvements. Most (especially in urban areas) have emergency preparedness plans that address issues such as redundancy of operations, public notification, and coordination with law enforcement and emergency response officials. However, many plans were developed to respond to natural disasters, domestic threats such as vandalism, and, in some cases, cyber attacks. Drinking water and wastewater utilities coordinated efforts to prepare for possible Y2K impacts on their computer systems, but these efforts focused more on cyber security than physical terrorism concerns. Thus, it is unclear whether previously existing plans incorporate sufficient procedures to address other types of terrorist threats. Utility officials are reluctant to disclose details of their systems or these confidential plans, since doing so might alert terrorists to vulnerabilities.

Water supply was one of eight critical infrastructure systems identified in President Clinton's 1998 Presidential Decision Directive 63 (PDD-63)[3] as part of a coordinated national effort to achieve the capability to protect the nation's critical infrastructure from intentional acts that would diminish them. These efforts focused primarily on the 340 large community water supply systems which each serve more than 100,000 persons. The Environmental Protection Agency (EPA) was identified as the lead federal agency for liaison with the water supply sector.

In response, in 2000, the EPA established a partnership with the American Metropolitan Water Association (AMWA) and American Water Works Association

(AWWA) to jointly undertake measures to safeguard water supplies from terrorist acts. AWWA's Research Foundation has contracted with the Department of Energy's Sandia National Laboratory to develop a vulnerability assessment tool for water systems (as an extension of methodology for assessing federal dams). The EPA is supporting an ongoing project with the Sandia Lab to pilot test the physical vulnerability assessment tool and develop a cyber vulnerability assessment tool. An Information Sharing and Analysis Center (ISAC) supported by an EPA grant became operational under AMWA's leadership in December 2002. It will allow for dissemination of alerts to drinking water and waste-water utilities about potential threats or vulnerabilities to the integrity of their operations that have been detected, and viable resolutions to problems.[4]

Some research on water sector infrastructure protection is underway. The Department of the Army is conducting research in the area of detection and treatment to remove various chemical agents. The Federal Emergency Management Agency (FEMA) is leading an effort to produce databases of water distribution systems and to develop assessment tools for evaluating threats posed by the introduction of a biological or chemical agent into a water system. The Centers for Disease Control and Prevention is developing guidance on potential biological agents and the effects of standard water treatment practices on their persistence. However, in the January 2001 report of the President's Commission on Critical Infrastructure Protection, ongoing water sector research was characterized as a small effort that leaves a number of gaps and shortfalls relative to U.S. water supplies.[5]

This report stated that gaps exist in four major areas, concerns that remain relevant and are guiding policymakers now:

- Threat/vulnerability risk assessments;
- Identification and characterization of biological and chemical agents;
- A need to establish a center of excellence to support communities in conducting vulnerability and risk assessment; and
- Application of information assurance techniques to computerized systems used by water utilities, as well as the oil, gas, and electric sectors, for operational data and control operations.

Less attention has been focused on protecting wastewater treatment facilities than drinking water systems, perhaps because destruction of them probably represents more of an environmental threat (i.e., by release of untreated sewage) than a direct threat to life or public welfare.

Vulnerabilities do exist, however. Large underground collector sewers could be accessed by terrorist groups for purposes of placing destructive devices beneath buildings or city streets. Damage to a wastewater facility prevents water from being treated and can impact downriver water intakes. Destruction of containers that hold large amounts of chemicals at treatment plants could result in release of toxic chemical agents, such as chlorine gas, which can be deadly to humans if inhaled and, at lower doses, can burn eyes and skin and inflame the lungs. Since the terrorist attacks, many utilities have switched from using chlorine gas for disinfection to alternatives which are believed to be safer, such as sodium hypochlorite or ultraviolet light. However, some consumer groups remain concerned that many wastewater utilities continue to use chlorine gas, including facilities that serve heavily populated areas. To prepare for potential accidental releases of hazardous chemicals from their facilities, 3,460 wastewater and drinking water utilities already are subject to risk management planning requirements under the Clean Air Act, but some observers advocate requiring federal standards to ensure that facilities using dangerous chemicals, such as wastewater treatment plants, use the best possible industry practices to reduce hazards.[6]

There are no federal standards or agreed-upon industry best practices within the water infrastructure sector to govern readiness, response to security incidents, and recovery. Efforts to develop protocols and tools are ongoing since the 2001 terrorist attacks. Wastewater and drinking water utility organizations are implementing computer software and training materials to evaluate vulnerabilities at large, medium, and small utility systems, and the EPA has provided some grant assistance for conducting vulnerability assessments. Out of funds appropriated in January 2002 (P.L. 107–117), the EPA awarded $51 million for vulnerability assessment grants to 449 large drinking water utilities, averaging $115,000 per utility. Out of subsequent appropriations, the EPA has been targeting grants to "train the trainers," delivering technical assistance to organizations such as the Rural Community Assistance Program and the Water Environment Federation that, in turn, can assist and train personnel at thousands of medium and small utilities throughout the country. With financial support from the EPA, water and engineering groups are developing voluntary physical security standards for drinking water and wastewater systems that could serve as a model for future EPA voluntary standards; the EPA is not currently authorized to require water infrastructure systems to undertake specific security measures or meet particular security standards.

The EPA has taken a number of organizational and planning steps to strengthen water security. The agency created a National Homeland Security Research Center within the Office of Research and Development to develop the scientific foundations and tools that can be used to respond to attacks on water systems. In September 2003, it created a Water Security Division, taking over activities initiated by a Water Protection Task Force after the September 11 terrorist attacks. The office is training water utility personnel on security issues, support the WaterISAC, and implement the agency's comprehensive research plan. The EPA has issued both a Water Security Research and Technical Support Action Plan, identifying critical research needs and providing an implementation plan for addressing those needs, and a Strategic Plan for Homeland Security.[7] The Strategic Plan, which is not limited to water security concerns, identifies four mission-critical areas on which the EPA intends to focus its homeland security planning: critical infrastructure protection; preparedness, response, and recovery; communication and information; and protection of EPA personnel and information.

There has been criticism of some of these EPA efforts, however. A preliminary review of the Research and Action Plan by a panel of the National Research Council identified some gaps, suggested alternative priorities, and noted that the Plan is silent on the financial resources required to complete the research and to implement needed countermeasures to improve water security.[8] The EPA's Inspector General recently issued an evaluation report on the Strategic Plan for Homeland Security, and concluded that the agency has not outlined how resources, activities, and outputs will achieve the water security program's goals. Moreover, the Inspector General said that EPA lacks fundamental components, such as performance measures, for monitoring program performance against goals.[9]

The EPA responded that long-term objectives for critical water infrastructure protection activities may be identified in a future, revised strategic plan.

Federal officials have been reassessing federal infrastructure vulnerabilities for several years. The Bureau of Reclamation's site security program is aimed at ensuring protection of the Bureau's 252 high- and significant-hazard dams and facilities, and 58 hydroelectric plants. After September 11, the Bureau committed to conducting vulnerability and risk assessments at 280 high-priority facilities. Risk assessments were completed at 156 of these in fiscal year 2002 and fiscal year 2003; the remaining facilities are to be completed in fiscal year 2004. These assessments resulted in recommendations now being implemented to enhance security procedures and physical facilities, such as additional security staffing, limited vehicle and visitor access, and coordination with local law enforcement agencies. The Corps implements a facility protection program to detect, protect, and respond to threats to Corps facilities, and a dam security program to coordinate security systems for Corps infrastructure. It also implements a national emergency preparedness program which assists civilian governments in responding to all regional/national emergencies, including acts of terrorism. Both agencies participate in the Interagency Committee on Dam Safety (ICODS), which is part of the National Dam Safety Program that is led by FEMA.

A February 2002 White House report[10] presented a national strategy for protecting the nation's critical infrastructures, and identified four water sector initiatives: identify high-priority vulnerabilities and improve site security; improve monitoring and analytic capabilities; improve information exchange and coordinate contingency planning; and work with other sectors to manage unique risks resulting from interdependencies. It also proposed establishing an ISAC for information sharing among dam operators. The strategy is intended to focus national protection priorities, inform resource allocation processes, and be the basis for cooperative public and private protection actions.

Department of Homeland Security

The newly created Department of Homeland Security (DHS, established in P.L. 107–297[11]) has a mandate to coordinate securing the nation's critical infrastructure, including water infrastructure, through partnerships with the public and private sectors. It is responsible for detailed implementation of core elements of the national strategy for protection of critical infrastructures. One of its tasks is to assess infrastructure vulnerabilities, an activity that wastewater and drinking water utilities have been doing since September 11, under their own initiatives and congressional mandates (P.L. 107–188, discussed below). The legislative reorganization did not transfer Corps or Bureau responsibilities for security protection of dams and other facilities, or the EPA's responsibilities to assist drinking water and wastewater utilities.

In December 2003, President Bush issued Homeland Security Presidential Directive/HSPD-7 which establishes a national policy for the federal government to identify, prioritize, and protect critical infrastructure as a part of homeland security.[12] The directive called for the DHS to integrate all security efforts among federal agencies and to complete a comprehensive national plan for critical infrastructure protection by December 2004. The document supersedes PDD-63, which started the process of federal protection of critical infrastructure even before the 2001 terrorist attacks.

Under HSPD-7, the EPA continues as the lead federal agency to ensure protecting drinking water and wastewater treatment systems from possible terrorist acts and other sabotage.

Appropriations

In P.L. 107–38—the 2001 Emergency Supplemental Appropriations Act, enacted one week after September 11—Congress appropriated $40 billion for recovery from, and response to, the terrorist attacks. The President allocated $20 billion of this total (about $30 million went to water infrastructure), and in October 2001, he requested allocation of the remaining $20 billion to be distributed by Congress. The request included $245 million for federal water infrastructure programs: $30 million for security at Bureau facilities; $139 million for security at Corps facilities; and $45.5 million to the EPA for drinking water vulnerability assessments. P.L. 107–117—the DoD and Emergency Supplemental Appropriations Act for fiscal year 2002—provided the full amounts requested for the Bureau and the Corps, and increased funding for the EPA—including $91 million to strengthen security at large drinking water systems through vulnerability assessments and other non-structural security efforts.

In July 2002, Congress approved a fiscal year 2002 supplemental appropriations bill that included $50 million more in EPA grants for vulnerability assessments by small and medium-size drinking water systems, and $108 million for security activities at Corps facilities (P.L. 107–206). However, on August 13, President Bush announced that he would not spend $5.1 billion of contingent emergency funds in the bill, including the EPA grant and Corps funds. (For information, see CRS Report RL31406, *Supplemental Appropriations for FY2002: Combating Terrorism and Other Issues*.)

The President's fiscal year 2003 budget requested $115 million for security at water infrastructure facilities, consisting of $28.4 million for the Bureau, $65 million for the Corps, and $22 million for the EPA including $15 million for vulnerability assessments at small- and medium-size drinking water systems. Final action on appropriations for these agencies was delayed until February 2003. In P.L. 108–7, Congress appropriated $85 million for water infrastructure security programs, approving the amounts requested for the EPA and the Bureau, but $30 million less than was requested for the Corps' facility security program. In P.L. 108–11, the fiscal year 2003 supplemental appropriations bill, Congress provided an additional $39 million for the Corps and $25 million for the Bureau, for increased security measures at their facilities.

For fiscal year 2004, Congress appropriated funds for water infrastructure security at levels requested by the Administration, including $32.2 million for the EPA to support utility vulnerability assessments and the WaterISAC (in P.L. 108–199), $12.9 million for the Corps, and $27.8 million for the Bureau (appropriations for the Bureau and the Corps are included in P.L. 108–137).[13] Appropriations for water infrastructure security have totaled $482.8 million since the September 11 attacks. The President's fiscal year 2005 budget requested $66.3 million for water security, consisting of:

- $11.1 million for the EPA (to support training and development of voluntary industry best practices for security; the request is $21 million less than the fiscal year 2004 request, largely due to the completion of vulnerability assessments by drinking water utilities, which the EPA had previously assisted with);

- $43.2 million for the Bureau ($15.4 million more than was requested for fiscal year 2004), intended to fund full implementation of the agency's physical security, personnel and information security, law enforcement program, and to advance the physical hardening improvements that were identified in the Bureau's security risk assessments in fiscal year 2002; and

- $12 million for the Corps (approximately the same as requested for fiscal year 2004) to cover non-project specific protective measures at Corps administrative buildings and other general use facilities. Also, the Corps budget requests an additional $72 million for security measures at various specific individual water resource projects around the country.

Policy Issues and Congressional Responses

Congress and other policymakers are considering a number of initiatives in this area, including enhanced physical security, communication and coordination, and research. Regarding physical security, a key question is whether protective measures should be focused on the largest water systems and facilities, where risks to the public are greatest, or on all, since small facilities may be more vulnerable. A related question is responsibility for additional steps because the federal government has direct control over only a limited portion of the water infrastructure sector. The adequacy of physical and operational security safeguards is an issue for all in this sector. One possible option for federal facilities (dams and reservoirs maintained by the Bureau and the Corps) is to restrict visitor access, including at adjacent recreational facilities, although such actions could raise objections from the public. Some operators of non-federal facilities and utilities are likewise concerned. As a precaution after September 11, New York City, which provides water to 9 million consumers, closed its reservoirs indefinitely to all fishing, hiking, and boating, and blocked access to some roads.

Policymakers also are examining measures that could improve coordination and exchange of information on vulnerabilities, risks, threats, and responses. This is a key objective of the WaterISAC and also of the Department of Homeland Security, which includes, for example, functions of the National Infrastructure Protection Center (NIPC) of the FBI that brings together the private sector and government agencies at all levels to protect critical infrastructure, especially on cyber issues.

One issue of interest is how the new Department is coordinating its activities with ongoing security efforts by other federal agencies and non-federal entities that operate water infrastructure systems—including its implementation of the comprehensive national plan required by the recent Presidential Directive/HSPD-7. This issue has arisen in recent weeks as a result of moves by the DHS to assert authority over water utility security, despite claims by the EPA that it is the lead federal agency. For example, the DHS is preparing guidance documents on how each infrastructure sector, including water systems, can protect itself from security threats, and DHS contractors have visited several water utilities and asked to view pertinent information, including the utilities' vulnerability assessments. EPA sources have said that the DHS contractors may not have authority to view the vulnerability assessments, but Department officials have reportedly cited

HSPD-7 as giving them authority to conduct water system inspections, due to its lead role in coordinating critical infrastructure protection. Since February, 2004, the two agencies have been working to clarify their roles in providing security to water utilities.

One particular communication/coordination issue concerns the extent of the EPA's ability to collect and analyze security data from water utilities, especially information in vulnerability assessments submitted under the Bioterrorism Preparedness Act (discussed below). EPA officials believe that the Act permits reviewing utility submissions for overall compliance and allows aggregation of data, but precludes the agency from asking for or analyzing data showing changes in security levels as a safeguard against unintended release of such information. Others, including the EPA's Inspector General, believe that the EPA has the authority and responsibility to review and analyze the information in order to identify and prioritize threats and to develop plans to protect drinking water supplies.

Among the research needs being addressed are tools for vulnerability and risk analysis, identification and response to biological/chemical agents, real-time monitoring of water supplies, and development of information technology. The cost of additional protections and how to pay for them are issues of interest, and policymakers continue to consider resource needs and how to direct them at public and private sector priorities. One issue of increasing importance to drinking water and wastewater utilities is how to pay for physical security improvements, since currently there are no federal funds dedicated to these purposes.

The 107th and 108th Congresses have conducted oversight on a number of these issues, and considered legislation to address various policy issues including government reorganization and additional appropriations. In May 2002, Congress approved the Public Health Security and Bioterrorism Preparedness and Response Act (P.L. 107–288). Title IV of that act requires drinking water systems serving more than 3,300 persons to conduct vulnerability analyses and to submit the assessments to the EPA. The legislation authorizes grant funding to assist utilities in meeting these requirements. (For information, see CRS Report RL31294, *Safeguarding the Nation's Drinking Water: EPA and Congressional Actions.*) Legislation authorizing the Bureau to contract with local law enforcement to protect its facilities also was enacted during the 107th Congress (P.L. 107–69).

In 2001, the House and Senate considered, but did not enact, legislation authorizing a six-year grant program for research and development on security of water supply and wastewater treatment systems (H.R. 3178, S. 1593). Some of the drinking water research provisions in these bills were included in the Bioterrorism Preparedness Act. In October 2002, the House approved a bill authorizing $220 million in grants and other assistance for vulnerability assessments by wastewater treatment utilities (H.R. 5169), but the Senate did not act on a related bill (S. 3037). In the 108th Congress, legislation authorizing vulnerability assessment grants to wastewater utilities (H.R. 866, identical to H.R. 5169 in the 107th Congress) was approved by the House on May 7, 2003, by a 413–7 vote. The Senate Environment and Public Works Committee approved related legislation on May 15, 2003 (S. 1039, S.Rept. 108–149). No further action has occurred, due in part to concerns expressed by some that the legislation does not require that vulnerability assessments be submitted to the EPA, as is the case with drinking water assessments required by the 2002 Bioterrorism Preparedness Act. Continuing attention to these issues by Congress is anticipated.

Security has become a permanent part of everyone's world, and the water sector is grappling with the challenges involved in viewing its services as potential targets and thinking through the consequences. For many in this sector, the first hurdle is realizing that its operations are vulnerable, whether to human-caused or natural disasters. Although the water sector is diverse, many of the known system vulnerabilities are common to most of its component parts, including contamination (especially of water and wastewater treatment systems), damage to physical assets (pumps and valves, for example), misuse of onsite chemicals, vulnerabilities of supervisory control and data acquisition (SCADA) and information technology (IT) systems, and loss of service to customers. The water sector reflects varying degrees of protection now, and in responding to the new security reality, system managers face a balancing act between external demands for security and internal resources to act and finance needed measures. How the federal government will guide, assist, and coordinate security measures of this sector will become clearer over time.

Notes

1. For additional information, see CRS Electronic Briefing Book on Terrorism, www.congress.gov/brbk/html/ebter1.html.
2. J. E. Hoover, "Water Supply Facilities and National Defense," *Journal of the American Water Works Association* 33 no. 11 (1941): 1861.
3. Presidential Decision Directive 63 "The Clinton Administration's Policy on Critical Infrastructure Protection," www.ciao.gov/resource/paper598.html (accessed January 5, 2004).
4. For additional information, see www.waterisac.org/aboutisac.asp (accessed January 5, 2004).
5. Critical Infrastructure Assurance Office, *Report of the President of the United States on the Status of Federal Critical Infrastructure Protection Activities*, January 2001, www.ciao.gov/resource/cip_2001_congrept.pdf (accessed January 5, 2004).
6. See, for example, Environmental Defense, *Eliminating Hometown Hazards, Cutting Chemical Risks at Wastewater Treatment Facilities,* December 2003, p. 14, www.environmentaldefense.org/documents/3357_EliminatingHometownHazards.pdf (accessed January 5, 2004).
7. U.S. Environmental Protection Agency, *Strategic Plan for Homeland Security*, September 2002, p. 62, www.epa.gov/epahome/downloads/epa homeland_security_strategic_plan.pdf (accessed January 5, 2004).
8. Water Science and Technology Board, *A Review of the EPA Water Security Research and Technical Support Action Plan: Parts I and II,* 2003, www.nap.edu/books/0309089824/html (accessed January 5, 2004).
9. Office of Inspector General, U.S. Environmental Protection Agency, *EPA Needs a Better Strategy to Measure Changes in the Security of the Nation's Water Infrastructure*, Report No. 2003–M–00016, Sept. 11, 2003, www.epa.gov/oig/reports/2003/HomelandSecurityReport2003M00016.pdf (accessed January 5, 2004).
10. Office of Homeland Security, *The National Strategy for the Physical Protection of Critical Infrastructures and Key Assets*, 2002, p. 90, www.whitehouse.gov/homeland/book/index.html (accessed January 5, 2004).

11. For current information on the Department, see CRS products identified at www.congress.gov/erp/legissues/html/isdhs2.html.

12. Homeland Security Presidential DirectiveHSPD-7, Critical Infrastructure Identification, Prioritization, and Protection, December 17, 2003, www.whitehouse.gov/news/releases/2003/12/20031217–5.html (accessed January 5, 2004).

13. Fiscal year 2004 appropriated amounts reflect a provision in P.L. 108–199, which mandated a 0.59 percent rescission to accounts and to each nondefense discretionary program, project and activity funded by that legislation as well as previously enacted fiscal year 2004 appropriations acts, including P.L. 108–137.

Chapter 14

Food Biosecurity: Food Supply and Bioterrorism[1]

Barbara Bruemmer

Food is an element of daily life, but, in our complex culture, we often overlook the role of food in basic survival. The threat of a bioterrorist attack on our food supply is an issue that we need to evaluate and analyze at every level of preparedness planning.

A compromised food supply would have physical, psychological, political, and economical consequences. The physical consequences may include inedible food and/or insufficient food. Distribution centers and retail outlets such as grocery stores could encounter disruptions in supplies and limitations in the ability to assess the safety of food. The service and hospitality industries, including sites of institutional food service, could be unable to obtain and deliver a viable product. If food is compromised with chemical or biological agents, the direct results could include significant morbidity and mortality, or the indirect results of hunger and inadequate nutrition. The psychological consequences could include the perception of an unsafe food supply and vulnerability to hunger and want. Food represents security, comfort, and the ability to provide basic needs to those who rely on others for protection and support. The long-term consequences could include aversion to a particular food or to an entire class of foods. The political consequences of any act of bioterrorism, including a compromised food supply, could include civil discord and diminished confidence in the government. Finally, there is the profound potential consequence to our economy. Our agricultural industries could be severely disrupted in the event of an attack on the food supply. Retail and commercial food vendors could face liability issues and loss of revenue. The economic impact could be of variable duration with lost consumer confidence and market image.

How the Food Supply Could Be Compromised

Food may be compromised in a terrorist attack by being the primary agent, such as by being a vessel to deliver a biological or chemical weapon, or as a secondary target, where the amount of food is not adequate to feed the population. As a primary agent, food may be contaminated with infectious or noninfectious biological agents or chemical weapons. Food contaminated with an infectious agent may be difficult to handle by traditional methods of product recall involving identification and destruction. The presence of contaminated food at a distribution center could lead to significant disruption in the flow of safe food to consumers. Consider the disruptions to postal service that occurred during the

2001 anthrax incidents. Alternate food distribution sites would need to be identified, prepared, and stocked. Consumers would need to be kept well informed of the response and be redirected to new facilities. Although we have a culture that provides people with exposure to a wide variety of foods, consumers may not be familiar with preparation of non-traditional foods, and might need assistance identifying substitutions in food choices.

The Centers for Disease Control and Prevention (CDC) classify the botulism toxin as a category A agent, the same category as smallpox, and notes that it is "the single most poisonous substance known" to humankind. Exposure to this toxin leads to muscle paralysis often requiring respiratory support and/or total parenteral nutrition, an extended time of recovery—from weeks to months—and has a high case-fatality rate.[2] Other biologic agents from the CDC's category B are often traditionally associated with food-borne illness such as Salmonella species, *E. coli* O157:H7, or *Shigella*. The current systems of detection are designed to identify outbreaks from food spoilage, poor food-handling practices, or other unintentional sources.

Should food be compromised, the first recommendation is to destroy potentially tainted food, but, in the event of widespread or unknown distribution, consumers may need to be extra cautious in the use of raw foods. Agents such as *E. coli* O157:H7 or Salmonella will be destroyed when foods are cooked to 160 degrees Fahrenheit. Should there be a risk of contamination with these agents, hand washing, safe food handling, avoidance of cross contamination, and thorough cooking to this temperature may diminish consumption of cross-contaminated items. However, botulism contamination would be more difficult to manage because the spores are very heat resistant. Again, destruction of contaminated food and appropriate cleansing of any exposed areas would be the first option, but destroying botulism toxin requires boiling for 15 minutes. Suspicious food should never be tasted until this has been done.

The intentional use of one of these agents may reasonably be mistaken for a normal episode of food poisoning because they are all common sources of food-borne illness. Preparedness planning, rapid communication, and central analysis may be necessary to distinguish the early phase of a hostile act from the normal fluctuation in the incidence of illnesses. The method in which an agent or agents could be disbursed would also impact surveillance and response. Epidemiologic methods rely on the histories provided by victims, assuming there is a point source of contamination. However, the introduction of an agent with multiple contamination points could compromise the ability to identify the contaminated food or foods and delay the detection of an attack.

Food may also be a secondary agent of terrorism. A terrorist attack may impact our ability to feed individuals by limiting access to food and water, by disrupting the flow of energy and therefore cooking fuels, or by causing significant casualties, leading to social disruption. The release of an infectious agent might lead to some type of forced and/or self-imposed quarantine to prevent spread of the agent or to avoid risk. The ability to feed people in these situations differs greatly from our traditional approach to disaster relief. Our emergency preparedness models assume that access to affected individuals will not be limited by the risk of contamination or spread of a biologic agent. The models assume that hungry people will seek assistance and have confidence in the food that is offered.

The National Academy of Sciences report "Making the Nation Safer: The Role of Science and Technology in Countering Terrorism" notes that food and water supply networks have a ready-made distribution system for the rapid and widespread introduction of chemical weapons.[3] The quality control systems of food production and distribution centers are not designed to deter and detect intentional contamination. Certain categories of food are more suitable for use in a bioterrorist attack. Canned or well-preserved items have a longer shelf life and thus would be more likely to be identified and recalled. However, production facilities for perishable items, such as milk, bread, fresh meats, and vegetables, would be more likely targets. Of these items, foods that are traditionally not cooked before consumption carry additional risks. Thus, our supply of dairy, fresh bread products, and fresh fruits and vegetables is particularly vulnerable. These foods are staples, thus a high level of vigilance is needed. This NCS report also notes the risk from unregulated diet supplements including vitamins, health supplements, and "natural" remedies. Recommendations from the National Academy of Sciences report include the following:

- The FDA should act promptly to extend hazard analysis and critical control point (HACCP) methodology to enable it to deal effectively with deliberate contamination of the food supply.
- The FDA should develop criteria for quantifying hazards in order to define the level of risk for various kinds of food-processing facilities. The results could then be used to determine the minimal level of protection required for making each type of facility secure.
- The FDA should convene panels of experts in major areas of food production to assess vulnerabilities and recommend corrective actions. This effort should be pursued with as much cooperation as possible from industry, but it should not be left to industry alone.[4]

Public Health Preparedness

The basic components of public health preparedness include the following: planning, surveillance, detection, response, and recovery. The U.S. Department of Agriculture (USDA), the Food and Drug Administration, the Federal Emergency Management Agency (FEMA), and the CDC, as well as state and local agencies, are all involved in our national response on food biosecurity (see Figure 14-1). Regarding prevention, federal legislation has been enacted to enhance the security of our food supply. The Public Health Security and Bioterrorism Preparedness and Response Act of 2002 includes Title III: Protecting the Safety and Security of the Food and Drug Supply.[5] The USDA Food Safety and Inspection Service has prepared the "Security Guidelines for Food Processors" for the inspection of plants that produce meat, poultry, and egg products.[6]

Response strategies to a bioterrorist attack are being developed but, as previously noted, are often based on models of natural disasters. Models need to include the unique needs of individuals in the event of a catastrophic attack. Surge capacity for emergency response teams, and medical and support personnel, is seriously limited.[7] It has been estimated that for every one legitimate victim presenting for treatment from a biological attack, 100 to 1,000 worried-but-well individuals will also present for assessment and reassurance.[8] The initial response strategies have identified a series of priorities targeting the highest risk events and agents. Thus, smallpox prevention strategies have been a high priority. Response strategies specific to food biosecurity must be integrated into the

FIGURE 14-1.   Federal Agencies Involved in Food Biosecurity

---

1. US Department of Agriculture and Homeland Security Council

PFSAP–Protection of the Food Supply and Agricultural Production
Responsibilities:
- Issues dealing with food production, processing, storage and distribution
- Threats against the agriculture sector and rapid response to threats
- Border surveillance and protection to prevent introduction of plant and animals pests and diseases
- Food safety activities concerning meat, poultry, and egg inspection, laboratory support, research, education and outbreaks of food-borne illness

Ready.gov
Responsibilities:
- Educate the public about how to be prepared in case of a national emergency-including a possible terrorist attack

---

2. US Department of Agriculture–USDA Food Safety and Inspection Service–FSIS

PrepNet–Food Threat Preparedness Network
Responsibilities:
- Ensures effective coordination of food security efforts
- Focuses of the group on preventive activities to protect the food supply
- Provides rapid response to threats

F-BAT–Food Biosecurity 'Action Team
Responsibilities:
- Assesses potential vulnerabilities along the farm-to-table continuum
- Provides guidelines to industry on food security and increased plant security
- Strengthens FSIS coordination and cooperation with law enforcement agencies
- Enhances security features of FSIS laboratories

---

3. Centers for Disease Control and Prevention–CDC

PulseNet–A national network of public health laboratories
Responsibilities:
- Performs DNA fingerprinting on food-borne bacteria
- Assists in the detection of food-borne illness outbreaks and traceback to their source
- Provides linkages among sporadic cases

Food Net–The Food-borne Diseases Active Surveillance Network
Responsibilities:
- Functions as the principal food-borne disease component of COO's Emerging Infections Program
- Provides active laboratory-based surveillance

Centers for Public Health Preparedness
Responsibilities:
Funds three types of centers including (a):
- Academic or comprehensive base centers link Schools of Public Health with state, local and regional bioterrorism preparedness and public health infrastructure needs.
- Specialty Centers of the national system of Centers for Public Health Preparedness focus on a Topic, professional discipline, core public health competency, practice setting or application of learning.

FIGURE 14-1.   continued

- Local Exemplar Centers develop advanced applications at the community level in three areas of key importance to preparedness for bioterrorism and other urgent health threats: integrated communications and information systems across multiple sectors, advanced operational readiness assessment, and comprehensive training and evaluation. These Centers work in collaboration with a variety of public and private partners at the local, state, and national levels, as well as, with the other academic and specialty centers."

---

4. Food and Drug Administration

<u>CFSAP—Center for Food Safety and Applied Nutrition</u>
Primary responsibilities include (b):
- "The safety of substances added to food, eg, food additives (including ionizing radiation) and color additives
- The safety of foods and ingredients developed through biotechnology
- Seafood Hazard Analysis and Critical Control Point (HACCP) regulations
- Regulatory and research programs to address health risks associated with foodborne chemical and biological contaminants
- Regulations and activities dealing with the proper labeling of foods (eg, ingredients, nutrition health claims) and cosmetics
- Regulations and policy governing the safety of dietary supplements, infant formulas, and medical foods
- Safe and properly labeled cosmetic ingredients and products
- Food industry postmarket surveillance and compliance
- Consumer education and industry outreach
- Cooperative programs with state and local governments
- International food standard and safety harmonization efforts"

Activities include response to the Public Health Security and Bioterrorism Preparedness and Response Act of 2002, Title III. Protecting Safety and Security of Food and Drug Supply. Section 302. Protection Against Adulteration of Food (c):
- "Directs the Secretary to improve linkages with other Federal, State and tribal food safety agencies"
- "Directs the Secretary to coordinate as appropriate on the research with CDC, NIH, EPA, and USDA"

---

5. Federal Emergency Management Agency (FEMA)

<u>Emergency Support Functions</u>
Responsibilities include those related to Emergency Support Function—Food. Identify food needs; ensuring that food gets to areas affected by lead agency: Food and Nutrition Service, USDA. (d) "A significant disaster or emergency may deprive substantial numbers of people access to food or the means to prepare food."

Agencies involved include:
- USDA-Food and Nutrition Service
- Department of Defense
- Department of Health and Human Services (DHHS)
- American Red Cross
- Environmental Protection Agency (EPA)
- FEMA
- GSA

FIGURE 14-1. continued

Notes

a. Centers for Disease Control and Prevention Centers for Public Health Preparedness. Programs in Brief, www.cdc.gov/programs/bio9.htm. Accessed April 7, 2003.

b. US Food and Drug Administration. Center for Food Safety and Applied Nutrition Overview, www.cfsan.fda.gov/programs/bio9.htm. Accessed April 7, 2003.

c. US Food and Drug Administration Center for Food Safety and Applied Nutrition. Public Health Security and Bioterrorism, Preparedness and Response Act of 2002 (PL107–188), www.cfsan.fda.gov/~dms/sec-ltr.html#sec302. Accessed April 7, 2003.

d. Federal Emergency Management Agency, US Department of Homeland Security. Federal Response Plan—ESF#11–Food Annex, www.fema.gov/rrr/frp/frpesf11.shtml. Accessed April 7, 2003.

national response during every phase. Scenarios surrounding quarantines, isolating contaminated food, and distribution of food to emergency personnel need to be tested under assumptions that would apply during a bioterrorist attack. These strategies and protocols then need to be disseminated to local public health officials and emergency response programs to meet regional needs. Have we planned scenarios for assisting a family if a mother has been exposed to radiation and should not breastfeed? Can we convey to a panicked public the need to identify and feed at-risk individuals, such as insulin-dependent diabetics?

Two of the strengths of our current system include the existence of consumer education materials on safe food-handling practices and a heightened awareness of safe food-handling practices.[9] The risk of potential food-borne contaminants, such as Salmonella, may be countered with good hygiene, avoidance of cross contamination, and appropriate cooking temperatures. Other response strategies include methods of disseminating information. Even if quarantine or self-selected isolation were to occur, continued access to the Internet, radio, or television could provide emergency bulletins, information on access to food, and preparation guidelines, if power is available.

However, the list of limitations and needs is long. The risks begin with our assumption that food is always available and is always safe. Often, basic nutrition texts for students in the United States examine food choices as driven by taste, convenience, price, etc, but do not specifically include survival.

Even though information on food safety is available, surveys of food safety practices indicate that inappropriate food-handling behaviors are widely prevalent, particularly in certain segments of the population. A survey of 1,620 randomly selected U.S. residents indicated a lack of routine hand washing by as much as 33 percent of respondents, with men, adults 18 to 29 years of age, and occasional food preparers, more likely to report unsafe practices.[10] The Behavioral Risk Factor Surveillance System survey conducted in 1995 and 1996 solicited information on food safety habits from respondents in eight states (n= 19,356). Nineteen percent reported not washing hands or cutting boards after contact with raw meat or chicken. Again, this report found unsafe practices more common in men than women.[11] However, a FoodNet survey of 7,493 adults in California,

Connecticut, Georgia, Minnesota, and Oregon in 1996–1997 reported a much higher rate of appropriate behaviors, including a 93 percent report of "almost always" washing hands and cutting boards after handling raw chicken—again, young adults were less likely to follow appropriate guidelines.[12]

Of great concern is the lack of basic food preparation skills where survival may necessitate the use of raw foods. There was a time when "ready-made clothing" was a commonly used term to describe clothing that had not been made in the home. In our culture, an "emergency meal" means going to the drive-through window of a fast-food outlet or a 24-hour minimart. We have a generation of adults who have been raised on microwave cooking and who consider food preparation a semi-entertaining event modeled after the activities of a television chef. The recommendations from the Department of Homeland Security for a three-day supply of nonperishable food emphasize the selection of foods that require no preparation and no cooking.[13] However, the recommendations from FEMA for long-term food supplies "in the unlikely event of a military attack or some other national disaster" are canned and dried food with bulk quantities of staples including wheat (20 pounds), powered milk (in nitrogen-packed cans, 20 pounds), corn (20 pounds), iodized salt (1 pound), soybeans (10 pounds), vitamin C (15 grams), per person, per month. These recommendations include obtaining a hand-cranked grain mill.[14] If this is indeed what will determine who survives a major attack, how many of our citizens will meet this standard? An actual assessment of the food-preparation knowledge and skills of our population is essential to providing federal and local emergency planners with information on which to base the reserves and plan response strategies.

Although initial efforts on prevention and preparedness have targeted food importation and production, similar HACCP procedures and security protocols should be considered at every step, from the farm to the consumer, for high-risk perishable foods. Security measures have been tightened at airports and over-the-counter drugs use tamper-proof packaging, yet fresh fruits and vegetables are routinely left exposed. For example, in 1984, restaurant salad bars in The Dalles, Oregon, were intentionally contaminated with Salmonella by a local religious commune.[15] There is always a trade-off in a free society, where the perception of a wholesome, healthy product is important for increasing the intake of fruits and vegetables, but an attack on our food supply might associate an otherwise healthful food with risk. The perception of risk is influenced by how much the individual considers the risk a consequence of a voluntary action, as compared with an involuntary action.[16] The concept of intentional harm to our food supply strikes at the very root of an American definition of peace and prosperity. Vigilance begins by challenging our complacency.

Registered dietitians, due to their training and scope of practice, are in a unique position to take a global approach to the provision of a safe food supply. RDs may be a key element of any public health preparedness plan and response. They can contribute in the arena of vigilance, preparedness, and response. In the event of an attack on our food supply, dietetics professionals could assist in the identification of subgroups of the population with unique nutritional risks, and could assist in the dissemination of information to those groups. Registered dietitians are trained in food safety, HACCP procedures, and food and nutrition education. Knowledge of correct food-handling practice for agents associated with food-borne illness would be valuable in times of crisis. These professionals are integrated into public health, health care, and food service management, and thus may provide a high level of expertise in assessing and responding to the physical, emotional, and economic threats to the food security of our country.

Notes

1.   This chapter was originally published as "Food Biosecurity: Food Supply and Bioterrorism," *Journal of the American Dietetic Association* (June 2003). An updated version will appear as a chapter in Edelstein, S. (ed). Nutrition in Public Health, 2nd ed., Jones & Bartlett Publishers, 2006.

2.   P. S. Mead, L. Slutsker, V. Dietz, L. F. McCaig, J. S. Bresee, C. Shapiro, P. M. Griffin, R. V. Tauxe, "Food-Related Illness and Death in the United States." *Emerg Infect Dis,* 5 (1999): 607–625, www.cdc.gov/ncidod/eid/vol5no5/mead.htm (accessed February 25, 2003).

3.   Committee on Science and Technology for Countering Terrorism, *Making the Nation Safer, the Role of Science and Technology in Countering Terrorism* (Washington, DC: National Academy Press, 2002).

4.   Ibid.

5.   Director, Center for Food Safety and Applied Nutrition, U.S. Food and Drug Administration, Letter, July 17, 2002. www.cfsan.fda.gov/~dms/sec-ltr.html (accessed October 18, 2002).

6.   Food Safety Insepction Service, *Security Guidelines for Food Processors,* May 2002, www.fsis.usda.gov/oa/topics/SecurityGuide.pdf (accessed February 25, 2003).

7.   Committee on Science and Technology for Countering Terrorism, *Making the Nation Safer.*

8.   Ibid.

9.   Food Safety and Inspection Service, *Food Safety Education and Consumer Information,* Washington, DC: US Department of Agriculture. www.fsis.usda.gov/OA/consedu.htm (accessed March 10, 2003); and T. Peregrin, "Bioterrorism and Food Safety: What Nutrition Professionals Need to Know to Educate the American public," *JAm Diet Assoc* 102 (2002): 14–16.

10.   S. F. Altekruse, D. A. Street, S. B. Fein, A. S. Levy. "Consumer knowledge of foodborne Microbial Hazards and Food-Handling Practices." *J Food Prof* (1996): 59–287–294.

11.   S. F. Altekruse, S. Yang, B. B. Timbo, F. J. Angulo, "A Multi-State Survey of Consumer Food-Handling and Food-Consumption Practices," *Am J Prey Med* 16 (1999): 216–221.

12.   B. Shiferaw; S.Yang; P. Cieslak; D. Vugia; R. Marcus; J. Koehler; V. Deneen; F. Angulo, "Prevalence of High-Risk Food Consumption and Food-Handling Practices Among Adults: A Multistate Survey, 1996–1997," *Journal of Food Professionals* 63 (2000): 1538–1543.

13.   U.S. Department of Homeland Security. *Make a Kit,* March 10, 2003, www.ready.gov/water_food.html.

14.   Federal Emergency Management Agency, *Emergency Food and Water Supplies,* July 28, 2002, www.fema.gov/library/emfdwtr.shtm.

15.   T. J. Torok; R. V. Tauxe; R. B. Wise; J. R. Livengood; R. Sokolow; S. Mauvais; K.A. Birkness; M. R. Skeels; J. M. Horan; L. R. Foster, "A Large Community Outbreak of

Salmonellosis Caused by Intentional Contamination of Restaurant Salad Bars," *Journal of the American Medical Association* 278 (1997): 389–395.

16.   P. Slovic, *The Perception of Risk* (London: Earthscan Publications Inc, 2000).

Section III

National and Local
Responses to the Threat

It is one of today's great paradoxes that the most powerful nation in the world, having invested more in its military and defense than any nation in history, faces the challenges described in the preceding sections of this volume. Clearly, organizing our domestic agencies to prevent and respond to terrorism has not always been a priority of public policy. The chapters in this section explore how this has changed in the last few years. In most cases, the authors call for greater intergovernmental and interagency cooperation, and emphasize the need for an effectively networked community of agencies and individuals committed to homeland security.

Louise Comfort begins the dialogue by exploring the concepts of individual, organizational, and collective learning in environments exposed to recurring risk, and proposes a model of "auto-adaption" to improve intergovernmental performance during extreme events such as natural disasters and terrorist attacks. Her analysis is followed by a chapter from Los Angeles County Deputy Sheriff John Sullivan, whose Terrorism Early Warning (TEW) Group provides public safety agencies with a cooperative vehicle for obtaining and assessing the information needed to manage threats and acts of terrorism. New TEWs are emerging across the nation, a testament to the effectiveness of the model Sullivan describes.

Reid Sawyer and Joseph Pfeiffer then recount the 9/11 lessons learned by the New York City Fire Department, highlighting the need to build capacity within first-responder organizations. Their chapter presents a framework for recognizing and addressing the need for change in an organization prior to a crisis, and examines themes such as crisis management in a first responder context, and how organizations should adapt to the changing security environment.

More lessons for first responders are provided in a chapter by former Oklahoma Governor Frank Keating, who reminds us that not all terrorist attacks are conducted by international non-state actors such as al-Qaida. Based on his experience as Governor during the April 19, 1995, Oklahoma City bombing, and his later participation in the *Dark Winter* exercise in 2002, Governor Keating provides useful conclusions and findings, and makes recommendations for first-responders to follow in the event of a terrorist attack.

Finally, Seth Jones and Chris Hornbarger debate the relative merits of the Department of Homeland Security, America's newest and most important experiment in interagency and intergovernmental coordination. Jones argues that until the Department of Homeland Security (DHS) has authority to "synthesize and analyze homeland security intelligence from multiple sources," it will not be able to fulfill its three primary objectives: (1) prevent terrorist attacks in the United States; (2) reduce America's vulnerability to terrorism; and (3) respond to any terrorist attacks and natural disasters. Jones contends that the effectiveness of DHS has been greatly marginalized because of the reluctance of the FBI and CIA to relinquish significant intelligence gathering powers.

In contrast, Chris Hornbarger argues that the nation's homeland security policies are on track, and that the next administration should stay the course. The first *National Strategy for Homeland Security*, in concert with other Presidential policies, has provided meaningful direction to the breadth of federal, state, local, and private sector homeland security activities. The *Strategy* does what successful strategies must: articulate ends (the *Strategy* names three); identify means (the *Strategy* provides an approach for allocating finite resources against an almost limitless array of vulnerabilities); and, most importantly, connect ends and means with ways (the *Strategy* provides the first blueprint for the institutional capacity to protect the homeland over the long-term).

However, as Hornbarger and the other authors of this volume clearly indicate, there is still a good deal of tough work ahead. The Department of Homeland Security remains a work-in-progress. Significant reform of the intelligence community will take years. But, thankfully, a vibrant community of agencies and individuals at the local, state, and federal levels are investing immense time and energy to meet the homeland security challenges of the future.

Chapter 15

Managing Intergovernmental Response to Terrorism and Other Extreme Events

Louise K. Comfort[1]

Etched indelibly in memory for most Americans is the searing image of United Airlines Flight 175 crashing into the South Tower of the World Trade Center (WTC) in New York City at 9:03 A.M. on September 11, 2001. Eighteen minutes earlier, American Airlines Flight 11 had crashed into the North Tower, and television cameras captured both towers engulfed in flames. Virtually anyone in the world with access to a television set has seen the powerful images, evoking horror in the minds of those who sympathized with the victims. To some, the images undoubtedly elicited admiration for the boldness of the act or acknowledgment of the singular goals of the perpetrators, but to all, they represented an extreme event, one that could not be addressed by routine measures. When the towers collapsed, virtually the whole world knew of the extraordinary impact of the coordinated attacks on the U.S. civilian targets. The security of major U.S. cities had been breached, and public agencies, charged with the legal responsibility to protect life, property, and continuity of operations, mobilized in response to the disaster.

For public agencies, the events of September 11 presented an extraordinary test of their capacity to function under the most severe conditions of disruption and destruction. Each of the public organizations and jurisdictions responsible for public security in New York, New Jersey, and Virginia had emergency plans, but none had imagined an event that would turn civilian airliners into weapons of mass destruction. The challenge lies, first, in recognizing the danger and anticipating the scope of the damage. Extreme events demand resources and skills from a wider range of organizations than those in the immediately affected area. More difficult is the task of integrating multiple agencies and jurisdictions into a smoothly functioning interorganizational, inter-jurisdictional response system under the urgent, chaotic conditions of full-scale disaster.

The need for integration intensifies as the number of organizations engaged in response operations increases, and the range of problems they confront widens. Since all organizations in the damaged area are affected, private and nonprofit actors, as well as public agencies, become participants in the response system. Some organizations may not have emergency plans, or may not have linked them to a larger community-wide response process. As the type and size of organizations involved in response operations varies, there emerges a wider disparity among the participants in their skills, knowledge, access to information, and equipment. Achieving coordinated action among a disparate group of actors depends fundamentally on their access to timely, valid information and their capacity for information search, exchange, absorption, and adaptation.

Reliable performance of information functions under stress is a critical factor in achieving coordination among a large and varied group of actors engaged in crisis response. This performance depends on at least three basic sets that influence the interaction among agents involved in the response to the event (Comfort, 1999). The first set includes the technical structure needed to support information search and exchange. The second set of conditions involves the organizational policies and procedures that shape action both within, and among, the participating organizations. The third set involves cultural openness to new information, new strategies for addressing an unimaginable set of problems, and willingness to adapt to extraordinarily difficult conditions. These three sets of conditions shape in fundamental ways the evolution of an interorganizational system in response to the event. Furthermore, the interaction among the agents shapes the next round of actions taken by each individual organization or agent. The result is the emergence of a complex, adaptive system that responds both to the demands from the environment, and the degree of pressure or support from other organizations within the system as it evolves.

The 9/11 events were extraordinarily complex. Three different sites were involved in the attacks, and simultaneous demands were made upon federal agencies from all three locations. At the same time, the evolving response system needed to integrate different state, regional, county and municipal agencies—as well as private and nonprofit organizations—with federal agencies into a coherent framework for action. The knowledge base to support response operations in such an event needs to be scalable. That is, it needs to provide specific information to support action by personnel operating at different sites within multiple jurisdictions, and between multiple levels of jurisdiction, simultaneously. Most public agencies have emergency plans, but they are not always current. Although some private companies and nonprofit organizations such as hospitals and schools have emergency plans, they often are not integrated with those of the public agencies to provide a comprehensive plan for a community, much less multiple communities in an affected region. Facilitating the evolution of response systems to extreme events in densely populated metropolitan areas is a major challenge in public policy and administration.

Mobilizing response operations across organizational and jurisdictional boundaries on a regional scale requires a collaborative effort among participating public, private, and nonprofit organizations that is not yet defined by current administrative policy and procedures. This chapter addresses the need to strengthen the capacity of the emerging response system in order to respond more effectively to threats on a regional scale.[2] In doing so, I will undertake five tasks. First, I will briefly discuss the difference between linear and nonlinear models in public policy and administration, and the conceptual shift to nonlinear operations in the dynamic context of disaster. Second, I will examine briefly the theoretical background of response systems in extreme contexts as complex adaptive systems, identifying their characteristics and modes of adaptation in changing environments. Third, I will use incidents from the 9/11 events to illustrate different modes of adaptation among the multiple agents involved in response operations. Fourth, I will discuss the potential of auto-adaptation to improve intergovernmental response to extreme events. Finally, I will conclude with recommendations for a preliminary model of auto-adaptation for intergovernmental and intersectoral response on a regional scale.

The Dynamic Context of Disaster

The effective mobilization of response to extreme events on a large scale is one of the least understood problems in public management. This process requires the rapid search, exchange, and absorption of valid information regarding sudden, damaging events, and must be transmitted through a network of organizations that crosses disciplinary, organizational, and jurisdictional boundaries. It requires pre-disaster planning among organizations to identify what information will be required and how this information may be accessed. It entails the rapid comprehension of danger that, under ordinary circumstances, is unimaginable. It requires the capacity to use that powerful insight to anticipate the spread of risk through an interdependent community, and to devise actions that will interrupt or limit the risk. It means discovering the "logic" that will govern the ensuing uncertainty in technical and organizational performance (Comfort, 1989). This is an inference process that functions more through the rapid recognition of signals and symbols (Feldman and March, 1981) and the use of mental models (Weick, 1995), than on rule-based reasoning (Hayes-Roth, Waterman, and Lenat, 1983).

Extreme events pose a distinct problem for theorists in public policy and administration. In the past, practicing managers preferred to consider these events rare occurrences, calling them "acts of God" or calculating the chances of occurrence versus the costs of mitigation in terms of defining "acceptable risk" (Kartez and Kelly, 1988). But when extreme events do occur, and public agencies fail to respond promptly and efficiently, the political as well as social and economic consequences are severe (Gawronski and Olson, 2000; Carley and Harrald, 1997). Public agencies bear the legal responsibility for the protection of lives, property, and continuity of operations, and local agencies bear the brunt of first response. Consequently, disaster management remains the quintessential function of government, and public managers at all levels of government are rethinking their odds on the probability of disaster.

The extraordinary losses incurred on September 11 compel a review of the capacity of government agencies to mitigate and respond to extreme events. While much work has been done to assess planning and response activities by municipal and federal agencies (Mileti, 1999; Platt et al., 1999; Sylves and Waugh, 1996), little attention has been given to structuring interorganizational response to extreme events on regional levels. Nor has there been careful study of how response systems, once constituted, could contribute to the ability of the region to manage recurring risk. The challenge to administrative theory and practice is how to design and support governmental systems that can adapt readily to the urgent demands and complex operating conditions in extreme events.

The standard administrative approach to solving complex problems has been to organize work involving multiple agents and tasks hierarchically (Simon, 1981; Newell and Simon, 1972). Hierarchy is used to establish control, specify tasks, allocate responsibilities and reporting procedures, and presumably, gain reliability and efficiency in work flow. This approach works reasonably well in routine circumstances when there is time to plan actions, train personnel, identify problems, and correct mistakes. Under the urgent, dynamic conditions of disaster, however, such procedures almost always fail. Carefully developed emergency plans may not fit the specific conditions of the disaster. Information required by disaster managers may be old or incomplete. Key personnel may be missing or unavailable for decisions. Under cumulative stress, hierarchical organizations tend to break down, and personnel are hindered by a lack of information, constraints on innovation, and an inability to shift resources and actions to meet new demands quickly (Comfort, 1999).

In extreme events, public organizations need the ability to adapt quickly and effectively to rapidly changing conditions. Such capacity relies on a continuous exchange of timely, valid information among multiple participants regarding their shared goal in dynamic operating conditions. The two types of operating environments—routine and extreme—illustrate the difference between linear and nonlinear systems in theory, and the difference between organized hierarchy and complex adaptive systems in practice. Routine environments assume a complete knowledge base with all relevant information available, so that organized hierarchy can apply known information efficiently to known problems. In this context, linear systems function well. Extreme environments, in contrast, acknowledge that all relevant information is not known, and that previously known conditions may be in a state of flux. Relations between organizations and their operating conditions are nonlinear, and actions must be based on incoming information integrated with known information to adapt effectively to the changing environment. This fundamental difference in operating conditions shifts the system's focus from control, based on known information, to continuous search-and-exchange processes to develop valid information as a basis for action.

The distinctive advantage of human organizations is that the individuals within them are able to learn. This ability to learn from incoming information and observation creates the potential for self-organizing agents or auto-adaptive systems in dynamic environments (Gell-Mann, 1994; Holland, 1995). An auto-adaptive system acknowledges the organizational and policy processes that contribute to change, learning, and innovation in dynamic environments (Peitgen, Saupe, and Jurgens, 1992; Argyris, 1993; Comfort, 1994), but considers these processes on a different scale, that of system-wide response to a massive event.

While the collapse of organizational capacity to act under extreme conditions has been documented in actual cases (Weick, 1993; Carley and Harrald, 1997; Comfort, 1999), the opposite phenomenon—the design and development of communities capable of innovative and responsible performance under threat of extreme danger—has not been studied systematically. There has been no rigorous effort to model the effects of the rapid spread of information regarding risk on the performance of communities under threat, or to estimate the economic costs and social benefits of making the investment in information technology and organizational training that would be necessary to achieve reliable performance in extreme events. This chapter examines modes of increasing the capacity of interorganizational systems to adapt to extreme events.

Theoretical Background

The concept of adaptation in interorganizational systems draws on findings from four distinct research themes in public administration and organizational theory. First, it is informed by the broadly interdisciplinary literature on complex adaptive systems

(Prigogine and Stengers, 1984; Kauffman, 1993; Holland, 1995; Axelrod, 1997; Axelrod and Cohen, 1999). A key concept in this literature is self-organization, or the ability to reallocate resources and action to meet changing demands from the environment (Kauffman, 1993). This capacity refers to change in behavior that is initiated by the actor, not imposed by any external force. Rather, the agent seeks change in order to achieve a better fit with its environment. Self-organization has been observed in physics (Bak and Chen, 1991), biology (Kauffman, 1993), and public policy (Comfort, 1999; Comfort and Sungu, 2001). Elinor Ostrom (1998) observed a similar process of collective learning among organizations operating in dynamic environments. Extending the concept of self-organization by a single agent to adaptation among a set of interacting organizations is critical to understanding the dynamics of response to extreme events.

Second, recent work on decision making under conditions of uncertainty offers a valuable perspective to adaptation in interorganizational systems. Karl Weick (1995; 2001), a psychologist, and his colleague Kathleen Sutliffe (Weick and Sutliffe, 2001), present the concept of sensemaking as a process of scanning the environment for information and using it to develop a plausible course of action in a difficult or shifting context. Gary Klein (1993) developed a more detailed model called recognition primed decision making, based on his observation of fire commanders directing operations in the dynamic context of a ground fire. Klein finds that fire commanders make decisions not on a basis of a rational review of alternative strategies, but on recognition of situations they have seen before. They craft a strategy of action from a repertoire of previous events that are similar to the situation they are confronting. Rhona Flin (1996) confirms this process of naturalistic decision making in her observations of emergency operations chiefs performing under stressful conditions. Weick and Roberts (1996) move from observations regarding decision making by single operations chiefs to the interaction among members of a crew on an aircraft carrier. Their concept of "heedful interrelating" refers to a state of mindful attention among a group of actors that evolves from common training, intense communication, and a distinct culture derived from shared experience. The authors use this concept to explain the high reliability in performance that is achieved by ordinary human actors in the dangerous operating environment of an aircraft carrier. Each of these concepts offers insight into decision making in difficult, dynamic conditions, but none addresses this process in the context of a region-wide interorganizational response system.

Third, research on uses of technology by social organizations documents the emergence of sociotechnical systems (Goodman and Sproull, 1990; Gell-Mann, 1994; Comfort, 1994). A sociotechnical system integrates humans, computers, and organizations in an interactive system that transmits, receives, stores, and acts on information from the environment. The capacity to learn from incoming information in a dynamic environment alters significantly the operating context of organizations responding to threat. An interorganizational response system depends on access to information and on the range and quality of the information available to operations personnel. This capacity can be enhanced by a technical infrastructure that establishes contact and communication with a wider range of sources of information and support to organizational personnel, but it can also be limited if the technical information infrastructure fails or if vital communications cannot be made. It is the interaction between human actors and technical infrastructure that extends or limits the operating capacity of the response system.

Fourth, modes of adaptation in interorganizational response systems depend on the initial conditions of the participant organizations. Four types of adaptation identified in an analysis of rapidly evolving response systems following earthquakes (Comfort, 1999) may be applicable to interorganizational systems emerging in response to other types of hazards, including terrorist attacks. This initial characterization gives a beginning classification of types of adaptation demonstrated by interorganizational systems under differing technical, organizational, and cultural conditions. Each type of adaptation can be characterized by technical, organizational, and cultural indicators. Technical indicators include measures of reliability for technical structures (e.g., transportation, electrical power, and communications). Organizational indicators include measures of organizational flexibility, such as adaptability to changing conditions, style of communication among members, and leadership or lack thereof. Cultural indicators include measures of openness and innovation, such as willingness to accept new concepts or initiate new patterns of action. The emerging systems vary in terms of their characterization by these indicators, and interaction among the three sets of conditions limits the system's capacity for adaptation to a damaged environment. The response systems reflect these limits, defined largely by the initial conditions in which the damaging event occurred.

The four types of adaptive systems identified in field studies of earthquake response systems, briefly, are: nonadaptive systems, emergent adaptive systems, operative adaptive systems, and auto-adaptive systems (Comfort, 1999). Nonadaptive systems are systems that are low on technical structure, low on organizational flexibility, and low on cultural openness to new information. They function under threat and are largely dependent upon outside assistance, but revert to previous status after the threatening event. Emergent adaptive systems are low on technical structure, medium on organizational flexibility, and medium on cultural openness to new concepts of operation and organization. These systems develop a mode of organization and action to cope with threat during disaster operations, but are unable to sustain collective action after the immediate threat passes. Operative adaptive systems are those that are medium on technical structure, medium on organizational flexibility and medium on cultural openness to new information. These systems function well in response to threat, but prove unable to translate methods of response into new modes of sustained operation and threat reduction. Auto-adaptive systems are those systems that are high on technical structure, high on organizational flexibility, and high on cultural openness to new information. Such systems represent a rare achievement, but in practice, these systems prove effective in response to threat and are able to transfer lessons learned from prior experience into a sustained reduction of threat. For threats of unbounded uncertainty, such as terrorism, the preferred type of adaptation is an auto-adaptive system that is able to learn from incoming information, reallocate its resources and attention, reorder its relationships with other entities, and act promptly to reduce the threat or respond to destructive acts.

While the concept of auto-adaptation fits the requirements for interorganizational response to extreme events, the conditions needed to support its development in practice and the dynamics by which it evolves have received little research attention. In order to apply this concept to a strategy of interorganizational response in extreme events, its characteristics need to be developed more fully. Auto-adaptation by a single actor is a form of individual learning, but it moves to group learning when it occurs in one organization, and to broader collective learning when it occurs in an interorganizational system. Auto-adaptation is a form of mutual adjustment among the component units of an organization and, again, among the component organizations of an interorganizational system. It depends upon creating a shared understanding of the goal to be achieved, and shared knowledge of the respective capacities and vulnerabilities among the participating units or organizations in the operational system. Auto-adaptation is a means of managing change of different types, at different rates among different units or agents, that allows the formation of a coherent strategy of action for the interorganizational system. This concept is directly relevant to understanding the dynamics involved in mobilizing response to extreme events that require exchange of information and resources, and collaboration among intragovernmental, intergovernmental, interjurisdictional, and intersectoral operational entities.

In addition to meeting the initial conditions stated above, an auto-adaptive system appears to move through five distinct phases in its response to extreme events. These phases are: (1) information search or scanning; (2) information exchange, or "heedful interrelating" with other agents in the system; (3) sensemaking, or selection of a plausible strategy of action, given the situation and resources available; 4) adaptation, or action taken to implement that strategy; and 5) evaluation of actions taken and modification of succeeding actions on basis of observed results. In the next section, I will present brief vignettes of auto-adaptation in situations when the response system did function well, as well as brief vignettes when it did not.

Modes of Adaptation to the 9/11 Events

While the full record of damaged conditions and actions taken during the intense hours, days, and weeks immediately following the 9/11 terrorist attacks is not yet complete, sufficient information regarding key aspects of the response is available to allow preliminary observations and interpretation. This analysis is based upon accounts of the events and actions taken from news reports, agency situation reports, and notes from interviews with key participants.[3] It is also important to set this analysis in administrative context. In terrorist incidents, two types of response operations are initiated simultaneously. The first is crisis management, or the effort to identify and pursue the perpetrators of the incident. Under the United States Government Interagency Domestic Terrorism Concept of Operations Plan (CONPLAN, 2001), the U.S. Department of Justice (DOJ) is designated as the lead agency for crisis management, and coordinates its work with other agencies involved in pursuing individuals who may have engaged in illicit activity. These agencies include the Federal Bureau of Investigation (FBI), the Central Intelligence Agency (CIA) when international agents are involved; the Immigration and Naturalization Service (INS), which governs entry and exit of foreign nationals across U.S. borders; and the Bureau of Alcohol, Tobacco, and Firearms (ATF), which tracks the entry of illegal substances across U.S. borders. These agencies operate within the bounds of security required for a criminal investigation.

The second type of response to a terrorist attack is consequence management, or the immediate mobilization of search and rescue operations to save the lives of people harmed by the incident, as well as disaster assistance to the people who suffered losses from the incident, and recovery and reconstruction of the damaged communities. The Federal Emergency Management Agency (FEMA) has lead responsibility for consequence management—

focusing first on lifesaving operations and second on assistance to the victims—along with recovery and reconstruction of the community. Under the Federal Response Plan, eight federal agencies in addition to FEMA play lead roles in disaster operations, with 25 federal agencies assigned responsibilities under 12 specified emergency support functions. The lead agencies include the Departments of Transportation (DOT), National Communications Service (NCS), Defense (DoD), Agriculture (USDA), Health and Human Services (HHS), Housing and Urban Development (HUD), the Environmental Protection Agency (EPA), and the General Accounting Office (GAO). Three departments have emergency support functions: The USDA has the primary support function for firefighting, carried out by its subunit, the U.S. Forest Service (USFS), as well as for food. FEMA is responsible for information management, as well as urban search-and-rescue operations (Federal Response Plan, 1999). The American Red Cross (ARC), a nonprofit organization, is designated as the lead agency for mass care.

This analysis addresses only consequence management operations, which are led by FEMA in conjunction with other civilian federal agencies and state and local governments. While the interaction between the DOJ agencies and FEMA is critical to the overall operation of the response to a terrorist attack, the records of the agencies supervised by the DOJ are not open for public review because the criminal investigation is still on-going.

The initial conditions in which the incidents occurred distinctively shaped the emergence of the response systems at the WTC and the Pentagon. At the WTC, the physical devastation was catastrophic. The attacks caused not only the collapse of the 110-story twin towers, with an estimated 20,000 people in the buildings at the time of the attacks, but also the complete or partial loss of 5 smaller buildings in the immediate area, and heavy damage to 12 other buildings in the roughly 6-square-block area in which the towers were located. In addition, the electrical power generation and distribution system for lower Manhattan was destroyed; the water distribution system, dependent upon electricity for pumping water, was disabled; gas pipelines were heavily damaged; and the telephone and telecommunications services were seriously disrupted.[4] The technical infrastructure that enabled people to live and work in this densely populated, interdependent, urban environment was decimated, and the site was appropriately dubbed "Ground Zero."

Organizationally, the New York City Fire and Police Departments responded immediately to the event. In terms of professional experience and training, both departments had seasoned, well-trained, and well-equipped personnel. Neither department, however, had ever confronted events as catastrophic as this. Both departments responded within their standard framework of operations for a major fire. But without an assessment of the interdependent effects of the collapse of the technical infrastructure needed to support their operations, the responders themselves became victims. The loss was greatest in the Fire Department, in which 343 fire personnel were lost. This number included personnel who were in the buildings seeking to rescue others when the towers collapsed, as well as departmental leadership on duty when their command post, established in the ground floor of the North Tower, was destroyed.

Culturally, the emergency-response departments of New York City have well-developed, coherent, professional beliefs and values regarding their departmental performance. Less well developed, however, was their awareness of the need for information from other departments in order to craft an effective strategy of action for this extraordinarily difficult event. With little experience in suppressing fire in 110-story buildings, the fire department did not consider the possible collapse of the buildings themselves. Without an assessment of the structural damage to the building and its state of fragility, standard departmental procedures placed their own personnel at risk.

At the Pentagon site, the Boeing 767 struck a section of the building that had just been reinforced against possible attack. The physical reinforcement of the building, including $10,000 windows and fire-resistant walls between sections of the building, limited the damage. Fortunately, the advanced structural design of the building largely confined the damage to one section, facilitating response and enabling the occupants of the other sections of the building to leave unharmed. Organizationally, Pentagon forces were both a target of the attack and a responder to the event. With personnel trained in battlefield management, the DoD was uniquely suited to respond to this event. Located in Arlington County, Virginia, the Pentagon site drew its first responders from the Arlington County Fire Department and the Fairfax County Search and Rescue Team. With familiarity developed from prior training and joint exercises, the local emergency-response agencies moved quickly to join operations with the DoD's Security Force, and together the two sets of agencies created an effective response system. In this unusual situation, federal forces integrated directly with county emergency-response teams without the usual intervening state jurisdiction. The markedly lower death toll at the Pentagon site, 184 persons, documented both less devastating conditions and a smoother interorganizational transition to response than at the WTC.

Auto-Adaptation in Practice

Elements of auto-adaptation were evident in local response at both sites, but the difference in the magnitude of disaster at the two sites affected the interaction between the local site-response sub-systems and the wider national response. The response to the WTC attacks involved a much larger loss of life, a far greater number of organizations, a significantly higher cost in damage, and a more profound impact on the economic, social, and emotional state of New York City, the state, and the nation. Responsible actors at both the Pentagon and WTC sites requested assistance from FEMA, and FEMA personnel responded promptly to both sets of requests. The response to the Pentagon site was managed by a joint federal-local task force and was largely under control within four days. The response to the WTC site was a much more complex operation that was still in progress six months after the attacks. This analysis will review the five phases of a preliminary model of auto-adaptation against actual practice, focusing on the response to the WTC site and the interactions among the participating jurisdictions as the more complex, dynamic set of operations.

Information Search

The interdependence among the response organizations' technical information infrastructure, their organizational procedures and capacity to assess accurately the risk to which they were exposed, and their willingness to explore alternative strategies in response to the extraordinary damage, is clear. This interdependence is vividly demonstrated by the mixed signals, costly delays, and painful misjudgments that exacerbated the loss of life in the 71 minutes that included the crash of United Flight 11 into the North Tower at 8:48

A.M., the second crash of American Airlines Flight 175 into the South Tower at 9:03 A.M., and the collapse of the South Tower at 9:59 A.M. The final collapse of the North Tower at 10:28 A.M. added a scant 29 minutes to potential evacuation time for the occupants of the North Tower.

In retrospect, it is difficult to portray the unimaginable horror that emergency personnel confronted as these events were unfolding. Information search was seriously limited, resulting in a severe lack of information as a basis for decision making in this urgent, uncertain, swiftly moving context. The communications infrastructure was disabled. Verizon's cables in the base of the North Tower were destroyed, and telephone communication lines were disrupted. As people turned to cell phones, the number of calls increased by more than 1,000 percent, overloading the base stations and rendering them useless. Police and fire personnel turned to radio communications, but their call channels were also overloaded. In this extremely dangerous environment, thousands of people frantically sought safety. Fire personnel entered the towers seeking to suppress the fires or guide the occupants to safety, but without adequate communication, they lost contact with departmental leadership and had little or no information about the growing instability of the towers. Information search at the site failed to provide a sufficiently timely assessment of this volatile set of conditions to support coordinated action. Departmental procedures developed for fires of lesser scale proved inadequate in this inferno.

Information Exchange

The capacity for information exchange is directly related to the performance of information search processes. On-scene at the WTC collapse, information exchange in the first hours after the attack was limited by the same failure of communications infrastructure that hindered information search. Without information exchange, coordination between the leaders of the response organizations and their personnel, as well as among organizations and between jurisdictions, was delayed and disrupted. The need for a joint information center among federal, state, municipal, and borough operations was acute, but the extraordinary physical destruction in the immediate area of the WTC complex made it difficult to find space close to operations to establish a joint information center. Separate jurisdictions established separate information centers, asserting that they were joint, but in fact presenting different accounts of operations to news and agency personnel. Conflicting reports hindered cooperation, and detracted from efforts to build trust and coordinate action among the agencies and jurisdictions in an extremely difficult, uncertain operations environment.

Among the federal agencies, information exchange reached the level of near auto-adaptation for agencies engaged in consequence management. At FEMA headquarters in Washington, DC, senior personnel activated the Emergency Operations Center immediately upon seeing the second plane crash into the South Tower on the television news. Personnel from HHS began to mobilize the Disaster Medical Assistance Teams (DMAT) and Disaster Mortuary Teams (DMORT) to respond first to New York, and minutes later, to the Pentagon. Secretary of Transportation Norman Y. Mineta quickly grounded all airplanes in U.S. airspace in order to prevent any further attacks. Army Corps of Engineers personnel recognized that debris removal would prove a major problem for New York, and planned ways in which they would offer their services to New York City personnel.

In Washington, DC and in the cities near New York, the physical information infrastructure remained intact. Communication lines were not damaged, and information was exchanged freely via telephone, fax, radio, and e-mail. Daily conference calls between FEMA's regional operating centers and headquarters maintained an open, two-way exchange of information that informed decisions at both locations. Twice-a-day briefings at FEMA headquarters kept both staff and leaders focused on actions planned and actions taken. In the intense first hours after the attacks, decisions were made and resources committed among agencies on the basis of verbal agreements. This informal process revealed the degree of common understanding among the senior personnel of the principal response agencies. It reflected a high degree of mutual respect, shared goals, and trust among responsible personnel gained from working together in previous disaster operations. This kind of information exchange represented "heedful interrelating" among the personnel, with participants paying careful attention to the actions and needs of the other agencies in order to achieve coordinated action among all participants in response operations. Even members of Congress set aside partisan differences to show a unified approach to counter this sobering national threat.

Problems did arise, however, in integrating information from the consequence management set of operations with reports from crisis management operations to present a comprehensive profile of disaster operations to President George W. Bush. At times, reports of the state of disaster operations were conflicting, or information presented to the public was not checked carefully. The result was apparent confusion among agency personnel and the public, with the unfortunate outcome of missed opportunities for detection in the anthrax cases or conflicting statements made regarding the level of risk to which postal workers or others were exposed. The credibility of the information processes is cumulative, with the quality of information exchanged dependent upon the degree of care taken in information search.

Sensemaking

The ability to act in difficult, urgent situations depends on sufficient understanding of the context to formulate a plausible strategy of action, given the existing constraints and available resources. This capacity depends, in turn, on the preceding processes of information search and information exchange. In coping with this seemingly incomprehensible event, few persons initially understood the danger to which they were exposed. Most painful were the accounts of security guards urging occupants of the South Tower to return to their desks after the North Tower was struck. In an effort to maintain order, and based on inadequate information, responsible managers informed employees that they could safely remain in the building and return to work. Precious minutes were lost in evacuating the building, as employees followed instructions instead of checking the validity of the information against their own perceptions (*New York Times,* September 12, 2001). The limitations of human cognitive capacity are nowhere more apparent than in the inability to absorb information that is startlingly divergent from one's previous experience (Cohen and Levinthal, 1990). The potential collapse of the towers was not recognized by managers, individuals, or emergency personnel in time to immediately implement the strategy of evacuation that appears obvious only in hindsight.

Away from the horror of burning buildings and failed infrastructure, federal-agency sensemaking spurred action in anticipation of requests for assistance. Federal officials, recognizing the extraordinary extent of damage, pre-positioned mobile emergency response support (MERS) units to send communications equipment to New York to facilitate immediate response.[5] From previous experience, senior officials recognized the type of assistance that would be needed for this demanding, urgent environment. They acted effectively to provide support to the on-scene managers, constructing meaning from a collage of prior disaster events. The contrast in ability to make sense out of this seemingly incomprehensible situation reflected not only the difference in experience between senior emergency management personnel and on-site security guards, but also the long-recognized observation that human problem-solving ability drops under stress (Miller, 1967; Weick, 1993; Comfort, 1999; Flin, 1996, 2001). In the actual context of disaster, the demands of the situation often exceed human problem-solving capacity.

Adaptation

Sensemaking represents a form of learning, the ability to construct meaning from perceptions that may be disparate or scattered, but that lead to recognition of a coherent strategy of action. The ensuing action constitutes a change from previous behavior that fits environmental demands more appropriately. Two incidents indicate adaptation of response units to urgent needs from the disaster environment. At the Pentagon, local emergency-response units from Arlington County and the FEMA-sponsored Urban Search and Rescue Team from Fairfax County responded immediately to the crash scene. Because the Department of Defense was the victim, the scene immediately became a federal disaster. Federal resources were made available to local managers, and the response system evolved essentially as a federal-local set of operations, with little involvement from the State of Virginia, despite formal requirements for state agencies to act as the intermediary between federal and local units. In this case, the experience and professional capacity of the local Arlington and Fairfax County responders, coupled with the immediacy of federal assistance, made formal intervention by state agencies located in Richmond, several hours away, virtually unnecessary.

The same situation prevailed in New York City, where federal agencies provided support directly to New York municipal agencies, without direct involvement of New York state agencies located in Albany, two hours away. The urgency and scope of assistance required in response operations in New York City demanded federal resources, and prior relationships between federal and municipal officials established the trust and collaboration essential to coordinate actions under the stress of this uncertain disaster environment. Prior procedures proved inappropriate, given the size and scope of this disaster. Taking reasoned action to save lives, reduce risk, assist those who had been harmed, and restore basic services in the damaged area meant adapting practice to this severely altered environment. Slowly, order emerged at both sites, but with significant adjustment of prior practices to meet the enormity of the tasks. These events indicate the need to review the role of state agencies in managing extreme events.

Interorganizational Learning

The final phase in adapting to a changed disaster environment includes evaluation of actions taken and modification of succeeding actions on the basis of observed results. This phase could initiate system-wide change as the action of one organization affects the performance of its near-neighbors in the response system, triggering a ripple of change throughout the interdependent set of organizations. It is too early to assess whether changes initiated by organizations, as they modified prior practice in this event will remain in place. To the extent that they do, these changes will represent learning among organizations in a permanent alteration of conditions that lead to the disaster. A candidate for this type of permanent change among organizations responsible for public security is the newly formed Department of Homeland Security (OHS). This office, as presently conceived, integrate functions of crisis and consequence management in a unified approach to reduction of risk and response to terrorist attacks or other types of threats. Although there is widespread recognition of the need to reduce the risk of threats to public security, the precise mechanisms for bringing about this reduction are not clear.

At issue is the balance between governmental authority used to protect the public good, and the rights of individuals to freedom from unwarranted breaches of their privacy. A secondary issue is interdependence among government agencies. Whether agencies currently operating under the DOJ would be limited in their functions of pursuing perpetrators of terrorist acts, by sharing information more widely with other governmental agencies, remains to be seen. Clearly, mutual adaptation among the agencies will occur over time, but the direction, rate, and intensity of this change will vary among the participant organizations, and with the scope of the continuing threat.

Equally important will be the evolution of the relationships among the jurisdictions in countering and responding to terrorist threats. Whether the emergence of direct federal-local relationships will continue or be replaced by wider, regional networks of preparedness and response, will depend on the interplay of threat and developing governmental capacity at state and local agencies. The lasting form of a response system for extreme events will certainly be intergovernmental, but the precise mix of federal-state-local participation will likely depend on public investment in building an information infrastructure sufficiently advanced to manage the intense flow of information search, exchange, and sensemaking among the respective governments needed to support coordinated action in risk reduction and response.

Auto-Adaptation in Inter-Governmental Relations

While instances of auto-adaptation occurred in response to the 9/11 events, they were largely spontaneous acts taken by different agencies at different levels of jurisdiction in fortuitous recognition of a chance to improve performance. These instances were intermittent, without the cumulative power of a systematic effort to create change in the performance of the whole system. To improve agency response in extreme events, it is essential to recognize the systemic functions inherent in intergovernmental performance. Further, this recognition needs to foster the emergence of an auto-adaptive system among the governmental agencies that would seek the best mode of action at each agency and jurisdictional level of operations, while simultaneously integrating these separate actions into a coherent strategy of action for the whole system. This requirement places an intensive load on shared knowledge, communications, and feedback, both within and among the agencies and jurisdictions. It means the articulation of a common goal that is accepted by all agencies and jurisdictions, such as protection of public security. It also means the development of a basic set of knowledge bases for each agency within a jurisdiction—and for each jurisdiction—that can guide operations on a daily basis, but that can be integrated across the interjurisdictional response system in an extreme event.

Accomplishing this change in intergovernmental performance means rethinking the public investment in governmental service. Systemic performance cannot be achieved by a hierarchical ordering of responsibilities and resources within and among jurisdictional boundaries. It requires the flexibility to reallocate resources and knowledge among agencies within a given jurisdiction and between the set of jurisdictions, in response to demands from the environment. To counter the threat of terrorism, for example, local governments not only need viable computational systems to manage risk at their respective levels, but also to integrate the specific knowledge of their jurisdictions with the broader knowledge of the intergovernmental system. The lack of such capacity, particularly at the regional level that includes municipalities, counties, and special districts, as well as major nonprofit and private institutions that serve a metropolitan region, was evident in the effort to mobilize response to the 9/11 events.

A Preliminary Model of Auto-Adaptation in Emergency Response

From this brief analysis, a beginning model of auto-adaptation in emergency response may be sketched. Auto-adaptation is a nonlinear process that depends on early recognition of indicators for change. In contrast to linear models that have clear demarcations of authority and specific tasks for different levels of operation, nonlinear models have overlapping authorities and multiple points of entry into, or exit from, an operations field. Instead of a step-wise progression through categorical stages of change, the organization may proceed with a cumulative assessment of changing conditions that warrant reconsideration of risk and reformulation of strategies that shift responsibilities for action according to need and capacity. Identifying, measuring, and monitoring a set of critical conditions that place a community or region at risk become primary methods of providing decision support to practicing managers in terms of reducing their exposure to risk and determining the need for preventive action.

Auto-adaptation is primarily a learning strategy. It depends on the development of a scalable knowledge base and information infrastructure to support interorganizational operations among the multiple agents that make up the potential response system. Although the exact form of this sociotechnical infrastructure is not yet defined, it would likely have the following characteristics:

Information Search

Search processes will be most effective if they are linked to current assessments of conditions and facilities vital to continuing operations in the community at risk. Establishing and maintaining the knowledge bases, and updating the technical requirements to conduct rapid information search and aggregation functions to provide comprehensive views of the state of vulnerability for the community, are the first steps in mobilizing that community's ability to manage its own risk.

Information Exchange

These processes are necessarily interorganizational, and the boundaries of the information exchange will be defined, in part, by the state of technical advancement of the infrastructure that supports it. More importantly, the quality and effectiveness of the information exchange will be defined by the organizational processes of training, receptiveness to incoming information that may be inconsistent with prior assumptions, and willingness to share information regarding actual performance. Instead of following traditional jurisdictional boundaries, information exchange will more likely be defined by regions that share similar types of risk, or are bounded by functional interdependencies such as transportation systems or electrical power and water-distribution systems.

Sensemaking

The capacity to interpret the signals and shifts in conditions of routine operations depends on the sociotechnical infrastructure that has been established for information search and exchange processes. It also depends on the cognitive capacity of those responsible for action. Understanding the limits of human cognitive capacity, and using technical means of decision support to augment this capacity in extreme situations, are fundamental to increasing the ability of an interorganizational system of governmental agencies to take timely, informed action in response to risk. This function is likely to be most effective when performed on a regional scale. Municipal governments are too limited to manage extreme events with only their resources. State governments may be inadequately informed regarding the specific details of operations in local governmental jurisdictions. National governments may be too broad to provide the specificity in action needed for effective risk reduction and response over the range of local regions exposed to risk. Regional systems of risk reduction and response are likely to emerge in metropolitan areas as the most effective balance between size, capacity, and specificity needed for effective action.

Adaptation

Particular forms of adaptation to manage extreme events are likely to continue to develop. The federal-local partnership proved effective in the 9/11 response at both the WTC and the Pentagon, but it is an expensive alternative. When costs are considered in assessing alternative forms of interorganizational response over the long term, increasing the capacity of regional networks may prove a more efficient, viable alternative. Most important will be fostering the dynamic of individual, intra-organizational, and interorganizational learning that leads to lasting change.

Auto-adaptation

The conceptual model of auto-adaptation is a system of interacting units, each performing at its own rate but adjusting performance to that of its near-neighbors in response to incoming information from the environment. Thus, information entering the system becomes immediately accessible throughout the system in a synergistic adaptation to threat and reallocation of resources and responsibilities to meet that threat. It is a system of continuous learning, and fosters initiative and responsible action at all governmental levels, through mutual adjustment and reciprocal exchange of information and resources. It is guided by a common goal of public security for the community, region, state, and nation.

Conclusion

Auto-adaptation offers a mode of improving intergovernmental coordination in response to extreme events. This model acknowledges that change in performance needs to occur within organizations, among organizations within a single jurisdiction, and between jurisdictions engaged in response to an extreme event. The model builds on the human ability to learn and adapt to new information, but acknowledges that this capacity can only occur with the support of an appropriate information infrastructure. Federal investment in building the information infrastructure at sub-national levels of government would yield a major return in increased capacity of the intergovernmental system to anticipate and respond to extreme events.

References

Argyris, C. *Knowledge for Action: A Guide to Overcoming Barriers to Organizational Change*. San Francisco: Jossey-Bass, 1993.

Axelrod, R. *The Complexity of Cooperation: Agent-Based Models of Competition and Collaboration*. Princeton, N.J.: Princeton University Press, 1997.

Axelrod, R., and M. Cohen. *Harnessing Complexity*. New York: The Free Press, 1999.

Bak, P., and K. Chen. "Self-Organized Criticality." *Scientific American* (1991): 46–53.

Carley, K., and J. Harrald. "Organizational Learning under Fire: Theory and Practice." *American Behavioral Scientist* 40 no. 3 (January 1997): 310–332.

Cohen, W. M., and D. A. Levinthal. "Absorptive Capacity: A New Perspective on Learning and Innovation." *Administrative Science Quarterly* 35 (1990): 128–152.

Comfort, L. "Governance under Fire: Organizational Fragility in Complex Systems." *Governance and Public Security*. Syracuse, NY: Syracuse University, 2002, pp. 113–127.

Comfort, L. K. *Shared Risk: Complex Systems in Seismic Response*. Amsterdam: Pergamon, 1999.

Comfort, L. K. "Self Organization in Complex Systems." *Journal of Public Administration Research and Theory* 4 no. 3 (July 1994): 393–410.

Comfort, L. K. "Interorganizational Coordination in Disaster Management: A Model for an Interactive Information System." National Science Foundation Grant #CES 88–04285, 1989. Final report, June 30, 1993.

Comfort, L. K., and Y. Sungu. "Organizational Learning from Seismic Risk: The 1999 Marmara and Duzce, Turkey Earthquakes." In *Managing Crises: Threats, Dilemmas and Opportunities*, ed. U. Rosenthal, L. K. Comfort, and A. Boin. Springfield, IL: Charles C. Springer Publishers, 2001, pp. 119–142.

Federal Emergency Management Agency. *Federal Response Plan*. Washington, DC: Federal Emergency Management Agency, 1999.

Feldman, M., and J. G. March. "Information in Organizations as Signal and Symbol." *Administrative Science Quarterly* 26 (1981): 171–86.

Flin, R. "Decision Making in Crises: The Piper Alpha Disaster." In *Managing Crises: Threats, Dilemmas, Opportunities,* ed. U. Rosenthal, A. Boin, and L. K. Comfort. Springfield, IL: Charles C. Thomas Publishers, 2001, pp. 103–118.

Flin, R. *Sitting in the Hot Seat: Leaders and Teams for Critical Incident Management.* Chicester: John Wiley and Sons, 1996.

Gawronski, V. T., and R. S. Olson. "'Normal' Versus 'Special' Time Corruption: An Exploration of Mexican Attitudes." *Cambridge Review of International Affairs* 16 no. 1 (2000): 344–361.

Gell-Mann, M. "Complex Adaptive Systems." In *Complexity: Metaphors, Models, and Reality*, ed. G. A. Cowan, D. Pines, and D. Meltzer. Reading, MA: Addison-Wesley, 1994, pp. 17–45.

Goodman, P., L. Sproull and Associates. *Technology and Organizations.* San Francisco: Jossey-Bass Publishers, 1990.

Hayes-Roth, F., D. Waterman, and D. Lenat. *Building Expert Systems.* Reading, MA: Addison-Wesley Publishing Company, 1983.

Holland, J. *Hidden Order: How Adaptation Builds Complexity.* Reading, MA: Addison Wesley Publishing Co., 1995.

Kartez, J. D. and W. J. Kelly. "Research Based Disaster Planning: Conditions for Implementation." In *Managing Disaster: Strategies and Policy Perspectives*, ed. L. K. Comfort. Durham, NC: Duke University Press, 1988, pp. 126–146.

Kauffman, S. A. *The Origins of Order: Self-Organization and Selection in Evolution.* New York: Oxford University Press, 1993.

Klein, G. A. "A Recognition-Primed Decision Making (RPD) Model of Rapid Decision Making." In *Decision Making in Action: Models and Methods*, ed. G. Klein, J. Orasanu, R. Calderwood, and C. Zsambok. Norwood, NJ: Ablex Publishing Corporation, 1993, pp. 138–147.

Mileti, D., ed. *Disasters by Design: A Reassessment of Natural Hazards in the United States.* Washington, DC: Joseph Henry Press, 1999.

Miller, G. "The Magical Number Seven, Plus or Minus Two: Some Limits on Our Capacity for Processing Information." *Psychology of Communication.* New York, NY: Basic Books, 1967, pp. 14–44.

Newell, A., and H. A. Simon. *Human Problem Solving.* Englewood Cliffs, NJ: Prentice Hall, 1972.

Ostrom, E. "A Behavioral Approach to the Rational Choice Theory of Collective Action." *American Political Science Review* 92 no.1 (1998): 1–22.

Peitgen, H., H. Jurgens, and D. Saupe. *Chaos and Fractals: New Frontiers of Science.* New York: Springer-Verlag, 1992.

Platt, R., et al. *Disasters and Democracy.* Washington, DC: Island Press, 1999.

Prigogine, I., and I. Stengers. *Order Out of Chaos.* 1977. Rpt. New York: Bantam Press, 1984.

Simon, H. A. *The Sciences of the Artificial*, 2nd ed. Cambridge, MA: MIT Press, 1981.

Sylves, R. T., and W. L. Waugh, Jr., eds. *Disaster Management in the U.S. and Canada: The Politics, Policymaking, Administration, and Analysis of Emergency Management,* 2nd ed. Springfield, IL: Charles C. Thomas, Publisher, 1996.

United States Government, *United States Government Interagency Domestic Terrorism Concept of Operations Plan,* January 2001, www.fema.gov.

Weick, K. *Making Sense of the Organization.* Malden, MA: Blackwell, 2001.

Weick, K. *Sensemaking in Organizations.* Thousand Oaks, CA: Sage Publications, 1995.

Weick, K. "The Collapse of Sensemaking in Organizations: The Mann Gulch Disaster." *Administrative Science Quarterly* 22 no. 3 (1993): 606–639.

Weick, K., and K. Roberts. "Collective Mind and Organizational Reliability: The Case of Flight Operations on an Aircraft Carrier Deck." In *Organizational Learning*, ed. M. D. Cohen and L. S. Sproull. Thousand Oaks, CA: Sage Publications, 1996, pp. 330–358.

Weick, K., and K. Sutliffe, *Managing the Unexpected*: *Assuring High Performance in an Age of Complexity*. San Francisco: Jossey Bass, 2001.

Notes

1. I wish to thank John R. Harrald and Joseph L. Barbera, coprincipal investigators of "Observing and Documenting the Interorganizational Response to the September 11 Attacks," National Science Foundation Grant #CMS0139309, for including me in their research team. This article reports findings from research conducted under this grant. I also acknowledge the assistance of Michael Carrigan and Naim Kapucu, graduate student assistants at the Graduate School of Public and International Affairs, University of Pittsburgh, for their careful and diligent work in conducting the content analysis of the *New York Times* reports and the FEMA situation reports for this case. Further, I thank the public managers from the Federal Emergency Management Agency, the U.S. Army Corps of Engineers, and the Department of Health and Human Services, who gave their time and thoughtful observations to this research. For reasons of professional confidentiality, they are not named.

2. In an essay published earlier (Comfort, 2002), I discussed the need to identify the potential points of breakdown, or fragility, in interorganizational systems that evolve rapidly in response to extreme events. In this essay, I address the converse need to strengthen the capacity of the emerging response system in order to respond more effectively to threats on a regional scale.

3. The analysis of this case study draws heavily upon the daily news reports published by the *New York Times,* September 12 to October 6, 2001; situation reports prepared by the Department of Health and Human Services and the Federal Emergency Management Agency, and semi-structured interviews with key operations personnel in the Federal Emergency Management Agency, the Department of Health and Human Services, and the U.S. Army Corps of Engineers. The report is also informed by observations from professional researchers who were engaged in studies of response to the World Trade Center-Pentagon Attacks but who have not yet published their findings. To protect the confidentiality of the respondents, names will not be identified.

4. Federal Emergency Management Agency, FEMA Situation Report #1, September 11, 2001 (Washington, DC: Federal Emergency Management Agency, 2001.)

5. Director of Operations, Federal Emergency Management Agency, Interview, January 28, 2002, Washington, DC.

Chapter 16

Terrorism Early Warning Groups: Regional Intelligence to Combat Terrorism

John P. Sullivan

Combating terrorism within the United States is of the greatest priority to preserving American liberties, lives, and the public peace. An effective national strategy to combat terrorism must include efforts to deter, prevent, and marshal effective response to terrorist incidents. This chapter describes an interagency model developed in Los Angeles County, California. The Terrorism Early Warning (TEW) Group provides public safety agencies with a cooperative vehicle for obtaining and assessing the information needed to manage threats and acts of terrorism.

Protecting a Region

Los Angeles County is home to over 10 million people. It contains 88 separate cities, including Los Angeles (the largest), Pasadena, and Long Beach. Reaching from the "desert to the sea," Los Angeles (LA) County is home to the Ports of Los Angeles and Long Beach, several airports including LAX, oil refineries, food distribution hubs, entertainment and cultural facilities, and a complex transportation system including railways, a subway, and freeways. All of this infrastructure is vulnerable to potential attacks or disruption. Protecting the people and infrastructure within the county is a full time job. The region is served by 43 local police agencies (including the Los Angeles Sheriff's Department and the Los Angeles Police Department), 35 fire departments, and 3 public health agencies, as well as numerous utilities, water systems, emergency management agencies, and their partners at the Federal and State levels.

Each agency in the region has a specific focus and expertise. Police officers and sheriff's deputies patrol neighborhoods. Fire departments provide fire suppression, hazardous materials response, urban search and rescue, and emergency medical services. Public health agencies monitor the health and progress of disease. Emergency management agencies coordinate major disaster responses to both natural occurrences and intentional attacks. In many ways, a terrorist attack is an intentional disaster. The Federal Bureau of Investigation (FBI) is the lead federal investigative agency for terrorism; the California Highway Patrol, a state agency, protects freeways and bridges; the United States Coast Guard protects the seaports; the Transportation Security Administration, and local and airport police, secure the airports; the Postal Inspection Service protects the mail; Immigration and Customs Enforcement secures the borders and ports; and the Coroner investigates deaths.

Each of these agencies has a role in prevention or response to terrorism. In fact, no single agency can do it alone. Comprehensive efforts to prevent and respond to attacks when they occur require many unique and specialized skills. Law enforcement and fire and health services, together with many government and private entities, have a role in securing the region. Each of these partners also has unique information requirements in order to perform its individual and collective tasks in a coordinated and effective manner.

To facilitate building upon the expertise and capabilities of the entire community, the Los Angeles TEW Group was established in 1996. The TEW brings together representatives of the Los Angeles Sheriff's Department, Los Angeles Police Department, FBI, Los Angeles Fire Department, Los Angeles County Department of Health Services, Los Angeles County Police,[1] as well as individual police and fire agencies, to develop the information and intelligence needed to coordinate terrorism prevention and response for all entities in Los Angeles County, and to link with surrounding counties and similar efforts across the nation.

The LA TEW includes a number of elements. The heart of the TEW is a full-time watch center where law enforcement, fire, and health analysts monitor regional and global threats. They field inquiries from local agencies regarding suspicious circumstances, analyze information they receive from a variety of sources, and share this information with all appropriate investigative and response agencies. In addition, the TEW holds a monthly meeting to foster coordination and skills development. It also coordinates a network of "Terrorism Liaison Officers" (TLOs) at each law enforcement, fire service, and health agency in the county. TLOs funnel threat information to the TEW for assessment, and bring actionable intelligence from the national level and the TEW back to field personnel. TLOs also coordinate with local businesses, industry, and utilities. Within this framework, community police are the first link to the public. The expertise and familiarity of beat officers and firefighters at a local firehouse is combined with strategic analysis and intelligence support from the TEW. The TEW can then gain an understanding of what's happening on the street, and can tell field personnel what to look for based upon global trends and specific threat information.

The TEW Model

The TEW model was first established in Los Angeles County in 1996 to address the challenges of terrorism. Prior to September 11, 2001, the TEW worked to stimulate regional participation, and was activated to manage specific threats (such as anthrax threats) or special events (such as the Y2K). On 9/11 the TEW was activated, making a transition into a full-time standing organization over the next few months. The TEW follows a networked approach, bringing together law enforcement, fire, health, and emergency management agencies to address the intelligence needs for terrorism and critical infrastructure protection.

The TEW model is based on the premise that intelligence is more than "secret information" about an adversary. Intelligence to address threats must go beyond simply describing the possible perpetrators. It must also provide investigators, emergency responders, city planners, and other authorities with accurate information about the situations they are managing or may face.

The TEW model describes this process as *"All Source/All Phase Fusion."* For the TEW, intelligence is derived from all potential sources, reflecting all phases of the information collection process. These could be classified sources, sensitive but unclassified sources, or open sources such as local newspapers or industry bulletins. The TEW assumes that useful information about any event is available from the smallest local source through the widest global sources. The trigger for an attack may be found in the local area, across the nation, in a foreign nation, in cyberspace, or in a combination of these factors.

To achieve this local through global fusion, the TEW relies on a process known as Intelligence Preparation for Operations (IPO). IPO combines a number of traditional intelligence procedures with its own TEW process (which includes evaluating trends and potentials, capabilities and intentions, and providing an operational net assessment).

The Los Angeles TEW is designed to provide operational intelligence for developing potential courses of action, helping decision makers move through the decision cycle (known as the Observe-Orient-Decide-Act Loop). It helps forecast potential events, and crafts meaningful courses of action for interagency, interdisciplinary response. It relies upon open source intelligence for scanning and monitoring trends that may influence training and doctrinal needs. Additionally, during an actual threat period or attack, the TEW provides consequence projection (forecasting) to identify potential courses of action to authorities.

TEW Organization

While monitoring trends or during an actual event, the TEW uses a "Net Assessment" process to determine the scope of an actual or potential event, and its possible impact.

Rather than just place representatives of various agencies into an unstructured environment and hope they effectively share information, the TEW is organized along functional lines. Thus, law enforcement officers, analysts, fire officers, public health and emergency medical practitioners, and subject matter specialists from a variety of disciplines are brought together to work as an integrated team. Full-time TEW personnel from law, fire, and health agencies are supplemented during surge periods from the broader response community.

The TEW is organized into six cells, as reflected in Figure 16-1.

- The *Officer-in-Charge (Unified Command) cell* provides direction, sets intelligence requirements, and is responsible for interacting with outside incident command entities.
- The *Analysis/Synthesis cell* takes in information from all sources and develops an information collection plan (including tasking requests for information to other parts of the TEW and outside agencies). The Analysis/Synthesis cell is also responsible for developing a complete picture of the situation, turning the TEW's analysis into actionable intelligence products (advisories, alerts, warnings, and mission folders to assist response).

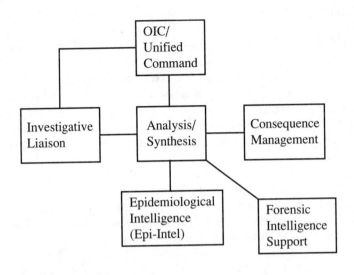

FIGURE 16-1. Los Angeles TEW Organization

- The *Consequence Management cell* makes an assessment of the law, fire, and health consequences of an event. This includes assessing and developing courses of action for response.
- The *Investigative Liaison cell* coordinates with criminal investigative entities (such as local law enforcement agencies) and the traditional intelligence community. This cell is the outreach component of the analytical process. This cell ensures that TEW information gets to the appropriate investigative entity—such as a joint terrorist task force—and that investigative information gets to the TEW so it can develop the strategic picture.
- *The Epidemiological Intelligence cell* is responsible for capturing the results of real-time disease surveillance and coordinating with the disease investigation. This includes helping prepare plans and procedures to protect food, water supply, and agricultural and veterinary sectors.
- Finally, the *Forensic Intelligence Support cell* exploits a range of technical means to support the TEW fusion process. These include chemical, biological, radiological, nuclear, and explosive reconnaissance, liaison with bomb squads, public health labs, hazardous material teams, the use of sensors and detectors, and geospatial tools (including mapping, imagery and Geographic Information System products).

TEW in Action

A TEW can play several complementary roles during various phases of terrorism prevention and response. Early in its evolution, the LA TEW was primarily an "integrating concept" for addressing emerging threats—including the potential for terrorism involving chemical, biological, radiological, or nuclear (CBRN) agents. From its inception, the LA TEW held a monthly meeting to develop a cooperative vehicle for addressing threats. As part of that process, the TEW conducted an on-going assessment of global terrorist trends and potentials.

Anthrax (or "white powder") threats were one specific threat identified by the TEW in the second half of 1998. A suspicious white powder was found in Wichita, Kansas on August 18, 1998 (four months before similar incidents began to happen in Los Angeles). The LA TEW recognized the possible significance of this event and reported it in the TEW's August "OSINTrep" (a monthly open source review of trends and potentials); it was also discussed at the August 27 TEW meeting. The Wichita incident turned out to be a hoax, and additional anthrax hoaxes were reported in the TEW's October, November, and December reports, and discussed at those months' meetings. As a result, the TEW was familiar with the issue and was able to serve as a catalyst for threat assessment and development of measured response protocols when a sequence of over four dozen anthrax hoaxes hit Los Angeles.[2]

After the 9-11 attacks, the TEW began operating as a standing intelligence watch center. By the time the nation was struck with actual anthrax attacks and an epidemic of white powder hoaxes in October 2001, the TEW had developed a comprehensive countywide protocol for conducting threat assessments and supporting field and laboratory personnel. Such assessments (available to support all law enforcement, fire, and health agencies in the county) are only one of the TEW's tasks.

A Real-Life Example of TEW

The following scenario extracted from TEW experience describes the TEW in action. (Specific events and actions are scrubbed for operational security.)

It's 0500 hours; the TEW starts its daily routine. Personnel report to work and begin reviewing reports, media sources, and leads to assess the current situation. Overnight, several leads have been faxed or e-mailed to the group. They include suspected reconnaissance of transit terminals, oil refineries, and cultural facilities. The leads are assessed in light of current threat information, entered into a database, and prioritized. One lead is particularly intriguing this morning. There has been a report to a local police agency of several (possibly Middle Eastern) men staying in a hotel room in a suburban city. The men avoid contact with other guests and are seen with documents believed to be jihadist literature. A TEW analyst from the Analysis/Synthesis cell contacts the reporting agency to confirm the report and gather additional information. The intake analyst obtains additional details on the men's identity and vehicle, and runs the information via several criminal justice information systems. The lead is designated high priority by the collection manager. Next, a liaison officer from the Investigative Liaison cell joins the analyst to form a team for follow up. The liaison officer contacts several investigative agencies including the Joint Terrorist Task Force (JTTF) to share the details and determine if there is a terrorist link. In the case of this particular lead, it is determined that the case will be referred to the JTTF. In many other leads processed by the analysts, no terrorist nexus will be found, or a criminal nexus not related to terrorism will be found and the lead will be referred by the Investigative Liaison cell to the appropriate investigative team for action.

At 0700 hours each day, all TEW cells join together for a net assessment meeting. All active leads are reviewed. Leads can be workable, non-workable due to insufficient information or lack of criminal nexus, monitored to determine if there is a terrorist nexus or link to another lead, or, in the case of events occurring in other jurisdictions, monitored for information only. Trends and potentials are then discussed in light of recent leads and global events. Inputs from all disciplines are solicited to ensure relevant threats and their possible impacts are identified. If a threat is discerned, the TEW then begins developing advisories, alerts, or warnings for dissemination to the response community. On-going workload (such as development or updates of response information folders or playbooks) is then prioritized.

If specific information is needed, or threat potentials are identified, a collection plan will be developed. Any necessary information will be channeled out to the field via the network of TLOs. Returning information from the field is then factored back into on-going assessments and analysis. General trend information on local leads and information requirements is given out in a weekly field report for line personnel (police officers, firefighters, health workers, etc). Global and strategic trends (the bigger picture) are discussed in the TEW weekly report directed to command personnel, analysts, and other TEWs.

This day-to-day routine also includes site visits to local infrastructure, briefings to field personnel and TLOs, and participation in exercises designed to build skills. If a threat matures or an attack occurs (locally or elsewhere), the TEW shifts out of its day-to-day "indications and warning" role. It conducts a "net assessment" of the circumstances. If the situation requires specialized local response, the TEW will begin developing a mission folder to provide operational intelligence support to the unified command. This support will ensure that field responders and investigators have the information they need.

Lessons Learned

During its eight years of evolution, the Los Angeles TEW has learned many valuable lessons. First, a team approach to analysis is essential to developing a comprehensive understanding of both the current situation and emerging threats. Traditional case analysis alone does not develop comprehensive situational awareness—especially during a critical incident involving multiagency, multidisciplinary field response. Case analysis alone is not enough to connect the dots and discern the complete picture. Case analysis is typically linear in fashion. It seeks to assemble a case for criminal prosecution but does not provide the operational intelligence needed to forge an effective interagency response.

Pulling together comprehensive situational awareness requires a standing team of personnel from several disciplines. These personnel must be organized to work as a functional team, not just individuals representing their agency or discipline. To see between the information seams, the team must work together regularly. Regular interaction allows an appreciation of context and builds the trust needed to explore alternative courses of action. Information from the top-down is not enough. Information must be obtained from the bottom-up (from field responders), and laterally (from other regions facing similar challenges). This requires the deployment of liaison officers knowledgeable in many facets of terrorist threats (such as the TEW's Investigative Liaison and Forensic Intelligence Support cells) to accurately assess the situation and get real-time information back to the TEW for assessment. Similarly, in order to get accurate and timely reports from field personnel, the TEW must maintain a two-way flow of information and be responsive to the information needs of field personnel. Field personnel need clear, concise things to look for, in order to become good information collectors. When field personnel report suspicious circumstances or provide a lead, the TEW must follow-up and get results back to the field to ensure continued reporting. All of this requires standardized procedures and training to ensure effectiveness. Continual communication is needed to maintain networked intelligence fusion.

Information technology is needed to help ensure this flow of information and to process the large quantity of potentially useful information. During day-to-day operations, activations (such as the TEW activation for the 2000 Democratic National Convention), and exercises, the benefits of technical means—such as chemical sensors and detectors, plume models, and geospatial visualization tools—have repeatedly shown their value. These tools help speed the achievement of situational understanding and assist in sorting through volumes of data to discern trends and connections among seemingly separate indicators. More data-mining, modeling, and visualization tools need to be added to the TEW's toolkit. To quickly determine what's happening during a major attack, all responding agencies need to share information. This demands development of collaborative tools and information technology. A network of TEWs throughout the nation could help achieve this.

Finally, the TEW has learned that it must remain nimble and adaptive to negotiate the dynamic threat environment. New tools, new partners, and continual exercising and skill development are needed to sustain integrated intelligence fusion.

The contemporary terrorist threat involves a series of adversaries linked in networks. These adversaries challenge our safety and our capacity to respond. Combating networks requires an understanding of networked threats, and developing network capabilities of our own. As the Markle Foundation Task Force on National Security in the Information Age noted:

> Participation in such networks can take many forms. Individuals act in a variety of roles, as part of changing organizations. In a national security infrastructure, local police officers, state health officials, and national intelligence analysts are all important actors in the network. Communities of practice—groups of participants in fields like public safety, transportation, agriculture, or energy—can also collectively act in a network. These communities benefit greatly from increased connections to those with similar roles in different organizations or at other levels. In addition, the collective community may come together as ad hoc workgroups, mobilized for specific tasks. Ad hoc workgroups evolve as they respond to a particular challenge.[3]

The First Markle Report essentially commented on the utility of the TEW concept as evolving in Los Angeles and elsewhere in California. Their observations mirror the LA TEW's experience:

> These participants are not distinguished by their relationship to a central gate-keeper, but by their relationship to one another. In a distributed, decentralized network, they can, will, and should form unique and utilitarian relationships in order to best support their particular role in national security, whether in prevention, analysis, response, or protection. This peer-to-peer collaboration allows federal, state, and local participants to draw upon the collective expertise of the community.[4]

The Markle Task Force also validated the TEW's view of the value of distributing counterterrorist capabilities, noting:

> In an environment of such great risks, empowerment of local actors will lead to better prevention or response management. What we face today is a global, multifaceted problem, and the tools for addressing the challenge may be dispersed among thousands of police officers, state public health officials, firefighters, emergency room staff, or soldiers.[5]

This is not the first national body to recognize the value of networked approaches such as the TEW to combat terrorism. For example, the Second Annual Report of the Gilmore Panel contained the following observations on cooperative assessment:

> **Threat Analysis Needs a Cooperative Vehicle**
> As has been noted elsewhere, threat analysis is critical in the determination of appropriate response. Because of the complexity of terrorism threats in general, and the CBRN threat in particular, threat analysis is most effectively conducted by multiple agencies, each of which brings its own special skills and strengths to the table. In Los Angeles County, the TEW has filled the previously wanting role of a medium for information transfer, joint analysis and incident net assessment and thus has proven to be an exceptionally useful mechanism.[6]

TEW Expansion

The TEW model is currently expanding to other jurisdictions. At the time of this writing, there are TEWs at various stages of evolution in Orange, San Bernardino/Riverside, San Diego, and Sacramento Counties in California. Others also exist in Pierce County (Tacoma), Washington; Tulsa, Oklahoma; Hennepin County (Minneapolis), Minnesota; the National Capital Region (DC, VA, MD); and New Orleans, Louisiana in addition to the initial Los Angeles (LA TEW) group.

These groups are evolving into a network, sharing common organization and doctrine, in order to share threat information and support each other during critical periods. Also, the Memorial Institute for the Prevention of Terrorism (Oklahoma City) and the U.S. Department of Homeland Security (Office of Domestic Preparedness) are sponsoring efforts to expand the TEW model into approximately 51 other cities throughout the United States.

To summarize some of the key points of the TEW concept:

- Local law enforcement agencies play key roles in preventing and responding to terrorism.
- Local law enforcement agencies have the ability to gather intelligence and criminal leads during the course of their routine public safety and policing missions.
- Local law enforcement agencies (police officers and sheriff's deputies) can contribute information and intelligence that, when collated and assessed, can lead to the prevention of terrorist acts and related crimes.
- Local agencies can feed this information to an integrated information-sharing and analysis grid that facilitates collaborative analysis.
- Regional TEWs can be a key node in a nationally distributed network for assessing and analyzing terrorist related information. This can be used to guide criminal investigations, as well as for contingency planning.
- Regional TEWs can be linked to each other and to state threat or warning centers, as well as to federal information fusion centers (such as the Terrorist Threat Integration Center, the National Joint Terrorist Task Force, or the CIA's Counterterrorism Center).

Challenges of Networked Fusion

While the LA TEW model has demonstrated that networked intelligence fusion is possible, a number of challenges remain. First among these are organizational and bureaucratic competition. Networked forms compete with existing security structures. Bureaucratic inertia slows movement toward collaboration both within and especially across disciplines (and jurisdictions). This is complicated by competition for funding and struggles for intergovernmental control. While the TEW is a good way to exchange information, some agencies prefer hoarding their knowledge to bolster their own organizational position.

Within a networked structure, the question of who is in control is unavoidable. Defining the relations between networked partners is essential to successful intelligence fusion. Not all information comes from the top. Much of the information necessary to understand the dynamics of a threat—indeed even recognize that there is a threat—is developed from the bottom-up (from cops on the beat or emergency room doctors faced with a mystery illness).

Finally, there is a tension between specialization and generalization. The TEW model fills a specialty niche. Some observers prefer a model that fuses intelligence for the traditional criminal and security services alone. In reality, both types of fusion are necessary. Criminal and security intelligence for terrorism and criminal enterprises of all sorts (such as narcotics, gangs, or organized crime) cannot fill all the intelligence needs for combating terrorism.

Conclusion

The LA TEW has successfully adapted over the past eight years to provide local regional intelligence fusion. When cops, firefighters and health practitioners come together to work as a team, they can pool their experience and expertise to recognize threats that they might individually miss. Together they can develop a comprehensive picture of the current situation, and anticipate future threats. These individuals enable the TEW model to provide a nimble capability that links federal, state, and local agencies so they can swiftly move information in all directions. New TEWs are emerging across the nation. By bringing together analysts and responders from all the services that have a role in responding to terrorism, a TEW allows a region to recognize threats, to possibly prevent an attack, and to develop effective responses to attacks that do occur.

Notes

1. Because of its size, there are several law enforcement agencies in Los Angeles County. The *Los Angeles Sheriff's Department* is the largest sheriff's department in the world. A deputy sheriff works for the County Sheriff's Department. In communities of Los Angeles County that have not incorporated into cities, the Los Angeles County Sheriff's Department provides law enforcement and operates the county jails and courts. The *Los Angeles Police Department (LAPD)* is an independent police agency specifically within the City of Los Angeles. On January 1, 1998, the *Los Angeles County Police* was established through a consolidation of the Los Angeles County Office of Public Safety (LACOPS), the former park police from the Department of Parks and Recreation and the safety police from the Departments of Health and Internal Services. It is the fourth largest law enforcement agency in the county of Los Angeles and one of the largest in the state of California.

2. A case study recounting this sequence is found in Appendix G of Advisory Panel to Assess Domestic Response Capabilities for Terrorism Involving Weapons of Mass Destruction, *Second Annual Report: Toward a National Strategy for Combating Terrorism* (Santa Monica, CA: RAND Corp., 2000). The Los Angeles Case Study is found at pp. 105–126 (Appendix G, G-1 to G-22). The report can be found on line at www.rand.org/nsrd/terrpanel/terror2.pdf.

3. See Markle Foundation Task Force on National Security in the Information Age, *Protecting America's Freedom in the Information Age* (New York: The Markle Foundation, 2002), p. 13. The report can be found on line at www.markletaskforce.org/documents/Markle_Report_Part1.pdf.

4. Ibid.

5. Ibid.

6. Advisory Panel to Assess Domestic Response Capabilities for Terrorism Involving Weapons of Mass Destruction, *Toward a National Strategy for Combating Terrorism.*

References

Advisory Panel to Assess Domestic Response Capabilities for Terrorism Involving Weapons of Mass Destruction, *Second Annual Report: Toward a National Strategy for Combating Terrorism,* Santa Monica, CA: RAND Corp., 2000. See especially the Los Angeles Case Study found at pp. 105–126, Appendix G, G-1 to G-22.

Arquilla, J., and D. Ronfeldt. *Networks and Netwars: The Future of Terror, Crime, and Militancy,* Santa Monica, CA: RAND Corp., 2001.

Bunker, R.J., ed. *Non-State Threats and Future Wars*, London: Frank Cass, 2003.

Markle Foundation Task Force on National Security in the Information Age. *Protecting America's Freedom in the Information Age.* New York: Markle Foundation, October, 2002.

Wilson, G. I., J. P. Sullivan, and H. Kempfer. "Fourth-Generation Warfare: It's Here, And We Need New Intelligence-Gathering Techniques for Dealing with It." *Armed Forces Journal International,* October, 2002, pp. 56–62.

Chapter 17

Strategic Planning for First Responders: Lessons Learned from the NY Fire Department

Reid Sawyer and Joseph Pfeifer[1]

On September 11, 2001, at precisely 8:46 A.M., I watched our world change forever as American Airlines Flight 11 aimed and crashed into the North Tower. Entering the Trade Center to take command, it appeared as if I were stepping into a war zone. The damage in the lobby was extensive. Untold numbers of people were severely injured and trapped. Seventeen minutes later a second plane crashed into the South Tower. We were faced with one of the largest rescue efforts of any fire department in the world.

Each and every firefighter responding to the World Trade Center knew that tens of thousands of people were in their greatest moment of need. In the minutes it took to respond, firefighters looked at the burning Towers and into their own hearts and souls, knowing they would be faced with the danger of climbing 110 stories and encountering fire to rescue those that could not get out. Nonetheless, they entered the buildings and began to climb the narrow stairs.

At 9:58, the South Tower collapsed. Our world in the lobby of the North Tower went black. In darkness, I radioed to the firefighters above. "Command to all units in Tower 1, evacuate the building!" While many of the firefighters assisting people heard the message, they were already dozens of floors above ground level. Little did we know that time was running out. What the world saw on television, I could not see. The area was covered with smoke and I did not know the South Tower had collapsed.

Then, at 10:28, after fighting our way out into the street, I heard the roar of the North Tower starting to collapse. The beautiful morning that was filled with sunshine turned black. After the collapse, in the darkness there was complete silence. It is like a first snowfall: you heard nothing, there were no radio communications, there was only an eerie silence. When I stood up, I saw the skeletons of the collapsed buildings.

20,000 people were saved that day.

2,749 people, including 343 firefighters, perished.

> *In the dust of the collapsed Towers, our world was in its darkest hour, but through the darkness a ray of light appeared. The silhouette of firefighters searching for those lost became a symbol for the world, not because so many were lost, but because so many were inspired to hope. Terrorism aims to take away that very hope. Those firefighters and rescue workers demonstrated to all that men and women will confront any danger, including terrorism, to protect life and care for one's fellow human beings.*
>
> —Deputy Assistant Chief Joseph Pfeifer,
> Fire Department of New York September 2005

Four years after that day, this story has been told many times. The pictures of that day and the subsequent memorials have filled our consciousness. Yet, even given the significant impact of that day, there is still much to learn from the events of September 11 that has not been explored. This chapter attempts to put a face on the extreme complexity of that day, and the challenges of preparing organizations for the next terrorist attack. However, the challenges do not solely revolve around preparing for terrorist attacks. Even on September 11 and the days that followed, the first responders of New York City had to remain prepared to answer other calls, to protect citizens from danger, and to fight other fires. This chapter will outline the issues and lessons learned from 9/11 and how the New York City Fire Department (FDNY) has adapted. However, these lessons are larger than the FDNY or the Fire Service; they apply to all first responders and emergency responders.

Challenges Defined: Innovation and Resilience In and After Crisis

The events of September 11 challenged emergency response organizations in an entirely new way. During the first 102 minutes of the 9/11 attacks, emergency responders in New York City, Washington, DC, and Pennsylvania had to adapt standard operating procedures to deal with unfolding events. The New York City Fire Department (FDNY), in particular, was faced with multiple terrorist attacks that caused a new type of fire and an emergency on an incomprehensible scale. While standard operating procedures provided a framework to operate within, they proved insufficient to meet the challenges that fateful Tuesday morning.

The attacks also forced emergency response organizations to consider their strategic planning in a new light. Many organizations have focused their strategic response on preventing future attacks or acquiring new equipment for handling chemical, biological, radiological, or nuclear (CBRN) attacks. However, equipment alone will not address the issue. Very little thought has been done to identify what skills and capabilities organizations need during the first hour after an attack, much less in the ensuing weeks and months. Most importantly, organizations responding to disasters and terrorist attacks need to adapt quickly to the new reality of the post-crisis situation. Implicit within this mandate is that top leadership and managers must prepare for critical decision-making and incident management. It is not enough to train first responders to use expensive new equipment if we do not also prepare them to make critical command decisions at large, complex incidents.

A crisis of the magnitude of 9/11 forces innovation and change. If an organization learns effectively from these innovations, however, it can reduce the negative impact of future major crises. Organizations that cannot adapt to the ongoing threat of terrorism will suffer a greater impact, and will struggle to meet every subsequent crisis. At the same time, first responder organizations must not let crisis response measures reduce their focus on their daily responsibilities or undercut their normal response capacity.

This is a difficult balance requiring long-term commitment, careful analysis and forward-looking vision. This chapter will explore these challenges by asking two questions at both the strategic and operational levels:

- How can organizations design emergency response procedures that can adapt readily to the demands of a terrorist attack or other crisis event?
- How do organizations develop their operational and strategic capacities to become resilient enough to withstand the stress of crisis and post-crisis events?

Given that we will never operate in a world of perfect information, crisis managers and strategic planners must make decisions for the future in the midst of tremendous uncertainty. Mistakes will be made, but if organizations are flexible, adaptive, and receptive to change, the mistakes will not lead to systemic failure during a crisis or the aftermath. While the goal is to "win" every crisis, reality tells us that this is a nearly impossible standard. Rather, we must not let any one crisis defeat us. This is our challenge as we move forward.

Dynamic Planning

Despite the best efforts of our national security apparatus, we do not know whether we are any safer today than before 9/11. U.S. and international counterterrorist professionals have arrested thousands of terrorist operatives, yet London and Madrid have witnessed their own horrifying attacks, with hundreds killed and wounded during near-simultaneous rush-hour transit system attacks. Other attacks in Casablanca, Turkey, Riyadh, and Bali, as well as the foiled ricin plots in London, paint the clear picture that terrorist threats remain pervasive and dangerous. Terrorism is fundamentally a strategy of surprise; enemies continue to emerge in new areas of operation and rapidly adapt to changes in their security environment. Four years after 9/11 we do not know who the next terrorist actor will be, when or how they will strike, or on what scale. The myriad of unknowns creates a complex landscape populated with hundreds of possible scenarios.

Many observers overlook the extent of the uncertainties surrounding the current terrorist threat, perhaps because the details of the 9/11 attacks have become such defining elements of our threat perception. We have so deeply internalized the specific information about the attacks—the name of the operatives involved in the attack, their backgrounds, their travel patterns, the plot details, their victims—that we do not stop to wonder about how the next attack, orchestrated by different people with a different plan, will occur.

Clearly, we can learn valuable lessons from investigating the 9/11 plot and our response, but relying too heavily on past events to plan for the future can be detrimental. This approach to meeting a new threat environment can produce false confidence that an organization's "improved" skills have actually succeeded in improving the organization's preparedness. Military historians often lament the fact that our armed forces, relying on after-action reviews to train personnel for future action, in effect, prepare to fight the past battle, not the next one. This phenomenon is happening now in our first responder organizations.

Many first responder organizations and managers assume they are prepared for the next terrorist attack because they have purchased new equipment and trained their personnel to use new gear and tools. For instance, the emergency response community has adapted to better respond to the "plane into a building scenario" and thus may feel "prepared" to counter the next terrorist attack. Alternatively, some organizations may suffer from a sense of inadequacy if they determine that they have not built enough capacity to respond to a plane/building scenario. Organizations functioning under these false assumptions continue to purchase equipment and seek out new training without a strategic vision that links means to ends. In reality, organizations should instead focus on evaluating their current capacity in terms of the risk they face within their particular environment.

For the past four years, cities like New York have revised their incident command procedures, individual departments are developing new emergency response plans, and agencies at all levels are conducting exercises to better prepare for an unknown future. However, even within this revised and energized context, many of the existing emergency response procedures wrongly assume:

- a predictable threat and response environment;
- that having standardized operating procedures eliminates uncertainty from a situation; and
- that organizations will have the time and capacity to assess and allocate resources, as well as to identify and correct errors before they occur.

These erroneous assumptions prompt the creation of static emergency response plans based on assumptions that, too often, are never revisited. The vast majority of plans work well during routine operations but often fail in a crisis, since a crisis often eliminates the relevance of standard assumptions made during planning. As Bertrand and Lajtha observe, many plans are "written as compliance gestures rather than realistic emergency operating guidelines. The vast majority of emergency response plans are out of date by the time they are published; are published in inappropriate formats; [and] remain unknown to key persons who are likely to become involved with the emergency."[2] Organizations test their emergency plans at drills and exercises using threat scenarios, but many scenarios lack the interjection of complex or dynamic changes that force decision makers into uncomfortable territory.

Additionally, many simulations portray a discrete threat: a singular event absent a responsive enemy. Such scenarios created on the basis of discrete threats create two dangerous conditions. First, non-dynamic threat scenarios tend to reinforce assumptions about the threat instead of challenging preconceived notions of the security environment, allowing trainees to escape the uncertainty of the "real world," where they must operate without perfect information, and where surprise can obviate assumptions in a moment. Second, the threat is rarely discrete, but is usually multistage, layered, and complex. Training against a discrete threat can lead us to overestimate our capabilities to respond to an extended crisis, and to underestimate our enemy's capabilities to attack. Continued training against these static scenarios ossifies thinking and allows complacency to emerge.

Instead, organizations must recognize that the threat is dynamic and is characterized by extensive uncertainty. To move beyond preparing for the last war, our training must challenge and test our assumptions about operating in complex environments, examine our operational and strategic constraints, and evaluate our capabilities to respond effectively to challenging, changing events. Taking this advanced approach, first responder organizations can begin to build flexibility to respond to real, dynamic threats.

Beyond Capacity Building

Although the nature of any given terrorist attack is unpredictable, any terrorist incident ultimately results in a fire, hazardous material release, a structural collapse, or a medical emergency, requiring that an effective incident command system be established. Therefore, capacity building within the context of homeland security requires more than the introduction of new personnel or equipment. (Incidentally, the structure of federal and state funding mechanisms for homeland security improvements allows organizations to purchase new equipment or train for new roles, but prohibits hiring new personnel to fill these new roles, which is a serious challenge for first responders, but beyond the scope of this chapter.) Basically, what is most central to this mission is how crisis managers will balance the demands of routine operations with the immeasurable risk of terrorism; the issues demand that first responder organizations must evaluate the opportunity costs of pursuing one endeavor over another. Terrorism preparedness is the ultimate insurance question; crisis mangers must ask themselves "How much of what type of 'insurance' should they 'purchase?'" First responders are not the only organizations asking these questions. Private firms, government agencies, and individual citizens have to question how much they can afford to focus on homeland security and security measures at the expense of other issues.

The prospect of the continuing terrorist threat to the United States is driving new spending for first responder training and equipment, but at the same time, first responder organizations must continue to perform their daily activities (law enforcement, firefighting, or emergency medical support).[3] First responder planners must therefore develop a strategy to prepare simultaneously both for their core missions and the new counterterrorism mandate. Since we do not have the luxury of creating a stand-alone terrorism response force in our cities, or even at the national level, first responders must plan to build resilience, and to integrate skills and resources strategically and methodically to meet their core and counterterrorist missions.

Building Core Competencies

We are beginning to see a disturbing trend of imbalanced capacity building in first responder organizations in the post-9/11 environment. Many groups are redefining their missions in terms of the terrorism threat. To meet new homeland security demands, many organizations are adding new tasks far beyond their core competencies, a challenging process at best, that often poses unforeseen complications. For instance, first responders that adopt expansive homeland security missions will conduct more training against possible CBRN threats. This requires that they familiarize themselves with new equipment to detect toxins and radiological particles, and process complicated information about the CBRN threat environment. These skills require a great deal of training and can perish without periodic retraining. The new equipment generates new maintenance and inspection requirements that, in turn, require additional training on how to maintain and inspect the new equipment. The organization must service these requirements with the same number of people as before. This dynamic alone adds a host of new stresses to the organization, even if a CBRN crisis never arises.

First responders will benefit from assessing and leveraging their core competencies, their unique set of strengths that are fundamental to their organization. When agencies add new tasks outside their existing competencies, they run the risk of diluting the organization's mission focus. The effects may not manifest themselves during routine operations, but in times of crisis, organizations revert to their true principal task (police protect and defend, fire departments respond to fires and hazardous material spills), and may fail at their new terrorist-related mission, leaving a gap in public protection. Organizations must seriously consider whether they need to reinvent themselves; most first responders already have the key skills necessary for successful terrorist response. To meet the terrorism threat, our police, fire, and emergency medical services can focus on developing new strategies to adapt existing infrastructure and use new technology, all while maintaining a high degree of proficiency in their core competencies.

One of the many lessons learned on 9/11 was that the FDNY's ability to respond to acts of terrorism is inextricably linked with its ability to respond to traditional firefighting and emergency medical incidents. The FDNY's conceptualization of how its core competencies support the counterterrorism mission is reflected in Figure 17-1.

The FDNY recognized that rather than adding core competencies to include specific counterterrorism skills, their existing core competencies to respond to fire, medical, hazardous materials, and structural collapse emergencies—guided by unified direction from incident commanders—can be employed to respond effectively to terrorist events, both conventional and unconventional. Ultimately, improving the ability of the FDNY to respond to the homeland security mission required only that incident commanders link existing skills to the threats of the new environment. Thus, increasing preparedness depends on the strengthening of core competencies—not the addition of new competencies beyond the scope of the department. Homeland security preparedness also reinforces day-to-day operational competencies that can then be employed effectively both at major disasters and terrorist attacks. The core competencies of fighting fires, delivering pre-hospital care, mitigating hazardous material, and performing technical rescue for building collapse—as well as the homeland mission—are all strengthened by every investment in planning, training, and equipment.

Each type of first responder organization has complementary skills to offer others, however, so the optimal outcome is recognized when first responder organizations recognize and acknowledge their own comparative advantages, and work in concert with sister organizations (e.g., fire with police) to create synergistic models of cooperation. This approach not only allows the contributors to build stronger, more capable organizations through focusing on their specific core missions, but ultimately presents a more effective terrorist response at the systemic level. Today's environment of robust federal homeland security funding has encouraged too many city organizations to adopt competitive positions, rather than cooperative ones, vying for funds to increase their individual organization's perceived ability to respond to terrorism. Using funds for ill-conceived change,

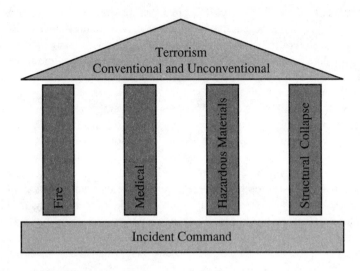

FIGURE 17-1.   FDNY Core Competencies

though, not only cheats the city of an optimally resilient first response system of complementary organizations, but may even dilute the ability of all involved to perform optimally at the individual level.

Innovation

Once a first responder organization has identified its core competencies, however, the task is only beginning. The organization must be innovative throughout the crisis and encourage members at all levels to find solutions outside standard operating procedure. Twenty-thousand people were saved on that fateful day because firefighters and other emergency personnel were able to cope with an extremely dangerous and complex situation. It was the actions on the ground in the first 102 minutes on 9/11 that proved critical to establishing command and control of the situation and to minimizing loss of life on all sides; this is why first responders must not fail to respond in crisis, no matter the shock of the situation.

The FDNY lost 343 members on 9/11, including the Chief of the Department, the First Deputy Commissioner, and other key leaders at all levels. Over 91 fire apparatus were destroyed, along with untold amounts of other equipment. Despite the loss of leadership and equipment and the tremendous shock to the organization, the fire department still had to lead and conduct the primary rescue mission. After the second tower fell, regaining command became imperative. Peter Hayden, then a Division Commander, now the Chief of the Department, gathered the firefighters at the scene, addressed them from atop the remains of a fire truck, and asked for a moment of silence. This moment was not only exceptionally meaningful, but allowed Chief Hayden to regain control of his personnel and begin rescue operations more systematically. It may seem like a small gesture, but because of the catastrophic loss and utter shock, the situation had long since eclipsed standard operating procedure. Chief Hayden's well-made decision to step back from the crisis to regroup was a valuable innovation that reflected his resiliency in command. It was on-site operational decisions—made without the guidance of standard operating procedure—that rebuilt department cohesion, which was critical for the rest of that day and the following weeks.

Another innovative decision at the operational level brought the private and public sectors together to address how to document the locations where victims, as well as equipment and significant wreckage, were found. The 16-acre World Trade Center site had few recognizable landmarks after the collapse. Rescuers could not accurately map the points in the rubble where they found victims, a key indicator of where to look for others. The FDNY brought together a team from the private sector to develop a mechanism to accurately record these positions in an efficient manner that would be manageable within the 10-story pile of debris. Firefighters defined the problem and guided the technological solution. Within three days, technical experts created and deployed to Ground Zero a global positioning system that worked in conjunction with a small handheld computer, which automatically captured time, date, and location of items. The new technology, developed in response to unexpected requirements identified by operational personnel, proved invaluable in assisting the recovery operations.

Strategic level innovation also occurred following 9/11. At the World Trade Center attack, the radio repeater system in the building failed and the point-to-point radios were not strong enough to penetrate the highest floors of the 110-story building. In the months following the attack, it was a FDNY Captain that came up with an innovative solution. He took spare radio parts, assembled them in a suitcase, and built a portable radio. This high wattage portable radio, called a "Post-radio," works with existing equipment, forming a dependable, portable communication system that is now brought to every major emergency. This example not only demonstrates the recognition of change but also shows readiness to adapt by implementing an innovative concept.

In the hours and days following that Tuesday morning, there were hundreds of other examples of innovation. Some of these innovations proved valuable and others did not. Nevertheless, it is impossible to overestimate the importance of the firefighters' willingness and ability to adapt to the changing situation and innovate throughout the crisis.

Building Resiliency

More broadly, we are finding that as terrorist attacks unfold, organizations are faced with an increasing level of stress that swiftly outstrips their capacity to respond. Further, the stress of the events and aftermath can push agencies beyond their capabilities to manage new preparedness initiatives. Thus, it becomes critical that senior managers be able to track carefully their organizations' well-being and cohesion on new initiatives. Helping their agencies develop resiliency in the face of these cumulative forces at the systemic level requires strategic planning and foresight, but once achieved, this will help their organizations scale their responses to meet emerging requirements in a crisis situation. This is often easier said than done, and the events of September 11, 2001, emphasize this point.

As 9/11 unfolded, the emergency services of New York City surged to meet the demands of the situation. What began initially as a two-alarm fire response, rapidly escalated to multiple fifth-alarms, and then progressed into a recall of all off-duty firefighters. Yet, at 8:46 A.M., when the first plane struck the North Tower, it was not clear that this was going to be the case. Within the 17 minutes a second plane crashed into the South Tower, the situation was extremely complex and dangerous, but the situation was manageable, even if at the extremes. However, when the towers collapsed, the situation exceeded the capacity of the entire City of New York to respond. Far beyond a city-wide response, the crisis required massive federal aid and assistance from many organizations. The lessons from that morning are clear: no matter what equipment organizations may possess, they must develop, test, and evaluate their ability to scale their response rapidly to an event as it unfolds, and be able to bear the initial shock of a terrorist event when their response capabilities are strained.

The ability to withstand increasing degrees of cumulative stress is critical for emergency responder organizations. Louise Comfort, a public policy professor at the University of Pittsburgh, makes use of "fragility curves" to illustrate this point.[4] Buildings and bridges are designed and modeled using fragility curves to determine the cumulative amount of stress over time a structure can withstand before failing. At its most basic level, first responder curves can be described through the examination of the following:

- physical capacity (number of apparatuses, number of people, amount of equipment);
- quality of people and training; and
- the ability to command in crisis.

This concept of fragility curves highlights two important points of analysis for any first responder organization to consider. First, how much stress over time can an organization currently withstand before failing? Second, how can an organization further develop its capacity to withstand greater amounts of stress in both the short and long term? In other words, how can an organization change the shape of its fragility curve?

An organization's physical capacities can be modeled by examining the routine operations and assessing the capacity of its core competencies. Within the field of emergency management, routine operating conditions have a high degree of normalcy based on general historic conditions, degree of experience in similar situations, and some amount of known information about the emergency. New York City constantly tracks its capacity for routine operations, recording statistics that can help identify minimal and maximum stress effects from normal operations, including the type and number of responses by size and response time. At the most basic level, organizations can model the amount of equipment and people that are available at any given time to respond to a problem of a given size. Developing a more nuanced analysis—to examine issues such as the duration of first responders on scene during a long crisis, minimal protective levels required for the non-affected areas, and the depth of skills needed for specific tasks associated with given terrorist events—would offer valuable tools for strategic planners. Once current capacities for stress are understood, a new model can be developed that incorporates an exogenous shock to the system, such as a terrorist attack—a far more dynamic emergency, which requires a much different approach and, potentially, scale of response.[5]

Understanding when an organization's capacity is outstripped is critical for effective crisis management. Without such knowledge, crisis managers cannot effectively lead their organizations, nor can the organizations effectively respond to the crisis at hand. For instance, if a subway attack were to occur on multiple subway lines in New York City, the fire and police departments would instantly be faced with a myriad of difficult issues. Are there enough ambulances to respond to the different trains? At what point will the emergency medical service "break"? After what level does the city need to activate mutual aid agreements for additional medical equipment from neighboring towns? Are there fires aboard any of the trains? If so, where are the trains located? Are there fires in the tunnels that run beneath the rivers, requiring specially trained rescue personnel? Do we have enough special operations personnel and equipment to respond to the situation?

The second factor of the stress curve—quality of training—is a critical component of preparedness on two levels. Firefighters need tactical and operational skills to use in their response to a particular terrorist attack, and organizational leaders need a deeper understanding of the strategic threat environment in order to better adapt the force to face new threats. The examples of innovation at Ground Zero, and the virtues of strategic deployment of core competencies against changing threats, demonstrate this priority.

The third dimension of the stress curve—the development of the ability to command in crisis—depends entirely on training individuals at all levels to act in the face of uncertainty. As Bertrand and Lajtha note, training crisis managers about uncertainty is important because "crises are characterized by the absence of obvious solutions, the scarcity of reliable information when it is needed, and the lack of time to reflect on and debate alternative courses of action."[6]

Uncertainty in Decision Making

While there are many books written on command and leadership in crisis, we wish to focus on one key aspect that is often overlooked in these discussions: the question of how to teach crisis managers to incorporate unexpected information during a crisis that they would otherwise naturally be inclined to overlook. The challenge in achieving this stems from the human cognitive bias to make decisions based on conceptual and experiential learning—i.e., to more easily process types of information in decision moments based on what they have learned and seen before. There is a good reason humans process information this way: it allows us to quickly assimilate key information in stressful situations and readily process it, which is a powerful tool as long as the stressful situation is the same or similar to ones we have been in before.

For instance, in a normal warehouse fire, commanders evaluate the stability of the burning structure based on previous warehouse fires they have witnessed (experiential learning), combined with knowledge gained from classroom type experiences (conceptual learning). Upon reaching the fire, experienced firefighters will look immediately for the key indicators of stress or damage to the building that, through experience and instruction, they know will indicate which parts of the building are safe to enter, where victims are likely to be trapped, and which routes are the safest for rescuers. A rookie firefighter in a warehouse fire does not know where to look first to identify these key factors, and must take precious time to assess every part of the fire before he can begin to make suggestions about how to approach it. The cognitive bias can backfire, though, when experienced firefighters respond to a fire in a type of structure they have never seen. Their natural tendency to seek out their known helpful indicators dominates, and they spend time scanning for those same types of signals, overlooking the signals that are the most relevant indicators of details of the new fire.

Much like the events of 9/11 outstripped the response capacity of emergency services due to their scale and complexity, they also pushed the crisis decision makers outside of any previous experiences or classroom knowledge. It would have been all too easy for the firefighters to have treated the situation as a high rise fire (albeit a complex one), a situation where buildings do not usually collapse. The FDNY chiefs recognized that a plane hitting the tower represented an exceptional emergency and created a host of issues that they could not foresee, and therefore they remained receptive to other abnormalities in the environment throughout the 102 minutes of crisis response. Under normal conditions, even working in complete blackness, firefighters do not abandon rescue operations. Yet on 9/11, decision makers escaped their cognitive biases. Even though they did not know the South Tower had collapsed, the resulting blackout in the North Tower lobby was a cue to them that the situation had changed and they ordered an unprecedented evacuation of a rescue operation. Their actions ultimately saved many of the firefighters' lives.

Training people to identify and assess the relevant indicators in a new environment, without clinging to preconceived lists of favorite indicators, is a challenge. Developing the capacity to imagine what might happen, evaluate the likelihood of outcomes, and choose the first best option, is a skill that can be developed with time and experience, but is missing in too many individuals. Militaries have grappled with this question since the beginning of organized combat, and have learned it can be encouraged through targeted training programs. One approach is to expose individuals (and organizations) to high-stress training in completely unfamiliar scenarios, and then rigorously reviewing with trainees the ways they gathered information to help them recognize threats, identify central problems, and make correct decisions. Ultimately, the goal is to help the trainees learn to keep their eyes and minds open to crucial elements in situations they have not experienced before. They learn to be willing and able to weigh all information for potential worth, including signals that may come from unexpected quarters. Their ability to imagine and even anticipate the unthinkable is critical to effective decision making during crises.

Reaching our Goal

Many of the current homeland security programs are still reacting to the al-Qaida threat of 2001, investing in more equipment, new equipment, or different training that may not be relevant to the actual terrorist threat environment, and therefore will offer only minimal improvement in preparedness—and, ironically, may actually undermine it.

Change during crisis is relatively easy; bureaucratic hurdles are suddenly removed, budgetary constraints no longer matter and organizations come together with a single purpose. But organizations in times of crisis must have the ability not just to respond to change, but to do so effectively. At the operational level, individuals must have the ability to rapidly assimilate far-ranging data beyond the scope of their past experience, quickly evaluate the data, and determine the course of action. Crisis managers must move beyond reactive scenario-based planning, and instead move towards predictive analysis to serve as a foundation for long-term improvements in organizational preparedness.

Innovation prior to crisis is a difficult but critical second challenge. Organizations must constantly evaluate the effectiveness of their structure and their performance as it relates to a dynamic threat environment shaped by vast unknowns that may stretch an organization to its limits with no notice. Organizations must build a forward-looking vision to help them imagine changes that they might make after a crisis, and to implement these changes before another crisis happens. The ability to make good choices at both the operational and strategic levels remains central to this process, and organizations and managers must constantly evaluate proposed change to focus efforts on the most viable and productive innovations.

This process will not always be foolproof, given the unpredictable nature of terrorism; we cannot know whether the next attack will be simple, or perhaps even more complex than 9/11. First responder groups will anticipate incorrectly and will make mistakes, but the potential gains from this type of anticipatory process are many. The use of dynamic threat scenario training to promote innovation within core competencies, even in the face of uncertainty, will help first responder organizations build their ability to address and withstand terrorist attacks. To use these abilities effectively, however, leaders must move beyond our traditional reactive behavior, and demand resilient and adaptive thought at both the strategic and operational levels to promote forward thinking in defining, planning, and implementing the vision for first responders' future development. The alternative is grim: we will continue to run poor exercises well and build false confidence in our abilities to respond to known threats. Following such an approach, we will find ourselves at sea when the world changes forever in front of our eyes one more time.

Notes

1. The authors would like to acknowledge Ms. Kate Marquis, fellow-in-residence at the Combating Terrorism Center at West Point, for her assistance with the development of this article, and Mr. Jarret Brachman, senior associate at the Combating Terrorism Center, for his editorial assistance.
2. Robert Bertrand and Chris Lajtha, "A New Approach to Crisis Management," *Journal of Contingencies and Risk Management* 10 no. 4 (December 2002): 184.
3. The scope of daily activities is not insignificant. For instance in 2004, the FDNY responded to 951,455 Fire Apparatus Responses; 1,285,836 EMS Unit Responses (runs); 6,205 Fires Investigated for Potential Arson/Cause and Origin; and 286,296 Fire Code Regulatory Inspections, *FDNY Annual Report 2004*.
4. Louise K. Comfort, "Rethinking Security: Organizational Fragility in Extreme Events," *Public Administration Review* 62 (September 2002): 102.

5. This is not to say that routine fires or other emergencies are not dynamic, only that terrorist attacks are so far out of the norm of daily operations, and of a different psychological and potentially physical dimension, that they are orders of magnitude more dynamic than a routine house fire.
6. Bertrand and Lajtha, "A New Approach," p. 185.

Chapter 18

Catastrophic Terrorism: Local Response to a National Threat

Governor Frank Keating

In June of 2001, I had the honor of taking the role of a state governor in an exercise that simulated the intentional release of the deadly virus smallpox in three U.S. cities. During the simulated 13 days of the game, titled *Dark Winter*, the disease spread to 25 states and 15 other countries. Fourteen participants playing roles—including that of the president, the National Security Council, and a seated Governor (played by me)—and 60 observers witnessed terror warfare in slow motion. Discussions, debates, and decisions focused on the public health response, lack of an adequate supply of smallpox vaccine, roles and missions of federal and state governments, civil liberties associated with quarantine and isolation, the role of the Department of Defense, and potential military responses to the anonymous attack. The scenario of that exercise was different from the real-life crisis we faced in Oklahoma on April 19, 1995, but the fundamental principles were the same. In both instances, our tasks as leaders of local, state, and federal agencies were to respond to a terrorist assault in ways that protected and preserved lives and property, ensured accountability and justice for those responsible for the attack, and protected the national security. I was honored to share my own experiences from Oklahoma City with the group, and I am equally honored to share my perspective with the American public.

In that respect, I want to review briefly what happened in Oklahoma City in 1995, and then relate the lessons we learned there to the experiences we shared at the *Dark Winter* exercise and to the issues surrounding an incident of this magnitude.

You will recall that a massive terror bomb was detonated at 9:02 A.M. on April 19, 1995, in front of the Alfred P. Murrah Federal Office Building in the heart of our community. It killed 168 people, injured hundreds more, and severely damaged many dozens of buildings. The rescue and recovery efforts that followed, along with the criminal investigation, were the most massive of their kind up to that time in American history. These efforts threw together, literally overnight, more separate agencies from the local, state, and federal governments than had ever worked cooperatively on a single task. The outcome could have been chaotic—it has been before when far fewer agencies tried to coordinate their efforts on much more discrete and manageable tasks. But the outcome in Oklahoma City was not chaos. Later, observers would coin the label "The Oklahoma Standard" to refer to the way our city, state, and nation came together in response to this despicable act.

I think that what happened in Oklahoma City in 1995 served as a model for the *Dark Winter* participants, and I believe it should also help guide the deliberations on a national policy for responding to catastrophic events on the American homeland. Simply put, we did it right in 1995. The principles behind the Oklahoma Standard can help govern our nation's future course in responding to the terrorist threat.

On April 19, 1995, every injured person was cared for promptly and with great skill and compassion—in fact, at the closest hospital to the blast site, every arriving ambulance was met by an individual physician assigned to a specific victim. Of several dozen victims deemed critically injured on that day, only one who made it to the hospital alive subsequently died.

Every deceased victim was recovered, and all remains were restored to the families for burial, promptly and with great sensitivity.

Key evidence that would lead to the apprehension, conviction, and eventual execution of the primary perpetrator of the crime was in law enforcement hands within minutes after the explosion. A local deputy sheriff found and recorded the serial number from the bomber's vehicle at almost the same moment that a state trooper was arresting the suspect some miles away. The criminal case built over the next few weeks was simply overwhelming. It assured our victims, and our society, of justice.

Finally, our national security was protected. In the months and years after the Oklahoma City bombing, local and federal authorities directed new attention to potentially dangerous domestic insurgent groups, defusing a number of similar terrorist plots before anyone was hurt. Congress also passed stronger antiterrorism legislation.

The *Dark Winter* scenario involved a foreign source of terrorism, not one of our own citizens. In *Dark Winter*, the weapon was bacterial rather than explosive. But in virtually every other respect, these two scenarios shared these key goals and principles:

- To protect, preserve, and save lives and property
- To hold accountable those responsible for terrorism
- To protect and advance America's interests and security

Those are the three fundamental challenges presented by any terrorist attack, from a bomb to a biological assault to the nightmare of a clandestine nuclear confrontation. I think it is instructive to compare how we pursued those goals in Oklahoma City with the outcomes of the *Dark Winter* scenario, and to look at how that comparison might reflect on future policy.

The conclusions drawn by a series of after-action analyses from Oklahoma City are remarkably similar. I will consolidate those conclusions into five basic findings, compare them to what we did (or did not do) at *Dark Winter*, and suggest resulting policy implications.

The Local Response

Recognize that in virtually every possible terrorism scenario, first responders will be local. In Oklahoma City, the true heavy lifting of the initial rescue and recovery operations, as well as the key evidence collection that led to a successful criminal prosecution, was the task of local fire, police, and emergency medical personnel. In fact, the real first responders were not even public employees; they were bystanders and coworkers of the trapped and injured, who often shrugged off their own injuries and got up out of the rubble to help others. The first Federal Emergency Management Agency (FEMA) Urban Search and Rescue Task Force did not reach Oklahoma City until late on the night of April 19—several hours after the last living victim had been extracted from the wrecked building. That task force, and the 10 that followed it, were absolutely essential to the successful recovery operations that followed, but it is important to note that even those FEMA Urban Search and Rescue Task Forces are drawn from local police and fire departments.

As an example, many of those task forces brought structural engineers to Oklahoma. They were able to work closely in planning the search and recovery operation with the local architect who had designed and built the Murrah Building in the 1970s. Who was better prepared and qualified for this crucial task? Neither party was; it was a true cooperative effort, blending federal and local resources to achieve outstanding results that allowed many hundreds of rescue workers to labor around the clock in a devastated and unstable structure, without serious injury to any of those involved.

In the *Dark Winter* scenario, as in virtually any real-world terrorist assault, the first responders will also be local. The federal government does not maintain rapid response teams in any area of expertise close enough to any potential terrorist target, save perhaps the White House, to allow them to be first on the scene. In *Dark Winter*, local private physicians and public health officials were the first to detect cases of smallpox. Local government and law enforcement agencies were the ones with the power to impose and enforce quarantines; curfews, and states of martial law; to disseminate information through local media; and to collate and forward epidemiological data to federal agencies such as the Centers for Disease Control in Atlanta. Local law enforcement would be the ones to discover, preserve, and secure any available crime scenes or evidence. As in Oklahoma City, the preponderance of personnel, vehicles, equipment and even the volunteer force of blood donors, Salvation Army canteen operators, and the people who showed up to do laundry for the FEMA Urban Search and Rescue Task Force members, will necessarily be drawn from local resources.

Teamwork

Insist that teamwork is not just desirable—it is possible. The after-action reports from Oklahoma City noted that agencies from various levels and jurisdictions that had not traditionally worked closely in the past, did so to a remarkable extent at the Murrah Building site, and in the ensuing criminal investigation. They even worked closely to overcome what was a huge potential initial hurdle—the conflicting purposes of those who were working through the rubble to extract the dead and those who saw the same rubble pile as a vast crime scene to be processed for evidence.

This is not to say that there were no conflicts. There were, but they were resolved in virtually every case, to the mutual satisfaction of all of those concerned. We have seen too many cases in the past where an investigative agency or a rescue unit squabbled in private (and sometimes in public) over "my crime scene" or "our rescue mission." That this natural source of conflict did not overwhelm or dissipate the Oklahoma City effort is a tribute to the good sense and reason of those involved.

The one central problem that emerged in Oklahoma City was that of communications. From the first response through the final body recovery, it was noted that the many radio frequencies and institutional policies in play all too often left many participants in the effort in the dark concerning vital decisions that should have been shared universally. This was remedied in part—but only in part—by the creation of a unified command center, which invited key representatives from all the agencies involved to frequent information briefings and discussions on tactics.

Ironically, local agencies were in some ways better equipped to overcome this communications gap than their federal counterparts, thanks to a quirk of geography. Because central Oklahoma is located dead center in what is called "tornado alley," our public safety and emergency medical agencies had planned and even drilled for a mass-casualty incident in the past. They had on hand mobile command posts with some (though not all) interlocking radio capabilities. They also had the distinct advantages of familiarity with each other's basic operating procedures, local geography, even which local companies might be able to bring a large crane to the site on that first night to begin the search for buried victims. Time after time, I saw federal officials turn to local fire and police personnel and ask for assistance that only they could give.

I want to encourage the readers of this chapter, and the general public, to visit the Oklahoma City National Memorial Institute for the Prevention of Terrorism (www.mipt.org), which was a direct outgrowth of our experiences in Oklahoma City and a co-sponsor of the *Dark Winter* exercise. No one else has more information, drawn directly from field experience, on how to blend the many levels of responders in as seamless a way as possible to react to a terrorist attack.

Information Assurance

The rapid and accurate flow of information—both internally among government agencies and externally to the public—is absolutely essential. Because the Murrah Building was located in downtown Oklahoma City, for all to see, we immediately stumbled into the right answer to the eternal question "How much do we tell the public?" That answer is simple—we tell them everything that does not need to be safeguarded for valid reasons of security.

I know you will all recall the steady, 24-hour broadcasts and news dispatches that came from Oklahoma City in the first days after the 1995 bombing. Our policy was to conduct regular media briefings on everything from body counts to alerts involving the composite drawings of the principal suspects in the bombing, and the results were positive in virtually all cases. Certainly many aspects of the criminal investigation were not disclosed in those early days. The Oklahoma City Fire Department and the Office of the Chief Medical Examiner carefully controlled release of information concerning the dead, to ensure that families were fully notified before victim identities were made public. We did not allow open media access to the interior site itself for reasons of safety and efficiency. But in almost every other instance, our decision was in favor of openness and candor, and the results are very clear. I continue to receive letters, many years later, from Americans who have a permanently positive impression of how the bombing was handled.

In the *Dark Winter* exercise, many decisions concerning the release of information went in a different direction. From my own service in Washington, I know there exists an instinct for secrecy, an urge to classify, that often bears little relation to the realities of the moment. This happened in *Dark Winter* too. I believe that was, and is, a mistake, especially in a situation where bioterrorism was involved. Americans expect and deserve to be told the truth by government at all levels when their safety is at stake. Certainly, I do not counsel revealing matters that would endanger national security or ongoing criminal investigations, but when the question is one between candor and secrecy in a matter of enormous public interest, and absent a clear and compelling reason for secrecy, candor should be the chosen option.

Our *Dark Winter* participants too often opted to conceal or obscure where openness would have done no harm—and where it would have increased public confidence. To cite a clear and compelling example of why this is true, contrast the high public approval of the FBI's successful identification and prosecution of Timothy McVeigh in the Oklahoma City bombing with the Bureau's present image problems related, in large part, to inept handling of documentation in that case. Simply put, the FBI was remarkably open—and praised—as it identified, caught, and prosecuted McVeigh; it was closed, and justifiably mistrusted, when it misplaced the files.

Government at all levels earns the trust of those it serves every day. It does not merit that trust if it is overly secretive.

Using Experts

Experts are called experts for a reason—rely on them. In Oklahoma City, the agency best equipped to handle the removal, identification, and processing of the 168 people killed in the bombing was the Office of the Chief Medical Examiner, which did an outstanding job. I recall at least one federal official with some experience in mass-casualty incidents assuring the staff from the medical examiner's office that they would "never" be able to identify all the victims. In fact, they did, with vast cooperation from local funeral directors, dentists, physicians, and many others, who worked countless hours at a most heartrending and often distasteful task. They were the experts, and they did their job well.

That was also true of the crane operators who helped remove the rubble, the federal agents who identified the explosive components, and many others. People work for many years to acquire skills; agencies involved in responding to a terrorist attack should let them do their jobs.

In *Dark Winter*, the obvious agency with the expertise to isolate and identify the smallpox microorganism was the Centers for Disease Control in Atlanta. The experts in potential delivery systems were chemists and physicists. Those best equipped to identify Iraqi origins for the terrorist act were from the intelligence field.

Conversely, those best qualified to assess what (and how) information is to be publicly released are the communications professionals. When a building is badly damaged by a bomb, engineers and architects play a central role; when germs are released on the public, doctors must be involved. In responding to any terrorist attack, supervising agencies should rely on the experts in their respective fields, and not seek to concentrate decision-making powers above and removed from the level where those experts can be heard.

Federal versus Local Responses

Resist the urge to federalize everything. Perhaps the strongest lesson from Oklahoma City—and perhaps the most worrisome outcome from the *Dark Winter* exercise—concerns the almost instinctive urge common to officials of federal agencies and the military to open the federal umbrella over any and all functions or activities. Simply put, the federal government all too often acts like the 500-pound gorilla.

In *Dark Winter*, we encountered this tendency as soon as state National Guard units were activated in response to the bioterrorist attack. The functions of those units—imposing curfews and quarantines and keeping public peace—were exclusively local. Still, many of the participants sought to call the Guard into federal service immediately. I want to thank Senator Nunn, who played the role of the president in the exercise, for resisting this temptation and deciding not to federalize the Guard.

Federalizing makes sense when the mission is largely federal—for example, a combat environment or an overseas deployment—but not when the mission remains largely local. I noted that I failed to see how a National Guard company, led by a local captain and staffed by local residents who had assembled at the local armory for duty, would perform in any different manner if it were formally inducted into federal service. My experience following the Oklahoma City bombing was that members of the Oklahoma Army and Air National Guards called to service did an excellent job under state control. In fact, the very first makeshift memorial to the dead was created near the Murrah Building site, along a security fence line, by Air Guard personnel who were mourning the deaths of their neighbors. The Guard blended well with other agencies, both local and federal. Its members took special pride in serving their Oklahoma neighbors as members of the *Oklahoma* Guard.

Certainly if a Guard formation cannot perform well, or if it requires specialized training or equipment to discharge its role in response to a terrorist incident, it should be promptly federalized. Equally surely, many components of the national response to an attack like that proposed in *Dark Winter* must be largely federal—from the gathering of intelligence that pointed to an Iraqi connection to the formulation for diplomatic and military responses. But that does not mean that every part of the broad response must or should originate at the federal level, or that federal officials should assume supremacy in every aspect of the response, or that the military response should trump the humanitarian response. It was a deputy sheriff who jotted down the number from a mangled truck axle that, ultimately, brought McVeigh to justice. It was a surgeon from a state hospital who crawled into the Murrah rubble to amputate a trapped victim's leg as local police officers and firefighters held lights and moved obstacles. Oklahomans carried the first injured out of the building on April 19, and three weeks later they recovered the last of the dead. They continue to staff mental health and counseling services—funded in part by federal sources—to help with the healing.

Conclusion

My experiences in Oklahoma City in 1995, and my participation in *Dark Winter* in 2001, both taught me some valuable lessons:

- Train and equip your first responders, for they are the front line in meeting the terrorist threat.
- Search for ways to support teamwork *before* an incident, and emphasize that teamwork after.
- Tell the truth, and be candid with the people we are working to protect and serve.
- Trust the experts to do what they know best.

And remember that the response to terrorism does not begin and end in Washington. Trust local governments, local agencies, and local citizens to do the right thing, because in the end, they are the real targets of terrorism, whether it's a bomb in front of a building filled with ordinary Americans or a germ unleashed on their neighbors.

Chapter 19

Terrorism and the Battle for Homeland Security

Seth G. Jones

Four years after 9/11, is the United States better prepared to prevent and respond to homeland security threats? Has the Department of Homeland Security (DHS) materially improved the coordination and analysis of intelligence on terrorist threats to the United States? Numerous recent government and think-tank reports concluded that U.S. counterterrorism coordination was abysmal before September 2001.[1] In June 2002, when it announced plans to establish the DHS, the White House envisioned it as one department to "synthesize and analyze homeland security intelligence from multiple sources [and] coordinate communications with state and local governments, private industry, and the American people about threats and preparedness."

However, this hope has not been realized. The DHS has struggled for relevance, and become increasingly sidelined in the analysis and dissemination of terrorism-related intelligence. Meanwhile, the CIA's homeland security role has been bolstered through its creation of a Terrorist Threat Integration Center in 2003 subsequently replaced by the national Counterterrorism Center in 2004, and the FBI has devoted substantial resources to improving its homeland security-related counterterrorism and intelligence capabilities.

The DHS's struggle to find its niche fulfills the following observation made in 1888 by Lord Bryce, a British historian and ambassador to the United States:

> There is among political bodies and offices—of necessity, a constant strife, a struggle for existence similar to that which Mr. Darwin has shown to exist among plants and animals. [T]his struggle stimulates each body or office to exert its utmost force for its own preservation, and to develop its aptitudes in any direction where development is possible.[2]

While the United States is better today at collecting, analyzing, and disseminating intelligence on terrorist threats to the homeland than it was prior to 9/11, little of this is attributable to the DHS. The FBI and CIA, supported by the White House and some in Congress, have strongly resisted handing over counterterrorism and intelligence responsibilities to the DHS.

A Leading Role for DHS?

To counter terrorist threats to the homeland, the United States must gather and assess intelligence about enemies planning attacks on American soil or on U.S. targets abroad.

Which individuals and organizations are planning attacks? Where are they located? What equipment and methods are they using? When are they likely to attack? Intelligence is critical for law enforcement organizations seeking to deter or prevent attacks from occurring. State and local police, the FBI, Coast Guard, and other organizations need sound information to monitor and arrest adversaries. The challenge is the large number of federal, state, local, and private sector actors involved in intelligence.

Consequently, the DHS was established in December 2002 to fulfill three primary objectives: (1) prevent terrorist attacks within the United States; (2) reduce America's vulnerability to terrorism; and (3) respond to any terrorist attacks and natural disasters that do occur. The DHS integrated a number of agencies, such as the Federal Emergency Management Agency (FEMA), Transportation Security Administration, Secret Service, and Coast Guard, in the largest federal government restructuring effort since the creation of the Department of Defense (DoD) after World War II. The DoD, FBI, Department of Justice, and CIA would still play important homeland security roles, but the DHS would be the focal point.

A critical DHS function would be analyzing and assessing terrorist threats to the United States, and better coordinating intelligence information. Of its four directorates, the Directorate of Information Analysis and Infrastructure Protection (IAIP) was intended to be the most important—tasked with coordinating and analyzing intelligence information about terrorist threats to the United States, assessing vulnerabilities to U.S. infrastructure, and disseminating information to the private sector and to relevant federal, state, and local officials. It would "fuse and analyze intelligence and other information pertaining to the homeland from multiple sources—including the CIA, NSA, FBI, INS, DEA, DOE, Customs, DOT, and data gleaned from other organizations." The Homeland Security Act of 2002, which officially created the DHS, did not mandate the IAIP to collect intelligence, though it could receive "raw intelligence" from the CIA and FBI and task other agencies to collect information.

The Struggle for Power

However, the CIA and FBI, eventually supported by the executive and legislative branches, strongly resisted handing over significant power to the DHS. Both agencies increased, rather than decreased, their homeland security functions. Despite initial backing from the White House and many on Capitol Hill, support for the DHS faded quickly. Most policymakers believed that either the DHS was unable to perform terrorist threat analysis adequately, or that other departments within the federal government could do it better.

CIA. The CIA increased its homeland security power through the creation, in May 2003, of the Terrorist Threat Integration Center (TTIC). The CIA has traditionally been the primary government agency dealing with terrorism, though it is barred from collecting intelligence or conducting operations within the United States. It established a Counterterrorism Center in 1986 under the Directorate of Operations to help combat international terrorist threats, including on its staff personnel from the broader intelligence community. Directorate of Intelligence officers served in its analytic components to provide regional and functional expertise, making it the first permanent unit at the CIA to combine analysis and operations.

September 11 highlighted for the intelligence community the need to improve coordination. A new interagency terrorism center with greater participation from throughout the U.S. government was more politically palatable than simply revamping the Counterterrorism Center. But under whose roof should it set up shop? One option was the DHS's Directorate of IAIP. However, CIA officials vigorously lobbied to keep the center under the jurisdiction of the Director of Central Intelligence (DCI), arguing that the CIA had the most competent terrorism analysts. DHS analysts had little experience in handling complicated legal and security intelligence matters, or in co-handling foreign and domestic intelligence. Furthermore, some argued that it would be most efficient to have a single agency—the CIA—with de facto control over both offensive capabilities (e.g., penetrating terrorist organizations and attacking them through preemptive strikes) and defensive capabilities (e.g., preventing future attacks by analyzing threats to the homeland).[3]

Therefore, the TTIC was created under the DCI, to coordinate and provide comprehensive analysis to the president and federal agencies on terrorist threats—the very task originally envisioned for the DHS. From the beginning, the TTIC was responsible for integrating and analyzing all terrorist threat information collected domestically and abroad in a central location, and housed a database of known and suspected terrorists that federal, state, and local officials across the country can access. It examined regional threats, such as Middle Eastern terrorist organizations, as well as functional threats, such as weapons of mass destruction (WMD) and cyber attacks. It was also responsible for putting together the president's daily threat matrix, and was staffed by several hundred representatives on assignment from the CIA, FBI, DHS, and other bodies from the Departments of Defense and State, such as the NSA, National Geospatial-Intelligence Agency (formerly the National Imagery and Mapping Agency), and Defense Intelligence Agency.

On August 27, 2004, President Bush issued Executive Orders 13354 and 13356, creating a new organization called the National Counterterrorism Center (NCTC), which subsumed TTIC's responsibilities on December 6, 2004.[4] The NCTC serves the newly-established Office of the Director of National Intelligence, and is responsible for (1) serving as the primary organization within the U.S. government for analyzing and integrating all intelligence possessed by the U.S. government pertaining to terrorism and counterterrorism, (2) conducting strategic operational planning for counterterrorism activities, (3) assigning operational responsibilities to lead agencies for counterterrorism activities, and (4) serving as a shared knowledge bank on known and suspected terrorists and international terror groups.[5]

FBI. The FBI has traditionally played the leading role in responding to terrorism within the United States, though it was severely criticized for being insufficiently proactive before 9/11. Since 2001, it has adopted a preemptive strategy, increased its counterterrorism resources, and established an Office of Intelligence, motivated in part by a desire to remain the lead counterterrorism agency for homeland threats.

The FBI's attempt to redefine itself from an agency that investigates crimes after they occur, to one that is proactive in gathering intelligence before attacks occur, is articulated in its reformulated vision statement, "FBI Vision 2010." Since 2001, the FBI has disrupted alleged terrorist cells in Buffalo, Detroit, and Portland, Oregon; charged nearly 200 suspected terrorist associates with crimes; and deported at least 500 suspected terrorists. FBI Director Robert Mueller has also tried to change the FBI's traditional system of decentralized management, in which significant power was in the hands of the 56 field offices, by increasing the number and importance of analysts and policymakers at head-quarters.[6]

When Director Mueller made counterterrorism the FBI's top priority, he implemented a major reorganization and increased resources for the Counterterrorism Division. More than 500 field agents were permanently shifted from criminal investigations to counterterrorism. On September 11, 2001, the FBI had roughly 635 agents working on counterterrorism issues full time; it now has more than 2,000.[7] The FBI established an Operations Center to serve as a clearinghouse for information sharing and collaboration. It created 66 Joint Terrorism Task Forces across the country, which include state and local law enforcement officers and FBI agents. Finally, it expanded its international counterterrorism presence in Southwest Asia, Southeast Asia, Africa, the Middle East, and Central Asia, by adding FBI legal attache (LEGAT) offices and deploying agents abroad. There are currently more than 50 LEGAT offices and several hundred FBI employees overseas. The FBI has played a key role in investigating recent terrorist bombings in Bali, Saudi Arabia, Turkey, and other countries. Given the rising threat from international terrorist organizations, and the increase in transnational organized crime, the FBI's overseas presence should and will continue to increase.

In January 2003, the FBI also bolstered its analytical capabilities by creating an Executive Assistant Director for Intelligence and an Office of Intelligence. The office is responsible for identifying emerging threats and crime problems that impact FBI investigations and overall strategies. It is the FBI's primary interface for coordinating intelligence on terrorist threats to the United States, and sharing information with the U.S. intelligence community, the legislative branch, foreign government agencies, state and local law enforcement, and the private sector, and also places the FBI in direct competition with the DHS.

Each FBI field office also has a Field Intelligence Group to centrally manage, execute, and coordinate the FBI's intelligence functions in that field office. The expectation is that a cadre of nationwide intelligence analysts will be built up over the next few years.

Left Out in the Cold

These developments have made it difficult for the DHS—particularly its Directorate of IAIP—to find a role for intelligence analysis and dissemination, and it has established little power and capability to do this.

One of its problems is that IAIP does not have significant analytical power; the FBI and CIA retain primary power for analyzing raw terrorist intelligence. This has left the DHS with a paucity of competent intelligence analysts, who have been much more willing to go to the CIA, FBI or intelligence bodies within the Departments of Defense and State.[8] Numerous reports on the DHS have given the impression of an organization that is in serious turmoil regarding personnel, facilities, infrastructure, and mission. Paul Redmond, IAIP's first assistant secretary, served for only a few months before resigning. As a Markle Foundation Task Force recently concluded, the DHS "does not appear to have taken the necessary steps to build the communications and sharing network required to deal with the threat, or to begin producing regular, actionable intelligence products for other agencies."[9] The one exception is infrastructure protection, in which the DHS performs vulnerability assessments of key U.S. infrastructure targets. The DHS inherited the

National Infrastructure Protection Center, formerly part of the FBI, which develops and distributes daily classified and unclassified infrastructure warnings.

Moreover, the DHS has had significant competition from other federal agencies in disseminating information to state and local authorities, the private sector, and other areas, despite President Bush's July 2003 Executive Order giving the Secretary of Homeland Security primary authority for sharing homeland security information. This is probably largely due to overlapping responsibilities. For example, the FBI is responsible for sharing intelligence information with state and local law enforcement through its Joint Terrorism Task Forces, but also disseminates information to state and local governments. Another cause may be proactive efforts by state and local governments. Senior intelligence officials have noted that some intelligence sharing between the CIA and state and local actors is initiated by the state and local entities.[10] And while the DHS and other agencies are trying to improve information-sharing, their efforts have been insufficient so far.[11]

Salvaging Homeland Security

The culture the CIA has developed over the years is effective for collecting and analyzing foreign intelligence information, penetrating foreign organizations and governments, and conducting covert attacks. The agency's work necessitates dealing with unsavory characters, protecting sources and methods used to gather information, and keeping a close hold on intelligence. It has rigid standards for employment, requiring prospective employees to take a polygraph and psychological examinations. Above all, it is deeply reluctant to share information. But this culture is at odds with what is needed for homeland security, and it raises concerns about the CIA's influence in domestic matters.[12] The CIA is not the agency best suited to analyze intelligence from both domestic and foreign sources, and quickly disseminate it as appropriate.[13]

Placing much of the power to collect and analyze data on homeland security threats with an agency that is fundamentally geared toward secrecy and has no legal domestic jurisdiction compromises homeland security. It is not that intelligence hasn't been—or wouldn't be—shared if there is a specific threat about an attack on the United States, but that important intelligence won't be shared efficiently with state, local, private sector, and health entities when the threat is more ambiguous.

Drawing clear jurisdictional boundaries and ensuring sufficient cooperation between the DHS and the FBI has proven the hardest challenge since the DHS was created. The FBI has a clear and legal domestic jurisdiction, a good working relationship with state and local actors, a Counterterrorism Division already in place, and proven willingness to become more proactive. It gathers information through its field offices, agents, and state and local law enforcement. Meanwhile, the DHS's Customs, Border Patrol, and Coast Guard components offer a goldmine of useful information, and should be officially authorized to collect domestic intelligence. These agencies constantly interact with people and goods at airports, seaports, land checkpoints, coastlines, and other border areas. Collected information can be coordinated through the NCTC, regardless of whether the FBI or another government agency is in charge of it.

In the years since 9/11, progress in intelligence sharing has come mostly in spite of the DHS, rather than as a result of its actions. While the DHS certainly has an important role to play in the collection of information and infrastructure protection, this is not the mandate initially envisioned by the White House and some in Congress. Fortunately, this is not a bad development. The DHS has little experience and few capabilities to take on its original mandate. It would accordingly be unwise to shift more power to the DHS. Rather, the FBI should be the lead agency for collecting, analyzing, and disseminating information on terrorist threats to the homeland, with support from the DHS, CIA, the NCTC, and the intelligence community as a whole.

Notes

1. These include reports by the Advisory Panel to Assess Domestic Response Capabilities for Terrorism Involving Weapons of Mass Destruction, a joint inquiry by the U.S. Senate Select Committee on Intelligence and U.S. House Permanent Select Committee on Intelligence, Brookings Institution, Council on Foreign Relations, and Markle Foundation.
2. Lord Bryce, *The American Commonwealth*, quoted in Hans J. Morgenthau, *Politics Among Nations: The Struggle for Power and Peace* (New York: A. A. Knopf, 1963), p. 171.
3. Interviews with senior intelligence officials, Washington, DC, August 6 and 13, 2003.
4. For more on this, see www.whitehouse.gov/news/releases/2004/08/20040827-5.html.
5. The NCTC has other responsibilities as well. See the *The National Counterterrorism Center: Implementation Challenges and Issues for Congress,* Congressional Research Service Report, March 24, 2005, www.fas.org/sgp/crs/intel/RL32816.pdf.
6. Dick Thornburgh, Testimony before the Subcommittee on Commerce, State, Justice, the Judiciary, and Related Agencies, House Committee on Appropriations, June 18, 2003.
7. Interview with senior FBI official, Washington, DC, February, 26, 2004.
8. John Mintz, "At Homeland Security, Doubts Arise Over Intelligence," *Washington Post*, July 21, 2003; Edward Alden, "U.S. Fails to 'Connect the Dots' By Pooling Its Terrorist Watch Lists," *Financial Times*, July 16, 2003; "September 11 and Today," *Christian Science Monitor*, July 29, 2003.
9. Markle Foundation Task Force, *Creating a Trusted Network for Homeland Security: Second Report of the Markle Foundation Task Force* (New York: Markle Foundation, 2003), p. 3.
10. Interview with senior intelligence official, Washington, DC, August. 6, 2003.
11. General Accounting Office, *Homeland Security: Efforts to Improve Information Sharing Need to Be Strengthened,* GAO-03-760 (Washington, DC: U.S. GAO, 2003).
12. Dan Eggen, "Center to Assess Terrorist Threat," *Washington Post*, May 1, 2003; Robert Bryant, John Hamre, John Lawn, John MacGaffin, Howard Shapiro, and Jeffrey Smith, "America Needs More Spies—Intelligence and Security," *Economist*, July 12, 2003.
13. Bruce Berkowitz, "A Fresh Start Against Terror," *New York Times*, August 4, 2003; Siobhan Gorman, "FBI, CIA Remain Worlds Apart," *National Journal*, August 1, 2003.

Chapter 20

National Strategy: Building Capability for the Long Haul

Chris Hornbarger

The United States shall guarantee to every State in this Union a Republican Form of Government, and shall protect each of them against Invasion; and on Application of the Legislature, or of the Executive (when the Legislature cannot be convened) against domestic Violence.
—*The Constitution of the United States of America*, Article IV, Section 4

The National Commission on Terrorist Attacks upon the United States (the 9/11 Commission) released its final report on July 22, 2004. The report arrived at a pivotal time. One thousand and forty-five days after 9/11, America seemed to have settled into a wary acceptance of continuous threat, according to some, or a dangerous complacency, according to others. One hundred and thirty-three days after a terrorist bombing in Madrid turned a national election, and only 103 days before our own presidential election, issues of national security divided the body politic more dramatically than at any other time since the Vietnam War. And just 10 days after the report's release, the Department of Homeland Security, citing information "chilling in its scope, in its detail, in its breadth," raised the national threat level from yellow to orange.[1] According to officials at the time, the terrorist threat against the United States was at its highest level since 9/11.[2]

Fear was the pervasive undercurrent of the last election. President Bush warned we have much to fear, yet offered an upbeat assessment of homeland security efforts to date.[3] Senator John Kerry charged the president with exploiting fear, yet said we have done too little, too slowly, and need a new homeland security strategy that takes bolder steps.[4] Against this backdrop, a variety of experts, panels, and critics have highlighted America's continued vulnerability to attack, with a few sounding dire warnings that disaster is imminent.[5]

After more than three years without a major attack on our soil, has national homeland security policy been effective? Or are we merely biding time? Have our national leaders charted a prudent and balanced course between security, liberty, and other national priorities? Or has official Washington gradually reverted to business-as-usual, with policy bounded by the perceived realm of the politically feasible, rather than the urgent demands of the threat?

The 9/11 Commission reviewed millions of pages of documents—many highly classified—and interviewed senior officials from the current and previous administrations, including both presidents.[6] Their report paints a remarkably complete and detailed picture, and is as close as the nation will ever get to a definitive account of what went wrong prior to 9/11. But on the whole, the Commission's recommendations are unsurprising, if not anti-climactic. Almost all have precedent in existing policy. What is most remarkable about the report's 41 recommendations, particularly the 28 which concern the homeland security policy area, is the degree to which they build on—rather than depart from—the policies of the last three years.[7]

National homeland security policy since 9/11 has properly focused on "first things first." The *National Strategy for Homeland Security (NSHS),* in concert with other national policies and strategies, has provided meaningful direction and coherence to the broad range of federal, state, local, and private sector activities essential to homeland security.[8] The *Strategy*, with the Department of Homeland Security (DHS) at its center, has for the first time clarified the "lines of business" for homeland security, thus beginning the urgent and complex task of aligning authority, responsibility, and resources to accomplish critical missions. In so doing, the *NSHS* has accomplished what all successful strategies must: articulate ends (the *Strategy* identifies three); identify means (the *Strategy* provides an approach for allocating finite resources against an almost limitless array of vulnerabilities); and, most importantly, connect ends and means with ways (the *Strategy* provides a blueprint for creating the institutional capacity to protect the homeland over the long-term). The first national strategy for homeland security has served the nation well, creating a foundation for the concerted, long-term effort to build a resilient homeland.

By the time this volume goes to print, Americans will have chosen a President to serve for the next four years, and the nation will have its best opportunity since 9/11 to dispassionately assess what we have and have not accomplished in homeland security, to adjust course, and to chart a way forward. We have made significant progress, but tough work lies ahead. DHS remains a work in progress. Deep reform of the intelligence community will take years. And persistent areas of systemic vulnerability still demand improvement on an urgent basis. Having successfully tackled "first things first," the nation needs an updated homeland security strategy to focus the national effort on the next steps.

This chapter draws five major conclusions. First, the magnitude of uncertainty in homeland security distinguishes it from other security and risk-management challenges. National strategy and policy must systematically reduce the uncertainty of three key variables—threat, vulnerability, and capability—and account for the relationships among them. Pursuing this is impossible without first building institutions, relationships, and processes that did not exist on 9/11. Second, distinguishing between the concepts of homeland security and national security has been a practical necessity for "phase one" of the war on terrorism. The President and nation will be best served in the future by a single strategy that integrates national security and homeland security policy, developed by separate but well-coordinated National Security Council (NSC) and Homeland Security Council (HSC) staffs. Third, the *NSHS* and related policies reflect the best concepts of good strategy. Fourth, this strategy provides a sound framework for the entire range of critical homeland security activities, not just those performed by DHS. And fifth, results of national homeland security policy so far have been generally positive, with certain exceptions that the nation and its leaders should address in an updated national strategy.

The Strategic Challenge of Homeland Security

> *Greater is our terror of the unknown.*
> —Titus Livius, Roman Historian

There is considerable risk in publishing the view that the national homeland security policies of the last three years have focused on the right priorities. But doing so is no more or less risky than the practical decisions that policymakers have had to make every day since 9/11. Officials have had little to go on. Lacking intelligence about where, when, or how our terrorist adversaries may seek to strike (or even who and how numerous our adversaries are); faced with a limitless array of targets to protect; armed with few serious quantitative models (and no comprehensive models) to assess the systemic vulnerabilities of our critical infrastructures; and absent precious little objective data to determine whether the marginal cost of any particular security investment exceeds the marginal benefit, national policymakers have relied primarily on judgment and common sense. Homeland security—like raising and maintaining a military, preparing for natural disasters, exploring space, or ensuring aviation safety—is about managing risk. But homeland security, unlike these otherwise comparable challenges, involves much greater uncertainty.

Patrick Lagadec and Erwan Michel-Kerjan, in their recent analysis of the 2001 anthrax attacks, highlight how the uncertainty of terrorist risk differs in an important way from other risks, such as natural hazards or technological failure:

> Since attackers will adapt their strategy as a function of their resources and their knowledge of the vulnerability of the entity they are attacking, the risk is thus the equilibrium resulting from a complex mix of strategies and counterstrategies developed by a range of stakeholders. The nature of the risk changes over time and it is continuously evolving, which leads to dynamic uncertainty. This dynamic uncertainty also makes efforts to quantitatively model the risk more challenging.[9]

A closely related challenge is that of risk-shifting, described as "the implications of the displacement of terrorist attack risk to less-fortified targets when security is improved at a particular target . . . [setting] terrorism risk apart from other natural catastrophe risks."[10] Theoretically, risk-shifting occurs in any interaction between opposing strategic actors. As a practical matter, the nature of catastrophic terrorism and the enormous breadth and depth of vulnerability inherent to a free society, means that risk-shifting is a significantly tougher problem today than it ever was during the great power competitions that have characterized the international security environment since the birth of the modern nation-state in 1648.[11]

Dynamic uncertainty and risk-shifting in homeland security are intuitively obvious, but their significance is often overlooked.[12] Policy thinkers have been inclined to draw analogies between the challenge of homeland security and other familiar problems, rather than assess the challenge on its own terms. Stephen Flynn, one of the best-known experts in the homeland security field, argues that we should model our homeland security efforts after the decades-old pursuit of perfect safety in civil aviation: accept some level of residual risk; fully integrate safety into all aspects of operations; and allow the government a role in providing incentives and disincentives for compliance.[13] James Steinberg, former Deputy National Security Advisor to President Clinton, has likened homeland security to fighting crime: the perpetrators are unknown, the targets frequently opportunistic, and the goal is zero crime even though eliminating crime is impossible.[14] The White House has also relied on analogy, likening the war on terrorism to the Cold War, and citing the National Security Act of 1947 to justify the need for the Homeland Security Act of 2002.[15]

These analogies are useful to a degree, but have important limitations when applied to homeland security. Aviation safety (versus aviation security) is primarily a discipline of known risks, specific hazards, well-understood contributing factors, a distinct operational environment, and comprehensive statistical data that provides the actuarial risk of nearly every conceivable event, as well as the marginal costs and benefits of specific safety measures.[16] Criminals and terrorists are motivated and deterred by very different factors, and crime (in all its varieties) occurs often enough to allow meaningful statistical analysis of trends and countermeasures.[17] Finally, while the threats of the Cold War and catastrophic terrorism have posed similar imperatives for reorganization of our security institutions, the threats are as different as they are alike. We had no doubt about the Soviet Union's identity, and we could measure its capabilities, confront and communicate with it directly, deter its actions with the credible threat of nuclear annihilation, and develop sophisticated warning systems to detect unambiguous signs of impending attack. Analogies disguise the significance of uncertainty in homeland security policy.

Homeland security's fundamental strategic question is: how does the nation make rational, reasonably objective choices about where, how thoroughly, and how fast to build specific capabilities and mitigate specific vulnerabilities, given that we cannot possibly build all needed capabilities and mitigate all vulnerabilities, everywhere, to 100 percent, at the same time? Simply stated, homeland security policy amounts to setting priorities. On this point, nearly every study, review, and task force report agree. The point on which they do not agree, and which few address, is how to accomplish this.

To set homeland security priorities systematically, we must reduce to a practical minimum the uncertainty of three key variables—threat, vulnerability, and capability—and understand and account for the relationship among them:

- *Understanding the threat* requires, at a minimum, "institutionalizing imagination" (in the words of the 9/11 Commission), which includes activities such as net assessment, modeling, and red-teaming—a technique in which the U.S. government would create a team that plays the role of the terrorists in terms of identifying vulnerabilities and planning attacks; rapid sharing and analysis of massive volumes of information ("connecting the dots"); and collecting, producing, and disseminating high-quality tactical intelligence.[18]
- *Prioritizing vulnerabilities* requires, at a minimum, comprehensive and scientific assessment of the nation's critical infrastructure and assets in a holistic way that cuts across sectors and agency boundaries.
- *Building and maintaining capabilities* (such as border security, emergency preparedness, or biodefense) requires, at a minimum, a disciplined requirements process, a uniform account structure, a programming and budgeting

system that shows exactly where homeland security dollars are going, and
objective criteria for measuring outcomes.
- *Accounting for the dynamic relationship of threat, vulnerability, and capability* requires a coherent and comprehensive strategic framework and process that synthesizes the above.[19]

A crude illustration may be useful. Figure 20-1 depicts the three key variables of threat, vulnerability, and capability. The y-axis represents the degree of certainty with regards to each variable (in other words, the extent of our knowledge about and understanding of each variable), and the chart depicts notional levels of certainty (for the Soviet threat during the Cold War, and for the threat of catastrophic terrorism today) in each of the three variables.

By its nature, the terrorist threat today entails greater uncertainty (in terms of our ability to know and understand) than the Soviet threat during the Cold War. To assess the Soviet threat, the United States built formidable intelligence capabilities—human intelligence (HUMINT), image intelligence (IMINT), signals intelligence (SIGINT), and so forth—well-suited to the threat they were built to understand and analyze. We had reasonable success pinpointing Soviet divisions and missile silos, assessing weapons capabilities and unit morale, obtaining plans, and sometimes discerning intentions. We also

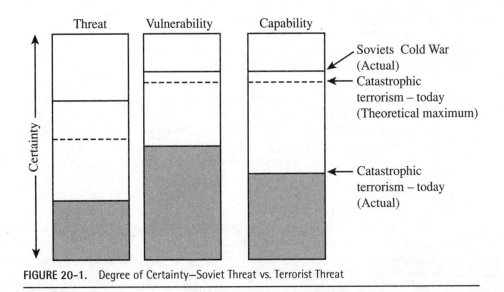

FIGURE 20-1. Degree of Certainty—Soviet Threat vs. Terrorist Threat

developed institutions such as the RAND Corporation, and sophisticated analytic models and branches of thought such as game-theory, to predict what the Soviets would do in all variety of circumstances and scenarios. We have no comparable institutional or academic effort underway with regards to terrorism. To be sure, we were taken by surprise many times during the Cold War—the Cuban missile crisis is a prominent example. But that crisis speaks as much about the *effectiveness* of our capabilities to detect the Soviet-era threat—locate it, understand it, and take action to defuse it—as it does about the *limitations* of those capabilities. By comparison, our current capabilities to discern the terrorist threat are not nearly as effective, relevant, or useful.

Our ability to assess our own vulnerability to terrorism fares better, but once again involves greater uncertainty than the Soviet threat. During the Cold War, the United States was able to triage our own vulnerabilities in much the same way we triaged the Soviets' vulnerabilities. We knew which cities, industrial sites, and missile silos they would prioritize as targets. We could reasonably estimate how our armored divisions would stack up against their armored divisions. The Cold War (force on force; red vs. blue) lent itself to complex, but nonetheless straightforward, methods of assessing our own vulnerabilities. On the basis of such assessments, we were able to make well-informed decisions about what capabilities to build: Army divisions that capitalized on mobility versus mass, B2 bombers that could evade radar, and command and control systems (such as a GPS satellite network) to support a battle doctrine of continuous, synchronized air, land, and sea operations. In short, we knew what our vulnerabilities were, but more importantly, we could reasonably predict which vulnerabilities our enemy would seek to exploit, and plan accordingly. Today, we can make no such reasonable prediction. We can assess the vulnerability of a chemical plant, or a port, or an aircraft, and figure out how to make each of them less vulnerable. But we have little to no capacity for assessing the vulnerabilities of all our chemical plants, ports, aircraft, and countless other targets, and figure out how to make this national target set, as a whole, less vulnerable, rather than simply diverting terrorist plans and shifting the risk, from target to target, sector to sector.

Lastly, we developed during the Cold War a reasonable proficiency at assessing our own capabilities to deal with both threat and vulnerability. To use my own profession as an example, the U.S. Army developed objective standards to determine whether an armor battalion was proficient and trained to conduct a deliberate attack, or whether it was not. We had a fair base of institutional experience on which to build these standards. We developed means (the National Training Center, lasers to simulate bullets in our weapons systems) to assess whether a battalion had met these standards. And with each new war, each new training event, each new weapon fielded, we adjusted and updated our standards. Most other national security institutions of the day developed similar methods to gauge their readiness to perform. But today, many if not most of the key institutions critical to homeland security have no comparable ability to determine whether they are meeting appropriate objective standards of proficiency or success (commonly referred to as "performance measures"). Some institutions (the Transportation Security Agency) are simply too new. Some institutions (the Customs Service, the FBI) have been measuring their success for decades against different metrics (number of shipments inspected, tons of drugs seized, number of successful prosecutions). And some institutions (FEMA, the Los Angeles Police Department, the National Disaster Medical System) are fortunately hampered by the problem that certain events (such as mass-casualty bioterrorism attacks) don't occur often enough to provide sufficient real-world experience from which to develop and refine benchmarks.

Finally, the dynamic relationship between each of these three variables, as discussed previously, is significantly more fluid than it was in the Cold War. Terrorists have far more flexibility than the Soviets to adjust their plans in response to their assessment of our vulnerabilities and capabilities.

The model above is simplistic. But it also usefully highlights another key point: we should attempt to define the theoretical maximum of certainty achievable in each of these three variables; and we should focus our efforts on raising our level of certainty—block by block, program by program—to this theoretical maximum. This is a decidedly unglamorous and workmanlike foundation for a national homeland security strategy, but it is useful. It is a relevant—indeed essential—question to ask how the nation can systematically increase the level of certainty in assessing the threat, our vulnerability to the threat, and our capabilities for assessing both threat and vulnerability.

Raising the bar in each of these areas is a tough task. It is also impossible to achieve without institutions and processes designed for the job. Such institutions and processes did not exist, or were woefully inadequate, on 9/11.[20] Nonetheless, many continue to assert that the historic reorganization endeavored since has been a distraction from "real" improvement in homeland security.[21] That argument only holds water in the short-term. Real improvement over the long haul cannot be pursued meaningfully without the right structures. That is not to say that organization and process are sufficient for building capability—it is only to say that they are essential. Richard Clarke, Counterterrorism Coordinator for both President Clinton and (until October 8, 2001) for President Bush— along with many others—are right to warn that past attempts to reorganize or create government agencies include unfulfilled promises and failure.[22] But past efforts also include important success stories, including the Department of Defense (DoD) and the other entities created by the National Security Act of 1947 (such as the Joint Chiefs of Staff, the Air Force, the Central Intelligence Agency, and the National Security Agency), NASA, the Centers for Disease Control (CDC), the Federal Emergency Management Agency (FEMA), the National Science Foundation, and the Defense Advanced Research Projects Agency (DARPA)—all of which are relevant to homeland security.[23]

National Security vs. Homeland Security

Understanding your business and acting within the disciplines of consent [are] the first imperatives for democratic leadership.[24]

—Arthur Schlesinger, Jr.

So far, this chapter has implicitly incorporated the idea that national security and homeland security are distinct, albeit closely related policy areas. The prevalent view is that this distinction is artificial and problematic for two primary reasons. First, the distinction is conceptually (or to use military parlance, doctrinally) unsound. Second, the distinction fundamentally hinders effective integration of our combined national efforts to defeat terrorism and protect the homeland. On their face, these arguments have some intrinsic merit. So why did President Bush divide duties between two separate coordinating councils, and publish separate national strategies for homeland security and national security?

As many have noted, our adversaries don't respect international boundaries, let alone how those boundaries affect the manner with which U.S. law may apply to their actions. Some, such as former Director for Central Intelligence John Deutch, as well as 9/11 Commission Executive Director Phil Zelikow, have argued that distinguishing between homeland security and national security is an artificial luxury that only the United States can contemplate, and that doing so complicates the already difficult task of interagency coordination.[25] The 9/11 Commission has cited the existence of a separate policy coordination council within the White House as one factor complicating unity of effort across the foreign-domestic divide.[26] Critics such as Stephen Flynn argue that treating homeland security as a separate policy area has reinforced the already problematic foreign-domestic breach in security affairs.[27] And Antulio Echeverria and Bert Tussing, in a monograph published by the Army War College, go so far as to assert that the establishment of the DHS has in fact *created* a division of responsibility in which the DoD focuses primarily beyond the nation's borders (although most security scholars accept that the DoD's outward focus was firmly entrenched long before the DHS, with roots dating back to Southern Reconstruction and *posse comitatus*).[28] Each of these arguments asserts that our defenses, like our enemies, should be united, and not bifurcated. The boldest formulation of this argument, and the point at which it begins to bear real utility, contends that distinguishing between homeland security and national security hinders priority-setting—which is more important to the nation, $3.1 billion for port and container security, or $3.1 billion for a squadron of 24 F-22 fighters? With two separate coordinating councils, how does one even pose, let alone answer, such a fundamental question?

Most of these arguments assert that the NSC staff should subsume the HSC staff, and that our concepts of national security should broaden to include the domestic efforts which have proven so important in the aftermath of 9/11. A revised NSC would be responsible for the full breadth of policy demanded by the terrorist threat, and would run a more streamlined interagency coordination mechanism, ensuring a better lash-up of homeland and national security policy. Such a streamlined council would conceivably be capable of generating a single, coherent national security strategy that encompasses our overseas and domestic actions in an integrated plan that "attack[s] terrorists and their organizations; prevent[s] the continued growth of Islamic terrorism; and protect[s] against and prepare[s] for terrorist attacks."[29] Reinforcing this view is the complaint that in the months following 9/11, department and agency officials at many levels spent too much valuable time in hastily convened, haphazardly organized interagency meetings of the newly-formed Office of Homeland Security (OHS).[30]

In the months following 9/11, distinguishing between national security and homeland security was a practical necessity. The executive branch's policy coordinating structure had to immediately tackle two urgent priorities: first, successfully prosecute an offensive war against al-Qaida; and second, begin the monumental work necessary to secure the homeland. Each of these priorities was of singular importance, and each represented an extraordinarily difficult undertaking. Just as importantly, each involved very different policy challenges and tools.

National security primarily involves a single constitutional jurisdiction (outside the sovereign territory of the United States); homeland security intersects directly with more than 87,000 federal, state, local, and tribal jurisdictions. The President's constitutionally enumerated powers in the national security arena are his most formidable (even considering

Congress' rarely exercised but exclusive power to declare war); the President's powers in the domestic arena are among the most circumscribed of chief executives of democratic governments.[31] National security policy aims to proactively create and seize opportunities; the goal of homeland security policy is primarily to deny opportunities to our adversaries. And even in the infrequent circumstance that national security policy *directly* impacts the daily lives of Americans (for example, base realignment and closure), it does so to a far less tangible degree than nearly all homeland security policies, which touch almost every aspect of American life—from obtaining a driver's license to electronically transferring funds; from boarding an airplane to attending a baseball game.

In the views of many, these distinctions only tend to deepen the foreign-domestic seam that complicates national security policy. But the foreign-domestic seam is not primarily a geographic divide, but rather a legal one. The Constitutional and statutory authorities that enable the executive to act so decisively outside our borders, are very different than the authorities that tend to constrain the executive within our borders. The legal protections afforded to citizens and non-citizens alike within the United States, change dramatically outside the United States. This is not an artificial, doctrinal distinction, but an inherent characteristic of sovereignty, and an essential feature of a system of government devoted to guaranteeing the liberty of its citizens.

Finally, national security policy is the responsibility of a "huddle" of key agencies. The National Security Act of 1947 established the President's war "huddle:" the Vice President, the Secretary of State, and the Secretary of Defense, advised by the Director of Central Intelligence and the Chairman of the Joint Chiefs of Staff.[32] Each of these officials and the agencies they lead has a primary (or only) mission of security and clear lines of statutory authority and responsibility; in particular, the Secretary of State for foreign affairs, and the Secretary of Defense for waging war. This tight organization and crisp delineation of authority and responsibility is a key ingredient to the President's ability to execute foreign and national security policy with the "unity . . . decision, activity, secrecy, and dispatch" which our founding fathers deemed essential.[33]

Homeland security involves a far more diverse collection of agencies, with overlapping authorities, and with primary or important missions other than security. Prior to 9/11, 11 of 14 cabinet departments (State, Treasury, Defense, Justice, Interior, Agriculture, Commerce, Health and Human Services, Transportation, Energy, and Veterans Affairs), plus a host of independent and subordinate agencies (for example, the CIA, the Environmental Protection Agency, and FEMA) bore substantial responsibility for key aspects of homeland security.[34] Eleven responsible cabinet departments is *not* a recipe for unity, decision, activity or dispatch.[35]

Encumbering the NSC and its staff with corralling, coordinating, and reforming this array, while simultaneously waging the offensive effort overseas, would have been ineffective at best, and foolhardy at worst. By appointing Tom Ridge as the first Homeland Security Advisor, the President created an official directly accountable to him on the important homeland security issues, allowing his National Security Advisor to focus the policy machinery of the NSC on toppling the Taliban and decimating al-Qaida while continuing to deal with top-priority national security issues like counterproliferation, Russia, China, and North Korea. It would not have made sense for the President to dilute the focus of his National Security Advisor and NSC staff by forcing them to assume responsibility for the enormous homeland security "to do list." It would not have made sense for the

President to ask the National Security Advisor to simultaneously oversee the near-doubling of her staff; expand and restructure the counterterrorism coordinator's office and create subordinate offices devoted to border security, biosecurity, and emergency preparedness; and become embroiled in the domestic politics that are inseparable from the homeland security challenge.[36]

This is not to say the NSC staff was not already in the business of homeland security. The 9/11 Commission report aptly outlines the steps the Clinton Administration took to address the issue—establishing a Coordinator for Counterterrorism (Clarke) with staff in the NSC, increasing funding for homeland security priorities, and creating an interagency Counterterrorism Security Group (CSG) of the top counterterrorism officials across the agencies to continuously evaluate day-to-day threats and actively manage the government's response.[37] The Clinton NSC also promulgated and actively coordinated implementation of a series of well-regarded and reasonably comprehensive Presidential Decision Directives (PDDs) that greatly clarified U.S. counterterrorism policy (PDD-39), established procedures for dealing with unconventional threats (PDD-62), created a framework and organizations (including novel partnerships with the private sector) to coordinate protection of the nation's critical infrastructure (PDD-63), and established procedures to ensure the continuity of government in the wake of a catastrophic attack (PDD-67).[38]

But in spite of these steps, the homeland security effort before and after 9/11 remained balkanized and largely incoherent. The task was simply too big, the diffusion of responsibility too broad, and the bureaucratic inertia too great for a small office within the White House to coordinate its entirety. Clarke disagrees, "I believed that adept White House coordination and leadership could get the many agencies all working on components of a consistent overall program."[39] But as the 9/11 Commission notes, years of aggressive and forceful coordination by the NSC staff were not sufficient to overcome agency resistance, nor convince the NSC principals to take steps more dramatic than those taken.[40]

Consider the following, which highlights the difference in the President's powers in the national security and homeland security arenas. The President was able to lead America into war with Iraq, largely on the basis of his own powers, yet he had no inherent authority as Chief Executive to reorganize the unitary executive branch he leads in the wake of 9/11. Should the National Security Advisor have been embroiled in the debate about civil service reform and collective bargaining rights for federal workers, not to mention Alaskan fisheries and FEMA's ability to deliver aid after floods—issues over which the President and Congress clashed and negotiated during the legislative process to create DHS? Should the NSC staff have extended their habitual working relationships with the armed services and intelligence committees of Congress to include the 26 committees and 62 subcommittees which claimed some jurisdiction over the DHS proposal?[41]

Aaron Wildavsky, in his 1966 article entitled "The Two Presidencies," incisively highlights the significance of the President's relatively diminished importance in domestic affairs, "The President's normal problem with domestic policy is to get congressional support for the programs he prefers. In foreign affairs, in contrast, he can almost always get support for policies that he believes will protect the nation—but his problem is to find a viable policy."[42] Wildavsky goes on to note that "it takes great crises . . . for Presidents to succeed in controlling domestic policy."[43] While 9/11 certainly qualifies as a great crisis, the challenge in the homeland security policy area is to effect policy to *prevent* crisis, not respond to it. Wildavsky's analysis (dated but still valid) demonstrates that the President's domestic policy proposals are more than twice as likely to fail in Congress as his defense policy proposals. This is the political reality of the homeland security policy area.

Contrast the President's domestic powers with those of his neighbor, the Canadian Prime Minister. The day he assumed office, Prime Minister Paul Martin used his authority as head of government, without Parliament's consideration or approval, to create a powerful new Ministry of Public Safety and Emergency Preparedness, modeled in part on DHS, that subsumed under a single roof Canada's justice ministry, intelligence agency, the Royal Canadian Mountain Police, a new consolidated border security agency, and Canada's agency for infrastructure protection and emergency preparedness.[44] The President's power to set domestic policy is far more constrained than his ability to set foreign policy, and far less substantial than the power wielded by leaders of other democratic nations. Encumbering the NSC with the homeland security challenge in the wake of 9/11 would have failed to recognize the relative dominance of Congress and the relative weakness of the presidency in domestic affairs, and would have necessarily caused the NSC to become substantially involved in an enormous range of tangentially related domestic policy issues. Passing the Homeland Security Act took a Republican gain in a bitterly contested mid-term Congressional election, and all of the institutional and rhetorical muscle of the presidency; whereas invading Afghanistan or Iraq did not.[45]

Another line of argument asserts that by merging national security and homeland security policy into a single discipline, agencies with long-standing core competencies in national security would then assume key responsibilities currently carried out by "civilian" agencies. Several have proposed shifting responsibility for border security to the DoD—which, after all, has primary responsibility for defending our sovereign territory and is proficient in using an economy of force to defend vast stretches of terrain. This argument misses key issues that distinguish a homeland security mission (border management) from a national security mission (defense of territory). Should the DoD be responsible for working with the auto industry to develop a public-private partnership to expedite and increase supply-chain predictability of high-volume, low-risk shipments of auto parts across the Ambassador Bridge from Ontario to Michigan?[46] Should the DoD embroil itself in the government's process to allocate federal highway funds to ensure that cross-border transportation infrastructure projects address the dual imperatives of security, and facilitating an ever-increasing volume of travel and trade? Should the DoD train soldiers to man inspection booths, pop trunks, and make arrests in Laredo? Should the DoD be responsible for developing immigration policy in coordination with the Departments of State, Justice, and Homeland Security? The DoD has no broad competency in these areas, which would dilute its core competency of conducting military operations. Border management is as much about trade facilitation as it is about security, and is a good example of the difference between homeland security policy issues and national security policy issues. An effective long-term border approach is not to layer security on top of an existing structure to facilitate trade, but rather to evolve the structure over time to treat security and facilitation of legitimate flows as two sides of the same coin.[47] That should not be the DoD's job.

On a final note, giving the DoD the primacy in homeland security affairs that it enjoys in national security affairs creates the significant risk that the DoD (the largest executive agency, with over 50 percent of the government's discretionary budget, power-ful protectors in the armed services committees, and a policy apparatus of unparalleled depth and bureaucratic savvy) will use its heft to outmuscle and outmaneuver "domestic" agencies on issues over which those agencies should appropriately be in the lead.

It is ironic that many of the same observers who criticize the DHS as a "wire dia-gram" fix that overemphasizes the value of centralization, assume that centralizing secu-rity policy coordination under the NSC will improve policy coordination and coherence. Neither the NSC or HSC staffs are "deep"—both include one or two staff members who are expert in their particular area and responsible for the policy issues in their particular portfolio, with peers who are expert in other areas and responsible for other issues. Whether the President has one council or two, he still needs one or two experts on immi-gration policy, one or two on transportation security, one or two doctors to work biode-fense, a handful of "old hands" on incident management, and so forth. Whether the President is served by one council or two, he must organize these experts into offices aligned with key agencies and missions, and these offices must coordinate with counter-part offices throughout the Executive Office of the President. A border directorate in the HSC, or a border directorate in the NSC, must still coordinate with the NSC's regional office for western hemisphere affairs. Finally, the notion that a separate HSC burdens the agencies with unnecessary meetings is not compelling. While the nascent OHS certainly had its growing pains, felt most acutely by those whom the OHS was charged with coor-dinating, it is inconceivable to imagine a post-9/11 Washington that was *not* host to a flurry of chaotic meetings. Three years after the attacks, the NSC and HSC have managed to delineate relatively clear, albeit overlapping, lines of policy responsibility, and have established a policy "rhythm" which is predictable, manageable, and effective.

Should the NSC and HSC merge now? One can make a reasonable case. The bur-den of interacting with Congress on homeland security issues has shifted from the White House to the DHS, and Congress is likely to follow the 9/11 Commission's recommenda-tion to establish a more sensible oversight structure.[48] The argument that two staffs basi-cally require the same number of experts as a single staff, also means a single staff would, at worst, face similar coordination challenges and at best, have an integrated executive secretary and administrative system to support their work.

These bureaucratic arguments are secondary, however, to the notion that an inte-grated staff would generate an integrated strategy that sets clear guidance on key strategic tradeoffs. Does preemption mitigate the threat beyond our shores, so there is less impera-tive to bolster security and possibly erode civil liberties at home; or does preemption cre-ate and inflame new adversaries and ultimately exacerbate the threat to the homeland? Does an overly assertive foreign and security policy irritate key allies and partners in a way that makes cooperation on less-visible homeland security issues (such as sharing watch list data, coordinating visa policy, or aligning laws on wiretapping) more difficult? Should the defense budget allocate fewer resources for protecting military bases so that greater resources can be devoted to protecting the nation's commercial infrastructure? These are critical questions that national strategy should deal with directly and unam-biguously.[49]

Two integrated, well-coordinated strategies can do the job. Indeed criticisms that the current *National Security Strategy* does not adequately address homeland security issues fail to recognize that this is by design. The *National Strategy for Homeland Security* directly addresses these issues, and a small team of NSC and OHS staff worked together in the autumn and winter of 2001 to establish the basic architecture of the two documents, determine their relationship to subordinate strategies like the *National Strategy to Combat Terrorism*, and develop the documents in tandem.[50] That said, two strategies are more likely to get bureaucratically sidetracked onto divergent paths (which is apt to happen given the preceding discussion of how homeland security and national security differ), and a single strategy is more likely to articulate the critical policy choices and set a clear direction through them.

Thus, the President and nation are best served by a single, integrated strategy, developed by separate but well-coordinated NSC and HSC staffs which are expert in their respective areas of policy responsibility, and staffed with veterans skilled at wielding the distinct policy tools available to the President for foreign policy, on the one hand, and domestic policy, on the other. Stated differently, a single national strategy will better provide clear policy direction. Separate NSC and HSC staffs will better ensure effective interagency coordination of policy, while ensuring an NSC with an organizational culture consistent with the President's formidable foreign policy powers, and an HSC that is fluent in navigating the complex intersection of homeland security and domestic policy.

What Makes Good Strategy?

> *We reject, on the other hand, the artificial definitions [of strategy] of certain writers, since they find no reflection in general usage.*
> —*Carl von Clausewitz*, On War[51]

Strategy is about getting important things done. Good strategy is that which accomplishes well-chosen ends, nothing more. Ultimately, *how* things get done is subordinate to whether they get done or not. That is not to say that the *how* (strategy) doesn't matter— to the contrary, strategy is essential to tackle all complex challenges, and to coordinate the activities of all complex organizations. It is only to say that our concepts of what strategy *is* or *is not* should recognize that the measure of strategy should be its effectiveness at accomplishing the task at hand, not whether it fits a particular definition or another.

Military strategists have criticized the *NSHS* for lacking a unifying strategic concept, such as "containment" for the Cold War, "engagement" for the 1990s, or "shape, respond, prepare" in the 1997 *National Military Strategy*. In this vein, Echevarria and Tussing's Army War College monograph proposes a "global defense-in-depth."[52] Grand strategic concepts like "defense-in-depth" are descriptive, but in fact have provided limited practical guidance to homeland security policymakers who, since 9/11, have had to make hundreds of individual decisions about which specific capabilities and vulnerabilities should warrant priority attention. The primary factors shaping these concrete decisions have been the criticality of the specific capabilities or vulnerabilities in question; to what extent focusing on them would bear a reasonable prospect of improving our safety; and to what extent focusing on them might divert effort from more important priorities. These decisions have helped set funding priorities, but just as importantly, have determined which issues deserve the time-consuming, hands-on interagency coordination of the HSC and HSC staff. Such coordination has been essential to driving progress on critical policy issues such as establishing the Terrorist Threat Integration Center (TTIC, which President Bush proposed in his 2003 State of the Union address and which he recently renamed the National Counterterrorism Center in Executive Order 13354), creating the Terrorist Screening Center (TSC) to integrate terrorist watch lists, developing a comprehensive national biodefense policy including initiatives such as BioShield and BioWatch, creating a new National Response Plan (NRP), and advancing cooperation with Canada and Mexico.

Ironically, under Governor Ridge's leadership (following substantial department and agency opposition to his proposal to consolidate border agencies), the HSC coordinated an interagency effort in the first two months of 2002 to develop a strategy for the "Border of the Future." This effort was entirely consistent with (if not as comprehensive as) Echevarria's and Tussing's "defense-in-depth" concept, and supplied much of the substance for the "smart borders" and international initiatives in the *NSHS*.[53] The Administration has made significant progress in advancing these initiatives, and has managed to sustain productive, pragmatic cooperation with allies and partners on a broad range of homeland security issues, in spite of the more visible and better-publicized disagreements over Iraq and the preemption strategy.[54] The United States has implemented "smart border" action plans with Canada and Mexico, reached agreements with more than 25 countries to put DHS inspectors in foreign ports, won adoption of transportation security initiatives at three successive G-8 Summits and the Asian Pacific Economic Conference (APEC), and convinced a skeptical European Union to share passenger data on international air travelers. The last three years have demonstrated that while the United States and its allies may differ on key issues of international security, including how best to fight terrorism, they recognize and are committed to sustained cooperation on policy issues in the homeland security domain. The Administration has been implementing, in practice if not in name, the "defense in depth" concept.

It is telling to compare the literature on grand strategy, military strategy, domestic policy strategy, and business strategy, and to look at examples of each. The variety and differences are striking. The lesson that emerges from such a comparison is that successful strategies take many forms. Good strategy fits the nature of the problem at hand, provides a vision, states clear objectives, organizes the effort of key actors, effectively harnesses the available resources, and creates synergy, producing a result greater than the sum of these parts. The form strategy takes is entirely subordinate to these qualities, and many forms have been successful. Furthermore, no consensus exists on which work best. Ernest May edited an entire volume of such widely divergent opinions with respect to National Security Council Resolution 68 (NSC-68), which many regard as a classic distillation of grand strategy, and others regard as a "deeply flawed document."[55] Not surprisingly, neither NSC-68, nor George Kennan's famous "Long Telegram," nor Sun Tzu's classic on the art of war, nor the corporate strategies taught at the Harvard Business School bear much resemblance to one another, yet each are famous and widely emulated as effective models.[56] The flexible mind embraces this variety, not rejects it. Bernard Brodie, in a speech at the Naval War College in 1958, captured this point vividly; "I think the so-often-repeated axiom that I quoted a moment ago—'methods change, but principles are unchanging'—has had on the whole an unfortunate influence on strategic thinking, encouraging, as it does, the lazy man's approach to novel problems."[57] In the same speech Brodie notes that history's preeminent military strategist, Carl von Clausewitz, deserves great credit rather than criticism for "leaving no 'system' of strategy, no method which can be indoctrinated by teachers and learned by students."[58]

This chapter has argued that the magnitude of uncertainty in homeland security distinguishes it from other security and risk-management challenges, and that homeland security is a distinct policy area. Given the unique nature of the challenge and the unique features of the policy area, and absent a fail-safe model, how should one shape a national homeland security strategy? Perhaps the best approach is that which Richard Neustadt and May suggest succinctly and directly, ". . . for any decision, the first step in analysis should be to take apart and thus define the situation that seems to call for action. . . . Put another way, [our advice] is nothing but an injunction to get the facts straight before acting."[59]

What were the essential facts about homeland security facing the President and his staff in the months following 9/11? This chapter has already touched on most:

- a clear understanding of the importance of the threat, but significant uncertainty and little specific knowledge about its exact nature;
- a clear understanding of the enormous breadth and depth of our vulnerability as an open society, but no way to take a risk-management approach to the whole of our vulnerability;
- a lack of real capacity to address both threat and vulnerability, and just as importantly, the inability to even assess our capacity;
- a recognition that the homeland security policy area is distinct from the national security policy area, and that the policy choices and tools available to the President differ in important ways than those available for foreign policy and national security;
- a recognition that state and local governments, as well as private sector institutions, bear important responsibilities for key activities;
- eleven cabinet departments and a score of independent and subordinate agencies with important homeland security responsibilities, none with the primary mission of homeland security, with semi-overlapping statutory authorities, a spotty record of cooperation, and no rational mechanism for distributing resources among them;
- no clear alignment of authority, responsibility, and resources;
- proof, both before and after 9/11, that aggressive coordination from the White House is necessary but not sufficient to coordinate policy and activities across such a broad and diverse variety of agencies; and
- an unmistakable lesson (department and agency opposition to Governor Ridge's January 2002 proposal to consolidate border agencies) that, notwithstanding the President's Constitutional role as head of the unitary executive branch, the President and his staff would not be able to effect bold institutional reform with a transparent, consensus-based, committee approach.[60]

From the perspective of the President and his advisors, these were the straight facts. From them, one other lesson is clear: abstract strategic concepts (containment, détente, engagement, preemption, layered defense) and vivid bumper-sticker phrases ("Germany first, Japan second;" "shape, respond, prepare;" "the best defense is a good offense") might be usefully descriptive but would not be sufficient. The President and the nation would require a strategy to deal with the preceding facts head-on. Dramatic institutional change would be critical. Regardless of the form the strategy might take, it would need to set a path to accomplish this reform and establish a practical and straight-forward framework within which to organize the national effort.[61]

The National Strategy for Homeland Security and the Case for DHS

It must be considered that there is nothing more difficult to carry out, nor more doubtful of success, nor more dangerous to handle, than to initiate a new order of things. For the reformer has enemies in all those who profit by the old order, and only lukewarm defenders in all those who would profit by the new.

—*Niccolo Machiavelli*, The Prince

The *National Strategy for Homeland Security* establishes a practical, straight-forward framework of six critical mission areas:

- *Intelligence and Warning,* which involves an integrated, government-wide approach to requirements, collection, analysis, production, and dissemination of classified and open-source information;
- *Border and Transportation Security,* which seeks to prevent terrorists and terrorist materiel from entering the country, and seeks to ensure that our border systems and the interconnected transportation network that straddles them, can securely and efficiently support the legitimate flow of people and goods;
- *Domestic Counterterrorism,* which focuses on intelligence and law enforcement efforts to identify terrorists and their supporters, prevent them from carrying out attacks within the United States, and apprehend and prosecute them;
- *Protecting Critical Infrastructure and Key Assets,* which involves identifying and prioritizing the nation's infrastructure; assessing criticality, consequence, and the connections among infrastructures; evaluating the marginal costs and benefits of protection measures; and synthesizing threat and vulnerability to prevent risk-shifting;
- *Defending Against Catastrophic Threats,* which emphasizes the detection, deterrence, prevention, and management of the consequences of terrorist use of weapons of mass destruction; and
- *Emergency Preparedness and Response,* which focuses on efforts to minimize the damage and rapidly recover from terrorist attacks which may occur.[62]

Each of these six critical mission areas is a main "line of business" that, like each of the operating divisions in a corporation, generates a distinct "output" critical to homeland security. Corporations attempt to align the cultures, responsibilities (or markets), resources, and outputs of their distinct operating divisions, subsidiaries, or brands to fulfill the corporation's fundamental responsibility of generating profits for its shareholders. Why should the government *not* have to do the same to fulfill its fundamental Constitutional responsibility of providing for the security of its citizens? To use a different term, each of the critical mission areas reflects a homeland security "core competency:" if the country performs all of these missions well, is it doing a good job of providing homeland security? The answer is "yes." If the country performs one of these missions poorly, is it doing a good job? The answer is "no." Defining how government thinks about and organizes for homeland security is not a semantic exercise, but a practical requirement.

Finally, the critical mission areas encompass the full range of homeland security activities, and provide a framework within which every federal homeland security dollar maps into one, and only one, line of business. Accordingly, the Office of Management and Budget (OMB) has organized the account structure of the entire federal budget to fit this framework, establishing for the first time a coherent means of managing homeland security resources. Critics have almost universally failed to appreciate the significance of this seemingly bureaucratic exercise. But anyone who has ever led a complex enterprise will agree that it is essential to know how much money the organization is spending, on what, when, and at the expense of what other priorities. On a smaller (though still massive) scale, this is what Secretary McNamara accomplished for the DoD in the 1960s with the Planning, Programming, and Budgeting System (PPBS) that, while often criticized, remains intact and has proven an essential tool for balancing near-term operational requirements with long-term, capital-intensive research and development. PPBS was essential to the DoD's effort during the 1970s and 1980s to "offset" Soviet military mass with American technological edge; it remains essential today for waging the war on terrorism while simultaneously transforming the military. OMB's effort to organize the federal budget according to the coherent *NSHS* framework, as a foundation for a disciplined and comprehensive programming and budgeting process in the DHS, and as a means to rationalize resources across agency lines, will prove equally significant over time.[63] Table 20-1 shows recent budgeting activity for each of the six critical mission areas.

The *NSHS* also includes four "foundations" that cut across the mission areas: law, science and technology, information sharing and systems, and international cooperation. Each of the foundations provides policy options and tools for each mission area, imposes constraints on the policy options in each mission area, and is useful for integrating policy and balancing resources across mission areas. For example, how much is the government spending on homeland security research and development, and which programs across all agencies deserve priority for funding? In the months immediately following 9/11, there was no way to answer that question.

From this straightforward framework a key question emerges: within each mission area, prior to the Homeland Security Act, were culture, authority, responsibility, and resources aligned?[64] The answer is "no" for five out the six critical mission areas: intelligence and warning (as the 9/11 Commission report highlights), border and transportation security, critical infrastructure protection, defending against catastrophic threats, and emergency preparedness and response. One can make the case that the sixth—domestic counterterrorism—suffered from the distinction between foreign and domestic intelligence. As this chapter has argued, the distinction between the two is a Constitutional necessity, and the manner in which we address it is not primarily structural, but a question of carefully tailoring legal authorities to balance the imperatives of security and liberty. The principal *organizational* challenge in the domestic counterterrorism mission area is not how responsibility is divided among federal agencies, but how responsibility is shared between federal, state, and local agencies.

TABLE 20-1. Federal Homeland Security Funding by National Strategy Mission Area (Budget authority, in millions of dollars)

Critical Mission Area	2002 Enacted	2002 Supplemental	2003 Enacted	2003 Supplemental	2004 Enacted	2005 Request
Intelligence and Warning[1]			125.1	86.0	268.7	474.1
Border and Transportation Security			15,170.8	1,859.0	15,322.5	17,074.6
Domestic Counterterrorism			2,509.2	522.6	2,994.1	3,419.8
Protecting Critical Infrastructure and Key Assets			12,893.1	388.3	12,571.0	14,060.0
Defending against Catastrophic Threats			2,428.4	201.1	2,827.2	3,358.2
Emergency Preparedness and Response			3,873.2	2,272.0	7,132.5	8,8802.4
Other			118.3	––	191.1	196.5
Total, Homeland Security 47,385.7 Budget Authority	20,620[2]	12,264[2]		37,118.2	5,329.0	41,307.1

1. Figures in the Intelligence and Warning (I&W) critical mission area include only unclassified data. Specific data for many I&W programs and activities remain classified.

2. Sources: *Fiscal Year 2004 President's Budget Summary Tables,* Table S-5; all other data from *Analytic Perspectives, Budget of the United States Government, Fiscal Year 2005,* pp. 25–39. (The National Strategy for Homeland Security established the framework of homeland security critical mission areas in 2002, therefore OMB did not organize homeland security budget data by critical mission area prior to Fiscal Year 2003).

Consider the example of one mission area—border and transportation security. At the time of the 9/11 attacks, five cabinet agencies shared responsibility:

- the Department of State's Bureau of Consular Affairs was responsible for issuing visas (which grant permission to foreign nationals to approach our borders), and was responsible for coordinating immigration policy with the Department of Justice (DOJ);
- the DOJ's Immigration and Naturalization Service (INS) was responsible for granting foreign nationals admission through our borders and for enforcing immigration law (including apprehension and deportation); INS' Border Patrol was responsible for patrolling between ports-of-entry to prevent illegal entry of people; and the DOJ's Executive Office of Immigration Review was responsible for adjudicating deportations;

- the Department of the Treasury's Customs Service was responsible for controlling the flow of goods across our border, and for patrolling between ports-of-entry to prevent the illegal entry of goods;
- if those goods happened to be food, plants, or animals, the Department of Agriculture's Animal and Plant Health Inspection Service (APHIS) was responsible for preventing illegal entry and safeguarding against disease; and
- the Department of Transportation (DOT) was responsible for the transportation system which straddles our ports-of-entry and connects 54 international airports in the United States' interior with the rest of the world, while DOT's Coast Guard guarded the waters within twelve nautical miles of our borders.

Border and transportation security is perhaps the most dramatic example, but each of the other mission areas suffered, to one degree or another, from a similar diffusion. For example, there was no credible national effort to advance homeland security research and development to protect against catastrophic terrorism (for example, detectors sophisticated enough to detect illicit radiological material but not so sensitive as to "trip" a port-of-entry shutdown every time a truck passes through an inspection lane carrying one of the thousands of industrial or medical devices that legitimately use low-grade radiological material). Such research was not the primary focus of any agency, but was a secondary or tertiary focus of multiple agencies.

Ensuring each "line of business" could generate the right "outputs" would require institutional change, and the President's proposal for DHS was the principal vehicle for affecting it. The Department's four major operational directorates (Border and Transportation Security, Information Analysis and Infrastructure Protection, Science and Technology, and Emergency Preparedness and Response) align directly with four of the six critical mission areas cited above.[65] An Undersecretary—appointed by the President, confirmed by the Senate, and equipped with clear statutory authority—heads each directorate, and the President now has a homeland security "huddle"—a manageable number of directly accountable Cabinet officials (enumerated in Title IX of the Homeland Security Act) with responsibility for the critical homeland security functions. Figure 20-2 provides an overview of this organizational structure.

Thus, the DHS does not represent a wire-diagram panacea or a "lesser-but-included" problem of national homeland security strategy. The rationalization and organization of the national homeland security effort into critical mission areas, and the corresponding alignment of resources, responsibility, and authority, establish a foundation for real institutional capacity that would be unachievable otherwise.[66]

The *NSHS* does more than simply provide a rationale for DHS: it includes more than 80 specific initiatives across all of the critical mission areas and foundations. Scholars such as Paul Light (2002) have commented on the "laundry list" nature of these initiatives, but again, the measure of strategy is whether it provides meaningful direction for action. The *Strategy's* straightforward framework, its success in providing a case for a Department that would align with that framework, and the substance of its initiatives, have created clear direction for immediate action. Only five-and-a-half months after proposing the DHS (about 14 months after 9/11), the President signed into law a Homeland Security Act that incorporated 90 percent of that for which he asked.

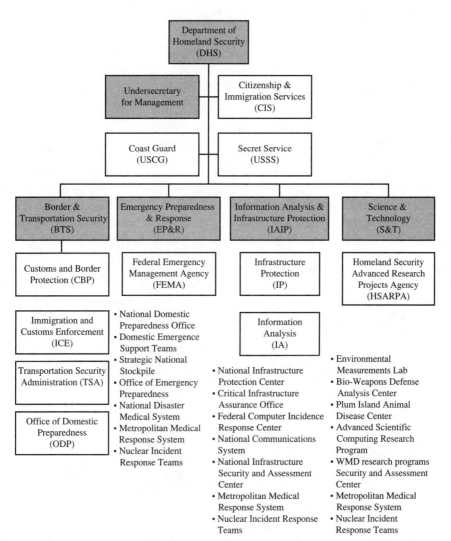

Department of Homeland Security (DHS)

- Undersecretary for Management
- Citizenship & Immigration Services (CIS)
- Coast Guard (USCG)
- Secret Service (USSS)

Border & Transportation Security (BTS)
- Customs and Border Protection (CBP)
- Immigration and Customs Enforcement (ICE)
- Transportation Security Administration (TSA)
- Office of Domestic Preparedness (ODP)

Emergency Preparedness & Response (EP&R)
- Federal Emergency Management Agency (FEMA)
  - National Domestic Preparedness Office
  - Domestic Emergence Support Teams
  - Strategic National Stockpile
  - Office of Emergency Preparedness
  - National Disaster Medical System
  - Metropolitan Medical Response System
  - Nuclear Incident Response Teams

Information Analysis & Infrastructure Protection (IAIP)
- Infrastructure Protection (IP)
- Information Analysis (IA)
  - National Infrastructure Protection Center
  - Critical Infrastructure Assurance Office
  - Federal Computer Incidence Response Center
  - National Communications System
  - National Infrastructure Security and Assessment Center
  - Metropolitan Medical Response System
  - Nuclear Incident Response Teams

Science & Technology (S&T)
- Homeland Security Advanced Research Projects Agency (HSARPA)
  - Environmental Measurements Lab
  - Bio-Weapons Defense Analysis Center
  - Plum Island Animal Disease Center
  - Advanced Scientific Computing Research Program
  - WMD research programs Security and Assessment Center
  - Metropolitan Medical Response System
  - Nuclear Incident Response Teams

Notes

1. The broad variety of DHS' subordinate entities means that no single methodology defines the "major operational elements" depicted in this chart. The chart attempts to depict DHS' major subordinate entities, measured loosely in terms of their place within the organizational hierarchy (such as the four major directorates), their size (such as CBP), their status as distinct entities (such as FEMA and the Secret Service), or the unique importance they bear on a particularly important mission (such as the Domestic Emergency Support Teams and entities or programs specifically transferred by name in the Homeland Security Act).

2. The chart largely depicts the organization of entities as of the effective date of their transfer to DHS—March 1, 2003. Since then, the Secretary of Homeland Security has used his statutory authority to reorganize the Department (a hard-fought provision which almost prevented Senate passage of the Homeland Security Act) and restructure, rename, and transfer these entities between directorates. That said, it is not an easy task to discern the current structure of DHS simply by browsing its website or scanning public documents. This in itself may say something about the speed and effectiveness (or lack thereof) with which DHS has integrated its constituent agencies.

3. The Nuclear Incident Response Teams (listed under the Emergency Preparedness and Response directorate) remain part of the Department of Energy, but act under the operational control of DHS when deployed.

4. The Homeland Security Act transferred the Strategic National Stockpile from the Department of Health and Human Services (HHS) to DHS' EP&R directorate, but subsequent legislation has since transferred the Stockpile back to HHS.

5. Refer to the Homeland Security Act of 2002 or Bush, The Department of Homeland Security, for the departments and agencies from which the entities depicted were transferred.

6. References: Homeland Security Act of 2002; DHS Strategic Plan; DHS FY2005 Budget in Brief.

FIGURE 20-2. Major Operational Elements of the Department of Homeland Security

Compare this to the National Security Act of 1947. President Truman, General Marshall, and others began actively discussing the need for military unification as early as 1943. World War II ended in 1945. The National Security Act, an ungainly compromise among interests bitterly at odds with one another, became law in 1947, and almost immediately needed amendment in 1949 to give the Secretary of Defense real authority.[67] Even then, it failed to effectively unify the services, requiring amendment in 1953, 1958, and finally in 1986 with the Goldwater-Nichols Act. In comparison, passage of the Homeland Security Act was lightning-fast, and the degree to which the Act conforms to the President's proposal is remarkable.

Undoubtedly, time will show that the President and Congress got some things wrong, and, as with the National Security Act of 1947, the Homeland Security Act will inevitably require amendment and adjustment. The creation of the DHS is significantly more complex than the creation of the DoD a half-century ago. The National Security Act essentially installed a Cabinet secretary and a staff above separate military departments that, to this day, retain their distinct missions, identities, and relative autonomy. By contrast, the creation of the DHS involves a far more difficult functional integration.[68] For example, while the DHS consolidates border agencies, it separates immigration services (in the Bureau of Citizenship and Immigration Services, within the DHS secretariat) from immigration enforcement (in the Bureau of Customs and Border Protection and the Bureau of Immigration and Customs Enforcement, both of which report to the Undersecretary for Border and Transportation Security).

Is the DHS an unmanageable behemoth, as Clarke and others assert?[69] Perhaps, but assessing the managerial challenge by totaling the DHS budget and counting its employees is grossly misleading.

Just two DHS entities (the Directorate of Border and Transportation Security and the U.S. Coast Guard) account for approximately 58 percent of the DHS' total budget authority and 87 percent of its employees.[70] The Directorate of Border and Transportation Security (BTS) controls approximately $15.9 billion of DHS' proposed Fiscal Year 2005 budget of $40.2 billion, and employs approximately 110,000 of DHS' 180,000 employees. But as discussed previously, the case for consolidating border security into a single organization is probably more compelling than the case for any other DHS element. Efforts to consolidate Customs and INS date back to the Hoover Administration.[71] While there are many criticisms of various elements of the DHS, critics of border agency consolidation have fallen silent, and the *9/11 Commission Report* and other studies embrace BTS' basic organization.[72] The Coast Guard accounts for approximately 19 percent of DHS' budget and approximately 46,000 employees, but has retained its distinct operational identity, and operates just as effectively under the DHS as it did under the DOT (just as the U.S. Secret Service operates as effectively under the DHS as it did under the Department of the Treasury). If anything, size is to the DHS' long-term advantage, because down the road it will allow the Department to reap the benefits of economies of scale (as the DoD does) that provide strategic flexibility and adaptability. Critiques of the DHS' size are not relevant; critiques of its complexity are.

Why didn't the President seek reform in the fifth critical mission area—intelligence and warning—mentioned above? The President's proposal and the Homeland Security Act included the Bureau of Information Analysis and Infrastructure Protection (IAIP), intended to integrate threat and vulnerability analysis as discussed in the first section of this chapter.

Subsequently, the President established the Terrorist Threat Integration Center (TTIC) to integrate terrorist threat analysis by the CIA, FBI, DoD, and DHS' IAIP. Arguably, seeking more substantial intelligence reform in the Homeland Security Act would have encumbered the proposal, complicated the legislative debate, and put passage of the Act at risk. Perhaps more importantly, pursuing bold intelligence reform while fighting an offensive war on terrorism, and prior to the report of the 9/11 Commission would have been extraordinarily difficult, possibly dangerous. In this case, the short-term requirements to maintain the mission effectiveness of the existing intelligence apparatus rightfully outweighed the long-term need to reform the intelligence community. The reform effort is underway now.[73]

Did the President propose DHS to forestall Congressional action (such as S.1534, the Department of National Homeland Security Act of 2001, submitted by Senator Lieberman on October 11, 2001)?[74] The record seems to say yes, but the question of whether the proposal itself and its timing were motivated solely or primarily by politics, seems unfair. Governor Ridge has publicly stated that the President's initial guidance to him gave him free rein to look hard at all areas of government, determine if reorganization or change was necessary, and make recommendations. Ridge wasted no time in doing so, proposing the creation of a consolidated border administration while the OHS was still building its staff and struggling to develop the four budget priorities outlined in the President's first post-9/11 State of the Union Address. Moreover, the President's proposal was significantly more comprehensive than any previously proposed, including the Hart/Rudman Commission's recommendation to create a National Homeland Security Agency, as well as Senator Lieberman's proposed bill.[75] Lastly, the President's proposal differed from previous proposals by fully shifting "operational" responsibilities out of the White House and into a Cabinet department, *strengthening* Congressional oversight. These facts seem to indicate that, while political considerations were likely crucial (for which presidential actions are they not?), policy considerations were equally important.

Has the DHS fulfilled its promise? No; and while no active politician is likely to say so, it will still take years before it begins to produce results greater than the sum of the 22 disparate agencies it subsumed and the handful of agencies to which it gave birth. The DoD has experienced significant growing pains over the years, but the fact that the nation acted upon the lessons of World War II, proved essential to the generation-long Cold War that ensued. While we may never know for sure, the fact that the nation acted quickly in the wake of 9/11 to create the DHS may well prove crucial to facing the challenges ahead. The DHS today is only a foundation, but establishing a foundation is necessary to build real capability. It may take 5, 6, even 10 years before the DHS is capable of ensuring that our systems for international trade don't grind to a halt in the wake of an attack using weapons of mass destruction. But it may take 6, 7, or 11 years before terrorists have the capability to develop and deliver such weapons. That the job will take years is no argument for not starting now. That the job will be difficult and complex is no argument for seeking a softer road.

Results—Is America Safe Enough?

> Do not confuse sécurité, the feeling of having nothing to fear and sûrete—the
> state of having nothing to fear.
>
> —*Marguerite-Marie Dubois*[76]

The degree to which the 9/11 Commission's recommendations are consistent with, rather than depart from, the framework and policies articulated in the *NSHS* is remarkable (particularly given that the President released the *NSHS* more than two years prior to the *9/11 Commission Report,* without the benefit of the exhaustive investigation the Commission conducted). The *9/11 Commission Report* implicitly embraces the DHS. A recent GAO report concludes that, taken together, the *NSHS* and the *National Strategy for Combating Terrorism (NSCT),* are generally aligned with the 9/11 Commission recommendations, only eight of which are not addressed by either strategy.[77] Two of those eight regard Congress' oversight structure, a problem the President cited in his DHS proposal, but which he identified as the responsibility of the legislative, not the executive branch.[78] Two others concern intelligence restructuring, which, as discussed earlier, the President deliberately opted to postpone—that said, the Commission's report recommends building the National Counterterrorism Center on the foundation of the TTIC, the creation of which the President directed in January 2003.

This GAO report only outlines a superficial analysis of which 9/11 Commission recommendations map onto which *NSHS* and *NSCT* recommendations. A more difficult and useful analysis would not only assess the alignment of initiatives published two years apart, but would evaluate the whole of presidential policy and executive branch activity in relationship to each 9/11 recommendation. Such an analysis would reveal that much of what the 9/11 Commission recommends is already underway, and builds on policy developed and promulgated over the last three years.

For example, the 9/11 Commission's fifteenth recommendation calls for an integrated system of screening points, including our transportation system and critical infrastructure.[79] On September 16, 2003, the President issued *Homeland Security Presidential Directive-6* (HSPD-6), which established the Terrorist Screening Center (TSC) and directed the Secretary of Homeland Security to develop guidelines to govern the use of terrorist screening information to support state, local, territorial, and tribal screening processes, and private sector screening processes that have a substantial bearing on homeland security. HSPD-6 also directed executive departments and agencies to conduct terrorist screening at "all appropriate opportunities."[80] The President's HSC staff coordinated a companion memorandum of understanding between the Secretary of State, the Attorney General, the Secretary of Homeland Security, and the Director of Central Intelligence, signed the same day, that provided further guidance on accomplishing the directives in HSPD-6.[81] Both the policy, and the effort to implement it, were well underway at the time the Commission released its report. Shortly after the *9/11 Commission Report,* on August 27, 2004, the President supplemented HSPD-6 with *HSPD-11— Comprehensive Terrorist-Related Screening Procedures,* which had been under development prior to the *9/11 Commission Report.*[82] A second example is the strong tie between the Commission's nineteenth recommendation (prioritizing critical infrastructure protection) and the *National Strategy to Physical Protection of Critical Infrastructure and Key Assets,* released in February 2003, as well as *HSPD-7—Critical Infrastructure Identification, Prioritization, and Protection,* released in December 2003.[83]

Moreover, the GAO analysis only looked at the initiatives in the critical mission area chapters; it did not assess the nearly 40 initiatives in the foundation chapters. Had it done so, it would have noted the strong overlap of many more areas of the *NSHS* and the *9/11 Commission Report.* For example, the Commission's seventeenth recommendation (international cooperation) relates strongly to the initiatives in the "International Cooperation" chapter of the *NSHS*, as well as the broad range of substantial initiatives achieved through the pragmatic (though not highly visible) international collaboration already outlined in this chapter.[84] Says President Clinton's former Deputy Secretary of Defense, John Hamre, ". . . it is my sense that international collaboration on domestic security issues is a quiet success story."[85]

So is America safe? The nation has expended enormous effort since 9/11. The United States has a new Cabinet department (DHS), a new military command (U.S. Northern Command), and a host of new institutions (the Transportation Security Administration, the National Counterterrorism Center, the Terrorist Screening Center, and the Homeland Security Advanced Research Projects Agency, to name only a few). Airlines have hardened their cockpit doors and the Transportation Security Administration has put air marshals on flights. The FBI has expanded its mission and hired over a thousand new agents dedicated to counterterrorism. In three successive G-8 summits, the United States has secured agreement on initiatives to ensure international transportation security, counter the proliferation of weapons of mass destruction, and prevent the smuggling and terrorist use of Man Portable Air Defense Systems (MANPADS). The Department of State has substantially tightened the process for obtaining visas. DHS has developed a National Incident Management System to standardize emergency response nationwide, and created a Homeland Security Operations Center linked to the White House, the rest of the executive branch, and all 50 states. The Department of Health and Human Services has bolstered the Strategic National Stockpile, which now contains enough smallpox vaccine for every American. State and local governments have developed new incident management procedures, conducted thousands of training exercises, and spent billions improving their emergency response capabilities. There are countless other concrete examples. America is safer.

But is America safe enough? According to the 9/11 Commission, "it is [not] possible to defeat all terrorist attacks against Americans, every time and everywhere."[86] So, how do we determine how safe is safe enough? According to Stephen Flynn, the answer is "something less than ironclad security. What is required is enough security to create a deterrent."[87] This does not seem a practical measure. While it is possible to deter terrorists from executing specific attacks against specific targets, ultimately deterrence is of limited utility against terrorists willing to die in the commission of their acts.[88] Later in his book, Flynn argues that "We have done enough when the American people can conclude that a future attack on U.S. soil will be an exceptional event that does not require wholesale changes to how we go about our lives. This means they should be confident that the measures in place are sufficient to confront the danger."[89] In practice, this approach requires that we simply continue to invest in homeland security until it crowds out investment in other priorities the public feels are more important. This likewise seems insufficient, since individual Americans have no real way of objectively assessing our vulnerability, and since Flynn argues that Americans are victim to a false sense of confidence. This chapter has offered a more tempered view—the only way to objectively approach the question of "how safe is safe enough" is to develop and execute a strategy that reduces the uncertainty of the threat and improves our ability to assess threats, vulnerabilities, and capabilities, and then effect appropriate action. Rhetorically, perhaps, Flynn is right—but it would be hard to craft policy calibrated on Americans' perceptions of their own safety. That said, a thorough analysis reveals that there is substantial room for improvement.

Not a single one of 27 visa-waiver countries met the United States' October 2004 deadline to embed biometric data into machine-readable passports. The United States requires visas of travelers from 19 countries of which Canada requires no visa, even though U.S. policy allows tens of thousands of people to cross the U.S.-Canada border every day without a passport. The DHS has yet to field an improved computer pre-screening system for air passengers. Recently, an internal DOJ report revealed that, as of April 2004, the FBI had not reviewed or translated more than 123,000 hours of audio recordings in languages associated with terrorists. While it has made progress, the TSC has yet to fully integrate terrorist watch lists maintained by several federal agencies. There is no international system to track lost and stolen passports. States continue to issue driver's licenses and other "breeder" documents which meet no independent scientific standards of security and integrity.[90] In 2003, a power outage across the northeastern United States revealed that localized attacks could cascade across fragile, interdependent infrastructures, at enormous economic cost. The failure to find weapons of mass destruction in Iraq has raised questions about the CIA, while long-standing cultural differences continue to inhibit information sharing and cooperation between the CIA and the FBI. And Congress is only just beginning the task of restructuring the intelligence community, which will take years to complete and is fraught with difficulty. There are other shortcomings as well. A sober assessment of our homeland security must acknowledge these realities. An updated national strategy must address them.

The Next National Strategy for Homeland Security

What should the next national strategy look like? This chapter has already recommended that the President should produce a single strategy that integrates the national security and homeland security imperatives. The homeland security substance of that document should chart a transition from "phase one" of the homeland security effort ("first things first," or building an essential framework and foundation for real institutional capacity) to "phase two:" shoring-up that framework across the board with solid programs, clearly-defined program objectives, and performance metrics that together work to reduce the uncertainty of threat, vulnerability, and capability.[91] This is not to imply that the process of building capability is just beginning—to the contrary, nearly every agency of government at the federal, state, and local levels has dramatically strengthened their capacity to carry out their homeland security responsibilities. But the challenge ahead requires new capabilities that did not exist prior to 9/11 (for example, the threat and vulnerability integration mission of the DHS' IAIP), and realistically, we are only now reaching the point where our efforts to build wholly new capabilities are beginning to bear fruit.

Beyond this macro-level recommendation on the form of the next strategy, and the policy scope it should embrace (both national security and homeland security), what substantive issues should the strategy address? The following are nine recommendations, which are far from a comprehensive treatment, but are important to (and representative of) the types of activities on which the strategy should provide guidance and effect action.

1. Strengthen the Relationship Between the Department of Defense and the Department of Homeland Security. Perhaps the most important practical step for effectively integrating national security and homeland security policy is to strengthen the DoD-DHS relationship. While the nation faces a single set of strategic risks, and a single array of adversaries, it lacks an integrated national contingency planning capability. The DHS is still building a "joint staff" to conduct planning for its statutory mission (responding to terrorist attacks at home), while the DoD conducts joint strategic planning for its statutory mission to fight wars abroad. But, while the DoD's planning incorporates potential "support" to the DHS and other federal agencies in the event of a domestic attack, and while the DoD has important statutory roles for domestic response under the Stafford Act, there is no national contingency planning process that integrates the highest level DoD and DHS plans.

There is no single plan for integrating DoD and DHS activities in the event of simultaneous catastrophic attacks on the homeland and major theater war overseas. The idea that the DoD's plans would prioritize its overseas missions, within the sovereign territory of other nations, and subordinate its contribution to the domestic response, on our own sovereign territory, would not and should not make any sense to the American people. Yet this is exactly the dynamic that the current set of planning processes encourages. The DoD treats assets (such as strategic airlift to move materiel, mobile hospitals to augment the HHS and VA contingency medical system, or military police for civil order) as tied to its overseas requirements, and will only consider the diversion of such assets for domestic purposes on a case-by-case basis in response to a specific agency request. The DoD will not commit to the allocation of such assets under the DHS or other agency plans. This is a recipe for chaos under the scenario painted above. The orientation of assets in contingency plans is the critical strategic question for guiding the long-term process of training, manning, and equipping government elements for specific missions.

It is also the critical strategic question driving the allocation of resources among response capabilities, and for balancing resources between near-term and long-term requirements. Accordingly, the OMB, working with the DHS and DoD, should supplement an interagency DHS-DoD strategic planning effort with a mechanism for integrating the Future Years Homeland Security Program (FYHSP) and the Future Years Defense Program (FYDP), and, if necessary, should develop a legislative proposal to cement this mechanism. The President should not continue the current practice of nesting separate budget and program review offices within the HSC and NSC, but should allow the OMB—which possesses real budget expertise and wherewithal—to effect such an integration.

The Defense Advanced Research Projects Agency (DARPA) and the Homeland Security Advanced Research Projects Agency (HSARPA) should establish a collaborative relationship on science and technology research that is relevant to both the DoD and DHS. Given that the nation faces one set of strategic risks, the DoD and DHS should establish a joint net assessment office, or at a minimum establish a collaborative relationship between the DoD Net Assessment Office (which under the leadership of Andy Marshall has proven extremely useful over the years) and a new DHS Net Assessment Office nested within IAIP or within the DHS Secretariat. Finally, the DHS should adopt the recommendation of James Carafano, Richard Weitz, and Alane Kochems to establish an Undersecretary for Policy to ensure the coherence of these efforts in partnership with the DoD's Undersecretary for Policy.[92]

2. Address the Cultural Aspect of Institutional Reform—Create "Jointness" in the Interagency. We learned the lesson with the DoD that integrating the military services ultimately required the Goldwater-Nichols reforms to create a culture and personnel system of "jointness." To effect the integration described above requires a similar effort. The President should propose, and the Congress should enact, a process to ensure that senior civilians (GS-15s and members of the Senior Executive Service) and senior military officers (Colonels and higher) within specific specialties, serve tours within the interagency planning apparatus described above, and in interagency entities such as the National Counterterrorism Center. The proposal should include a provision for a National Homeland Security University, which should share the campus at Fort McNair with the long-standing National Defense University. Finally, the DHS should continue its efforts to integrate the disparate personnel systems of the DHS as rapidly as possible, and should ensure that its joint strategic planning capability includes the most talented experts from across its subordinate entities.

3. "Institutionalize Imagination." As the 9/11 Commission asserted in one of its major conclusions, dealing with the threat requires more than planning for our response, but requires imagining the scenarios to which we might be forced to respond.[93] As former Deputy Secretary of Defense John Hamre has noted:

> The missing ingredient in homeland defense today is thoughtful hypothesis formulation. We really don't know for which needles we are looking in the vast haystacks of information. We have a tendency to let the past provide the hypotheses for the future. We are busily connecting the dots that would find the nineteen terrorists who perpetrated the tragedies of September 11, and instead we should be anticipating the concepts and plans of the next terrorist cells.[94]

But how should we accomplish this? First, we should devote the resources necessary to effect intelligence reforms similar to those the 9/11 Commission recommended, and which Congress is currently debating. But secondly, the next strategy should clear up the confusion surrounding DHS' IAIP element. With a National Counterterrorism Center, IAIP is not the government's center of excellence for integrating terrorist intelligence. Instead, IAIP should capitalize on its unique mission to synthesize threat and vulnerability analysis by developing a "core competency" in creative assessment and sophisticated modeling of the threat-vulnerability nexus. IAIP should also build on its unique and holistic understanding of national vulnerability to develop the executive branch's premier independent "red teaming" capability. Many have noted that IAIP has struggled to establish itself within the well-defined domain of terrorism intelligence players. It should cease struggling, and instead establish itself as an intelligence entity that uses its statutory access to terrorism intelligence to operate and think *outside of* the standard counterterrorism community. As Hamre observed, "Data mining is more about hypotheses than it is about technology."[95]

4. Articulate an Overarching Information Architecture for Homeland Security. While technology and data analysis is not sufficient for imagining the threat, it is essential for identifying specific threats, and for building a net assessment grounded in empirical data. The need to "connect the dots" has been cited repeatedly since 9/11, but today, departments and agencies continue to overhaul their existing data systems with a stove-piped approach that avoids effective integration with the systems of other agencies until the latter stages of development. Even the complex "system-of-systems" applications the DHS is fielding, such as US-VISIT, are not being built according to an overarching architecture which spans agency boundaries. The roadblock encountered by the DHS' proposed system for screening airline passengers (the Computer Assisted Passenger Prescreening System—II, or CAPPS-II), after two-and-a-half years of development, is in part a reflection of this. While the CAPPS-II development team was extraordinarily proactive in effecting coordination with other agencies, the system they developed was ultimately a casualty of the fact that the HSC had never coordinated a document which outlined, as a matter of Administration policy, (1) the key parameters for how various systems should address legal and policy questions such as privacy, or (2) a vision, philosophy, or blueprint to guide how various systems should connect with one another.

The HSC, in collaboration with the NSC and OMB, need to coordinate a macro-level vision for an interagency information architecture to drive the parallel development of complex systems. For example, the U.S. Government needs a single "risk-assessment" engine such as that which the National Targeting Center administers (and CAPPS-II would have administered); a single "name-checking" engine such as that which the Terrorist Screening Center administers; a single "biometric-checking" engine such as those the DHS is developing and which relate to legacy systems like the FBI and INS fingerprint databases; a single "terrorist identity" engine such as those administered by the NCTC (formerly TTIC), the Defense Intelligence Agency, and the Joint Interagency Task Force-Counterterrorism (JITF-CT); and a single "metadata" (data about data) standard to ensure disparate systems can talk with one another. The architecture needs to establish the relationship of these components to individual department and agency systems, and provide an integrated interagency mechanism for navigating the complex maze of the differing statutory authorities agencies posses for gathering, processing, sharing, and maintaining information.

Finally, the proposal must tie this architecture to a cross-cutting program management mechanism in the OMB. Under the current approach, the U.S. Government will be no further along 10 years from now in its ability to determine whether a piece of terrorist information it legally possesses relates to any other piece of terrorist information the government legally possesses.

5. Renew the PATRIOT Act "Sunset" Provisions. Technology aside, connecting the dots will be impossible without the PATRIOT Act provisions that enable the sharing of information between intelligence and law enforcement agencies. As reflected in the chapters of this volume, there is a great deal of opinion (much of it ill-informed and distorted) circulating about the PATRIOT Act. Important provisions of the Act are set to expire in December 2005, unless Congress renews them. The Act has been a critical factor in lowering the long-standing "wall" between the intelligence and law enforcement communities, and is one of the most significant elements of the government's ability to prevent another 9/11. The Act updates wiretap laws written in the telephone age, gives the government authorities to fight terrorism which it already possessed to fight organized crime and drugs, and includes substantial provisions for judicial oversight.

Critics argue that the Act grants the government alarming new powers to invade the privacy of citizens, such as secretly obtaining financial information or accessing library records. Fear that the government will abuse these powers has combined with other concerns (Guantanamo detainees, military tribunals, the designation of American citizens captured on U.S. soil as enemy combatants, and the Abu Ghraib prison scandal) to fuel a perception that our government has pursued security at the expense of liberty, and ceded its international moral authority on human rights. Whether this is true or not, what is happening in the public debate over the PATRIOT Act is instructive: when it comes to civil liberties, credibility and perception matter as much as policy—as they should. "Trust us" does not cut it for too long, nor should we expect it to. It would be unfortunate, perhaps tragic, if the Administration's sluggish awakening to that lesson endangers PATRIOT Act provisions that are essential to preventing the next 9/11. The next National Strategy should seek to set the debate about the PATRIOT Act in an objective context, and should include strong measures (such as that which the President recently took under Executive Order 13353) to reestablish public confidence in the government's commitment to protect civil liberties.

   6. Develop the Components Necessary to Perform National Risk Management Across the Full Breadth of Threat and Vulnerability. The preceding discussion has already touched on key elements of this initiative (net assessment, "red-teaming," threat-vulnerability integration, and information sharing), but a less obvious element is the need for concrete, objective performance measures to assess homeland security "outputs" and evaluate agency capabilities. For example, how much security is enough at chemical plant X versus nuclear power plant Y versus port infrastructure Z? Many have written on the need for such metrics, and the *NSHS* also calls for them. The alignment of activities, core competencies and resources to support mission-related outcomes must be complemented by real performance measurement systems. Homeland security involves an array of linkages between multiple agencies at the federal, state, and local levels. Measuring the robustness of these linkages is crucial for identifying areas of fragility that could lead to particularly catastrophic cascading events, such as widespread power outages or domino effect impacts on food supply, emergency preparedness, or information distribution systems.[96] Also, there is not yet a comprehensive set of preparedness standards for measuring first responder capacities, identifying gaps in those capacities, and evaluating progress toward achieving performance goals.[97] In order to assist key agencies in assessing progress towards implementing homeland security efforts, the HSC in collaboration with the OMB should pursue on a priority-basis the development and coordination of performance measures, and link them with agency budgets and strategic planning documents and systems, such as the National Response Plan and National Incident Management System.

   7. Lead International Cooperation to Establish a Multilateral Watch List Mechanism. The security and integrity of the international transportation system is a global public good. The security of the United States is compromised not only when terrorists travel from Charles DeGaulle Airport to LaGuardia, but when they travel from Myanmar to Hamburg. Currently, the United States and many allies and partners possess identifying information on tens of thousands of terrorists and terrorist supporters, but have no mechanism for ensuring that a terrorist traveling through a port-of-entry in one country is not the same person on the terrorist watch list of another, all while safeguarding the integrity of each country's data (some of which, because it is tied to intelligence sources and methods, is among the most sensitive data that countries possess). The United States should lead an international effort to establish a multilateral watch list mechanism, which will act as a repository for encrypted versions (according to a randomly generated encryption key produced by an automated engine under multilateral administration and control) of each participating country's data. Participating countries would bounce encrypted versions of air manifests (filtered through the same automated encryption key) off this repository, and a "hit" would alert the country that owns the terrorist identifying data and allow that country to initiate coordination and appropriate action with the querying country, according to arrangements negotiated in advance between the two. Nations would have an incentive to join because participation would increase their individual national security. For example, Germany's security would be increased when Singapore intercepts a terrorist on America's watch list.

The system should also provide for "silent hits," in which the country which owns the terrorist identifying information can specify that the querying country would receive a "no response" even if the manifest record matches. In other words, the country which owns the terrorist identifying information is solely and always responsible for initiating coordination with other countries in the event of a "hit." This provision would encourage cautious participants worried that individuals or terrorist insiders with access to the system from other countries would "game" the system by intentionally submitting false queries, thereby gleaning highly-sensitive information about what other countries know and don't know. Participants would still have an incentive to join, since the "silent hit" provision would protect their information as it protects others' information, and since theoretically it would also increase their security. For example, Poland's security would be increased when Great Britain secretly begins to monitor a terrorist suspect who "hits" on Great Britain's watch list when a terrorist travels through Warsaw. In practice, countries would likely use this provision very sparingly, since the diplomatic consequences of a terrorist carrying out an attack after a participating country remained silent on a "hit" would be considerable. While the "silent hit" provision would provide a strong incentive for countries to join at the outset, over time, participants will likely shift to the alternative strategy of withholding a small subset of identities from the multilateral mechanism. As the multilateral system leads to the apprehension of terrorists, and as faith in its integrity increases over time, participants will withhold names less frequently.

8. *Lead an International Effort to Build a Global Trading System Resilient to Catastrophic Terrorism.* The United States has made impressive strides advancing pragmatic cooperation within the international community to improve the security of international transportation and trading systems. That said, there is one area in which the dire warnings of Stephen Flynn and others is on target—that the global trading system is dangerously vulnerable to catastrophic terrorism, that the United States and the world would suffer irreparable harm from such an attack, and that the United States has placed insufficient emphasis on the problem. In part, this is a product of the difficulty of the challenge. Solving the problem is not as simple as unilaterally requiring corporations to embed GPS transmitters and chemical detectors in shipping containers, nor attaching radiological detectors on the cranes used to unload cargo ships in ports-of-entry. Solving the problem requires *every significant country* in the international trading system to do the same. The difficulty of such an endeavor is enormous, but it is essential. It is also achievable if the United States focuses on the goal, and brings its wherewithal as the world's largest economy and a technology leader, to bear.

In the meantime, Flynn and others are right to declare that spending in border and transportation security has been insufficient—the agencies which the BTS includes have a decent track record of providing a security return on the dollar invested, and could meaningfully improve security with additional resources. The federal investment is worth it. Finally, Flynn is right in asserting that the federal government must be willing to intervene in the marketplace more aggressively than the first George W. Bush Administration has been willing to do. U.S. corporations, let alone foreign corporations that do substantial business with the United States, will not make the type of dramatic supply chain security improvements Flynn rightfully calls for without a government impetus, and a U.S.-led international effort will lack credibility unless our government is willing to set the bar for global standards of transportation security. The next national strategy should articulate a long-term vision for achieving this goal, and propose specific initiatives that provide stronger incentives for corporations to make the substantial investments required, strengthen the market penalties for failing to make those improvements, and supplement private investment with government investment.

9. Extend North American Security Cooperation. Finally, the next strategy should seek to accelerate and extend the cooperation established between the United States, Canada, and Mexico, to enhance North American security while improving the efficiency of legitimate flows. Ultimately, American security depends on a coordinated North American effort, and we should view our relationships with Canada and Mexico primarily through this lens. The United States has tended to place its diplomatic focus (and its diplomatic talent) on everywhere else but North America. It can no longer afford to do so. The threat of global terrorism makes Canada and Mexico as strategically important as any country in Europe and Asia.

A "Maginot line" border strategy that focuses border enforcement efforts at our land borders is a recipe for failure and will not protect the country from terrorists. We have failed to control the 1,700 mile-long U.S.-Mexican border against drug smuggling and waves of illegal immigrants, let alone a terrorist cell consisting of a handful of sophisticated, motivated persons, or the handful of shipments required to move terrorist materiel. We will never be able to satisfactorily control the 3,000 mile-long U.S.-Canada border, the longest undefended border in the world, regardless of the accuracy of our entry-exit tracking system (US-VISIT) and regardless of the sophistication of our surveillance systems. A team of terrorists is many times smaller than the daily marginal rate of error in a complex "system-of-systems" such as US-VISIT and the other border management systems to which it links. At a minimum, the United States and Canada should establish complementary systems to track the entry and exit of foreign nationals to the North American *continent*, rather than attempt to track them crossing the permeable U.S.-Canada border.

Canada should develop the equivalent of the U.S. Terrorist Screening Center, and both the U.S. and Canadian centers should serve as complementary components of a foundation for a continental network of screening points similar to that which the President directed in HSPD-6, supplemented with HSPD-11, and which the 9/11 Commission recommends. While it may take some time for Mexico to develop the institutional capacity to field an equivalent system, and while such an endeavor poses political challenges to both Canada and Mexico, we should use the breadth of our diplomatic relationship with both countries to provide incentives for pursuing solutions such as these that would provide real improvement in security, and disincentives for not pursuing them.

A more robust agenda for North American cooperation should also contain "next logical steps" for building on the substantial border cooperation steps already taken, and extend collaboration into such important areas as aviation security, incident management and emergency preparedness, and biodefense. For example, such coordination would aim to establish integrated procedures for detecting and responding to animal or human disease outbreaks (e.g., SARS or Mad Cow disease) that could be indicators of a biological attack. To use another example, such coordination would seek to synchronize complementary independent scientific standards for ensuring the security and integrity of identification and "breeder" documents issued by the respective countries.[98]

Conclusion

When considered together, these elements provide useful areas of guidance for an integrated homeland security strategy for the future. As Paul Light—a noted historian of government successes and failures (2002)—observed, "achievement appears to be firmly rooted in a coherent policy strategy. The government's top ten achievements [over the last 50 years] center on a mostly unified regulatory or spending strategy that is anchored in a relatively clear description of the problem to be solved and is supported by enough resources, budgetary or administrative, to succeed."[99] Light goes on to note that throughout its history, the federal government has "largely succeeded by tackling problems and setting audacious goals that were seen as nearly insurmountable . . . There are times when government must embark on endeavors without absolute knowledge of its ultimate success. Those endeavors involve both great risk and great reward, and may be the truest measure of a society's greatness."[100] Clearly, the challenges facing the nation today involve both great risks and rewards. A comprehensive, long-term strategic approach will ultimately determine our ability to respond to these challenges with increasing sophistication and success.

It has been only four years since America awoke to the strategic reality of this age—that a handful of individuals, armed with little more than cunning and resolve, can carry out catastrophic attacks on our own soil. Regardless of our eventual success against al-Qaida and the broader war on terror, this strategic reality will not go away anytime soon. Homeland security is thus a permanent requirement. The difficulties are staggering, but the costs are perhaps more so. More than 200 years ago, Alexander Hamilton penned a famous Federalist Paper to argue that the Constitution would protect against conflict at home, so that geography could protect the nation from conflict abroad. Times have clearly changed. But Hamilton's warning remains prophetic:

> *Safety from external danger is the most powerful director of national conduct. Even the ardent love of liberty will, after a time, give way to its dictates. The violent destruction of life and property incident to war—the continual effort and alarm attendant on a state of continual danger, will compel nations the most attached to liberty, to resort for repose and security, to institutions, which have a tendency to destroy their civil and political rights. To be more safe they, at length, become willing to run the risk of being less free.*
> —Alexander Hamilton, *Federalist Paper No. 8*

Acknowledgments

The views expressed herein are those of the author and do not purport to reflect the position of the United States Military Academy, the Department of the Army, or the Department of Defense.

Notes

1. Senior intelligence officials, background briefing. Office of the Press Secretary, Department of Homeland Security, August 1, 2004, at www.dhs.gov/dhspublic. Since the President issued Homeland Security Presidential Directive-3 (HSPD-3) establishing the Homeland Security Advisory System on March 12, 2002, the United States has raised its national threat level from yellow to orange six times: (1) from September 10 to 24, 2002—around the first anniversary of the 9/11 attacks; (2) from February 7 to 27, 2003—to coincide with the end of the Hajj, an important Muslim religious period; (3) from March 17, 2003 to April 16, 2003—in conjunction with the U.S. invasion of Iraq; (4) from May 20 to 30, 2003—in the wake of terrorist bombings in Saudi Arabia and Morocco; (5) from December 21, 2003 to January 9, 2004—in conjunction with increased terrorist "chatter" over the holiday period; and (6) from August 1, 2004 to present—for the financial services sector in New York and Washington (the first time an orange alert was confined to a specific region and economic sector), as a result of specific, credible intelligence.

2. David Johnston and Douglas Jehl, "CIA Sends Terror Experts to Tell Small Towns of Risk," *New York Times*, July 18, 2004.

3. In addition to President Bush's public statements, the administration has released several documents that aim to comprehensively articulate the White House's assessment of national homeland security efforts, including *Progress Report on the Global War on Terrorism*, September 2003; and *President George W. Bush: A Remarkable Record of Achievement*, August 2004. See www.whitehouse.gov.

4. See www.johnkerry.com/issues/homeland_security.

5. In addition to the *9/11 Commission Final Report*, recent assessments include Stephen Flynn, *America the Vulnerable: How our Government is Failing to Protect Us from Terrorism* (New York: Harper Collins Publishers, 2004); and, to some extent, Richard A. Clarke, *Against All Enemies: Inside America's War on Terror* (New York: Free Press, 2004). A series of both positive and negative assessments, prepared by the Republican and Democratic members, respectively, of the House Select Committee on Homeland Security, can be accessed through the House of Representatives Website. Less recent assessments include Michael O'Hanlon, Peter Orszag, Ivo Daalder, I.M. Destler, David Gunter, James Lindsay, Robert Litan, and James Steinberg, *Protecting the American Homeland: One Year On* (Washington, DC: Brookings Institution Press, 2002); Gary Hart and Warren B. Rudman, *America: Still Unprepared, Still in Danger* (New York: Council on Foreign Relations Press, 2002); and the two most recent reports of the Advisory Panel to Assess Domestic Response Capabilities for Terrorism Involving Weapons of Mass Destruction (the Gilmore Commission), *Implementing the National Strategy* and *Forging America's New Normalcy: Securing Our Homeland, Preserving our Liberty* (Santa Monica,

CA: The RAND Corp., 2002 and 2003). Several other documents evaluate the performance of the Department of Homeland Security in particular, including The Century Foundation, *The Department of Homeland Security's First Year: A Report Card* (New York: The Century Foundation, 2004). These assessments of homeland security policy are outnumbered by the recent series of works offering critical assessments of the Bush administration's foreign and national security policies (including Clarke, *Against all Enemies,* and Anonymous, *Imperial Hubris* [Dulles, VA: Brassey's, Inc., 2004] among many others. These latter works, while relevant, are outside the scope of this chapter.

6. National Commission on Terrorist Attacks upon the United States, *The 9/11 Commission Report* (New York: W.W. Norton & Company, 2004), p. xv.

7. See the Appendix of this volume for a summary of the 9/11 Commission recommendations. Views differ on which issues fall in the "homeland security" policy area and which in the "national security" policy area or indeed whether such a distinction is artificial and problematic. I address that issue later in this chapter. My count of 28 includes recommendations 13 to 41 and is based on the practical standard of which issues, as of today, the HSC (as established in the Homeland Security Act of 2002) coordinates, and which issues the NSC (as established in the National Security Act of 1947) coordinates. It is important to note, however, that many of these issues (for example, terrorism financing, terrorist travel, and intelligence) straddle the charters and membership of both councils, and both councils play a coordinating role.

8. The *National Strategy for Homeland Security* was the first in a series of complementary strategies developed in tandem and released by the White House after 9/11. Members of the NSC and HSC staffs coordinated the basic architecture of how these strategies would fit together in the autumn and winter of 2001. The other strategies are, in order of release, the *National Security Strategy of the United States*, September 2002; the *National Strategy to Combat Weapons of Mass Destruction*, December 2002; the *National Strategy for Combating Terrorism*, February 2003; the *National Strategy for the Physical Protection of Critical Infrastructures and Key Assets*, February 2003; and the *National Strategy to Secure Cyberspace*, February 2003. Several additional strategies, developed by lead agencies and coordinated with the White House and other relevant agencies, establish or articulate national policy. Among these are, for example the *National Money Laundering Strategy*, 2003; and the classified *National Military Strategic Plan for the War on Terrorism*, October 2002. For a general description of how these strategies fit together as a coherent whole, see the *National Strategy for Homeland Security*, p. 5. In addition, the President has issued 12 Homeland Security Presidential Directives (HSPDs) to implement or build upon various elements of these strategies, and has, from time to time, used major speeches to make significant statements of policy or launch major initiatives. For a chronological listing of significant presidential homeland security policy documents since 9/11, see the Appendix of this volume.

9. Patrick Lagadec and Erwan Michel-Kerjan, "A Framework for Senior Executives to Meet the Challenge of Interdependent Critical Networks Under Threat: The Paris Initiative, Anthrax and Beyond" (draft), Center for Risk Management and Decision Processes, The Wharton School, University of Pennsylvania, 2004, p. 7, grace. wharton.upenn.edu/risk.

10. RAND Center for Terrorism Risk Management Policy, *Terrorism Risk Management Theory and Policy*, 2004, www.rand.org/multi/ctrmp/pubs/theory.html.

11. A growing body of scholarship is beginning to describe the theoretical contours of a fundamentally new international system. See Robert Cooper, *The Breaking of Nations: Order and Chaos in the Twenty-First Century* (New York: Atlantic Monthly Press, 2003).

12. The *National Strategy for Homeland Security* incorporates the notion of dynamic uncertainty on page 2 (in the paragraph entitled "Reduce America's Vulnerability") and in the chapter entitled "Threat and Vulnerability," pp. 7–10.

13. Stephen Flynn, *America the Vulnerable: How our Government is Failing to Protect us from Terrorism* (New York: Harper Collins Publishers, 2004), pp. 60–64.

14. James B. Steinberg, "Necessary Priorities for Homeland Security: Framing a Comprehensive Strategy" in *Planning to Win: A Report on Homeland Security*, ed. Aspen Strategy Group (Aspen, CO: Aspen Strategy Group, 2002), pp. 24–25.

15. George W. Bush, *The Department of Homeland Security* (Washington, DC: The White House, 2004), pp. 6–7.

16. See the Web sites of the National Transportation Safety Board, which tracks aviation incidents for the Department of Transportation, and the National Response Center, which tracks hazardous material incidents for the U.S. Coast Guard, www.ntsb.gov/aviation/Stats.htm, and www.nrc.uscg.mil/stats.html, respectively.

17. Since the mid-1990s, the New York City Police Department's primary strategic management tool to predict and prevent crime, Compstat, has relied on extensive crime statistics, updated weekly, from across the city's precincts. The Compstat model has been adopted by many police departments nationwide. For a glimpse at the richness of crime data, see the Bureau of Justice statistics Web site, www.ojp.gov/bjs/welcome.html.

18. See National Commission on Terrorist Attacks upon the United States, *9/11 Commission Report*, pp. 344–348, for discussion of the "institutionalization of imagination."

19. For a cogent description of this requirement, see Center for Strategic and International Studies, *Meeting the Challenges of Establishing a New Department of Homeland Security: A CSIS White Paper* (Washington, DC: CSIS, 2002), pp. 6–7.

20. A variety of sources provide good overviews of the gaps and shortcomings in government homeland security capabilities prior to 9/11. Of note: chapters three, six and eleven of the *9/11 Commission Report*; Bush, *The Department of Homeland Security*; Ashton B. Carter and John P. White, ed., *Keeping the Edge: Managing Defense for the Future* (Cambridge, MA: The MIT Press, 2000), particularly chapter one; United States Commission on National Security/21st Century (the Hart-Rudman Commission), *Road Map for National Security: Imperative for Change* (Alexandria, VA: U.S. Commission on National Security/21st Century, 2001), as well as the study addendum; and Richard A. Falkenrath, Robert D. Newman, and Bradley A. Thayer, *America's Achilles' Heel: Nuclear, Biological, and Chemical Terrorism and Covert Attack* (Cambridge, MA: The MIT Press, 1998).

21. For the starkest version of this argument, see Richard A. Clarke, *Against All Enemies,* (New York: Free Press, 2004), p. 249.

22. Ibid.

23. With the exception of the agencies created by the National Security Act and FEMA, these examples are drawn primarily from Paul Light, *Government's Greatest Achievements: From Civil Rights to Homeland Security* (Washington, DC: The Brookings Institution, 2002), pp. 62–164. To be fair, in other writings Light has drawn careful distinctions between these examples and DHS, but the history of government organization provides examples of both success and failure that are relevant to homeland security and the creation of DHS.

24. Arthur Schlesinger, Jr., "Democracy and Leadership," *The Cycles of American History* (Boston: Houghton Mifflin Company, 1986), p. 430.

25. See John Deutch, Arnold Kanter, Brent Scowcroft, with Chris Hornbarger, "Strengthening the National Security Interagency Process," in *Keeping the Edge,* ed. Ashton B. Carter and John P. White (Cambridge, MA: MIT Press, 2001), pp. 268–9, and Philip Zelikow "Homeland Security: The White House Plan Explained and Examined" (A Brookings Institution forum with Richard A. Falkenrath, James B. Steinberg, Ruth A. David, Michael E. O'Hanlon, Peter R. Orszag, and Philip Zelikow, September 4, 2002), www.brookings.edu/comm/events/20020904homeland.htm.

26. National Commission on Terrorist Attacks, *9/11 Commission Report,* pp. 400–403.

27. Flynn, *America the Vulnerable,* p. 51.

28. Antulio J. Echevarria II and Bert B. Tussing, *From "Defending Forward" to a "Global Defense-in-Depth:" Globalization and Homeland Security* (Carlisle, PA: Strategic Studies Institute, 2003), p. 10.

29. 9/11 Commission, *9/11 Commission Report,* p. 363.

30. There is some confusion between the terms Office of Homeland Security (OHS) and Homeland Security Council (HSC). President Bush, using his maximum legal authority, established OHS and HSC by Executive Order 13228 of October 8, 2001, "Establishing the Office of Homeland Security and the Homeland Security Council." The order created an office (OHS) within the Executive Office of the President, headed by an Assistant to the President for Homeland Security (commonly referred to as the Homeland Security Advisor) to coordinate homeland security policy in much the same manner that the NSC coordinates national security policy. The President appointed Tom Ridge as the first Homeland Security Advisor. Because the government lacked real capability for key homeland security tasks, Executive Order 13228 arguably gave the OHS numerous responsibilities normally the province of agencies subject to direct congressional oversight. While White House Counsel drew a careful legal line (and successfully defended its interpretation in federal court) to ensure that the Office of Homeland Security would restrict its activities to advising the President and coordinating policy (hence retaining the prerogative of executive privilege), the Office's level of coordination in some areas, by necessity, extended down to very detailed, specific levels. Executive Order 13228 also created a council (the HSC) consisting of the President; the Vice President; the Attorney General; the Secretaries of the Treasury, Defense, Health and Human Services, Transportation; the Directors of FEMA, FBI, and CIA; and the Homeland Security Advisor. The order also provided that certain high-level members of the President's and Vice President's staffs (such as the White House Chief of Staff and the National Security Advisor) could attend HSC meetings, and other officials would be invited to attend as appropriate: the Secretaries of State,

Agriculture, Interior, Energy, Labor, Commerce, and Veterans Affairs; the Administrator of the EPA; certain high-level Presidential advisors; and other officials as necessary. Prior to the President's June 6, 2002, proposal to create the DHS, there were a growing number in Congress who advocated ensconcing the OHS in statute, both to give the OHS real authority (particularly budget authority), and to strengthen Congressional oversight. The President's proposal for the DHS shifted the vast majority of OHS' operational responsibilities to a department, led by a Senate-confirmed Secretary, and subject to Congressional oversight, leaving the OHS with the White House staff's appropriate role to advise the President and coordinate policy across agencies. Nonetheless, the effort to codify the OHS in statute and make it a quasi-independent entity similar to the Office of Management and Budget, persisted. Thus, during the legislative process, the President's staff worked with Congress to incorporate a provision in the Homeland Security Act (Title IX) that would ensconce the HSC in statute, but, using language analogous to that used in the National Security Act of 1947, would give the President and future Presidents broad latitude in structuring the staff that would support the HSC. After the President signed the Homeland Security Act into law on November 25, 2002, the OHS, mirroring the long-standing practice of the NSC staff, began referring to itself as the HSC staff. As with the NSC, the term HSC is now frequently used to refer to both the council itself, and the staff that supports it. While the Homeland Security Advisor, the HSC staff, and most others no longer refer to the "Office of Homeland Security," the President has issued no order or directive abolishing the term.

31. The fact that the President's powers are weaker than those enjoyed by the chief executives of most other democratic countries is by constitutional design, and reflects the founding fathers' concern that a unitary executive would replicate the tyranny of the British monarchy—a concern that remains strong in American political culture. American's apprehension about combining foreign and domestic intelligence is remarkable when compared to our closest allies, both politically and culturally (Great Britain, Canada, and Australia), which all have organizations which either combine foreign or domestic intelligence into a single ministry (Canada and Australia), or which are devoted to domestic intelligence (Great Britain's MI-5).

32. *Public Law 235–61 Stat. 496; U.S.C. 402: The National Security Act of 1947,* as amended in 1949, 1953, 1958, and 1986.

33. Alexander Hamilton, "Federalist Paper No. 70: Concerning the Constitution of the President: The Same Subject Continued in Relation to the Unity of the Executive, with an Examination of the Project of an Executive Council," in *The Essential Federalist and Anti-Federalist Papers,* ed. David Wootton (Indianapolis, IN: Hackett Publishing Company, Inc., 2003), p. 277.

34. Bush, *The Department of Homeland Security,* p. 9.

35. For students of military strategy, consider Clausewitz's famous dictum that the maximum number of maneuver elements a commander can effectively control in combat is five. No military commander could imagine commanding 11 subordinate maneuver elements, notwithstanding the fact that a commander's relative power over his units far exceeds the President's power over his Cabinet and bureaucracy. For proof of this

point, turn to Richard Neustadt's classic treatise, *Presidential Power and the Modern Presidents* (New York, The Free Press, 1990).

36. It is interesting to consider that Tom Ridge is perhaps the first Assistant to the President who was a nationally recognized politician (indeed, considered a likely pick for Vice President) when he joined the White House staff. Many factors likely affected the President's selection of Ridge, but among them was probably the notion that a former Congressman and Governor was appropriate given the extraordinary degree to which homeland security policy intersects with domestic policy. Ridge, a national political figure, could also serve the role of reassuring the American public, which had never before been the job of Presidential advisors but which was consistent with the substantial "operational" responsibilities the President assigned to Ridge in Executive Order 13228. Moreover, Ridge could theoretically use his stature to act with implicit authority, given that Presidential staff rarely have any formal authority, to coordinate the activities of the executive branch on an equal footing with the President's Cabinet. It is useful to evaluate the President's selection of Ridge through the lens of Neustadt's thesis in *Presidential Power*.

37. President Bush maintained the Counterterrorism Security Group (CSG) in National Security Presidential Directive-1 (NSPD-1), though he adjusted its responsibilities and added a supervisory layer between himself and the CSG. The CSG convenes via video-teleconference at least once a day, and meets at least once a week.

38. William Jefferson Clinton, Presidential Decision Directive-39 (PDD-39), "U.S. Policy on Counterterrorism," June 21, 1995; PDD-62, "Protection Against Unconventional Threats to the Homeland and Americans Overseas" (unclassified extract), May 22, 1998; PDD-63, "Critical Infrastructure Protection," May 22, 1998; PDD-67, "Enduring Constitutional Government and Continuity of Government," October 21, 1998.

39. Clarke, *Against All Enemies,* p. 249.

40. National Commission on Terrorist Attacks upon the United States, *9/11 Commission Report,* p. 213.

41. Bush, *The Department of Homeland Security*, p. 9.

42. Aaron Wildavsky, "The Two Presidencies," *Trans-Action* 4 no. 2 (December 1966), rpt. in ed. Aaron Wildavsky, *Perspectives on the Presidency* (Boston, MA: Little, Brown and Co., 1975), p. 448.

43. Ibid., pp. 448–9.

44. Paul Martin, "Changing Government: Prime Minister Announces Appointment of Cabinet," press release, Canada Privy Council Office, Ottawa, Ontario, Canada, December 12, 2003, www1.pm.gc.ca/eng/news.asp?id=2.

45. The second volume of Henry Kissinger's biography provides a vivid illustration of the substantial difference between the President's domestic and foreign policy powers. On page 1, 124, Kissinger asserts that President Nixon, distracted by the Watergate scandal and sapped of credibility and potency in domestic affairs, increasingly turned to foreign policy, both in the Middle East and with China, to bolster his presidency. Nixon was able to effectively exercise the presidency's foreign policy powers, even though he was crippled domestically. See Henry Kissinger, *Years of Upheaval* (Boston, MA: Little, Brown and COmpany, 1982).

46.   Examples include programs which the DHS' Bureau of Customs and Border Protection administers, including the Customs-Trade Partnership on Terrorism (C-TPAT), which provides incentives to companies to improve their supply-chain security from point of origin to destination, and the Free and Secure Trade (FAST) program, an initiative developed by the United States and Canada as part of the U.S.-Canada Smart Border Declaration and Action Plan, and subsequently expanded to the U.S-Mexican border. FAST requires participating corporations to adopt supply-chain security measures, subject their truck drivers to background checks by the DHS and the Canadian Border Security Agency (CBSA), and electronically transmit their shipping manifests to the Bureau of Customs and Border Protection (or the CBSA if transiting into Canada). In exchange, FAST shipments are pre-cleared by Customs officials, are subject to a lower rate of random inspection, and the trucks (equipped with transponders) are able to pass across the border without stopping.

47.   In this respect, the argument Stephen Flynn makes in *America the Vulnerable* (that we should integrate security into the global trading and transportation system like we integrate safety into aviation) is relevant and useful.

48.   National Commission on Terrorist Attacks, *9/11 Commission Report,* p. 421. Since the writing of this chapter, both the House of Representatives and the Senate have passed resolutions restructuring the homeland security and intelligence oversight committees, effective with the convening of the 109th Congress. Senate Resolution 445 changed the Senate Committee on Governmental Affairs to the Senate Committee on Homeland Security and Government Affairs, currently chaired by Senator Susan Collins (R-ME). House Resolution 5 changed the House Select Committee on Homeland Security to the House Committee on Homeland Security, currently chaired by Representative Chris Cox (R-CT).

49.   This point is akin to the argument in Anonymous, *Imperial Hubris.* Anonymous also ties homeland security to our policy on Israel and Palestine and our failure to achieve energy self-sufficiency.

50.   Again, see Bush, *National Strategy for Homeland Security*, p. 5 for a description of how the *NSS, NSHS,* and subordinate strategies relate to one another.

51.   Carl von Clausewiz, *On War* (NJ: Princeton University Press, 1976), p. 128.

52.   Echevarria and Tussing, *From Defending "Forward,"* p. 3.

53.   *National Strategy for Homeland Security*, pp. 21–23 and 59–61. At the time, Executive Order 13228, establishing the Office of Homeland Security, and Homeland Security Presidential Directive-1 (HSPD-1), "Organization and Operation of the Homeland Security Council," defined the operation of the HSC Deputies Committee.

54.   To some extent, the division of responsibility between the HSC and NSC on international issues has helped maintain this pragmatic undercurrent of homeland security cooperation, though it requires constant and sometimes complicated coordination with the regional bureaus in the NSC and State Department.

55.   Ernest May, *American Cold War Strategy: Interpreting NSC-68* (Boston, MA: Bedford/St. Martin's, 1993), pp. 16–17.

56.   For example, see Robert S. Kaplan and David P. Norton, *The Strategy-Focused Organization: How Balanced Scorecard Companies Thrive in the New Business Environment* (Boston, MA: Harvard Business School Press, 2001). The Web site of Yale University's Grand Strategy Project captures this range: "Traditionally believed

to belong to and best-developed in the politico-military and governmental realms, the concept of grand strategy applies—and [the International Security Studies program] believes is essential—to a broad spectrum of human activities, not least those of international institutions, non-governmental organizations, and private businesses and corporations;" www.yale.edu/iss/grandstrategyproject.html.

57. Bernard Brodie, "Strategy as an Art and Science," *Naval War College Review,* September 18, 1958, www.au.af.mil/au/awc/awcgate/theorists/brodie1.htm.

58. Ibid.

59. Ernest R. May and Richard E. Neustadt, *Thinking in Time: The Uses of History for Decision Makers* (New York: The Free Press, 1986), p. 37. The historical method May and Neustadt outline has enormous utility to a solid analysis of the homeland security problem. For example, comparing the "likenesses" and "differences" between homeland security and the analogies discussed in the first section of this chapter is an extremely instructive exercise that underscores the point that analogies disguise the degree of uncertainty in homeland security. Outlining the "known," "uncertain," and "presumed" as May and Neustadt suggest (first as we understood the facts on 9/11, and as we understand them now in the wake of the 9/11 Commission Report), is equally instructive.

60. Critics who assert that the President proposed the DHS purely for political purposes should consider that Governor Ridge and the OHS staff, and perhaps more importantly, the White House Chief of Staff and the Office of the Vice President (who were appropriately and closely monitoring the efforts and growing pains of the nascent OHS), heeded the criticism of the departments and agencies: that the OHS staff was "shooting from the hip" and not thinking *comprehensively enough* about how to organize for homeland security.

61. That said, several evaluations of the *National Strategy for Homeland Security* have lauded its conceptual clarity and substantive content. The ANSER Institute for Homeland Security: "the Strategy should be judged against its declared intent, and not against an academic concept of how a strategy should be designed. Does [the *NSHS*] provide a useful framework to understand what must be done, who must do it, and what actions are required to get started? Our judgment is 'Yes.'" (Dave McIntyre, *The National Strategy for Homeland Security: Finding the Path among the Trees* [Arlington, VA: ANSER Institute for Homeland Security, 2002]; Peter Orszag, former economist in the Clinton Administration: ". . . as an economist I'm particularly heartened by the general approach in the strategy of weighing costs and benefits. In particular, language like 'it is not practical or possible to eliminate all of the risks.' There will always be some level of risk that cannot be mitigated without the use of unacceptably large expenditures I think is exactly right" (Brookings Institution, "Homeland Security: The White House Plan Explained and Examined," September 4, 2002); Stephen Flynn: "The logic underpinning the strategy is laudable," (*Creating the Department of Homeland Security: Rethinking the Ends and Means* [New York: The Century Foundation, 2002]); the GAO: "On the whole, the *National Strategy for Homeland Security* and the *National Strategy for the Physical Protection of Critical Infrastructures and Key Assets* address the greatest number of the desirable characteristics [of any effective national strategy]" (GAO, *Combating Terrorism: Evaluation of Selected Characteristics of National Strategies Related to Terrorism*, GAO-04-408T,

[Washington, DC: GAO, February 3, 2004]); Frank Hoffman, in this volume: "The strategy . . . is remarkable compare to typical Beltway policy pronouncements. Unlike most strategic documents, the homeland security strategy goes well beyond platitudes and generalities. It does not shy away from identifying ends, and articulates many steps towards those goals. Even more startling, it talks about priorities."

62. Bush, *National Strategy for Homeland Security*, pp. viii-xii.

63. Titles VII and VIII of the Homeland Security Act reinforce this resource structure, and mandate a Future Years Homeland Security Program analogous to the DoD's Future Years Defense Program.

64. A variety of critics and scholars have noted that the President issued the *National Strategy for Homeland Security after* he proposed the DHS, and cite this fact as evidence that it was merely a sales document for the DHS proposal. In fact, a small team in the President's HSC staff, led by Richard Falkenrath (then Special Assistant to the President and Senior Director for Policy and Plans in the HSC; later the Deputy Homeland Security Advisor), developed the framework of the *National Strategy for Homeland Security* and many of its initiatives prior to beginning work on the DHS proposal, then shifted gears to work on the DHS and Homeland Security Act, and then returned its focus to the strategy. Incidentally, this same team prepared the earlier border consolidation proposal upon which much of the design of the BTS was based. That the strategy so thoroughly incorporates the DHS proposal is not an artifact of after-the-fact packaging, but a reflection of the conceptual clarity that ties the strategy and the DHS together.

65. The President's proposal named the science and technology bureau Chemical, Biological, Radiological and Nuclear Terrorism, consistent with the "catastrophic threat" mission area articulated in the *National Strategy for Homeland Security*. See Bush, *The Department of Homeland Security*, p. 2.

66. The former Deputy National Security Advisor to President Clinton, James Steinberg, agrees: "Establishing the necessary priorities for homeland security must flow from a strategic framework that sets out an overall concept and a plan for implementation. . . . The challenge we face is to maintain a balance between meeting the urgent short-term threat while preparing ourselves for a long-term challenge of meeting a constantly changing and dynamic threat" (Aspen Institute, *Planning to Win: A Report on Homeland Security from the Aspen Strategy Group*, pp. 32–33).

67. See Amy Zegart, *Flawed by Design* (Palo Alto, CA: Stanford Univeristy Press, 2000).

68. Bush, *The Department of Homeland Security*, pp. 1–3. See also U.S. Congress, *Public Law 107–296—Homeland Security Act of 2002*, November 25, 2002. For overviews on the complexity of creating DHS, see Michael E. O'Hanlon; Peter R. Orszag; Ivo H. Daalder; I. M. Destler; David L. Gunter; James M. Lindsay; Robert E. Litan; James B. Steinberg, *Protecting the American Homeland: One Year On* (Washington, DC: Brookings Institution Press, 2002) pp. ix-xxxvii; Ivo H. Daalder; I. M. Destler; Paul C. Light; James M. Lindsay; Robert E. Litan; Michael E. O'Hanlon; Peter R. Orszag, James B. Steinberg, *Assessing the Department of Homeland Security* (Washington, DC: Brookings Institution Press, 2002); and Center for Strategic and International Studies, *Meeting the Challenges of Establishing a New Department of Homeland Security: A CSIS White Paper* (Washington, DC: CSIS, 2002).

69. Clarke, *Against All Enemies*, p. 251.

70. United States Department of Homeland Security. *Budget in Brief: Fiscal Year 2005* (Washington, DC: Department of Homeland Security, 2004), pp. 18–69.

71. President Hoover proposed border consolidation in his 1929 State of the Union Address, and proposed nearly identical plans to Congress in 1930 and 1932. The Customs Service commissioned the McKinsey Company in 1948 to develop a border consolidation proposal. In 1972, President Nixon proposed Government Reorganization Plan #2, which sought to consolidate border responsibility under the Department of the Treasury. In 1973, 1977, 1985 and 1993, the Government Accountability Office issued reports calling on consolidation. In 1974, the OMB proposed that Customs exercise single-agency management of the U.S.-Mexico border. In 1977, President Carter's Reorganization Project proposed a single border management agency. In 1981, former Attorney General Griffin Bell proposed transferring the Border Patrol to Customs. In 1983, the presidentially chartered Grace Commission recommended a single border agency. In 1988, Senate Bill 2205 and House Bill 4230 would have consolidated Customs, INS, and the Coast Guard under the Department of the Treasury. In 1993, President Clinton's National Performance Report issued a report titled *Improved Border Management* called for creation of a single, independent border agency if existing agencies did not effect substantial improvements within two years. Finally, the Hart/Rudman Commission's 2001 report called for creation of a National Homeland Security Agency with sole responsibility for border management.

72. The degree to which the policy community has accepted the intrinsic merit of border consolidation is remarkable given the near unanimous agency opposition to OHS' January 2002 proposal for a federal border agency. This is similar to the Goldwater-Nichols Act of 1986, which all of the military services vehemently opposed at the time, but which they now tout as a critical step towards achieving jointness. The conventional wisdom is that this is an endemic Washington phenomena that reflects the parochialism of self-interested agencies seeking to protect agency equities and turf. However, I judged that there was more than mere parochialism motivating agency opposition to the OHS' original border proposal. Rather, departments and agencies rightfully fight for the ability to carry-out their statutory authority. This is what we expect them to do–aggressively ensure they can do their job. Until the Congress changes an agency's statutory role, the agency will understandably fight to protect the authorities and subordinate entities (many of which agencies took the initiative to create) that enable it to fulfill that role. This is why broad institutional change is so difficult to initiate within the executive branch. Not because officials are primarily narrow-minded and turf-conscious, but because good people are doing everything they can to carry out their unique responsibilities, and usually don't have the luxury of time to step back and thoroughly consider the benefits of adjusting or shifting those responsibilities.

73. Since completion of this article, the Congress passed S. 2845, the Intelligence Reform and Terrorism Prevention Act of 2004. The President signed the act, which became Public Law 108–458, on December 17, 2004.

74. See Clarke, *Against All Enemies,* p. 250. The text of Senator Lieberman's proposed bill, S.1534, the Department of National Homeland Security Act of 2001, see thomas.loc.gov/cgi-bin/query/z?c107:S.1534.

75. United States Commission on National Security/21st Century (the Hart-Rudman Commission), *Road Map for National Security: Imperative for Change* (Alexandria, VA: U.S. Commission on National Security/21st Century, 2001), pp. 14–23. In response to the Hart/Rudman final report, Representative Mac Thornberry (R-TX) introduced H.R. 1158, the National Homeland Security Agency Act of 2001, on March 21, 2001.

76. Marguerite-Marie Dubois, cited in David Jablonsky, "The State of the National Security State," in *Parameters, Winter 2002–2003* (Carlisle, PA: U.S. Army War College, 2003), p. 17.

77. United States Government Accountability Office (GAO), *Homeland Security: Observations on the National Strategies Related to Terrorism*, GAO-04-1075T (Washington, DC, 2004).

78. Bush, *The Department of Homeland Security*, p. 9.

79. National Commission on Terrorist Attacks, GAO, *9/11 Commission Report,* p. 387.

80. Bush, Homeland Security Presidential Directive-6, September 16, 2003.

81. The Secretary of State, the Attorney General, the Secretary of Homeland Security, and the Director of Central Intelligence, *Memorandum of Understanding on the Integration and Use of Screening Information to Protect against Terrorism* (unclassified extract) (Washington, DC: The Department of Justice, 2003).

82. Additionally, the Intelligence Reform and Terrorism Prevention Act of 2004 includes Sections 7211 to 7214, giving the federal government the authority to establish minimum national standards for the integrity, security, and data on social security cards, birth certificates, and drivers' licenses. While little attention has been paid to these sections, the Section 7211–7214 provisions will greatly facilitate implementation of both HSPD-6 and HSPD-11 and enable the Terrorist Screening Center to perform its mission.

83. National Commission on Terrorist Attacks, 9/11 Commission Report, p. 391, and Bush, Homeland Security Presidential Directive-7 (HSPD-7), "Critical Infrastructure Identification, Prioritization, and Protection," December 17, 2003.

84. National Commission on Terrorist Attacks, *9/11 Commission Report,* p. 390.

85. Hamre, p. 22.

86. National Commission on Terrorist Attacks, *9/11 Commission Report,* p. 365.

87. Flynn, *America the Vulnerable,* p. 15.

88. See Russell D. Howard, "Preemptive Military Doctrine: No Other Choice against Transnational, Non-State Actors," in *Through Alternative Lenses: Current Debates in International Relations,* ed. Daniel J. Kaufman, Jay M. Parker, Patrick V. Howell, and Kimberly C. Field (Boston, MA: McGraw-Hill, 2004).

89. Flynn, *America the Vulnerable,* p. 164.

90. Since completion of this chapter, and as noted earlier, the Intelligence Reform and Terrorism Prevention Act of 2004 (S.2845, P.L. 108–458) became law on December 17, 2004, and includes Sections 7211 to 7214, giving the federal government the authority to establish minimum national standards for the integrity, security, and data on social security cards, birth certificates, and drivers' licenses. While little attention has been paid to these sections, the Section 7211–7214 provisions will greatly facilitate imple-

mentation of both HSPD-6 and HSPD-11, enable the Terrorist Screening Center to perform its mission, and over time will directly address the wide disparity of standards in state-issued "breeder" identification documents. See also the Congressional Research Service, *Report RL32722—Intelligence Reform and Terrorism Prevention Act of 2004: National Standards for Drivers' Licenses, Social Security Cards, and Birth Certificates,* Washington, DC: Library of Congress, 6, 2005).

91. There have been a broad range of studies, articles, and reports criticizing the *National Strategy for Homeland Security* and the DHS for a lack of performance metrics (and this chapter adds to that chorus), but it's important to note that developing and applying performance metrics requires that you first have the organizations right, and that those organizations have some track-record of objective performance data (as noted earlier in the second section of this chapter). The *Natiunal Strategy for Homeland Security* discusses the need for performance measures, but rightfully states that the development of specific performance measures is not the province of presidential strategy, but of agencies with operational responsibilities, expertise, and experience. The OMB, HSC, DHS and the other agencies with substantial homeland security responsibilities have made the development and application of such measures a priority in implementing the strategy, but absent some foundation, they are in many cases starting from scratch or close to it. That said, this chapter argues that the development and implementation of objective performance measures is critical to the next phase of the homeland security effort, and are particularly essential to ensuring that DHS evolves along the right path.

92. James Jay Carafano, *Homeland Security Dollars and Sense #1: Current Spending Formulas Waste Aid to States* (Washington, DC: The Heritage Foundation, 2004).

93. National Commission on Terrorist Attacks, *9/11 Commission Report,* pp. 339–348.

94. John J. Hamre, "Homeland Defense: A Net Assessment," in *Planning to Win: A Report on Homeland Security* (Aspen, CO: Aspen Strategy Group, 2002), p. 20.

95. Ibid., p. 19.

96. Normal J. Rabkin, Testimony before the Subcommittee on National Security, Emerging Threats, and International Relations, Committee on Government Reform, House of Representatives, September 22, 2004.

97. Ibid., p. 16.

98. Thus, the Secretary of Homeland Security and Canada's Minister of Public Safety and Emergency Preparedness would seek to align the authorities of the U.S. federal government to set minimum national standards for birth certificates, social security cards, and drivers' licenses (authorities granted to the federal government in Sections 7211–7214 of P.L. 108–458, the Intelligence Reform and Terrorism Prevention Act of 2004) with similar authorities and standards in Canada. Such an effort would be typical of the type of laborious, detailed, unglamorous (yet extremely meaningful) U.S.-Canadian coordination that has been underway since 9/11, and which is absolutely essential to both countries' security.

99. Paul Light, *Government's Greatest Achievements: From Civil Rights to Homeland Security* (Washington, DC: The Brookings Institution, 2002), p. 63.

100. Ibid., p. 65.

References

Advisory Panel to Assess Domestic Response Capabilities for Terrorism Involving Weapons of Mass Destruction [Gilmore Commission]. *First Annual Report to Congress, Assessing the Threat.* Arlington, VA: RAND Corporation, 1999.

———. *Fifth Annual Report to Congress, America's New Normalcy: Securing Our Homeland, Protecting Our Liberty.* Arlington, VA: RAND Corporation, 2003.

———. *Fourth Annual Report to Congress, Implementing the National Strategy.* Arlington, VA: RAND Corporation, 2002.

———. *Second Annual Report to Congress, Toward a National Strategy for Combating Terrorism.* Arlington, VA: RAND Corporation, 2000.

———. *Third Annual Report to Congress, For Ray Downey.* Arlington, VA: RAND Corp., 2001.

Allison, Graham. *Nuclear Terrorism: The Ultimate Preventable Catastrophe.* New York, NY: Times Books, 2004.

American Enterprise Institute. "The Battle for Ideas in the U.S. War on Terrorism." Conference transcript. Washington, DC: American Enterprise Institute, October 29, 2001, www.aei.org/events/filter.,eventID.364/transcript.asp.

Anonymous. *Imperial Hubris: Why the West is Losing the War on Terror.* Washington, DC: Brassey's, Inc., 2004.

Aspen Institute. *Planning to Win: A Report on Homeland Security from the Aspen Strategy Group,* 2002, www.aspeninstitute.org/bookdetails.asp?i=55&d=112.

Brodie, Bernard. "Strategy as an Art and Science" *Naval War College Review,* 1959, www.au.af.mil/au/awc/awcgate/theorists/brodie1.htm.

Brookings Institution. "Homeland Security: The White House Plan Explained and Examined." A Brookings Institution forum with Richard A. Falkenrath, James B. Steinberg, Ruth A. David, Michael E. O'Hanlon, Peter R. Orszag, and Philip Zelikow, September 4, 2002, www.brookings.edu/comm/events/20020904homeland.htm.

Bush, George W. *Biodefense for the 21st Century,* April 28, 2004.

———. Executive Order 13221. October 8, 2001.

———. Executive Order 13228. October 8, 2001.

———. Executive Order 13284, "Amendment of Executive Orders, and Other Actions, in Connection With the Establishment of the Department of Homeland Security." January 23, 2003.

———. Executive Order 13286, "Amendment of Executive Orders, and Other Actions, in Connection With the Transfer of Certain Functions to the Secretary of Homeland Security." February 28, 2003.

———. Executive Order 13311, "Homeland Security Information Sharing." July 29, 2003.

———. Executive Order 13323, "Assignment of Functions Relating to Arrivals in and Departures From the United States." December 20, 2003.

———. Executive Order 13353, "Establishing the President's Board on Safeguarding Americans' Civil Liberties." August 27, 2004.

———. Executive Order 13354, "National Counterterrorism Center." August 27, 2004.

———. Executive Order 13355, "Strengthened Management of the Intelligence Community." August 27, 2004.

———. Executive Order 13356, "Strengthening the Sharing of Terrorism Information to Protect Americans." August 27, 2004.

―――. *Fact Sheet: G-8 Secure and Facilitated International Travel Initiative.* June 9, 2004. www.g8usa.gov/f_060904g.htm.

―――. *G8 Action Plan: Enhance Transport Security and Control of Man Portable Air Defense Systems (MANPADS).* 2003. www.g8.fr/evian/english/navigation/news/news_update/enhance_transport_security_and_control_of_man-portable_air_defence_systems_-_man-pads_-_a_g8_action_plan.html.

―――. *G-8 Secure and Facilitated International Travel Initiative.* June 9, 2004. www.white-house.gov/news/releases/2004/06/20040609.

―――. *G-8 Transportation Security Initiative.* June 26–27, 2002. www.useu.be/Categories/Transportation/June2602G8TransportSecurity.html.

―――. Homeland Security Presidential Directive-1 (HSPD-1), "Organization and Operation of the Homeland Security Council." October 29, 2001.

―――. Homeland Security Presidential Directive-3 (HSPD-3), "Homeland Security Advisory System." Washington, DC: The White House, March 12, 2002.

―――. Homeland Security Presidential Directive-5 (HSPD-5), "Management of Domestic Incidents." February 28, 2003.

―――. Homeland Security Presidential Directive-6 (HSPD-6), "Integration and Use of Screening Information to Protect against Terrorism." September 16, 2003.

―――. Homeland Security Presidential Directive-7 (HSPD-7), "Critical Infrastructure Identification, Prioritization, and Protection." December 17, 2003.

―――. Homeland Security Presidential Directive-8 (HSPD-8), "National Preparedness." December 17, 2003.

―――. Homeland Security Presidential Directive-9 (HSPD-9), "Defense of United States Agriculture and Food." February 3, 2004.

―――. Homeland Security Presidential Directive-11 (HSPD-11), "Comprehensive Terrorist-Related Screening Procedures." August 27, 2004.

―――. Homeland Security Presidential Directive-12 (HSPD-12), "Policy for a Common Identification Standard for Federal Employees and Contractors." August 27, 2004.

―――. *National Security Strategy of the United States.* 2002.

―――. *National Strategy for Combating Terrorism.* 2003.

―――. *National Strategy for Combating Weapons of Mass Destruction* (unclassified version; also referred to as Homeland Security Presidential Directive-4). 2002.

―――. *National Strategy for Homeland Security.* 2002.

―――. *National Strategy for the Physical Protection of Critical Infrastructures and Key Assets.* Washington, DC: The White House, 2003.

―――. *National Strategy to Secure Cyberspace.* 2003.

―――. *Securing our Homeland: Strengthening the Nation.* 2002.

―――. State of the Union Address. January 29, 2002.

―――. State of the Union Address. January 27, 2003.

―――. *The Department of Homeland Security.* Washington, DC: The White House, 2004.

―――. *United States-Canada Smart Border Declaration: Building a Smart Border for the 21st Century on the Foundation of a North American Zone of Confidence.* Ottawa, Ontario, Canada: The Office of Homeland Security jointly with the Office of the Deputy Prime Minister, December 12, 2001, www.dfait-maeci.gc.ca/anti-terrorism/declaration-en.asp, and associated Action Plan, accessible at www.dfait-maeci.gc.ca/anti-terrorism/actionplan-en.asp.

———. *United States-Mexico Border Partnership*. Mexico City, Mexico: The Secretary of Governance, 2002.

Carafano, James Jay. *Homeland Security Dollars and Sense #1: Current Spending Formulas Waste Aid to States*. Washington, DC: The Heritage Foundation, 2004. www.heritage.org/ Research/HomelandDefense/wm508.cfm

Carafano, James Jay, Richard Weitz, and Alane Kochems. *Department of Homeland Security Needs Undersecretary for Policy*. Washington, DC: The Heritage Foundation, 2004. www.heritage.org/Research/HomelandDefense/bg1788.cfm

Carter, Ashton B. "The Architecture of Government in the Face of Terrorism." *International Security* 26 no. 3 (Winter 2002).

Carter, Ashton B., and John P. White, eds. *Keeping the Edge: Managing Defense for the Future*. Cambridge, MA: The MIT Press, 2000.

Carter, Ashton B., and William J. Perry. *Preventive Defense: A New Security Strategy for America*. Washington, DC: Brookings Institution Press, 1991.

Center for Strategic and International Studies. *Meeting the Challenges of Establishing a New Department of Homeland Security: A CSIS White Paper*. Washington, DC: Center For Strategic and International Studies, 2002.

Century Foundation. *The Department of Homeland Security's First Year: A Report Card*. New York: The Century Foundation, 2004.

Clarke, Richard A. *Against All Enemies: Inside America's War on Terror*. New York: Free Press, 2004.

Clausewitz, Carl von., (edited and translated by Michael Howard and Peter Paret). *On War*. Princeton, NJ: Princeton University Press, 1976.

Clinton, William Jefferson. Presidential Decision Directive-39 (PDD-39), "U.S. Policy on Counterterrorism." June 21, 1995.

———. Presidential Decision Directive-62 (PDD-62), "Protection Against Unconventional Threats to the Homeland and Americans Overseas (unclassified extract)." May 22, 1998.

———. Presidential Decision Directive-63 (PDD-63), "Critical Infrastructure Protection." May 22, 1998.

———. Presidential Decision Directive-67 (PDD-67), "Enduring Constitutional Government and Continuity of Government." October 21, 1998.

Congressional Budget Office. *Federal Funding for Homeland Security*. Washington, DC: Congressional Budget Office, April 30, 2004. www.cbo.gov.

Congressional Quarterly Researcher. *Civil Liberties Debates* 13 no. 37 (October 24, 2003).

———. *Cybersecurity* 13 no. 33 (September 26, 2003).

———. *Homeland Security: Two Years After 9/11, Are We Safer?* 13 no. 31 (September 12, 2003).

———. *Policing the Borders* 12 no. 7. (February 22, 2002).

———. *Presidential Power* 12 no. 40 (November 15, 2002).

———. *Re-examining 9/11* 14 no. 11 (June 4, 2004).

———. *Smallpox Threat* 13 no. 5 (February 7, 2003).

Cooper, Robert. *The Breaking of Nations: Order and Chaos in the Twenty-first Century*. New York: Atlantic Monthly Press, 2003.

Cordesman, Anthony H. *The 9/11 Commission Report: Strengths and Weaknesses*. Washington, DC: Center for Strategic and International Studies, 2004, www.csis.org/press/wf_2004_0730.pdf.

Daalder, Ivo H.; I. M. Destler; Paul C. Light; James M. Lindsay; Robert E. Litan; Michael E. O'Hanlon; Peter R. Orszag, James B. Steinberg. *Assessing the Department of Homeland Security*. Washington, DC: Brookings Institution Press, 2002.

Echevarria, Antulio J., II, and Bert B. Tussing. "From 'Defending Forward' to a 'Global Defense-in-Depth:' Globalization and Homeland Security." Carlisle, PA: Strategic Studies Institute, 2003.

Falkenrath, Richard A., Robert D. Newman, and Bradley A. Thayer. *America's Achilles' Heel: Nuclear, Biological, and Chemical Terrorism and Covert Attack*. Cambridge, MA: The MIT Press, 1998.

Flynn, Stephen. *America the Vulnerable: How Our Government Is Failing to Protect us from Terrorism*. New York: Harper Collins Publishers, 2004.

———. *Creating the Department of Homeland Security: Rethinking the Ends and Means*. New York: The Century Foundation, 2002. www.cfr.org/pdf/HomeSecur_Flynn.pdf.

Gaddis, John Lewis. *Strategies of Containment: A Critical Appraisal of Postwar American National Security Policy*. New York: Oxford University Press, 1982.

———. *Surprise, Security, and the American Experience*. Cambridge, MA: Harvard University Press, 2004.

Hoffman, Bruce. *Inside Terrorism*. New York: Columbia University Press, 1998.

Howard, Russell D. "Preemptive Military Doctrine: No Other Choice Against Transnational, Non-State Actors," in *Through Alternative Lenses: Current Debates in International Relations,* ed. Daniel J. Kaufman, Jay M. Parker, Patrick V. Howell, and Kimberly C. Field. Boston, MA: McGraw-Hill, 2004.

Jablonsky, David. "The State of the National Security State," *Parameters* 32 no. 4 (2003): 4–20.

Kaplan, Robert S. and David P. Norton. *The Strategy-Focused Organization: How Balanced Scorecard Companies Thrive in the New Business Environment*. Boston: Harvard Business School Press, 2001.

Kettl, Donald F., with T. Alexander Aleinikoff; E. Marla Felcher; Anne Khademian; and Gregory F. Treverton. *The Department of Homeland Security's First Year: An Assessment*. The Century Foundation Press, 2004.

Kissinger, Henry. *Years of Upheaval*. Boston, MA: Little, Brown and Company, 1982.

Korb, Lawrence J. *A New National Security Strategy In An Age of Terrorists, Tyrants, and Weapons of Mass Destruction*. Washington, DC: Council on Foreign Relations Press, 2003.

Kunreuther, Howard and Erwann Michel-Kerjan. *Dealing with Extreme Events: New Challenges for Terrorism Risk Coverage in the U.S.* Philadelphia, PA: Center for Risk Management and Decision Processes, 2004. grace.wharton.upenn.edu/risk/.

Lagadec, Patrick and Erwan Michel-Kerjan. "A Framework for Senior Executives to Meet the Challenge of Interdependent Critical Networks Under Threat: The Paris Initiative, "Anthrax and Beyond," Draft. Center for Risk Management and Decision Processes, The Wharton School at the University of Pennsylvania, 2004. grace.wharton.upenn.edu/risk/.

Light, Paul C. *Government's Greatest Achievements: From Civil Rights to Homeland Security*. Washington, DC: Brookings Institution Press, 2002.

Locher, James R. III. "Taking Stock of Goldwater-Nichols." *Joint Force Quarterly* (Autumn 1996): 10–17.

Markle Foundation. *Protecting America's Freedom in the Information Age: A Report of the Markle Foundation Task Force on National Security in the Information Age*. New York: The Markle Foundation, 2002.

————. *Creating a Trusted Network for Homeland Security: Second Report of the Markle Foundation Task Force*. New York: The Markle Foundation, 2003.

Martin, Paul. "Changing Government: Prime Minister Announces Appointment of Cabinet." Press release. Canada Privy Council Office, Ottawa, Ontario, Canada, December 12, 2003, www1.pm.gc.ca/eng/news.asp?id=2.

————. *Securing an Open Society: Canada's National Security Policy*, Canada Privy Council Office, Ottawa, Ontario, Canada, 2004.

May, Ernest R. and Richard E. Neustadt. *Thinking in Time: The Uses of History for Decision Makers*. New York: The Free Press, 1986.

May, Ernest R., ed. *American Cold War Strategy: Interpreting NSC-68*. Boston: Bedford/St. Martin's, 1993.

McIntyre, Dave. *The National Strategy for Homeland Security: Finding the Path among the Trees*. Arlington, VA: ANSER Institute for Homeland Security, 2002.

National Commission on Terrorist Attacks Upon the United States. *The 9/11 Commission Report: Final Report of the National Commission on Terrorist Attacks Upon the United States*. New York, NY: W.W. Norton & Company, Inc., 2004.

————. *The 9/11 Investigations: Staff Reports of the 9/11 Commission*. New York: Public Affairs, L.L.C., 2004

National Response Center. "Statistics: Incident Type Per Year—1997–2003." www.nrc.uscg.mil/stats.html.

National Transportation Safety Board. "NTSB Reports Increase in Aviation Accidents in 2003." NTSB Press Release SB-04-09, March 22, 2004. www.ntsb.gov/aviation/Stats.htm.

Neustadt, Richard E. *Presidential Power and the Modern Presidents: The Politics of Leadership from Roosevelt to Reagan*. New York: The Free Press, 1990.

Office of Management and Budget. *Analytical Perspectives, Budget of the United States Government, Fiscal Year 2004*. Washington, DC: Office of Management and Budget, 2003. www.whitehouse.gov/omb/budget/fy2004/.

————. *Analytical Perspectives, Budget of the United States Government, Fiscal Year 2005*. Washington, DC: Office of Management and Budget, 2004. www.whitehouse.gov/omb/budget/fy2005/.

————. *Budget of the United States Government, Fiscal Year 2004*. Washington, DC: Office of Management and Budget, 2003. www.whitehouse.gov/omb/budget/fy2004/.

————. *Budget of the United States Government, Fiscal Year 2005*. Washington, DC: Office of Management and Budget, 2004. www.whitehouse.gov/omb/budget/fy2005/.

O'Hanlon, Michael E.; Peter R. Orszag; Ivo H. Daalder; I. M. Destler; David L. Gunter; James M. Lindsay; Robert E. Litan; James B. Steinberg. *Protecting the American Homeland: One Year On*. Washington, DC: Brookings Institution Press, 2002.

RAND Center for Terrorism Risk Management Policy. *Publication and Research: Terrorism Risk Management Theory and Policy,* 2004. www.rand.org/multi/ctrmp/pubs/theory.html.

Rosenzweig, Paul, Alane Kochems, and James Jay Carafano. *The Patriot Act Reader: Understanding the Law's Role in the Global War on Terrorism*. Washington, DC: The Heritage Foundation, 2004.

Thompson, Larry D. "9/11 Commission Findings: Sufficiency of Time, Attention, and Legal Authority," Testimony to the House Permanent Select Committee on Intelligence, August 11, 2004. www.brookings.edu/views/testimony/20040811thompson.htm.

Turner, Jim. Report of the Minority Members of the House Select Committee on Homeland Security, *Securing our Homeland, Strengthening our Liberties*, 2004. www.house.gov/hsc/democrats.

———. Report of the Minority Members of the House Select Committee on Homeland Security, *Winning the War on Terror*, 2004. www.house.gov/hsc/democrats.

United States Commission on National Security/21st Century (the Hart-Rudman Commission). *Road Map for National Security: Imperative for Change*. Alexandria, VA: U.S. Commission on National Security/21st Century, 2001.

United States Congress. *H.R. 1158: The National Homeland Security Agency Act of 2001*. U.S. Congress, March 21, 2001.

United States Congress. *Public Law 107–296—Homeland Security Act of 2002*. U.S. Congress, November 25, 2002.

United States Congress. *Public Law 108–458—The Intelligence Reform and Terrorism Prevention Act of 2004*. U.S. Congress, 2004.

United States Congress. *Public Law 235–61 Stat. 496; U.S.C. 402: the National Security Act of 1947,* as amended in 1949 (63 Stat. 579; 50 U.S.C. 401 et seq.). U.S. Congress, 1949.

United States Congress. *S.1534: The Department of National Homeland Security Act of 2001*. U.S. Congress, October 11, 2001.

United States Department of Homeland Security. *Initial National Response Plan*. Washington, DC: Department of Homeland Security, 2003.

———. *Budget in Brief: Fiscal Year 2005*. Washington, DC: Department of Homeland Security, 2004.

———. *National Incident Management System*. Washington, DC: Department of Homeland Security, 2004.

———. *Securing our Homeland—U.S. Department of Homeland Security Strategic Plan*. Washington, DC: Department of Homeland Security, 2004.

United States Department of Justice. *FY 2003 Performance and Accountability Report*. Washington, DC: U.S. Department of Justice, 2004. www.justice.gov/ag/annualreports/ar2003/index.html#appendices.

———. *Report from the Field: The USA PATRIOT Act at Work*. Washington, DC: U.S. Department of Justice, 2004. www.lifeandliberty.gov/docs/071304_report_from_the_field.pdf.

United States Environmental Protection Agency. *Chemical Emergency Preparedness and Prevention: Evaluations and Studies*. Washington, DC: Environment Protection Agency, 2004. yosemite.epa.gov/oswer/ceppoweb.nsf/content/evalandstudy.htm#databases.

United States Government Accountability Office. *9/11 Commission Report: Reorganization, Transformation, and Information Sharing*. GAO-04-1033T. Washington, DC: U.S. Government Accountability Office, 2004.

———. *Combating Terrorism: Evaluation of Selected Characteristics of National Strategies Related to Terrorism*. GAO-04-408T. Washington, DC: U.S. Government Accountability Office, 2004.

————. *Homeland Security: Observations on the National Strategies Related to Terrorism*. GAO-04-1075T, Washington, DC: U.S. Government Accountability Office, 2004.

Wildavsky, Aaron. "The Two Presidencies," *Trans-Action* 4 no. 2 (December 1966). Reprinted in Aaron Wildavsky, ed. *Perspectives on the Presidency*. Boston, MA: Little, Brown and Co, 1975.

Zegart, Amy. *Flawed by Design: The Evolution of the CIA, JCS, and NSC*. Palo Alto, CA: Stanford University Press, 2000.

Section IV

Public Security and Civil Liberties

Amid the flurry of activity meant to protect America from future terrorist attacks, we face an additional challenge of maintaining a balance between freedom and security. Clearly, in reacting to global terrorism, we cannot allow our freedoms to be diminished. As Benjamin Franklin so aptly put it, "They that can give up essential liberty to obtain a little temporary safety, deserve neither liberty nor safety."

Amanda J. Dory begins this section by arguing that civil defense measures taken during the Cold War should again be implemented. The civil security approach she proposes seeks to empower the average American citizen to engage in activities useful for strengthening homeland security. Efforts are needed—particularly in areas of risk education, preparedness, warning, and protective actions—in order to build the capacity and resolve of individuals, neighborhoods, and communities to endure and prevail against adversaries who deliberately seek to instill fear and undermine Americans' confidence in themselves and in their government. Public support and participation, notes Dory, is crucial to homeland security.

This is followed by two chapters written specifically for this book, covering the need to ensure freedom of the press in the new security environment. Dr. Jim Robbins provides an overview of contemporary "freedom of the press" issues and challenges, particular with regard to saturation coverage of terrorist attacks on the U.S. homeland. Elizabeth Robbins explores government-media relations, arguing that a symbiotic, even co-dependent, relationship will result in more efficient dispersal of higher quality public information—a critical element in an effective response to national crises.

Finally, this section on civil liberties addresses the debate over the USA PATRIOT Act, passed by Congress on October 24, 2001, and signed into law by President George W. Bush two days later. Because the Act provided broad new powers to various agencies of the federal government—particularly in the area of gathering information about communications, financial transactions, and other activities—it has become a focal point in the struggle to maintain civil liberties while increasing the nation's security. This section illustrates the contemporary debate by providing three diverse—yet complementary—perspectives on the PATRIOT Act. Nancy Chang calls it an attack on the Bill of Rights, while Brian Hook, Margaret Peterlin, and Peter Walsh contend that intelligence and information sharing among governmental agencies will not occur without many of the provisions in the Act. In the middle of these two opposing viewpoints, Roger Golden takes a nuanced approach toward the issue of establishing a healthy balance between freedom and security. He notes that, for now, we have witnessed a shift toward security with the potential loss of a degree of the freedom, but American history suggests that a shift in the other direction is likely once the threat to security is perceived as sufficiently reduced.

This collection of chapters highlights just a few of the most important components of the debate over how to effectively maintain a balance between freedom and security. From the surveillance of internet communications to restrictions on what the media can report in the global war on terrorism, few public debates have been more central to American values than maintaining this balance. How we eventually resolve this debate will certainly have lasting implications for the long-term health of the entire republic.

Chapter 21

American Civil Security: The U.S. Public and Homeland Security

Amanda J. Dory

Has homeland security planning effectively prepared today's U.S. public for future terrorist attacks? The war on terrorism pursued abroad—the offensive component of homeland security—seeks to disrupt and defeat terrorists beyond U.S. borders. Yet, with officials at the highest level consistently sending the message that the threat of terrorism within U.S. borders is not going away anytime soon, it is time to create a common defense: a more resilient U.S. population that is better prepared to survive and cope with future attacks, as well as their economic and psychological consequences here at home.

Since the September 11 attacks, the U.S. public has faced a new learning curve with each succeeding crisis—anthrax letters, sniper attacks, monkey pox, SARS, and power-grid failures—first trying to determine whether terrorism is involved in each instance, and then how to deal with the problem at hand. Efforts to educate the public about the range of terrorist threats, our vulnerabilities to terrorism, and ways to respond during attacks have been limited, confusing, and at times, even contradictory. This reflects the pursuit of other homeland security priorities; an intellectual debate on whether terrorism represents one hazard among many or a unique phenomenon; and diverging views as to whether the U.S. public needs to be reassured, scared into taking action, or a bit of both.

The stakes are too high to rely on a patchwork of cumulative learning from events still to come. Deficiencies in Americans' emergency preparedness have been made sufficiently apparent. Evacuation plans are lacking at every level, from families and businesses up through state governments. A comprehensive warning system does not exist by which to reach the public to provide guidance on what to do in an emergency. Individuals have little basis for making informed decisions in the face of an event involving chemical, biological, radiological, or nuclear (CBRN) effects. Procedures to undertake mass vaccinations or to distribute medical countermeasures have not been rehearsed. Perhaps most ominous, the U.S. public lacks confidence in information provided by authorities. As evidenced by the federal "Ready" campaign's devolution into a duct-tape frenzy that coincided with raising the homeland security threat level to orange for the first time in the spring of 2003, the public's capacity to absorb unfamiliar information in a stressful environment is not optimal. The communication of uncertain threats and equally uncertain response plans, combined with media treatment long on hype and short on science, breeds the kind of public fear and confusion that undermine the public's confidence in itself and in the U.S. government, thus furthering terrorists' goals.

Renewed attention to individual Americans, and their contribution to and participation in domestic security, might best be called "civil security," a term that harkens back to the Cold War U.S. civil defense effort, but is firmly grounded in the current homeland security context. Civil security refers to measures undertaken to reduce the U.S. public's vulnerability to the physical, psychological, and economic impacts of terrorism, as well as measures to enable individuals to minimize damage and recover from terrorist attacks in the United States. Civil security thus parallels the Bush administration's broad definition of homeland security,[1] but with particular emphasis on the American public. Civil security requires increased efforts by the full range of homeland security players; individuals must participate in civil security on their own behalf, while governments pursue it for their constituents, and businesses address it with their employees. By enhancing individual understanding of terrorism's risks as well as effective, specific, protective action responses, a comprehensive approach to civil security can further steel Americans against future terrorist attacks.

Why Civil Security?

In the inaugural *National Strategy for Homeland Security,* the Bush administration articulated a sweepingly inclusive vision of a partnership for homeland security: "The [a]dministration's approach to homeland security is based on the principles of shared responsibility and partnership with the Congress, state and local governments, the private sector, and the American people."[2] In considering the public's role in dealing with terrorism, however, decision makers tend to view American individuals, not as partners, but as either potential attack victims or panicked masses. Rather than paying attention to individuals directly, government decision makers, often at the federal level, tend to view state and local governments and/or emergency responders as proxies for the people.

Increased government attention to the role of the public is crucial for a number of reasons. First, terrorist attacks target public confidence (in itself and in the government), individual American lives, and the American way of life more broadly. Americans risk becoming victims of future terrorist attacks, not only from possibly being in the wrong place at the wrong time but also from the economic and psychological fallout that would result from such attacks. As the September 11 attacks revealed, terrorism's reverberations reach far beyond the death toll, resulting in billions of dollars of economic loss and incalculable national distress. Because terrorism directly affects individuals and their livelihood, preparations to address the consequences of terrorism cannot be divorced from the very people these measures are ultimately intended to benefit.

Second, public support and cooperation are critical throughout any crisis, both for emergency response and for long-term recovery. For example, the public's failure to comply with authorities' instructions to quarantine themselves in their homes or in a designated facility, could prolong or worsen an incident involving contagious biological agents such as smallpox. Similarly, spontaneous evacuations in areas surrounding a radiological, or "dirty bomb," explosion could complicate authorities' decontamination efforts. On the other end of the evacuation spectrum, refusal to comply with directions to evacuate promptly could also endanger lives and hinder emergency responses. A recent study revealed that, if directed to do so, 90 percent of respondents nationwide would not comply with a directive to evacuate immediately during a crisis and would instead seek out additional information or otherwise prolong or avoid rapid departure.[3] Increasing the public's willingness and ability to respond appropriately to terrorist attacks and to return to normalcy thereafter is clearly in the interests of individuals, the private sector, and all levels of government alike.

Third, the U.S. population provides the financial resources needed for homeland security through tax dollars paid to federal, state, and local governments, and through security costs that businesses pass on to consumers. Devoting these resources to homeland security, at an estimated cost of $100 billion annually,[4] results in very real and tangible trade-offs from other priority areas such as education, health, and Social Security benefits. Officials at all levels of government thus have to justify and build public support, not only for decisions on how much domestic security is enough, but also for the ensuing winners and losers in the resource allocation process.

Based on statements by national leaders, public participation in homeland security efforts clearly counts on a rhetorical level. In Atlanta in late 2001, in a major speech dealing with homeland security, President George W. Bush stated, "[W]e are a nation awakened to danger. . . . Our nation faces a threat to our freedoms and the stakes could not be higher. . . . This new era requires new responsibilities, both for the government and for our people."[5] Similarly, Secretary of Homeland Security Tom Ridge referred to the U.S. citizen as "the ultimate stakeholder," and the need to "empower citizens to play a more direct role" in homeland security.[6] To date, these new roles and responsibilities for the people have yet to be articulated in detail, allowing the misperception that governments are exclusively charged with maintaining homeland security to continue.

Lessons Learned from Civil Defense

An historical precedent for educating and involving the U.S. public directly in homeland defense efforts can be found in civil defense measures taken during the Cold War. From the early 1950s until 1994, when Congress pulled the plug on the program at the end of the Cold War, civil defense comprised a variety of programs including public shelters, stockpiles of supplies, radiological detection devices, education, training, warning systems, and so forth. The goal of Cold War civil defense was to enable the greatest number of Americans to survive a Soviet nuclear attack on the United States, should one occur. Through outreach and educational activities, the government provided the public with a basic understanding of the nature of the Soviet threat, the nation's vulnerability to nuclear attack, and potential consequences if one were to occur. Certain aspects of the civil defense program were quite sound, including its comprehensiveness, voluntary nature, strong focus on education, distribution of costs throughout society (to federal, state, and local governments and to individuals), and patriotic linkage to a larger sense of community and civic duty.

Civil defense was not without flaws, however. Resources for the civil defense program waxed and waned over time, and its focus shifted significantly to reflect the changing threat environment, as well as the views of the U.S. executive and legislative leadership on how to deter the Soviet Union using a combination of offensive (strategic nuclear forces) and defensive (civil defense) measures. Late in the Kennedy administration, the shift to a doctrine of mutually assured destruction, premised on the ability to inflict horrendous losses on civilian populations, undercut the strategic rationale for a civil defense program designed to protect the public—a discontinuity that continued for two decades. As for the public itself—ostensibly the most important constituency the program was designed to serve—the vast majority of the U.S. population did little or nothing, responding to civil defense with a mixture of indifference, fear, anger, and occasional support. Some believed that nothing useful could be accomplished, while others were in denial and failed to acknowledge the threat; still others considered a program that might not save all people to be immoral. Thus, civil defense failed to attract the enduring public interest and support necessary to realize the goal of a nation prepared to survive a Soviet nuclear attack.

Unfortunately, in the collective consciousness, memories of civil defense have been boiled down to a duck-and-cover bumper sticker, tinged with ridicule, rather than a more balanced assessment. As former senators Gary Hart (D-CO) and Warren Rudman (R-NH) stated in a recent task force report, "The contemporary security environment mandates that we put this anti–civil defense bias behind us."[7] Although imperfect, the Cold War civil defense program nonetheless had a clear focus on the people as a strategic national resource, and on the necessity and desirability of their participation to promote domestic security.

A Modest Proposal: Civil Security

A comprehensive and updated effort comparable to that employed by the United States in the face of the Soviet threat has yet to emerge in today's threat environment, in which attacks on U.S. soil have already occurred and future ones are anticipated. Based on lessons from Cold War civil defense, several characteristics of a program designed to increase the U.S. public's resilience and ability to cope with terrorist attacks today are apparent. They include

- *effectiveness*, the capability to save lives;
- *flexibility*, a capacity to evolve in tandem with changes in the security environment;
- *inclusiveness*, the ability to address a tremendously diverse U.S. population;
- *comprehensiveness*, an expansive conception that accounts for the public before, during, and after terrorist incidents; and
- *affordability*, a burden-sharing arrangement that distributes and rationalizes costs among stakeholders in homeland security.

An underlying tension within the emerging homeland security field of expertise is the extent to which terrorism, and the responses it requires, are distinct from other man-made and natural disasters. The debate can be grossly simplified by dividing it into two camps that roughly correspond to the national security community—which tends to focus on the uniqueness of deliberate terrorist attacks relative to accidents and natural phenomena—and the disaster response community—which emphasizes the similarity of responses (for example, roles played by emergency managers and first responders) across the full range of hazards, referred to as "all hazards" by practitioners.

Three aspects of terrorism make it difficult to add terrorism neatly into the all-hazards spectrum of disasters. First, through the deliberate use of CBRN effects, terrorist attacks have the potential to significantly increase the casualty levels historically associated with other types of disasters and accidents. Second, as adaptive adversaries, terrorists not only have the ability to change tactics as an attack unfolds, but also can "reload" rapidly[8] and/or pursue multiple attacks simultaneously—characteristics that do not apply to natural hazards and accidents. Third, terrorist attacks are criminal acts and, as such, include the additional complications of securing a crime scene and conducting an investigation during the response phase. Although the debate may seem arcane at first glance, it directly influences how the government encourages the public to think about terrorism and prepare for terrorist attacks—that is, whether terrorism is just another disaster or whether it requires unique treatment.

An effective civil security effort should split the difference, so to speak, by building on the all-hazards foundation, recognizing that aspects of emergency response are indeed applicable across the board, yet elements particular to terrorism require distinct protective actions as well as specialized preparations. The chart in Figure 21-1 summarizes how needed detection capabilities, protective actions, and protective equipment can differ depending on whether an incident is conventional (involving explosives alone) or has CBRN effects.

A "one size fits all" response to terrorist attacks is misleading and potentially dangerous in a dynamic, complex, and scenario-dependent threat environment. An effective civil security approach would entail informing the public as to which responses are the most effective against which threats and in what circumstances specialized preparedness items may be required. For example, Americans need to understand that sealing windows and doors with duct tape and plastic is a useful protective action only in specific situations, such as attacks involving chemical effects, and must be followed promptly by venting the affected area after contaminated external air has dissipated. Similarly, particulate masks can provide limited protection in situations involving radioactive dust, certain viruses (depending on size), and aerosolized chemical agents, but they are useless against chemical vapors. Meanwhile, biological incidents are fundamentally different from other attacks because the effects evolve gradually and are not immediately detectable. A one-size-fits-all preparedness campaign and checklist obscures these important distinctions; a far-reaching educational campaign is the only way that individuals will be able to grasp these differences.

To address the role of the U.S. public in homeland security before, during, and after terrorist attacks, at least four key components are needed in a contemporary civil security approach: risk education, preparedness, warning, and protective actions. These same components all have some precedent in the Cold War civil defense program, but obviously require retooling for a new set of adversaries with an expanded arsenal of weapons of mass destruction.

Risk education refers to an interrelated approach to encourage Americans to play an active and supportive role in defense against terrorism: the processes of risk assessment (assessing threats and vulnerabilities in an integrated way), risk psychology (how people think about terrorism), and risk communication (adapting information to how people learn best about risk). Inspiring public support requires a realistic portrayal of risk that is accurate and draws a fine line between hyping the threat to spur people to action and trivializing it to provide them false reassurances. Risk education provides the foundation of civil security and is a fundamental prerequisite to enable individuals to minimize damage and recover from terrorist attacks. It can provide the impetus for Americans to undertake voluntary emergency preparedness activities. It can also serve as the basis for individuals to make informed decisions during an emergency, and take protective actions expediently if official warnings with recommended actions are not immediately available.

Preparedness provides a way for individuals, communities, and institutions to translate risk awareness into action. Preparedness can consist of a range of activities, including developing and practicing contingency plans (such as communication, evacuation, or sheltering), participating in education and awareness activities, providing first aid and emergency response training, and stockpiling emergency supplies. Preparedness serves as a bridge between risk education (which occurs in advance of an event) and taking protective actions during a crisis. Preparedness for all hazards (such as stockpiling three days' worth of food and water) may be applicable and useful during a crisis triggered by a terrorist attack. There are several preparedness items that are not all-hazards in nature, however, including respiratory protection, duct tape and plastic, and certain kinds of medical countermeasures. These would only be relevant for attacks (or accidents) involving CBRN effects.

Warning aims to save lives and to reduce the costs of disasters by giving guidance on specific actions to take in a crisis. In contrast to risk education, federal, state, and local government officials issue warnings with urgency in a crisis environment via predominantly privately operated communications channels (such as television, radio, telephone, and wireless devices). Unlike the advance notice of an escalating crisis that likely would have preceded a Soviet attack during the Cold War, terrorist attacks are designed to surprise; thus, warnings are more likely to be issued during, and immediately following, a terrorist incident rather than in advance. Precisely because official guidance may not be immediately available during an attack or its immediate aftermath, individuals must be empowered with the knowledge and capacity to make their own decisions on the spot.

Protective actions consist of steps that individuals and communities can take to save lives and to reduce losses when an event occurs. The ultimate test of civil security is the effectiveness of protective actions—that is, what people actually do in a crisis. Examples of protective actions include different forms of sheltering, evacuation, and quarantine (voluntary or mandatory); using individual protective equipment such as respiratory equipment or protective clothing; and using a variety of medical countermeasures including vaccines, antidotes, antibiotics, and potassium iodide. Risk education, preparedness, and warning are all intended to improve the public's knowledge and its ability to respond in ways that reduce loss of life during a terrorist attack through effective protective actions. The chances for successful protective actions can also be increased through the existence of plans for how the actions are to be executed, and advance communication of the content of such plans to potentially affected parties (notably the public) to build understanding and confidence.

Figure 21-1 shows when different protective actions would be relevant for CBRN terrorist attacks, underscoring that a standardized approach does not work for the range of potential scenarios.

Collectively, these four interactive elements can reinforce one another as part of a comprehensive civil security approach that focuses on the U.S. public under the larger homeland security umbrella.[9] As described, civil security components provide the tools to maximize the odds for physical survival of a terrorist attack. They can also serve to mitigate the psychological and economic consequences of terrorist threats or acts. Household and business preparedness activities, for example, can provide reassurance in addition to their practical value. Similarly, warnings that are targeted for specific populations at risk can avoid unnecessarily dampening economic activity in areas where precautions are unwarranted.

FIGURE 21-1. Terrorist Attacks and Individual Protective Actions

Types of Attach	Detection Capability	Short-term Protective Action (s)	Individual Protective Equipment	Medium-Term Response	Related Historical Experience
Conventional					
• Delivery: vehicle, plane, suicide bomber, building attach	• Explosive-sniffing dogs • Explosion	• N/A • Medical care for victims	• N/A	• Recovery and reconstruction	• U.S. Sept. 11, 2001; Oklahoma City (1995)
Chemical					
• Types: blister agents, nerve agents, pulmonary agents • Delivery : airborne (aerosol, vapor), foodborne, or waterborne; attach on chemical facility or transit	• Limited sensor detection capability deployed[1] • Explosion • Victims evident or present for medical care	• Some medical countermeasures • Decontamination for immediately exposed individuals • Expedient shelter-in-place for several hours (duct tape, sheeting), then venting • Evacuate (from downwind area if time available)	• Expedient: N95 or p100 particulate masks • Specialized: escape hoods, chemical respirators, protective clothing and hoods	• Venting buildings and homes for airborne agents • Decontamination of surfaces and buildings for persistent agents[3]	• U.S.: Baltimore, Md., chlorine train accident (2001) • World: Mississauga, Canada (1979); Bhopal, India (1984); Tokyo, Japan (1995)
Biological					
• Types: bacteria (e.g., anthrax), virus (e.g., smallpox), toxins (e.g., ricin)	• Epidemiological monitoring • Limited sensor detection capability deployed[1]	• Medical countermeasures (e.g., vaccination, antibiotics) for affected individuals • Mass Vaccination	• Expedient: N95 or P100 particulate masks	• Decontamination of surfaces and buildings[3]	• U.S. New York City smallpox epidemic (1946), Oregon salmonella poisoning (1984), anthrax mail attack (2001)

FIGURE 21-1. continued

• Delivery: airborne, food-borne, or waterborne; human or animal transmission	• Anthrax detection at several postal facilities • Victims present for medical care	• Voluntary quarantine in home (shielding) in outbreak area • Government-directed quarantine for particular area	• Specialized: escape hoods, protective clothing and hoods	• Vaccination to prevent future outbreaks	• World: Sverdlosk, Soviet Union, anthrax (1979)
Radiological • Effects blast, radioactive contamination • Delivery: bomb, food-borne or waterborne	• Radiation detection devices at transit points and other locations • Explosive • Victims present for medical care	• Decontamination for immediately exposed individuals	• Expedient: N95 or P100 particulate masks • Specialized: Protective suits for nuclear industry workers	• Decontamination of surfaces and buildings[3]	• World: Goiania, Brazil, cesium poisoning (1987)
Nuclear • Effects blast/initial radiation, electromagnetic pulse (EMP); fallout • Delivery: nuclear or cruise missile, attack on nuclear power plant	• Explosion • Disruption of electronic devices by EMP • Radiation detection devices	• Shelter-in-place, preferably undergrounds (days or longer—depends on proximity to attack location) • Evacuate (from downwind areas if time available) • Potassium iodide to protect thyroid • Decontamination of affected individuals	• Specialized: protective suits for nuclear industry workers	• Long-term evacuation from affected areas • Medical monitoring for individuals • Decontamination of surfaces of buildings many not be possible	• U.S.: Three Mile Island, N.Y. (1979) • World Hiroshima and Nagasaki, Japan 91945); Chernobyl, Soviet Union (1986)

1. The Department of Homeland Security Biowatch program has a limited detection capability in some 30 unspecified location, while the Department of Defense has a parallel detection system at some 200 U.S. installations. The national laboratories and at least one specialized National Guard team are also involved in pilot detection efforts.

2.. In any cases, specialized equipment is available to industrial workers and the military but not the general public.

3.May or may not be economically feasible depending on the agent and extent of contamination.

Making it Work

Creating a civil security focus within current homeland security efforts is not a Herculean undertaking. What it does require is a clear sponsor within the federal structure, a modicum of funding, sustained attention, and participation by all stakeholders in homeland security. A quintessential lesson learned from the experience of Cold War civil defense is that bureaucratic success requires a dedicated and identifiable sponsor with assured access to senior government officials. To advance civil security concerns in the short term, the most effective structural solution would be the creation of a small civil security liaison office within the immediate Office of the Secretary of Homeland Security. This office would join counterparts in the front office that have been created for the other homeland security stakeholders, including a special assistant for the private sector, a legislative affairs office, and an office responsible for state and local government coordination. There is also current debate about moving the Office of Domestic Preparedness (formerly part of the Department of Justice), which liaises with the emergency responder community, to be a component of the secretary's office.

Although the Department of Homeland Security (DHS) already has an Office of Public Affairs, it primarily uses media channels to represent the work of the entire department and of its key officials; the public affairs office is not designed to be a two-way conduit for risk education. Communications skills are critical for a civil security program, but they need to be buttressed by additional technical knowledge and a mandate for coordination across the DHS organization (and also with other agencies) to address issues relating to risk education, preparedness, warning, and protective actions in an integrated way. The term "liaison office" is used deliberately to underscore the two-way communication with the U.S. public that is needed for civil security, much in the same way the current DHS office that deals with state and local issues serves as a liaison.

The work of the civil security liaison office should be twofold. First and foremost, the office must be charged with connecting the dots—that is, developing linkages among diverse activities that have direct impact on the entire U.S. population so that, from the public's perspective, a coherent game plan is provided to instruct people in how to respond to a terrorist attack and how their capabilities will be supported by governmental resources. Second, in terms of philosophical approach, the liaison office should acknowledge the merits of the all-hazards approach as a foundation, but at the same time take responsibility for making it clear to the public which types of preparedness activities and protective actions are relevant for different kinds of terrorist attacks, particularly for each of the CBRN constituent parts (chemical, biological, radiological, and nuclear). An added benefit of this all-hazards "plus" approach is that it can allow changes in emphasis in the future as the nature of the threat evolves. In periods when the threat recedes, preparedness for a terrorist attack can be deemphasized relative to other hazards (i.e., natural disasters) and vice versa, thus providing programmatic flexibility and sustainability over time.

Four existing federal efforts under the purview of the DHS are logical pillars that can support a civil security program: the Ready terrorism preparedness campaign, the Citizens Corps initiative, the Emergency Alert System (EAS), and the Strategic National Stockpile (SNS). Theses are currently managed by different parts of the DHS and the Centers for Disease Control and Prevention (CDC), with little vision of how they interrelate from the public's perspective. The civil security liaison office could provide that vision without necessarily assuming operational responsibility for all of the programs.

The Ready campaign initiative debuted in March 2003, and comprises a Web site, public service announcements, and a toll-free information number. The Web site is off to a good start, with 15.5 million unique page views. In addition, the toll-free telephone number that callers can use to request an informational brochure has received 130,000 calls.[10] With a U.S. population of 290 million, however, a great deal more remains to be done, especially for those without Internet access. Launched as a result of a private foundation grant (with close to $3 million in start-up funds provided by the Sloan Foundation), federal funding is now required to sustain the campaign over time to ensure the continued expansion of risk awareness and preparedness among the U.S. population. Current and future administrations, as well as Congress, must ensure that the campaign receives adequate resources to reach more Americans, to fine-tune its messages, and to measure its effectiveness through surveys and focus groups on a continuing basis. Short-term priorities include translation of Ready content into multiple languages, the addition of specific CBRN scenarios (historical and hypothetical) to the Web site to improve individuals' understanding of how terrorist attacks could potentially unfold, and interactive functionality to allow two-way dialogue with the public. To reach a greater number of Americans, DHS must also focus on reaching people in nontraditional ways, including making use of such locations as grocery stores, banks, gas stations, and other facilities that most people have to visit in the course of their daily lives.

The second existing program, the Citizens Corps initiative, is an umbrella structure with distinct community-based functions: fostering volunteer service, which regroups well-known existing programs such as Neighborhood Watch and Community Emergency Response Training, and facilitating education and outreach. The latter involves establishing a new structure altogether—Citizens Corps Councils—at state and local levels. These councils mirror similar efforts used to mobilize and reach Americans during the Cold War civil defense days. In a short period of time, the Citizens Corps initiative has managed to attract a healthy number of federal and nonfederal partners[11] that share the goal of helping communities prevent, prepare for, and respond to disasters. To date, 50 state and territory councils and 770 local councils have been formed.[12] These councils, with a grassroots flavor that can give them relevance and credibility within local communities, can serve as two-way conduits in the risk education and risk communication process. For the program to succeed, however, administrations must propose—and Congress must approve—the nominal funding required over time to supplement and sustain the organizational capabilities and human resources provided by dedicated local volunteers, and the educational and training activities they sponsor in the community. Unfortunately, the initiative did not receive congressional funding for fiscal year 2003, despite the administration's request for $100 million. For fiscal year 2004, the administration requested $181 million; in September 2003, Congress approved $40 million.

The third existing building block for a civil security program is the EAS, a leftover warning system from Cold War civil defense days that provides warnings via radio and television. The EAS is jointly managed by the Federal Emergency Management Administration (now located within DHS), the National Oceanographic and Atmospheric Administration (NOAA)—NOAA Weather Radio is a key channel for warnings—and the Federal Communications Commission. The lack of complete ownership by any single entity, however, has produced both bureaucratic inertia and friction over time. In addition, the EAS urgently needs updating to accommodate and incorporate the proliferation of communications devices and media beyond traditional television and radio outlets. On the receiving end, individual Americans need to think about how warnings can reach them 24 hours a day, seven days a week (even in the event of a power outage), and acquire appropriate devices to receive such warnings. Even so, it is possible or even likely that, in the early minutes and hours following a future terrorist attack, the U.S. public will have to respond as best as possible on its own, without immediate access to considered advice from local, state, or federal officials. This situation underscores the need for better risk education up front so that individuals are equipped with information that can improve their ability to survive.

For protective actions, the SNS, an essential source of specialized CBRN medical countermeasures, is truly a national treasure. Managed for DHS by the CDC, the SNS provides capabilities and supplies that can be deployed on short notice to assist state governments if requested. SNS "push packages" contain antibiotics, vaccines, and other medical supplies, and are located in multiple undisclosed locations across the country. Materials in the SNS must continue to be expanded based on evolving threat information. Countermeasures developed for military use must also be explored for their civilian relevance and potential inclusion in the SNS. Beyond the existence of the stockpile, developing state, community, and individual plans is indispensable to successfully execute protective actions such as evacuation, sheltering inside or outside the home, and quarantine. Public understanding of the plans in which they will be involved is also essential, and can be conveyed as part of the risk education process. The current effort to update and expand the Federal Response Plan—which lays out roles for federal agencies in disasters of all kinds—to make it a National Response Plan involving stakeholders beyond the federal level, provides an opportunity for state and local governments to develop and/or update protective action plans.[13] Such plans then need to be communicated to members of the public so that they are not revealed for the first time in a crisis situation when anxieties and the potential for miscommunication are high.

Building Mutual Government and Public Trust

The American people need a clear advocate at the federal level who will focus on their interests before and throughout a terrorist attack, in contrast to activities such as critical infrastructure protection, port security, and border security that benefit Americans but do not directly involve them for the most part. Public opinion surveys since September 11, 2001, consistently show that a significant portion of the U.S. population is concerned about terrorism. According to an August 2003 survey, 76 percent of the respondents were concerned about the possible occurrence of additional terrorist attacks; the figure was even higher in New York City.[14] This level of concern was matched by a strong sense of community and a desire to help in local emergency planning. Yet, new initiatives such as the Ready campaign and the Citizens Corps are still largely unknown to the U.S. public, and few individuals, families, and communities have developed recommended emergency plans. For example, the Columbia University survey found that only 23 percent of respondents had a basic emergency plan and supplies, while a DHS-sponsored survey showed that 20 percent considered themselves prepared for a terrorist event.[15]

The civil security approach proposed here seeks to bridge two gaps: the gap between idle concern and useful action by Americans and the gap between rhetoric about the importance of the citizen stakeholder in homeland security and the tangible results to date. Efforts to improve risk education, preparedness, warning, and protective actions and to recognize the linkages between these components, can strengthen the ability and resolve of individuals, neighborhoods, and communities to endure and prevail against adversaries who deliberately seek to instill fear and undermine Americans' confidence in themselves and in their government. Civil security also provides an outlet for individual participation in, and contribution to, homeland security. Several existing programs described here can serve as building blocks for a civil security program. If linked together conceptually and adequately funded, these measures could improve the population's resilience and ability to respond in the event of future terrorist attacks on the United States.

About 40 years ago, at the height of the Berlin crisis, President John F. Kennedy declared, "To recognize the possibilities of nuclear war in the missile age, without our citizens knowing what they should do and where they should go if bombs begin to fall, would be a failure of responsibility."[16] Today's stakeholders in homeland security—federal, state, and local governments; the private sector; individuals; and communities—must collectively face up to this responsibility as well. Such an effort will require clear vision and strong leadership in two directions—from the federal level down, and from individual Americans up—to create a more resilient population in the face of terrorist adversaries with intentions to inflict widespread harm.

Notes

1. The Bush administration defines homeland security as "a concerted national effort to prevent terrorist attacks within the United States, reduce America's vulnerability to terrorism, and minimize the damage from attacks that do occur." Office of Homeland Security, *National Strategy for Homeland Security,* July 2002, p. 2, www.dhs.gov/interweb/assetlibrary/nat_strat_hls.pdf (accessed October 2, 2003).
2. Ibid.
3. National Center for Disaster Preparedness, *How Americans Feel About Terrorism and Security: Two Years After 9/11* (New York: Mailman School of Public Health, Columbia University, 2003), p. 10, www.ncdp.mailman.columbia.edu/How_Americans_Feel_About_Terrorism.pdf (accessed October 2, 2003). Hereinafter cited as terrorism survey.
4. Office Homeland Security, *National Strategy for Homeland Security,* p. xii.
5. George W. Bush, "This New Era Requires New Responsibilities," *Washington Post,* November 9, 2001.
6. Tom Ridge, Remarks, "Homeland Security from the Citizen's Perspective Meeting," Council on Excellence in Government, Washington, DC, September 16, 2003.
7. Gary Hart and Warren B. Rudman, *America Still Unprepared—America Still in Danger* (New York: Council on Foreign Relations, 2002, p. 16, www.cfr.org/pdf/Homeland_Security_TF.pdf (accessed October 2, 2003).
8. For a discussion of the reload phenomenon, see Richard Danzig, *Catastrophic Bioterrorism: What Is to Be Done?* (Washington, DC: National Defense University Press, 2003), sec. 1.

9. See Amanda Dory, *Civil Security: Americans and the Challenge of Homeland Security* (Washington, DC: CSIS, 2003), www.csis.org/isp/civilsecurity.pdf (accessed October 29, 2003).

10. Office of Public Affairs, Department of Homeland Security (DHS), communication with author, Washington, DC, June 2, 2003.

11. At the July 2003 National Citizens Corps Conference in Washington, DC, the National Oceanographic and Atmospheric Administration, the Environmental Protection Agency, and the Department of Education signed on as new federal partners, with the Departments of Homeland Security, Health and Human Services, and Justice established as charter partners. Nonfederal affiliate programs involved nine organizations, including the American Red Cross, Jaycees, and the Points of Light Foundation.

12. Office of Citizens Corps, Department of Homeland Security, communication with author, Washington, DC, September 29, 2003.

13. Homeland Security Presidential Directive/HSPD-5, February 2003, www.whitehouse.gov/news/releases/2003/02/20030228–9.html (accessed October 2, 2003).

14. Terrorism survey. Other surveys have been done by Harvard University's School of Public Health, Department of Homeland Security, and the Gallup organization.

15. Terrorism survey; ORC Communications Survey commissioned by Department of Homeland Security and presented at National Citizens Corps Conference, Washington, DC, July 2003.

16. John F. Kennedy, Radio and Television Report to the American People on the Berlin Crisis, July 25, 1961, www.cs.umb.edu/jfklibrary/jfk_berlin_crisis_speech.html (accessed October 2, 2003).

Chapter 22

Terrorists, the Media, and Homeland Security

James S. Robbins

Bin Laden realizes very well that the media war is as important as the military one he is fighting against the United States.[1]
—Abd al-Rahman al-Rashid, al-Qaida Spokesman

Twenty years ago in his groundbreaking anthology *Terrorism, the Media and the Law*, Dr. Abraham H. Miller wrote that contemporary terrorism is a stepchild of the media, an *enfant terrible* with a penchant for taking hostages.[2] Since then scholars and policy makers have debated the extent to which media coverage enables or encourages terrorism.[3] Proponents of the thesis that media coverage is incidental to terrorism point out that terrorist tactics have existed for centuries, long before the advent of what we recognize as mass media. While modern information dissemination techniques and technologies did not create the phenomenon of terrorism, contemporary mass media have magnified the impact of what had previously been isolated acts of political violence by small groups of people. Over the past twenty years, both the media and terrorism have expanded, evolved, and become more diverse and influential. This has given new opportunities to radical political actors to promote their causes through media-enabled terrorism. Network feeds off network; terrorists understand that information strategies are central to the practice of their craft. Muwaffaq al-Jammal, head of the Hizballah Information Center, observed, "Information is one of the most important weapons in this age, and it is part and parcel of any war or battle with the enemy. Without information, no battle is complete."[4]

Terrorists are naturally attracted to engagement in the information domain. While they must necessarily adopt asymmetric strategies against their enemies in the field of military conflict, in the global media space they are on a level playing field. Terrorists can command as much press coverage as the institutions and societies they seek to undermine. Media competition is low cost, low risk, and allows terrorists to present themselves and their movement in the most favorable light possible. Terrorists pursue sophisticated information strategies on many levels, addressing disparate audiences. They adopt the methods one would see in any political or propaganda campaign, such as message discipline, spin, and getting the right information in the hands of the right people. Overall they have been very successful. The mass media may not have created terrorism, but they have turned some of its practitioners into malevolent superstars.

The basic symbiosis between terrorism and the media has not changed since the phenomenon first came under study; reporters want a story, and terrorists want an audience. In fact terrorists want to reach multiple audiences simultaneously. Terrorists seek not only to maximize press coverage but also to manage the interpretation of their attacks, the meaning, symbolism, and implications for their own power and influence. They also seek to elucidate the legitimacy and justice of their cause. Most research focuses on the intended effects of terrorist violence on its victims, i.e., creating public dismay and intimidating decision makers. But terrorists also seek to attract sympathizers, recruits, and political support, as well as raise morale and promote cohesion within their group. This is particularly important in a widely dispersed network where day-to-day communications and personal contact are problematic. The terrorist, who is fundamentally weak, uses violence to demonstrate strength and thereby attract followers. A recent al-Qaida publication noted that motivating the target population of potential sympathizers is difficult:

> The Mujahedin must understand that most people are preoccupied with the life of this world and are running after their daily bread . . . . The Mujahedin must create such conditions [of support] by means of quality operations such as September 11 and by means of organized media efforts.[5]

Usama bin Ladin explained that the significance of the 9/11 attacks was showing the Muslim world that his movement was capable of punishing the world's preeminent power. "When people see a strong horse and a weak horse," he said, "by nature they will like the strong horse."[6] So the same event has multiple purposes and can be interpreted various ways through different lenses, with different effects. Terrorist violence inside the United States is intended not only to terrify but also to captivate. Actions that are barbaric to us are praiseworthy to others, and coverage is the common coin. A terrorist would agree with playwright Brendan Behan when he observed, "All publicity is good, except an obituary notice."

Organizing for Information War

Terrorist media relations are part of a general conception of information operations that includes agitation, propaganda, and indoctrination, focused both internally and externally. Al-Qaida's information operations are (or were, before 9/11) under the supervision of a major division called the "Information Committee."[7] The Information Committee was divided into subunits including Computers, Foreign Relations, Photography, Phonetics, Translation, and Microfiche. The committee head, originally Kuwait-born Sulyman Abu Gaith, was required to have five years work experience, have Jihad combat experience, be not less than thirty years old and physically fit, have a working knowledge of Islamic law, be "[sincere] of his manner of speaking, large hearted, mild tempered, [with the ability] to plan ahead, [be] correct in opinion, smart and clever." He also had to be able to maintain secrecy, since his unit would serve as an interface between the terrorist cells and the outside world, and operational security is always an imperative. Note that Abu Gaith was not informed of the 9/11 attacks before they happened, and only learned about them while watching them on television with the al-Qaida leadership. An event that size did not need a prearranged media strategy; it created its own coverage.

General message guidance for the committee included stressing the importance of the jihad as a means of promoting change, exposing the flaws in arguments of al-Qaida's enemies, maintaining relations with sympathetic Islamic groups (with a view toward bringing them into the fold), preventing internal criticism of the movement except through accepted channels, and obeying central guidance when conveying major policy provisions (i.e., sticking to the talking points). The al-Qaida Information Committee coordinated "all of the scientific, legal, and Jihad capabilities . . . in order to construct one line in front of the alliance of the infidel and the ugly ones." Maintaining message discipline can be understandably difficult in decentralized terrorist networks. It is also hard to confirm what information is being released because of the number of media outlets that report on terrorism with varying records of accuracy and fidelity to their sources.

Terrorist groups in the developing world often do not have ready access to free media, since in many countries, particularly in the Middle East, the media is under state supervision or control. Information operations in closed societies takes the form of underground activity—the surreptitious distribution of leaflets, letters, sermons, audio and video tapes, CDs, and other media. Such information reaches fewer people, but those who receive it are more likely to be active consumers. In 1998 al-Qaida produced a lengthy strategy paper, "Incite the Believers," detailing such a campaign in Saudi Arabia.[8] It envisioned:

> a comprehensive information program for incitement under the supervision of a group of knowledge seekers and propagandists. Its objective is to find a wide base of Muslims inside the Arabian Peninsula, in specific, and the Islamic nation, in general, that believes in implementing the required Jihad in the sake of Allah and to push back the Jews and the Crusaders.

The 124-page document, posted on several Web sites, contained minute details on objectives, justification, and means of pursuing the struggle against the Saudi regime and its Western supporters.

Exploiting the Free Press

Terrorists face fewer challenges spreading the word in open societies, where they can exploit the dynamics of the free press. This has never been difficult; terrorism has everything reporters want—violence, human drama, jeopardy, story lines, exotic and charismatic characters, and good visuals.[9] With the advent of cable television, securing coverage has become even easier. The media are under tremendous pressure for content. The expression "twenty-four-hour news cycle" misstates the condition of contemporary media. The news cycle used to be twenty-four hours, culminating with the evening newscast. But with the advent of around-the-clock news coverage there is no cycle, just a continuous renewal, a continuum punctuated by morning deadlines for the press and evening deadlines for the networks, but nevertheless driven by the agenda-setting power of the ceaseless stream of cable news. In the words of one viewer, cable news is like a great white shark: "They never sleep and are always hungry."[10]

The demands of the continuum have sharpened the competition between journalists. They face time limits and pressure for breaking the scoop, which means there is no longer a choice between waiting several hours for the regular newscast or interrupting regular programming. Hot stories can now go on the air immediately. This can lead to reporting rumor—such as the allegations about terrorist strikes hitting the U.S. Capitol and a car bomb exploding at the State Department on September 11, 2001.[11]

Nevertheless, when journalists need instant information, terrorists are there to help. According to al-Qaida spokesman Abd al-Rahman al-Rashid, one of the objectives of the terrorist information strategy is to enable and facilitate "immediate media response to the event."[12] Al-Qaida's information warriors are conscious of their role as the prime source of information about their organization. "The [story] is essentially based on the source," he said. "All right, we are a source and provide the media men with the news. . . . The Mujahedin do not have in general any problem in making their voice reach any newspaper or channel."[13]

Terrorists use access control as a means of shaping coverage. They can give exclusives to reporters they wish to court, such as granting interviews with top leaders or allowing journalists to accompany teams on attacks. This adds value and authenticity to the stories and promotes the career of the journalist. Terrorists can also control coverage by denying access, depending on the results of prior collaborations. Al-Rashid noted that they differentiate messages intended for international consumption and for the Arab press. In addition, they do not like to work directly with media outlets that have a history of negative stories about the Mujahedin. They monitor sources closely to see how they are covered. Furthermore, al-Qaida has an important asset in Usama bin Ladin. Any new material released by bin Ladin will find an immediate audience with the global press. Al-Rashid noted that the al-Qaida leader has no particular desire to seek publicity, but in fact he is their most important on-air talent, immediately recognizable, invoking strong emotions, and highly marketable.

The al-Qaida–affiliated Abu Sayyaf Group (ASG) has an excellent record of maximizing coverage by catering to the interests of the media. The ASG has exploited the strong tradition of freedom and independence of the Philippine press and, despite being neither the largest nor the longest active terrorist group in the country, receives the most coverage. The relationship of the ASG with the press gives the group a competitive advantage over other groups. For example, in 2000 President Joseph Estrada launched a military offensive against the Moro Independent Liberation Front (MILF), at the time a better established and more significant threat to the Philippines than the ASG. But most press coverage went not to Estrada's offensive but to an ASG raid of the Sipadan and resulting hostage crisis and negotiations. According to an analysis of the event, "The greater news attention given to the Abu Sayyaf follows traditional news values—the story had more drama and more excitement than the largely invisible international terrorist cells. The story was easier to sell, and TV exploited the visual elements. The competition for scoops was so sharp that media TV correspondents were instructed not to return to Manila for so long as the competing network's team stayed on site."[14]

Terrorists will also seek more direct influence over the media. They have no particular respect for journalistic integrity or independence. They will seek out coreligionists, sympathetic reporters and organizations, and appeal to their pre-existing biases, seeking favorable treatment. Penetrating news organizations and attempting to extend their influence is simply another field of endeavor, another arena of jihad. The Al Jazeera network is a case in point. Qatar-based Al Jazeera started out in 1996 as a liberal alternative to the state-controlled media in the Middle East. During Operation Enduring Freedom it became the primary vehicle for al-Qaida to release videotapes of Usama bin Ladin, Ayman al Zawahiri, Abu Gaith and others. This led to charges that Al Jazeera was in league with the terrorists. From al-Qaida's point of view, they were simply executing their script, seeking the outlet that would best reach its target audiences, primarily Muslims in the region, and secondarily the rest of the world. Al Jazeera was the first twenty-four-hour all-news network in the Arab world, thus a natural conduit. Chief news editor Ibrahim Helal said, "If we can reach [U]sama, or [U]sama can reach us, it's just journalism."[15] For Al Jazeera, the key motivation was the scoop, and it made the network famous.

But there was some evidence that even by 2000 the Al Jazeera newsroom had begun to tilt toward a more sympathetic view of terrorism. With the advent of the "second intifadah" in Israel in 2000, Palestinian terrorists began to be called *fedayeen* (fighters for peace), and those who were killed *shuhada* (martyrs). Munir Mawari, a Yemeni journalist who worked at Al Jazeera from 2000 to 2003, estimates that 50–70 percent of the people who work there are either members or sympathizers of Islamic fundamentalist groups.[16] Many had close links to HAMAS, the Egyptian Muslim Brotherhood, and other terrorist organizations. "We watched them while they worked and we used to say that they were preparing 'breaking news' on a terrorist attack that would take place a few hours later," Mawari said. His colleagues had the information about attacks in advance and only had to wait "in order to add on the casualty figures."[17] He believes that al-Qaida chose to work with Al Jazeera because of the sympathies of the people working there. Yet, the journalists could argue that they have simply developed good sources, and if they are given information in advance it only reflects their good work. Al Jazeera Moscow Bureau Chief Abram Khazam rejects the notion that anyone in his network is complicit with Al-Qaida, and insists that Usama bin Ladin is "a product of the United States. I am sure of it because through him the United States could invade Afghanistan, come to Central Asia for a long time, and occupy Iraq. Now I do not care whether he exists or not."[18]

Not all terrorist groups view reporters as potential allies. Even media-savvy al-Qaida has periodically denounced the Western media (or, as they call it, the "Jewish press") and refused requests for interviews. The Taliban were even more suspicious of journalists and often treated reporters as espionage agents. Covering the Taliban was dangerous; nine journalists were killed in Afghanistan in 2001, most notably on November 19, 2001, when Taliban fighters executed four journalists taken from a convoy in Nangarhar Province. In July 2004 Mullah Omar, in a letter faxed to newspapers, blamed journalists for the deaths of two Taliban commanders, alleging they later worked with authorities revealing what they had learned during interviews. He said that "journalists who work for infidel forces deserve to be killed, and they should be murdered."[19] Mullah Omar may have believed he had cause for concern: Taliban Deputy Interior Minister Mohammed Khaksar, who claimed to have been an informant for Western intelligence services, stated that he was contacted by agents disguised as journalists "two or three times" before the war.[20] As well, al-Qaida sent two assassins disguised as journalists to kill Afghan resistance leader Ahmed Shah Massoud on September 9, 2001. These blurred lines emphasize the dangerous business of reporting the terrorist beat.[21]

The Power of Visuals

Compelling images are critical for the media. A good picture or video segment can make a story. As previously noted, this is another of the attractive features of terrorism as news. The Popular Front for the Liberation of Palestine (PFLP), which had pioneered terrorist hijacking in 1968, demonstrated the power of images when they hijacked three passenger aircraft on September 9, 1970, flew them to Dawson's Field in the Jordanian desert, and three days later, having assembled the press, blew the aircraft up. It marked the advent of the age of the mass media–terrorism symbiosis.

While some media outlets restrict the type of images they transmit (for example, the video of the beheading of journalist Daniel Pearl, or other similar bloody scenes), terrorists can create events that are too compelling to resist. For example, many raised ethical qualms about printing disturbing photos from the 9/11 attacks, particularly the images of trapped people leaping from the flaming World Trade Towers. One study of 22 newspapers nationwide showed that although the editorial staffs had misgivings, 18 of them decided to run the photos. The authors noted that

> despite being concerned with reader response and invasion of privacy, the overwhelming reason the photography editors said they published the disturbing photographs was because they contributed to the overall story about the attacks. A few editors remarked that they would not run such disturbing images but that the immensity of the attacks prompted them to reevaluate their reasoning.[22]

One can conclude that in the case of a particularly gruesome attack on the homeland, particularly involving chemical, biological, or nuclear weapons, the media will show as much as they believe the public can tolerate.

Terrorists do not need to rely on the media to frame the visuals of their events. They produce their own videos and other images with sometimes crude but increasingly sophisticated production values. These may take the form of video suicide notes, images of beheadings or other killings, or films of combat, particularly ambushes against vehicles. Chechen guerrillas have been particularly active in making and distributing videos of their operations against Russian forces. Hizballah uses homemade videos of its attacks to prove that they took place in the face of possible Israeli denials.[23] A Pakistani production company called al-Sahab ("the Clouds") has produced and distributed many of the post-9/11 al-Qaida videos. The videos are sent through channels to outlets such as Al Jazeera or the Middle East Broadcasting Centre (MBC) in Bahrain. If the networks fail to run them (as sometimes happens), the videos can be posted to Web sites where they are frequently picked up by other conventional media outlets. For example, in December 2003, numerous Jihadist Web sites carried links to an al-Sahab multimedia production, "The Martyrs of the Confrontations in the Arab Peninsula," a tribute to the terrorists killed by Saudi authorities. The tapes included rereleases of statements from bin Ladin, which initially garnered much more attention and publicity than the videos warranted.

Of course imagery can work both ways. The same media that publicize the effects of terrorist violence will also show the comeuppance of those who commit it. Scenes such as the capture of al-Qaida treasurer and operations planner Khalid Sheikh Mohammed in March 2003 in Rawalpindi help strip some of the romance from terrorism. The image of the unshaven, overweight, and despondent terrorist mastermind in a shabby room in his underwear spoke for itself. It illustrated to those who would emulate him that there is a definite downside to the lifestyle of the international terrorist. Likewise, the image of Saddam Hussein being taken from his spider-hole was a necessary antidote to some of the more fanciful tales of his directing the violence in Iraq from a secret headquarters.

Web-Based Terrorism

The Internet and World Wide Web are ideal vehicles for terrorist communication. The Web is secure and easy to access, has global reach, and facilitates inexpensive entrée to the media. The Web acts as a gateway to the major press outlets, either directly or through smaller media organs. Despite some misgivings, mainstream journalists increasingly use the Web to conduct research and gather information. Al-Qaida has been active in this area for many years. In 1997 Saudi opposition leader Muhammad al-Masri became chairman of the "Ummah Trust," a British umbrella group that supported the "Islamic Gateway Project" (www.ummah.net), which gave radicals such as bin Ladin access to the Web. Al-Masri was instrumental in disseminating al-Qaida's 1996 Declaration of War through a network of fax machines. He "personally supervised the translation and distribution of the English-language version," which was uploaded to the Web and reprinted in the Western press.[24] His group regularly distributes information to "fraternal media outlets," primarily newspapers owned by sympathizers in Europe and North America. Al-Masri is straightforward about his objectives; he stated that the Islamic Gateway "exists to benefit the struggle for re-establishment of Islamic Rule over the planet, *insha'llah*."[25]

Iraqi terrorist groups have opened Web sites and traded information on publicly accessible Internet forums, where reporters can follow them from anywhere in the world. One example is the al-Faruq Brigades Yahoo group, linked to the increasingly popular al-Qaida–affiliated "Global Islamic Media Center," which apparently has no existence outside the Web.[26] However, the proliferation of jihadist Web sites and the resulting lack of central control have led to a splintering of the message and focus of the radical movement. This is understandable; the same strengths that allow terrorists to exploit the Web (low cost, ease of access, and equal ability to reach any Web-based media consumer) also allow other similar groups to erect and sustain a Web presence without the message control that al-Qaida had identified as a priority. An August 2004 posting on the "Global Islamic Media Center" site called for the creation of "a unified, Islamic media front on a global scope in a coordinated fashion." The posting noted, "In fact, such a front does exist but in an unsatisfactory, weak, dispersed, unacceptable, uncoordinated, and disorganized manner."[27]

The Impact on the Homeland

Al-Qaida can take credit for making terrorism a dominant news story. One measure of the impact of al-Qaida on press coverage is the frequency with which mention is made of its leader. Figure 22-1 shows the number of articles referring to Usama bin Ladin in *USA Today*, the *New York Times*, the *Washington Post* and the *Los Angeles Times*, by month, from August 2001 to July 2004. In August 2001, references to bin Ladin numbered 30 across the four papers (surprisingly, about one a day even before the attacks). Two months later articles referring to bin Ladin reached a high of 1,914 (61 per day, or about 15 per newspaper per day). This was the most attention that had ever been paid to the terrorist leader and his message.

After coverage peaked in October 2001, references to bin Ladin declined steeply until increasingly slightly in May 2002, following the appearance of videotapes of the al-Qaida leader in April (see Figure 22-2). Coverage of bin Ladin then flattened out, with occasional peaks linked to specific events.

References in September 2002 more than doubled over the previous month due to the anniversary of 9/11, and al-Qaida engineered a successful media event by releasing a tape of Usama bin Ladin on September 9 in which the group made its first public admission that it had planned and executed the attacks. In early October, Ayman al Zawahiri appeared in a taped announcement of the beginning of a fall offensive by al-Qaida, and

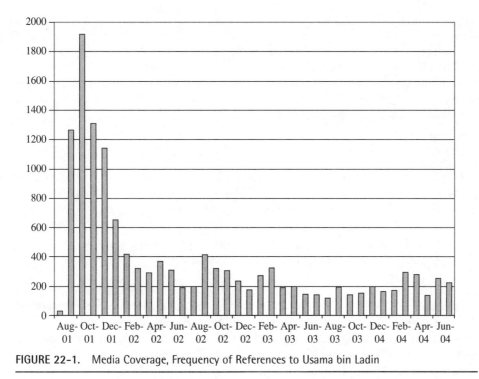

FIGURE 22–1. Media Coverage, Frequency of References to Usama bin Ladin

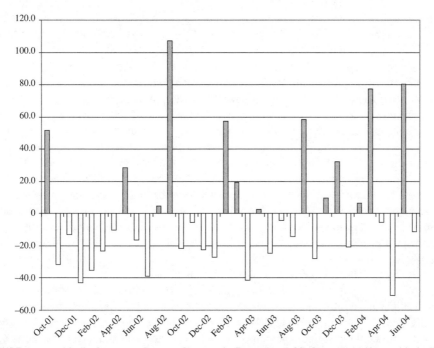

FIGURE 22–2. Media Coverage, Percent Changes in Frequency of References to Usama bin Ladin

though coverage remained higher than usual, it still eroded during this period. Bin Ladin's name appeared more frequently during the lead-up to the war in Iraq, again in September 2003 (though less than half as frequently as September 2002), and coverage rose during the 9/11 Commission hearings and after the final report was issued.

However, from the summer of 2002 to the summer of 2004 references to bin Ladin declined overall, and from April 2003 to February 2004 the numbers stayed below 200 per month. When they have recently exceeded this level it has little to do with current al-Qaida operations and more with echoed references to the 9/11 attacks. Bin Ladin still enjoys about six times the press attention he got before September 2001, but references have dropped 90 percent from their peak.

Measuring the extent of coverage is one matter; knowing how it affects the public is another. There are numerous methodological challenges in measuring the impact of media coverage.[28] At base, one must demonstrate:

1. That people are paying attention to the coverage; and
2. How and to what degree they are affected by it.

Independent data indicates that the public tends to pay close attention to coverage of domestic terror attacks. A 1995 Pew Center survey showed that 58 percent of Americans followed news of the Oklahoma City "very closely," compared to the 23 percent average score for any story, and against the general drift toward not following the news closely at all.[29] A similar Pew survey from December 2001 showed that the percentage of Americans who followed coverage of terrorist attacks "very closely" peaked in mid-October at 78 percent, declining to 60 percent by December. (Note that public attention peaked simultaneously with the intensity of coverage.) The domestic terrorism story garnered far more attention than U.S. overseas military operations—only 44 percent followed operations in Afghanistan "very closely."[30] Data also shows that the public can be affected by watching coverage. A Pew survey in October 2001 showed an aggregate 69 percent agreed or strongly agreed with the statement that "It's frightening to watch news about terrorism." This had declined from a high of 77 percent in mid-September.[31]

From this data one may at least conclude that events such as 9/11 lead simultaneously to media coverage and to public anxiety. The Pew data from the fall of 2001 indicate that coverage heightens anxiety, but it should also be noted that heightened public interest can in turn lead to more press coverage as the market meets demand for news. This is a methodological quandary since it establishes a recursive relationship between the variables that might be difficult to disaggregate. Note that one study of response to media coverage of terror attacks in Israel showed greater anxiety levels in those exposed to news coverage than those not exposed.[32] This is a good example of a controlled approach to studying the phenomenon. However, from the terrorist's point of view, the finer points of social science may be irrelevant to the fact that they get the publicity they are seeking.[33]

A basic analytical question is whether levels of public anxiety co-vary with coverage. Even this descriptive effort can be a difficult proposition. Major news and research organizations have only sporadically conducted polls on public feelings about terrorism, usually tied to breaking events. However, some polls have been conducted over long enough time to allow for comparisons. Two sets of data, one from a series of polls conducted by CNN/Time Magazine (Figure 22-3) and another from the Pew Center (Figure 22-4) were compared to an index derived from the data on references to Usama bin Ladin,

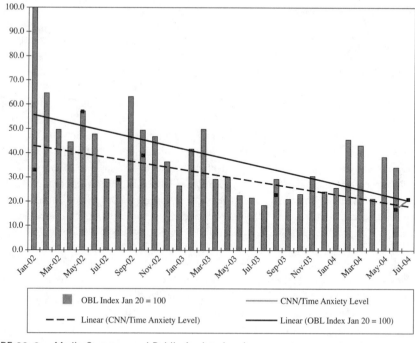

FIGURE 22-3. Media Coverage and Public Anxiety Levels

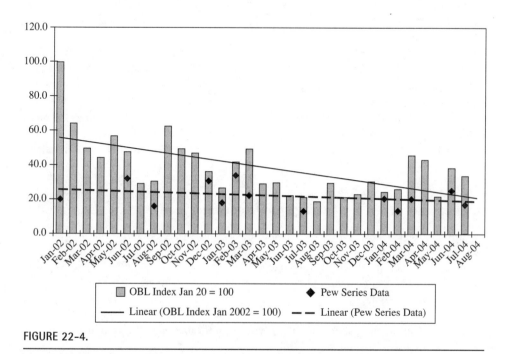

FIGURE 22-4.

with January 2002 set as 100.[34] In both sets, the poll numbers indicate the percentage of Americans who believed an attack on the United States in the next twelve months was "very likely." The data show broad trends of declining coverage and declining attack anxiety levels (less so in the Pew set, which is basically flat). Perhaps more revealing, the anxiety data from individual surveys, though regrettably sparse, tends to track movements of press attention to bin Ladin (again, less so in the Pew data).[35]

As of this writing (August 2004) terrorists have not carried out a major attack on the United States since 9/11. It is certain that they are seeking to strike. Violent action is the primary means by which they legitimize themselves and their cause. Their followers want to see them engage in direct confrontation with the United States, and the longer they wait, the less relevant they become. Terrorist groups such as al-Qaida face the same dilemma as the government in the period between attacks (as Major Elizabeth Robbins notes in her article in this volume)—they have to devise ways to maintain the media's attention.

Al-Qaida has attempted to fill this void and raise public levels of concern by issuing threats of impending attacks. In a 53-minute tape released in February 2003 Usama bin Ladin claimed that a large strike would take place soon led by him personally, and that he would "die in the eagle's belly," a reference widely believed to refer to an attack on the U.S. homeland. In June 2003, Al-Qaida spokesman Abu-Muhammad al-Ablaj stated that an attack was near. In the fall of 2003, Abu Salma al Hijazi, another spokesman and self-described lieutenant to Usama bin Ladin, stated that "a huge and courageous strike" would take place during or very near the approaching Ramadan. He estimated 100,000 people would die. Al-Ablaj also stated separately that the group would strike a mortal blow at the United States during Ramadan, and that active planning had been under way for a month. "Time is running fast," he said. "We are preparing for a great day in the Arab region and in a place in the Western countries that Abu-Abdallah [Usama bin Ladin] referred to in his message to the American people." He added, "Either it does not happen and we are lying, or it happens and we are telling the truth."

None of these attacks came about, and some of the participants in the Jihadist chat rooms showed signs of disillusionment. One online al-Qaida sympathizer complained that "Our houses are full of rice, flour, and dates" in anticipation of the attacks, and "the Muslims morale is low" because nothing happened during Ramadan in spite of the many threats. "This is precisely what Muslims do not need," he concluded.[36] The hollow threats also have created a credibility gap with the media, which does not give them as much coverage as they did initially. Without action, al-Qaida will be unable to maintain its reputation.

Implications of Press Coverage for Homeland Security: The DC Snipers

Al-Qaida has specialized in the spectacular attack, usually a series of near-simultaneous blows intended to disrupt, paralyze, and astonish. Such attacks are difficult to carry out but guarantee widespread media coverage. However, terrorists do not need to go to such extraordinary lengths to secure publicity. A 1987 study[37] showed that factors that can increase coverage include:

- The unique event. The press will be more interested in an unusual type of attack than something familiar.

- The event of long duration, such as a hostage drama. One of history's most successful acts of terrorism was the Iranian hostage crisis. The event was closely choreographed to maximize press coverage, with great success. The *Washington Post* ran 916 articles on Iran in 1980, compared to 134 in 1978 during the much more significant Iranian revolution. The crisis spawned "America Held Hostage," later called "Nightline," secured Ted Koppel's career, and showed other journalists what was possible.[38]
- The domestic terror event, which will invariably receive more coverage than violence committed overseas.

A telling case that was unique, lengthy, and domestic was the October 2002 Beltway Sniper incident.[39] The first shots were fired the evening of October 2, 2002, and the gunmen, John Mohammed and Lee Malvo, were apprehended on October 24. During their three-week period of activity, Mohammed and Malvo conducted fourteen attacks, killing ten people and wounding three. Most dramatic was the initial period from 5:40 P.M. October 2 to 9:15 P.M. October 3, in which they carried out seven attacks, killing six people.[40] These attacks played to the three biases identified above. They were unusual (in manner of attack, and in scope), sustained over a three week period (and would have gone longer had the gunmen not been caught), and took place within the United States, significantly in the nation's capital.

The total number of casualties over these three weeks was small compared to the 9/11 attacks, but the coverage nationwide was excessive. Cable news viewership rose 40 percent during the operation period, and 91 percent of respondents to a USA TODAY/CNN/Gallup Poll said that they were following the case "very" or "somewhat" closely.[41] Compare this result to the Pew data noted above, that similar attention to 9/11 coverage peaked at 78 percent. Newspaper editors at the annual Associated Press Managing Editors Conference took cable news to task for sensationalizing the story, and in the words of one editor, "trying to take 15 minutes of news and stretch it into a three-hour window."[42] However, newspapers also covered the story excessively, to the limits of their medium. Using the same index used to measure articles referring to Usama bin Ladin, 1,502 stories were filed in October 2002 dealing with snipers or shooting in Washington, 19 percent more than ran about bin Laden in September 2001.[43]

The *Washington Post* naturally gave the story total exposure. It was literally front-page news every day from October 4 through the time the gunmen were captured. Front-page coverage alone averaged two stories per day, ranging from one to four. Over 206,000 words were published in news, features, analyses, editorials, opinion pieces and letters relating to the attacks and their effects. Average coverage was over 10,000 words per day. Coverage tended to spike the day after attacks, with some exceptions—the highest level of coverage was October 17, with over 22,000 words and three front-page articles. This came in the middle of what turned out to be a four-day lull in attacks, the longest period without an attack during the operation. A seven-day moving average of words printed shows that coverage climbed for two weeks before leveling out at around 12,500 words per day.

Volume of coverage was driven in part by regular news briefings by the investigation team, even when there was nothing to report. As Paul Fahri of the *Post* put it,

> The relationship between the police and the news media in such situations is often symbiotic—both sides have something to gain by keeping the story

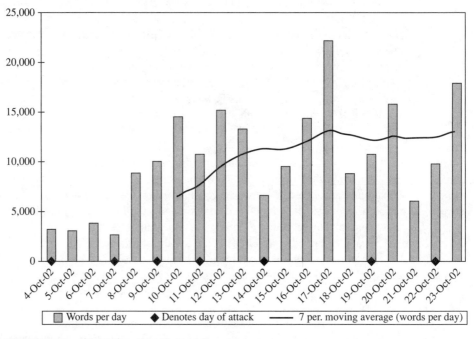

FIGURE 22-5. Washington Post "Sniper" Coverage

"alive." The live news briefing is partly a public service, partly an exercise in community hand-holding, partly an attempt at group crime-solving. There's some grandstanding, too. And the ratings are boffo.[44]

Fahri noted that, if nothing else, regular briefings allow authorities to address rumors that are usually rampant during crises.[45]

The shootings were the most important media event of 2002, and this was achieved without an active information strategy on the part of the gunmen. The only statements they left were cryptic, such as a tarot card with the statement "Dear Policeman: I am God," which did not convey their radical Jihadist message. The gunmen's motives were unambiguous in the copious letters and drawings Lee Malvo later made in prison. One of them shows a drawing of the Twin Towers burning with a plane flying toward them, a self-portrait of Malvo as a sniper labeled "Believer" and a drawing of Usama bin Ladin labeled "prophet." A caption reads, "JIHAD ISLAM UNITE RISE!"[46] In another the White House is seen through a sniper scope, with the messages "Sep. 11 we will ensure will look like a picnic to you," and "You will bleed to death little by little."[47] The lack of an obvious message led to a great deal of speculation as to the gunmen's motives, most of which ironically pointed away from radical Islam.[48]

Nevertheless, the operation was very successful. A poll of area residents conducted by the *Washington Post* in the third week of the attacks showed that 50 percent of respondents were either somewhat or very fearful of falling victim to the gunmen.[49] Comparable nationwide data from September 2002 polls by CNN/USAToday, Gallup, and Fox News showed that the generic level of concern that one could personally fall victim to a terror attack ranged from 20–38 percent. The *Post* poll also showed that 19 percent of respondents said they had no worries about being victimized, compared to 25–57 percent in the September national polls. Forty percent of respondents in the *Post* poll said that the shootings made them feel personally more threatened than either the 9/11 attacks or the fall 2001 anthrax attacks. Half the respondents said that they had altered their behavior.

Another report said that public response to the sniper attacks was greater than to 9/11 because of the sheer randomness of the attacks.[50] Anyone could be a victim. Press coverage focusing on self-defense measures encouraged this type of thinking and some commentary bordered on the ridiculous. In one case, a former police detective cautioned listeners to "avoid loitering anywhere, to carry something in front of us as a shield—even our folded arms would do—and to walk at a 45-degree angle."[51] Dr. Harvey Goldstein, a psychologist who teaches classes to law enforcement agencies including the Secret Service, noted,

> Another radio show told of service station customers who would not take the time to fill up their gas tanks, but were buying just enough fuel to keep going, afraid to linger at the pump and afford an easy target—as if a few seconds would discourage the shooter. In fact, we are much more likely to be killed in a car accident than by a sniper, but we don't abandon our cars because of it.[52]

Mohammed and Malvo generated the climate of fear they had intended. And they showed that attacks do not have to be "spectacular" to dominate the news. However, a more significant finding of the *Post* poll was not the anxiety the attacks generated, but the sense of rage. Seventy-five percent of the respondents said that they were angered by the attacks. When broken down by gender, the poll showed that among men, three-fourths reported anger to the level of outrage. This is a critical finding. The people of Washington, though proportionately more fearful than the rest of the country over possibly falling victim to terrorist violence, were not gripped by a European fatalism, a sense of helplessness in the face of events beyond their control. They were much more likely to be angry, and anger can be mobilized and lead to action. The attacks did not weaken public resolve, but made citizens more resolute.

This finding should help shape future research on the question of the impact of terrorist events and the attendant media coverage on populations. If researchers only ask people if they are "terrorized" (i.e., asking if the enemy has achieved their objective), that is all we will learn. Research design that seeks fear and despair will probably find it, but this approach will magnify the negative impact of terrorism.

A broader approach is necessary to understand the phenomenon, and translate understanding into policy. Terrorism can incite numerous emotions, many of which have implications for responses at every level (strategic, operational and tactical). Anger is not an emotion that terrorists want to generate. Yet it can be pervasive and enduring. Three years after the 9/11 attacks few Americans probably would describe themselves as still feeling fear because of it (though they may have trepidation over possible future attacks). However, mentioning the attacks still conjures a visceral hatred of Usama bin Ladin and al-Qaida from almost every segment of the population. Future terrorist attacks on the U.S. homeland of any kind will undoubtedly receive saturation coverage from the media. But the attackers would be mistaken to believe that this would automatically be translated into a sense of national despair. A more likely outcome would be a combination of fear, sorrow, and resolve to take whatever action was necessary to end the terrorist threat.

Notes

1. Abd-al-Rahman al-Rashid, "Interview," *Al-Majallah*, October 13, 2002, pp. 30–32.
2. Abraham H. Miller, "Terrorism, the Media and the Law: A Discussion of the Issues," in *Terrorism, the Media and the Law*, ed. Abraham H. Miller (Dobbs Ferry, NY: Transnational Publishers, 1982).
3. See for example Miller, "Terrorism, the Media, and the Law"; Robert G. Picard, *Media Portrayals of Terrorism* (Ames: Iowa State University Press, 1993); Yonah Alexander and Richard Latter, eds. *Terrorism and the Media* (New York: Brassey's, 1990); Brigitte L. Nacos, *Mass-Mediated Terrorism: The Central Role of the Media in Terrorism and Counterterrorism* (New York: Rowman & Littlefield Publishers, 2002); and Stephen Hess and Marvin Kalb, eds., *The Media and the War on Terrorism* (Washington, DC: Brookings Institution Press, 2003).
4. Muwaffaq al-Jammal, "Interview," *Damascus Al-Ba'th*, July 12, 1999, p. 13.
5. Translated in "JTIC/MEMRI Joint Investigation; Jihad on the Web, Part II," *Jane's Terrorism and Insurgency Centre,* March 18, 2004, http://gtic.janes.com.
6. Bin Laden tape, made probably mid-November 2001, released December 13, 2001.
7. AFGP-2002–000078.
8. AFGP-2002–002883/SUB-00956.
9. To an extent, the media is biased toward creating anxiety on any type of story, not just terrorism. While overall risk factors in American life have declined dramatically over the past century, media coverage tends to focus on sensational areas of risk far out of proportion to what people actually experience. A good discussion of this phenomenon is found in Jane Spencer and Cynthia Crossen, "Fear Factors: Why do Americans Feel that Danger Lurks Everywhere?" *The Wall Street Journal*, April 24, 2003. The government also plays a role; the author notes that since the advent of the color-coded alert system in March 2002, "the Homeland Security department has never designated the U.S. to be at less than a 'significant' risk for terrorist attacks—level yellow. (The two lower levels, green and blue, haven't been used, and even the safest level—green—warns that the risk is 'low,' not zero.)"
10. Jon Sinton, of Atlanta, quoted in Bruce Schwartz, "Poll Finds Appetite for Sniper Coverage," *USA TODAY*, October 23, 2002. Sinton further stated that "(Often) there is no news there, and these guys are pounding the drum. It is better to wait for the evening (network) news when they have it all sorted out."
11. Stephen Jukes, "Real Time Responsibility: Journalism's Challenges in an Instantaneous Age," *Harvard International Review*, Summer 2002.
12. Abd-al-Rahman al-Rashid, "Interview."
13. Ibid.
14. Melinda Quintos de Jesus, "Media Coverage of Terrorism: The Philippine Experience" (Center for Media Freedom and Responsibility, 2002).
15. Mohammed el-Nawawy and Adel Iskandar, *Al-Jazeera: How the Free Arab News Network Scooped the World and Changed the Middle East* (Cambridge, MA: Westview Books, 2002), p. 148.

16. Magdi Allam, "I Will Tell You How al Jazeera has Changed from Being a Nonconfessional Broadcaster to Being an Islamic Militant," *Milan Corriere della Sera*, May 4, 2004, p. 8.

17. Ibid.

18. "Is it a private property? Al-Jazeera versus al-Qaida," *Almaty Novoye Pokoleniye*, May 1, 2004.

19. Abdul Wadood Baig, "Mullah Omar; We Will Soon Achieve Major Successes; The United States Got Mufti Shamzai and Nek Mohammed Martyred," *Karachi Islam*, July 19, 2004, p. 1, 6.

20. Peter Baker, "Defector Says Bin Laden Had Cash, Taliban In His Pocket," *The Washington Post*, November 30, 2001.

21. On the other hand, in December 2003, Pakistan arrested two French journalists who had interviewed Mullah Omar, charging them with violating immigration laws. See, "Two French Journalists Arrested for Interviewing Mullah Omar," *Karachi Ummat*, December 18, 2003, p. 1, 7.

22. Renee Martin Kratzer and Brian Kratzer, "How Newspapers Decided to Run Disturbing 9/11 Photos," *Newspaper Research Journal* 24 no. 1 (Winter 2003): 43. Note that there were also images of the bodies of the people who jumped after impact that were not run in any newspapers or magazines but could be found on the World Wide Web.

23. Muwaffaq al-Jammal, "Interview." p. 13.

24. "Saudi Opposition Figure Takes Over Global Islamic Internet Organization," Foreign Bureau Information Service, July 9, 1997. Hereafter cited as FBIS.

25. Ibid.

26. "Iraq: Anti-US Resistance Groups Proliferate, Use Media to Push Agendas," FBIS Media Analysis, July 18, 2003.

27. "Al-Qa'ida-Affiliated Website Urges Coordinated Internet Strategy," FBIS, August 3, 2004.

28. There is a very good discussion of the methodological issues in Richard W. Shaffert, *Media Coverage and Political Terrorists: A Quantitative Analysis* (New York: Praeger, 1992).

29. *Public Tunes Out Recent News* (Washington, DC: Pew Research Center for the People & the Press, May 19, 1994).

30. *Terrorism Transforms News Interest; Worries Over New Attacks Decline* (Washington, DC: Pew Research Center for the People & the Press, December 18, 2001).

31. *Attacks at Home Draw More Interest than War Abroad* (Washington, DC: Pew Research Center for the People & the Press, October 22, 2001).

32. See Michelle Sloan, "Responses to Media Coverage of Terrorism," *The Journal of Conflict Resolution* 44 no. 4 (August 2000): 508–522.

33. For a critical discussion of the issues in analyzing data of this type, see Robert G. Picard, "News Coverage as the Contagion of Terrorism," in *Media Coverage of Terrorism: Methods of Diffusion*, ed. A. Odasuo Alali and Kenoye Kelvin Eke, (London: Sage Publications, 1991), p. 49–62.

34. This date was chosen because it avoids distortions caused by the hyper-coverage of the fall of 2001.

35. This is a very limited approach, which can yield at best a descriptive conclusion. A robust study of this nature would involve more systematic collection of anxiety data at

set periods unrelated to terrorist activity, ideally involving large samples and a sub-group of respondents who would participate over the life of the survey to enable more rigorous data analysis.

36.   "Jihadist Chatrooms Criticize Bin Ladin, False Threats, Arab Leaders," FBIS, December 5, 2003.

37.   Micael X. Delli Carpini and Bruce A. Williams, "Television and Terrorism: Patterns of Presentation and Occurrence, 1969 to 1980," *The Western Political Quarterly* 40 no. 1 (March 1987): 45–64.

38.   Robert A. Friedlander, "Iran: The Hostage Seizure, the Media, and International Law," in *Terrorism, Media, and the Law,* ed. Abraham H. Miller (Dobbs Fery, NY: Transnational Publishers, 1982), pp. 51–66.

39.   Note that use of the term "sniper" is probably misplaced with respect to John Mohammed and Lee Malvo. They lacked the specialized training that one associates with military snipers. Early law enforcement focus on trained snipers is partly to blame for this moniker. Though colloquially used, and probably embedded in the public mind, the word *gunmen* is preferable and used herein.

40.   This includes the first shots fired, which hit a store window but did not kill or injure anyone.

41.   Bruce Schwartz, "Poll Finds Appetite for Sniper Coverage," *USA TODAY*, October 23, 2002.

42.   Joe Strupp, "Newspaper Editors Criticize TV Sniper Coverage**,**" *Editor and Publisher*, October 23, 2002.

43.   Note that of the three factors noted above, the 9/11 attack lacked duration.

44.   Paul Farhi, "The Reassuring Routine Of 'No-News' Briefings," *The Washington Post*, October 9, 2002.

45.   Countering rumor is an important part of any government information operation.

46.   Fairfax County Courts, *Commonwealth of Virginia v. Lee Boyd Malvo, a/k/a John Lee Malvo*, exhibit 65–057.

47.   Ibid., exhibit 65–117.

48.   Dana Priest and Brooke A. Masters gave a good overview of the issue in "Experts Look for Link To Al-Qaida Attacks; Officials Say Sniper Probably Is Unaffiliated," *The Washington Post*, October 16, 2002. Richard Roeper of the *Chicago Sun-Times* represented the politically correct version of events, denying the possibility that the snipers were motivated by radical Islamic sympathies even after their capture in "Right-wingers can't take getting sniper fact wrong," *Chicago Sun-Times*, November 5, 2002. Roper singled out the analysis by the author ("Who Is the Sniper? Behind the Evil," *National Review Online*, October 15, 2002), that concluded that the perpetrator was "an active member of al-Qaida, a bin Laden sympathizer, or someone motivated by the same type of hatred."

49.   Richard Morin and Claudia Deane, "Half of Area Residents In Fear, Post Poll Finds; Many Alter Routines as a Safety Measure," *The Washington Post,* October 24, 2002.

50.   Monte Reel, "A Region Running Scared? Response May Be Excessive, but Situation Is Unique, Experts Say," *The Washington Post*, October 19, 2002, p. A01.

51.   Harvey Goldstein, "News We Should Lose; Due to Circumstances Within Our Control We're Encouraging the Sniper," *The Washington Post*, October 13, 2002.

52.   Ibid.

Chapter 23

Leadership through Media

Elizabeth L. Robbins

Government decision makers frequently see media relations as a necessary—and some-times unnecessary—evil. This attitude is understandable given the sometimes fractious nature of government-media relations. However, when properly managed, the media offer solutions to public officials governing during domestic crises. This chapter offers sugges-tions on how to craft government-media relations strategies that serve the needs of gov-ernment while acknowledging that media are more interested in ratings and circulation than the public good.

This symbiotic relationship collides over control of information and its effects; thus, successful governance requires understanding and aligning the motivations of both par-ties. In theory, government-media relations could be neutral; in fact, there are strong cur-rents of negativity. The political culture and media's "watchdog" obligation have combined such that journalists have adopted an adversarial relationship as their profes-sional norm, the product of which is generally mutual mistrust.

Fortunately, many government officials understand that a bunker mentality is dysfunc-tional. When officials avoid media or approach them with caution, they damage their ability to govern. Government cannot afford to distance itself from those who possess the dominant ability to communicate with citizens—an ability that enables strategic, operational, and tacti-cal success. Since good governance requires media coverage and media's appetite for stories is both insatiable and capricious, this chapter explores how to maximize this relationship dur-ing two domestic homeland security circumstances: crisis and inter-crisis.

Crisis Motivations and Effects

In a crisis brought about by spectacular or large-scale violence, mass media effects are a force multiplier for the government.[1] When the public feels threatened, people turn to the mass media for information. Even when the Federal Communications Commission exercises its system of mandatory emergency broadcasts for television and radio, the stations that carry these brief and highly unusual messages are almost entirely privately owned and operated. Therefore, most information and comfort is conveyed by nongovernment sources.

What most citizens seek is an assessment of personal risk and an emotional con-nection to the event. Television is the most popular primary news source due to ease of access and compelling visuals, followed by radio, Web sites, and print. Given these usage and ownership patterns, government outreach to the media is the most efficient, cost-effective way to convey critical messages.

The government need not establish and secure communications systems parallel to the private sector. Many terrorists seek publicity for their acts, thus they are unlikely to attack existing private sector systems.[2] Even those few terrorists who eschew publicity will likely find less symbolic.[3] In addition, worst-case scenarios, such as blackout or nuclear detonation, will equally affect both government and private hardware and capabilities, forcing the government to respond with expanded law enforcement contact. Therefore, at no cost to the government, market forces provide effective mass communications systems with variety, redundancy, and geographic dispersal. In addition, concerning two-way communication, instead of establishing outreach mechanisms to gauge public sentiment, government leaders can rely on initial media output to determine whether they are providing the right type and amount of government services.

This profusion of media sources, coupled with widely available means of communication, such as the Internet, cellular phones, satellite phones, short-wave radio, and digital cameras, means that some crisis information will quickly reach citizens no matter the type or size of attack. The question for government officials is, *what* information needs to be presented in *which manner?*

Immediately following an attack on the homeland, government officials at the local, state, and federal levels will want to issue immediately actionable guidance. Citizens need to be advised of their relative safety, followed by recommendations on whether they should change locations or remain in place. Families will try to regroup, so the public needs information on the feasibility of such efforts given rescue and recovery operations. Next, government seeks to establish who is in charge. In particular, city, state, and federal officials want to establish their utility and operational competence. Press briefings will focus on previous preparations and current actions, implying that a disciplined network of government agencies is aggressively solving the people's problems. Intergovernment turf battles and resource competitions should give way to cooperation and unity, at least temporarily.

Local officials will attempt to control the crisis battle space in order to facilitate first-response operations. However, this should not extend to efforts to control information. Arguments for prohibiting media from crisis scenes include providing casualties with privacy and respect, avoiding the broadcast of specifics prior to family notification, preventing terrorists from coordinating follow-up attacks, protecting sensitive information (such as the compromise of military capability), protecting ongoing military and intelligence agency operations, and minimizing embarrassment due to inaccurate reporting or government gaffes. Other arguments include preventing mass hysteria, reducing imitative attacks, and denying terrorists status and legitimacy.[4]

The other, often unstated argument for restraining media coverage is to earn time for policymakers. The "CNN Effect," a term coined during the Gulf War for instantaneous and continuous news coverage, can put pressure on the decision cycle of government officials.[5] In addition, crisis media coverage tends to consist of reporting (providing facts and emotional reactions) rather than journalism (presenting information in context and explaining its meaning). When the media convey the extent of a crisis without contextualizing it, leaders may feel compelled to act before they are ready.

Despite these well-intentioned arguments, true information control is no longer possible. Video and digital cameras, as well as wireless Internet devices and camera cell phones, are routinely carried by regular citizens as well as first responders. Officials should assume that visuals and on-the-scene testimonials will be immediately disseminated. Preventing such information from swiftly reaching the media is nearly impossible,[6] as took place when cell phone camera images were broadcast by the mainstream media immediately following the

July 7, 2005 attack in London. As with post-9/11 coverage, when the media withheld images of identifiable corpses, market forces and community standards will influence the media to cover casualties with discretion. Concerning sensitive information, government agencies can request that media act with voluntary restraint, but the government is largely unable to compel legal compliance by formally censoring media output. Given this new reality, officials must aggressively pursue policies that positively impact media coverage.

It is generally believed that media relations during a crisis are the most problematic aspect of homeland security information operations. The fear is that the media will obscure the government's focused, deliberate message or reveal sensitive information that impairs government operations. But in fact, immediately following an attack, media motivations closely mirror those of the government.

Ultimately, media outlets are businesses seeking to maximize profits. Most profits are generated from advertising, and advertising revenues are tied to the number and demographic of consumers. To provide subject matter that attracts the largest audience, news media must provide truthful, relevant, timely information. Postcrisis consumers want actionable, immediate guidance, thus the media seeks out the most credible and accessible experts—typically, government officials, who are concurrently motivated to establish their utility and operational competence. Unless government officials are unprepared and avoiding exposure, the potential for conflict is minimal; the media will seek to link government officials with the American public.

The media's profit-driven public service impetus is augmented by individual ambition. Even when the corporate profit incentive is largely discarded—such as post-9/11 when some broadcasters did not run advertisements for several days—individual journalists are motivated by professional recognition and fame. Despite personal risk, individual journalists may flock to a crisis to burnish professional credentials.

Without much initial information, the media will struggle to contextualize crisis coverage. Organizing techniques for packaging stories are known as frames. Common frames are human interest (profiles of grief/courage/resolve), good vs. evil (victims and perpetrators), and horse race (who's ahead, who's behind). Immediately following an attack, the media will pursue human interest frames as they interview survivors and responders. Subsequently, media will pursue a good vs. evil framework to support local victims, to support government as citizens reflexively fall behind elected leadership, and to attempt to fix responsibility. In general, the media will go to the limit of what is known and move beyond into speculation, as occurred when the national media quickly and inaccurately fixed responsibility on Muslim extremists for the 1995 Oklahoma City bombing. Such media speculation, however unfair, can spur public and perpetrator responses that assist in identifying and apprehending the responsible parties.

Therefore, during crisis conditions, the government seeks to efficiently reach the public, and the media is anxious to assist. But following an attack, within hours or days, these motivations diverge as media cooperation and voluntary restraint dissolve. The true challenge for government officials is in maintaining media interest, and thereby public commitment, after fear abates.

Inter-crisis Motivations and Effects

The primary reason that the public consumes news is to further their personal and collective security. If the public learns of a significant threat, demand surges for follow-up media coverage and support mobilizes (at least initially) for those responsible for providing security.[7] Since the government is best able to address the public's most pressing concern, this is government's primary advantage in the postcrisis tussle of government-media relations.

But government's power is limited to the level of public concern, and maintaining this concern is difficult without new attacks or new threats. Publicizing a series of threats that do not materialize into attacks may erode public and media confidence—even though the threat may have been dire. This power to select news content is media's principal power. Given a planet's worth of intriguing story possibilities, most media are staffed to produce only a handful of original stories for a fickle consumer base with many other news options. In addition, the press faces structural limits: television and radio can broadcast only one lead story, and newspapers have limited front-page space. The humorist Will Rogers famously underscored the media's "gatekeeper" function by stating, "All I know is just what I read in the papers."[8]

When the media fails to report, citizens may forget that government officials are still closely engaged in homeland security issues. As public life normalizes but terrorist threats remain, the government is caught between two competing motivations—to allow domestic life to resume its routines by reducing terror about future threats, or to spur action and political will. The government is motivated to prepare citizens for various contingencies, to establish the cultural norm of vigilance, to support government workers, and to publicize target hardening (and thereby deterring attacks). Most importantly, the government must provide rationale to translate public sentiment that "something must be done" into political and financial support for government action.

However, as the public feels safer, it becomes more tolerant of government criticism. The media complies, using this opportunity to freshen up and improve the marketability of the homeland security story-line. The "good vs. evil" frame—i.e., the government vs. the terrorists—will have played out; ostensibly, in order to perform their watchdog function, the media will turn on those previously framed as heroes. For example, in August 2004, the Bush administration won positive publicity and spurred preventative action by raising the terror threat level in response to fresh intelligence from a captured enemy laptop. Yet within a few days, the media adopted the story line that the administration was manipulating public fears during an election year.[9] Producing such an opinion-based and mostly speculative story requires scant research and effort, plus creates the type of controversy that is good for ratings.

The media will also pursue politicization of homeland security issues driven by the internal bureaucratic politics of various government agencies. Government efforts to establish utility and operational competence may be, in appearance or in fact, less driven by the public interest than a desire to expand power. Since various levels and functions of government compete against each other for missions and resources, inevitably some officials will make their case directly to the citizenry either openly or through leaks and providing background interviews. While the media are uniquely positioned to publicize the opportunity costs of preparation against the probability of attack or the funding of other government programs, it is easier to write stories that chronicle interagency maneuvering using the horse race frame.

Therefore, unless there is a new crisis, market forces encourage the media to drift from publicizing homeland security efforts. Regardless of political or public service leanings, the primary media bias is toward stories that appeal to consumers. Few homeland security efforts provide the visuals essential for television coverage—the primary news source for most Americans. For instance, a Treasury Department team that uses their computer terminals to disrupt a terrorist financial network provides little visual value to a television producer. In addition, when the government subsequently publicizes this effort at a press conference, the news is not particularly "new" because the situation is no longer evolving. Success is by definition old news. Even worse, the media view such news with skepticism because they cannot perform their watchdog function of investigating and substantiating the government's claims. Lastly, if the media does cover the story, it will receive single-day, soft coverage because the operation is complete; such inconsistent story lines deny government the repeated coverage required to achieve broad public consciousness and support.

Meanwhile, the government's need to mobilize political will extends beyond domestic politics to include the broader strategic function of public diplomacy. Since many forms of domestic media reach foreign audiences, the media can serve unwittingly as a strategic enabler for government by helping to gain and maintain world support, as well as to provide an alternative view to favorable coverage of adversaries. For instance, following 9/11, Usama bin Ladin was not portrayed by the U.S. government or domestic media as a sympathetic figure.[10] This unfavorable perspective stood in contrast to positive international perspectives, but U.S. media did not sustain this story line.

Diminishing coverage of homeland security is one indicator that the media have different opinions than government of what it means to win the information war. In fact, most journalists view the fight as bypassing government censorship and control. In addition, the media may believe that the government is withholding news that is politically unfavorable, and some journalists will try to further their own convictions by using coverage to influence politics or policy. Lastly, some journalists believe that "balanced" coverage means routinely publicizing the philosophy and ideas of terrorists—the approach of "Why do they hate us? Are we to blame?" As Dr. James S. Robbins suggests in this volume, publicity is precisely what terrorists seek in order to terrorize the public and win recruits and sympathizers. The good news for government is that the media tend to downplay terrorist motives and goals in favor of more sensationalistic coverage of terrorist events. During the intercrisis period, the terrorists face the same dearth of coverage as the government.

Policy Solutions for Government Officials

An analysis of contemporary government-media relations suggests a number of initiatives through which this relationship can be improved for mutual benefit. These include assembling a crisis information dissemination team, providing selective members of the media with "crisis credentials" and establishing crisis roles and responsibilities.

Assemble the Crisis Information Dissemination Team

Despite widespread concern that media coverage is "the oxygen of terrorism,"[11] government officials must embrace the reality that a significant terrorist attack will receive non-stop domestic and international media coverage. To provide the public with the most useful post-attack coverage, the government should aggressively earmark and train any officials who are likely to be involved in information dissemination.

The media are free to decide how they will collect their information; as one German television and print journalist wryly observed, the media are "free to be lured this way and that."[12] But given the media's vital public information capabilities, the government should regard media representatives as part of its first-response team. The best-case scenario would be to establish government–media relationships in an inter-crisis period in order to develop mutual trust and cooperation, and to allow both parties to test the relationship when the stakes are low. Such trust may pay dividends in terms of balanced coverage and cooperation should the government need to request a delayed release of information.[13] Since limited numbers of media representatives can be allowed access to a crisis scene, local governments should proactively establish a means to "crisis-credential" local journalists who will be allowed access to crisis scenes; as required, these sources can feed to national media.

Some journalists will not embrace such a system; cooperation with government is viewed as compromising journalistic professional ethics. However, when offered access, most journalists will accept it while simultaneously complaining about coercion.[14] William Dean Singleton, chief executive officer of MediaNews, warns, "I think it's very dangerous for the press ever to make deals with the government." But given the need to occasionally cooperate, he agrees that the media should share this fact with the public in order to maintain their contract with consumers who want journalism to watch over government, not serve as its agent.[15] Therefore, in this situation, most credible news organizations will choose to crisis-credential some journalists while allowing others to report what they can without government involvement.

However, crisis-credentialing media and providing them access may not be embraced within the government. Government service generally does not reward risk-taking, and since 9/11, the stakes seem much higher. As noted by Jack Nelson, the former Washington bureau chief of the *Los Angeles Times*, "mushrooming government secrecy" has resulted in federal officials increasingly curbing reporters' physical freedom to seek out information, and mounds of documents are newly classified out of the reach of reporters.[16]

Cooperation requires courage and trust on the part of both parties, and establishing such a mutually beneficial relationship requires upfront effort and continuous dialogue. For instance, the government should arrange background discussions with the media in order to open the lines of communication, share expectations and ground rules, and explore their distinct roles in information warfare.[17] While responsible journalists are not combatants or tools of the government, government agencies must feel confident that journalists will not knowingly endanger individuals or ongoing covert operations. Concurrently, journalists must have confidence that government will not withhold information unless its release would truly compromise national security.[18] It is the obligation of media to work with the appropriate government agency when considering the publication of potentially sensitive information, and it is the obligation of the government, when necessary, to make a compelling argument against its release.

In addition, government officials need to appreciate that some negative coverage has beneficial effects. For instance, media skepticism about government preparations may prompt the public to weigh the costs and consequences of preventative and response measures; given limited resources, the public should understand the limitations of public officials and their own responsibilities. In addition, as Howard Kurtz of the *Washington*

Post reveals, even when skeptical stories are written about government policy, they receive less prominent placement than government declarations.[19] Therefore, such stories may be less damaging than public officials fear.

To familiarize emergency workers with media professionals operating within their midst, journalists and simulated media scenarios should be incorporated into training exercises. Government workers at all levels should practice interview techniques, establishing and staying on message, and limiting comments to the scope of one's job. Similarly, these training exercises serve media by spurring them to become familiar with government command structure as well as to purchase and to practice usage of special protective equipment that will promote access to biological or nuclear crises. Actual embedding, such as when journalists lived and moved with U.S. Forces during Operation Iraqi Freedom, is a reasonable media approach only when journalists cannot provide their own transportation or physical protection, or when they require long-term access to a restricted area or government team. Most officials need not plan for this contingency.

In addition, all parties must understand that media access does not authorize unrestricted reporting; thus, the government should establish parameters that are acceptable to both parties. The standard should be "why release," rather than "why," understanding that reasonable people can disagree about what constitutes a threat to operational security.[20] According to Kathryn Kross, the Washington bureau chief for CNN during Operation Iraqi Freedom (OIF), "They must balance our need to be where the action is with the needs of the military [or government] to operate undisturbed."[21] During OIF, journalists who chose to embed signed a binding contract with the government, agreeing to abide standard ground rules or risk revocation of media credentials.[22] Figure 23-1 provides excerpts from these ground rules, edited for homeland security scenarios.

Establish Crisis Roles and Responsibilities

The media will provide a platform to the first emergency workers or government officials who will grant them an interview. Therefore, given a network of responsible government agencies, leaders must predetermine roles and responsibilities. Ideally, spokesmen are established at each government level who work with their networked public affairs specialists in order to present a consistent, coordinated message. Establishing chains of command across functional boundaries is beyond the scope of this article but is clearly essential

When preparing command teams, government agencies must ensure that their primary public affairs officer is established as a special staff officer with full access to key decision makers. In addition, a deputy public affairs officer should be similarly informed so that "the thread of continuity, familiarity, and accessibility are not lost with the press or with the circumstances of the incident . . . because of exhaustion or improper backup."[23]

This access will ensure that the public affairs office can authoritatively speak for its agency, and the agency is perceived as informative and responsive. The Department of Homeland Security (DHS) has struggled with this issue itself:

> "Answering the complaints, Dennis Murphy, director of public affairs for border and transportation security, concedes that there have been issues with responsiveness . . . 'It's the age-old struggle between the operational side of the house and the press side of the house,' he says. Much like the Pentagon or

the CIA, Murphy explains, DHS must weigh every public response with its impact on national security, and that conflict naturally slows down the process of releasing information. 'We want to get the word out quickly, to be responsive, but operations folks want to make sure that we're not saying too much. It's a constant tug and pull.'"[24]

FIGURE 23-1.   Sample Ground Rules for Crisis-Credentialed Media

- All interviews with government officials will be on the record. Security at the source is the policy. Interviews with first responders are authorized upon completion of missions.
- Embargoes may be imposed to protect operational security. Embargoes will only be used for operational security and will be lifted as soon as the operational security issue has passed.
- The following categories of information are immediately releasable:
  - Information on and location of domestic terrorist targets previously under attack
  - Approximate figures and images of civilian casualties
  - Responding government agencies: names, origins (hometowns, etc..), and activities
  - Types of material or equipment being used, in general terms
  - International response efforts (search and rescue teams, International Red Cross, etc.) and donated materials (bottled water, decontamination equipment, etc.)
  - Operation code names
  - Service members' and government workers' names and home towns, given individual consent
- The following categories of information require prior approval from the Public Affairs Office since release may jeopardize operations or endanger lives:
  - Postponed, cancelled, future and ongoing offensive operations to capture or kill terrorists; extra precautions in reporting will be required at the commencement of an operation in order to maximize operational surprise
  - Individuals detained, captured, or killed; images or other visual media showing a detainee's recognizable face, nametag, or other identifying feature, or their custody procedures or interviews with authorities; media interviews with detainees
  - Numbers of responding military and law enforcement personnel, rules of engagement, and force protection measures (except those that are visible or readily apparent)
  - Intelligence collection and special operations units, to include activities, location, tactics, techniques, or procedures
  - Effectiveness of enemy electronic warfare, camouflage, cover, or deception
  - Names of first responders who are killed, missing, or injured until next of kin notification is complete
  - Images or other visual media showing a deceased's recognizable face or nametag or other identifying feature or item
  - Media visits to medical facilities will be in accordance with applicable medical facility regulations, standard operating procedures, operations orders, and instructions by attending physicians.

"I (insert name)_____, a (insert job description) _____, an employee of _____(insert news organization), have read the aforementioned media ground rules and agree, with my signature, to abide by them. I also understand that violation of these ground rules is cause for the revocation of my media accreditation with _____."

The DHS has recently codified the importance of the public affairs function in the final draft of its National Response Plan. However, local government officials may feel constrained by the many layers of control the plan imposes. For instance, following an "Incident of National Significance," DHS will create a temporary Joint Field Office (JFO) to serve as a coordination center for responding federal, state, local, tribal, nongovernmental, and private-sector organizations. The JFO will establish a Joint Information Center (JIC), where public affairs professionals from each of these agencies will:

> " . . . work together to provide critical emergency information, crisis communications, and public affairs support. The JIC serves as a focal point for the coordination and dissemination of information to the public and media concerning incident prevention, preparedness, response, recovery, and mitigation. . . . The JIC develops, coordinates, and disseminates unified news releases." [25]

Clearly, the federal government will assist localities by managing media inquiries that might otherwise hinder ongoing operations or be misrouted to the wrong level and function of government. In addition, when time is needed to develop viable solutions, local and state officials can reduce pressure on themselves by directing media inquiries to this clearinghouse. However, each level and agency of government retains an obligation to communicate with and provide leadership to their constituencies, and relinquishing all such power to a central agency is likely to be professionally and politically disastrous.

Prepare Draft Products

Public affairs officers should pre-prepare templates. These include press statements with generic information about the region and its resources, a series of daily updates that the government could be expected to provide given various contingencies (natural disaster, conventional bombing, biohazard, etc.), and draft crisis Web pages.

To provide the most accurate information, counter inaccurate reporting, and provide rumor control, government Web sites (both intranet and Internet) require dedicated personnel and manning to post daily or hourly updates. Lead agencies should be linked from the Web site of the appropriate level of government (city, county, state, or federal). The primary function of an agency Web site is to serve a dissemination function for crisis facts, government remediation efforts, and government contact information. A secondary function is to channel the potential outpouring of national and international support into means useful to the affected community. An optional, tertiary function is to establish a place for community members to post thoughts and images as part of the healing process. These crisis Web sites should augment routine public information sites such as the DHS preparation primer at www.ready.gov.

Expand Capabilities

During inter-crisis periods, government public affairs offices handle many fewer media inquiries than during a crisis. Accordingly, hardware capacity such as phone banks and computer servers should be expanded and allowances made to accommodate crisis surge capacity; ideally, computer networks should be backed up at an alternate site. Also, additional government personnel should be cross-trained to staff the public affairs function during crises.

Since the public information function is vital to good governance in crisis, plans must accommodate when government headquarters are the target of a terrorist attack. For instance, following the 9/11 Pentagon attack, much of the building was evacuated—to include the Army's central public affairs office; within hours, the Army recovered by switching operations to an existing satellite Army public affairs office located several miles away. Local government should establish the same options, either by equipping several different locations, or by purchasing mobile command centers with the capability to communicate with the media and to monitor output.

Shape News Stories

A terrorist event never occurs in a vacuum; thus, leaders must aggressively set the parameters that will assist media with contextualizing the news. Leadership matters, and the media will often follow the lead of top government leaders. For example, the morning of September 12, 2001, President Bush stated to the press, "The deliberate and deadly attacks which were carried out yesterday against our country were more than acts of terror. They were acts of war."[26] The paradigm that the nation was at war was promptly mirrored by the media with front page headings such as "America Attacked: The Investigation; Acts of War; Bush vows Full Assault, Says 'Good Will Prevail'" and "Bush: 'They Can't Hide.'"[27]

In contrast, President Clinton shared a different interpretation of the 1993 World Trade Center bombing, stating that he'd set in motion "the full, full resources of the federal law enforcement agencies—all kinds of agencies, all kinds of access to information—at the service of those who are trying to figure out who did this and why."[28] Accordingly, mainstream media mirrored his perspective with headlines such as "Clinton: Don't 'Overreact,' Urges calm after bombing" and "Clinton vows investigation of New York explosion."[29]

As the government communicates with the media, it can directly assist in packaging and story preparation if it is aware of the media's preferred frames. Quotes that emphasize the cowardliness of terrorists and the innocence of civilian casualties play directly into the good vs. evil frame. As the crisis fades and a horse race frame is adopted, the government can provide information that while an attack was horrifying and significant, it could have been worse, and future such attempts will be thwarted by government safeguards now in place.

The government can also directly influence news quality by engaging their own officials and scientists. Directly after a crisis, news media will provide unceasing coverage. In particular, cable news and talk shows may fill airtime with guests of questionable expertise. Public affairs officers should maintain updated lists of actual experts, some of whom may be recently retired from government service, and notify cable and network news producers of their availability. Preparation of these experts should be tied into the overall response plan as well as training exercises.

Finally, government should consider institutionalizing their communications techniques. Routine outreach such as a daily or weekly press briefing may be useful, even when there is nothing new to share (see below). For example, the much-maligned color-coded threat alert system initiated in January 2003 by the (then) Office of Homeland Security, is brilliant policy. While not offering many specifics, the existence of the system forces the media and the public to maintain a sense of insecurity that promotes political engagement. In addition, threat level changes earn top nationwide coverage, and should something untoward occur, government officials receive credit for having communicated previously their situational awareness.

Market News Stories

In order to prove that the government is doing anything at all, government public information officials must aggressively market stories. In addition, to generate public support for the homeland defense effort, officials need to shape coverage by engaging in the strategically placed communication known familiarly as "propaganda." The first step is to master the press release and video news release (VNR), as many news agencies are heavily dependent on them for story ideas. Drawing on public relations and advertising, another popular tactic is to create "pseudo-events"—circumstances that are staged solely for publicity.[30] Such events include showcasing the particular date that a new system, capability, or team is established as well as publicizing the subsequent anniversaries of these capabilities or the precipitating terrorist attacks. More common efforts include press conferences, official speeches, interviews, government facility tours, and radio and television talk shows. Colorful specifics such as capturing terrorists, disrupting cells, or exposing plots will facilitate the best results, but most coverage generated by pseudo-events will not receive top billing due to its forced nature. Officials should be aware that public interest limits the number of these PR "silver bullets," and a low volume of pseudo-events increases the news value of each one.

Alternatively, government may consider the special form of advertising known as the public service announcement (PSA). Possible PSA formats include television, radio, billboards, public transportation, magazines, and newspapers. Benefits include focusing attention on a specific complex issue and reaching underserved populations such youth and non-English speakers. The PSA serves to issue pure government information, with media assistance, without infringing on media news room independence.

Monitor Media Output

Some public affairs personnel must be devoted to monitoring media output during crisis and inter-crises periods. The press serves as a two-way medium between government and the citizenry, and it is the most efficient method of determining the concerns of the public and refocusing strategic communications plans. Monitoring should extend not only to news stories but to media trade Web sites. For instance, in an effort to counter government secrecy, in January 2004 The Reporters Committee for Freedom of the Press established "Behind the Homefront," a daily Weblog intended to assist journalists with "information access and free press issues."[31] In addition, citizen Weblogs and discussion boards offer candid perspectives on government response efforts.

More importantly, media output must be monitored because access works both ways. The First Amendment of the U.S. Constitution grants the press the freedom to publish, not the freedom to access government at will. Since the government controls something of value to journalists, government officials should not hesitate to use it as a lever. The government should, in the words of President Ronald Reagan, "trust, but verify." If the media fail to adhere to guidelines, or if they write stories that are untruthful or inflammatory, government public affairs officers should feel no obligation to feed their fire. Robert Johnson, the former Transportation Security Administration director of public affairs, was accused of blacklisting journalists by failing to call them back or include them in press events. Now the director of public affairs at the Department of Transportation, Johnson stated in his own defense, "We managed reporters based on how they wanted to be managed. Those who came at us guns a'blazing, story done before talking to us, they were managed in such a way as to protect our position as much as possible. Those who were willing to give us a fair hearing were given fair treatment."[32] Journalists who feel mistreated are welcome to file Freedom of Information Act (FOIA) requests, and await responses.

Conclusion

Government agencies should aggressively manage government-media relations as an essential element of leadership. A symbiotic, even codependent, relationship will result in more efficient dispersal of higher-quality public information. Any definition of success following a terrorist attack includes "reduction of terror," and responsive public officials utilizing media will quickly reassure citizens and focus collective efforts. During crises, government and media relations are closely aligned, thus the government simply must be prepared to work efficiently with media. The central challenge for government is maintaining media interest and public support during the lull between crises.

Notes

1. Robert G. Picard, *Media Portrayals of Terrorism: Function and Meaning of News Coverage* (Ames, IA: Iowa State University Press, 1993), p. 8.
2. Ibid, p. 7.
3. At the date of this writing, those responsible for the September–October 2001 anthrax-transmitting letters to NBC News, the *New York Post,* Senator Leary, and Senator Daschle, as well as the October 2001 hoax letter to the *New York Times,* have neither claimed responsibility nor been brought to justice. The FBI investigation, while incomplete, indicates that the letters may be a possible case of "homegrown" terrorism motivated by an economic desire to spur drug sales [Susan Schmidt and Joby Warrick, "FBI Investigates Possible Financial Motive in Anthrax Attacks" *Washington Post,* December 21, 2001]. In any case, what is noteworthy about this incidence of media terrorism was that it was not designed to disrupt news operations nor did it have that effect.
4. Picard, *Media Portrayals,* p. 9.
5. Warren P. Strobel, "The CNN Effect," *American Journalism Review* 18 (May 1996).
6. Robert Plummer, "US Powerless to Halt Iraq Net Images," *BBC News Online,* May 8, 2004, www.bbc.co.uk.
7. Picard, *Media Portrayals,* p. 43.
8. Doris A. Graber, *Media Power in Politics* (Washington, DC: CQ Press, 1984), p. 61.

9.   Governor Ridge raised the threat level at an August 1, 2004, press conference. As an example of media coverage, two days later, the *New York Times* published "Federal, State and Local Officials Step Up Security Efforts in Wake of New Threats." A total of five days later, the *Times* began a series of critical articles, editorials, and op-eds, including "Across America, Terror Alert Raises Skepticism as Well as Fear" and "Spin Again: What, Us Worry? The New State of Disbelief," *New York Times,* August 7, 2004.

10. Brigitte L. Nacos, "Terrorism as Breaking News: Attack on America," *Political Science Quarterly* 118 no. 1 (2003): 41.

11. Margaret Thatcher, as quoted in Nacos, "Terrorism as Breaking News," p. 23.

12. Mark Blaisse, "Reporters' Perspectives," *Terrorism and the Media,* ed. David A. Paletz and Alex P. Schid (Newbury Park, CA: Sage Publications, 1992), p. 139.

13. On October 10, 2001, National Security Adviser Condoleezza Rice placed a conference call to the news chiefs of ABC, CBS, NBC, CNN, and Fox News. Her request to limit broadcast of a publicly available tape (Al-Jazeera possessed and broadcast the entire tape) was reluctantly heeded. Detailed in Adam Clymer, *Journalism, Security, and the Public Interest: Best Practices for Reporting in Unpredictable Times* (Washington, DC: The Aspen Institute, 2003), p. 14.

14. Jonathan Alter, "In Bed with the Pentagon," *Newsweek*, March 10, 2003, p. 45.

15. Clymer, *Journalism, Security, and the Public Interest,* p. 14.

16. Jack Nelson, "U.S. Government Secrecy and the Current Crackdown on Leaks" (working paper, The Joan Shorenstein Center on the Press, Politics, and Public Policy, Fall 2002), p. 9.

17. U.S. Department of State, Guidelines for United States Government Spokespersons during Terrorist Incidents quoted in *Terrorism: The Media and the Law,* ed. Abraham H. Miller (Dobbs Ferry, NY: Transnational Publishers, Inc, 1982), p. 150.

18. Nelson, "U.S. Government Secrecy," pp. 20–22.

19. Howard Kurtz, "Ultimately, Newspapers Can't Move the Earth," *Washington Post,* August 22, 2004.

20. Andrew Bushell and Brent Cunningham. "Suddenly the Pentagon Grants Access to the Action, But the Devil's in the Details," *Columbia Journalism Review,* March/April 2003.

21. Ibid.

22. Coalition Force Land Component Command (CFLCC) Ground Rules Agreement, February 2003.

23. U.S. Department of State, p. 151.

24. U.S. Department of Defense, Dennis Murphy quoted in "Analysis: Department of Homeland Security—Media Takes DHS to Task over Efficiency of Its Press Office." *PR Week (US),* March 22, 2004, p. 9.

25. Department of Homeland Security, "National Response Plan, Final Draft," June 30, 2004, p. 47.

26. George W. Bush, Remarks by the President in Photo Opportunity with the National Security Team, September 12, 2001, www.whitehouse.gov/news/releases/2001/09/20010912-4.html.

27. William C. Rempel. "America Attacked: The Investigation; Acts of War; Bush Vows Full Assault, Says 'Good Will Prevail.'" *Los Angeles Times,* September 13, 2001; John Marelius, "Bush: 'They Can't Hide,'" *San Diego Union-Tribune,* September 13, 2001.

28. Susan Page, "Clinton: Don't 'Overreact,' Urges Calm after Bombing," *New York Newsday*, March 2, 1993.

29. Ibid; "Clinton Vows Investigation of New York Explosion." UPI, February 27, 1993.

30. Daniel J. Boorstin, *The Image: A Guide to Pseudo-Events in America* (New York: Harper Colophon Books, 1961).

31. The Web site can be found at www.rcfp.org/behindthehomefront. Lucy Daglish, "The Ups and Downs of Covering the Homefront," *News Media and the Law*, Winter 2003, p. 3.

32. "Analysis: Department of Homeland Security—Media takes DHS to Task over Efficiency of Its Press Office." *PR Week (US)*, March 22, 2004.

Chapter 24

The USA PATRIOT Act: What's So Patriotic About Trampling on the Bill of Rights?

Nancy Chang[1]

Just six weeks after the September 11 terrorist attacks on the World Trade Center and the Pentagon, a jittery Congress—exiled from its anthrax-contaminated offices and confronted with warnings that more terrorist assaults were soon to come—capitulated to the Bush Administration's demands for a new arsenal of antiterrorism weapons. Over vigorous objections from civil liberties organizations on both ends of the political spectrum, Congress overwhelmingly approved the Uniting and Strengthening America by Providing Appropriate Tools Required to Intercept and Obstruct Terrorism Act, better known by its acronym, the USA PATRIOT Act.[2] The House vote was 356 to 66, and the Senate vote was 98 to 1. Along the way, the Republican House leadership, in a raw display of force, jettisoned an antiterrorism bill that the House Judiciary Committee had unanimously approved and that would have addressed a number of civil liberties concerns.[3] The hastily-drafted, complex, and far-reaching legislation spans 342 pages. Yet it was passed with virtually no public hearing or debate, and it was accompanied by neither a conference nor a committee report. On October 26, the Act was signed into law by a triumphant President George W. Bush.[4]

The USA Patriot Act Confers Vast and Unchecked Powers to the Executive Branch

Although a number of its provisions are not controversial, the USA PATRIOT Act nevertheless stands out as radical in its design. To an unprecedented degree, the Act sacrifices our political freedoms in the name of national security and upsets the democratic values that define our nation by consolidating vast new powers in the executive branch of government. The Act enhances the executive's ability to conduct surveillance and gather intelligence, places an array of new tools at the disposal of the prosecution, including new crimes, enhanced penalties, and longer statutes of limitations, and grants the Immigration and Naturalization Service (INS) the authority to detain immigrants suspected of terrorism for lengthy and, in some cases, indefinite periods of time. At the same time that the Act inflates the powers of the executive, it insulates the exercise of these powers from meaningful judicial and Congressional oversight.

It remains to be seen how the executive will wield its new authority. However, if the two months that have elapsed since September 11 serve as a guide, we should brace ourselves for a flagrant disregard of the rule of law by those charged with its enforcement. Already, the Department of Justice (DOJ) has admitted to detaining more than 1,100 immigrants, not one of whom has been charged with committing a terrorist act and only a handful of whom are being held as material witnesses to the September 11 hijackings.[5] Many in this group appear to have been held for extended time periods under an extraordinary interim regulation announced by Attorney General John Ashcroft on September 17 and published in the Federal Register on September 20.[6] This regulation sets aside the strictures of due process by permitting the INS to detain aliens without charge for 48 hours or an uncapped "additional reasonable period of time" in the event of an "emergency or other extraordinary circumstance." Also, many in this group are being held without bond under the pretext of unrelated criminal charges or minor immigration violations, in a modern-day form of preventive detention. Chillingly, the Attorney General's response to the passage of the USA PATRIOT Act was not a pledge to use his new powers responsibly and guard against their abuse but instead was a vow to step up his detention efforts. Conflating immigrant status with terrorist status, he declared: "Let the terrorists among us be warned, if you overstay your visas even by one day, we will arrest you."[7]

Furthermore, the Administration has made no secret of its hope that the judiciary will accede to its broad reading of the USA PATRIOT Act just as pliantly as Congress acceded to its broad legislative agenda. In a letter sent to key senators while Congress was considering this legislation, Assistant Attorney General Daniel J. Bryant, of DOJ's Office of Legislative Affairs, openly advocated for a suspension of the Fourth Amendment's warrant requirement in the government's investigation of foreign national security threats.[8] The Bryant letter brazenly declares:

> As Commander-in-Chief, *the President must be able to use whatever means necessary to prevent attacks upon the United States;* this power, by implication, includes the authority to collect information necessary to its effective exercise . . . . The government's interest has changed from merely conducting foreign intelligence surveillance to counterintelligence operations by other nations, to one of preventing terrorist attacks against American citizens and property within the continental United States itself. The courts have observed that even the use of deadly force is reasonable under the Fourth Amendment if used in self-defense or to protect others . . . . Here, for Fourth Amendment purposes, the right to self-defense is not that of an individual, but that of the nation and its citizens . . . . *If the government's heightened interest in self-defense justifies the use of deadly force, then it certainly would also justify warrantless searches.*[9]

Suspension of Civil Liberties

The Administration's blatant power grab, coupled with the wide array of antiterrorism tools that the USA PATRIOT Act puts at its disposal, portends a wholesale suspension of civil liberties that will reach far beyond those who are involved in terrorist activities. First, the Act places our First Amendment rights to freedom of speech and political association in jeopardy by creating a broad new crime of "domestic terrorism," and by denying entry to noncitizens on the basis of ideology. Second, the Act will reduce our already lowered expectations of privacy under the Fourth Amendment by granting the government enhanced surveillance powers. Third, noncitizens will see a further erosion of their due process rights as they are placed in mandatory detention and removed from the United States under the Act. Political activists who are critical of our government or who maintain ties with international political movements, in addition to immigrants, are likely to bear the brunt of these attacks on our civil liberties.

Silencing Political Dissent

Section 802 of the USA PATRIOT Act defines for the first time a federal crime of "domestic terrorism" that broadly extends to "acts dangerous to human life that are a violation of the criminal laws" if they "appear to be intended . . . to influence the policy of a government by intimidation or coercion," and if they "occur primarily within the territorial jurisdiction of the United States."[10] Because this definition is couched in such vague and expansive terms, it may well be read by federal law enforcement agencies as licensing the investigation and surveillance of political activists and organizations based on their opposition to government policies. It also may be read by prosecutors as licensing the criminalization of legitimate political dissent. Vigorous protest activities, by their very nature, could be construed as acts that "appear to be intended . . . to influence the policy of a government by intimidation or coercion." Further, clashes between demonstrators and police officers and acts of civil disobedience—even those that do not result in injuries and are entirely nonviolent—could be construed as "dangerous to human life" and in "violation of the criminal laws." Environmental activists, antiglobalization activists, and antiabortion activists who use direct action to further their political agendas are particularly vulnerable to prosecution as "domestic terrorists."

In addition, political activists and the organizations with which they associate may unwittingly find themselves the subject of unwanted government attention in the form of surveillance and other intelligence-gathering operations. The manner in which the government implements the Act must be carefully monitored to ascertain whether activists and organizations are being targeted selectively for surveillance and prosecution based on their opposition to government policies. The First Amendment does not tolerate viewpoint-based discrimination.[11]

Furthermore, Section 411 of the Act poses an ideological test for entry into the United States that takes into consideration core political speech. Representatives of a political or social group "whose public endorsement of acts of terrorist activity the Secretary of State has determined undermines United States efforts to reduce or eliminate terrorist activities" can no longer gain entry into the United States.[12] Entry is also barred to noncitizens who have used their "position of prominence within any country to endorse or espouse terrorist activity," if the Secretary of State determines that their speech "undermines United States efforts to reduce or eliminate terrorist activities."[13]

Tolling the Death-Knell on Privacy

The USA PATRIOT Act[14] launches a three-pronged assault on our privacy. First, the Act grants the executive branch unprecedented, and largely unchecked, surveillance powers, including the enhanced ability to track e-mail and Internet usage, conduct sneak and peek searches, obtain sensitive personal records, monitor financial transactions, and conduct nationwide roving wiretaps. Second, the Act permits law enforcement agencies to circumvent the Fourth Amendment's requirement of probable cause when conducting wiretaps and searches that have, as "a significant purpose," the gathering of foreign intelligence. Third, the Act allows for the sharing of information between criminal and intelligence operations and thereby opens the door to a resurgence of domestic spying by the Central Intelligence Agency.

1. Enhanced Surveillance Powers. By and large, Congress granted the Administration its longstanding wish list of enhanced surveillance tools, coupled with the ability to use these tools with only minimal judicial and Congressional oversight. In its rush to pass an antiterrorism bill, Congress failed to exact in exchange a showing that these highly intrusive new tools are actually needed to combat terrorism and that the Administration can be trusted not to abuse them.

The recent decision in *Kyllo v. United States*[15] serves as a pointed reminder that once a Fourth Amendment protection has been eroded, the resulting loss to our privacy is likely to be permanent. In *Kyllo,* the Supreme Court concluded that the use of an advanced thermal detection device that allowed the police to detect heat emanating from marijuana plants growing inside the defendant's home constituted a "search" for the purposes of the Fourth Amendment and was presumptively unreasonable without a warrant. The Court placed great weight on the fact that the device was new, "not in general public use," and had been used to "explore details of a private home that would previously have been unknowable without physical intrusion."[16] Implicit in the Court's holding is the principle that once a technology is in general public use and its capabilities are known, a reasonable expectation of privacy under the Fourth Amendment may no longer attach. Several of the Act's enhanced surveillance tools, and the civil liberties concerns they raise, are examined below.

Sneak and Peek Searches: Section 213 of the Act authorizes federal agents to conduct "sneak and peek searches," or covert searches, of a person's home or office that are conducted without notifying the person of the execution of the search warrant until after the search has been completed. Section 213 authorizes delayed notice of the execution of a search warrant upon a showing of "reasonable cause to believe that providing immediate notification . . . may have an adverse result."[17] Section 213 also authorizes the delay of notice of the execution of a warrant to conduct a seizure of items where the court finds a "reasonable necessity" for the seizure.

Section 213 contravenes the "common law 'knock and announce' principle," which forms an essential part of the Fourth Amendment's reasonableness inquiry.[18] When notice of a search is delayed, one is foreclosed from pointing out deficiencies in the warrant to the officer executing it and from monitoring whether the search is being conducted in accordance with the warrant. In addition, Section 213, by authorizing delayed notice of the execution of a warrant to conduct a seizure of items, contravenes Rule 41(d) of the Federal Rules of Criminal Procedure, which requires that, "The officer taking property under the warrant shall give to the person from whom or from whose premises the property was taken a copy of the warrant and a receipt for the property taken or shall leave the copy and receipt at the place from which the property was taken."

Under Section 213, notice may be delayed for a "reasonable period." Already, DOJ has staked out its position that a "reasonable period" can be considerably longer than the seven days authorized by the Second Circuit Court of Appeals in *United States v. Villegas*[19] and by the Ninth Circuit Court of Appeals in *United States v. Freitas*.[20] DOJ states in its *Field Guidance on New Authorities (Redacted) Enacted in the 2001 Anti-Terrorism Legislation*[21] that "[a]nalogy to other statutes suggest [*sic*] that the period of delay could be substantial if circumstances warrant" and cites in support of this proposition a case that found a 90-day delay in providing notice of a wiretap warrant to constitute "a reasonable time." Notably, Section 213 is not limited to terrorism investigations; it extends to all criminal investigations, and is not scheduled to expire.

Access to Records in International Investigations: Section 215[22] is one of several provisions in the USA PATRIOT Act that relaxes the requirements, and extends the reach, of the Foreign Intelligence Surveillance Act of 1978 (FISA).[23] Under Section 215, the Director of the FBI or a designee as low in rank as an Assistant Special Agent in Charge may apply for a court order requiring the production of "any tangible things (including books, records, papers, documents, and other items)" upon his written statement that these items are being sought for an investigation "to protect against international terrorism or clandestine intelligence activities."[24] A judge presented with an application under Section 215 is required to enter an order if he "finds that the application meets the requirements of this section."[25]

Notably absent from Section 215 is the restriction in the FISA provision it amends that had required the government to specify in its application for a court order that "there are specific and articulable facts giving reason to believe that the person to whom the records pertain is a foreign power or an agent of a foreign power."[26] Now, under Section 215, the FBI may obtain sensitive personal records by simply certifying that they are sought for an investigation "to protect against international terrorism or clandestine intelligence activities." The FBI need not suspect the person whose records are being sought of any wrongdoing. Furthermore, the class of persons whose records are obtainable under Section 215 is no longer limited to foreign powers and their agents, but may include United States citizens and lawful permanent residents, or "United States persons" in the parlance of the FISA.[27] While Section 215 bars investigations of United States persons "solely upon the basis of activities protected by the first amendment to the Constitution," it does nothing to bar investigations based on other activities that tie them, no matter how loosely, to an international terrorism investigation.[28]

The FISA provision that was amended by Section 215 had been limited in scope to "records" in the possession of "a common carrier, public accommodation facility, physical storage facility, or vehicle rental facility."[29] Section 215 extends beyond "records" to "tangible things" and is no longer limited in terms of the entities from whom the production of tangible things can be required.[30] A Congressional oversight provision will require the Attorney General to submit semiannual reports on its activities under Section 215.[31] Section 215 is scheduled to expire on December 31, 2005.

Tracking Internet Usage: Under Section 216 of the Act, courts are required to order the installation of a pen register and a trap and trace device[32] to track both telephone and Internet "dialing, routing, addressing and signaling information"[33] anywhere within the United States when a government attorney has certified that the information to be obtained is "*relevant* to an ongoing criminal investigation."[34] Section 216 states that orders issued under its authority cannot permit the tracking of the "contents of any wire or electronic communications." However, in the case of e-mail messages and Internet usage, the Act does not address the complex question of where the line should be drawn between "dialing, routing, addressing and signaling information" and "content." Unlike telephone communications, where the provision of dialing information does not run the risk of revealing content,[35] e-mail messages move together in packets that include both address and content information. Also, the question of whether a list of Web sites and Web pages that have been visited constitutes "dialing, routing, addressing and signaling information" or "content" has yet to be resolved.

By providing no guidance on this question, Section 216 gives the government wide latitude to decide what constitutes "content." Of special concern is the fact that Section 216 authorizes the government to install its new Carnivore or DCS1000 system, a formidable tracking device that is capable of intercepting all forms of Internet activity, including e-mail messages, Web page activity, and Internet telephone communications.[36] Once installed on an Internet service provider (ISP), Carnivore devours *all* of the communications flowing through the ISP's network—not just those of the target of surveillance but those of all users—and not just tracking information but content as well. The FBI claims that through the use of filters, Carnivore "limits the messages viewable by human eyes to those which are strictly included within the court order."[37] However, neither the accuracy of Carnivore's filtering system nor the infallibility of its human programmers has been demonstrated. While Section 216 requires the government to maintain a record when it utilizes Carnivore, this record need not be provided to the court until 30 days after the termination of the order, including any extensions of time.[38] Section 216 is not scheduled to expire.

2. Allowing Law Enforcement Agencies to Evade the Fourth Amendment's Probable Cause Requirement. Perhaps the most radical provision of the USA PATRIOT Act is Section 218, which amends FISA's wiretap and physical search provisions. Under FISA, court orders permitting the executive to conduct surreptitious foreign intelligence wiretaps and physical searches may be obtained without the showing of probable cause required for wiretaps and physical searches in criminal investigations. Until the enactment of the Act, orders issued under FISA's lax standards were restricted to situations where the gathering of foreign intelligence information was *"the* purpose" of the surveillance.[39]

Under Section 218, however, orders may be issued under FISA's lax standards where the primary purpose of the surveillance is criminal investigation, and the gathering of foreign intelligence information constitutes only "a *significant* purpose" of the surveillance.[40] As a result, Section 218 allows law enforcement agencies conducting a criminal investigation to circumvent the Fourth Amendment whenever they are able to claim that the gathering of foreign intelligence constitutes "a significant purpose." In doing so, Section 218 gives the FBI a green light to resume domestic spying on government "enemies"—a program that reached an ugly apex under J. Edgar Hoover's directorship.

In the seminal case of *United States v. United States District Court for the Eastern District of Michigan (Keith)*,[41] the Supreme Court rejected President Richard Nixon's ambitious bid for the unchecked executive power to conduct warrantless wiretaps when investigating national security threats posed by *domestic* groups with no foreign ties. The Court recognized that national security cases reflect "a convergence of First and Fourth Amendment values not present in cases of 'ordinary' crime."[42] With respect to the First Amendment, the Court wisely observed that "[o]fficial surveillance, whether its purpose be criminal investigation or ongoing intelligence gathering, risks infringement of constitutionally protected privacy of speech" because of "the inherent vagueness of the domestic security concept . . . and the temptation to utilize such surveillances to oversee political dissent."[43]

With respect to the Fourth Amendment, the Court acknowledged the constitutional basis for the President's domestic security role but refused to exempt the President from the Fourth Amendment's warrant requirement.[44] The Court explained that the oversight function assumed by the judiciary in its review of applications for warrants "accords with our basic constitutional doctrine that individual freedoms will best be preserved through a separation of powers and division of functions among the different branches and levels of Government."[45]

Notably, the Keith Court declined to examine "the scope of the President's surveillance power with respect to the activities of *foreign* powers, within or without this country."[46] To fill the vacuum left in the wake of the Keith decision, in 1978 Congress enacted FISA, which is premised on the assumption that Fourth Amendment safeguards are not as critical in foreign intelligence investigations as they are in criminal investigations. The Supreme Court has yet to rule on FISA's constitutionality. However, both the Fourth and Ninth Circuits have cautioned that applying FISA's lax standards to criminal investigations raises serious Fourth Amendment concerns. In *United States v. Truong Dinh Hung,* the Fourth Circuit held that "the executive should be excused from securing a warrant only when the surveillance is conducted *'primarily' for foreign intelligence reasons,*" because "once surveillance becomes *primarily a criminal investigation,* the courts are entirely competent to make the usual probable cause determination, and because, importantly, individual privacy interests come to the fore and government foreign policy concerns recede when the government is primarily attempting to form the basis for a criminal prosecution."[47] In a similar vein, the Ninth Circuit held in *United States v. Johnson* that "the investigation of criminal activity cannot be the primary purpose of [FISA] surveillance" and that "[FISA] is not to be used as an end-run around the Fourth Amendment's prohibition of warrantless searches."[48]

The constitutionality of Section 218 is in considerable doubt. The extremist position staked out by DOJ in the Bryant Letter, which argues that "[i]f the government's heightened interest in self-defense justifies the use of deadly force, then it certainly would also justify warrantless searches," would undermine the separation of powers doctrine.[49] Until the Supreme Court weighs in on this matter, the government will find itself in a quandary each time it seeks to prosecute a criminal defendant based on evidence that, although properly obtained under the lesser showing required by Section 218, does not meet the probable cause showing required by the Fourth Amendment. Should the government decide to base prosecutions on such evidence, it will run the risk that the evidence will be suppressed under the Fourth Amendment exclusionary rule.[50] Section 218 is scheduled to expire on December 31, 2005.

3. Sharing of Sensitive Criminal and Foreign Intelligence Information. Section 203 of the USA PATRIOT Act authorizes the disclosure, without judicial supervision, of certain criminal and foreign intelligence information to officials of the FBI, CIA, and INS, as well as other federal agencies, where receipt of the information will "assist the official . . . in the performance of his official duties."[51] Section 203(a) permits the disclosure of matters occurring before a grand jury—a category that is as boundless in scope as the powers of a grand jury to subpoena records and witnesses.[52] Section 203(b) permits the disclosure of recordings of intercepted telephone and Internet conversations.[53] And Section 203(d) permits the disclosure of foreign intelligence obtained as part of a criminal investigation.[54]

While some additional sharing of information between agencies is undoubtedly appropriate given the nature of the terrorist threats we face, the Act fails to protect us from the dangers posed to our political freedoms and our privacy when sensitive personal information is widely shared without court supervision. A cautionary tale can be found in the 1976 report of the Senate's Church Committee, which revealed that the FBI and CIA had spied on thousands of law-abiding citizens, from civil rights workers to anti-Vietnam War protestors, who had been targeted solely because they were believed to harbor politically dissident views.[55] Section 203(a) is not scheduled to expire. Subsections (b) and (d) of Section 203, however, are scheduled to expire.

Stripping Immigrants of Constitutional Protections

The USA PATRIOT Act deprives immigrants of their due process and First Amendment rights through two mechanisms that operate in tandem. First, Section 411 vastly expands the class of immigrants who are subject to removal on terrorism grounds through its broad definitions of the terms "terrorist activity," "engage in terrorist activity," and "terrorist organization." Second, Section 412 vastly expands the authority of the Attorney General to place immigrants he suspects are engaged in terrorist activities in detention while their removal proceedings are pending.

1. Expanding the Class of Immigrants Subject to Removal. Section 411 vastly expands the class of immigrants that can be removed on terrorism grounds.[56] The term "terrorist activity" is commonly understood to be limited to premeditated and politically motivated violence targeted against a civilian population.[57] Section 411, however, stretches the term beyond recognition to encompass any crime that involves the use of a "weapon or dangerous device (other than for mere personal monetary gain)."[58] Under this broad definition, an immigrant who grabs a knife or makeshift weapon in the midst of a heat-of-the-moment altercation or in committing a crime of passion may be subject to removal as a "terrorist."

The term "engage in terrorist activity" has also been expanded to include soliciting funds for, soliciting membership for, and providing material support to a "terrorist organization," even when that organization has legitimate political and humanitarian ends and the noncitizen seeks only to support these lawful ends.[59] In such situations, Section 411 would permit guilt to be imposed solely on the basis of political associations protected by the First Amendment.[60]

To complicate matters further, the term "terrorist organization" is no longer limited to organizations that have been officially designated as terrorist and that therefore have had their designations published in the Federal Register for all to see.[61] Instead, Section 411 now includes as "terrorist organizations" groups that have never been designated as terrorist if they fall under the loose criterion of "two or more individuals, whether organized or not," which engage in specified terrorist activities.[62] In situations where a noncitizen has solicited funds for, solicited membership for, or provided material support to an undesignated "terrorist organization," Section 411 saddles him with the difficult, if not impossible, burden of "demonstrat[ing] that he did not know, and should not reasonably have known, that the act would further the organization's terrorist activity."[63] Furthermore, while Section 411 prohibits the removal of a noncitizen on the grounds that he solicited funds for, solicited membership for, or provided material support to a designated "terrorist organization" at a time when the organization was not designated as a "terrorist organization," Section 411 does *not* prohibit the removal of a noncitizen on the grounds that he solicited funds for, solicited membership for, or provided material support to an undesignated "terrorist organization" *prior* to the enactment of the Act.[64]

2. Detention at the Attorney General's Decree. At the same time that Section 411 vastly expands the class of immigrants who are removable on terrorist grounds, Section 412 vastly inflates the Attorney General's power to detain immigrants who are suspected of falling into that class.[65] Upon no more than the Attorney General's unreviewed certification that he has "reasonable grounds to believe" that a noncitizen is engaged in terrorist activities or other activities that threaten the national security, a noncitizen can be detained for as long as seven days without being charged with either a criminal or immigration violation.[66] This low level of suspicion falls far short of a finding of probable cause and appears even to fall short of the "reasonable and articulable suspicion" that supports a brief investigatory stop under the Fourth Amendment.[67]

If the noncitizen is charged with an immigration violation, he is subject to mandatory detention and is ineligible for release until he is removed, or until the Attorney General determines that he should no longer be certified as a terrorist.[68] While the immigration proceedings are pending, the Attorney General is required to review his certification once every six months.[69] However, Section 412 does not direct the Attorney General to inform the noncitizen of the evidence on which the certification is based or to provide the noncitizen with an opportunity to contest that evidence at an Immigration Judge hearing or other administrative review procedure. Instead, Section 412 limits the noncitizen's ability to seek review of the certification to a habeas corpus proceeding filed in federal district court, appeals from which must be filed in the Court of Appeals for the District of Columbia.[70] Since habeas proceedings are civil rather than criminal in nature, the government has no obligation under the Sixth Amendment to provide noncitizens with free counsel in such proceedings.[71]

Even where a noncitizen who is found removable is deemed eligible for asylum or other relief from removal, Section 412 does not permit his release.[72] Further, in the event that the noncitizen is found removable, but removal is "unlikely in the reasonably foreseeable future"—most likely because no other country will accept him—he may be detained for additional periods of six months "if the release of the alien will threaten the national security of the United States or the safety of the community or any person."[73] Only habeas review of such a determination is available under Section 412.[74]

The Due Process Clause "applies to all 'persons' within the United States, including aliens, whether their presence is lawful, unlawful, temporary, or permanent."[75] Yet, Section 412 exposes immigrants to extended, and, in some cases, indefinite, detention on the sole authority of the Attorney General's untested certification that he has "reasonable grounds to believe" that a noncitizen is engaged in terrorist activities. It remains to be seen what evidentiary safeguards, if any, the Attorney General will build into his regulations implementing Section 412. It also remains to be seen how rigorous federal court habeas reviews of such certifications will be and to what extent the courts will demand that the

Attorney General base his certification on objective evidence. Nevertheless, it is hard to avoid the conclusion that the Act will deprive noncitizens of their liberty without due process of law.[76]

3. Political Implications of the USA PATRIOT Act for Immigrants. In short, immigrants who engage in political activities in connection with any organization that has ever violated the law, risk being certified as terrorists, placed in mandatory detention, and removed, whether on a technical immigration violation or on terrorism grounds. Immigrants cannot protect themselves from such risks by simply avoiding association with organizations that have been designated as "terrorist organizations," because the Act broadens that term to include undesignated groups. Nor can immigrants protect themselves from such risks by limiting themselves to activities that are protected by the First Amendment, such as soliciting membership for, soliciting funds for, and providing material support to a "terrorist organization" toward the goal of furthering the organization's lawful ends, because the Act broadens the term "engage in terrorist activity" to include these activities. Ironically, in the post-USA PATRIOT Act world, immigrants who are intent on avoiding such risks should refrain from any associations with organizations that could potentially be deemed terrorist, even if their association is strictly confined to activities that further the humanitarian and peace-oriented goals of the organization, such as training members of such a organization on how to present international human rights claims to the United Nations, representing such an organization in peace negotiations, and donating humanitarian aid to such an organization.

Will the Judiciary Rein in the Executive and Uphold the Bill of Rights?

Our commitment to the Bill of Rights and to the democratic values that define this nation has been put to the test by the events of September 11. Already, Congress and the Administration have demonstrated their eagerness to sacrifice civil liberties in hopes of gaining an added measure of security. The task of upholding the Bill of Rights—or acquiescing in its surrender—will soon fall to the judiciary, as lawsuits testing the constitutionality of the USA PATRIOT Act wind their way through the courts.

In what we have come to regard as some of the most shameful episodes in our history, the judiciary has consistently bowed to the wishes of the political branches of government in times of crisis by finding the state interest in national security to be paramount to all competing interests. During World War I, the Supreme Court upheld the conviction of socialist Eugene Debs for expressing his opposition to World War I, refusing to recognize his nonviolent, antiwar advocacy as speech protected by the First Amendment.[77] More recently, following the bombing of Pearl Harbor during World War II, the Supreme Court upheld an executive order mandating the internment of more than 100,000 Japanese-Americans and Japanese immigrants based solely on their ancestry, refusing to recognize their preventive detention as a violation of the Equal Protection Clause.[78]

The extent to which the judiciary will defer to the Administration's views on the troubling First and Fourth Amendment issues presented by the USA PATRIOT Act, will tolerate ethnic and ideological profiling by the Administration as it implements the Act, and will allow the due process rights of immigrants in detention to be eroded remains to be seen. Certainly, the more anxious the times become, the more likely the judiciary will be to side with the Administration—at least where judges are convinced that the measures are vital to the national security, are not motivated by discriminatory intent, and tread as lightly as possible upon civil liberties. The recent words of Supreme Court Justice Sandra Day O'Connor, who so often figures as the swing vote on pivotal decisions, do not hold out hope for a vigorous defense of our political freedoms by the judiciary. Following a visit to Ground Zero, where the World Trade Center once stood, the Justice bleakly predicted, "We're likely to experience more restrictions on personal freedom than has ever been the case in this country."[79]

Notes

1. Nancy Chang is the Senior Litigation Attorney at the Center for Constitutional Rights, a progressive nonprofit legal and educational organization in New York City. This article is an excerpt from her book, *Silencing Political Dissent: How Post-September 11 Antiterrorism Measures Threaten Our Civil Liberties* (New York: Seven Stories Press, 2002).

2. Uniting and Strengthening America by Providing Appropriate Tools Required to Intercept and Obstruct Terrorism Act of 2001, Pub. L. No. 107–56.

3. Adam Clymer, "Antiterrorism Bill Passes; U.S. Gets Expanded Powers," *New York Times,* Oct. 26, 2001, p. A1; Robin Toner and Neil A. Lewis, "House Passes Terrorism Bill Much Like Senate's, but With 5-Year Limit," *New York Times,* Oct. 13, 2001, p. B6; Jonathan Krim, "Anti-Terror Push Stirs Fears for Liberties; Rights Groups Unite To Seek Safeguards," *Washington Post,* Sept. 18, 2001, p. A17; Mary Leonard, "Civil Liberties," *Boston Globe,* Sept. 21, 2001, p. A13.

4. Adam Clymer, "Bush Quickly Signs Measure Aiding Antiterrorism Effort," *New York Times,* Oct. 27, 2001, p. B5.

5. Amy Goldstein, et al., "A Deliberate Strategy of Disruption," *Washington Post,* Nov. 4, 2001, p. A1.

6. See 66 Federal Register 48334–35, Sept. 20, 2001. Congress denied the Attorney General's request for the codification of this interim regulation in the USA PATRIOT Act and limited to seven days the time aliens suspected of terrorist activity can be detained without charge. Although the interim regulation would appear to be in tension with the Act, it has not yet been rescinded. This interim regulation appears to have been drafted with the holding of *County of Riverside v. McLaughlin,* 500 U.S. 44 (1991), in mind. In *County of Riverside,* the Supreme Court considered the Fourth Amendment rights of individuals who had been arrested without a warrant and placed in detention. The Court ruled that after such an arrestee has been held in detention for 48 hours, the burden shifts to the government to show a bona fide emergency or an extraordinary circumstance for failing to provide the arrestee with a judicial probable cause determination. In marked contrast to the arrestees in *County of Riverside,* all of whom were arrested based on a probable cause finding by the arresting officer, the interim regulation has been drafted to support the detention of any noncitizen in this country, even when a basis for suspecting him of a criminal or immigration violation is entirely lacking.

7. Dan Eggen, "Tough Anti-Terror Campaign Pledged," *Washington Post,* Oct. 26, 2001 p. A1.

8. This undated letter was sent to Senators Bob Graham, Orrin Hatch, Patrick Leahy, and Richard Shelby. A copy of this letter is on file with the author.

9. Bryant Letter at p. 9 (emphasis added).

10. USA PATRIOT Act § 802, amending 18 U.S.C. § 2331.

11. See *R.A.V. v. City of St. Paul*, 505 U.S. 377 (1992).

12. USA PATRIOT Act § 411(a), amending 8 U.S.C. §1182(a)(3)(B)(i)(IV)(bb).

13. USA PATRIOT Act § 411(a), amending 8 U.S.C. §1182(a)(3)(B)(i)(VI).

14. Out of concern for the dangers that the USA PATRIOT Act's enhanced surveillance procedures pose to our privacy, and over the strong objections of the Administration, Congress has scheduled some—though not all—of these procedures to sunset, or expire, on December 31, 2005. See USA PATRIOT Act § 224(a). However, Congress has exempted from the operation of any sunset clause: (1) foreign intelligence investigations that began before the sunset date, and (2) offenses that began or occurred before the sunset date. See USA PATRIOT Act § 224(b).

15. 121 S. Ct. 2038, 2046, 2001.

16. *Ibid.*

17. USA PATRIOT Act § 213, amending 18 U.S.C. § 3103a. The definition of the term "adverse result" in Section 213 is borrowed from a statute establishing the standards under which the government may provide delayed notice when it searches stored e-mail and other wire and electronic communications—searches that are not nearly as intrusive as physical searches of one's home or office. The term is defined in 18 U.S.C. § 2705(a)(2) as: "(A) endangering the life or physical safety of an individual; (B) flight from prosecution; (C) destruction of or tampering with evidence; (D) intimidation of potential witnesses; or (E) otherwise seriously jeopardizing an investigation or unduly delaying a trial."

18. *Wilson v. Arkansas*, 514 U.S. 927, 929 (1995).

19. 899 F.2d 1324, 1337 (2d Cir. 1990).

20. 800 F.2d 1451, 1456 (9th Cir. 1986).

21. *See* www.cdt.org/security/011030doj.

22. USA PATRIOT Act § 215, amending 50 U.S.C. §§ 1862 and 1863.

23. 50 U.S.C. § 1801 *et seq.*

24. USA PATRIOT Act § 215, amending 50 U.S.C. 1862(a)(1).

25. USA PATRIOT Act § 215, amending 50 U.S.C. § 1862(c)(1).

26. *See* 18 U.S.C. § 1862(b)(2)(B), prior to its amendment by USA PATRIOT Act § 215.

27. FISA defines the term "United States persons" to include United States citizens and lawful permanent residents. *See* 50 U.S.C. § 1801(i).

28. USA PATRIOT Act § 215, amending 50 U.S.C. § 1862(a)(1).

29. *See* U.S.C. § 1862(a), prior to its amendment by USA PATRIOT Act § 215.

30. USA PATRIOT Act § 215, amending 50 U.S.C. § 1862.

31. USA PATRIOT Act § 215, amending 50 U.S.C. § 1863.

32. Pen registers record telephone numbers of outgoing calls. *See* 18 U.S.C. § 3127(3). Trap and trace devices record telephone numbers from which incoming calls originate. *See* 18 U.S.C. § 3127(4).

33. USA PATRIOT Act § 216(c)(3) amending 18 U.S.C. § 3127(4) (emphasis added).

34. USA PATRIOT Act § 216(b) amending 18 U.S.C. § 3123(a).

35. In the case of orders for pen registers and trap and trace devices, the Electronic Communications Privacy Act of 1986 demands only "a certification by the applicant that the information likely to be obtained is relevant to an ongoing criminal investiga-

tion." 18 U.S.C. §§ 3122(b)(2). *See also Smith v. Maryland*, 442 U.S. 735 (1979). However, providing telephone dialing information does not reveal the contents of telephone communications.

36. USA PATRIOT Act §216 (b) amending 18 U.S.C. § 3123(a)(3)(A).

37. *Internet and Data Interception Capabilities Developed by the FBI*, Statement of Dr. Donald M. Kerr, Assistant Director, Laboratory Division, July 24, 2000.

38. USA PATRIOT Act § 216(b) amending 18 U.S.C. § 3123(b)(3).

39. 50 U.S.C. §§ 1804(a)(7)(B) and 1823(a)(7)(B) (emphasis added).

40. USA PATRIOT Act § 218, amending 50 U.S.C. §§ 1804(a)(7)(B) and 1823(a)(7)(B) (emphasis added).

41. 407 U.S. 297 (1972).

42. 407 U.S. at 313.

43. 407 U.S. at 320.

44. *Ibid.*

45. 407 U.S. at 317.

46. 407 U.S. at 309 (emphasis added).

47. *United States v. Truong Dinh Hung*, 629 F.2d 908, 915 (4th Cir. 1980) (emphasis added).

48. *United States v. Johnson*, 952 F.2d 565, 572 (9th Cir. 1992).

49. *See supra* Note 8 and the accompanying text.

50. The exclusionary rule is a judicially created rule that bars prosecutors from using incriminating evidence obtained in violation of the Fourth Amendment to prove guilt. See, e.g., *Mapp v. Ohio*, 367 U.S. 643, 655, 1961.

51. USA PATRIOT Act § 203(a), (b), and (d). The information that may be shared must involve either "foreign intelligence or counterintelligence," as that term is defined in the National Security Act of 1947, at 50 U.S.C. § 401a, or "foreign intelligence information," as that term is defined in Section 203(a)(1), (b)(2)(C), and (d)(2).

52. USA PATRIOT Act § 203(a), amending Rule 6(e)(3)(C) of the Federal Rules of Criminal Procedure.

53. USA PATRIOT Act § 203(b), amending 18 U.S.C. § 2517(6).

54. USA PATRIOT Act §§ 203(d) and 905(a).

55. Select Committee to Study Governmental Operations with Respect to Intelligence Activities, *Intelligence Activities and the Rights of Americans, Final Report of the Senate Select Committee to Study Governmental Operations with Respect to Intelligence Activities,* 94th Cong., 2nd Sess. (1976).

56. Under the Immigration and Nationality Act (INA), noncitizens who have or are engaged in "terrorist activities" or activities that threaten the national security are subject to removal from the United States. *See* 8 U.S.C. § 1227(a)(4)(A) and (B).

57. Since 1983, the United States government has defined the term "terrorism," "for statistical and analytical purposes," as the "premeditated, politically motivated violence perpetrated against noncombatant targets by subnational groups or clandestine agents, usually intended to influence an audience." *See Patterns of Global Terrorism 2000,* United States Department of State, Introduction (April 2001).

58. USA PATRIOT Act § 411(a), amending 8 U.S.C. §1182(a)(3)(B)(iii)(V)(b).

59. USA PATRIOT Act § 411(a), amending 8 U.S.C. §1182(a)(3)(B)(iv)(IV)(bb) and (cc), (V)(bb) and (cc), and (VI)(cc) and (dd).

60. The Supreme Court has described guilt by association as "alien to the traditions of a free society and the First Amendment itself." *NAACP v. Claiborne Hardware Co.,* 458 U.S. 886, 932 (1982). *See also Healy v. James,* 408 U.S. 169, 186 (1972).

61. USA PATRIOT Act § 411(a) amended 8 U.S.C. §1182(a)(3)(B)(vi)(I) to include as a "terrorist organization" any foreign organization so designated by the Secretary of State under 8 U.S.C. § 1189, a provision that was introduced in the Antiterrorism and Effective Death Penalty Act of 1996. As of October 5, 2001, 26 organizations had been designated as foreign terrorist organizations under 8 U.S.C. § 1189. *See* 66 Federal Register 51088–90 (Oct. 5, 2001). In order to qualify as a designated "foreign terrorist organization" under 8 U.S.C. §1182(a)(3)(B)(vi)(I), the Secretary of State must find that "(A) the organization is a foreign organization; (B) the organization engages in terrorist activity; and (C) the terrorist activity of the organization threatens the security of United States nationals or the national security of the United States." *See* 8 U.S.C. § 1189(a)(1)(A)-(C).

    In addition, USA PATRIOT Act § 411(a) amended 8 U.S.C. §1182(a)(3)(B)(vi)(II) to include as a "terrorist organization" any domestic or foreign organization so designated by the Secretary of State in consultation with or upon the request of the Attorney General under Section 411. On December 5, 2001, the Secretary of State, in consultation with the Attorney General, designated 39 groups as Terrorist Exclusion List organizations under this provision. *See* 66 Federal Register 63619–63620 (Dec. 7, 2001). In order to qualify as a designated "terrorist organization" under 8 U.S.C. §1182(a)(3)(B)(vi)(II), a "finding" must be made that the organization engages in one or more of the "terrorist activities" described in 8 U.S.C. § 1182(a)(3)(B)(iv)(I)-(III). These activities consist of: (1) "commit[ting] or incit[ing] to commit, under circumstances indicating an intention to cause death or serious bodily injury, a terrorist activity;" (2) "prepar[ing] or plan[ning] a terrorist activity;" and (3) "gather[ing] information on potential targets for terrorist activity." *See* 8 U.S.C. § 1182(a)(3)(B)(iv)(I)-(III).

62. USA PATRIOT Act § 411(a), amending 8 U.S.C. §1182(a)(3)(B)(vi)(III). In order to qualify as an undesignated "terrorist organization" under 8 U.S.C. §1182(a)(3) (B)(vi)(III), "a group of two or more individuals, whether organized or not," must engage in one or more of the "terrorist activities" described in 8 U.S.C. § 1182(a)(3)(B)(iv)(I)-(III). *See supra* Note 59.

63. USA PATRIOT Act § 411(a), amending 8 U.S.C. § 1182(a)(3)(B)(iv)(IV)(cc), (V)(cc), and (VI)(dd).

64. USA PATRIOT Act § 411(c)(3)(A) and (B).

65. USA PATRIOT Act § 412(a), adding 8 U.S.C. § 1226A(a).

66. USA PATRIOT Act § 412(a), adding 8 U.S.C. § 1226A(a)(3) and (5).

67. *See, e.g., Terry v. Ohio,* 392 U.S. 1, 20–22 (1968).

68. USA PATRIOT Act § 412(a), adding 8 U.S.C. § 1226A(a)(2).

69. USA PATRIOT Act § 412(a), adding 8 U.S.C. § 1226A(a)(7).

70. USA PATRIOT Act § 412(a), adding 8 U.S.C. § 1226A(b)(1) and (2)(A)(iii) and (iv).

71. *See INS v. Lopez-Mendoza,* 468 U.S. 1032 (1984).

72. USA PATRIOT Act § 412(a), adding 8 U.S.C. § 1226A(a)(2).

73. USA PATRIOT Act § 412(a), adding 8 U.S.C. § 1226A(a)(6).

74. USA PATRIOT Act § 412(a), adding 8 U.S.C. § 1226A(b)(1).

75.   See *Zadvydas v. Davis,* 121 S.Ct. 2491, 2500 (2001).

76.   While the USA PATRIOT Act does not explicitly authorize the use of secret evidence in immigration proceedings, its provisions are certain to encourage its use. Since 1996, the INA has explicitly provided for the use of such evidence in removal proceedings before the Alien Terrorist Removal Court. *See* 8 U.S.C. § 1531 *et seq.* In addition, the INS has long taken the position that it is authorized to use secret evidence in bond proceedings. *See, e.g., Al Najjar v. Reno,* 97 F.Supp.2d 1329 (S.D.Fl. 2000); *Kiareldeen v. Reno,*71 F.Supp.2d 402 (D.N.J. 1999).

77.   *See Debs v. United States,* 249 U.S. 211, 1919.

78.   *See Korematsu v. United States,* 323 U.S. 214, 1944.

79.   Linda Greenhouse, "In New York Visit, O'Connor Foresees Limits on Freedom," *New York Times,* Sept. 29, 2001, p. B5.

Chapter 25

The USA PATRIOT Act and Information Sharing Between the Intelligence and Law Enforcement Communities

Brian H. Hook, Margaret J. A. Peterlin, and Peter L. Welsh

The nature of the threat to United States national security, especially, the nature of the threat posed by terrorist operations has changed fundamentally in the past decade. Shortly after the September 11 attacks, Ambassador Paul Bremer, who headed the National Commission on Terrorism, observed that the "threat of terrorism is changing dramatically. It is becoming more deadly and it is striking us here at home."[1] Contemporary terrorism traces its roots to the acts of political violence, such as the murder of eleven Israeli athletes at the Munich Olympics in 1972, committed in Western Europe during the late 1960s and 1970s. However, as Ambassador Bremer argues, today's terrorists have little in common with the pragmatic terrorists of the Cold War era.[2]

Much of the terrorist activity during the 1960s and 70s was inspired by Marxist-Leninist ideology, and the terrorists who acted in furtherance of that ideology did so principally to draw attention to their cause and gain certain worldly political concessions. Also, these groups were motivated by secular rather than apocalyptic ends. For example, they sought to drive the United States out of Western Europe, to compel Britain to withdrawn from Northern Ireland, or to undermine NATO.[3] By gaining attention through terrorist acts, the old school of terrorists believed that they could increase support among the general public in the West for their ideology. Moreover, these groups were quick to claim responsibility for a terrorist attack and would often release a document seeking political concessions consistent with Marxist ideology. By proceeding with the purpose of persuading the public in the West of the rightness of their cause and commending its widespread adoption, these early terrorist groups were necessarily constrained in the level of terror they could inflict. By inflicting human casualties, earlier terrorist groups ran the risk of alienating people from their cause. They, therefore, adopted certain limitations on the destruction they were prepared to inflict.[4] As Ambassador Bremer has noted, "[t]here was a self-constraint built into the terrorists' acts and the number of casualties they were willing to inflict."[5]

Today's predominate terrorist threat comes from militant Islam. Of the 19 foreign terrorist organizations listed by the State Department, 10 are Islamic organizations.[6] The groups that have launched the terrorist campaign against America are driven by a profound hatred of Western religion and Western civilization. These terrorists are not, moreover, motivated principally by pragmatic political goals. In the words of Ambassador Bremer: "[T]hese men do not seek a seat at the table; they want to overturn the table and kill everybody at it."[7] As such, they are not amenable to calculated or deterrent measures. Islamic terrorists have defined a mode of total war in which their military inferiority to the West is overcome by an indirect confrontation with the West.

This strategy was detailed in *The Quranic Concept of War,* published in 1979 by S.K. Malik, a militant Pakistani brigadier.[8] Arguing in favor of terror as a strategy for war, Malik writes: "[T]error struck into the hearts of the enemies is not only a means, it is the end in itself. Once a condition of terror into the opponent's heart is obtained hardly anything left is to be achieved. It is the point where the means and ends meet and merge. Terror is not a means of imposing decision upon the enemy; it is the decision we wish to impose upon him."[9] Today's terrorists are opposed to Western liberalism, as such, and seek the destabilization or destruction of pro-Western governments.[10]

The threat from escalating terrorist attacks is also an imminent one. As Yossef Bodansky argues in his biography, *Bin Laden,* Islamic extremists are "determined to ensure that [the] malaise that had already destroyed Christendom did not penetrate and similarly corrupt and destroy the modern world. All means, including the use of violence and terrorism, were justified to prevent such corruption."[11] Given the eagerness with which certain Islamic terrorists are seeking weapons of mass destruction, moreover, there evidently is insufficient time for liberal democratic mores to counteract extremist Islam.[12] The current circumstances, by and large, rule out proceeding by political or diplomatic half-measures.

Combating such a network presents entirely new challenges to Western governments and to the intelligence and law enforcement communities in the West. Because of the need to defend on all fronts against a terrorist attack, homeland security has an unusually great need for highly efficient and sophisticated intelligence and law enforcement operations. Ambassador Bremer explains:

> The terrorists take advantage of two important asymmetries. First, in the fight against terrorism, defenders have to protect all of their points of vulnerability around the world; the terrorist has only to attack the weakest point. This lesson was brought home to the U.S. government when Al-Qaeda attacked the American embassies in Nairobi and Dar es-Salaam in August, 1998, two embassies thought to be in little danger and, thus, ill-protected. Secondly, the costs of launching a terrorist attack are a fraction of the costs required to defend against it. To shoot up an airport, a terrorist needs only an AK-47 assault rifle; defending that same airport costs millions of dollars. The September 11 attacks probably cost less than $2 million and caused over $100 billion in damage and business disruption. Thus, the new terrorism reverses the conventional wisdom that, in military operations, the offense must be three times as strong as the defense. How, then, are we to fight this new and increasingly dangerous threat? The proper objective of a counter-terrorist policy is to prevent attacks before they happen. So, more than in any other field of foreign and national security affairs, success in the fight against terrorism depends on having good intelligence.[13]

Gaining and making effective use of "good intelligence" against this new threat, moreover, requires a change in the operational structure of intelligence and law enforcement agencies as well as more effective modes of cooperation between the agencies.

Many have argued—even before the events of September 11—that the intelligence and law enforcement communities are not institutionally capable of meeting the new terrorist threat. Just one month before the World Trade Center bombing, for example, a CIA veteran who spent nine years in the Directorate of Operations for the Middle East wrote in the *Atlantic Monthly* that "Westerners cannot visit the cinder-block, mud-brick side of the Muslim world—whence bin Laden's foot soldiers mostly come—without announcing who they are. No case officer stationed in Pakistan can penetrate either the Afghan communities in Peshawar or the Northwest Frontier's numerous religious schools, which feed manpower and ideas to bin Laden and the Taliban, and seriously expect to gather useful information about radical Islamic terrorism—let alone recruit foreign agents."[14] Another CIA veteran pointedly identified a related problem: "the CIA probably doesn't have a single truly qualified Arabic-speaking officer of Middle Eastern background who can play a believable Muslim fundamentalist who would volunteer to spend years of his life with shitty food and no women in the mountains of Afghanistan. For Christ's sake, most case officers live in the suburbs of Virginia. We don't do that kind of thing."[15]

Information sharing between the law enforcement and intelligence communities is especially critical in the new fight against terrorism.[16] Considerable emphasis has recently been placed on the fact that the war on terrorism is precisely that, a war.[17] As Ambassador Bremer argues, intelligence is crucial to winning this war on terrorism. But so, too, is law enforcement. Indeed, the on-the-ground fight against terrorism has much in common with a criminal investigation. In fighting this war, the United States, by and large, is not engaging an enemy that is massed on a battlefield and that may be defeated by conventional forces utilizing standard wartime intelligence capabilities. It is insufficient to destroy and/or confiscate the enemy's battlefield capabilities and disperse its troops. Rather, rooting out the secretive, diffuse cells of today's terrorists—particularly, those that may remain in the United States—requires tactics that are similar to those employed in certain criminal investigations. The neutralization of the threat posed to those cells may involve the arrest of the individuals involved. The intelligence and law enforcement communities must, therefore, work together with a level of coordination not previously achieved in the history of the two communities.

Brief History of Interagency Information Sharing

The USA PATRIOT Act promotes greater cooperation and information sharing between the intelligence and law enforcement communities. In doing so, the PATRIOT Act does not overturn the *status quo ante* with respect to coordination between intelligence and law enforcement. Although restricted in certain particular respects (such as grand jury secrecy, for example) and often plagued by political infighting and bureaucratic inefficiencies, there is nevertheless a long history in America of cooperation and information sharing between the CIA and the FBI.[18] The PATRIOT Act, moreover, does not change qualitatively the law or policy with regard to cooperation or information sharing between the law enforcement and intelligence communities. The relevant provisions of the PATRIOT Act are consistent with preexisting law. Indeed, most of the provisions of the PATRIOT Act have generally been in effect by executive order for at least twenty years.[19] What the PATRIOT Act principally seeks to correct is the bureaucratic friction that has too often existed between these two agencies.[20]

Origins of the Separation of Law Enforcement and Intelligence

The law enforcement and intelligence functions of the United States have, for the most part, been allocated between the Federal Bureau of Investigation, on the one hand, and the Central Intelligence Agency, National Security Agency, and military intelligence organizations on the other hand. The separation between the law enforcement and intelligence communities was established partly out of a concern for protecting civil liberties but significantly as a result of bureaucratic compromises.

Originally called simply the Bureau of Investigations, the Federal Bureau of Investigation was established in 1908 by Attorney General Charles Joseph Bonaparte. The Bureau of Investigations came into its own during World War I, when it coordinated attempts to infiltrate and suppress radical organizations, such as the International Workers of the World movement.[21] The FBI's formal intelligence-gathering efforts were, moreover, started shortly thereafter in the immediate wake of several terrorist acts committed by certain of these same radical groups in the summer of 1919.[22] In response to those attacks, the Bureau of Investigations started the General Intelligence Division which was formally organized on August 1, 1919 and headed from the outset by the young J. Edgar Hoover.[23] In the ensuing years, the General Intelligence Division developed into extensive and sophisticated counterintelligence operation.[24] By the end of World War II, the FBI was engaged in significant efforts to combat foreign espionage both at home as well as abroad.[25] The FBI's counterintelligence efforts, while conducted mostly by means of law-enforcement tactics, were nevertheless far-reaching in scope.[26] One of the FBI's main counterintelligence functions during the post-World War II era, for example, was the "surveillance of hostile foreign diplomats and their premises."[27] Given the breadth of the FBI's postwar counterespionage efforts, moreover, conflicts with the other intelligence agencies—especially, the newly formed National Intelligence Authority (precursor to the NSA) and Central Intelligence Group (precursor to the CIA)—were inevitable.[28] In 1946, J. Edgar Hoover attempted to persuade President Truman to place the nascent Central Intelligence Group under the direct control of Hoover and the FBI.[29] Truman, however, refused.[30] The President explained to others, at the time, that he did not want to place one man (particularly, J. Edgar Hoover) in charge of law enforcement and domestic and foreign intelligence.[31]

Although concerns about placing the main federal law enforcement and intelligence powers in the hands of one person account, in part, for the modern-day division of authority between the FBI and the CIA, those concerns do not suggest that information sharing or coordination between the FBI and the CIA pose any threat to civil liberties. As Angelo Codevilla has argued, "In realty and contrary to conventional wisdom, the CIA has *no* weapons with which to threaten civil liberties. The FBI, not the CIA, has the power of arrest. The FBI, not the CIA, can work with federal and state prosecutors. Nevertheless, the myth that the division of responsibility for [counterintelligence] has something to do with safeguarding civil liberties is an enduring one."[32] Rather than serving a legitimate concern for the protection of civil liberties, Codevilla has suggested that the separation of the intelligence and law enforcement communities was, in some significant part, the result of "a series of bureaucratic compromises" and that the stakes in the ensuing struggles "were simply pieces of bureaucratic turf."[33]

The allocation of the pieces of bureaucratic turf between the law enforcement and intelligence communities has occurred in several stages during the postwar era. There are at least three stages to this process: (1) the establishment of the Central Intelligence Agency and the National Security Agency in 1947; (2) the activities of the Church Committee; and (3) the era of the Reagan administration.

The Postwar Era—The National Security Act of 1947

The CIA and NSA were established as separate government agencies with passage of the National Security Act of 1947. The Act, moreover, includes the original mandate granted to the Director of Central Intelligence.[34] Notably, Section 103–3 of the National Security Act, specifying the "Responsibilities of Director of Central Intelligence," provides, in relevant part, that the Director of Central Intelligence shall "collect intelligence through human sources and by other appropriate means, except that the Agency shall have no police, sub-poena, or law enforcement powers or internal security functions."[35] The term "internal security functions" has no clear meaning under the Act and the term has been used liberally by critics of the CIA to attempt to limit the agency's powers.[36] According to one source, "[t]he statutory language regarding the authorities and functions of the new Central Intelligence Agency was left intentionally vague. In part this reflected the bureaucratic sensitivities involved in specifying in the law the DCI's roles and missions in regard to other agencies, and, in part, the desire to avoid wording that other governments might find offensive."[37]

The Turmoil of the 1970s—The Rockefeller Commission and Church Committee

Certain high-profile cases involving domestic intelligence gathering, and subsequent political scrutiny of those cases, have further defined the postwar allocation of power between the CIA and FBI. In June 1975, the Commission on CIA Activities Within the United States, also known as the Rockefeller Commission, released its final report to the President. Shortly thereafter, the Senate Select Committee to Study Governmental Operations With Respect to Intelligence Activities, known as the Church Committee (after its chairman, Senator Frank Church) released its report on the CIA.[38] The Rockefeller Commission and Church Committee reports detailed a number of activities that both reports characterized as abuses of the CIA's statutory authority. For example, the Rockefeller Commission found that, between 1952 and 1973, the CIA conducted a mail intercept program that involved the U.S. government opening thousands of letters sent to and from persons living within the United States.[39] The Commission also found that the CIA established a Special Operations Group to conduct surveillance of American dissident groups.[40] The efforts of the Special Operations Group, dubbed Operation CHAOS, resulted in the collection of significant information and materials on domestic dissident groups.[41] Cold War partisans seized on such abuses of intelligence collection techniques to demonize the CIA. These attacks on the CIA, however, had at least as much to do with the role that the CIA played in its foreign intelligence operations, and how those operations fit within the Cold War political *gestalt,* than with domestic intelligence activities, as such.[42]

More importantly, the Rockefeller Commission and the Church Committee did not rule out information sharing between the law enforcement and intelligence communities and, indeed, recommended *greater* coordination between the CIA and the FBI. Although both the Rockefeller Commission and Church Committee relied on a somewhat simplistic or anachronistic conceptual framework that contemplates that the CIA's activities could be strictly limited to what the Commission frequently refers to as "foreign intelligence matters,"[43] both bodies also acknowledged the need for some significant measure of coordination between the law enforcement and intelligence communities. Indeed, the Church Committee observed that there has been a long history of coordination between the CIA and FBI and recommended still closer coordination between the agencies, especially in their counterintelligence efforts:[44]

> *Coordination between CIA and FBI counterintelligence units is especially critical.* The history of CIA-FBI liaison has been turbulent, though a strong undercurrent of cooperation has usually existed at the staff level since 1952 when the Bureau began sending a liaison person to the CIA on a regular basis. The sources of friction between the CIA and FBI in the early days revolved around such matters as the frequent unwillingness of the Bureau to collect positive intelligence for the CIA within the United States or to help recruit foreign officials in this country. In 1970 an essentially minor incident resulted in an order from FBI Director Hoover to discontinue FBI liaison with the Central Intelligence Agency. Although informal communications between CIA and FBI staff personnel continued, it was not until the post-Hoover era that formal liaison relations were reestablished. *Today, there is still a need for closer coordination of FBI and CIA counterintelligence efforts.*[45]

The Rockefeller Commission's report, moreover, observed that the National Security Act "was intended to promote coordination, not compartmentation [*sic*] of intelligence between government departments."[46] In addition, the Commission's report states that "legitimate domestic CIA activities occasionally cross the path of FBI investigations. Daily liaison is therefore necessary between the two agencies."[47] The Commission also recommends that "[t]he Director of Central Intelligence and the Director of the FBI should prepare and submit for approval by the National Security Council a detailed agreement setting forth the jurisdiction of each agency and providing for effective liaison with respect to all matters of mutual concern."[48]

The Reagan Era

Much of the information sharing policy embodied in the USA PATRIOT Act has been in effect for at least twenty years, pursuant to an Executive Order issued by President Reagan. In December 1981, President Reagan issued Executive Order 12333 on "United States Intelligence Activities." Executive Order 12333 was intended to clarify the relationship amongst the various intelligence agencies of the United States Government. The Order includes as one of its goals, "to the greatest extent possible consistent with applicable United States law and this Order, and with full consideration of the rights of United States persons, all agencies and departments should seek to ensure full and free exchange of information in order to derive maximum benefit from the United States intelligence effort."[49] The Order contains many of the same policies embodied in the PATRIOT Act. For example, the Order provides that the Director of Central Intelligence shall "coordinate foreign intelligence and counterintelligence relationships between agencies of the Intelligence Community and the intelligence or internal security services of foreign governments . . . "[50] The Order further provides that the collection by the CIA of "foreign intelligence or counterintelligence within the United States shall be coordinated with the FBI" and that the CIA shall, "without assuming or performing any internal security functions, conduct counterintelligence activities within the United States in coordination with the FBI."[51] The Order defines both "counterintelligence" and "foreign intelligence" to include gathering information on "international terrorist activities."[52] The Order also provides that the FBI shall conduct "counterintelligence activities outside of the United States in coordination with the CIA" and that the FBI shall conduct "within the United States, when requested by officials of the Intelligence Community designated by the President, activities undertaken to collect foreign intelligence or support foreign intelligence collection requirements of other agencies within the Intelligence Community . . ."[53]

Information Sharing and the USA PATRIOT Act

The following section provides a brief overview of the provisions of the PATRIOT Act that relate to information-sharing between the intelligence and law enforcement communities.

Section 203—Section 203 of the PATRIOT Act amends Rule 6 of the Federal Rules of Criminal Procedure, governing grand jury secrecy, to permit disclosure of certain information presented before a grand jury. Prior to the PATRIOT Act, law enforcement officials were generally restricted by Rule 6 of the Rules of Criminal Procedure from sharing information provided to a grand jury with members of the intelligence community. While it is important to prevent evidence presented to a grand jury from leaking to the general public, there is little reason to prevent intelligence officials from gaining access to such information on a confidential basis.[54] Section 203 of the PATRIOT Act now permits disclosure of "matters involving foreign intelligence or counterintelligence" occurring before a grand jury to "any Federal law enforcement, intelligence, protective, immigration, national defense or national security official in order to assist the official receiving that information in the performance of his official duties." The information disclosed may only be used, moreover, "as necessary in the conduct of that person's official duties subject to any limitations on the unauthorized disclosure of such information." Section 203 also permits law enforcement to disclose the contents of any wire, oral or electronic communication, or evidence derived therefrom, to any other federal law enforcement, intelligence, protective, immigration, national defense or national security official.

Section 901—Amends section 103 of the National Security Act of 1947, which sets forth the DCI's role as head of intelligence, to provide that the Director of Central Intelligence shall provide assistance to the Attorney General to ensure that information derived from electronic surveillance or physical searches under the Foreign Intelligence Surveillance Act [FISA] is "disseminated so it may be used efficiently and effectively for foreign intelligence purposes."[55] Section 901 clarifies, however, that the DCI shall have "no authority to direct, manage, or undertake electronic surveillance or physical search operations pursuant to [FISA] unless otherwise authorized by statute or executive order."

Section 902—Clarifies that the definition of the term "foreign intelligence," under the National Security Act, shall also include "international terrorist activities." The term "counterintelligence" under the Act already included "international terrorist activities" within its definition.[56]

Section 903—States the sense of Congress that "officers and employees of the intelligence community of the Federal Government, acting within the course of their official duties, should be encouraged, and should make every effort, to establish and maintain intelligence relationships with any person, entity or group for the purpose of engaging in lawful intelligence activities."

Section 905—Amends the National Security Act of 1947 to add a new section, titled "Disclosure of Foreign Intelligence Acquired in Criminal Investigations; Notice of Criminal Investigations of Foreign Intelligence Sources." This new section provides, *inter alia,* that "the Attorney General, or the head of any other department or agency of the Federal Government with law enforcement responsibilities shall expeditiously disclose to the Director of Central Intelligence . . . foreign intelligence acquired by an element of the Department of Justice or an element of such department or agency, as the case may be in the course of a criminal investigation."

Section 906—This section requires that, not later than February 1, 2002, the Attorney General, the DCI and the Secretary of the Treasury jointly submit to Congress a report on the feasibility and desirability of reconfiguring the Foreign Terrorist Asset Tracking Center and the Office of Foreign Assets Control of the Department of Treasury to provide for the "effective and efficient analysis and dissemination of foreign intelligence relating to the financial capabilities and resources of international terrorist organizations."

Section 907—Requires that no later than February 1, 2002, the Director of Central Intelligence, in consultation with the Director of the FBI, submit to the appropriate committees of Congress a report on the establishment and maintenance within the intelligence community of an element for purposes of producing timely and accurate translations of foreign intelligence to be shared with all other elements of the intelligence community.

Section 908—Requires the Attorney General, in consultation with the DCI, to develop a program to provide training to certain officials in the Federal, State and Local governments who are not ordinarily engaged in the collection, dissemination, and use of foreign intelligence. Such training would seek to assist these officials in "identifying foreign intelligence information in the course of their duties, and utilizing foreign intelligence information in the course of their duties, to the extent that the utilization of such information is appropriate for such duties."

These sections represent the main provisions of the Act that allow for increased information sharing. They do not define the limits of the Act's impact on the relationship between the law enforcement and intelligence communities, however. In addition to providing for greater information sharing, for example, the PATRIOT Act also expands many of the FBI's surveillance powers.[57] Any analysis of information sharing must consider the scope and quantity of information shared. Limited sharing presents a different, and perhaps less challenging, question than more-expansive sharing.

Intelligence Collection as Distinguished from Information Sharing

Central to the issue of information sharing between the intelligence and law enforcement communities is how, rather than whether, these communities should share information. Furthermore, of paramount importance is how the information is collected in the first instance, and this shifts the inquiry to one of tracking the use of information and the mechanics and methods of surveillance.[58] As discussed earlier, the history of intelligence collection has included episodes of overreaching.[59] Even if that was not the case, a call for oversight is not inherently an accusation. Rather, it is the civic obligation of both Congress and the citizenry. In our view, the notion that a rule of law is preferred over rule by man properly includes the corollary that scrutinizing that law is not the same as scrutinizing the man.

A wide variety of oversight methods exist to vet intelligence collection, and the Act employs these methods to different degrees and in different contexts. Over time the question will become whether the combination of power granted to the intelligence and law enforcement communities and the oversight applied have resulted in the proper balance between liberty and security in that same area. This section considers, among the possibilities, three oversight tools as well as a discussion of how those oversight tools were or were not applied to a particular provision of the act.[60] This section also considers how the oversight tools may affect the manner and extent of cooperation between the intelligence and law enforcement communities. The three oversight tools discussed immediately below are judicial involvement, congressional oversight, and sunset provisions.

Since these tools are broadly equivalent, two general considerations are raised. First, each oversight option includes a different accompanying cost. For law enforcement this normally means that the employed option slows the process in some more or less acceptable way.[61] If the process is not slowed, then already strained resources are reprogrammed in order to meet the oversight requirement. These potential drawbacks can be conveniently reduced to two phrases: mission compromise and manpower drain. A third potential drawback is the overdissemination of sensitive information and the risk of compromising the usefulness of that information.[62] In order to "smoke them out of their holes," we must first discover the location of the hole and then strike when we know they are there.[63] That cannot be done, however, if the terrorists know what we know.[64] These three shape the adaptability of a particular oversight tool to reducing the risk associated with a specific collection technique.

Second, some of the oversight options present standard controversies. For instance, it tends to be the uncommon prosecutor that believes the exclusionary rule does anything more useful than complicate an already unfortunate situation. Another common concern is that congressional oversight rarely occurs.[65] This chapter does not address such controversies. Instead, the focus is on the appropriateness of the pairing of the power granted and the oversight tool selected.

Judicial Involvement

The Act's provisions task the judiciary repeatedly. Few of these tasks are new, however. Most of them are mere extensions of a common task to a new item. Some are reductions of the judiciary's role. One example is the involvement of the judiciary in section 209. This section removed stored communications (or yet unopened voicemails) from the definition of "wire communication," as found in 18 U.S.C. section 2510(1). Previously, law enforcement needed a wiretap order to access stored, unopened e-mail. To some, section 209 rationalizes the treatment of stored voice and nonvoice communications. To others, rationality demanded that access to such communications require a wiretap order. If wiretap orders unduly slow the pursuit of information that can be too easily deleted by a potential defendant, then one must look to another of the tools to resolve a lingering concern. Of the remaining options, congressional oversight hearings, FOIA requests, and media coverage are the only practical options. Those with concerns should, moreover, focus their efforts in one of these three areas.

Section 216 authorizes courts to grant pen register and trap and trace orders that are valid nationwide. The controversy surrounding (and nearly consuming) this "Carnivore" provision abated only after a requirement that a complete recording of the information extracted, to include the agents involved, and the configuration of the device during its use would be provided to the relevant judge 30 days after termination of the order. Advocates of the report hope it serves as a bulwark against the improper capture of content under an order that allows only for the capture of addressing information, in the same manner that a trap and trace order for telephones allows only for the capture of dialing information. This report, occurring *ex parte,* does not endanger any classified information and therefore does not threaten to compromise the mission.

Opponents of the reporting requirement may contend that it is a manpower drain, despite the fact that it appears that the FBI generates the report already and is simply required to provide a copy to the judge. Still, the balance may not yet be ideal. Depending on the duration of the initial trap and trace order, a report submitted 30 days after termination may not be sufficient. A more cautious approach would link the interval of the order and the reporting interval. For example, if an initial order is for one year, the reporting requirement could be every three months during the order, with the final report due 30 days after termination. When an initial order is for one month, the final report may be sufficient as the only report. Again, it is impossible to predict whether such an adjustment will be necessary, though it is an option that could improve oversight while remaining sensitive to the mission concerns.

One concern with judicial involvement as an oversight tool relates to the need to contain information. In order to engage clandestine organizations, it is often necessary to have meaningful limits on the use and dissemination of information.[66] The Act sought to correct a too-strict approach. A too-loose approach would lead to an equally ineffectual effort. The first of two possible responses is to limit dissemination by limiting judicial involvement in the process. The second is to limit dissemination through the use of tight controls within the judiciary. A first moderate step may be to require the use of sealed documents before adopting outright limitations on the role of the judiciary.

Congressional Oversight

The Act may rejuvenate the art of congressional oversight. Among the options, congressional hearings may compromise the mission the least. This is because most hearings occur *ex post*. Missions would be either accomplished or abandoned by the time testimony began. The reality that hearings occur after-the-fact also tends to negate the overdissemination concern. When methods of intelligence gathering are under review, classified hearings are certainly available. Those who malign congressional oversight as ineffectual should consider redirecting their energies to sharpening this tool. The unalterable need for greater information sharing means that the United States no longer has the luxury of simply separating law enforcement and intelligence agencies. Separation is a security risk.

Lack of oversight is a potential liberty risk, however. One obstacle to even classified oversight hearings is that they are not costless. While they may not generate the costs
associated with mission compromise or overdissemination, they will be a manpower
drain. For those with concerns, this inconvenience is likely to be seen as the exchange for
increases in surveillance powers. Members might express impatience when agents or
appointees claim unavailability for hearings. This security-liberty pairing means that these
agencies must do more on both fronts. The complete obligation to the American people
means that the agencies will be responsive to congressional requests and inquiries.

Sunset Provisions

The sunset provision applies to many, but not all, of the surveillance provisions of the bill.
Interestingly, it does not apply to the controversial section 216, discussed *supra*. The sunset provisions evoked heated negotiations. Having a sunset may mean that law enforcement and intelligence agencies are less likely to realign their bureaucracies as necessary
to maximize their information-sharing potential. New operating procedures need to be
written, disseminated, and translated into behaviors for the Act to have its intended beneficial result. If agents believe the basis for such efforts will disappear in a short span of
time, they may approach the task with an inadequate amount of zeal. Or, more realistically, they may have to rush the process so as to benefit from the provision. Rushed procedures may not be the most secure.

A sunset provision can serve several purposes. First, it has the potential to encourage the good habit of congressional engagement on both sides. Congress has an incentive
to discover whether it wants to renew the powers, and agencies have an incentive to win
renewal. Second, a sunset can be an encouragement for agencies to take additional care in
crafting their initial operating procedures. During this period, these careful procedures can
become rooted practices. Once rooted, the practices are less likely to change even if the
provisions are later made permanent. The result of this could be that additional sunsets are
not needed because a sunset was first used. Third, the sunset can be an absolute backstop
to any concerns. Legislative inertia works against passage. If the powers prove to be inherently problematic, they will most likely expire. Of course, this point loops back to one of
the disadvantages of sunsets: Inherently helpful powers can also expire.

In comparing these two viewpoints, the internal conflict of using a sunset in this circumstance becomes apparent. Several large bureaucracies need to dramatically and
quickly alter operational methods while at the same time ensuring that they do so in a
careful fashion so as both to accomplish and demonstrate that they remain institutionally
sensitive to liberty concerns.

Other Oversight Tools

Beyond the three oversight tools of judicial involvement, congressional oversight, and
sunset provisions, there are other options. Lawmakers can apply the exclusionary rule to
evidence obtained in a manner that violates the law.[67] This puts the impetus for oversight
in the hands of defense attorneys. As mentioned previously, some debate the value of the
exclusionary rule. *Mens rea* requirements increase the quality of proof necessary to
receive a search warrant or wiretap order. Overreaching is not just less likely, it is less pos-

sible, when a judge must be presented with probable cause that a person *knowingly* contributed money to a terrorist organization.

The next three oversight tools rely on action by the citizenry to be effective. The first creates a civil cause of action for willful disclosures of information that extends beyond what the statute allows.[68]

Freedom of Information Act (FOIA)[69] requests provide another opportunity for citizens to educate themselves as to how the agencies are operating. Amendments to FOIA that overreach the legitimate need to restrict access to government records should be resisted. To date, it appears that the Department is evaluating FOIA in light of the present security environment. On October 12, 2001, Secretary Ashcroft released a new FOIA memorandum in which he announced a change in the legal standard the department would use to determine whether it will defend an agency's decision on a particular FOIA request.[70]

The last tool needs no greater explanation than simply identifying it: press coverage.

In sum, the mere fact that law enforcement and intelligence agencies are sharing information does not raise concerns. Increased cooperation is necessary to restore security. Hand in hand, however, comes the realization that we do not have the luxury of structural separation as an alternative to vigorous oversight. Each relevant group—Congress, the agencies (to include the new Office of Homeland Security[71]), and the citizenry—must become more involved in security and more involved in oversight.

Conclusion

The coordination and information sharing contemplated by the USA PATRIOT Act between elements of the intelligence community, including the CIA and the FBI, is consistent with existing law governing the activities of law enforcement and the intelligence community. America's history includes periods of cooperation and information sharing between the CIA and the FBI. In addition, although the method by which government officials conduct surveillance and gather information has significant implications for civil liberties, the simple sharing of information between two elements of the intelligence community, or between the intelligence community and the law enforcement community, does not necessarily threaten civil liberties. Information can be shared in a manner consistent with the protection of civil liberties. It is the nature and techniques of the surveillance that matter most. Who performs the surveillance may also matter, but the conditions of the performance are of the most critical importance.[72]

Moreover, it is also possible that the participation of multiple government agencies in the same intelligence operation, far from threatening civil liberties, might serve instead to check potential overreaching by individuals within any one of the agencies.[73] In the end, the focus of attention should be principally on the techniques by which intelligence is gathered domestically, not on whether other members of the intelligence community are permitted to view the intelligence gathered as a result of those operations.

Notes

1.   L. Paul Bremer III, Testimony before the Senate Select Committee on Intelligence, June 8, 2000.

2. Ibid.

3. The Baader-Meinhoff group in Germany, *Action Directe* in France, the Red Brigades in Italy, the Irish Republican Army, and the Palestine Liberation Organization were all animated by such practical agendas.

4. It also bears emphasizing that these terrorist groups only threatened Americans when they were outside the country.

5. L. Paul Bremer III, Speech to the Heritage Society, Washington, DC, July 12, 2000.

6. Abu Sayyaf Group; Armed Islamic Group; Hamas; Harakat ul-Mujahidin; Hizballah; Islamic Group; Islamic Movement of Uzbekistan; Al-Jihad; Palestinian Islamic Jihad; and Al-Qaeda. U.S. Department of State, *Foreign Terrorist Organizations* (Washington, DC: Department of State, 2001).

7. L. Paul Bremer III, "A New Strategy for the New Face of Terrorism," *National Interest,* No. 65-S (Thanksgiving 2001): 24.

8. S. K. Malik, *The Quranic Concept of War,* quoted in Yossef Bodansky, *Bin Laden* (Roosevelt, CA: Prima Publishing, 1999), p. xv.

9. Ibid.

10. See, *e.g.,* Norman Podhoretz, "Israel Isn't the Issue," *Wall Street Journal,* September 20, 2001.

11. The Ayatollah Khomeini popularized the view in the Muslim world that America is oriented principally around money-making and that such an orientation makes "prostitution [the] community's way of life." One follower of Khomeini's described America as "a collection of casinos, supermarkets, and whore-houses linked together by endless highways passing through nowhere," quoted in Bodansky, *Bin Laden,* p. xiii. Accordingly, Islamic fundamentalists have long sought an end to what they consider unjust occupation of Muslim lands by those who they view as corrupt Westerners.

12. See, *e.g.,* Paul A. Rahe, *Republics: Ancient and Modern,* vol. 2 (Chapel Hill: University of North Carolina Press, 1994), pp. 85–104.

13. Bremer, "A New Strategy for the New Face of Terrorism," p. 25.

14. Reuel Marc Gerecht, "The Counterterrorist Myth," *The Atlantic Monthly*, July/August 2001.

15. Ibid.

16. Bremer, "A New Strategy for the New Face of Terrorism," p. 25.

17. See, *e.g.,* "Getting Serious," *Wall Street Journal,* September 13, 2001; Douglas W. Kmiec, "War Crimes Are Different," *Wall Street Journal,* November 15, 2001.

18. See,*e.g.* Edward Jay Epstein, *The Assassination Chronicles: Inquest, Counterplot and Legend* (New York: Carrol & Graf, 1992); Curt Gentry, *J. Edgar Hoover: The Man and His Secrets* (New York: Plume, 1991), p. 418; *Final Report of the Select Committee to Study Governmental Operations with Respect to Intelligence Activities,* vol. 1 (Washington, DC: GPO 1976), p. 440. Hereinafter cited as *Report of the Church Committee.*

19. See Executive Order 12333, United States Intelligence Activities, December 3, 1981.

20. See Gentry, *J. Edgar Hoover,* p. 410 *ff.* See also Stewart Baker, "Dangerous Secrets," *Wall Street Journal,* October 5, 2001 ("[T]he grand jury rules have the effect of putting Justice in a position of primacy among the agencies. [Prior to passage of the PATRIOT Act] the Justice Department [could] make exceptions to the no-sharing rule,

but only for CIA analysts who agree to work as prosecutors' assistants, and so long as prosecutorial goals take precedence over intelligence ones.").

21. Gentry, *J. Edgar Hoover,* p. 70 *ff.*
22 . Ibid.
23. Ibid.
24. Angelo Codevilla, *Informing Statecraft: Intelligence for a New Century* (New York: The Free Press, 1992), p. 134 *ff.*
25. Ibid.
26. Committee on the Role and Capabilities of U.S. Intelligence, *Preparing for the 21st Century: An Appraisal of U.S. Intelligence* (Washington, DC: GPO, March 1996), p. A-4; *see also* Codevilla, Informing Statecraft, p. 136.
27. Ibid.
28. Gentry, *J. Edgar Hoover,* p. 326–27.
29. Ibid.
30. Ibid.
31. Gentry, *J. Edgar Hoover; cf. Report to the President by the Commission on CIA Activities within the United States* (Washington, DC.: GPO, 1975), p. 11. Hereinafter cited as the Report of the Rockefeller Commission.
32. Codevilla, *Informing Statecraft,* p. 136.
33. Ibid.
34. See 50 U.S.C. 403 *et seq.*
35. 18 U.S.C. 403–403.
36. See, *e.g.,* Report of the Rockefeller Commission, pp. 10–11.
37. Committee on the Role and Capabilites of U.S. Intelligence, *Preparing for the 21st Century*, p. A-4.
38. The House Select Intelligence Committee, known as the Pike Committee, conducted a parallel investigation as well.
39. Report of the Rockefeller Commission, pp. 20–21.
40. Ibid., pp. 23–24.
41. Ibid; *see also, Report of the Church Committee*, p. 436.
42. See, *e.g.* "Unspooking Spooks," *Wall Street Journal,* September 18, 2001; Tom Clancy, "How We Got Here," *Wall Street Journal,* September 18, 2001.
43. Notably, the Report of the Rockefeller Commission recommends that Section 403 of the National Security Act be amended to "[m]ake explicit that the CIA's activities must be related to *foreign* intelligence" (p. 12). In so recommending, the commission lost sight of the fact that the CIA has an important role to play in domestic counterintelligence.
44. The focus of counterintelligence is on developing capabilities to thwart clandestine threats to national security. See Abraham N. Shulsky and Gary J. Schmitt, *Silent Warfare: Understanding the World of Intelligence,* 2nd ed. (Washington, DC: Brassey's, 1993). Counterterrorism is closely analogous to, and arguably, subsumed within counterintelligence. *See* Executive Order 12333, at "3.4(a).
45. Report of the Church Committee, p. 440 (emphasis added).
46. Report of the Rockefeller Commission, p. 22.
47. Ibid., p. 38
48. Ibid., p. 39.

49.   Executive Order 12333, at '1.1.

50.   Ibid. at '1.5. The intelligence community is defined by the order to include both the CIA and the intelligence elements of the FBI (Executive Order 12333, at "3.4(f).

51.   Ibid., at '1.8(a) and (d).

52.   Ibid., at '3.4(a) and (d).

53.   Ibid., at '1.14.

54.   See, *e.g.,* Stewart Baker, "Dangerous Secrets," *Wall Street Journal,* October 5, 2001.

55.   For more detailed discussion of FISA and changes to FISA effected by the USA PATRIOT Act, see Tom Gede, Montgomery N. Kosma and Arun Chandra, "Developing Necessary and Constitutional Tools for Law Enforcement" (Federalist Society White Paper on Anti-Terrorism Legislation: Surveillance and Wiretap Laws, November 2001), p. 6 *ff.,* www.fedsoc.org.

56.   50 U.S.C. 401a(3); *Cf.* Executive Order 12333, at "3.4(a).

57.   See Gede, Kosma and Chandra, "Developing Necessary and Constitutional Tools for Law Enforcement," p. 62.

58.   See Ibid.

59.   Report of the Rockefeller Commission, pp. 23–24.

60.   The last two options, available to the at-large citizenry, were not aspects of particular provisions.

61.   This concern was raised throughout the Conference Committee negotiations.

62.   This concern was also raised throughout the Conference Committee negotiations.

63.   President Bush, interview by CNN, www.cnn.com/2001/us/09/15/bush/terrorism.

64.   This point has been emphasized as recently at December 1, 2001, by Israeli Prime Minister Sharon in an interview with Chris Matthews following another act of war by a group of terrorists; this time the victims were inhabitants and visitors to Zion Square in Jerusalem.

65.   Donald R. Wolfensberger, "Congressional Oversight: Rules of the Road Less Traveled," (speech, Oversight Workshop United States Congress, June 28, 1999). Wolfensberger characterized Congressional oversight as "the road less traveled" and explained the political disincentives that keeps it that way.

66.   Report of the National Commission on Terrorism, Countering the Changing Threat of International Terrorism (Washington, DC: GPO, June 2000).

67.   In determining whether to exclude, courts "evaluate the circumstances of [a] case in the light of the policy served by the exclusionary rule . . . " *Brown v. Illinois*, 422 U.S. 590, 604 (1975). "[T]he rule is calculated to prevent, not repair. Its purpose is to deter—to compel respect for the constitutional guaranty in the only effectively available way—by removing the incentive to disregard it . . . [D]espite its broad deterrent purpose, the exclusionary rule has never been interpreted to proscribe the use of illegally seized evidence in all proceedings or against all persons." " *Id.* at 599–600 (citations omitted). The exclusionary rule has its limitations . . . as a tool of judicial control . . . [In] some contexts the rule is ineffective as a deterrent . . . Proper adjudication of cases in which the exclusionary rule is invoked demands a constant awareness of these limitations . . . [A] rigid and unthinking application of the . . . rule . . . may exact a high toll in human injury and frustration of efforts to prevent crime. *Terry v. Ohio,* 392 U.S. 1, 13–15 (1968). Three exceptions to the exclusionary rule have emerged: the independent source exception, the attenuation exception, and the inevitable discovery

exception. *People v. LoCicero* (*After Remand*), 453 Mich. 496, 508–509 (1996) (citations omitted). In *Nix v. Williams*, 467 U.S. 431, 442–43 (1984), the United States Supreme Court explained the deterrent purpose of the exclusionary rule. The Court stated: "The core rationale consistently advanced by this Court for extending the exclusionary rule to evidence that is the fruit of unlawful police conduct has been that this admittedly drastic and socially costly course is needed to deter police from violations of constitutional and statutory protections. This Court has accepted the argument that the way to ensure such protections is to exclude evidence seized as a result of such violations notwithstanding the high social cost of letting persons obviously guilty go unpunished for their crimes. On this rationale, the prosecution is not to be put in a better position than it would have been in if no illegality had transpired. By contrast, the derivative evidence analysis ensures that the prosecution is not put in a worse position simply because of some earlier police error or misconduct."

68.   *See* section 223 of the Act.

69.   5 U.S.C. section 552.

70.   FOIA Post, "New Attorney General FOIA Memorandum Issued," www.usdoj. gov/oip/foiapost/2001foaipost19.htm. Under the new standard—sound legal basis— the releasing department's decision will be defended if it is based on a sound legal and factual footing. The previous standard was a "foreseeable harm" standard. These standards should be compared to determine the net effect on the amount of information that is released. Whether a more or less open government is preferred is a normative question for each citizen to answer individually.

71.   This office should consider including an oversight role as it establishes its procedures. As the central information clearinghouse, based on a flowchart created by the administration, this office may be in a good position to monitor the monitors. Additionally, the executive branch may consider altering the executive order that modeled the office after the National Security Council; Thomas Ridge, serving in the same capacity as National Security Adviser Condoleezza Rice, is not a cabinet secretary and is not required to appear before Congress. *See* Mark Preston, "Ridge Rebuffs Hill Requests," *Roll Call,* November 5, 2001.

72.   If the CIA were to conduct domestic operations, or begin to task the FBI, then alarm we consider overly cautious here might be demanded. Just as restrictions on military assistance to domestic authorities have continuing validity (and contain reasonable exceptions) so may restrictions on the domestic operation of the CIA. *See* 18 U.S.C. 1385, commonly called the *Posse Comitatus* Act.

73.   The goals of Executive Order 12333, which provides guidelines for coordination among the different elements of the United States intelligence community, include "fostering analytical competition among appropriate elements of the Intelligence Community" and "ensuring that appropriate mechanisms for competitive analysis are developed so that diverse points of view are considered fully and differences of judgment within the Intelligence Community are brought to the attention of national policymakers" (Executive Order 12333, at '1.1(a), 1.5(k)).

Chapter 26

What Price Security?
The USA PATRIOT Act and
America's Balance Between
Freedom and Security

Roger Dean Golden

It is a melancholy reflection that liberty should be equally exposed to danger whether the government have too much power or too little.
—James Madison in a letter to Thomas Jefferson, October 17, 1788[1]

On September 11, 2001, terrorists crashed jetliners into the two World Trade Center towers in New York City and the Pentagon in Washington, DC These attacks were successful in many ways. Of course, there was the immediate devastation of some 3,000 people killed, with thousands more wounded. Billions of dollars in property damage also resulted from the attacks. In the weeks that followed, more effects were evident. Americans truly were terrorized and traumatized, realizing that they were not safe in their own homeland. While the lives of those closest to the tragedies were changed radically, virtually all Americans felt some emotional effect from the attacks. In addition, the American economy, already beginning to falter, was dealt a severe blow. Certainly, if the terrorists' goal was to punish America, their success was significant.

However, the terrorists may have accomplished an even greater long-term victory, with implications for the future of all Americans. As a reaction to the September 11th attacks, Congress rapidly passed the USA PATRIOT Act on October 24, 2001, and President Bush signed it into law two days later.[2] This Act provided broad new powers to various agencies of the federal government, particularly in the area of gathering information that might lead to the arrest of terrorists or prevent future terrorist acts. Among other issues, the USA PATRIOT Act addresses intelligence gathering related to communications, funding, and other activities of possible terrorists.

The weighty question is, to what degree does this new Act infringe upon the freedoms of American citizens? Does this Act allow the federal government to intrude in an unacceptable manner into the private lives of Americans? Does it diminish the civil liberties that Americans hold dear? Does it represent a shift toward increasing security while taking away freedom? If this Act has resulted in a loss of freedom and reduced civil liberties for Americans, then have not the terrorists accomplished an even greater long-term victory as a result of their attacks? Have we conceded a portion of victory to the terrorists by sacrificing freedom to increase security?

The Balance Between Security and Freedom

They that can give up essential liberty to obtain a little temporary safety deserve neither liberty nor safety.

—Benjamin Franklin

Freedom and security may be viewed on a continuum, with the assumption that as one is increased the other may decrease. A nation that has total freedom may be characterized by anarchy, with minimum security for individuals in the state. Every person is free to do as he pleases, with no restrictions by the state. In such a nation, one person may use his freedom to the detriment of other people, resulting in anarchy. On the opposite end of the spectrum, a state may best be able to ensure maximum security only by severely limiting the freedoms of individuals. The state may seek to protect its citizens by controlling their lives. Such a state may ultimately constitute a dictatorship. This totalitarian state is the type of state pictured in George Orwell's novel *1984*. A model of this continuum for a nation reflecting a healthy balance between security and freedom is represented in Figure 26-1.

However, as freedom is increased, security is decreased and the nation moves toward anarchy. Conversely, as security is increased, freedom is decreased, and the nation moves toward dictatorship. Thus, one might argue that America has historically found a healthy balance between freedom and security. However, due to reactions to the recent crisis of terrorism, the fulcrum in America has moved toward security. Consequently, as security has increased, freedom has decreased, and America may be moving toward an unhealthy balance. The model would be adjusted to reflect this movement in Figure 26-2.

Has America experienced an unhealthy shift in the balance between freedom and security as a result of the reactions to the terrorism of September 11, 2001? Champions of civil liberty argue that such a shift has taken place and that America is moving toward dictatorship. An examination of the USA PATRIOT Act from an American historical perspective may prove useful in determining whether this fear is plausible.

The Origins of Freedom

Is life so dear, or peace so sweet, as to be purchased at the price of chains and slavery? Forbid it, Almighty God! I know not what course others may take; but as for me, give me liberty or give me death!

—Patrick Henry, March 23, 1775

In 1776, America's Founding Fathers wrote in the Declaration of Independence: "We hold these truths to be self-evident, that all men are created equal, that they are endowed by

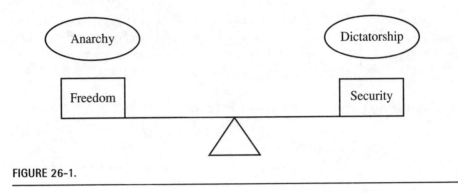

FIGURE 26-1.

their Creator with certain inalienable rights, that among these are life, liberty and the pursuit of happiness . . . " With this statement, the founding fathers expressed the heritage that was to be American—a heritage of liberty bestowed by the Creator himself. Infringement of this liberty was the reason given for the thirteen colonies revolting against the King of England and declaring their independence as the United States of America. The Declaration of Independence was enacted on July 4, 1776, and signed by representatives of the thirteen states, who pledged their lives, their fortunes, and their sacred honor to support this document and the liberty it proclaimed.

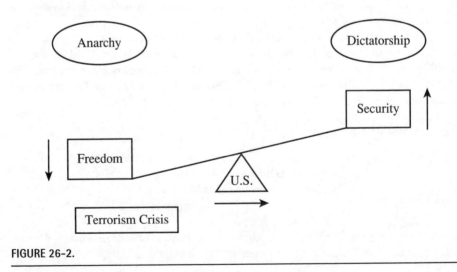

FIGURE 26-2.

This principle of preeminent liberty was codified by the Founding Fathers in the governing document that they wrote to establish the basic law for America, The United States Constitution. The Constitution was completed on September 17, 1787. The preamble to the Constitution states:

> We the People of the United States, in Order to form a more perfect Union, establish Justice, insure domestic Tranquility, provide for the common defence, promote the general Welfare, and *secure the Blessings of Liberty to ourselves and our Posterity,* do ordain and establish this Constitution for the United States of America. *(Emphasis added.)*

The objective of the Constitution was to establish the overall system of government that would defend the security of the people and provide domestic peace and welfare. However, the greater goal of the Constitution was the securing of liberty. The purpose of the law was so that liberty might be protected. Thus, a healthy balance was established between security and liberty in the Constitution.

In order to clarify the liberties which the Founding Fathers believed to be the unalienable rights of all Americans, the U.S. Congress added the first ten amendments to the Constitution, ratified on December 15, 1791 (just four years after the signing of the Constitution). The Bill of Rights, as these ten amendments have commonly been called, provides for specific rights and freedoms to be guaranteed to Americans. The first amendment rights include freedom of religion, freedom of speech, freedom of the press, freedom to assemble peacefully, and freedom to petition the government for redress of grievances. The second amendment provides the right to bear arms. The fourth amendment provides "[t]he right of the people to be secure in their persons, houses, papers, and effects, against unreasonable searches and seizures." The fifth amendment provides that no person shall be "deprived of life, liberty, or property, without due process of law." Amendment 9 recognizes that there are rights that even the Constitution may not enumerate: "The enumeration in the Constitution, of certain rights, shall not be construed to deny or disparage others retained by the people." Thus, the forefathers established the importance of civil liberties, with the principle that the Constitution and the body of law were there for the protection of the rights of the citizens.

Over the course of America's history, the body of law established by the U.S. Congress and interpreted by the courts has sought to maintain a proper balance between security and liberty. If security is threatened by a crisis, Congress may enact a law that represents a shift toward security at the cost of reduced freedom. This shift toward security may also be effectuated by a presidential executive order or other actions of the executive branch. However, if a law is too intrusive on liberty, it is likely that the Supreme Court will invalidate the law, moving the fulcrum back toward freedom, even at the cost of a potential reduction in security. Congress may also pass laws expanding or guaranteeing freedom, moving the balance toward freedom with possible reductions in security. Certainly, the fulcrum has shifted from time to time in one direction or the other. Historians might disagree as to the degree the fulcrum has shifted toward freedom or toward security, but examples of movement in both directions can be cited.

In 1928, writing the majority decision in *Olmstead v. U.S.,* Justice Louis Brandeis introduced the "right to privacy," which had not been specifically listed in the Constitution. Brandeis wrote, "To protect that right, every unjustifiable intrusion by the government upon the privacy of the individual, whatever the means employed, must be deemed a violation of the Fourth Amendment." Brandeis considered the right to privacy as "the right to be left alone—the most comprehensive of rights, and the right most valued by civilized men."[3] With this Supreme Court decision, the fulcrum moved toward increased freedom. Yet, the decision made it more difficult for the federal government to gather information that might ensure security. The right to privacy has subsequently been regarded to be as fundamental as the other civil liberties specifically enumerated in the Bill of Rights.

There are also examples of the fulcrum moving toward security at the cost of freedom. One of the most glaring examples was the treatment of Japanese-American citizens during World War II. After the Japanese attacked Pearl Harbor on December 7, 1941, the U.S. experienced great fear, particularly in the West, where citizens thought Japan would attack next. On February 14, 1942, President Roosevelt issued Executive Order 9066, which ordered Japanese residents to be taken from their homes and placed in camps supervised by the War Relocation Authority. More than 120,000 Japanese were placed in austere conditions in these camps, even though two-thirds of these Japanese people were American citizens. There was no evidence of a threat, or even disloyalty, by any of these Japanese people. Yet the Executive Order was not canceled until 1944, and the camps were not completely closed until March 1946.[4] The U.S. Supreme Court upheld these incarcerations. The fulcrum had shifted toward supposed security for Americans in general, while resulting in a total loss of freedom for thousands of Japanese-Americans.

In January 2001, Tampa, Florida used face-recognition cameras to scan the crowds at the Super Bowl. Faces were to be matched by computer with faces of known criminals, hopefully leading to arrest of those criminals. After the Super Bowl, the cameras were moved to the Ybor City region of Tampa, where police continued to try to identify criminals.[5] Civil libertarians protested this technique as an invasion of privacy, but the cameras were only removed after they proved ineffective in leading to the apprehension of criminals. Consideration is being given to use of similar face-recognition technology in airports and seaports to try to identify terrorists attempting entry into the United States. Opponents argue that this technology deprives Americans of the right to privacy, moving the fulcrum toward security at the cost of freedom.

American history includes many other examples of movement in one direction or the other. U.S. Representative Jerrold Nadler said that the United States has often limited civil rights during wartime, including the 1798 Alien Sedition Act, the 1917 Espionage Act and Palmer raids, COINTEL during the Vietnam War, and McCarthyism during the Cold War. He also noted that America has had to apologize for each of these cases.[6] Over time, America has continued to seek a healthy balance between freedom and security. Crisis has usually been the impetus for any moves toward security. Such is the case with the USA PATRIOT Act and other federal government actions following the September 11, 2001, terrorist attacks.

The USA PATRIOT Act

We're likely to experience more restrictions on personal freedom than has ever been the case in this country.

—Supreme Court Justice Sandra Day O'Connor, after a visit to Ground Zero,
the site of the terrorist attacks on the World Trade Center in New York[7]

The USA PATRIOT Act is actually 167 pages of documents, primarily modifying existing
laws on a variety of subjects. The title is an acronym for "Uniting and Strengthening
America by Providing Appropriate Tools Required to Intercept and Obstruct Terrorism."
The Act's primary focus is to grant the federal government increased powers for surveillance and intelligence gathering on individuals residing in the United States. These individuals may include both citizens and noncitizens. Other provisions of the Act cover a
variety of issues related to the war on terrorism.

With the anthrax scare in full swing and many lawmakers shut out of their offices, the
Act passed Congress with virtually no debate. According to Senator Russell Feingold, the
only senator voting against the bill, most senators were very unaware of the details of the
Act.[8] U.S. Representative Jerrold Nadler said that the version of the bill approved by the
House Judiciary Committee had been thrown out, with House Republican leaders and
Attorney General John Ashcroft crafting a new version. Although only two copies of the
lengthy new bill were printed at 10 A.M., the bill passed the House three hours later by an
overwhelming majority vote of 356 to 66.[9] In fact, the bill could only be understood by comparing it to the several other laws it amended. Critics of the bill contend that the federal executive department used this opportunity to railroad through many intrusive practices
Congress had refused to allow in the past. Senator Feingold said, "There is no doubt that if
we lived in a police state it would be easier to catch terrorists. That would not be America."[10]

The Act addresses a number of different areas in order to provide tools for the government to combat terrorism within the United States. Title I discusses antiterrorism funding and philosophical issues. Title I, Sec 102 (b) states: "It is the sense of Congress that
the civil rights and civil liberties of all Americans, including Arab-Americans, Muslim-
Americans, and Americans from South Asia, must be protected, and that every effort must
be taken to preserve their safety."[11] Thus, Congress stated their intention to maintain the
balance between security and freedom. However, critics of the Act argue that, in spite of
those stated intentions, the Act severely infringes on the civil liberties of all Americans.

Title II of the Act provides for enhanced surveillance procedures. Authority to intercept wire, oral, and electronic communications is expanded if these communications may
be related to terrorism or computer fraud and abuse. This title includes 25 separate sections, providing significant new authority for the government to monitor all forms of communication, including postal mail, e-mail, voice mail, telephone, and computer
communications. Search warrants will be easier to obtain, more powerful, broader in
scope, and will provide for warrants to be valid for longer periods of time. Typical language of this title indicates that the Federal Bureau of Investigation "may make an application for an order requiring the production of any tangible things (including books,
records, papers, documents, and other items) for an investigation to protect against international terrorism or clandestine intelligence activities."[12]

One statute revised by the USA PATRIOT Act is the Foreign Intelligence
Surveillance Act (FISA) of 1978. Congress passed FISA after learning that the FBI had
performed extensive surveillance on American citizens during the previous two decades.
FISA severely restricted domestic surveillance, establishing guidelines for when and how
wiretaps could be performed on American citizens. FISA was an example of Congress

moving the fulcrum toward liberty at the possible cost of security. The USA PATRIOT Act significantly loosens some of the restrictions of FISA, moving the fulcrum back toward security at the potential cost of freedom.

For example, the USA PATRIOT Act allows "roving" wiretaps that can follow a person wherever he goes, including a neighbor's computer, a library computer, his home or office computer, or any phone he may use. Critics argue that the new provision may violate the Fourth Amendment to the Constitution, which prohibits unreasonable searches and requires that warrants "particularly describ[e] the place to be searched, and the persons or things to be seized." Under the USA PATRIOT Act, national search warrants may be requested, whereas previously, separate warrants had to be obtained for every jurisdiction. The USA PATRIOT Act also changed the Electronic Communications Privacy Act (18 U.S.C. sec 2703) so that nationwide search warrants can be issued for voice mail and e-mail. The only probable cause that is required is a reasonable suspicion that a person may be acting for a foreign power. Search warrants are powerful, and can be enforced immediately, even against resistance.[13]

Wiretapping authority is also broadened by the USA PATRIOT Act. FISA allowed wiretaps only if a federal judge determined that the target individual had probably committed a serious crime, with those crimes specifically listed. The USA PATRIOT Act added a number of crimes related to terrorism and cybercrime to the list justifying wiretapping. In addition, an Internet service provider may be required to gather information such as Web sites visited or e-mail headers.[14] Critics argue that, once such broad access is allowed to an individual's communications, there is no way to ensure that the agency gathers only information relevant to an investigation or that information will not be used to harm individuals who are not involved in terrorism. Therefore, the right to privacy may have been significantly diminished by the USA PATRIOT Act.

Title III of the USA PATRIOT Act addresses "International Money Laundering Abatement and Anti-Terrorist Financing." The Act contends that money laundering totaling more than $600 billion annually permits funding of terrorism and international crime. This portion of the Act is designed to "increase the strength of . . . measures to prevent, detect, and prosecute international money laundering and the financing of terrorism."[15] The Act includes new authority to gather information, seize funds, and levy heavy criminal penalties, including fines and prison time, for money laundering. Areas of concern for civil liberty activists include new requirements for financial institutions such as banks to gather additional information and report more information to government agencies. Securities brokers and dealers are required to report activities that they judge to be "suspicious."[16] Many of the new provisions represent changes to the "Bank Secrecy Act," removing some of the privacy Americans have historically had in their financial transactions and arrangements.

Title IV of the USA PATRIOT Act provides measures to protect the borders of the United States. The State Department and the Immigration and Naturalization Service (INS) are provided more access to the criminal records of persons attempting to enter the United States. The U.S. Attorney General is given $2 million for an "integrated automated fingerprint identification system for ports of entry and overseas consular posts." The Act includes an extensive definition of terrorism and provides for mandatory detention of any suspected terrorist. The criterion for detention is "reasonable grounds" to believe that the person "is engaged in any . . . activity that endangers the national security of the United States."[17]

Title V aims to remove obstacles to investigating terrorism. Section 504 provides for more coordination and sharing of information between intelligence and law enforcement officials. Section 505 provides broader authority to obtain telephone bills and records and financial records. Sections 507 and 508 give authority to collect educational records. In each case, information previously considered private can be more readily obtained by federal agencies.[18]

Title VI provides financial benefits for victims of terrorism, public safety officers, and their families and does not appear to contain any civil liberty issues. Title VII expands information sharing between federal, state, and local law enforcement agencies. The Act provides $150 million to the Bureau of Justice Assistance to establish and operate "secure information sharing systems to enhance the investigation and prosecution abilities of participating enforcement agencies in addressing multi-jurisdictional terrorist conspiracies and activities." Critics fear a "big brother" type of government gathering all kinds of information on its citizens and using this information for wrong purposes.[19]

Title VIII strengthens criminal laws against terrorism. Statutes of limitation are removed for certain terrorism offenses. Maximum penalties are increased. Domestic terrorism, cyberterrorism, bioterrorism, terrorism conspiracies, and terrorism as racketeering are addressed. Even harboring of terrorists and providing material support for terrorists are discussed, with new penalties including fines and up to ten years in prison.[20]

Title IX discusses improved intelligence against terrorism, amending the National Security Act of 1947 to make clear the responsibilities and authorities for various federal agencies in dealing with terrorism. The Director of Central Intelligence is given broader authority to gather intelligence that possibly relates to terrorist activities. Requirements for reporting to Congress on intelligence gathering activities are softened.[21]

Title X includes a number of miscellaneous provisions, including efforts to provide some protections for civil liberties. Section 1001 says that the "Inspector General of the Department of Justice shall designate one official who shall review information and receive complaints alleging abuses of civil rights and civil liberties by employees and officials of the Department of Justice."[22] Section 1002 expresses the sense of Congress that "in the quest to identify, locate, and bring to justice the perpetrators and sponsors of the terrorist attacks . . . the civil rights and civil liberties of all Americans, including Sikh-Americans, should be protected."[23]

Reactions to the USA PATRIOT Act

I don't think the American public has even begun to grasp the kind of sacrifices we've been called to make in civil liberties in this war on terrorism.
—Vermont Law School Professor Stephen Dycus[24]

Since the USA PATRIOT Act became law, many voices have been raised in criticism of the Act, alleging that Americans have suffered serious loss of civil liberties. A statement by Nancy Chang, senior litigation attorney at the Center for Constitutional Rights in New York, is representative of the level of concern:

To an unprecedented degree, the Act sacrifices our political freedoms in the name of national security and upsets the democratic values that define our nation by consolidating vast new powers in the executive branch of government. The Act enhances the executive's ability to conduct surveillance and gather intelligence, places an array of new tools at the disposal of the prosecution, including new crimes, enhanced penalties, and longer statutes of limitations, and grants the Immigration and Naturalization Service (INS) the authority to detain immigrants suspected of terrorism for lengthy, and in some cases indefinite, periods of time. And at the same time that the Act inflates the powers of the executive, it insulates the exercise of these powers from meaningful judicial and Congressional oversight.[25]

Ms. Chang believes that the Act gives the federal government "unchecked surveillance powers" related to e-mail, Internet, and personal and financial records. She sees the Act as violating both First and Fourth Amendment rights, as well as virtually dismantling the right to privacy.[26]

The Electronic Frontier Foundation (EFF) expresses similar concerns, stating, "The civil liberties of ordinary Americans have taken a tremendous blow with this law, especially the right to privacy in our online communications and activities." The EFF says that many of the provisions are aimed at nonviolent cybercrimes that do not involve terrorism at all. Specific concerns include increased surveillance, overly broad provisions, and "spying" on Americans by the CIA and the FBI. EFF is also concerned about the lack of accountability to Congress, which may lead to misuse of the new powers.[27]

On November 18, 2002, a three-judge federal panel upheld provisions of the USA PATRIOT Act allowing expanded wiretap and other information collecting and sharing by the Justice Department and U.S. Intelligence Agencies. This decision by the panel stopped efforts of the Foreign Intelligence Surveillance Court to restrict surveillances by the FBI and the Justice Department. After the latest decision, Attorney General John Ashcroft quickly increased surveillance on terrorist suspects. Civil liberties advocates assailed the decision as allowing the government to eavesdrop on telephone conversations, read private e-mail, and search private property, even if there is no evidence of wrongdoing by the targeted individual.[28] The American Civil Liberties Union (ACLU) argued that the ruling violates rights to free speech and due process and said that the ruling would give the government free reign for "intrusive surveillance warrants."[29]

The ACLU has joined with the American Bookseller's Foundation for Free Expression, the Electronic Privacy Information Center, and the American Library Association's Freedom to Read Foundation to file suit against the Department of Justice (DOJ). These organizations allege that the DOJ refuses to release information concerning what actions it has taken under provisions of the USA PATRIOT Act. Of particular concern is the seizing of records from bookstores and libraries even when no criminal activity has been demonstrated. The DOJ says it cannot release the information due to possible detriment of national security. The plaintiffs want to build a case that information is being gathered unnecessarily and used improperly.[30]

Attorney General Ashcroft has said, "I don't have the power to erode the Constitution. I wouldn't do it if I could." However, Ashcroft also said, "We don't need any leads or preliminary investigations" to send undercover agents into public meetings or public places, including churches or mosques "under the same terms and conditions of any member of the public."[31] The government only needs a "reasonable indication," rather than the previous standard of probable cause.[32] Chairman of the House Judiciary Committee

James Sensenbrenner disagreed, stating, "We can have security without throwing respect for civil liberties into the trash heap. We don't have to go back to the bad old days when the FBI was spying on people like Martin Luther King." Roger Pilon of the Cato Institute went further, stating, "This is now an executive branch that thinks it's a law unto itself."[33]

Some Congressmen are not satisfied with the Executive Branch's actions under the USA PATRIOT Act. Senator Richard Durbin said the bill represented a "leap of faith, born of fear. This administration, this Department of Justice, has abused that faith." Senator Patrick Leahy, chairman of the Senate Judiciary Committee, has threatened subpoenas if the Justice Department does not give the requested information. House Judiciary Committee Chairman James Sensenbrenner has echoed the threat of subpoenas.[34]

Supporters of the USA PATRIOT Act contend that the expanded authorities are needed to protect the security of Americans. They are not opposed to civil liberties, but "Dead people have no civil liberties at all."[35] The *Village Voice* has quoted Attorney General Ashcroft as saying, "To those who scare peace-loving people with phantoms of lost liberty, my message is this: Your tactics only aid terrorists, for they erode our national unity and diminish our resolve. They give ammunition to America's enemies."[36] Associate Deputy Attorney General David Kris told the Senate Judiciary Committee, "What is at stake is nothing less than our ability to protect this country from foreign spies and terrorists."[37]

Supporters of the Act point out that we are at war, and the old standards no longer apply. With the crisis surrounding U.S. security, reasonable suspicion is a more realistic standard than the probable cause standard, which refers to mere criminal activity, not terrorism. Supporters cite the case of one terrorist, Zacarias Moussaoui. The government was actually arguing over whether to search Moussaoui's computer, even though he was not even in the country legally and could certainly not be considered a U.S. person.[38]

Writing in *The American Criminal Law Review,* Jennifer M. Collins notes that the events of September 11 changed reality. Collins notes that there has been a strong separation between law enforcement and the foreign intelligence community for the 50 years of the CIA's existence. Now, however, Collins cautiously argues that the ongoing danger of terrorism justifies "lowering the wall of separation between the grand jury and other agencies of the government to improve coordination and the sharing of national security information—with the goal of safeguarding the nation's security and its citizens."[39]

One recurring theme of supporters of increased government authority is that without adequate power, the government cannot protect the very liberty Americans hold dear. Laurence Tribe, of Harvard Law School, noted that "civil liberties are not only about protecting us from our government. They are also about protecting our lives from terrorism." Supporters also cite the example of President Abraham Lincoln's emergency actions during the Civil War. When Lincoln suspended the writ of *habeas corpus,* he justified the action with the statement, "Must a government, of necessity, be too strong for the liberties of its own people, or too weak to maintain its own existence?"[40] Supporters argue that, without the additional authorities given to government by the USA PATRIOT Act, the government will not have the tools of power to defend the lives—much less the freedom—of Americans.

Conclusion

For rulers are not a terror to good works, but to the evil. Wilt thou then not be afraid of the power? Do that which is good, and thou shalt have praise of

the same: For he is the minister of God to thee for good. But if thou do that which is evil, be afraid; for he beareth not the sword in vain: for he is the minister of God, a revenger to execute wrath upon him that doeth evil.
—*The Holy Bible,* King James Version, Romans 13:3–4

The USA PATRIOT Act certainly represents a shift toward security even at the cost of potential loss of freedom. However, the majority of Americans appear willing to accept this shift. In a February 2002 Greenberg poll, 62 percent of those responding agreed, "Americans will have to accept new restrictions on their civil liberties if we are to win the war on terrorism." In late September 2001, a NBC/*Wall Street Journal* poll found 78 percent of respondents approving surveillance of Internet communications. Sixty-three percent of respondents to a Harris poll approved camera surveillance on streets and public places. In 1998, Chief Justice William Rehnquist recognized that a national crisis can shift the balance between freedom and security toward security, "in favor of the government's ability to deal with the conditions that threaten the national well-being."[41]

However, as time passes and the events of September 11, 2001, begin to diminish, the mindset of the American people may change. A November 2001 Investor's Business Daily poll found 58 percent of respondents worried about losing "certain civil liberties in light of recently passed antiterrorism laws." By March 2002, a *Time*/CNN poll found 62 percent of respondents concerned that "the U.S. Government might go too far in restricting civil liberties."[42] Americans in general may be willing to accept some loss of freedom so long as the government uses the new powers to consistently target the "evil doers" of terrorism. However, if Americans believe their own personal civil liberties have been unnecessarily or overly limited, active opposition is likely to increase.

Does America still have a healthy balance between freedom and security? At this point, the fulcrum has shifted toward security with the potential loss of a degree of the freedom previously enjoyed by Americans. Whether this shift toward security will have significant permanent effects obviously remains to be seen. If America follows historical patterns, the people will force the fulcrum back toward freedom once the threat to security is perceived as sufficiently reduced. In the meantime, to the extent that any degree of freedom is lost for Americans, the terrorists will have achieved some measure of victory.

Notes

1. James Madison, "The Question of a Bill of Rights," Letter to Thomas Jefferson, October 17, 1788, www.constitution.org/jm/17881017_bor.htm (accessed December 2, 2002).
2. Mary Minow, "The USA PATRIOT Act," *Library Journal* 127 (October 1, 2002): 52–55.
3. Grawwroats.org, Your Right to Privacy, www.rightoprivacy.com (accessed November 15, 2002).
4. Roy Webb, "Japanese-American Internment Camps During World War II," www.lib.utah.edu/spc/photo/9066/9066.htm (accessed November 25, 2002).
5. Electronic Privacy Information Center, Face Recognition, www.epic.org/privacy/facerecognition (accessed November 25, 2002).

6. Jane Adas, "New York Congressman Nadler Calls USA PATRIOT Act Extreme Danger to Civil Rights," *The Washington Report on Middle East Affairs* 21 (August 2002): 57–58.

7. Justice Sandra Day O'Connor quoted in Nick Gillespie, "What Price Safety?: Freedom for Safety," *Reason* 34 (October 2002): 24–26.

8. Minow, "USA PATRIOT Act."

9. Adas, "New York Congressman Nadlen."

10. Senator Russell Feingold quoted in Alisa Solomon, "Things We Lost in the Fire," *The Village Voice* 7 (September 11–17, 2002): 32–36.

11. "USA PATRIOT Act," H.R. 3162, 107th Cong., 1st sess., October 24, 2001, p. 10, www.epic.org/privacy/terrorism/hr3162.pdf.

12. Ibid., 25.

13. Minow, "USA PATRIOT Act."

14. Ibid., 52–55.

15. "USA PATRIOT Act," 37.

16. Ibid., p. 71.

17. Ibid., pp. 103–106.

18. Ibid., pp. 119–26.

19. Ibid., p. 132.

20. Ibid., pp. 132–49.

21. Ibid., pp. 150–54.

22. Ibid., p. 154.

23. Ibid., p. 155.

24. Steven Dycus quoted in Gina Holland, "Government Surveillance Powers Scrutinized," *The Montgomery Advertiser,* November 20, 2002.

25. Nancy Chang, "The USA PATRIOT Act: What's So Patriotic About Trampling on the Bill of Rights?" Chapter 24 of this volume.

26. Ibid.

27. Electronic Frontier Foundation, EFF Analysis of the Provisions of the USA PATRIOT Act, www.eff.org/Privacy/Surveillance/Terrorism_militias/20011031_eff_usa_patriot_analysis.html (accessed November 26, 2002).

28. Holland, "Government Surveillance."

29. Curt Anderson, "Ruling Expands Wiretap Powers," *Montgomery Advertiser,* November 19, 2002.

30. Steven Zeitchik, "Groups Sue over Patriot Act," *Publishers Weekly* 249 (October 28, 2002): 16.

31. Nat Hentoff, "Citizens Resist War on the Bill of Rights," *Free Inquiry* 22 (Fall 2002): 13–14.

32. Joe Feuerherd, "September 11: A Year Later—Congress Questions Patriot Act Policies," *National Catholic Reporter* 38 (September 6, 2002): 7.

33. Hentoff, "Citizens Resist War on the Bill of Rights."

34. Jess Bravin, "Leahy Warns Justice Department on New Powers," *Wall Street Journal*, September 11, 2002.

35. Minow, "USA PATRIOT Act."

412 *Public Security and Civil Liberties*

36. Nat Hentoff, "The Sons and Daughters of Liberty," *Village Voice* 47 (July 2, 2002): 34. Note that this quote is reported by the *Village Voice,* which may be a biased source. The context of the alleged quote is not provided in the article.
37. Bravin, "Leahy Warns Justice Department."
38. Richard Lowry, "A Better Bureau," *National Review* 54 (July 1, 2002): 28–30.
39. Jennifer M. Collins, "And the Walls Came Tumbling Down: Sharing Grand Jury Information with the Intelligence Community under the USA PATRIOT Act," *The American Criminal Law Review* 39 (Summer 2002): 1261–1286.
40. Mackubin Thomas Owens, "Liberty & Security: A Prudential Balance," *National Review On-line,* www.nationalreview.com/comment/comment-owens120401.shtml (accessed December 1, 2002).
41. John B. Gould, "Playing With Fire: The Civil Liberties Implications of September 11th," *Public Administration Review* 62 (September, 2002): 74–79.
42. Ibid.

Section V

Lessons Learned

Within virtually every field of study, scholars seek to draw on experiences from the past to identify lessons for the future. This final collection of chapters offers a variety of research-based insights in several key areas of homeland security, including protecting the nation's critical infrastructure and preventing (and responding to) a bioterrorism incident. Randy May's chapter offers important insights on preventing communications blackouts in times of extreme emergency. Drawing on lessons learned from September 11, 2001 and the great Northeast blackout of 2003, May emphasizes the need for redundant networks and suggests a number of practical and policy recommendations for national, state, and local authorities. Clearly, the need for getting this right is paramount.

Vincent Covello and his colleagues follow with an analysis of the communication challenges that could result from a bioterrorism event. By examining New York City's response to the West Nile Virus in 1999–2000 as an example of "risk communication"—a science-based approach for communicating effectively in emergency situations—their chapter highlights important issues of roles, responsibilities, and managing the perception of risk among a community's members.

Kelly Hicks's chapter highlights the important role of the private sector, a theme raised by several other authors in this volume. Drawing lessons from how commercial industries played a major role in battling the SARS epidemic in Hong Kong during 2003, Hicks provides important recommendations for American business leaders, whose support in homeland security has never been more vital than now. Finally, in keeping with the theme of bioterrorism in the previous two chapters, Thomas Glass and Monica Schoch-Spana offer their insights on how to vaccinate a city against panic. Their analysis concludes with five categories of very practical recommendations for a city of any size or topography.

Throughout these selections, a common theme emerges—one that many of us have known since childhood: Knowledge, in its many forms, is empowering. By examining and reflecting upon past experiences (both our own and those of others, such as the people of Hong Kong), a growing number of experts have dedicated themselves to the construction of a knowledge base to support homeland security. In doing so, they are helping our elected officials, defense and security personnel, and emergency-preparedness forces develop new ways of responding to the terrorist threat with increasing sophistication.

Chapter 27

Preventing a Communications Blackout: The Need for Telecom Redundancy

Randolph J. May

Communications networks are the central nervous system of modern American society. If we lose our ability to communicate over these networks in any significant way, it is not an exaggeration to say that, in effect, our country breaks down. From banking to farming, from manufacturing to retailing, almost every aspect of private commercial activity depends on smoothly functioning, interdependent communications. This is true as well, of course, for the functioning of government at all levels.

If America's communications networks suddenly failed in any significant way, or worse yet, failed in the middle of a national emergency such as a terrorist attack, the harm to the nation in social and economic terms would be immense. Government personnel would be unable to communicate internally within their agencies or with other government departments and agencies. Emergency response teams—fire, medical, and police— would be unable to do their work. Even if the physical damage accompanying such a communications blackout was not substantial, the loss of the ability to communicate could be catastrophic.

What happened on September 11, 2001 should have taught us a very important lesson: Our telecommunications system is most likely to fail precisely when we need it most—and we must do what we reasonably can do to protect ourselves from the loss of the ability to communicate. This is especially so with regard to government agencies. In today's environment, they must be able to carry on their vital functions, which range from emergency response and disaster relief to protecting food safety to ensuring the continuation of government functions integral to our commercial life, such as keeping the Securities Exchange Commission, Department of Commerce, and the like up and running.

The Administration's white paper, *The National Strategy for the Physical Protection of Critical Infrastructures and Key Assets,* released in February 2003, states what should be obvious: "Critical infrastructures rely upon a secure and robust telecommunications infrastructure. Redundancy within infrastructure is critical to ensure that single points of failure in one infrastructure will not adversely impact others."[1]

In a May 2002 Report entitled "National Strategy for Critical Infrastructure and Cyberspace Security," the major associations representing the nation's communications service providers concluded:

One issue that needs further but *quick* examination is the need to create greater *redundancy* in our telecommunications infrastructure, particularly *diversity* of egress and ingress in buildings with major telecommunications facilities. Having backup telecommunications systems that are located in the same part of a building and that go in and out of the building through the same pipes may create a false sense of security.[2]

For whatever reasons, apparently now, eighteen months after that report and more than three years after September 11, 2001, it appears more still needs to be done in the way of achieving redundancy through diverse routing to protect our communications infrastructure. For example, a December 2003 report from the Markle Foundation entitled *Creating a Trusted Network for Homeland Security* concludes that the government "does not appear to have taken the necessary steps to build the communications and sharing network required to deal with the [terrorist] threat."[3] The Markle report suggests the formation of what it calls a Systemwide Homeland Analysis and Resource Exchange (SHARE) Network, with the first attribute being "no single points of failure."[4] By this, the authors mean the existence of "multiple and redundant communications pathways."[5]

To be sure, since September 11, progress has been made in upgrading and securing our communications infrastructure. But more needs to be done, and it is especially important that the federal government itself takes steps to ensure that it has built into the communications networks upon which it relies sufficient redundancy to maintain the availability and continuity of communications in times of crisis.

The Lessons of September 11 and the Great Northeast Blackout of 2003

The events of both September 11, 2001 and August 14, 2003 provide important lessons about the need for telecommunications networks that will remain operable at all times.

The September 11 Experience

The government and the private sector—and especially our citizens at large—responded effectively and heroically to the September 11, 2001 terrorist attack. Nevertheless, events like the September 11 attacks call into question whether, in similar circumstances, the government's ability to continue to function effectively may be impaired by the lack of ability to communicate satisfactorily due to communications transmission facilities becoming inoperable.[6] Indeed, the Administration's *National Strategy* paper states: "Lessons learned from the September 11 attacks indicate that the most pressing problems to be addressed regarding emergency services include . . . telecommunications problems, such as the lack of redundant systems."[7] The *National Strategy* paper goes on to say that, "DHS will work with state and local officials to develop redundant emergency response networks to improve communications availability and reliability especially during a major disruption."[8]

Recall the events of that Tuesday morning, and it is easy to understand the importance that should be placed on the availability of redundant communications networks. News alerts began flashing across Web pages, television, radio, and wire services that America was under attack. As the first reports were disseminated over the public media, telephones began to ring—not just in New York and Washington, DC where the attacks occurred—but across the entire nation.

People immediately began calling friends and loved ones. In a nation of more than 292 million people, everyone was making—or trying to make—telephone calls.[9] Indeed, within minutes of the first television reports of the attacks, tens of millions of telephone calls began flooding the nation's local and long-distance networks. Available capacity was overwhelmed, and many calls simply did not go through.[10] Often, there was no way to distinguish urgent and necessary calls from those that were not. On some occasions, police, medical, and other emergency crews just had to "wait their turn" to get through.[11]

In New York, all the telephone traffic poured into a system that was suddenly hit by physical damage to essential phone lines and switching equipment. When the World Trade Center towers collapsed, fiber optic cables beneath the buildings were crushed.[12] A Verizon central switching office for local telephone traffic was adjacent to the towers and sustained massive damage from the towers' falling debris. Flooding knocked out its backup power generators. At that time, the Verizon hub on West Street was attempting to serve 4.5 million data circuits and 300,000 phone lines.[13]

Cell phones, which many people consider a form of "backup" system, proved at key points unreliable as an alternate means of communications. Not only was there damage to the cell phone antennas on the World Trade Center towers, but the abnormally heavy amount of traffic made it extremely difficult to get calls through.[14]

Fortunately, in the immediate aftermath of the attacks, telephone service providers were largely able to keep 911 calls going through. Verizon provided additional circuits to city agencies—including police and fire departments—and undertook extraordinary efforts to keep communications traffic flowing to the extent possible. Other service providers, including non-wireline companies, rushed to provide specialized wireless communications equipment to emergency response teams.[15] Still other companies trucked in cellular towers.[16] By this combination of admirable efforts, the 911 system more or less functioned throughout the crisis.

In the days immediately following September 11, a new problem became apparent—the failure of communications due to the lack of truly redundant systems. What happened to New York's financial services industry offers the most telling example because of its location near Ground Zero in Lower Manhattan. The modern financial services industry is almost totally dependent on secure electronic voice and data communications. Many banks and brokerage houses had hundreds—if not thousands—of voice, facsimile, and data lines installed in individual offices. Most of these companies assumed they were prepared for a disruption to their telecommunications networks, in part because in the months leading up to the "Year 2000" computer/telecom scare, they had installed backup systems. These supposedly "redundant" systems were installed out of concern that serious computer code errors would surface at the click-over to Y2K, errors which had the potential to cause major system failures.[17]

The fact is that during the September 11 aftermath these much-touted backup systems did not function as effectively as expected for the financial services industry. For example, the Bank of New York had several backup systems in place and dual-access in and out of its Manhattan buildings before September 11. They still lost communications capability due to all their backup systems being connected through a commonly-connected central office.[18] The failure of the backup systems to meet expectations was perhaps best summed up by Thomas F. Costa, chief operating officer of the Government Securities Clearing Corporation. In an October *New York Times* article, Costa noted that "everyone had redundant telecommunications facilities, but a lot of them turned out to be routed through the same phone company offices."[19]

In other words, although most financial services companies had purchased transmission facilities from alternate carriers for the provision of telephone, fax and data services, the lines often entered the building through the same central conduit. And even in the event those lines entered the building through a separate point, many of the lines converged in the same right-of-way under the street or ran to a single exterior communications hub. When that single hub, or the right-of-way or conduit, was knocked out, all the backup lines went down with it.[20]

The September 11 experience provides valuable lessons concerning the way that telecommunications facilities should be set up and routed to be redundant in the sense of true diversity, rather than only redundant in some incomplete sense. The World Trade Center attacks demonstrated that the final constricted local links through major telecom hubs are an easy target, and far too vulnerable. A well-placed hit can trigger a systemwide failure. Indeed, one month after the attacks, thousands of businesses and residents of Manhattan still had not had their basic telephone service restored.

Lack of true redundancy attributable to the routing of facilities through a shared central communications hub was not unique to New York, of course. As reported in the *Wall Street Journal* post-9/11: "All across the country, towns and smaller cities rely on only one hub, meaning that they could lose touch completely if that hub were wiped out. In many larger cities, phone traffic is funneled in very concentrated routes in and out of town."[21]

The Great Northeast Blackout

On August 14, 2003, in connection with the Great Northeast Blackout, the United States again experienced a number of communications network problems. Shortly after 4 P.M., at the peak of power usage on that hot summer day, an 800-megawatt surge of electricity ripped across the northeastern power grid, creating the worst blackout in the country's history. Within nine seconds, approximately 50 million Americans lost electrical power. All of New York City went dark, along with parts of eight states and sections of Canada. While this massive power failure did not result in the human carnage of September 11, it once again underscored the need for survivable telecommunications networks.

During the extended blackout, critical backup systems worked for the most part. But there were many telling failures. For example, New York's 911 emergency-call system was disrupted three different times for 7, 11, and 14 minutes respectively.[22] In Detroit, a communications breakdown forced 911 operators to handwrite emergency notes out to police officers on the street, as well as to fire and emergency medical services. When the lights went out in August, police across Metro Detroit discovered many cell phones didn't work, and officers had too few reliable radios.[23] In Canada, some police officers had to go to pay telephones to communicate with dispatchers when cell phones and onboard computers crashed.[24]

In affected areas, usage of landline facilities immediately soared. These lines continued working in most places because telephone companies had backup power systems in place and landline telephones most often run off electric current in the actual phone line. They do not depend on an outside source of electricity to function. Although backup generators kept cell sites operational initially, heavy volume overwhelmed capacity. And the unusually large number of calls drained cell site backup batteries. As a result, thousands of cell phone towers and transmitters lost power within hours, causing widespread outages.

This August blackout, although it caused huge financial losses, fortunately did not lead to a wider catastrophe. But the widespread disruption of community and other services we take for granted shows just how critical telecommunications is to our daily social and economic life and, of course, to our safety and security.

The Need for Truly Redundant Communications Networks

The events surrounding the September 11 attacks and the August 14 electricity blackout demonstrate the need for telecommunications networks that will remain operable at all times and with sufficient capacity available to handle peak call volumes. Certainly, putting in place policies and programs that promote the availability and maintenance of diverse, truly redundant communications networks throughout the nation should be a high priority of government. And, as important as it is to maintain the viability of effective communications for the private sector, it is especially important that the government adopt and implement policies that ensure its own buildings and installations remain up and running. To do this, offices that house government officials must be served by diverse, truly redundant communications networks, so that, to the maximum extent feasible, the myriad government functions can continue without disruption.

The nation cannot afford a breakdown in communications within critical government sectors. "Emergency-essential" government bodies—such as the Center for Disease Control (CDC), the Federal Emergency Management Agency (FEMA), and other units within the Department of Homeland Security such as the Coast Guard, Secret Service, and Transportation Security Administration—can never afford to lose touch. They must always be able to communicate seamlessly among themselves and with the White House and Congress, as well as with police, fire, and medical services around the country.

The American people understand this. A September 2003 survey found that 86 percent of Americans believe the federal government should have the ability to use two physically distinct methods for telephone and computer communications. Strikingly, four in five Americans believe such a system needs to be installed soon—within a year or two.[25] These results are consistent across demographic and ideological groups. Whether the next crisis is a blackout or a terror attack, or something else, Americans do not want the public servants searching for, and standing in line to use, a (hopefully) working pay telephone or running to find the nearest (hopefully) working Kinko's fax and data services.

The experience of the few companies that maintained connectivity during the September 11 crisis provide a valuable example of the importance of diverse routing and redundant facilities to the safeguarding of communications capability. Companies such as British American Business, NCIC Computer Consulting, and YWCA Retirements Fund were all located within several blocks of Ground Zero. Yet, unlike their neighbors, their phone lines remained fully operational. They also maintained Internet access.

What these companies shared in common was a fixed-wireless backup system, which relied on small transceivers on the roof of their buildings that route traffic back to independent switching centers located in buildings wholly separate from the switching center of the incumbent wireline provider. Thus, unlike most backup networks, these fixed wireless communications systems were separate from the regular landlines, and the traffic was routed through separate facilities. So, these wireless networks were not disrupted on September 11 by high call volumes or the physical damage to switching hubs and major fiber optic cables.

Yet, in terms of true redundancy of telecommunications networks, many federal agencies apparently still are not significantly better prepared today than the financial services industry was at the time of the September 11 attacks. Many federal agency buildings and installation locations apparently do not currently have true telecommunications network redundancy installed in their buildings. Served by a single connection running through a single outside communications central office or switching hub, many are too vulnerable. If that single in-out link were to go down, all communications in or out of that location would be disrupted.

More Needs to Be Done Now to Increase Security

The *National Strategy* white paper released in February 2003 stated that telecommunications assets showed remarkable resiliency in the face of the September 11 attacks and aftermath and that progress had been made since then to further enhance the security and reliability of the telecommunications infrastructure. It nevertheless recognized that the nation still faces significant challenges in protecting its critical information infrastructure.

More specifically, the white paper recognized that redundancy, which is so crucial to maintaining the effective operability of communications, is compromised to the extent that communications users rely on service providers who have concentrated their facilities in the same location like "telecom hotels, collocation sites, or peering points."[26] The paper faulted the Telecommunications Act of 1996 for encouraging the sharing of communications networks rather than the construction of new facilities by virtue of "requir[ing] incumbent carriers to allow their competitors to have open access to their networks."[27] Indeed, as of February 2003, the white paper reports that, while networks are increasingly interconnected, "the industry's physical assets are increasingly concentrated in *shared* facilities."[28] Obviously, by definition, *shared* facilities are not *redundant* facilities.

Existing regulations concerning emergency planning for federal agencies, drafted prior to September 11, 2001, fail to address the issue of encouraging redundancy. In 1999 FEMA issued a federal preparedness circular (FPC) mandating continuity of operations "to ensure continuity of essential Federal functions under all circumstances."[29] Unfortunately, this FPC does not explicitly address redundant telecommunications networks in federal buildings. Rather, it focuses on the importance of having fully functioning secondary buildings for federal agencies to move into at the time of an emergency.[30] The Government Information Security Act requires federal agencies to annually report on what each is doing to protect federal information security.[31] However, this act does not address the need or benefit of redundant telecommunications networks to carry that information securely in the event of an emergency such as those previously addressed.

The federal government currently has two nationwide systems to deal with emergencies, crises, or war: the GETS system for landline communications and the WPS system for wireless communications. GETS stands for the Government Emergency Telecommunications Service, and it supports national security and emergency preparedness requirements for the use of public, defense, or federal telephone networks by government departments, agencies, and other authorized users.[32] GETS, which was designed to supply all available telephone resources during any type of emergency, uses three major types of networks:

1. The major long-distance networks provided by IECs (AT&T, MCI, and Sprint);
2. The local networks provided by LECs and wireless carriers; and
3. Government-leased networks, including the Federal Telecommunications System (FTS 2000), the Defense Switched Network (DSN), and the Diplomatic Telecommunications Service (DTS).[33]

For a federal agency or emergency service personnel to access GETS they must have a universal access number using any type of communications equipment: telephone (wireline or wireless), fax, or modem. GETS allows the user to bypass normal traffic congestion and dropped calls through such controls as trunk queuing, trunk subgrouping, trunk reservation, NS/EP identification, and priority signaling.

Wireless Priority Service (WPS) is the wireless industry's mechanism for addressing the emergency services access problem. The National Communications System (NCS) implemented the WPS in areas of the eastern United States in January, 2003 and plans to expand to full nationwide capability through 2003.[34] Since May 2002, limited WPS has been available in the metro regions of Washington, DC, and New York City. As of January 2003, WPS is available in thirteen major metropolitan areas.[35] The NCS states that this ensures that in times of emergency and disaster, "national security and emergency preparedness users will have the ability to gain priority access to the next available cellular channel to place their call."[36] According to NCS:

> To facilitate the completion of critical calls during these high usage events, WPS enables NS/EP personnel with WPS to access the next available wireless channel before subscribers who are not engaged in NS/EP functions. Priority calls *will not* preempt calls in progress and WPS *will not* guarantee the completion of priority calls. Additionally, WPS users *will not* monopolize all available wireless resources.[37]

The GETS and WPS programs are, of course, valuable, indeed critical, components of an overall broader effort to ensure that emergency and safety-related personnel have available the communications capabilities they need in times of crisis. They are not programs inherently designed to ensure the redundancy of facilities, however; rather, they establish and implement orders of priority for designated personnel to gain priority access to facilities that are still operable. Of course, if the telecommunications facilities connecting the government site to the outside public or private networks are inoperable, these priority-setting regimes are ineffective.

Recommended Actions for Increasing the Reliability and Security of Communications Networks Serving Government Officials

Changes in government policy are needed to increase the level of reliability and security of our nation's telecommunications infrastructure, especially relating to communications infrastructure upon which the continuation of vital federal functions are dependent. *First*, a targeted policy should require the federal government to focus in a systematic way on the need for truly redundant communications facilities at buildings and installations where federal agencies are located. In order for communications facilities to be considered truly redundant, they should be required to meet the following requirements:

- The point at which the alternative communications facilities enter and exit the building should be physically separate, by a significant distance, from the facilities of the incumbent provider.
- The alternative facilities should use a separate right-of-way between the building and the routing center.
- The alternative services should utilize a physically separate switching or routing center.[38]

There needs to be some form of mandate, probably implemented through a regulation, bulletin, or guideline, issued by the Department of Homeland Security or GSA, requiring federal agencies to move in this direction. After all, maintaining the ability to communicate is as much a "safety and security feature" as a properly tested sprinkler.

Establishing new requirements for buildings that house federal offices is not unusual, of course. Such installations are already regulated in myriad ways, from energy conservation to recycling to environmental preservation. Here are a few more typical examples:

- Buildings leased by the federal government must meet seismic safety standards.[39]
- Federal agencies must provide safe, healthy working conditions, including proper lighting, guard rails, indoor air quality, fire safety, elevators, etc.[40]
- Buildings must be inspected for asbestos. If asbestos is discovered, it must be dealt with according to government code and building occupants must be notified.[41]
- Water fountains and faucets must meet quality standards such as limits on lead content.[42]
- Federal buildings must have suitable facilities for the blind and otherwise physically disabled.[43]
- Gasses, such as carbon monoxide and nitrogen dioxide, are highly controlled.[44] Operators of enclosed parking garages are required to install exhaust fans.
- Fire, plumbing, mechanical and electrical systems are heavily regulated through building codes.[45]

It would be appropriate, of course, for a new mandate to provide sufficient leeway so that, in its implementation, the costs and benefits of achieving redundancy over time and in what priority may be taken into account. Obviously, there are many locations where it is more urgent to have in place truly redundant facilities (say, the Center for Disease Control) than others (say, the Consumer Product Safety Commission), and the new guideline should be sufficiently flexible to allow for an appropriate balancing of interests.[46]

Second, the Telecommunications Act of 1996 should be implemented in a way that does not tilt so far in the direction of encouraging the sharing of existing communications facilities as opposed to encouraging investment in new facilities. The National Strategy paper observed pointedly that the implementation of the 1996 act had, in fact, had the effect of encouraging sharing rather than investment.[47] In addition, a federal court reviewing the FCC's network sharing rules found them to be unlawful because they required virtually unlimited facilities sharing, despite the fact that "[e]ach unbundling of an element imposes costs of its own, spreading the disincentive to invest in innovation and creating complex issues of managing shared facilities."[48] With excessive mandatory sharing at below-market regulated prices, "the incentive to invest plainly declines."[49] In this respect, the DC Circuit followed the earlier Supreme Court decision holding unlawful the FCC's first set of sharing rules for requiring excessive sharing.[50] There, Justice Breyer explained that when providers know that competitive advantages will be dissipated by the sharing requirement, investment in new facilities is curtailed.[51]

Despite the previous judicial reversals, the FCC's most recent iteration of its network sharing rules continues to tilt too far toward unbridled mandatory facilities sharing.[52] As long as this is the case, the incentive for both new competitors and incumbents to invest in new facilities is diminished, thereby reducing the availability of redundant networks. The discouragement of investment in new facilities adversely impacts the reliability and security of communications networks for all users, including officials housed in federal office buildings.

Conclusion

In addition to other lessons, September 11 and the recent Northeast blackout should have taught us the importance of our federal agencies having in place secure and reliable communications facilities in times of crisis or distress. Indeed, the security of the United States and the safety of its citizens depend upon the development, adoption, and implementation of policies that spur federal agencies to have available truly redundant communications facilities. While such policies properly may take into account the different missions of the various agencies, their functions, and their reliance on communications, it is important that, in accordance with the recommendations contained in this paper, the nation move with steadfastness in the direction of increasing true redundancy of communications networks.

Acknowledgments

The views expressed are exclusively the author's and do not necessarily reflect those of the Progress and Freedom Foundation, its officers, or Board of Directors. The author would like to thank Sam Ryan, President, Keybridge Communications, LLC, for providing helpful research assistance on this paper.

Notes

1. Department of Homeland Security, *The National Strategy for the Physical Protection of Critical Infrastructures and Key Assets* (Washington, DC: Department of Homeland Security, 2003), p. 49.
2. Information and Communications Sector Coordinators, *"The National Strategy for Critical Infrastructure and Cyberspace Security"* (Paper, Department of Homeland Security, May 2002).
3. Markle Foundation, *Creating a Trusted Network for Homeland Security* (New York: The Markle Foundation, 2003).
4. Ibid, p. 17. The authors may have been striving for a name for the system that resulted in a catchy acronym when they came up with the "Systemwide Homeland Analysis and Resource Exchange (SHARE) Network." But obviously the emphasis on multiple pathways with no single points of failure means the system does not rely on shared facilities in the sense that compromises security and reliability through lack of redundancy.
5. Ibid.
6. Chairman Harvey L. Pitt, Remarks at the Securities Industry Association Annual Meeting, November 9, 2001, www.sec.gov/new/speech/spch521.htm.
7. Department of Homeland Security, *The National Strategy for the Physical Protection of Critical Infrastructures and Key Assets*, p. 43.
8. Ibid., p. 44.
9. "Verizon Reports Cellular, Landline Cells Double During Peak of Today's Tragedy," press release, September 11, 2003, reports that on September 11, calls to Verizon's cellular and landline networks doubled from their peak normal volumes. Calls reached twice the normal daily volumes of 115 million calls in New York City and 35 million calls in the nation's capital.
10. Lisa Guernsey, "An Unimaginable Emergency Put Communications to the Test," *New York Times,* September 20, 2001, www.nytimes.com/2001/09/20/technology/circuits/20INFR.html.
11. Shawn Young and Dennis K. Berman, "Trade Center Attack Shows Vulnerability of Telecom Network"; "Damage to Verizon Facility Snarled City's Phones"; "A Legacy Monopoly?"; "Lasers Across Hudson River," *Wall Street Journal*, October 19, 2001.
12. See Guernsey, "An Unimaginable Emergency."
13. See Ibid.
14. See Ibid.
15. Dennis K. Berman, "Disaster Gives New Life to Wireless Telecom Firms; By Sending Data Through Air, Struggling Start-Ups Link Cut-Off Manhattan Clients," *Wall Street Journal,* October 3, 2001.
16. Guernsey, "An Unimaginable Emergency."
17. Michael Vatis, *Cyber Attacks During The War on Terrorism: A Predictive Analysis* (Institute for Security Technology Studies at Dartmouth College, 2001).

18. Sandeep Junnarkar, "Lessons: Keeping Networks Alive in New York," *Cnet.com,* August 28, 2002, news.com.com/2009-1001-954796.html. The article quotes Donald Monks, senior VP at the Bank of New York, "We had all the redundancies, only to find out that several central offices in the current configuration nationwide were connected to each other: As a result of these dual connections, it's not buying you any redundancy from the position of failure of the senior central office."

19. Saul Hansell and Riva D. Atlas, "Disruptions Put Bank of New York to the Test," *New York Times*, October 6, 2001, www.nytimes.com/2001/10/06/business/06BONY. html.

20. Key government buildings, for example, a federal courthouse, still relied solely on backup services fortuitously available from a facilities-based telecommunications provider that offered services over a network physically separated from the disabled network of the incumbent provider.

21. See Young and Berman, "Trade Center Attack."

22. Lukas Alpert, "911 Dispatchers in Detroit, New York Lost Some Communication During Blackout," Associated Press, August 17, 2003.

23. Ronald J. Hansen, "Homeland Security Gaps Plaque Metro Area," *Detroit News,* October 31, 2003. However, progress in the Detroit police department's communications came over the next eighteen months with an installation of a radio system operated by the Michigan State police that allows communications between all Michigan police departments.

24. See Alpert, "911 Dispatchers."

25. Gary Andres and Michael McKenna, *The American Survey,* September 2003.

26. Department of Homeland Security, *National Strategy,* p. 48.

27. Ibid. I would say it was as much the implementation of the 1996 Act by the FCC as the statute itself that is to blame for encouraging reliance on sharing of common facilities rather than construction of new, separate networks. For a strong judicial rebuke by a federal appeal court of the FCC's overly expansive network sharing mandates, see *United States Telecom Ass'n v. FCC,* 359 F. 3d 554 (DC Cir. 2004).

28. Department of Homeland Security, *National Strategy,* p. 48.

29. Federal Emergency Management Agency, *Federal Preparedness,* Circular 65, no. 6 (Washington, DC: GPO, 1999).

30. Ibid.

31. Government Information Security Reform, 44 U.S.C. §§3531-3535, 2000.

32. See the Government Emergency Telecommunications Services (GETS), www.ncs. gov/nc-pp/html/new-gets.htm. Hereafter cited as GETS.

33. Ibid.

34. National Communications System, "NCS Begins Deployment of Nationwide Wireless Priority Service," press release, January 21, 2003.

35. Limited WPS available in Atlanta; Birmingham, AL; Boston; Jacksonville, FL; Louisville, KY; Memphis, TN; Miami; Mobile, AL; Nashville, TN; New Orleans; Norfolk, VA; Philadelphia and Richmond, VA.

36. Ibid.

37. National Communications System, "Wireless Priority Service (WPS)," wps.ncs. gov/carriers_body.html.

38. In July 2004, the New York Public Service Commission issued an order directing telecommunications carriers offering services in New York State to take a number of steps to strengthen their telecommunications networks, including identifying and reporting to the commission which of their central office buildings were equipped with "dual entrance cable facilities," as well as demonstrating that critical circuits were reasonably distributed between the two entrances where dual-cable entrances exist. Moreover, all facilities-based carriers serving Manhattan will be asked to provide data per central office building showing the costs for adding a dual-cable entrance to those buildings in Manhattan housing central office switching equipment and currently lacking a dual-entrance facility. See New York Public Service Commission, "NYPSC Takes Steps to Strengthen Telecommunications Network Reliability," news release,July 28, 2004. The NYPSC's focus on dual-entrance and physically separate facilities is consistent with the type of network redundancy urged here for government installations.

39. Executive Order 12,699, 55 Fed. Reg. 835, January 5, 1990.

40. 29 C.F.R. § 1910.39, 2003.

41. 29 C.F.R. § 1910.1001, 2003.

42. 29 C.F.R. § 1910.1025, 2003.

43. 42 U.S.C. §§ 4151 et seq., 2003.

44. 42 U.S.C. §§ 7521 et seq., 2003.

45. GETS.

46. While the focus of this chapter is on ensuring the security and reliability of communications, it should be noted that with diverse systems federal agencies also may save money. When a second telecommunications provider is introduced that provider can compete with the original provider on price, quality, and other terms of service. With two telecommunications network providers, an agency could route voice and data traffic to whichever system is more economical at a given time.

47. Department of Homeland Security, *National Strategy,* p. 48.

48. *United States Telecom Association v. FCC*, 290 F3d 415, 427, DC Cir. 2002.

49. Ibid. at 424.

50. *AT&T Corporation v. Iowa Utilities Board*, 119 S. Ct. 721, 1999.

51. Ibid. at 753.

52. Randolph J. May, "The Triennial Review Scorecard: A Disappointing Grade," *Progress on Point,* release 10.14, September 2003, www.pff.org/publications/communications/pop10.14triennialscorecard.pdf. Not surprisingly, the FCC's still overly expansive network sharing mandates, *United States Telecom Ass'n v. FCC,* were again held unlawful by the same DC Circuit appeals court in March 2004. See 359 F. 3d 554, DC Cir. 2004. Until the FCC meaningfully reduces the current mandates for facilities-sharing, investment in new networks will not be as robust as it would otherwise be.

Chapter 28

Risk Communication, the West Nile Virus Epidemic, and Bioterrorism: Responding to the Communication Challenges Posed by the Intentional or Unintentional Release of a Pathogen in an Urban Setting

Vincent T. Covello, Richard G. Peters, Joseph G. Wojtecki,
and Richard C. Hyde

The West Nile virus epidemic is a useful case study for examining the communication challenges posed by the appearance of a new infectious disease in an urban setting.[1] Effective communication is critical to the successful resolution of any type of health, safety, or environmental controversy.[2] High-concern situations involving risk create substantial barriers to effective communication[3] and evoke strong emotions, such as fear, anxiety, distrust, anger, outrage, helplessness, and frustration.[4] When the communication environment becomes emotionally charged, the rules for effective communication change. Familiar and traditional approaches often fall short or can make the situation worse.[5]

A body of communication theory, known as risk communication, offers insights into how crises and high-concern situations alter the usual rules of communication.[6] Risk communication science also provides a set of principles for meeting the challenges posed by the New York City West Nile Virus epidemic.[7]

The Risk Communication Perspective

The National Academy of Sciences defines risk communication as "an interactive process of exchange of information and opinion among individuals, groups, and institutions. It involves multiple messages about the nature of risk and other messages—not strictly about risk—that express concerns, opinions, or reactions to risk messages or to legal and institutional arrangements for risk management."[8] The scientific literature on risk communication addresses the problems raised in the exchange of information about the nature, magnitude, significance, control, and management of risks.[9] It also addresses the strengths and weaknesses of the various channels through which risk information is communicated: press releases, public meetings, hotlines, Web sites, small group discussions, information exchanges, public exhibits and availability sessions, public service announcements, and other print and electronic materials.[10]

Early risk communication research centered on debates about the health or environmental risks associated with waste disposal, toxic chemicals and heavy metals, air and water pollution, nuclear power, electric and magnetic fields, oil spills, food additives, radon in homes, and biotechnology.[11] Little attention was paid to risks caused by exposure to pathogens or to health belief models developed for addressing personal risk-taking behavior (e.g., smoking, alcohol consumption, and drug addiction).

Evaluation studies have consistently demonstrated the effectiveness of risk communication practices in helping stakeholders achieve major communication objectives: providing the knowledge needed for informed decision making about risks; building or rebuilding trust among stakeholders; and engaging stakeholders in dialogue aimed at resolving disputes and reaching consensus.[12] The evaluation literature has also demonstrated the major barriers to successful risk communication,[13] including conflict and lack of coordination among stakeholders and inadequate risk communication planning, preparation, resources, skill, and practice.

Government officials, industry representatives, and scientists often complain that nonexperts and lay people irrationally respond to risk information and do not accurately perceive and evaluate risk information.[14] Representatives of citizen groups, worker groups, and individual citizens, in turn, often question the legitimacy of the risk assessment or risk management process. They have argued that government officials, industry representatives, and scientists are often uninterested in citizens' concerns or unwilling to take actions to solve seemingly straightforward problems. These conflicts are often exacerbated by complex, confusing, inconsistent, or incomplete risk messages;[15] lack of trust in information sources;[16] selective and biased reporting by the media; and psychological factors (heuristics) that affect how risk information is processed.[17]

Effective risk communication is a professional discipline whose application requires knowledge, planning, preparation, skill, and practice.[18] It is a two-way, interactive process that respects different values and treats the public as a full partner.[19] As part of this process, nonexperts acquire information about the risk in question and about the assessment and management of the risk. Experts and risk management authorities acquire, in turn, information about the interests and concerns of stakeholders.[20]

Despite this interactive perspective, evaluation studies indicate that personnel from many agencies and organizations involved in risk controversies lack the knowledge, sensitivity, and skills needed for effective risk communication.[21] They adhere to the "decide, announce, defend" (DAD) model and proceed with limited understanding of the various stakeholders' values and concerns. They often fail to recognize and adapt to the fact that many people and groups use health, safety, and environmental risks as proxies or surrogates for other more general social, economic, political, or cultural concerns and agendas.

They initiate risk communication efforts with inadequate resources, unclear objectives, and little or no information or evaluation on:

- Who is perceived to be most trustworthy
- Who is best suited to communicate risk messages
- What messages are most effective
- What messages are most respectful of different values and worldviews
- What messages raise moral or ethical issues
- What messages are most respectful of process
- Where, when, and how the risk information should be communicated

Risk Communication Theoretical Models

Risk communication is based on four theoretical models that describe how risk information is processed, how risk perceptions are formed, and how risk decisions are made.[22] Together, these models provide a foundation for thinking about and coordinating effective communication in high-concern situations.

The Risk Perception Model

Many factors affect how risks are perceived, and these factors can alter risk perceptions in varying degrees of magnitude.[23] To date, at least 15 risk perception factors have been identified that have direct relevance to risk communication (see Table 28-1).[24] These factors play a large role in determining levels of concern, worry, anger, anxiety, fear, hostility, and outrage, which, in turn, can significantly change attitudes and behavior.[25] For example, levels of concern tend to be most intense when the risk is perceived to be involuntary, inequitable, not beneficial, not under one's personal control, associated with untrustworthy individuals or organizations, and associated with dreaded adverse, irreversible outcomes.

Because of the intense feelings that such perceptions can generate, the risk communication literature often refers to these characteristics as "outrage" factors.[26] Research indicates that an individual's perception of risk is based on a combination of hazard (e.g., mortality and morbidity statistics) and outrage.[27] When present, outrage factors take on strong moral and emotional overtones, predisposing an individual to react emotionally, which can, in turn, significantly amplify levels of perceived risk.

Risk perception research suggests that specific activities should ideally be undertaken as part of a risk communication effort.[28] First, it is important to collect and evaluate empirical information obtained through surveys, focus groups, or interviews about stakeholder judgments of each of the risk perception factors (in particular trust, benefits, control, fairness, and dread). Sustained interaction and exchange of information with stakeholders about identified areas of concern is also necessary. To organize effective risk communication strategies, shared understanding of interested or affected parties regarding stakeholder perceptions and the expected levels of concern, worry, fear, hostility, stress, and outrage is necessary.

TABLE 28-1.   Risk Perception Factors

- **Voluntariness.** Risks perceived to be involuntary or imposed are less readily accepted and perceived to be greater than risks perceived to be voluntary.
- **Controllability.** Risks perceived to be under the control of others are less readily accepted and perceived to be greater than risks perceived to be under the control of the individual.
- **Familiarity.** Risks perceived to be unfamiliar are less readily accepted and perceived to be greater than risks perceived to be familiar.
- **Equity.** Risks perceived as unevenly and inequitably distributed are less readily accepted than risks perceived as equitably shared.
- **Benefits.** Risks perceived to have unclear or questionable benefits are less readily accepted and perceived to be greater than risks perceived to have clear benefits.
- **Understanding.** Risks perceived to be poorly understood are less readily accepted and perceived to be greater than risks from activities perceived to be well understood or self-explanatory.
- **Uncertainty.** Risks perceived as relatively unknown or that have highly uncertain dimensions are less readily accepted than risks that are relatively known to science.
- **Dread.** Risks that evoke fear, terror, or anxiety are less readily accepted and perceived to be greater than risks that do not arouse such feelings or emotions.
- **Trust in institutions.** Risks associated with institutions or organizations lacking in trust and credibility are less readily accepted and perceived to be greater than risks associated with trustworthy and credible institutions and organizations.
- **Reversibility.** Risks perceived to have potentially irreversible adverse effects are less readily accepted and perceived to be greater than risks perceived to have reversible adverse effects.
- **Personal stake.** Risks perceived by people to place them personally and directly at risk are less readily accepted and perceived to be greater than risks that pose no direct or personal threat.
- **Ethical/moral nature.** Risks perceived to be ethically objectionable or morally wrong are less readily accepted and perceived to be greater than risks perceived not be ethically objectionable or morally wrong.
- **Human vs. natural origin.** Risks perceived to be generated by human action are less readily accepted and perceived to be greater than risks perceived to be caused by nature or "Acts of God."
- **Victim identity.** Risks that produce identifiable victims are less readily accepted and perceived to be greater than risks that produce statistical victims.
- **Catastrophic Potential.** Risks that produce fatalities, injuries, and illness grouped spatially and temporally are less readily accepted and perceived to be greater than risks that have random, scattered effects.

The Mental Noise Model

This model focuses on how people process information under stress and how changes in how information is processed affect their communication. When people are in a state of high concern because they perceive a significant threat, their ability to process information effectively and efficiently is severely impaired.[29] When people feel that what they value is being threatened, they experience a wide range of emotions, ranging from anxiety to anger. The emotional arousal and/or mental agitation generated by these strong feelings create mental noise. Exposure to risks associated with negative psychological attributes (e.g., risks perceived to be involuntary, not under one's control, low in benefits, unfair, or dreaded) are also often accompanied by severe mental noise,[30] which, in turn, can interfere with a person's ability to engage in rational discourse.

The Negative Dominance Model

The negative dominance model describes the processing of negative and positive information in high-concern situations. In general, the relationship between negative and positive information is asymmetrical, with negative information receiving significantly greater weight. The negative dominance theory is consistent with a central theorem of modern psychology that people put greater value on losses (negative outcomes) than on gains (positive outcomes).[31] One practical implication of negative dominance theory is that a negative message should ideally be counterbalanced by a larger number of positive or solution-oriented messages.[32]

Another practical implication of negative dominance theory is that communications that contain negatives—e.g., the words *no*, *not*, *never*, *nothing*, *none*, and other words with negative connotations—tend to receive closer attention, are remembered longer, and have greater impact than positive messages.[33] As a result, the use of unnecessary negatives in dialogue with stakeholders in high-concern situations can be highly detrimental, having the unintended effect of drowning out positive or solution-oriented information or undermining trust by stating an absolute that is impossible to defend or maintain. More specifically, risk communications are most effective when they focus on what is being done, rather than on what is not being done.

The Trust Determination Model

A common thread in all risk communication strategies is the need to establish trust.[34] Only when trust has been established can other goals, such as education and consensus-building, be achieved. Trust can only be built over time and is the result of ongoing actions, listening, and communication skill.[35] Because of the importance of trust in resolving risk controversies, a significant part of the risk communication literature focuses on the application of a trust determination model to particular scenarios. To establish or maintain trust, third-party endorsements from trustworthy sources should ideally be undertaken, as well as the use of four trust-determination factors: caring and empathy; dedication and commitment; competence and expertise; and honesty and openness.[36] Evaluation studies indicate that individual or small-group settings, such as information exchanges and public workshops, are the most effective venue for communicating these trust factors.[37]

The principle of trust transference states that a lower-trusted source typically takes on the trust and credibility of the highest-trusted source that takes the same position on the issue.[38] Surveys indicate that certain organizations and individuals, including citizen advisory groups, health professionals, safety professionals, scientists, and educators, are perceived to have high to medium trust on health, safety, and environmental issues.[39] An advantage of being from a trusted group is that it enables a person to communicate effectively, even when communication barriers exist. However, individual trust overrides organizational trust. Trust in individuals from a highly trusted organization may significantly increase or decrease depending on how they present themselves (verbally and nonverbally) and how they interact with others.[40]

Perceptions of trust are decreased by actions or communications that indicate: disagreements among experts; lack of coordination among risk-management organizations; insensitivity by risk-management authorities to the need for effective listening, dialogue, and public participation; an unwillingness to acknowledge risks; an unwillingness to disclose or share information in a timely manner; and irresponsibility or negligence in fulfilling risk-management responsibilities.[41]

New York City's West Nile Virus Response: Risk Communication in Practice

The first outbreak of West Nile virus in New York City occurred in late summer of 1999. By the following summer, the New York City Department of Health had developed a detailed response plan that included public education and outreach.[42] The three objectives for the public education and outreach plan were: (1) to improve the public's awareness of risk for disease; (2) to improve the public's participation in eliminating potential breeding sites; and (3) to provide timely and accurate information related to insecticide spraying. Channels of communication included television and radio public service announcements; press releases, extensive media outreach, and announcements during the scheduled daily mayoral press conferences; brochures and fact sheets, prepared in 10 to 15 languages; posters placed throughout the city; bill inserts mailed with the cooperation of city utilities, including the Consolidated Edison Company of New York and the Water Department; phone lines staffed and answered 24 hours a day, seven days a week, at the height of the outbreak, including the handling of more than 150,000 calls; a Web site that included general information, a question-and-answer section, forms for reporting standing water and dead birds, insecticide fact sheets, and press releases issued during the outbreak; and a limited number of town-hall public meetings.

The primary spokespersons were the New York City Health Commissioner and the mayor. In the outer boroughs, the borough president often assumed the mayor's role. The majority of the press releases addressed spraying and included telephone numbers to call for more information. Print materials, generally written at a high school reading level, contained information about personal protective behavior (e.g., sheltering-in-place and protection against mosquitoes) and included a request that the public assist government agencies by eliminating sources of standing water where mosquitoes might breed.

In general, the New York City risk communication effort related to the West Nile Virus epidemic was far-reaching, resource intensive, competently handled, and effective. At the same time, several areas for improvement can be noted.

New York City officials were clearly aware of risk perception factors and took these factors into account in their decisions. However, apparently little effort was made to collect, analyze, and evaluate empirical information—such as that obtained through surveys and focus groups—about stakeholder judgments of each of the major risk perception factors. Furthermore, the full range of communication channels, such as information exchanges and information workshops for engaging stakeholders in sustained interaction about identified areas of concern, were not exploited. Official spokespersons were apparently not informed about stakeholder perceptions or about various stakeholder groups' expected levels of concern, fear, hostility, or outrage.

In addition, public concern over the city's decision to use pesticides (e.g., malathion in 1999) for vector control, as well as the controversial decision to engage in aerial spraying by highly visible helicopters, underscores what appears to be an initial failure by city officials to ascertain the risk perceptions of an expanded circle of stakeholders, including wildlife experts and environmental groups.

The communication materials produced by city officials were highly informative. However, from a mental noise perspective, they also contained many more messages than could be easily comprehended by the intended audience. In addition, these materials contained inadequate repetition and visualization. For example, explanatory charts and graphs were generally absent, as were video tapes about the effects of the West Nile. Finally, most of the risk communication materials produced by the city were several school grade-levels higher than recommended.

Analysis of West Nile virus case study material indicates an apparent lack of attention to the unequal weights given to negative and positive information in high-concern situations. For example, many of the communications focused more on what was not being done by city authorities, or on what would not be done, than on what was being done and what would be done. In addition, negative messages (e.g., the decision to spray pesticides from helicopters and the decision to cancel a concert at Central Park) were not simultaneously counterbalanced by a larger number of positive or solution-oriented messages. The case study materials also provide little evidence that the positive or solution-oriented messages that were offered were the product of sustained interaction and dialogue with a wide range of stakeholders.

In general, city officials effectively communicated the four trust determination factors. Importantly, New York City officials and their families remained in the city during the outbreak. Given the controversial nature of pesticide spraying, early coordination and work with recognized wildlife and environmental groups and experts could have established credible third parties. It is not clear whether third-party endorsements (e.g., from faculty at major New York universities or medical schools) were solicited as part of the communication effort.

Additional factors compounded trust problems. The telephone hotlines, while answered 24 hours a day, were, in some cases, staffed by personnel in remote locations who were inadequately trained in risk communication. Communication directed to sensitive populations—such as asthmatics—about spraying locations and schedules was neglected. Additionally, town-hall meetings were overutilized, while more effective small-group activities, such as information exchanges and public workshops, were underutilized. Disagreements and lack of coordination among risk-management organizations, such as the lack of attention given by public health authorities at the city, state, and federal level to early warning messages by wildlife experts at the Bronx Zoo, facilitated mistrust.

A Bioterrorist Event—A Prospective Example of Risk Communication Practice

Many urban areas are preparing for an unprecedented crisis–a bioterrorist event.[43] A bioterrorist event in an urban area of North America presents an extraordinary requirement for risk communication planning, preparation, and practice.

Several factors could compound a bioterrorism event: the element of surprise, the use of an unseen lethal biological agent, the presence of an unknown perpetrator, the likelihood of widespread simultaneous attacks, and the probable delayed detection and reaction by public health agencies. Given the expected level of high concern, and the possibility of fear leading to panic, the application of sound risk communication principles will be imperative.

A bioterrorist event would likely trigger the full set of the risk perception factors. These factors amplify the perceived magnitude of risk levels unprecedented in the history of crisis communication. The perception factors that would most likely be amplified include involuntariness, uncontrollability, unfamiliarity, unfairness, lack of understanding, uncertainty, dread, ethical/moral violations, and distrust in institutions. All would combine to intensify the perceived risk.

A number of actions could be taken to modify the public's risk perceptions in response to a possible bioterrorist event. The trust the public has in the emergency responders is critical to the effectiveness of any postevent response. Such trust should be established well in advance of the event. Case studies, such as the Chemical Industry's Responsible Care program, indicate that proactive community outreach is one of the most effective means for achieving this goal.[44]

A domestic bioterrorist event is so horrible to contemplate that many people would likely adopt a mindset of denial, which could exacerbate the emotional and behavioral consequences of an actual bioterrorist event. By introducing the potential for a bioterrorist attack in a measured, progressive, and interactive manner—such as through school programs and student take-home assignments—familiarity can be established in advance of an event. Although the attackers will control the specific circumstances by which a bioterrorism attack creates terror, a legitimate sense of control can be given to those under threat, especially in advance of an attack, by public education, by public participation in the preparation process, and by providing the public a voice in the decisions that will affect them. A citizen advisory panel, comprised of community members respected by and credible with their peers, can be an effective mechanism for gaining constructive public participation and dialogue about possible high-concern situations.[45]

The intensity of emotions evoked by a bioterrorist event would predictably result in extreme levels of mental noise. In an unprepared context, communication could be virtually shut down. To avert this potential, all relevant emergency response organizations must be committed to producing communications—from the preparatory stage to final resolution—that are clear and concise and based on sound risk communication principles. Extensive communication training and practice opportunities, including scenario development, must be provided in advance of the crisis event.

In line with negative dominance theory, bioterrorism risk should include communications free of unnecessary negatives, offer a larger number of positive or solution-oriented messages, and focus on what is being done rather than on what is not being done in response to the potential event. Extensive risk communication training and practice opportunities must be provided in advance of the crisis event.

Unless conveyed by trusted sources, the most competently prepared communication materials will fall short in a high-concern situation. Those responsible for public communication in the event of a bioterrorist attack need to consider the trustworthiness of institutions, as indicated by surveys and focus groups, the trustworthiness of individual spokespersons, and the inclusion of trusted third-party voices in support of key messages.

Conclusion

Emerging illness and bioterrorism present extraordinary communication challenges. However, it is possible to develop an effective risk communication strategy for such events. It would be a serious error to underestimate the importance of developing, by consensus among organizations, the final version of a risk communication strategy and plan. The planning, preparation, and practice must begin now.

Notes

1. U.S. General Accounting Office, *West Nile Virus Outbreak: Lessons for Public Health Preparedness* (Washington, DC: U.S. Government Printing Office, 2000).

2. V. T. Covello, D. B. McCallum, M. T. Pavlova,"Principles and Guidelines for Improving Risk Communication," in *Effective Risk Communication: The Role and Responsibility of Government and Nongovernment Organizations,* ed. V. Covello, D. McCallum, and M. Pavlova (New York, NY: Plenum Press, 1989), pp. 3–16; National Research Council (NCR), *Improving Risk Communication* (Washington, DC: National Academy Press, 1989); P. Slovic, "Perception of Risk," *Science* 236 (1987): 280–85.

3. V. T. Covello, "Risk Perception, Risk Communication, and EMF Exposure: Tools and Techniques for Communicating Risk Information," in *Risk Perception, Risk Communication, and Its Application to EMF Exposure: Proceedings of the World Health Organization/ICNRP International Conference (ICNIRP 5/98)* , ed. R. Matthes, J. Bernhardt, and M. Repacholi (Vienna, Austria: International Commission on Non-Ionizing Radiation Protection, 1998), pp. 179–214; B. Fischhoff, "Risk Perception and Communication Unplugged: Twenty Years of Progress," *Risk Analysis* 15 no. 2 (1995): 137–45.

4. V. T. Covello and P. M. Sandman, "Risk Communication: Evolution and Revolution," in *Solutions to an Environment in Peril*, ed. A. Wolbarst (Baltimore: Johns Hopkins University Press, 2001), pp. 164–78; P. M. Sandman, "Hazard Versus Outrage in the Public Perception of Risk," in *Effective Risk Communication: The Role and Responsibility of Government and Nongovernment Organizations,* ed. V. Covello, D. McCallum, and M. Pavlova (New York: Plenum Press, 1989), pp. 45–49.

5. Covello, et al, 1989; NRC, 1989.

6. NRC, 1989; Covello and Sandman, 2001.

7. Covello, et al, 1989; NRC, 1989; National Research Council, *Understanding Risk: Informing Decisions in a Democratic Society* (Washington, DC: National Academy Press, 1996).

8. Covello, 1998.

9. NRC, 1989; Covello and Sandman, 2001.

10. E. B. Arkin, "Translation of Risk Information for the Public: Message Development," in *Effective Risk Communication: The Role and Responsibility of Government and Nongovernment Organizations,* ed. V. Covello, D. McCallum, and M. Pavlova (New York: Plenum Press, 1989), pp. 127–35.

11. Covello et al., 1989; J. Baron, J. C. Hershey, and H. Kunreuther, "Determinants of Priority for Risk Reduction: The Role of Worry," *Risk Analysis* 20 no. 4 (2000): 413–28; C. Chess,K. L. Salomone, B. J. Hance, and A. Saville."Results of a National

Symposium on Risk Communication: Next Steps for Government Agencies," *Risk Analysis* 15 no. 2 (1995): 115–25; J. Burger, K. K. Pflugh, L. Lurig, L. A.Von Hagen, and S. Von Hagen. "Fishing in Urban New Jersey: Ethnicity Affects Information Sources, Perception, and Compliance," *Risk Analysis* 19 no. 2 (1999): 217–29; S. J. Elliot, D. C. Cole, P. Krueger, N. Voorberg, and S. Wakefield,"The Power of Perception: Health Risk Attributed to Air Pollution in an Urban Industrial Neighborhood," *Risk Analysis* 19 no. 4 (1999): 621–33; D. Grobe, R. Douthitt, and L. Zepeda, "A Model of Consumers' Risk Perceptions Toward Recombinant Bovine Growth Hormone (rbGH): The Impact of Risk Characteristics," *Risk Analysis* 19 no 4. (1999): 661–73; M. K. McBeth and A. S. Oakes, "Citizen Perception of Risks Associated with Moving Radiological Waste," *Risk Analysis* 16 no 3. (1996): 421–27; T. L. McDaniels, R. S. Gregory, D. Fields. "Democratizing Risk Management: Successful Public Involvement in Local Water Management Decisions," *Risk Analysis* 19 no. 3 (1999): 497–509.

12. NRC, 1989; Covello, 1998; G. Morgan, B. Fischhoff, A. Bostrom, L. Lave, and C. J. Atman, "Communicating Risk to the Public," *Environmental Science and Technology* 26 no. 11 (1992): 2048–56.

13. Covello et al., 1989; Fischhoff, 1995; Chess et al., 1995.

14. Covello et al., 1989; S. Jasanoff, "Bridging the Two Cultures of Risk Analysis," *Risk Analysis* 13 no. 2 (1993): 123–29.

15. Covello et al., 1989.

16. O. Renn and D. Levine, "Credibility and Trust in Risk Communication," in *Communicating Risks to the Public*, ed. Kasperson and Stallen (Dordrecht, the Netherlands: Kluwer Academic Publishers, 1991).

17. U.S. Environmental Protection Agency, *Public Knowledge and Perceptions of Chemical Risks in Six Communities: Analysis of a Baseline Survey* (Washington, DC: USGPO, 1990); L. Sjoberg, "Factors in Risk Perception," *Risk Analysis* 20 no. 1 (2000): 1–11; N. D. Weinstein, "Why It Won't Happen to Me: Perceptions of Risk Factors and Susceptibility," *Health Psychology* 3 (1984): 431–57.

18. NRC, 1989.

19. NRC, 1989; NRC, 1996.

20. Nelkin D, "Communicating Technological Risk: The Social Construction of Risk Perception," *Annual Review of Public Health* 10 (1989): 95–113.

21. Fischhoff, 1995; Chess et al, 1995.

22. Covello, 1998; Covello and Sandman, 2001.

23. Slovic, 1987; Covello, 1998; G. O. Rogers, "The Dynamics of Risk Perception: How Does Perceived Risk Respond to Risk Events?" *Risk Analysis* 17 no. 6 (1997): 745–57; A. Wildavsky and K. Dake, "Theories of Risk Perception: Who Fears What and Why," *Daedalus* 112 (1990): 41–60; O. Renn, W. J. Bums, J. X. Kasperson, R. E. Kasperson, and P. Slovic, "The Social Amplification of Risk: Theoretical Foundations and Empirical Applications," *Journal of Social Science Issues* 48 (1992): 137–160.

24. NRC, 1989; Slovic, 1987; Sandman, 1989.

25. Slovic, 1987; Sandman, 1989.

26. Sandman, 1989.

27. Ibid.

28. B. Fischhoff, "Helping the Public Make Health Risk Decisions," in Covello, McCallum, and Pavlova (1989): 111–16; B. B. Johnson, "'The Mental Model' Meets 'The Planning Process': Wrestling with Risk Communication Research and Practice," *Risk Analysis* 13 no. 1 (1993): 5–8; R. Wilson and E. Crouch, "Risk Assessment and Comparisons: An Introduction," *Science* 236 (April 17, 1987): 267–70.

29. NRC, 1989; Baron et al, 2000; Fischhoff, 1989.

30. K. Neuwirth, S. Dunwoody, and R. J. Griffin, "Protection Motivation and Risk Communication," *Risk Analysis* 20 no. 5 (2000): 721–33; A. H. Maslow, *Motivation and Personality* (New York: Harper and Row, 1970); L. Gould and C. Walker (eds.). *Too Hot to Handle* (New Haven, Conn.: Yale University Press, 1982).

31. Maslow, 1970.

32. Covello, 1998.

33. Ibid.

34. Renn and Levine, 1991; P. Slovic, "Trust, Emotion, Sex, Politics, and Science: Surveying the Risk-Assessment Battlefield," *Risk Analysis* 19 no. 4 (1999): 689–701; R. G. Peters, V. T. Covello, and D. B. McCallum, "The Determinants of Trust and Credibility in Environmental Risk Communication: An Empirical Study," *Risk Analysis* 17 no. 1 (1997): 43–54.

35. Peters, Covello, and McCallum, 1997.

36. Slovic, 1999.

37. Covello, 1998; Fischhoff, 1989.

38. Covello, 1998.

39. U.S. EPA, 1990.

40. NRC, 1989; Chess et al., 1995.

41. Covello et al., 1989; Chess et al., 1995.

42. New York City Department of Health, *Comprehensive Arthropod-borne Disease Surveillance and Control Plan 2000* (New York, 2000).

43. National Research Council, *Chemical and Biological Terrorism: Research and Development to Improve Civilian Medical Response* (Washington, DC: National Academy Press, 1999); J. Lederberg, *Biological Weapons: Limiting the Threat* (Cambridge, MA: MIT Press, 1999).

44. S. Santos, V. T. Covello, and D. B. McCallum, "Industry response to SARA Title III: Pollution Prevention, Risk Reduction, and Risk Communication," *Risk Analysis* 16 no. 1 (1996): 57–65.

45. F. M. Lynn, and G. J. Busenberg, "Citizen Advisory Committees and Environmental Policy: What We Know, What's Left to Discover," *Risk Analysis* 15 no. 2 (1995): 147–61.

Chapter 29

How Business Can Defeat Terrorism: Global Financial Firms[1] Battle the SARS Outbreak in Hong Kong

Kelly J. Hicks

Imagine a terrorist group has just deployed a deadly, highly infectious disease in a densely populated financial "capitol city." It starts through means of a vector, an infected human "drone," whose itinerary includes key landmarks such as exchanges and major public buildings. To cause further confusion as to the source, he stays in an international hotel among guests—mostly businessmen—from twenty foreign countries. By the time three days have passed, hundreds of people worldwide are infected with—and dying from—a virus of an unknown type, which has no cure. Take away the terrorist intrigue, and you have the current SARS global pandemic that is now threatening the Asian economy and the global business environment.

Since the outbreak of SARS in 2003, the World Health Organization (WHO) has carefully monitored the possibility of another outbreak in several countries, especially China. Early in 2004, what appeared to be an outbreak of SARS took place in Beijing's National Institute of Virology. While the outbreak did not spread widely, it highlighted several important lessons learned. For one, SARS is a containable disease if authorities act quickly. Also, biosafety, or proper handling of the virus for study, must be ensured. Lastly, a sound strategy for laboratory research and speed of diagnosis of the virus must be put in place. These SARS-related factors apply just as much in the handling of a bio terror attack. If authorities enact proactive measures such as China has learned to do since the 2003 outbreak, they can swiftly diagnose and contain potentially devastating anthrax or other attacks. By setting up internal emergency-response and patient-evacuation procedures, businesses can also be better prepared to combat bioterror attacks. This chapter describes the circumstances and important lessons learned from the 2003 SARS outbreak.

The Challenges

SARS, or Severe Acute Respiratory Syndrome, hit Hong Kong in March 2003, with 350 infected cases and 13 deaths (91 cases in Singapore with 2 deaths and 10 cases with no deaths in Taiwan) by the 30th of the month. Hospitals, which were fighting to understand the disease and its causes, became spreading mechanisms for SARS. The virus hit medical staff particularly hard, impacting their ability to respond effectively. The intensive-care unit capacity in all of Hong Kong at the time was only 3,000 beds, and there were only a limited number of SARS respirators and related equipment. This fact, coupled with the direct threat to health-care workers, brought the dreadful realization to the community's leaders that if the daily infection rate continued at pace, Hong Kong's hospitals would be at full capacity by June.

Also by late March, highly sensational reports about the disease began appearing in the media. The causes of infection by SARS were not clear, the media were conjecturing about the disease being airborne (which it was not), and people began to panic. When a rumor circulated about an infection in a nearby building, part of a trade floor in a famous brokerage firm grabbed their belongings and headed home. What management realized at that moment was that they were facing a possibly catastrophic major business disruption if an infection broke out in that firm, or if just the fear of an outbreak caused people to refuse to come to work.

As this ball begins to roll in the financial markets, the consequences can be dramatic. For example, in a margin call, say a firm has a number of futures positions on its books, which require payment due to an external factor that affects the price. If that firm fails to make its margin payment, the reaction from the rest of the trading community is severe. Thinking that firm is out of cash, they stop trading with that firm; they go against that firm in other ways as well, creating a domino effect. This can break a financial institution quickly. If the stock exchange falls victim to an outbreak or mass panic, the financial impact to the greater community is worse. Once this happens enough times, a regional economy is threatened. This, incidentally, underscores one of the main aims of bioterrorism—to wreck the economy and thus the society of an adversary.

As the number of SARS cases in Hong Kong increased, sometimes dramatically— as in the case of almost the entire housing estate of Amoy Gardens, with several hundred infections in a matter of days—the pressure on management of major corporations and financial institutions became intense. Medical restrictions imposed locally and internationally meant that people could not travel without special medical clearance, or in many cases, without prior quarantine for a period of days. This meant that bankers could no longer see clients in certain locations (compounding this, there were reports that SARS could be easily caught onboard aircraft). This inability to travel effectively posed another potential threat to business, especially in terms of reputation.

Also, information about the treatment of SARS revealed an especially grave threat to the survival of unborn children, the solution to which was involuntary abortion under a certain gestational age. Given this threat to pregnant women, expecting mothers and their spouses were sent home from work. This posed another threat not only to business but also to morale of the work force. To top it all off, Hong Kong's lucrative tourism ceased, schools closed, restaurants and other public places closed, and there was a run on grocery stores. By the beginning of April, Hong Kong was in serious distress.

The Responses

The private sector—particularly financial institutions—and the public sector responded to the crisis in different ways, from which important lessons can be drawn.

The Financial-Sector Level

Major banks and other multinational businesses in Hong Kong took an aggressive approach in dealing with the threats posed by SARS to their people and their business. The most important theme to stress here is that the *fear* of the disease was much greater than the actual possibility of infection. This meant that people were physically afraid of coming out into public, commuting to work on public transportation, and sitting near coworkers in crowded offices. Firms had to creatively determine approaches to instill confidence in the employees so as to avoid workplace panic and possibly a major business disruption.

Very early in the outbreak, many firms formed SARS task forces, composed of members from human resources, security, business divisions, legal, head office, public relations, technology, and business continuity groups. Firms also communicated among one another to ensure best practices and share information. These SARS task forces were linked globally with their sister offices so that senior management could stay abreast of the developing situation.

SARS taskforces began the process of tackling health and psychological issues. They developed approaches such as management tool kits designed to enable managers to completely brief their people on all medical developments, as well on as how to respond to an outbreak in the firm. From the beginning, it was evident that decisive leadership and information from the very top were essential in managing the growing fear of the disease among employees. As noted earlier, this fear actually became more of a threat than the chances of contracting the disease itself.

The fear of the disease presented a threat to continued business, but if managed decisively and openly, a "come to work" environment could be maintained. The human resources/wellness departments of the member firms of the financial sector provided surgical masks to all employees for use in the office on a nonmandatory basis, as well as to wear while commuting to and from work. The building management departments increased the number of daily cleanups in the workplace, adding bleach cleaning to all surfaces per government advisories. The SARS task forces of the various financial firms also published a daily bulletin to all employees, helping them to stay abreast of accurate medical information, infection statistics, where to receive medical advice, etc.

As a lesson learned, there was a balance struck between providing complete vs. excessive information. An example of this was that some of the medical information in circulation was not confirmed. It was therefore necessary to limit communications to just the known facts and therefore be able to avoid having to go back and try to repeatedly adjust the bulletins.

The daily bulletin also provided useful information about checking for symptoms of SARS, key phone numbers to call at the task force, etc. Another confidence-building measure put in place by firms was to authorize a taxi subsidy for employees who routinely take public transportation to and from work. This also decreased the risk of exposure of firm employees to ill persons, thereby reducing the risk to the workforce. Firms also brought in medical experts such as local and International SOS doctors,[2] to provide daily medical advice and prescreening for travelers, and to address all employees in English and Cantonese on a frequent basis. Again, the psychological impact of the disease was worse than the disease itself, creating a level of tension and fear that required extraordinary measures to contain.

As part of risk management and business continuity, businesses prepositioned executives in other regional offices in order to prequarantine them so they could effectively meet with clients or pick up trading from a desk that has visibility on that data. However, even after quarantine and other measures, some clients still refused to meet with people from Hong Kong. Again, the fear of the disease was greater than the disease itself—giving way to illogical reactions.

While the human resources/wellness and executive office personnel worked to manage the people side of the threat, technology worked behind the scenes to bolster and upgrade the firm's capability to support the contingencies put in place in case of an outbreak within the office. Many firms have global technology architectures, allowing businesses to share data globally. With a disease being carried to hotels and public buildings—as it would in a bioterror attack—and the local populace in fear of coming to work, the contingency was to arrange for assistance from other regional offices to provide handoff on trade settlements and other vital functions for financial firms.

One particular need that the fear of SARS created was to potentially work from home or other offsite locations—including other regional offices. If the disease spread widely within the community, strict quarantining and lack of access to public buildings would severely impact the ability to conduct business. Therefore, dial-in capacity was increased to be able to handle about 30 percent of the workforce, concentrating on the key personnel and working downward. Offsite locations proved to be an effective means of prequarantining a segment of the workforce. Mingling of the workforce could be controlled or prevented, enabling certain business functions to continue in event of an outbreak in the main corporate offices.

Many firms have a business continuity off-site facility. Off-sites normally consist of a data center specially built in a location on a redundant power grid and with backup database servers, in case of a failure of the main campus data center. Normally a data center for a financial institution has a scaled-down version of a dealing floor, complete with the traders' personalized desktops and a settlement and funding team colocated in the same facility. Firms that invested in an offsite center had the added safety net of being able to operate or manage risk if an outbreak occurred in their main facility—an important lesson for a variety of other sectors as well.

At the Hong Kong–Government Level

The local government in Hong Kong began a public campaign of personal hygiene awareness, as well as implementing cleaning of streets and public facilities. One of the first actions the Hong Kong Government took was to close all schools in late March. Schools remained closed for more than one month. When schools resumed on April 28, strict daily temperature-taking procedures were implemented to ensure students' safety.

The Hong Kong airport authority implemented a 100 percent temperature-taking program for all departing travelers. Anyone with a temperature above 38 degrees Celsius was refused boarding and further medically screened. The airport also installed infrared screeners for all arriving passengers, to detect elevated body temperatures. These measures were implemented at the border crossing points between Hong Kong and Shenzhen, China. Hospitals set up SARS-only wards, strictly sealing them off from the rest of hospitals. Moreover, only government hospitals were authorized to treat SARS victims—no suspected SARS case could go to a private hospital. In this manner, the disease was localized to the extent possible within the centers best suited to treat it. Medical personnel who retired or were privatized were also invited to return to medical duty in SARS hospitals. This helped reduce the tremendous stress on the already stretched medical staff in the government hospitals.

The health department worked in conjunction with local universities' biological research departments, as well as the World Health Organization (WHO) and the Centers for Disease Control (CDC). Aggressively, these entities cooperated and coordinated their efforts toward isolating the suspected virus that causes SARS. The WHO and CDC assisted Hong Kong, Singapore, and Canada in their efforts against SARS. Unfortunately, China refused to cooperate for nearly a month, covering up their seriously high number of cases, and blocking WHO support to Taiwan for political reasons (China's massive failure to safeguard its people by dealing with SARS head-on will cost dearly in the attraction of business investment from abroad).

Conclusion/Lessons Learned—*Can Bioterrorism Be Defeated?*

Bioterrorism can be defeated. Large-scale acts of bioterrorism, such as SARS-like outbreaks, can be effectively contained if the appropriate measures are put in place quickly. SARS has not gone away; it will be endemic in some areas until there is a vaccine discovered that is effective against it. In the case of some bioterror diseases, vaccines or antibacterials can be brought to bear, along with other public and commercial measures to combat them. Therefore, terrorists will likely try to obtain and use unusual diseases that would be more difficult to contain.

However, SARS has been greatly reduced in Hong Kong and Singapore, where aggressive measures were put in place early on to combat its spread. Because of this, the WHO lifted travel restrictions to these locations relatively quickly. After the WHO dropped Hong Kong, Singapore, and China from the list of affected countries, business began to resume, and air travel volumes rose surprisingly quickly. Another key factor in containing or defeating a bioterror attack, as the SARS epidemic proved, is the ability to successfully conquer the *fear* of the disease within the community. This is important because it is probably the greatest lesson learned and is of future value to authorities and businesses if they have to face a bioterror attack.

There are examples in the SARS pandemic of how bioterrorism can have a more deadly impact. Nations with weak political systems or a weak national health care infrastructure are prime candidates for a devastating hit. The two most vivid examples are China and Taiwan. SARS continues to affect China, where the government delayed admitting the disease for months and did not begin taking measures against it until it had become a serious health threat and an international embarrassment. Many feel that a healthy China translates into robust global business growth. The effect of the SARS mishandling in China on international confidence is serious. Economists predict a slowing of the Chinese economy for 2003 as a result.[3]

Taiwan is still struggling to contain SARS, where the infections and deaths continue. The Taiwanese government actively quarantined suspected cases from the beginning. However, the infection spread by more than 50 cases per day. The reason for the difficulty in containing the disease seems to be that Taiwan lacks the means to prevent cross-infection within its hospitals. If the WHO had had early access to Taiwan's health authorities, they may have been able to help prevent some medical mistakes with the disease. Further compounding the difficult situation in Taiwan, some doctors and other medical staff refused to come to work for fear of infection. Again, the reaction to just the fear of the disease showed how damaging even a small-scale outbreak from a bioterror attack could be.

In closing, the SARS pandemic provided the world with a stark lesson in how a bioterrorist attack could unfold, as well as how nations, cities, and the financial sector could respond—and, hopefully, recover. Equally stark—and unsettling—SARS gave terrorist groups a direct insight as to where weaknesses exist in security, government, policy, medical infrastructure, and financial resilience of many nations and regions. So, in combating bioterrorism, success depends on two key things: nations having a robust medical infrastructure and the political will to be transparent and cooperate internationally.

Notes

1. The two main entities that battled SARS in Hong Kong were the Hong Kong government and the "commercial sector." Within each of these were multiple players, especially within the commercial sector. In order to present the story about SARS consistently, this chapter more narrowly defines the commercial sector as the financial sector (of which there are hundreds of firms that consist of similar structures and dealt with the outbreak along similar paths).

2. International SOS is a group of local doctors who meet certain certifications. One of their functions is to form a pool of recommended doctors and medical professionals for expatriate communities.

3. Goldman Sachs Group, *Japan Strategy Flash,* "SARS Scenarios and Sector Implications," April 28, 2003.

Chapter 30

Bioterrorism and the People: How to Vaccinate a City against Panic

Thomas A. Glass and Monica Schoch-Spana

Bioterrorism policy discussions and response-planning efforts have tended to discount the capacity of the public to participate in the response to an act of bioterrorism, or they have assumed that local populations would impede an effective response. Fears of mass panic and social disorder underlie this bias. Although it is not known how the population will react to an unprecedented act of bioterrorism, experience with natural and technological disasters and disease outbreaks indicates a pattern of generally effective and adaptive collective action. Failure to involve the public as a key partner in the medical and public-health response could hamper effective management of an epidemic and increase the likelihood of social disruption. Ultimately, actions taken by nonprofessional individuals and groups could have the greatest influence on the outcome of a bioterrorism event. Five guidelines for integrating the public into bioterrorism response planning are proposed: (1) treat the public as a capable ally in the response to an epidemic, (2) enlist civic organizations in practical public health activities, (3) anticipate the need for home-based patient care and infection control, (4) invest in public outreach and communication strategies, and (5) ensure that planning reflects the values and priorities of affected populations.

With more sophisticated awareness of the challenges posed by an epidemic caused by an act of biological terrorism (bioterrorism), the definition of a "first responder" to such an event is necessarily evolving. Infectious disease and infection control specialists, emergency department physicians and nurses, public health officials, epidemiologists, laboratorians, and hospital administrators are now seen as the frontline professionals (Henderson, 1999).

The current, professionalized model of the response to bioterrorism, however, has largely cast the civilian population as nonparticipants. Rare are the calls to prepare the public to respond in their own right (Dobbs, 2001; Taylor, 2000). Likely contributing to the neglect of the public's role in a response to bioterrorism is the assumption that the general public tends to be irrational, uncoordinated, and uncooperative in emergencies—not to mention prone to panic. Such a view, we argue, will lead public health professionals and emergency managers to miss the opportunity to harness the capacities of the civilian population to enhance the effectiveness of a large-scale response.

As demonstrated by community reactions to the terrorist attacks in New York and Washington, DC, the power of the public to respond effectively to disasters should not be underestimated. In New York, individual volunteers and organized groups converged on the epicenter of destruction to offer aid and support, despite hazardous conditions and uncertainty about the risks of further attack or structural collapse of the World Trade Center towers (Barry, 2001). Volunteers responded rapidly and in large numbers to help in search-and-rescue efforts while professional operations were yet to be put in place. Since the attacks, affected communities have been organizing through local government; relief groups; and civic organizations, such as churches, neighborhood associations, and labor organizations. A catastrophic epidemic caused by a bioterrorist attack could produce similar crisis conditions, although of a wholly different nature that will require the participation of nonprofessionals in the emergency response. Preparedness programs would benefit now from discussions about how to capitalize on the effectiveness and resourcefulness of nonprofessionals, especially in the identification, surveillance, and containment of an outbreak, and, potentially, in caring for large numbers of casualties. To that end, we offer five guidelines for enhancing the planning for responses to bioterrorism by improving the integration of the lay public (Table 30-1). In the "Conclusion" section, we offer a preliminary assessment of the general public's responses to the currently unfolding anthrax threat, as the responses bear upon the proposed guiding principles.

Recognize that Panic is Rare and Preventable

Discussion of how the general public might respond after a bioterrorist attack typically focuses on the possibility of mass panic, psychological trauma, and social disorder. Creating panic is among the probable goals of those who plan acts of bioterrorism (Wyatt, 2000). Expert guides on the health consequences of a bioterrorist attack predominantly focus on negative psychological reactions and aberrant social behaviors (World Health Organization, 2001; Holloway, et al, 1997; DiGiovanni, 1999). Constructive or salutary responses are rarely highlighted. Scenarios for response exercises routinely feature rioting, looting, and vigilantism (cf. Dark Winter, 2001; O'Toole, 1999).

There is a widespread belief that panic and civil unrest are likely in the aftermath of a bioterrorist attack, although it is not known how the general population will react to an unprecedented biological attack. However, research on population responses to a wide range of natural and technological disasters suggests that there is a tendency toward adaptability and cooperation and that lawless behavior is infrequent (cf. Quarentelli, 2001; Dynes & Tierney, 1994; Fischer, 1994; Johnson, 1987). Precipitate, unreasoning fear has been found in such rare circumstances as entrapment in a burning structure from which there is no visible means of escape. A study of the 1918 Spanish influenza pandemic suggests that, in a catastrophic epidemic, the general response of the public is also one of resourcefulness, civility, and mutual aid (Crosby, 1989).

The view that panic is the "natural" response of groups in extreme peril ignores the fact that behavioral responses are context sensitive. Collective behavior changes over time and in relation to external events. This suggests that, in times of disaster, panic may be "iatrogenic": that is, the actions of emergency managers may determine the extent and duration of panic, to the extent it exists. For example, public reactions to an outbreak of meningitis (Bray, 1996) suggest that infectious disease and infection control specialists who routinely deal with contagion can help prevent panic by using the mass media and personal outreach in neighborhoods and at people's workplaces to provide credible, practical information on how to minimize the risk of disease transmission. Public information

TABLE 30-1.   Five Guidelines to Improve Planning for and the Response to Release of a Biological Weapon by Increasing the Involvement of the Public

---

Guideline, specific step(s) for implementation

Recognize that panic is rare and preventable
- Create a positive, constructive role for the general public
- Release timely, accurate public information, including instruction in personal protective measures

Enlist the general public as a capable partner
- Use civic organizations to assist with information dissemination, outbreak monitoring, and medication distribution

Think beyond the hospital for mass-casualty care
- Develop plans for home-based patient care and infection control as part of plans for a communitywide response to deal with mass casualties
- Involve lay and alternative care providers
- Use family, neighbors, and community groups to identify patients, disseminate information and therapies, and assist affected individuals in obtaining treatment

Provide information, which is as important as providing medicine
- Plan a health communication strategy that empowers the general public
- Produce multilingual and culturally relevant health information
- Educate the educators; use local spokespersons to disseminate information
- Be timely and forthcoming with information about the limits of what is known

Assume that the public will not "take the pill" if it does not "trust the doctor"
- Educate the public, before an attack, about what is being done to prepare and respond
- Ensure open flows of information during an attack through mass media outlets and interpersonal exchanges (e.g., town meetings, workshops, chat rooms)
- Build nonadversarial relations with the press and respond to media requests for information
- Create participatory decision-making processes by including the public, especially in discussions about how to allocate scarce resources and institute epidemic controls that compromise civil liberties

---

strategies aimed at demystifying the world of microbes, as well as instruction in personal protective practices, reinforce the public's sense of control and would be important steps toward "vaccinating" the public against panic. This argument is bolstered by research on factors known to provoke and amplify worry, fear, helplessness, and anger in threatening situations (cf. Covello, et al, 2001; Bennett, 1999).

The image of a panicked mob makes exciting footage in disaster movies, but it obscures a broad range of possible public reactions. The empirical study of collective behavior during disasters documents stress, fear, depression, and other negative responses, but it also points to emergent patterns of action that show cooperation, adaptiveness, and resourcefulness. Often, behavior that is not sanctioned by officials is erroneously defined as panic, rather than as an effective response of resourceful people acting in concert. Officials may be inclined to see a "command-and-control" model of disaster management as the only rational approach. In 1979, when a partial meltdown occurred at the nuclear power plant at Three Mile Island (south of Harrisburg, Pennslyvania), almost 40 percent of the population within 15 miles of the nuclear plant evacuated the area on their own. In the absence of clear information or leadership from public safety officials, residents made the reasonable decision to remove themselves from a situation of unknown and potentially significant risk, and they did so effectively and without evidence of panic (Clarke, 1999).

Further protection against social disorganization and panic is provided by deeply ingrained norms of civility and sociality. For instance, panic was rare in the stairwells of the World Trade Center when it was bombed in 1993 (Aguirre, Wenger and Vigo, 1998). The calm and orderly evacuation of the towers was aided by the fact that people in the buildings knew each other from working together and sharing the same office floor. Because of these social ties and the perception that exits and stairways were accessible, groups of office workers cooperated in vacating the building calmly and efficiently. Initial reports about the evacuation of the World Trade Center during the attack that occurred on September 11, 2001 suggest that people's responses were equally clearheaded and cooperative. The study by Aguirre, Wenger and Vigo (1998) and other studies have shown that standards of civil behavior prevail even in the most challenging circumstances. Social chaos does not occur in disaster situations because people tend to respond in accordance with their customary norms and roles (e.g., the able-bodied assist the impaired, supervisors assume responsibility for the safety of those they supervise, and friends look out for friends) (Johnson, 1987). This finding suggests that plans for a response to bioterrorism should attempt, whenever possible, to recognize and capitalize on existing social relations. For example, if quarantine should be necessary, establishing cohorts of individuals who are already known to one other in some capacity might be better than creating clusters of strangers.

History demonstrates that large-scale, fatal epidemics of previously unknown disease can create significant social disruption early in the outbreak. Such disruption can include unwarranted fear of exposure to the disease, suspicion of others, and stigmatization of individuals or groups who have become infected or are presumed to be carriers of disease. However, these effects tend to become less severe as communities develop routines and strategies for coping, even during epidemics of such horrific diseases as the plague in 14th-century Europe and HIV/AIDS today (Strong, 1990). This finding suggests that effective communication strategies will be needed early during the outbreak and that substantial planning may be necessary far in advance of an incident.

Enlist the General Public as a Capable Partner

Emergency services personnel, when focused on executing their professional duties, tend to think of the public as passive bystanders who are dispensable to the business of response. To the extent that medical resources exceed the medical needs of a specific event, this view is reasonable. At the scene of a traffic accident, for example, members of the general public are separated from the response operation by the familiar barrier of yellow tape. By definition, however, a disaster is an event that generates casualties in excess of available resources (Quarentelli, 1998). In those specific circumstances, this "yellow-tape phenomenon" is vestigial. Data show that ordinary, nonprofessional citizens are capable of full and useful participation in times of crisis (Dynes & Tierney, 1994; Quarentelli, 1996). In general, nonprofessionals in the immediate vicinity have saved the majority of people rescued in disasters, greatly aiding the work of the professionals who respond (Shears, 1991).

It makes little sense to talk about the "general public" as if it is a single entity, in the same way that it makes little sense to talk about a single U.S. health care "system." The general public is comprised of an interconnected matrix of networks and subnetworks organized around social institutions and relationships. Individuals are members of organizations and groups whose social ties, resources, communication links, and leadership structures might be used to facilitate a better and more coordinated response after a terrorist attack. Examples of these networks include civic networks (e.g., churches, social clubs, and schools), occupational networks (e.g., businesses, labor unions, and professional organizations), and information networks (e.g., libraries and Internet chat rooms and bulletin boards). Each network can be thought of as a potential conduit for organizing or facilitating public responses that are beneficial. For example, church groups might distribute antibiotics, convene vaccination meetings, or arrange visits to the homes of people who are ill. Social groups, such as the Kiwanis or Rotary Clubs, might activate phone trees to gather case reports, trace contacts, or disseminate instructions on appropriate use of medications.

Planning for bioterrorism response has not, to date, defined a role for the public in disease surveillance, even though the general public historically has been an accurate source of reports of infectious disease outbreaks (Hugh-Jones, 1976; Mohle-Boetani, et al, 2000). Rumor-reporting systems and emergency telephone hotlines—two channels of information from the general population—have been invaluable to epidemiological investigations and efforts to trace contacts, and they have been important sources of information on the adverse effects of vaccines and antibiotics administered to control outbreaks (Lowe, Evans & Myers, 2000; Heymann, et al, 1999). As suggested by the Spanish influenza pandemic of 1918, the role of the general public in providing outbreak data becomes all the more critical in the context of a catastrophic epidemic (Schoch-Spana, 2000). Health care providers and institutions may be so consumed with caring for casualties that they will not be able to devote sufficient time or resources to the tracking of new cases of disease (Noji, 1996).

Not only is it possible to imagine networks of public responders that can aid in information dissemination, outbreak monitoring, resource distribution, and even patient care, but, in the midst of a collective crisis, a positive and active role for community groups and individual citizens provides a potential antidote to panic and other adverse psychological effects (Holloway, et al., 1997; Covello, et al., 2001). In times of crisis, having a constructive role to play engages people in a common mission and provides a sense of control in periods of grave uncertainty.

Think Beyond the Hospital for Mass-Casualty Care

Much planning for bioterrorism response has been guilty of double myopia. First, it has assumed that the formal hospital system will be capable of managing the disaster alone. Second, it has assumed that the general public is incapable of playing a role in the medical response. During the past decade, mergers, downsizing, workforce shortages, and the shift toward outpatient services have reduced the number of hospital beds drastically in all major medical marketplaces. The existing network of hospitals probably would not be capable of adequately caring for the people affected by a large-scale bioterrorist attack.

Because hospitals function according to a "just-in-time" management principle for nursing, medicine, and equipment, they typically do not have the capacity to handle patient loads that are greater than projected (O'Toole, 2001). Hospitals, in general, lack the capacity to cope with an unexpected surge of patients. In the aftermath of a significant bioterrorism event, overburdened hospitals may be forced to turn patients away, discharge those who are the least ill, and ration finite supplies and personnel; each of these responses occurred during the 1918 influenza pandemic (Schoch-Spana, 2000).

Plans have been made at the national level, as part of the Domestic Preparedness Program, for the mobilization of military teams and mobile medical care facilities; however, in most major U.S. cities, in even a small outbreak of epidemic disease, hospital-bed capacity could be exceeded quickly (Tucker, 1997; Department of Health and Human Services, 2000). Whatever partnerships might be imagined between clinics, hospitals, the Veterans Administration hospital system, and other inpatient care systems, hospitals could plausibly reach the limits of their functional capacity. What is needed is a plan that includes the possibility of home-based treatment and supportive care arrangements to augment hospital-based care. The majority of victims of the Spanish influenza outbreak of 1918, for example, were cared for at home by family, neighbors, Red Cross volunteers, visiting nurses, and hospital social workers, among others (Spoch-Spana, 2000).

Information on responses to infectious disease emergencies is not, however, the only source of evidence in favor of a decentralized response. Professional health services are only a small percentage of the total care that patients receive on a regular basis. Family members and other lay nonprofessionals provide the vast majority (70 to 90 percent) of routine care in communities (Suzman, 2000; Kovar, et al, 1989). Emergency plans for distributing to the general public resources and information about nutrition, sanitation, infection control, and the care of seriously ill persons could be of great value in a response to bioterrorism. For instance, a network of community information centers was critical to the functioning of Israel's emergency health system during the Persian Gulf War in 1991; these centers dispensed medical information, medication instructions, and reports indicating which hospitals, clinics, and pharmacies were open (Sachs, et al., 1991).

Provide Information, Which is as Important as Providing Medicine

Review of relevant historical examples suggests that effective leadership and delivery of clear, credible, and timely information both during and after a bioterrorist attack would be critical components of a response. In the face of uncertainty, the general public would need reassurance, descriptions of the response measures under way, instruction in personal and collective protective measures, and messages of hope. Infectious disease professionals (along with emergency managers) would have a critical role in helping to distribute this information in a timely and credible manner, which might significantly lessen the impact of a bioterrorist attack (Holloway, et al., 1997; Reynolds, 2000). On the other hand, the release of inaccurate, confusing, or contradictory information by leaders and/or the media has the potential to increase levels of fear, panic, and demoralization, as well as to discredit authorities. Moreover, failures of communication among government officials, health experts, and citizens can create misunderstanding, suspicion, and resistance that ultimately inhibit efforts to halt the spread of disease (Risse, 1992; Edison, 1992).

Considerable resources are required to disseminate information to the public in an emergency, as was demonstrated during a recent outbreak of West Nile virus in New York City in 1999 (Fine, 2001). Health officials and emergency managers conducted a massive campaign to educate the public through daily press conferences, regular media releases, a telephone hotline, Web site updates, multilingual brochures and fliers, and personal contact at the epicenter of the outbreak. This campaign severely strained existing human resources, underscoring the problem of surge capacity for health departments. Telephone hotline staff, 25 to 75 of whom were required per shift, answered telephone calls for 24 hours each day and fielded a total of 1.15 million inquiries during a period of seven weeks. A significant bioterrorist attack certainly would generate more calls than were made in the New York City area during the West Nile virus outbreak. Gathering data on the most frequently asked questions could be one step toward building a more responsive public information strategy.

A bioterrorist attack is likely to produce a climate of grave uncertainty and insecurity. As has been the case in historic epidemics, the general public will try to make sense of the experience of sudden, widespread disease (Rosenberg, 1989). Questions such as "Why?" "Why me?" "What next?" and "How and when will this end?" will abound. Public health officials should anticipate the need to provide accurate and timely information about the nature of the attack and the steps that are being taken to mitigate its effects. Reporting systems that track the scope of the epidemic will be critical to these efforts. At the same time, health authorities should also be open and candid about the limits of available information and resources. To the extent that the general public perceives that public health officials are failing to provide accurate appraisals of the outbreak's scope and impact, a credibility gap will open rapidly, causing individuals to seek alternative (and perhaps less accurate) sources of information.

Evidence from the public health response to the recent anthrax outbreaks illustrates the deleterious impact on public trust that can result from what John Schwartz of the *New York Times* has referred to as the "spin-control" model of public information release (Schwartz, 2001)—that is, a risk-averse approach that avoids full and complete disclosure in order to minimize potential negative political consequences of actual or perceived errors with respect to a response.

Public health officials should also expect requests to list specific steps that individuals can take to lower their risk of either being exposed to infectious agents or transmitting them. Along with the need for a pharmaceutical stockpile of vaccines and antibiotics, there is an urgent need for an information stockpile, including public service announcements about infectious disease concepts (e.g., contagion and the value of vaccination), infection control procedures to be followed at home, and information for the public in the event of the need for quarantine. Official spokespersons need to be prepared to discuss both the benefits and the risks of epidemic control measures while clearly advocating the need for recommended actions (Mullin, et al., 2001). Health officials and hospital administrators need to be prepared to indicate which hospitals and clinics are capable of taking patients and where other critical medical resources exist (Sachs, et. al., 1991). Efforts to provide adequate information will undoubtedly be complicated by the shifting sands of what is known and the interruptions in the flow of information that characterize all public emergencies.

The Public Will Not Take the Pill if It Does Not Trust the Doctor

Stopping a disease outbreak will require that public health professionals and government leaders carefully nurture the general population's trust and confidence in the institutions of public health and government and their actions, especially if large-scale disease containment measures are necessary. After a bioterrorist attack, public trust could be a fragile, yet essential, asset. The issue of trust bears significantly on two critical aspects of the medical and public health response to bioterrorism: (1) the choice of strategies for effective communication with the public, and (2) the processes for debating, as a society, some of the more ethically complex dimensions of disease containment.

Although there is a tendency to view the media as an impediment to emergency response, a bioterrorist attack would necessitate a close working relationship between the media, decision makers, and those involved in response operations. Given the speed with which news reports circulate today, and given the importance of the media in shaping public responses, health departments and hospitals would need to be responsive to media requests for information (Heymann, et al., 1999; Gushulak, 1994). An important step toward maintaining an effective, nonadversarial relationship with the press is to have more routine interactions with reporters, producers, and editorial boards before periods of crisis. During an emergency, health professionals could then build on their relationship with the media to effectively disseminate an accurate account of events, provide vital disease control information, and communicate the rationale and justification for the necessary medical and public health responses.

Mass media outlets can get vital information to the largest numbers of people the most quickly. However, the mass media and the Internet are insufficient. Additional communication strategies would be critical to enlisting the public as partners in implementing epidemic controls. Multilingual materials and culturally relevant messages that are endorsed and delivered by persons who have local respect and authority can help ensure that control measures are successfully disseminated to all sectors of a diverse community (DiGiovanni, 1999; Freimuth, et al., 2000). Direct personal contact has the most significant effect on a person's willingness to trust and act on health-related information (Covello, et al., 2001; Freimuth, et al., 2000). Public outreach strategies of health departments and emergency services should include interpersonal exchanges of information—for example, town meetings and public workshops. On the other hand, the realities of an outbreak of a disease that is propagated by person-to-person transmission would require alternatives to such public meetings. Under those circumstances, means of remote communication (e.g., "telephone trees," Internet-based communications, and newsletters) would be important alternatives.

The extent to which the general public supports large-scale, potentially disruptive disease containment measures may also depend on the transparency and accessibility of the decision-making process. Accounts of historic epidemics demonstrate that extreme containment measures, such as quarantine, can be perceived as being more problematic than the disease itself. During an outbreak of polio in 1916 in a Long Island community, a large citizens' group protested the sometimes forcible removal of sick children from the care of parents to an isolation hospital (Risse, 1992). Enlisting the public as partners in disaster response would likely require the use of participatory decision-making bodies, such as citizen advisory panels, for responses that require a community's ethical judgment (e.g., setting priorities for use of scarce medical resources, such as antibiotics and vaccines) (Covello, et al., 2001). Strategies for public discourse and a participatory and transparent decision-making process in the midst of an epidemic might involve enlisting leaders of local religious organizations or labor groups to provide feedback about proposed epidemic control measures.

Conclusion

Resourceful, adaptive behavior is the rule rather than the exception in communities beset by technological and natural disasters as well as epidemics. As planning for responses to acts of bioterrorism evolves, it is important to develop strategies that enlist the public as essential and capable partners. The recent terrorist attacks in New York and Washington, DC draw attention to the important role of nonprofessional individuals and groups in the immediate and long-term response to disasters with mass casualties that cannot be contained within a perimeter of yellow tape. Involving the general public will require, in part, raising public awareness of their roles and responsibilities after a biological attack.

The complexity of people's reactions to the anthrax-tainted letters discovered after the 9/11 tragedies further undermines any simple notions we might have about the general population's ability to cope with a bioterrorism crisis. What began as a single case of inhalational anthrax had become, by late November, an outbreak with 23 total cases of infection and five deaths, disrupting Congress, the Supreme Court, and the U.S. Postal Service. The exhortations of news editors, politicians, and pundits that urged the public not to panic and to go about their daily routines suggest how fearful decision-makers were about the potential for public hysteria. A preliminary assessment of events, however, indicates a temperate, if complex, response by the general public.

In the aftermath of the September 11 attacks, increases in the purchase of gas masks and ciprofloxacin were quickly seen. What was described as "panic buying" in some reports may have been a reasonable attempt to acquire protection in the face of stark, proven vulnerability to terrorism. Moreover, what appears to some as panic may be evidence of the public's resourcefulness when advice from professionals is confusing or nonexistent. Concerns about providing children with gas masks that fit and with correct doses of antibiotics also suggest that the public is not prone to panic but has a deep-seated need to seek protection for the most vulnerable members of society.

Health officials' warnings about the potential dangers of off the shelf respirators and personal drug stockpiles have also met a generally receptive audience. Seven of 10 individuals who were surveyed in a Gallup poll conducted on October 21, 2001 indicated that they had *not* thought about buying a gas mask or obtaining a prescription for antibiotics (Benedetto, 2001). This and a second poll characterize the response of the general public as one of "reasoned calm" and "reluctance to panic" (Benedetto, 2001; Cooper, 2001). Closer proximity to danger has not yet given rise to unreasoning fear and erratic behavior. In late October, a poll of Florida residents found that over 50% had little or no concern about contracting anthrax (Mozingo, 2001). Reports of mass testing and prophylaxis at affected work sites indicate that the process was orderly, as hundreds and sometimes thousands of individuals waited in line for their turn (Povich & Brune, 2001).

Increased vigilance regarding personal safety has resulted in a significant burden on professional responders. During October 2001, the Federal Bureau of Investigation investigated 12,500 suspected anthrax attacks, many of which were reports by concerned citizens about harmless substances (Levine, 2001). The health care system has also fielded an increasing number of demands for diagnostic tests by individuals who fear they may have been exposed to anthrax (Daniel, 2001). However, when seen in the context of conflicting reports from experts about the nature of the threat, as well as vague and nonspecific government alerts about additional possible attacks, the level of public concern appears measured and reasonable.

In short, evidence that the public cannot be trusted with full, accurate disclosure of what is known about a bioterrorist threat is lacking. The events of September 11, 2001 and after further undermine the view that the public is prone to panic, incapable of effective participation, and inclined to respond irrationally. How the public responds to this and any future threat of bioterrorism may depend, to a considerable degree, on how and to what extent decision makers activate strategies that "vaccinate" against the risk that the public will distrust them, will rely on misinformation, and will be excluded from participation in decision making.

References

Aguirre, B. E., D. Wenger, and G. Vigo. "A Test of the Emergent Norm Theory of Collective Behavior," *Sociological Forum* 13 (1998): 301–20.

Barry, D. "Determined Volunteers Camped Out to Pitch In," *New York Times,* 23 September 2001.

Benedetto, R. "Poll Finds Anthrax Fear but No Panic," *USA Today,* 23 October 2001.

Bennett, P. "Understanding Responses to Risk: Some Basic Findings." In *Risk Communication and Public Health,* ed. P. Bennett and K. Calman. Oxford: Oxford University Press, 1999, pp. 3–19.

Bray, J. "Public Information," *Nursing Standards* 11 (1996): 17.

Clarke, L. *Mission Improbable: Using Fantasy Documents to Tame Disaster.* Chicago: University of Chicago Press, 1999.

Cooper, R. "Response to Terror: The Anthrax Threat: Polls Find People Calm, Apprehensive," *Los Angeles Times,* 28 October 2001.

Covello, V. T., R. G. Peters, J. G. Wojtecki, et al. "Risk Communication, the West Nile Virus Epidemic, and Bioterrorism: Responding to the Communication Challenges Posed by the Intentional or Unintentional Release of a Pathogen in an Urban Setting," *Journal of Urban Health* 78 (2001): 382–91.

Crosby, A. W. *America's Forgotten Pandemic: The Influenza of 1918.* Cambridge: Cambridge University Press, 1989.

Daniel, M. "Health Officials Work to Avoid Outbreak of Fear," *Boston Globe,* 20 October 2001.

Department of Health and Human Services. *Hospital Preparedness for Mass Casualties, Final Report.* Washington, DC: American Hospital Association, 2000. www.ahapolicyforum.org/policyresources/MOdisaster.asp (accessed August 30, 2001).

DiGiovanni, C., Jr. "Domestic Terrorism with Chemical or Biological Agents: Psychiatric Aspects," *American Journal of Psychiatry* 156 (1999): 1500–1505.

Dobbs, M. "A Renaissance for U. S. Civil Defense?" *Journal of Homeland Security,* January 15, 2001. www.homelandsecurity.org/journal/Articles/Dobbs_July01.htm (accessed July 7, 2001).

Dynes, R. R., and K. J. Tierney, eds. *Disasters, Collective Behavior and Social Organization.* Newark: University of Delaware Press, 1994.

Edison, W. G. "Confusion, Controversy and Quarantine: The Muncie Smallpox Epidemic of 1893," *Indiana Magazine of History* 86 (1992): 374–98.

Fine, A., and M. Layton. "Lessons from the West Nile Viral Encephalitis Outbreak in New York City, 1999: Implications for Bioterrorism Preparedness," *Clinical Infectious Disease* 32 (2001): 277–82.

Fischer, H. W. *Response to Disaster: Fact Versus Fiction and Its Perpetuation.* Lanham: University Press of America, 1994.

Freimuth, V., H. W. Linnan, and P. Potter. "Communicating the Threat of Emerging Infections to the Public," *Emerging Infectious Diseases* 6 (2000): 337–47.

Gushulak, B. "Paradigms and Public Health: International Disease Control in the Information Age," *Canadian Journal of Public Health* 85 (1994): 374–77.

Henderson, D. A. "The Looming Threat of Bioterrorism," *Science* 283 (1999): 1279–82.

Heymann, D. L., D. Barakamfitiye, M. Szczeniowski, et al. "Ebola Hemorrhagic Fever: Lessons from Kikwit, Democratic Republic of the Congo." Supplement 1. *Journal of Infectious Diseases* 179 (1999): S283–86.

Holloway, H. C., A. E. Norwood, C. S. Fullerton, et al. "The Threat of Biological Weapons: Prophylaxis and Mitigation of Psychological and Social Consequences," *Journal of the American Medical Association* 278 (1997): 425–27.

Hugh-Jones, M. E. "Epidemiological Studies on the 1967–1968 Foot-and-Mouth Disease Epidemic: The Reporting of Suspected Disease," *Journal of Hygiene* 77 (1976): 299–306.

Johns Hopkins Center for Civilian Biodefense, Center for Strategic and International Studies, ANSER, et al. "Dark Winter: Bioterrorism Exercise, Andrews Air Force Base, June 22–23, 2001." Script. www.hopkins-biodefense.org/DARK%20WINTER.pdf (accessed July 1, 2001).

Johnson, N. R. "Panic and the Breakdown of Social Order: Popular Myth, Social Theory, and Empirical Evidence," *Sociological Focus* 20 (1987): 171–83.

Kovar, M. G., G. Hendershot, and E. Mathis. "Older People in the United States Who Receive Help with Basic Activities of Daily Living," *American Journal of Public Health* 79 (1989): 778–79.

Levine, S. "Disseminating Dread: Pranksters, Disgruntled Americans Perpetrate Hoaxes," *Washington Post,* 26 October 2001.

Lowe, G., M. R. Evans, and P. Myers. "Help—We Need a Helpline! A Public Health Audit Case Study," *Journal of Public Health Medicine* 22 (2000): 129–32.

Mohle-Boetani, J. C., S. B. Werner, S. H. Waterman, et al. "The Impact of Health Communication and Enhanced Laboratory-Based Surveillance on Detection of Cyclosporiasis Outbreaks in California," *Emerging Infectious Diseases* 6 (2000): 200–203.

Mozingo, J. "State Not in Panic, Poll Finds," *Miami Herald,* 25 October 2001.

Mullin, S., B. Reynolds, J. Gadd, et al. "How New York City Responded to an Emerging Infection," *Journal Health Communications* (2001): 1–9.

Noji, E. K. "Disaster Epidemiology," *Emergency Medical Clinicians of North America* 14 (1996): 289–300.

O'Toole, T. "Smallpox: An Attack Acenario," *Emerging Infectious Diseases* 5 (1999): 540–46.

O'Toole, T. Testimony. FEMA's Role in Managing Bioterrorist Attacks and the Impact of Public Health Concerns on Bioterrorism Preparedness. Hearing before U. S. Senate Committee on

Government Affairs, Subcommittee on International Security, Proliferation, and Federal Services, July 23, 2001, www.hopkins-biodefense.org/pages/library/fema.html.

Povich, E., and T. Brune. "America's Ordeal: Anxiety on Capitol Hill," *Newsday,* 18 October 2001.

Quarantelli, E. L. "Basic Themes Derived from Survey Findings on Human Behavior in the Mexico City Earthquake," *International Sociology* 11 (1996): 481–99.

Quarantelli, E. L. "The Sociology of Panic." In *International Encyclopedia of the Social and Behavioral Sciences*, ed. N. Smelser and P. B. Baltes. New York: Pergamon, 2001, pp. 11020–30.

Quarantelli, E. L., ed. *What Is a Disaster? Perspectives on the Question.* New York: Routledge, 1998.

Reynolds, B. "Stop the Panic: Understanding the Psychology of a Bioterrorism Disaster." Paper. National Bioterrorism Preparedness and Response Initiative, Centers for Disease Control and Prevention, regional meeting, Philadelphia, May 16–17, 2000. www.bt.cdc.gov/Regional MeetingSlides/AgendaPhillyDay2.asp (accessed August 21, 2001).

Risse, G. B. "Revolt Against Quarantine: Community Responses to the 1916 Polio Epidemic, Oyster Bay, New York," *Transactions and Studies of the College of Physicians of Philadelphia* 14 (February 1992): 23–50.

Rosenberg, C. E. "What Is an Epidemic? AIDS in Historical Perspective," *Daedalus* 118 (1989): 1–17.

Sachs, Z., Y. L. Danon, R. Dycian, et al. "Community Coordination and Information Centers During the Persian Gulf War," *Israeli Journal of Medical Science* 27 (1991): 696–700.

Schoch-Spana, M. "Implications of Pandemic Influenza for Bioterrorism Response," *Clinical Infectious Diseases* 31 (2000): 1409–13.

Schwartz, J. "Efforts to Calm the Nation's Fears Spin Out of Control," *New York Times,* 28 October 2001.

Shears, P. "Epidemiology and Infection in Famine and Disasters," *Epidemiological Infections* 107 (1991): 241–51.

Strong, P. "Epidemic Psychology: A Model," *Sociology of Health and Illness* 12 (1990): 249–59.

Suzman, R. *Older Americans 2000: Key Indicators of Well-Being.* Hyattsville, Md.: National Center for Health Statistics, 2000.

Taylor, E. R. "Are We Prepared for Terrorism Using Weapons of Mass Destruction: Government's Half Measures," *Policy Analysis* 387 (2000): 1–19.

Tucker, J. B. "National Health and Medical Services Response to Incidents of Chemical and Biological Terrorism," *Journal of the American Medical Association* 278 (1997): 362–68.

World Health Organization (WHO). *Health Aspects of Chemical and Biological Weapons.* 2nd ed. Geneva, Switzerland: WHO, 2001.

Wyatt, H. W. The Role and Responsibility of the Media in the Event of a Bioterrorist act. *Journal of Public Health Management Practices* 6 (2000): 63–67.

Appendix A

National Strategies, Presidential Directives, Significant Presidential Initiatives, and Selected Executive Orders Related to Homeland Security (Since 9/11)

October 8, 2001	Executive Order 13228—Establishing the Office of Homeland Security and the Homeland Security Council
October 16, 2001	Executive Order 13231—Critical Infrastructure Protection in the Information Age
October 29, 2001	Homeland Security Presidential Directive-1 (HSPD-1)—Organization and Operation of the Homeland Security Council
October 29, 2002	HSPD-2—Combating Terrorism Through Immigration Policies
March 12, 2002	HSPD-3—Homeland Security Advisory System
June 6, 2002	Presidential speech proposing the Department of Homeland Security, accompanied by *The Department of Homeland Security,* outlining the proposal
July 16, 2002	*National Strategy for Homeland Security*
September 20, 2002	*National Security Strategy of the United States*
December 11, 2002	*National Strategy for Combating Weapons of Mass Destruction* (unclassified companion to a classified HSPD/National Security Presidential Directive (NSPD) on this subject)
January 28, 2003	State of the Union Address, including President Bush's announcement to create the Terrorist Threat Integration Center, and his proposal for Project BioShield

January 23, 2003	Executive Order 13284—Amendment of Executive Orders, and Other Actions, in Connection With the Establishment of the Department of Homeland Security
February 14, 2003	*National Strategy for Combating Terrorism*
February 14, 2003	*National Strategy for the Physical Protection of Critical Infrastructures and Key Assets*
February 14, 2003	*National Strategy to Secure Cyberspace*
February 28, 2003	Executive Order 13286—Amendment of Executive Orders, and Other Actions, in Connection With the Transfer of Certain Functions to the Secretary of Homeland Security
February 28, 2003	HSPD-5—Management of Domestic Incidents
July 29, 2003	Executive Order 13311—Homeland Security Information Sharing
September 16, 2003	HSPD-6—Integration and Use of Screening Information to Protect against Terrorism
December 17, 2003	HSPD-7—Critical Infrastructure Identification, Prioritization, and Protection
December 17, 2003	HSPD-8—National Preparedness
December 30, 2003	Executive Order 13323—Assignment of Functions Relating to Arrivals in and Departures From the United States
February 3, 2004	HSPD-9—Defense of United States Agriculture and Food
April 28, 2004	*Biodefense for the 21st Century* (unclassified companion to a classified HSPD on this subject)
August 27, 2004	Executive Order 13353—Establishing the President's Board on Safeguarding Americans' Civil Liberties
August 27, 2004	Executive Order 13354—National Counterterrorism Center
August 27, 2004	Executive Order 13355—Strengthened Management of the Intelligence Community
August 27, 2004	Executive Order 13356—Strengthening the Sharing of Terrorism Information to Protect Americans
August 27, 2004	HSPD-11—Comprehensive Terrorist-Related Screening Procedures
August 27, 2004	HSPD-12—Policy for a Common Identification Standard for Federal Employees and Contractors

Appendix B

Recommendations of the 9/11 Commission

1. The U.S. government must identify and prioritize actual or potential terrorist sanctuaries. For each, it should have a realistic strategy to keep possible terrorists insecure and on the run, using all elements of national power. We should reach out, listen to, and work with other countries that can help. (367)
2. If Musharraf stands for enlightened moderation in a fight for his life and for the life of his country, the United States should be willing to make hard choices too and make the difficult, long-term commitment to the future of Pakistan. Sustaining the current scale of aid to Pakistan, the United States should support Pakistan's government in its struggle against extremists with a comprehensive effort that extends from military aid to support for better education, so long as Pakistan's leaders remain willing to make difficult choices of their own. (369)
3. The President and the Congress deserve praise for their efforts in Afghanistan so far. Now the United States and the international community should make a long-term commitment to a secure and stable Afghanistan, in order to give the government a reasonable opportunity to improve the life of the Afghan people. Afghanistan must not again become a sanctuary for international crime and terrorism. The United States and the international community should help the Afghan government extend its authority over the country, with a strategy and nation-by-nation commitments to achieve their objectives. (370)
4. The problems in the U.S.–Saudi relationship must be confronted, openly. The United States and Saudi Arabia must determine if they can build a relationship that political leaders on both sides are prepared to publicly defend—a relationship about more than oil. It should include a shared commitment to political and economic reform, as Saudis make common cause with the outside world. It should include a shared interest in greater tolerance and cultural respect, translating into a commitment to fight the violent extremists who foment hatred. (374)
5. The U.S. government must define what the message is, what it stands for. We should offer an example of moral leadership in the world, committed to treat people humanely, abide by the rule of law, and be generous and caring to our neighbors. America and Muslim friends can agree on respect for human dig-

nity and opportunity. To Muslim parents, terrorists like bin Ladin have nothing to offer their children but visions of violence and death. America and its friends have a crucial advantage—we can offer these parents a vision that might give their children a better future. If we heed the views of thoughtful leaders in the Arab and Muslim world, a moderate consensus can be found. (376)

6.   Where Muslim governments, even those who are friends, do not respect these principles, the United States must stand for a better future. One of the lessons of the long Cold War was that short-term gains in cooperating with the most repressive and brutal governments were too often outweighed by long-term setbacks for America's stature and interests. (376)

7.   Just as we did in the Cold War, we need to defend our ideals abroad vigorously. America does stand up for its values. The United States defended, and still defends, Muslims against tyrants and criminals in Somalia, Bosnia, Kosovo, Afghanistan, and Iraq. If the United States does not act aggressively to define itself in the Islamic world, the extremists will gladly do the job for us. Recognizing that Arab and Muslim audiences rely on satellite television and radio, the government has begun some promising initiatives in television and radio broadcasting to the Arab world, Iran, and Afghanistan. These efforts are beginning to reach large audiences. The Broadcasting Board of Governors has asked for much larger resources. It should get them. The United States should rebuild the scholarship, exchange, and library programs that reach out to young people and offer them knowledge and hope. Where such assistance is provided, it should be identified as coming from the citizens of the United States. (377)

8.   The U.S. government should offer to join with other nations in generously supporting a new International Youth Opportunity Fund. Funds will be spent directly for building and operating primary and secondary schools in those Muslim states that commit to sensibly investing their own money in public education. (378)

9.   A comprehensive U.S. strategy to counter terrorism should include economic policies that encourage development, more open societies, and opportunities for people to improve the lives of their families and to enhance prospects for their children's future. (379)

10.   The United States should engage other nations in developing a comprehensive coalition strategy against Islamist terrorism. There are several multilateral institutions in which such issues should be addressed. But the most important policies should be discussed and coordinated in a flexible contact group of leading coalition governments. This is a good place, for example, to develop joint strategies for targeting terrorist travel, or for hammering out a common strategy for the places where terrorists may be finding sanctuary. (379)

11.   The United States should engage its friends to develop a common coalition approach toward the detention and humane treatment of captured terrorists. New principles might draw upon Article 3 of the Geneva Conventions on the law of armed conflict. That article was specifically designed for those cases in which the usual laws of war did not apply. Its minimum standards are generally accepted throughout the world as customary international law. (380)

12. Our report shows that al Qaeda has tried to acquire or make weapons of mass destruction for at least ten years. There is no doubt the United States would be a prime target. Preventing the proliferation of these weapons warrants a maximum effort—by strengthening counterproliferation efforts, expanding the Proliferation Security Initiative, and supporting the Cooperative Threat Reduction program. (381)

13. Vigorous efforts to track terrorist financing must remain front and center in U.S. counterterrorism efforts. The government has recognized that information about terrorist money helps us to understand their networks, search them out, and disrupt their operations. Intelligence and law enforcement have targeted the relatively small number of financial facilitators—individuals al Qaeda relied on for their ability to raise and deliver money—at the core of al Qaeda's revenue stream. These efforts have worked. The death or capture of several important facilitators has decreased the amount of money available to al Qaeda and has increased its costs and difficulty in raising and moving that money. Captures have additionally provided a windfall of intelligence that can be used to continue the cycle of disruption. (382)

14. Targeting travel is at least as powerful a weapon against terrorists as targeting their money. The United States should combine terrorist travel intelligence, operations, and law enforcement in a strategy to intercept terrorists, find terrorist travel facilitators, and constrain terrorist mobility. (385)

15. The U.S. border security system should be integrated into a larger network of screening points that includes our transportation system and access to vital facilities, such as nuclear reactors. The President should direct the Department of Homeland Security to lead the effort to design a comprehensive screening system, addressing common problems and setting common standards with systemwide goals in mind. Extending those standards among other governments could dramatically strengthen America and the world's collective ability to intercept individuals who pose catastrophic threats. (387)

16. The Department of Homeland Security, properly supported by the Congress, should complete, as quickly as possible, a biometric entry-exit screening system, including a single system for speeding qualified travelers. It should be integrated with the system that provides benefits to foreigners seeking to stay in the United States. Linking biometric passports to good data systems and decision-making is a fundamental goal. No one can hide his or her debt by acquiring a credit card with a slightly different name. Yet today, a terrorist can defeat the link to electronic records by tossing away an old passport and slightly altering the name in the new one. (389)

17. The U.S. government cannot meet its own obligations to the American people to prevent the entry of terrorists without a major effort to collaborate with other governments. We should do more to exchange terrorist information with trusted allies, and raise U.S. and global border security standards for travel and border crossing over the medium and long term through extensive international cooperation. (390)

18. Secure identification should begin in the United States. The federal government should set standards for the issuance of birth certificates and sources of

identification, such as drivers' licenses. Fraud in identification documents is no longer just a problem of theft. At many entry points to vulnerable facilities, including gates for boarding aircraft, sources of identification are the last opportunity to ensure that people are who they say they are and to check whether they are terrorists. (390)

19. Hard choices must be made in allocating limited resources. The U.S. government should identify and evaluate the transportation assets that need to be protected, set risk-based priorities for defending them, select the most practical and cost-effective ways of doing so, and then develop a plan, budget, and funding to implement the effort. The plan should assign roles and missions to the relevant authorities (federal, state, regional, and local) and to private stakeholders. In measuring effectiveness, perfection is unattainable. But terrorists should perceive that potential targets are defended. They may be deterred by a significant chance of failure. (391)

20. Improved use of "no-fly" and "automatic selectee" lists should not be delayed while the argument about a successor to CAPPS continues. This screening function should be performed by the TSA, and it should utilize the larger set of watchlists maintained by the federal government. Air carriers should be required to supply the information needed to test and implement this new system. (393)

21. The TSA and the Congress must give priority attention to improving the ability of screening checkpoints to detect explosives on passengers. As a start, each individual selected for special screening should be screened for explosives. Further, the TSA should conduct a human factors study, a method often used in the private sector, to understand problems in screener performance and set attainable objectives for individual screeners and for the checkpoints where screening takes place. (393)

22. As the President determines the guidelines for information sharing among government agencies and by those agencies with the private sector, he should safeguard the privacy of individuals about whom information is shared. (394)

23. The burden of proof for retaining a particular governmental power should be on the executive, to explain (a) that the power actually materially enhances security and (b) that there is adequate supervision of the executive" use of the powers to ensure protection of civil liberties. If the power is granted, there must be adequate guidelines and oversight to properly confine its use. (394)

24. At this time of increased and consolidated government authority, there should be a board within the executive branch to oversee adherence to the guidelines we recommend and the commitment the government makes to defend our civil liberties. (395)

25. Homeland security assistance should be based strictly on an assessment of risks and vulnerabilities. Now, in 2004, Washington, DC, and New York City are certainly at the top of any such list. We understand the contention that every state and city needs to have some minimum infrastructure for emergency response. But federal homeland security assistance should not remain a program for general revenue sharing. It should supplement state and local resources based on the risks or vulnerabilities that merit additional support. Congress should not use this money as a pork barrel. (396)

26. Emergency-response agencies nationwide should adopt the Incident Command System (ICS). When multiple agencies or multiple jurisdictions are involved, they should adopt a unified command. Both are proven frameworks for emergency response. We strongly support the decision that federal homeland security funding will be contingent, as of October 1, 2004, upon the adoption and regular use of ICS and unified command procedures. In the future, the Department of Homeland Security should consider making funding contingent on aggressive and realistic training in accordance with ICS and unified command procedures. (397)

27. Congress should support pending legislation which provides for the expedited and increased assignment of radio spectrum for public safety purposes. Furthermore, high-risk urban areas such as New York City and Washington, DC, should establish signal corps units to ensure communications connectivity between and among civilian authorities, local first responders, and the National Guard. Federal funding of such units should be given high priority by Congress. (397)

28. We endorse the American National Standards Institute's recommended standard for private preparedness. We were encouraged by Secretary Tom Ridge's praise of the standard, and urge the Department of Homeland Security to promote its adoption. We also encourage the insurance and credit-rating industries to look closely at a company's compliance with the ANSI standard in assessing its insurability and creditworthiness. We believe that compliance with the standard should define the standard of care owed by a company to its employees and the public for legal purposes. Private-sector preparedness is not a luxury; it is a cost of doing business in the post-9/11 world. It is ignored at a tremendous potential cost in lives, money, and national security. (398)

29. We recommend the establishment of a National Counterterrorism Center (NCTC), built on the foundation of the existing Terrorist Threat Integration Center (TTIC). Breaking the older mold of national government organization, this NCTC should be a center for joint operational planning and joint intelligence, staffed by personnel from the various agencies. The head of the NCTC should have authority to evaluate the performance of the people assigned to the Center. (403)

30. The current position of Director of Central Intelligence should be replaced by a National Intelligence Director with two main areas of responsibility: (1) to oversee national intelligence centers on specific subjects of interest across the U.S. government and (2) to manage the national intelligence program and oversee the agencies that contribute to it. (411)

31. The CIA Director should emphasize (a) rebuilding the CIA's analytic capabilities; (b) transforming the clandestine service by building its human intelligence capabilities; (c) developing a stronger language program, with high standards and sufficient financial incentives; (d) renewing emphasis on recruiting diversity among operations officers so they can blend more easily in foreign cities; (e) ensuring a seamless relationship between human source collection and signals collection at the operational level; and (f) stressing a better balance between unilateral and liaison operations. (415)

32. Lead responsibility for directing and executing paramilitary operations, whether clandestine or covert, should shift to the Defense Department. There it should be consolidated with the capabilities for training, direction, and execution of such operations already being developed in the Special Operations Command. (415)

33. Finally, to combat the secrecy and complexity we have described, the overall amounts of money being appropriated for national intelligence and to its component agencies should no longer be kept secret. Congress should pass a separate appropriations act for intelligence, defending the broad allocation of how these tens of billions of dollars have been assigned among the varieties of intelligence work. (416)

34. Information procedures should provide incentives for sharing, to restore a better balance between security and shared knowledge. (417)

35. The President should lead the government-wide effort to bring the major national security institutions into the information revolution. He should coordinate the resolution of the legal, policy, and technical issues across agencies to create a "trusted information network." (418)

36. Congressional oversight for intelligence—and counterterrorism—is now dysfunctional. Congress should address this problem. We have considered various alternatives: A joint committee on the old model of the Joint Committee on Atomic Energy is one. A single committee in each house of Congress, combining authorizing and appropriating authorities, is another. (420)

37. Congress should create a single, principal point of oversight and review for homeland security. Congressional leaders are best able to judge what committee should have jurisdiction over this department and its duties. But we believe that Congress does have the obligation to choose one in the House and one in the Senate, and that this committee should be a permanent standing committee with a nonpartisan staff. (421)

38. Since a catastrophic attack could occur with little or no notice, we should minimize as much as possible the disruption of national security policymaking during the change of administrations by accelerating the process for national security appointments. We think the process could be improved significantly so transitions can work more effectively and allow new officials to assume their new responsibilities as quickly as possible. (422)

39. A specialized and integrated national security workforce should be established at the FBI consisting of agents, analysts, linguists, and surveillance specialists who are recruited, trained, rewarded, and retained to ensure the development of an institutional culture imbued with a deep expertise in intelligence and national security. (425)

40. The Department of Defense and its oversight committees should regularly assess the adequacy of Northern Command's strategies and planning to defend the United States against military threats to the homeland. (428)

41. The Department of Homeland Security and its oversight committees should regularly assess the types of threats the country faces to determine (a) the adequacy of the government's plans—and the progress against those plans—to protect America's critical infrastructure and (b) the readiness of the government to respond to the threats that the United States might face. (428)

Epilogue

As this book goes to press, the United States is absorbing the horror of the terrorist attacks in London and asking questions about the security of our own public transportation systems. Within the past year, we have endured various new terrorist watch alerts, with special concern for our nation's financial infrastructure and prominent landmarks, while Congressional hearings and high-profile arrests throughout 2004 highlighted the complex and ongoing struggle to identify those who would do harm to America and prevent them from doing so. From a review of the 9/11 Commission Report and the recent public debate about the Commission's recommendations on reforming the intelligence community, we clearly have much to do to secure the homeland.

To further heighten our sensitivity to these issues, one of the most hotly contested presidential elections in recent memory has just taken place. As the campaign speeches indicated, homeland security was clearly a major topic during this election. However, neither political party has a perfect record in the area of national security nor can we expect them to. Indeed, as the chapters in this volume illuminate, political affiliation has little bearing on the responsibility or capability of Americans to secure our homeland. Clearly, homeland security requires an educated workforce, informed policy making, and a public-private partnership at all levels of commerce and public life, regardless of who wins a presidential election. By addressing the debate surrounding many of the most critical challenges facing the country today, this volume should hopefully prove useful to any administration.

Bibliography

Aguirre, B. E., D. Wenger, and G. Vigo. "A Test of the Emergent Norm Theory of Collective Behavior. " *Sociological Forum* 13 (1998): 301–20.

Alali, A. O., and K. K. Eke, eds. *Media Coverage of Terrorism: Methods of Diffusion.* London: Sage Publications, 1991.

Alexander, Y., and R. Latter, eds. *Terrorism and the Media.* New York: Brassey's, 1990.

Argyris, C. *Knowledge for Action: A Guide to Overcoming Barriers to Organizational Change.* San Francisco: Jossey-Bass, 1993.

Arquilla, J., and D. Ronfeldt, eds. *In Athena's Camp: Preparing for Conflict in the Information Age.* Santa Monica, CA: RAND Corp., 1998.

_____, eds. *Networks and Netwars: The Future of Terror, Crime, and Militancy.* Santa Monica, CA: RAND Corp., 2001.

Art, R. J., and P. M. Cronin. *The United States and Coercive Diplomacy.* Washington, DC: United States Institute of Peace, 2003.

Axelrod, R. *The Complexity of Cooperation*: *Agent-Based Models of Competition and Collaboration.* Princeton, NJ: Princeton University Press, 1997.

Axelrod, R., and M. Cohen. *Harnessing Complexity.* New York: The Free Press, 1999.

Baird, Z., and J. Barksdale. *Protecting America's Freedom in the Information Age,* Report of the Markle Foundation Task Force. New York: The Markle Foundation, 2002.

Bak, P., and K. Chen. "Self-Organized Criticality." *Scientific American* (1991): 46–53.

Benedetto, R. "Poll Finds Anthrax Fear but No Panic." *USA Today,* October 23, 2001.

Benjamin, D., and S. Simon. *The Age of Sacred Terror.* New York: Random House, 2002.

Bennett, P. 1999. "Understanding Responses to Risk: Some Basic Findings." In *Risk Communication and Public Health,* edited by P. Bennett and K. Calman, pp. 3–19. Oxford: Oxford University Press, 1999.

Birkler, John, et al. *The U. S. Coast Guard's Force Modernization Program.* Santa Monica, CA: RAND Corp., 2004. www.rand. org/publications/MG/MG114/ MG114. pdf.

Blaisse, M. "Reporters' Perspectives." In *Terrorism and the Media,* edited by David A. Paletz and Alex P. Schid. Newbury Park, CA: Sage Publications, 1992.

Brackett, D. W. *Holy Terror: Armageddon in Tokyo.* New York: Weatherhill, 1996.

Bremer, L. Paul, III. 2001. "A New Strategy for the New Face of Terrorism." *National Interest* 65-S (2001).

Bunker, R. J., ed. *Non-State Threats and Future Wars.* London: Frank Cass, 2003.

Burke, J. 2004. "Al Qaeda." *Foreign Policy* (May/June 2003).

Bushell, A., and B. Cunningham. "Suddenly the Pentagon Grants Access to the Action, but the Devil's in the Details." *Columbia Journalism Review*, March/April 2003.

Caffera, P. J. "The Air Industry's Worst Nightmare." *Salon,* November 25, 2002, www.salon. com.

Cambone, S. A. *A New Structure for National Security Policy Planning.* Washington, DC: Government Printing Office, 1996.

Campbell, K. M., and Michele A. Flournoy. *To Prevail: An American Strategy for the Campaign Against Terrorism.* Washington, DC: Center for Strategic and International Studies, 2001.

Carley, K., and J. Harrald. "Organizational Learning under Fire: Theory and Practice." *American Behavioral Scientist* 40 no. 3 (January 1997): 310–32.

Carr, C. "Terrorism as Warfare." *World Policy Journal* 13 (Winter 1996–1997): 1–12.

Carus, W. S. "The Rajneeshees." In *Toxic Terror: Assessing Terrorist Use of Chemical and Biological Weapons,* edited by Jonathan B. Tucker, pp. 55–70. Cambridge, MA: MIT Press, 2000.

Chang, N. *Silencing Political Dissent: How Post-September 11 Antiterrorism Measures Threaten Our Civil Liberties.* New York: Seven Stories Press, 2002.

Cilluffo, F. J. *Combating Chemical, Biological, Radiological, and Nuclear Terrorism: A Comprehensive Strategy,* Washington, DC: Center for Strategic and International Studies, 2001.

Cilluffo, F. J., and C. H. Gergely. "Information Warfare and Strategic Terrorism." *Terrorism and Political Violence* 9 no. 1 (Spring 1997): 84–94.

Cilluffo, F. J., S. Cardash, and G. N. Lederman. *Combating Chemical, Biological, Radiological, and Nuclear Terrorism: A Comprehensive Strategy: A Report of the CSIS Homeland Defense Project.* Washington, DC: Center for Strategic and International Studies Press, 2001.

Clarke, L. *Mission Improbable: Using Fantasy Documents to Tame Disaster.* Chicago: University of Chicago Press, 1999.

Clutterbuck, Richard. *Living with Terrorism.* London: Faber & Faber, 1975.

Codevilla, A. *Informing Statecraft: Intelligence for a New Century.* New York: The Free Press, 1992.

Cohen, W. M., and D. A. Levinthal. "Absorptive Capacity: A New Perspective on Learning and Innovation." *Administrative Science Quarterly* 35 (1990): 128–52.

Collins, J. M. "And the Walls Came Tumbling Down: Sharing Grand Jury Information with the Intelligence Community under the USA PATRIOT Act." *The American Criminal Law Review* 39 (Summer 2002): 1261–86.

Comfort, L. K. "Governance under Fire: Organizational Fragility in Complex Systems." In *Governance and Public Security*, pp. 113–27. Syracuse, N. : Syracuse University, 2002.

_____. "Interorganizational Coordination in Disaster Management: A Model for an Interactive Information System." National Science Foundation Grant #CES 88-04285. 1989. Final Report, submitted June 30, 1993.

_____. "Self Organization in Complex Systems." *Journal of Public Administration Research and Theory* 4 no. 3 (July 1994): 393–410.

_____. *Shared Risk: Complex Systems in Seismic Response.* Amsterdam: Pergamon, 1999.

Comfort, L. K., and Y. Sungu. "Organizational Learning from Seismic Risk: The 1999 Marmara and Duzce, Turkey Earthquakes." In *Managing Crises: Threats, Dilemmas and Opportunities*, edited by U. Rosenthal, L. Comfort and A. Boin, pp. 119–42.

Springfield, Ill. : Charles C. Springer Publishers, 2001.

Committee on the Role and Capabilities of U. S. Intelligence. *Preparing for the 21st Century: An Appraisal of U. S. Intelligence.* Washington, DC: GPO, 1996.

Cooper, R. "Response to Terror: The Anthrax Threat: Polls Find People Calm, Apprehensive." *Los Angeles Times,* October 28, 2001.

Covello, V. T., R. G. Peters, J. G. Wojtecki, et al. "Risk Communication, The West Nile Virus Epidemic, and Bioterrorism: Responding to the Communication Challenges Posed by the Intentional or Unintentional Release of a Pathogen in an Urban Setting." *Journal of Urban Health* 78 (2001): 382–91.

Crenshaw, M. "The Causes of Terrorism." *Comparative Politics* 13 (July 1981): 397–99.

Crosby, A. W. *America's Forgotten Pandemic: The Influenza of 1918.* Cambridge: Cambridge University Press, 1989.

Daalder I. H., and I. M. Destler. "Advisors, Czars and Councils: Organizing for Homeland Security." *The National Interest* (Summer 2002): 66–78.

Daalder, I. H., et al. *Protecting the American Homeland, One Year On.* Washington, DC: Brookings Institution, 2003.

Daalder, I. H., J. M. Lindsay, and J. B. Steinberg. *The Bush National Security Strategy: An Evaluation.* Washington, DC: Brookings Institution, 2002. www.brookings. edu/ views/papers/daalder/20021004. htm.

Dacey, R. F. "Computer Security: Progress Made, but Critical Federal Operations and Assets Remain at Risk." Statement before the Subcommittee on Government Efficiency, Financial Management and Intergovernmental Relations. Committee on Government Reform. House of Representatives. November 19, 2002.

Danzig, R. *Catastrophic Bioterrorism: What Is to Be Done?* Washington, DC: National Defense University Press, 2003.

DiGiovanni, C., Jr. 1999. "Domestic Terrorism with Chemical or Biological Agents: Psychiatric Aspects." *American Journal of Psychiatry* 156 (1999): 1500-1505.

Dobson, C., and R. Payne. *The Terrorists, Their Weapons, Leaders and Tactics.* New York: Facts on File, 1982.

Dynes, R. R., and K. J. Tierney, eds. *Disasters, Collective Behavior and Social Organization.* Newark, Del. : University of Delaware Press, 1994.

Edison, W. G. "Confusion, Controversy and Quarantine: The Muncie Smallpox Epidemic of 1893." *Indiana Magazine of History* 86 (1992): 374–98.

Edler Baumann, C. *Diplomatic Kidnappings: A Revolutionary Tactic of Urban Terrorism.* The Hague: Nijhoff, 1973.

Elliott, P. *Brotherhoods of Fear.* London: Blandford, 1998.

el-Nawawy, M., and A. Iskandar. *Al-Jazeera: How the Free Arab News Network Scooped the World and Changed the Middle East.* Boulder, Colorado: Westview Books, 2002.

Epstein, E. J. *The Assassination Chronicles: Inquest, Counterplot and Legend.* New York: Carrol and Graf, 1992.

Falkenrath, R. A. "Confronting Nuclear, Biological and Chemical Terrorism," *Survival* 40 no. 3 (Autumn 1998).

Federal Emergency Management Agency. *Federal Response Plan*. Washington, DC: FEMA, 1999.

Feldman, M., and J. G. March. "Information in Organizations as Signal and Symbol." *Administrative Science Quarterly* 26 (1981): 171–86.

Fields, G. "War Game Scenario Shows Economic Impact of Terror." *Wall Street Journal*, Dec. 4, 2002.

Fine, A., and M. Layton. "Lessons From the West Nile Viral Encephalitis Outbreak in New York City, 1999: Implications for Bioterrorism Preparedness." *Clinical Infectious Disease* 32 (2001): 277–82.

Fischer, H. W. *Response to Disaster: Fact Versus Fiction and its Perpetuation*. Lanham, Md. : University Press of America, 1994.

Flin, R. *Sitting in the Hot Seat: Leaders and Teams for Critical Incident Management*. New York: John Wiley and Sons, 1996.

_____. "Decision Making in Crises: The Piper Alpha Disaster." In *Managing Crises: Threats, Dilemmas, Opportunities,* edited by U. Rosenthal, A. Boin and L. K. Comfort, pp. 103–18. Springfield, Ill. : Charles C. Thomas Publishers, 2001.

Flynn, S. E. "America the Vulnerable." *Foreign Affairs* (January/February 2002): 60–74.

_____. *America the Vulnerable*. New York: Harper Collins, 2004.

_____. "Beyond Border Control." *Foreign Affairs* (November/December 2000): 57–68.

_____. "Border Security, A Decade of Malign Neglect." In *How Did This Happen? Terrorism and the New War,* edited by J. F. Hoge, Jr., and G. Rose. New York: Public Affairs, 2002.

_____. *Creating the Department of Homeland Security: Rethinking the Ends and Means*. Issue brief. Washington, DC: The Century Foundation Homeland Security Project, 2002.

Freimuth, V., H. W. Linnan, and P. Potter. 2000. "Communicating the Threat of Emerging Infections to the Public." *Emerging Infectious Diseases* 6 (2000): 337–47.

Gale, S., and L. Husick. "From MAD to MUD: Dealing with the New Terrorism." Foreign Policy Research Institute, February 2003.

Gavel, D. 2002. "Can Nuclear Weapons Be Put Beyond the Reach of Terrorists?" *Kennedy School of Government Bulletin,* Autumn 2002.

Gawronski, V. T., and R. S. Olson. "'Normal' Versus 'Special' Time Corruption: An Exploration of Mexican Attitudes." *Cambridge Review of International Affairs* 16 no. 1 (2000): 344–61.

Gede, T., M. N. Kosma and A. Chandra. *Developing Necessary and Constitutional Tools for Law Enforcement*. Federalist Society White Paper on Anti-Terrorism Legislation: Surveillance and Wiretap Laws, November 2001. www.fedsoc. org.

Gell-Mann, M. 1994. "Complex Adaptive Systems." In *Complexity: Metaphors, Models, and Reality*, edited by G. A. Cowan, D. Pines, D. and D. Meltzer. Reading, MA: Addison-Wesley, 1994.

Gentry, C. *J. Edgar Hoover: The Man and His Secrets*. New York: Plume, 1991.

George, A., et al. *Limits of Coercive Diplomacy*. Boston: Little, Brown, 1972.

Gerecht, R. M. "The Counterterrorist Myth." *Atlantic Monthly*, July/August 2001.

Gleick, E. "Human Error May Have Caused the Crash but the FAA May Also Tolerate High Risk for Low Cost Airlines." *Time*, May 27, 1996.

Goodman, P., L. Sproull and Associates. *Technology and Organizations*. San Francisco: Jossey-Bass Publishers, 1990.

Gould, J. B. "Playing With Fire: The Civil Liberties Implications of September 11th ." *Public Administration Review* 62 (September 2002): 74–79.

Goure, D., and J. M. Ranney. *Averting the Defense Train Wreck in the New Millennium,* Washington, DC: Center for Strategic and International Studies, 1999.

Graber, D. A. *Media Power in Politics.* Washington, DC: CQ Press, 1984.

Greenberg, J. "Suicide Planner Expresses Joy Over His Missions." *New York Times*, May 9, 2002.

Gunaratna, R. *Inside Al Qaeda: Global Network of Terror.* New York: Columbia Press, 2002

Gushulak, B. "Paradigms and Public Health: International Disease Control in the Information Age." *Canadian Journal of Public Health* 85 (1994): 374–77.

Halberstam, D. *War in Time of Peace.* New York: Simon and Schuster, 2001.

HAMAS Communique No. 125. *Filastin al-Muslimah* (London), August. FBIS-NES-95-152, August 8, 1995.

HAMAS statement. *BBC Summary of World Broadcasts*, July, 23, 2000.

Hamre, J. J. "Homeland Defense: A Net Assessment." In *Planning to Win,* edited by the Aspen Strategy Group. Colorado: Aspen Institute, 2002.

Hart, G., and W. B. Rudman. *America: Still Unprepared, Still in Danger.* New York: Council on Foreign Relations, December 2002.

Hayes-Roth, F., D. Waterman, and D. Lenat. *Building Expert Systems*. Reading, Mass. : Addison-Wesley Publishing Company, 1983.

Henderson, D. A. "The Looming Threat of Bioterrorism." *Science* 283 (1999): 279–82.

Hess, S., and M. Kalb, eds. *The Media and the War on Terrorism*. Washington, DC: Brookings Institution Press, 2003.

Heymann, D. L., D. Barakamfitiye, M. Szczeniowski, et al. "Ebola Hemorrhagic Fever: Lessons from Kikwit, Democratic Republic of the Congo." *Journal of Infectious Diseases.* Supplement 1. 179 (1999): S283–6.

Heymann, P. "Dealing with Terrorism: an Overview." *International Security* 26 no. 3 (2001): 24–39.

Hoffman, B. *'Holy Terror': The Implications of Terrorism Motivated by a Religious Imperative*. RAND Document P-7834. Santa Monica, CA: RAND Corp., 1993.

_____. *Inside Terrorism,* New York: Columbia University Press, 1998.

_____. *Terrorism and Weapons of Mass Destruction: An Analysis of Trends and Motivations*. RAND Document P-8039. Santa Monica, CA: RAND Corp., 1999.

Hoffman, F. G. "Transform *Security*, Not Just Defense," *Strategic Review,* Spring 2001.

Hoge, J. F., Jr., and G. Rose. *How Did This Happen? Terrorism and the New War*. New York: Public Affairs, 2002.

Holland, J. *Hidden Order: How Adaptation Builds Complexity*. Reading, Mass. : Addison Wesley Publishing Co., 1995.

Holloway, H. C., A. E. Norwood, C. S. Fullerton, et al. "The Threat of Biological Weapons: Prophylaxis and Mitigation of Psychological and Social Consequences." *Journal of the American Medical Association* 278 (1997): 425–27.

Homer-Dixon, T. *The Ingenuity Gap: Facing the Economic, Environmental, and Other Challenges of an Increasingly Complex and Unpredictable World*. New York: Vintage, 2002.

_____. "The Rise of Complex Terrorism." *Foreign Policy* (January/February 2002): pp. 52–56.

Horowitz, M., and D. Reiter. "When Does Aerial Bombing Work? Quantitative Empirical Tests, 1917–1999." *Journal of Conflict Resolution* 45 (April 2001): 147–73.

Hroub, K. *Hamas: Political Thought and Practice.* Washington, DC: Institute for Palestine Studies, 2000.

Hugh-Jones, M. E. 1976. "Epidemiological Studies on the 1967–1968 Foot-and-Mouth Disease Epidemic: The Reporting of Suspected Disease." *Journal of Hygiene* (London) 77 (1976): 299–306.

Huntington, S. P. *The Third Wave: Democratization in the Twentieth Century.* Norman: University of Oklahoma Press, 1991.

Inbar, E. *Rabin and Israel's National Security.* Baltimore: John's Hopkins University Press, 1999.

Institute for Counter-Terrorism. *Countering Suicide Terrorism.* Herzliya, Israel: ICT, 2001.

Isenberg, D. *Less Talk, More Walk: Strengthening Homeland Security Now.* Washington, DC: Center for Defense Information, 2002.

Jenkins, B. M. *International Terrorism.* Washington, DC: RAND Corp., 1985.

_____. *Protecting Public Surface Transportation against Terrorism and Serious Crime: An Executive Overview.* San Jose: The Mineta Transportation Institute, 2001.

_____. "Will Terrorists Go Nuclear?" RAND Report P-5541. Santa Monica, CA: RAND Corp., 1975.

Jenkins, B. M., and L. N. Gersten. *Protecting Public Surface Transportation Against Terrorism and Serious Crime: Continuing Research on Best Security Practices.* San Jose: Norman Y. Mineta International Institute for Surface Transportation Studies, 2001.

Jenkins, B. M., et al. *Protecting Surface Transportation: Systems and Patrons from Terrorist Activities: Case Studies of Best Security Practices and a Chronology of Attacks.* San Jose: Norman Y. Mineta International Institute for Surface Transportation Studies, 1997.

Jervis, R. *Perception and Misperception in International Politics.* Princeton, NJ: Princeton University Press, 1976.

Johnson, N. R. 1987. "Panic and the breakdown of social order: popular myth, social theory, and empirical evidence." *Sociological Focus* 20 (1987): 171–83.

Jukes, S. "Real Time Responsibility: Journalism's Challenges in an Instantaneous Age." *Harvard International Review,* Summer 2002.

Karasik, T. *Toxic Warfare.* Santa Monica, CA: RAND Corp., 2002.

Kartez, J. D., and W. J. Kelly. 1"Research Based Disaster Planning: Conditions for Implementation." In *Managing Disaster: Strategies and Policy Perspectives,* edited by L. K. Comfort . Durham, NC: Duke University Press, 1988, pp. 126–46.

Kaufmann, C. D. "Possible and Impossible Solutions to Ethnic Civil Wars." *International Security* 20 (Spring 1996): 136–75.

_____. "When All Else Fails: Ethnic Population Transfers and Partitions in the Twentieth Century." *International Security* 23 (Fall 1998): 120–56.

Kauffman, S. A. *The Origins of Order: Self-Organization and Selection in Evolution.* New York: Oxford University Press, 1993.

Kauvar, G. B. "Transportation Security." *Issues in Science and Technology,* Fall 2002, p. 6.

Kay, D. "WMD Terrorism: Hype or Reality." In *The Terrorism Threat and US Government Response: Operational and Organizational Factors,* edited by James M. Smith and William C. Thomas. Boulder, CO: US Air Force Academy, INSS Book Series, 2001.

Kidwell, D. "Drug Ring Busted at Airport," *Miami Herald,* August 26, 1999.

Klein, G. A. "A Recognition-Primed Decision Making (RPD) Model of Rapid Decision Making." In *Decision Making in Action: Models and Methods,* edited by G. Klein, J. Orasanu, R. Calderwood, and C. Zsambok, pp. 138–47. Norwood, NJ: Ablex Publishing Corporation, 1993.

Kosiak, S. M. *Funding for Defense, Homeland Security and Combating Terrorism Since 9-11: Where Has All the Money Gone?* Washington, DC: Center for Strategic and Budgetary Assessments, 2003.

_____. *Overview of the Administration's FY2005 Request for Homeland Security.* Washington, DC: Center for Strategic and Budgetary Assessments, 2004.

Kovar, M. G., G. Hendershot, and E. Mathis. 1989. "Older People in the United States Who Receive Help with Basic Activities of Daily Living." *American Journal of Public Health* 79 (1989): 778–79.

Kramer, M. "Fundamentalist Islam at Large: Drive for Power." *Middle East Quarterly* 3 (June 1996): 37–49.

_____. "The Moral Logic of Hizballah." In *Origins of Terrorism,* edited by Walter Reich. New York: Cambridge University Press, 1990.

Kratzer, R. M., and B. Kratzer. "How Newspapers Decided to Run Disturbing 9/11 Photos." *Newspaper Research Journal* 24 no. 1 (Winter 2003).

Kunreuther, H., G. Heal, and P. Orszag. "Interdependent Security: Implications for Homeland Security and Other Areas." Policy Brief 108, 2002. www.brookings. org/comm/policybriefs/pb108. htm.

Kydd, A., and B. F. Walter. 2002. "Sabotaging the Peace: The Politics of Extremist Violence." *International Organization* 56 no. 2 (2002): 263–96.

Laqueur, W. *The Age of Terrorism.* Boston: Little, Brown, 1987.

Lavoy, P. R., S. D. Sagan and J. J. Wirtz, eds. *Planning the Unthinkable: How New Powers Will Use Nuclear, Biological and Chemical Weapons.* Ithaca: Cornell University Press, 2000.

Lebow, R. N. *Between Peace and War: The Nature of International Crisis.* Baltimore, MD: Johns Hopkins University Press, 1981.

Lee, J. "Progress Seen in Border Tests of ID System." *New York Times,* February 7, 2003.

Leitenberg, M. "The Widespread Distortion of Information on the Efforts to Produce Biological Warfare Agents by the Japanese Aum Shinrikyo Group: A Case Study in the Serial Propagation of Misinformation." *Terrorism and Political Violence* 11 no. 4 (Winter 1999).

Levine, S. "Disseminating Dread: Pranksters, Disgruntled Americans Perpetrate Hoaxes." *Washington Post,* October 26, 2001.

Lewis, B. *The Assassins.* New York: Basic Books, 1968.

Lowe, G., M. R. Evans, and P. Myers. "Help—We Need a Helpline! A Public Health Audit Case Study." *Journal of Public Health Medicine* 22 (2000): 129–32.

Lowry, R. "A Better Bureau." *National Review* 54 (July 1, 2002).

Loy J. M., and R. G. Ross. "Global Trade: America's Achilles' Heel." *Defense Horizons No. 7*. Washington, DC: Center for Technology and National Security Policy, 2002.

Makovsky, D., and A. Pinkas. "Rabin: Killing Civilians Won't Kill the Negotiations." *Jerusalem Post*, April 13, 1994.

Markle Foundation. *Creating a Trusted Network for Homeland Security*. Second Report of the Markle Foundation Task Force. Washington, DC: Markle Foundation, 2003.

Merari, A. "The Readiness to Kill and Die: Suicidal Terrorism in the Middle East." In *Origins of Terrorism* edited by Walter Reich. New York: Cambridge University Press, 1990.

Sloan, M. "Responses to Media Coverage of Terrorism." *The Journal of Conflict Resolution* 44 no. 4 (August 2000): 508–22.

Mileti, D., ed. *Disasters by Design: A Reassessment of Natural Hazards in the United States*. Washington, DC: Joseph Henry Press, 1999.

Miller, A. H. "Terrorism, the Media and the Law: A Discussion of the Issues." In *Terrorism, the Media and the Law* edited by Abraham H. Miller. Dobbs Ferry, NY: Transnational Publishers, 1982.

Miller, G. "The Magical Number Seven, Plus or Minus Two: Some Limits on Our Capacity for Processing Information." In *Psychology of Communication,* pp. 14–44. New York: Basic Books, 1967.

Mishal, S., and A. Sela. *The Palestinian Hamas*. New York: Columbia University Press, 2000.

Mohle-Boetani, J. C., S. B. Werner, S. H. Waterman, et al. "The Impact of Health Communication and Enhanced Laboratory-based Surveillance on Detection of Cyclosporiasis Outbreaks in California." *Emerging Infectious Diseases* 6 (2000): 200–203.

Nacos, B. L. *Mass-Mediated Terrorism: The Central Role of the Media in Terrorism and Counterterrorism*. New York: Rowman & Littlefield Publishers, 2002.

_____. Terrorism as Breaking News: Attack on America. *Political Science Quarterly,* 118, no. 1, 2003.

National Academy of Sciences. "Assessment of Technologies Deployed to Improve Aviation Security: Second Report: Progress Toward Objectives." 2002. Summary available at www.books. nap. edu/books/NI000396/htm/7. html.

National Commission on Terrorism. *Countering the Changing Threat of International Terrorism*. Washington, DC: GPO, 2000.

National Commission on Terrorist Attacks Upon the United States. *The 9/11 Commission Report*. New York: Norton, 2004.

National Research Council. Committee on Science and Technology for Countering Terrorism. *Making the Nation Safer, the Role of Science and Technology in Countering Terrorism*. Washington, DC: National Academy Press, 2002.

Nelson, J. "U. S. Government Secrecy and the Current Crackdown on Leaks." Working paper. The Joan Shorenstein Center on the Press, Politics, and Public Policy. Fall 2002.

Newell, A., and H. A. Simon. *Human Problem Solving*. Englewood Cliffs, NJ: Prentice Hall, 1972.

Niebuhr, R. *Moral Man and Immoral Society*. New York: Scribner, 1960.

Noji, E. K. "Disaster epidemiology." *Emergency Medical Clinicians of North America* 14 (1996): 289–300.

Nusse, A. *Muslim Palestine: The Ideology of Hamas*. Amsterdam: Harwood Academic, 1998.

O'Harrow, R., Jr. "Intricate Screening of Fliers in Works." *Washington Post*, February 1, 2003.

O'Neill, R. *Suicide Squads*. New York: Ballantine Books, 1981.

O'Toole, T. "Smallpox: An Attack Scenario." *Emerging Infectious Diseases* 5 (1999): 540–46.

Ostrom, E. "A Behavioral Approach to the Rational Choice Theory of Collective Action." 1998.

Paletz, D. A. and A. P. Schid, eds. *Terrorism and the Media*. Newbury Park, CA: Sage Publications, 1992.

Pape, R. A. *Bombing to Win: Air Power and Coercion in War*. Ithaca, NY: Cornell University Press, 1996.

_____. "Why Economic Sanctions Do Not Work." *International Security* 22 (Fall 1997): 90–136.

Parachini, J. V. "Comparing Motives and Outcomes of Mass Casualty Terrorism Involving Conventional and Unconventional Weapons." *Studies in Conflict & Terrorism* 24 (2001).

Pasternak, J. "FAA, Airlines Stalled Major Security Plans." *New York Times*, December 14, 2002.

Peitgen, H., H. Jurgens, and D. Saupe. *Chaos and Fractals: New Frontiers of Science*. New York: Springer-Verlag, 1992.

Picard. R. G. *Media Portrayals of Terrorism: Function and Meaning of News Coverage*. Ames: Iowa State University Press, 1993.

Pillar, P. 2001. *Terrorism and U. S. Foreign Policy*. Washington, DC: The Brookings Institution Press, 2001.

Platt, R., et al. *Disasters and Democracy*. Washington, DC: Island Press, 1999.

Polzin, S. "Security Considerations in Transportation Planning." *Southeastern Transportation Center.* 2002.

Post, J. M. "Terrorist Psycho-Logic: Terrorist Behavior as a Product of Psychological Forces." In *Origins of Terrorism*, edited by Walter Reich. New York: Cambridge University Press, 1990.

Povich, E., and T. Brune. "America's Ordeal: Anxiety on Capitol Hill. *Newsday,* October 18, 2001.

Prigogine, I., and I. Stengers. *Order Out of Chaos*. 1977. Rpt. New York: Bantam Press, 1984.

Przeworski, A., M. E. Alvarez, Jose Antonio Cheibub, and Fernando Limongi. *Democracy and Development: Political Institutions and Well-Being in the World, 1950–1990*. Cambridge: Cambridge University Press, 2000.

Public Citizen. "Delay, Dilute and Discard: How the Airline Industry and the FAA have stymied Aviation Security Recommendations." 2001. www.citizen. org.

Quarantelli, E. L. "Basic Themes Derived from Survey Findings on Human Behavior in the Mexico City Earthquake." *International Sociology* 11 (1996): 481–99.

_____, ed. *What Is a Disaster? Perspectives on the Question*. New York: Routledge, 1998.

_____. "The Sociology of Panic." In *International Encyclopedia of the Social and Behavioral Sciences* edited by N. Smelser and P. B. Baltes, pp. 11020–30.

New York. : Pergamon, 2001,

Quintos de Jesus, M. *Media Coverage of Terrorism: The Philippine Experience,* Center for Media Freedom and Responsibility, 2002.

Rapoport, DC *Assassination and Terrorism.* Toronto: CBC Merchandising, 1971.

_____. "Fear and Trembling: Terrorism in Three Religious Traditions." *American Political Science Review* 78 (September 1984): 655–77.

Reagan, R. *An American Life.* New York: Simon and Schuster, 1990.

Reich, W., ed. *Origins of Terrorism.* New York: Cambridge University Press, 1990.

Risse, G. B. "Revolt Against Quarantine: Community Responses to the 1916 Polio Epidemic, Oyster Bay, New York." *Transactions and Studies of the College of Physicians of Philadelphia* 14 (February 1992): 23–50.

Rose, G. "It Could Happen Here: Facing the New Terrorism." *Foreign Affairs,* March–April 1999.

Rosenberg, C. E. "What is an Epidemic? AIDS in Historical Perspective." *Daedalus* 118 (1989): 1–17.

Sachs, Z., Y. L. Danon, R. Dycian, et al. "Community Coordination and Information Centers During the Persian Gulf War." *Israeli Journal of Medical Science* 27 (1991): 696–700.

Sallinger, R. 2003. "Explosive Traces Evade DIA Security." News4, www.news4Colorado. com/global/story. asp?s=1142555.

Sauvagnargues, P. "Opposition Candidate." Agence France Presse, August 14, 1994.

Schalk, P. "Resistance and Martyrdom in the Process of State Formation of Tamililam." in *Martyrdom and Political Resistance*, edited by Joyed Pettigerw, pp. 61–83. Amsterdam: VU University Press, 1997.

Schelling, T. *Arms and Influence.* New Haven, Conn. : Yale University Press, 1966.

Schmid, A. P., and A. J. Jongman. *Political Terrorism.* New Brunswick, N. J. : Transaction Books, 1988.

Schoch-Spana, M. "Implications of Pandemic Influenza for Bioterrorism Response." *Clinical Infectious Diseases* 31 (2000): 1409–13.

Schwartz, J. "Efforts to Calm the Nation's Fears Spin out of Control." *New York Times,* October 28, 2001.

Sciolino, E. "Saudi Warns Bush." *New York Times,* January 27, 2002.

Select Committee to Study Governmental Operations with Respect to Intelligence Activities. *Intelligence Activities and the Rights of Americans, Final Report of the Senate Select Committee to Study Governmental Operations with Respect to Intelligence Activities.* 94th Congress, 2nd Session, 1976.

Shaffert, R. W. *Media Coverage and Political Terrorists: A Quantitative Analysis.* New York: Praeger, 1992.

Shears, P. "Epidemiology and Infection in Famine and Disasters." *Epidemiological Infections* 107 (1991): 241–51.

Shiqaqi, K., et al. *The Israeli-Palestinian Peace Process.* Portland, OR: Sussex Academic Press, 2002.

Shulsky, A. N., and G. J. Schmitt. *Silent Warfare: Understanding the World of Intelligence.* 2nd ed. Washington DC: Brassey's, 1993.

Simon, H. A. *The Sciences of the Artificial.* 2nd ed. Cambridge, MA: MIT Press, 1981.

Simon, S., and D. Benjamin. "America and the New Terrorism." *Survival* 42 no. 1 (Spring 2000).

Slovic, P. *The Perception of Risk.* London: Earthscan Publications Inc., 2000.

Spencer, J., and C. Crossen. "Fear Factors: Why Do Americans Feel that Danger Lurks Everywhere?" *The Wall Street Journal,* April 24, 2003.

Sprinzak, E. "Rational Fanatics," *Foreign Policy* 120 (September/October 2000): 66–73.

St. John, P. *Air Piracy, Airport Security, and International Terrorism.* New York: Quorum Books, 1991.

Stern, J. "The Protean Enemy." *Foreign Affairs,* July–August 2003.

_____. *The Ultimate Terrorists.* Cambridge: Harvard University Press, 1999.

Strobel, W. P. "The CNN Effect." *American Journalism Review* 18 (May 1996).

Strong, P. "Epidemic Psychology: A Model." *Sociology of Health and Illness* 12 (1990): 249–59.

Suzman, R. *Older Americans 2000: Key Indicators of Well-being.* Hyattsville, MD: National Center for Health Statistics, 2000.

Sylves, R. T., and W. L. Waugh, Jr., eds. *Disaster Management in the U. S. and Canada: The Politics, Policymaking, Administration, and Analysis of Emergency Management.* 2nd ed. Springfield, IL: Charles C. Thomas, Publisher, 1996.

Szyliowicz, J., and P. Viotti. "Transportation Security." *Transportation Quarterly* 51 (1997): 79–95.

Task Force on National Security in the Information Age. *Protecting America's Freedom in the Information Age.* Washington, DC: Markle Foundation., 2002.

Taylor, E. R. "Are We Prepared for Terrorism Using Weapons of Mass Destruction: Government's Half Measures." *Policy Analysis* 387 (2002): 1–19.

Transportation Research Board. *Deterrence, Protection, and Preparation: The New Transportation Security Imperative.* Special Report 270. Washington, DC: TRB, 2002.

Tuchman, B. W. *The Proud Tower.* New York: Macmillan, 1966.

Tucker, J. B. "National Health and Medical Services Response to Incidents of Chemical and Biological Terrorism." *Journal of the American Medical Association* 278 (1997): 362–68.

_____, ed. *Toxic Terror: Assessing Terrorist Use of Chemical and Biological Weapons.* Cambridge, MA: MIT Press, 2000.

Tyson, A. "Al Qaeda, Resilient and Organized," *Christian Science Monitor,* March 7, 2002.

U. S. Department of State. "Guidelines for United States Government Spokespersons during Terrorist Incidents." In *Terrorism: The Media and the Law,* edited by Abraham H. Miller. Dobbs Ferry, NY: Transnational Publishers, Inc., 1982.

U. S. Department of Transportation. *Audit of Federal Aviation Administration's Airport Security Program.* Washington, DC: U. S. DOT, 1993

U. S. Environmental Protection Agency. 2003. *EPA Needs a Better Strategy to Measure Changes in the Security of the Nation's Water Infrastructure.* Report No. 2003-M-00016. September 11, 2003, www.epa. gov/oig/reports/2003/HomelandSecurity Report2003M00016. pdf.

U. S. General Accounting Office. *Transportation Security: Post-September 11th Initiatives and Long-Term Challenges.* GAO 03-616T. Washington, DC: GAO, 2003.

Vatis, M. *Cyber Attacks during The War on Terrorism: A Predictive Analysis.* Hanover, N. H. : Institute for Security Technology Studies at Dartmouth College, 2001.

Wald, M. L. "A Plan for Screening at Airports Is Dropped." *New York Times,* July 25, 2004, section 5.

Waterman, S. Huge U. S. Aviation Gap. UPI, Washington Politics and Policy Desk, 2003. www.upi. com.

Water Science and Technology Board. *A Review of the EPA Water Security Research and Technical Support Action Plan: Parts I and II.* 2003, www.nap. edu/books/ 0309089824/html.

Weick, K. "The Collapse of Sensemaking in Organizations: The Mann Gulch Disaster." *Administrative Science Quarterly* 22 no. 3 (1993): 606–39.

_____. *Making Sense of the Organization.* Malden, MA: Blackwell Business, 2001.

_____. *Sensemaking in Organizations.* Thousand Oaks, CA: Sage Publications, 1995.

Weick, K., and K. Roberts. "Collective Mind and Organizational Reliability: The Case of Flight Operations on an Aircraft Carrier Deck." In *Organizational Learning*, edited by M. D. Cohen and L. S. Sproull, pp. 330–58. Thousand Oaks, CA: Sage Publications, 1996,

Weick, K. and K. Sutliffe, *Managing the Unexpected*: *Assuring High Performance in an Age of Complexity.* San Francisco: Jossey Bass, 2001.

Wilson, G. I., J. P. Sullivan, and H. Kempfer. "Fourth-Generation Warfare: It's Here, and We Need New Intelligence-Gathering Techniques for Dealing With It." *Armed Forces Journal International* (October 2002): 56–62.

Winner, L. 2002. "Complexity, Trust and Terror." *Tech Knowledge Revue* 3. 1. www. praxagora. com/stevet/netfuture/2002/Oct2202_137. html#1.

World Health Organization (WHO). *Health Aspects of Chemical and Biological Weapons.* 2nd ed. Geneva, Switzerland: WHO, 2001.

World Islamic Front. "Jihad Against Jews and Crusaders." February 23, 1998.

Wright, R. *Sacred Rage*. New York: Simon and Schuster, 2001.

Wyatt, H. W. "The Role and Responsibility of the Media in the Event of a Bioterrorist Act." *Journal of Public Health Management Practices* 6 (2000): 63–67.

Recommended Online Resources

Annotated Research Bibliographies

Annotated Bibliography of Government Documents Related to the Threat of Terrorism and the
Attacks of September 11, 2001.
www.odl.state.ok.us/usinfo/terrorism/911.htm

Bibliography of Future Trends in Terrorism: A Report by the Library of Congress, Federal
Research Division.
www.loc.gov/rr/frd/pdf-files/Future_trends.pdf

Center for Terrorism Studies (Maxwell Air Force Base)
c21.maxwell.af.mil/cts-ref.htm#bibliographies

Terrorism and Counterterrorism: An Annotated Bibliography (Dr. James Forest, USMA
Combating Terrorism Center).
www.teachingterror.com/bibliography

University of Texas at Arlington, Bibliography on Terrorism and Homeland Security Research
Resources.
libraries.uta.edu/dillard/subfiles/bibterror.htm

Primary Documents

AOPA Online. "General Aviation and Homeland Security" and "Regulatory Brief: FAA and TSA
Security Direct Final Rules," 2003. www.aopa.org/whatsnew/regulatory/reg_security.html

Federal Emergency Management Agency, U.S. Department of Homeland Security. Federal
Response Plan: ESF#11-Food Annex.
www.fema.gov/rr/frp/frpesf11.shtm

Federal Emergency Management Agency. Emergency Food and Water Supplies.
www.fema.gov/library/emfdwtr.shtm

Homeland Security Funding, FY 2004
www.whitehouse/omb/budget/fy2004/tables.html

ICAO. "Aviation Security Plan of Action," 2002.
www.icao.org

Joint Inquiry into Intelligence Community Activities before and after Terrorist Attacks of
September 11, 2001, July 2003.
www.gpoaccess.gov/serialset/creports/911.html

National Invasive Species Council (NISC). "National Management Plan: Executive Summary."
www.invasivespecies.gov/council/execsumm.shtml

Office of Homeland Security (OHS), "National Strategy for Homeland Security," July 2002.
 www.dhs.gov/interweb/assetlibrary/nat_strat_hls.pdf.
The Maritime and Transportation Security Act.
 www.uscg.mil/hq/g-m/mp/mtsa.shtml
The National Strategy for the Physical Protection of Critical Infrastructures and Key Assets.
 www.whitehouse.gov/pcipb/physical.html
The National Security Strategy of the United States of America.
 www.whitehouse.gov/nsc/nss.html
The National Strategy for Combating Terrorism.
 www.whitehouse.gov/news/releases/2003/02/20030214-7.html
The National Strategy for Homeland Security.
 www.whitehouse.gov/homeland/book/index.html
The National Strategy to Secure Cyberspace.
 www.whitehouse.gov/pcipb
The White House. "Protection Against Unconventional Threats to the Homeland and Americans
 Overseas." Presidential Decision Directive-62 (PDD-62).
 www.ojp.usdoj.gov/odp/docs/pdd62.htm
The White House. "The Clinton Administration's Policy on Critical Infrastructure Protection:
 Presidential Decision Directive-63."
 www.ciao.gov/resource/paper598.html
The White House. "United States Policy on Counterterrorism," Presidential Decision Directive-39
 (PDD-39).
 www.ojp.usdoj.gov/odp/docs/pdd39.htm
The White House. December 17, 2003 Homeland Security Presidential Directive/Hspd-7, Critical
 Infrastructure Identification, Prioritization, and Protection.
 www.whitehouse.gov/news/releases/2003/12/20031217-5.html
The White House. Securing the Homeland and Strengthening the Nation.
 www.whitehouse.gov/omb/fy2004/homeland.html
U.S. Environmental Protection Agency. *Strategic Plan for Homeland Security,* 2002.
 www.epa.gov/epahome/downloads/epa_homeland_security_strategic_plan.pdf
U.S. Food and Drug Administration Center for Food Safety and Applied Nutrition. Public Health
 Security and Bioterrorism, Preparedness and Response Act of 2002 (PL107-188).
 www.cfsan.fda.gov/~dms/sec-ltr.html#sec302
United States Government Interagency Domestic Terrorism Concept of Operations Plan.
 www.fbi.gov/publications/conplan/conplan.pdf

Online Reports

9-11 Commission Report (National Commission on Terrorist Attacks Upon the United States).
 www.9-11commission.gov
 www.gpoaccess.gov/911
2003 Annual U.S. State Department Report, Patterns of Global Terrorism, April 2004.
 www.state.gov/s/ct/rls/pgtrpt/2003
A Military Assessment of the al Qaeda Training Tapes, June 28, 2003
 www.strategypage.com/articles/tapes/5.asp
After September 11th Essays, by the Social Science Research Council.
 www.ssrc.org/sept11/essays
Al-Salama, Abdullah Ali. *Military Espionage in Islam.*
 www.skfriends.com/bin-laden-terrorist-manual.htm

CDI Primer: Terrorist Finances.
 www.cdi.org/terrorism/finance_primer-pr.cfm
Centers for Disease Control and Prevention Centers for Public Health Preparedness. Programs in
 Brief.
 www.cdc.gov/programs/bio9.htm
Counterterrorism Intelligence Capabilities and Performance Prior to 9/11.
 www.fas.org/irp/congress/2002_rpt/hpsci_ths0702.html
Creating a Trusted Network for Homeland Security: A Report by the Markle Foundation Task
 Force on National Security in the Information Age, December 2003.
 www.markletaskforce.org
Critical Infrastructure Assurance Office. *Report of the President of the United States on the Status
 of Federal Critical Infrastructure Protection Activities.* January 2001.
 www.ciao.gov/resource/cip_2001_congrept.pdf
CRS Electronic Briefing Book on Terrorism.
 www.congress.gov/brbk/html/ebter1.html
Cybersecurity: Getting it Right, by Daniel Wolf, U.S. National Security Agency.
 www.nsa.gov/ia/Wolf_SFR_22_July_2003.pdf
Dark Winter: Bioterrorism Exercise, 2001. Johns Hopkins Center for Civilian Biodefense, Center
 for Strategic and International Studies, ANSER, et al.
 www.hopkins-biodefense.org/dark winter.pdf
Deepwater modernization program.
 www.uscg.mil/deepwater
Department of Health and Human Services. Hospital preparedness for mass casualties: Final
 report (August 2000).
 www.ahapolicyforum.org/policyresources/MOdisaster.asp
Dobbs, M. "A renaissance for U.S. civil defense?" *Journal of Homeland Confronting Biological
 Weapons,* January 15, 2001. www.homelandsecurity.org/journal/Articles/Dobbs_July01.htm
Drug Enforcement Agency (DEA). "Drug Trafficking in the United States," 2003.
 www.dea.gov./concern/drug_trafficking.html
Freeman, Lawrence. "Out of Nowhere—Bin Laden's Grievances," BBC Online, 2001.
 www.bbc.co.uk/history/war/sept_11/build_up_05.shtml
Garden, Timothy. "Security and the War Against Terrorism," 2002.
 www.tgarden.demon.co.uk/writings/articles/2002/020320riia.html
Gilmore Commission Reports on Terrorism.
 www.rand.org/nsrd/terrpanel
Gilmore Commission. "First Annual Report to the President and the Congress of the Advisory
 Panel to Assess Domestic Response Capabilities for Terrorism Involving Weapons of Mass
 Destruction, I: Assessing the Threat." (December 15, 1999).
 www.rand.org/nsrd/terrpanel/terror.pdf
Hart, Gary and Warren B. Rudman, *America Still Unprepared—America Still in Danger,* New
 York: Council on Foreign Relations, 2002.
 www.cfr.org/pdf/Homeland_Security_TF.pdf
Media Interactions with the Public in Emergency Situations: Four Case Studies.
 www.loc.gov/rr/frd/pdf-files/Media_Interaction.pdf
Myers, Richard B. "Fighting Terrorism in an Information Age." U.S. Department of State,
 International Information Programs, August 19, 2002.
 usinfo.state.gov/regional/nea/sasia/text/0819info.htm
National Center for Disaster Preparedness, Mailman School of Public Health, Columbia
 University, "How Americans Feel About Terrorism and Security: Two Years After 9/11."
 www.ncdp.mailman.columbia.edu/How_Americans_Feel_About_Terrorism.pdf

National Infrastructure Protection Center. "Homeland Security Information Update: Al Qaeda Chemical, Biological, Radiological, and Nuclear Threat and Basic Countermeasures," *Information Bulletin* 03-003, February 12, 2003. www.nipc.gov/publications/infobulletins/2003/ib03-003.htm

Newsome, Bruce. *Mass-Casualty Terrorism: Second Quarterly Forecast by the University of Reading Terrorism Forecasting Group,* June 13, 2003. www.rdg.ac.uk/GSEIS/University_of_Reading_Terrorism_Forecast_2003Q2.pdf

Parachini, John. "Combating Terrorism: Assessing Threats, Risk Management, and Establishing Priorities." Statement before the House Government Reform Subcommittee on National Security, Veterans Affairs, and International Relations, July 26, 2000. cns.miis.edu/pubs/reports/paraterr.htm

Phelps, Mark. "Do SAMs Pose a Real Threat to Civil Aviation?" *Aviation International News,* 2003. www.iasa.com.au/folders/Security_Issues/dosamspose.html

President's Commission on Critical Infrastructure. National Strategy for the Physical Protection of Critical Infrastructure and Key Assets, 2003. www.iwar.org.uk/eip/resources/physical-cip/national-strategy.htm

Project Megiddo: An FBI Strategic Assessment of the Potential for Domestic Terrorism. permanent.access.gpo.gov/lps3578/www.fbi.gov/library/megiddo/megiddo.pdf

Protecting America's Freedom in the Information Age: A Report by the Markle Foundation Task Force on National Security in the Information Age, October 2002. www.markletaskforce.org

Report by the Subcommittee on Terrorism and Homeland Security, House Permanent Select Committee on Intelligence. intelligence.house.gov

Specially Designated Nationals (SDN) and Blocked Persons List (U.S. Dept. of Treasury). www.ustreas.gov/offices/enforcement/ofac/sdn/index.html

Terror.net: How Modern Terrorism Uses the Internet, by Gabriel Weimann. www.usip.org/pubs/specialreports/sr116.html

Terrorism and Organized Crime in the TriBorder Region of Latin America. www.loc.gov/rr/frd/pdf-files/TerrOrgCrime_TBA.pdf

Terrorist Financing Rewards Program (U.S. Dept. of Treasury). www.ustreas.gov/rewards/terrorismlist.html

Terrorism: Near Eastern Groups and State Sponsors. www.fas.org/irp/crs/RL31119.pdf

Terrorism, the Future, and U.S. Foreign Policy. www.fas.org/irp/crs/IB95112.pdf

Tyson, Ann. "Al Qaeda Broken, but Dangerous," *Christian Science Monitor,* June 24, 2002. www.csmonitor.com/2002/0624/p01s02-usgn.htm

U.S. Commission on National Security/21st Century. "Road Map for National Security: Imperative for Change." Phase III report, 2001. www.nssg.gov/PhaseIIIFR.pdf

U.S. Department of Homeland Security. Make a Kit. www.ready.gov/water_food.html

U.S. General Accounting Office, "Combating Terrorism: Analysis of Federal Counterterrorist Exercises," *Briefing Report to Congressional Committees,* GAO/NSIAD-99-157BR. www.gao.gov/archive/1999/ns99157b.pdf

Whine, Michael. "The New Terrorism," 2002. www.ict.org.il/articles/articledet.cfm?articleid=427

Who Becomes a Terrorist and Why? The Sociology and Psychology of Terrorism. www.loc.gov/rr/frd/pdf-files/Soc_Psych_of_Terrorism.pdf

Yost, Patrick M. and Harjit Singh Sandhu. "The *hawala* Alternative Remittance System and its Role in Money Laundering," Interpol General Secretariat, January 2002. www.interpol.int/Public/FinancialCrime/MoneyLaundering/hawala/default.asp.

Recommended Web Sites

A Citizen's Resource Website, U.S. Department of Homeland Security.
    www.ready.gov
America's War Against Terrorism (University of Michigan).
    www.lib.umich.edu/govdocs/usterror.html
ANSER Institute For Homeland Security.
    www.homelandsecurity.org
Behind the Homefront (The Reporters Committee for Freedom of the Press).
    www.rcfp.org/behindthehomefront
British American Security Information Council: Network on European and Transatlantic Security.
    www.basicint.org/netsindx.htm
CIA Factbook on Intelligence.
    www.cia.gov/cia/publications/facttell/index.html
Center for Arms Control and Non-Proliferation: Terrorism Prevention.
    www.armscontrolcenter.org/terrorism/handbook
Center for Defense Information: Terrorism Project.
    www.cdi.org/terrorism
Center for Nonproliferation Studies: Terrorism.
    cns.miis.edu/research/terror.htm
Center for the Study of Terrorism and Political Violence.
    www.st-and.ac.uk/academic/intrel/research/cstpv
Combating Terrorism Center, U.S. Military Academy.
    www.dean.usma.edu/departments/sosh/CTC
Countering the Changing Threat of International Terrorism.
    www.fas.org/irp/threat/commission.html
Customs-Trade Partnership Against Terrorism (C-TPAT).
    www.customs.gov/xp/cgov/import/commercial_enforcement/ctpat.html
FEMA Emergency Management Library.
    www.fema.gov/gems/index.jsp
George Washington University: The National Security Archive.
    www.gwu.edu/~nsarchiv
GlobalSecurity.org.
    www.globalsecurity.org
Government Emergency Telecommunications Services (GETS).
    www.ncs.gov/nc-pp/html/new-gets.htm
Government Publications on Terrorism.
    www.lib.umd.edu/GOV/terrorism.html
Henry L. Stimson Center: Chemical and Biological Terrorism.
    www.stimson.org/cwc/terror.htm
Homeland Security Project.
    www.homelandsec.org
International Policy Institute for Counter-Terrorism.
    www.ict.org.il

International War on Terrorism (Air War College, U.S. Air University).
　　www.au.af.mil/au/awc/awcgate/cps-terr.htm
INTERPOL—the International Criminal Police Organization (ICPO).
　　www.interpol.int
Lexington Institute.
　　www.lexingtoninstitute.org
Library of Congress, Federal Research Division: Terrorism Studies.
　　www.loc.gov/rr/frd/terrorism.htm
Library of Congress: "Remembering 9/11" Resources.
　　www.loc.gov/loc/lcib/0209/index.html
Marshall Center Information Resource on Terrorism.
　　www.marshallcenter.org
Memorial Institute for the Prevention of Terrorism.
　　www.mipt.org
MI5: The British Internal Security Service.
　　www.mi5.gov.uk
National Security Council.
　　www.whitehouse.gov/nsc
RAND Corporation Web site.
　　www.rand.org
Terrorist Group Profiles.
　　www.terrorism/com/terrorism/Groups2.shtml
Teaching Terror: An online resource guide for the study of terrorism and counterterrorism.
　　www.teachingterror.com
Terrorist Group Profiles.
　　library.nps.navy.mil/home/tgp/tgpndx.htm
The Network of Terrorism (U.S. Department of State).
　　usinfo.state.gov/products/pubs/terrornet
U.S. State Department Terrorism Information.
　　usinfo.state.gov/topical/pol/terror
White House Web Site on Homeland Security.
　　www.whitehouse.gov/homeland
Winning the War on Terrorism (U.S. Department of State).
　　usinfo.state.gov/is/international_security/terrorism.html

Index

Beirut, Lebanon, U. S. Marines barracks bombing, 85
Beltway sniper incident, 2002, media coverage, 348–351
Bill of Rights, 378–379, 403
bin Laden, Usama
   fatwa to kill Americans, 76
   finances, 9–10
   media coverage, 344–346
biological agents production, 50
biological terrorism, 46–47, 130–131
   casualty care planning, 446–447
   food supply security, 206–213
   information dissemination, 448–449
   lessons learned from SARS outbreak, 441–442
   public reaction, 444–446
   public responders, 446–447
   recommendations for response planning, 53–55, 443–452
   risk communication, 431–432
   vulnerability of the United States, 53–55
   (*See also* CBRN threat; invasive species)
Bioterrorism Preparedness Act of 2002, 203
blackouts and telecommunications, 417–422
border security
   assessment, 150–161
   Directorate of Border and Transportation Security, 292
   funding, 153
   responsibilities, pre-9/11, 289–290
   security policies and actions, 159–160
   weaknesses, 143–144
   (*See also* homeland security)
Bremer, Paul, 384–385
budget of homeland security, 153–154, 201, 288
   Department of Homeland Security, 121
bus terrorist attacks, 129–130
(*See also* Israel; surface transportation security)
Bush administration
   national security policy, 145, 150–152
   security organizations, 157

C
Canada-United States cooperation, 302–303
CAPPS (Computer Assisted Passenger Prescreening System), 113, 115–116, 149–150
cargo, maritime
   security systems, 145, 147
   vulnerability to attack, 182–184
   (*See also* sea-container security)

casualties of terrorism
   bioterrorism, care planning, 446–447
   mass casualties, 7
   terrorist tactics, 24–25
CBRN (chemical, biological, radiological, nuclear) threat, 31–39
   counterterrorism policy, 38–39
   Irish Republican Army, 37–38
   al-Qaida, 32–33, 37
   studies of, 34–35
   technical hurdles, 36–38
   terrorist access to, 12–13
   warnings by U. S. policy makers, 34
   (*See also* biological terrorism)
censorship (*see* government-media relations)
Centers for Disease Control (CDC), 209
charities, Islamic, financing of terrorism, 10
Chechen rebels, attack statistics, 79, 99
chemical attacks, 33, 130–131
   al-Qaida's interest in, 32–33
   (*See also* CBRN threat)
chlorine gas
   terrorist use, 36
   wastewater facility security and, 198–199
Church Committee, 1976, 388–389
CIA (Central Intelligence Agency)
   history, 387–390
   homeland security powers, 267–268
Citizens Corps initiative, 334
civil defense
   lessons learned from, 327–328
   (*See also* civil security)
civil liberties vs. national security
   history, 401–404
   public opinion, 410
   USA PATRIOT Act and, 369–379
civil security, 325–336
   recommendations, 328–333
Coast Guard, 148–149, 154
coercion strategy, 75–77
   assessments of terrorism effectiveness, 83–86, 92–93
commercial aviation security (*see* aviation security)
communication of risk (*see* risk communication)
communication of security information, 178–179
   Department of Homeland Security, 179–181
communications networks (*see* telecommunications networks viability)
companies
   response to SARS outbreak, 439–440